Palgrave Macmillan Transnational History Series

Series Editors
Akira Iriye
Department of History
Harvard University
Cambridge
MA, USA

Rana Mitter
Department of History
University of Oxford
Oxford, UK

This distinguished series seeks to develop scholarship on the transnational connections of societies and peoples in the nineteenth and twentieth centuries; provide a forum in which work on transnational history from different periods, subjects, and regions of the world can be brought together in fruitful connection; and explore the theoretical and methodological links between transnational and other related approaches such as comparative history and world history.

Editorial board
Thomas Bender, University Professor of the Humanities, Professor of History, and Director of the International Center for Advanced Studies, New York University
Jane Carruthers, Professor of History, University of South Africa
Mariano Plotkin, Professor, Universidad Nacional de Tres de Febrero, Buenos Aires, and member of the National Council of Scientific and Technological Research, Argentina
Pierre-Yves Saunier, Researcher at the Centre National de la Recherche Scientifique, France
Ian Tyrrell, Professor of History, University of New South Wales

More information about this series at
http://www.springer.com/series/14675

Torsten Weber

Embracing 'Asia' in China and Japan

Asianism Discourse and the Contest for Hegemony, 1912–1933

Torsten Weber
DIJ German Institute for Japanese Studies
Tokyo, Japan

Palgrave Macmillan Transnational History Series
ISBN 978-3-319-87960-4   ISBN 978-3-319-65154-5   (eBook)
https://doi.org/10.1007/978-3-319-65154-5

© The Editor(s) (if applicable) and The Author(s) 2018
Softcover re-print of the Hardcover 1st edition 2018
This work is subject to copyright. All rights are solely and exclusively licensed by the Publisher, whether the whole or part of the material is concerned, specifically the rights of translation, reprinting, reuse of illustrations, recitation, broadcasting, reproduction on microfilms or in any other physical way, and transmission or information storage and retrieval, electronic adaptation, computer software, or by similar or dissimilar methodology now known or hereafter developed.
The use of general descriptive names, registered names, trademarks, service marks, etc. in this publication does not imply, even in the absence of a specific statement, that such names are exempt from the relevant protective laws and regulations and therefore free for general use.
The publisher, the authors and the editors are safe to assume that the advice and information in this book are believed to be true and accurate at the date of publication. Neither the publisher nor the authors or the editors give a warranty, express or implied, with respect to the material contained herein or for any errors or omissions that may have been made. The publisher remains neutral with regard to jurisdictional claims in published maps and institutional affiliations.

Cover illustration: detail from two-page illustration of Sun Yat-sen's Greater Asianism speech of 1924, as portrayed in the Chinese *Dongya lianmeng huabao* journal, March 1941 (see Fig. 7.2). Courtesy of Waseda University Library

Printed on acid-free paper

This Palgrave Macmillan imprint is published by Springer Nature
The registered company is Springer International Publishing AG
The registered company address is: Gewerbestrasse 11, 6330 Cham, Switzerland

To my parents

Series Foreword

The *Palgrave Macmillan Transnational History Series* is designed to encourage research and writing in transnational history, that is, the study of the modern era that is not constrained by the focus on nations. Most studies of modern history are still confined to conceptual frameworks that privilege sovereign states and their interactions with one another. We believe, however, that such frameworks tend to lose sight of the fact that human beings have many identities besides their nationality that have preceded the birth of modern states. Identities such as gender, race, age and physical as well as psychological conditions have long existed, none of which is equatable with nationality. People interact with one another across national boundaries as women, for instance, or as children, Muslims and the physically handicapped. These are all important identities in terms of which individuals relate themselves to one another.

Many such identities are presented as dichotomies; young and old, men and women, sick and healthy, 'whites' and 'coloured', and so on. This is a way to enable humans to make sense of each other both within and across national boundaries.

'Asia' is another example. 'Asia' or 'the East' stands in contrast to 'the West'. Just like other dichotomies, 'Asia' or 'the East' is defined as that part of the world that is not 'the West' 'Asians' or 'Easterners' divide the world with 'non-Asians' or 'non-Easterners', of whom there are not only 'Westerners' but also 'Southerners', the former usually referring to Europeans and Americans and the latter to people in Africa. Where the

Middle East and South America fit is not always clear, and sometimes they are put in the category of 'the West', and at other times in 'the East'. But historically, the most influential reference point for 'Asia' has been what is called 'the West'.

It is not surprising that, just as people in 'the West' have developed their identity as 'Westerners', those in 'Asia' have also been fascinated by the question of what makes them 'Asians'. Discourses on 'Asia' and 'Asians' have long existed, but they became politically significant in the nineteenth and twentieth centuries as Europeans and Americans augmented their economic and military power, in the process also spreading their ideas of the world and of history to the rest of the world. In response, thinkers and publicists in Asia developed their own perspectives on humanity, seeking to locate themselves in relation to the West.

This book focuses on such discourses in China and Japan in the early decades of the twentieth century, in particular from the 1910s to the 1930s. This was the time when Chinese and Japanese thinkers, publicists, and educators wrote a great deal about the meaning of 'Asia'. Many of them were 'Asianists' in that they rebelled against the influence of Western thought that had begun to penetrate Asian countries and sought to resuscitate what they believed to have been an indigenous, authentic tradition. Hence the vogue of 'Asianism'. This book examines this phenomenon and recaptures the environment in which Chinese and Japanese writers were engaged in asserting the authenticity of the 'Asian' tradition.

At that time, it was a losing battle. Both China and Japan continued their societies' 'modernization', which was tantamount to Westernization. Worse, a 'Westernized' Japan went to war against a 'Westernizing' China, with tragic consequences for both. But it is worth recalling that story today, at the beginning of the twenty-first century when 'the rise of Asia' is once again developing as a way to understand world affairs. But this time the idea of Asia's rise seems to be gaining more influence in view of what many consider the loss of influence of the United States in world affairs.

It would be premature to consider such a phenomenon as more than a temporary circumstance. It may well be that in the decades to come, Asia and the West may both 'rise' or, alternatively, 'decline'. Whatever happens, it will be a world in which there will be far more extensive interactions and intermingling among people of different regions and cultures. More and more people may end up being intermixed so there may be no such thing as 'Asia' or 'Asianism' left in the world. To comprehend this development, it will be important to go back to the 'Asianism' discourse of a century ago. This book will provide an essential guide to such understanding.

Cambridge, USA
Oxford, UK

Akira Iriye
Rana Mitter

Preface

The embrace of 'Asia', as studied in this book, occurred in the first half of the twentieth century and refers to the ways and motivations of Japanese and Chinese who started to accept and utilize the newly coined concept of Asianism as a useful instrument in their rhetorical toolboxes. The discourse that unfolded around the neologism, called *Ajiashugi* in Japanese and *Yazhou zhuyi* in Chinese—which I refer to as Asianism discourse—often concerned itself with defining and defying hierarchies regarding China's and Japan's place in East Asia, in Asia, vis-à-vis the 'West', or globally. But not all participants in this discourse prioritized the nation (usually their own); some were less interested in the nation than in promoting different political, social, or cultural agendas, such as liberalism, Christianity, and democracy, while a few others were true Asiaphile, Chinese Japanophile, or Japanese Sinophile transnationalists. Asianism discourse therefore was a contest for hegemony on two different, if interlinked, levels. It was a contest for discursive hegemony regarding the real, true, or best conception of Asianism and simultaneously it was a rhetorical expression of the ideological or pragmatic contest for political hegemony within a social group, a country, or a region, or in the world.

As this book aims to demonstrate, Asianism understood as a political concept played an important role in facilitating this contest within and between China and Japan in the first decades of the twentieth century and particularly from 1912 to 1933, when Asianism discourse peaked in the transnational Sino-Japanese public sphere. Of course, there were also contests for hegemony within and between China and Japan before 1912 and after 1933. While Asianist ideas had circulated well before the early 1900s, Asianism as a concept, however, only emerged in mainstream public discourse around 1912. After 1933, the concept lost much of its discursive attraction as it became integrated into official propaganda in Japan, its empire, and parts of China. But Asianism was no concept of only temporary significance. As discussed in some detail in the conclusion of this book, Asianism has re-emerged in the twenty-first century as an instrument in the contest for hegemony, in particular regional hegemony, between China and Japan. It continues to influence public political discourse in various fields, including diplomacy, domestic politics, and sociopolitical ideas. Sinocentric conceptions of Asianism aim at justifying a leading role for China in the region, while Japan-centred conceptions often represent the opposite claim: they reject such claims from China and implicitly assert a renewed Japanese leadership. Some debaters use Asianism to criticize the neoliberal global order and to promote transnational civil society cooperation as well as historical reconciliation in East Asia, but others reduce Asianism's Asia to a profitable market or defend imperialist-hegemonic conceptions of Asianism that had been widespread in the 1930s and 1940s. Asianism has thus re-emerged in today's 'history wars' between the two countries as one of the preferred concepts utilized by historical revisionists in a similar way to how it was used as a propaganda instrument in Japan's war against China (and the Allies). This book leads us back to the origins of this dispute, when Asianism first appeared as a key concept in public political discourse in China and Japan, but also links its historical analysis to the present-day contest for hegemony in East Asia.

A decade ago, Asianism (or Pan-Asianism) was catapulted to the centre of scholarly attention when three excellent English-language books on the topic were published almost simultaneously. Eri Hotta studied Asianism as ideology in Japan's war from 1931 to 1945; Cemil Aydin focused on Asianism as an anti-Western ideology that appealed to East and West Asian Asianists alike; and an edited volume by Sven Saaler and Victor Koschmann demonstrated the width and diversity of historical topics into which Asianism extends (all published in 2007). Only shortly before, the first monographs centrally concerned with Asianism had appeared in China (Wang Ping 2004) and in Japan (Yamamuro 2006). A decade later, Asianism has become a topic that is rarely absent from any teaching curriculum in Japanese Studies, Chinese Studies, East

Asian Studies and international or global history programmes as well as Asian and international politics courses. Many of the research results of the above-mentioned publications are still valid today and some authors have continued to make important contributions to the field, such as the two-volume documentary history of Asianism edited by Sven Saaler and Christopher Szpilman (2011) and two massive volumes written and edited by Matsuura Masataka in Japanese (2010, 2013). Some questions, however, have remained unanswered or, as new sources have become available, need to be re-addressed: why and how did 'Asia' become an *ism* and how did the emergence of a new concept affect the political debate in Japan and China? How far did Asianism extend into public discourse in both countries beyond the level of elites? Was Asianism an ideology that can be fully understood by exclusively studying affirmations of the concept? Which insights can we gain if we comprehend Asianism as discourse and include criticisms and negations of the concept in our analysis? How does our understanding of Asianism change when we enlarge the scope of analysis spatially beyond contributions made by Japanese in the Japanese language to a transnational discursive space that pays more attention to non-Japanese participation? This book results from my efforts to provide answers to these and related questions. In addition, it addresses questions that have arisen because new sources have become available during the past decade. In fact, many of the contributions to Asianism discourse studied in this book have, to the best of my knowledge, never been studied before and even fewer are part of the canon of Asianism studies. While I cannot claim to give final answers to all of the questions posed above, I hope to contribute to develop the field further into the next, hopefully equally fruitful, decade of studies on Asianism, Asia consciousness, and the contest for hegemony within and between China and Japan.

Parts of this book previously appeared in *Asia after Versailles: Asian Perspectives on the Paris Peace Conference and the Interwar Order, 1919–1933*, ed. Urs Matthias Zachmann, Edinburgh: Edinburgh University Press 2017 and *Pan-Asianism: A Documentary History 1860–2010*, Vol. 2, ed. Sven Saaler and Christopher W.A. Szpilman, Boulder: Rowman & Littlefield 2011. I thank the respective publishers for their permission to use them.

Finally, a short note on conventions: Japanese, Chinese, and Korean names are rendered in their usual order, with the family name preceding the given name. Chinese names and words are transcribed according to the Pinyin system, except for names that are commonly rendered in English using different transcriptions, such as Sun Yat-sen (Sun Zhongshan) and Chiang Kai-shek (Jiang Jieshi). Similarly, macrons are omitted in commonly known Japanese place names, such as Tokyo (Tōkyō), Kyoto (Kyōto), Osaka (Ōsaka), and Kobe (Kōbe). Translations are my own, if not otherwise indicated.

Tokyo, Japan   Torsten Weber

Acknowledgements

The research and writing of this book was made possible by the generous support of a number of individuals and institutions whom I wish to thank. First, I wish to express my deepest gratitude to my *Doktorvater* Wolfgang Seifert. His interest in my research, his encouragement, and his support have been the greatest motivation to finish my doctoral dissertation, on which this book is based. At Heidelberg University, I also thank Gotelind Müller-Saini for agreeing to act as the second reader of the dissertation and for her invaluable feedback and support. Urs Matthias Zachmann introduced me to Wolfgang Seifert and encouraged me during different phases of research and writing, for which I am very grateful. At Leiden University, where this project started, I wish to thank my former colleagues Els van Dongen, Christian Uhl, Joel Joos, Ethan Mark, Rikki Kersten, Axel Schneider, Annika Pissin, Chiara Brivio, Lewis Mayo, Paramita Paul, Lena Scheen, Jeroen Groenewegen, Curtis Anderson Gayle, Motoe Sasaki, Kiri Paramore, Chris Goto-Jones, Michael Laver, Marc Matten, Viren Murthy, Esther van Eijk, and Carolien Stolte. I also thank Matsuda Kōichirō, Yonetani Masafumi, Hiraishi Naoaki, Hirakawa Hitoshi, Andrea Germer, Matthias Koch, Sven Saaler, Inoue Toshikazu and the participants of the Japan Foundation intellectual exchange programme on the Taishō period for sharing their insights and for inspiring conversations on my research. On various occasions and at various locations, many others have generously used their time to provide feedback on my work, including Kawashima Shin, Cemil Aydin, Prasenjit Duara, Sun Ge, Wang Hui, Kevin M. Doak, Sheldon Garon, Tosh Minohara,

Tze-ki Hon, Evan Dawley, Craig Smith, Chris Szpilman, Roger Brown, Michael Schneider, Dick Stegewerns, Naoko Shimazu, John LoBreglio, Juljan Biontino, Ulrich Flick, Takamichi Sakurai, Kuniyuki Terada, Haruko Sakaguchi, Sebastian Conrad, Mahon Murphy, Marc Frey, Nicola Spakowski, Maria Framke, Esther Möller, Joann Huifen Hu, Stefan Hübner, Stefani Jürries, Sönke Kunkel, Christoph Meyer, Alexander Thies, Joanna Wu, Ronald Saladin, Hanno Jentzsch, Steffen Heinrich, and Axel Klein. I am very grateful to everyone for sharing his or her thoughts and time to discuss my project with me.

I am deeply indebted and very grateful to Akira Iriye and Rana Mitter for accepting my book to be included in this series. At Palgrave and Springer I thank Molly Beck, Oliver Dyer, and Velvizhi Mari for their kind support. I am extremely grateful to Tessa Carroll who proofread the manuscript most professionally and thoughtfully and to Marie Berg and Miki Aoyama who helped to prepare the final manuscript for submission.

The pages of this book could not have been filled without the patient and tireless assistance of the staff of many libraries in Europe and Asia. I am very grateful to everyone who ordered, copied, or shipped materials, in particular Yoko Horikoshi as well as Ursula Flache and Sigrid Francke of the German Institute for Japanese Studies in Tokyo, Paul Wijsman and Hanno Lecher at Leiden University, and Lara Christianson at Jacobs University Bremen.

Only second to sources are resources that enabled me to conduct research at various places, including several stays in Japan and trips to China. I gratefully acknowledge the financial support of the *Nederlandse Organisatie voor Wetenschappelijk Onderzoek* (NWO), the German Institute for Japanese Studies (DIJ), the Japan Foundation, and the *Deutsche Forschungsgemeinschaft* (DFG). I also thank the JaDe Foundation for the Promotion of German–Japanese Scientific and Cultural Relations for the honour of being selected as their prizewinner in 2014. In addition, research and teaching positions at Leiden University, Heidelberg University, Jacobs University Bremen, and Freiburg University enabled me to survive while researching and writing this book. Special thanks are due to the DIJ Tokyo and its former and current directors, Florian Coulmas and Franz Waldenberger, for supporting this project from its earliest to its final stages.

Along the way, many others have generously supported my studies and the research which led to writing this book, including: R. Gary Tiedemann, formerly of SOAS; Jin Guangyao of Fudan University

Shanghai; the friendly and supportive staff at the *Nichi-Ran Gakkai* in Tokyo, particularly Willem Remmelink; Karin Aalderink and Ilona Beumer at Leiden University and Bianca-Maria Bergmann and Rena Dickel at Jacobs University.

Finally, I could not have completed this book without the continuous love, support, and friendship I have received from my parents, my sister, and my best friends Michael and Neil. Thank you so much for everything throughout all those years.

CONTENTS

1 Introduction 1

2 Studying Asianism: The Impact and Legacy of Takeuchi Yoshimi 31

3 Asia Becomes an *ism*: Early Chinese and Japanese Asianism 63

4 Asianism During World War One: Macro-Nationalism or Micro-Worldism? 107

5 The Racialization of 'Asia' in the Post-Versailles Period 167

6 The Regionalization of 'Asia': Asianism from Below and Its Failure 229

7 Asianism From Above: The Realization of 'Asia' in Manchuria 267

8 Conclusion: Continuing Antagonisms and Asianism Today	319
Appendix	337
Glossary	339
Bibliography	347
Index	391

List of Figures

Fig. 2.1	White Peril cartoon. 'Doitsu Kōtei no manako ni eijitaru Kōjinshu Dōmei' [The Alliance of Yellow Peoples as reflected in the eyes of the German Emperor], *Yomiuri Shinbun* (1900)	51
Fig. 4.1	Ninagawa Arata (1918)	119
Fig. 5.1	Cover of the Japanese journal *Nihon oyobi Nihonjin* (1924)	182
Fig. 5.2	Sun Yat-sen and his interpreter Dai Jitao during Sun's famous speech on Greater Asianism in Kobe (1924)	201
Fig. 6.1	Nagatomi Morinosuke (mid-1920s)	250
Fig. 7.1	'Wangdao yu badao' [Rule of Right and Rule of Might] cartoon, *Dongya lianmeng huabao* [East Asian League Pictorial], February 1941	282
Fig. 7.2	'Heyi yao shixian Da Yazhou zhuyi?' [How can Greater Asianism be realized?] illustration, *Dongya lianmeng huabao* [East Asian League Pictorial], March 1941	283
Fig. 7.3	Cover of the Japanese journal *Dai Ajiashugi* [Greater Asianism], August 1933	292

CHAPTER 1

Introduction

I suspect that just as plants exist for the sake of animals, and animals exist for the sake of human beings, so perhaps the 'East' (Tōyō) exists for the sake of Europeans.[1]
—Tokutomi Sohō (1886)

The glory of Europe is the humiliation of Asia! The march of history is a record of the steps that lead the West into an inevitable antagonism to ourselves.[2]
—Okakura Tenshin (1902)

This book examines how Asianism became a key concept in mainstream political discourse in China and Japan and how it was used both domestically and internationally in the contest for political hegemony. I argue that, from the early 1910s to the early 1930s, this contest changed Chinese and Japanese perceptions of 'Asia', from a concept that was foreign-referential, foreign-imposed, peripheral, and mostly negative and denied (in Japan) or largely ignored (in China) to one that was self-referential, self-defined, central, and widely affirmed and embraced. These changes were facilitated by the emergence of 'Asia' as a central geographical, cultural, racial, and political category in Japanese and Chinese published discourse. As an *ism*, Asianism not only elevated 'Asia' as a geographical concept with culturalist-racialist implications to the status of a full-blown principle (Jp. shugi/Ch. zhuyi), but also encouraged its proposal and discussion vis-à-vis other political doctrines of the time, such as nationalism, internationalism, and imperialism. By the late 1920s,

© The Author(s) 2018
T. Weber, *Embracing 'Asia' in China and Japan*,
Palgrave Macmillan Transnational History Series,
https://doi.org/10.1007/978-3-319-65154-5_1

a great variety of conceptions of Asianism had emerged which terminologically and conceptually paved the way for the appropriation from above of 'Asia' discourse from the early 1930s onwards.[3] By then—against the background of increasing military penetration of Asia by Japan—transnational Chinese-Japanese Asianism discourse and practice had largely become defunct. In this sense, in Japan the period under analysis (roughly the Taishō era, 1912–1926) forms an important turning point of 'Asia' discourse and constitutes a link between the official pro-Westernist orientation of the Meiji period and the ideologization of 'Asia' from the early Shōwa period onwards. In China, the close association of affirmative views of 'Asia' with Sun Yat-sen (1866–1925), the founder of the Chinese Republic in 1912, provided the conceptual equipment with which Japanese attempts at a monopolization of Asianism could be challenged. Chinese cooperation and collaboration with Japan, especially from the 1930s onwards in Manchuria, Nanjing, and elsewhere, would also be difficult, if not impossible, to imagine without the official embrace of 'Asia' by the founding father of modern China and his disciples after his death.

Topic and Scope

Studying Asianism (Jp. Ajiashugi, Ch. Yaxiya zhuyi/Yazhou zhuyi) as a key concept in the transnational political discourse of China and Japan from 1912 to 1933, this book examines how and why Asianism was utilized in the contest for hegemony within the changing world order. The *temporal* limitations of this study are informed by shifts in published political discourse: in 1912, the first year of the reign of the Taishō emperor in Japan and the first year of the Chinese Republic, a Chinese newspaper published an article with the title 'Da Yaxiya zhuyi lun' (On Greater Asianism). This article would be republished several times in the following years and decades in Japan and may therefore be seen as the origin of transnational Chinese-Japanese public discourse on Asianism. In 1933, two years after the so-called Manchurian Incident and one year after the founding of Manchukuo (Jp. Manshūkoku, Ch. Manzhouguo), the *Dai Ajia Kyōkai* (Greater Asia Association) was founded in Tokyo. Its founding symbolized the end of transnational[4] and civil society-driven discourse on Asianism 'from below'. Asianism, or at least specific conceptions thereof, now became appropriated 'from above'[5] by government and military representatives. Manchukuo functioned as the locus of its assumed first implementation.[6] In the sense of a widely circulated and hotly disputed negotiation of the content and significance of Asianism as a key concept that terminologically unified extremely diverse conceptions of Asia, 1912 marks the beginning of transnational Asianism discourse and 1933 its end. It was during these two decades that previous notions of Asian commonality and solidarity as expressed in terms such as 'same culture, same race' (Jp. dōbun dōshu, Ch. tongwen tongzhong), 'to raise Asia' (Jp. kō A, Ch. xing Ya), or 'White Peril' were terminologically and conceptually subsumed under the neologism 'Asianism'. Simultaneously, with the introduction of the term Asianism as a politico-cultural principle or doctrine, discussions about the 'question of Asia' in China and Japan ceased to be a prerogative of scholars such as Kang Youwei (1858–1927) or Liang Qichao (1873–1929) in China and of radical interest groups such as the Fukuoka-based *Genyōsha* or the *Kokuryūkai* in Japan. By the mid-1910s, Asianism as a political concept had entered the mainstream of public discourse in both countries. Politicians, educators, bureaucrats, poets, and others now joined influential thinkers as part of a wider debate that analysed, proposed, or dismissed Asianism as a viable alternative or a supplement to other political concepts such as internationalism, nationalism, or cosmopolitanism.

The *spatial* focus of this study lies in the transnational public sphere consisting of Chinese–Japanese interactions and exchanges. With greater publishing activities (and a more stable political and economic environment) in Japan, many of these Chinese and Japanese contributions to Asianism discourse from 1912 to 1933 were published in Japan and in the Japanese language. However, the mutual reception of Chinese, Japanese, and other contributions testifies to the fact that these publications were part of a larger discourse that transcended the borders of Japan. In fact, some of the most influential contributions to Asianism discourse in Japan, such as the 'Greater Asianism' proposal of 1912, the Mahan–Chirol dispute of 1913 on Japanese Asianity and assimilability (see Chap. 3), as well as Sun Yat-sen's influential Kobe speech on Greater Asianism in 1924 (see Chap. 5), have non-Japanese origins and protagonists. Obviously, Asianism discourse in Japan was connected to other parts of Asia and to other parts of the world, not only with regard to its content but also physically; most strongly, this influence came from Chinese thinkers and activists who contributed their own original conceptions of Asianism or discussed those proposed by their Japanese counterparts, who in turn rediscussed the Chinese reactions. At no time were these contributions unrelated to the shifting regional hierarchy, in which

China declined and Japan rose. On the contrary, the renegotiation of regional order, including regional hegemony, was an essential impetus that drove Chinese-Japanese Asianism discourse during the period under study.

In order to analyse this functional dimension of Asianism discourse, first and foremost this study seeks to understand how contemporary thinkers and activists in both countries defined and discussed Asianism. Who affirmed, analysed, criticized, and rejected the content of the concept or its viability and for what reasons? How did thinkers and activists interpret and employ Asianism to position themselves within public political discourse? How was 'Asia' as a concept re-evaluated and politicized? Why did disinterest in or negative perceptions of 'Asia' gradually change into more widely and openly articulated affirmations of the existence and significance of 'Asia' in mainstream political discourse in Japan and China during the 1910s and 1920s? In other words, how and why did an increasing number of Japanese and Chinese embrace 'Asia' from the early 1910s through the early 1930s?[7] Of course, this embrace of 'Asia' must not be misunderstood as representing in all cases an expression of sympathetic feelings; rather, to some, this process of affirmatively integrating 'Asia' into their discursive toolbox was much less a sympathetic embrace than a stranglehold. Thus, some only embraced 'Asia' to choke or backstab it, to exploit the concept theoretically, or, in practice, to claim Asia's resources for personal, national, or ideological reasons. Others may have felt that for geopolitical or other reasons they had no choice and reluctantly embraced 'Asia', while yet others were driven by sincere feelings of solidarity and friendship. And, although in decreasing numbers, at least in public, even by the 1930s some Japanese continued to refuse to welcome or embrace 'Asia' at all—and voiced their opposition. Their contributions make up an important part of what I understand by *Asianism discourse* (which this book studies) as opposed to *Asianism* (the focus of most other works on this topic) as a mere sequence of affirmations of the concept.

It is through the lens of Asianism that this book approaches the research questions posed above and, more generally, sheds new light on our understanding of Japanese and Chinese consciousness of 'Asia'.[8] Asianism in the widest sense can be defined as a concept that affirms the existence and significance of 'Asia'. The study of Asian history or Asian culture would fall into this category, as would the holding of Asian Games or the Asian Cup sports competitions. In each of these cases, the use of the term Asia may have political implications, but it may also—or primarily—be employed for the mere sake of the convenience of geographical demarcation. This book, however, is informed by a narrower definition which understands Asianism as a key concept with explicit political connotations around which a dispute over the significance of 'Asia' evolved in China, Japan, and other parts of Asia. Historically, Asianism in this narrower sense often, though not always, coincided terminologically with the 'Asia doctrine' or 'Asia principle'[9] (Jp. Ajiashugi, Ch. Yaxiya zhuyi/Yazhou zhuyi) or its variants 'Greater Asia principle' (Jp. Dai Ajiashugi, Ch. Da Yaxiya zhuyi/Da Yazhou zhuyi) and 'Pan-Asia principle' (Jp. Han Ajiashugi, Ch. Fan Yaxiya zhuyi/Fan Yazhou zhuyi).[10] Asianism in this literal sense as the principle (Jp. shugi, Ch. zhuyi) or doctrine (*ism*) of 'Asia'[11] constitutes a crystallization of 'Asia' discourse, as it elevates 'Asia' to the status of a principle or of an *ism*. While 'Asia' as the 'East' may primarily indicate the regional dimension—which, of course, includes culturalist and political implications, too—'Asia' as a principle or doctrine primarily displays a political dimension. It challenges other *ism*s of the times, including their spatial orientations, such as Japanism (Jp. Nipponshugi, Ch. Riben zhuyi), Euro-Americanism (Jp. Ōbeishugi, Ch. Ou-Mei zhuyi), Internationalism, Worldism (Jp. Sekaishugi, Ch. Shijie zhuyi), statist nationalism (Jp. Kokkashugi, Ch. Guojia zhuyi), ethnic nationalism (Jp. Minzokushugi, Ch. Minzu zhuyi), civic nationalism (Jp. Kokuminshugi, Ch. Guomin zhuyi)[12] as well as imperialism, militarism, and many others. While, consequently, the elevation of 'Asia' to the status of a principle disputed the importance or suitability of other political concepts, Asianism did not necessarily stand in opposition to all of them. As the case studies in the following chapters will demonstrate, in some conceptions Asianist thought and practice was envisioned, for example, as coinciding with or supplementing different forms of nationalism or internationalism.

Consequently, the argumentation in this book rests on the observation that, despite its partial conflation with—in the case of China—cultural Sinocentrism or a formula for wartime collaboration or—in the case of Japan—imperialism and wartime propaganda, Asianism historically functioned as a multifaceted and complex political concept that could represent a variety of diverse political agendas. It therefore deserves to be examined in its own right. In particular, I question the characterization and dismissal of Asianism *in toto* as (semi-)official Japanese ideology.[13] In my view, this interpretation is informed and, indeed, predetermined by the anachronistic and teleological study of a small range of exclusively Japanese wartime affirmative conceptions of Asianism. Other affirmative conceptions of Asianism, as advanced by Japanese and non-Japanese utopian-internationalist or socialist thinkers, as well as critical analyses and rejections of the concept by leftist-liberal or nationalist thinkers, have frequently been excluded from the rich body of sources available for the study of Asianism. Drawing on theories of conceptual history, this book proposes to expand the scope of sources to include a more diverse range of interpretations of Asianism as well as critiques and rejections of the concept in order to grasp more comprehensively the controversial character of transnational political discourse in China and Japan centring on Asianism from the early 1910s through the early 1930s.

LIMITATIONS

While the topic and scope as addressed above aspire to extend the conventional framework within which most scholarship has engaged with Asianism, naturally this book has its limits too. First, the focus on Asianism as a concept in mainstream political discourse means that other 'Asia' discourse and Asianist practice that does not centrally concern itself with the discussion, examination, or critique of Asianism, such as academic 'Asia' discourse or Asianist practices at pan-Asian sports or cultural events, remain outside the scope of this study. Second, the transnational expansion of the spatial scope of this study focuses on Japan and China. It excludes Western Asia by and large and neither Korea and Taiwan (as parts of the Japanese Empire) nor India are treated as central references. This focus on Japan and China is mainly due to the prominence and relevance of Japanese and Chinese contributions to Asianism discourse. Third, despite its focus on agency beyond, or rather 'below', the level of so-called great thinkers, this study, too, is based on a somewhat privileged body of sources, namely those that were published and widely distributed in Japan and China from the early 1910s to the early 1930s and that are still accessible to researchers today. Consequently, although it hopes to make a contribution to the 'democratization' of the canon of intellectual history (see Chap. 2) and to our understanding of politico-intellectual debate below the epistemological elite of society, this book can by no means claim to study the *vox populi* of Japan's 'Asia' discourse. Lastly, the perspective chosen, that is, to provide a comprehensive analysis of the negotiation of a concept within its politico-intellectual context, poses a limit to the exhaustive character of this study. At various points a more detailed or in-depth examination of the background of participants or debate may appear desirable. It is hoped that my microscopic focus on one concept in a pluralistic perspective will facilitate and encourage future in-depth research on aspects, thinkers, activitists, and conceptions that have been dealt with here in a more comprehensive manner.

THEORY AND METHODS: CONCEPTS AND DISCOURSE

One basic premise of this study is the assumption that Asianism did not exist as an isolated concept whose meaning changed linearly over time or, worse, did not change at all. Rather, this book aims to demonstrate that Asianism—as soon as it appeared on the stage of mainstream political discourse during the early 1910s—provoked a heated debate on its content, its significance, and its practicability. The analysis of Asianism therefore requires the inclusion of its politico-intellectual contexts provided by other ideas and by the political, economic, and social conditions in which these were formulated. In addition, as mentioned above, this book explicitly focuses on *one* concept: Asianism. However, it deals not only with a multitude of different conceptions of this concept[14] but also includes voices of dissent, in order to gain a more nuanced picture of what contemporaries understood by Asianism, how they voiced their criticism, and which alternatives they proposed. Consequently, this study of Asianism—while based on theoretical-methodological assumptions of conceptual history—does not constitute a conceptual history of Asianism in the traditional sense of examining different affirmations (positive uses) of one concept over time. Rather, it extends its analytical scope to that of a historical discourse analysis. My definition of discourse, consequently, is informed by the way concepts are perceived to function within discourses. Replying to critics of his classical approach of conceptual history,[15] Reinhart Koselleck (1923–2006), the doyen of German conceptual history (Begriffsgeschichte), has proposed in his later works that studies of concepts and discourse analyses should be viewed as supplementary, not opposing, methodologies. As he argued:

> Every concept *eo ipso* refers to its context. Especially without counter-concepts, super- and sub-concepts, accompanying and side-concepts no concept can be analysed. [...] In particular parallel concepts necessitate

asking not only semasiological questions of univocal meanings but also onomasiological questions of different terms with the same meaning. The transition to so-called discourse analysis is a natural result.[16]

Discourse, here, refers to the literal meaning of the term, derived from the Latin word *discurrere* which denotes a process of 'running to and fro'. Political discourse, therefore, refers to a unified or unifiable body of materials that expresses an exchange and negotiation of opinions, usually involving some degree of controversy, on issues of political relevance. In other words, by Chinese and Japanese political discourse I understand the mesh of arguments put forward publicly in China and Japan with the intention of influencing the domestic or foreign policies of either or both countries.[17] Chinese and Japanese 'Asia' discourse, therefore, combines a regional focus (on China and Japan) with a topical focus (on 'Asia') and refers to that mesh of arguments regarding Chinese and Japanese views and policies towards 'Asia'. Similarly, references to Asianism as a key concept form the unifying element in Asianism discourse. This straightforward definition of discourse does not, of course, dismiss the validity and relevance of alternative views of discourse, most notably Michel Foucault's emphasis of social practices, strategies, and inherent power relations.[18] Doubtless, the sources available to contemporary observers of and participants in Asianism discourse in the 1910s and 1920s are determined by the existing structures and power relations of knowledge production and distribution. The same is true for the work of any historian today whose access to sources is further limited by resources which again may be viewed as resulting from imbalances of power. In this sense, all forms of social practices, including the analysis of historical discourse itself, follow Foucault's logic of discursive constitution. This dimension is to be kept in mind in the context of this study of politico-intellectual history that focuses on the aspect of discourse as an exchange of views centring on a common concept that, like an assembly of intertwined threads, interweaves arguments which compete for hermeneutic and political hegemony.

What are concepts and how do they function in political discourse? According to Gallie's 'contestability thesis', conceptual disagreement is a natural and constitutive part of political discourse. Concepts are, in Gallie's words, 'in the nature of the case contestable, and will, as a rule, be actually contested by and in another use of it, which in the nature of the case is contestable, and will … and so on'.[19] Gallie, however, does not propose abandoning any efforts to define, understand, and analyse such concepts on the grounds of their contestability. Rather, he suggests that most, if not all, such contested concepts share a common core meaning which facilitates their definition. Following Gallie, Gaus has proposed distinguishing the so-defined and inherent 'abstract, ideal notions' (concept) from its various 'particular interpretations and realizations' (conceptions).[20] In other words, 'competing views represent alternative "conceptions" of the same "concept"' and 'in spite of their disagreements about how the concept might be defined, they are nonetheless debating the same idea'.[21] The analysis of political concepts requires an analysis of the political discourse that these concepts are part of for exactly this reason.

With regard to the functional aspects of political concepts, Terence Ball has observed that concepts deployed in political discourse are usually not elevated linguistic representations of abstract philosophical ideas, but must rather be seen as 'tools of persuasion and legitimation, badges of identity and solidarity' and, sometimes, may even function as 'weapons of war'. As such, political concepts are 'in the thick of partisan battles for "the hearts and minds of men"'.[22] 'To study the history of political concepts', Ball concludes, 'is to revisit old battlefields and reconstruct the positions and strategies of the opposing forces'.[23] In other words, political concepts cannot be reduced to their meaning *prima facie*, but must also be comprehended as strategies of communicating political agendas. For Asianism discourse this means that 'Asia' constitutes only one, albeit very important, aspect of that discourse. The appeal of Asianism as a political concept, however, also lay in its potential use as a tool to promote different political agendas that sometimes had little to do with 'Asia' itself, such as the contest for party leadership. In addition, based on Ball's definition, Heywood's distinction between 'value-laden' normative concepts and 'descriptive or positive concepts' appears helpful in understanding how concepts function as tools, although I would argue that one and the same political concept can contain both normative and descriptive aspects.[24] The 'value-laden' aspects which refer to 'moral principles and ideals' are more likely to appeal to 'the hearts', while the 'descriptive' aspects which refer to 'an objective and demonstrable existence' are more likely to appeal to the 'minds'.[25] In the context of the study of Asianism, Koschmann has introduced a corresponding distinction, namely between 'the rationalist extreme of Pan-Asianism', on the one hand, and 'culturalist pan-Asianists', on the other, who proposed 'highly intuitive, naturalistic, or culturalist visions of Asia'.[26] As we shall see below, the coexistence of both aspects in the concept of Asianism has contributed to the emergence of a great variety of conceptions of Asianism, many of which were actually opposed to each other, despite common terminology.

In more general terms, Reinhart Koselleck has argued that modern political and social concepts display the following three characteristics.[27] *Demokratisierung* (democratization) of political and social vocabularies indicates the popularization of an otherwise highly specialized discourse which only involves an inner circle of informed people with access to information that is not available openly. *Ideologiesierbarkeit* (capacity to be employed as ideology) indicates the extent to which concepts may be incorporated into ideologies. Finally, *Politisierung* (politicization) indicates both the political content and the potential function of concepts to become, as Ball put it, a 'tool of persuasion' in political dispute. As the case studies in the following chapters display, Asianism corresponds to all three characterizations: first, unlike more elevated and theoretical academic 'Asia' discourse,[28] Asianism quickly became a concept that facilitated the debate on 'Asia' in Japan and China among vast portions of the educated population, ranging from 'ordinary' readers of newspapers to scholars, journalists, other professional writers, and politicians; second, as Chap. 7 will address in detail, from the early 1930s onwards Asianism became part of the official state ideology that first promoted Japanese imperialism under Asianist slogans and later sought to justify pro-Japanese collaboration in China; thirdly, Asianism, as has been addressed above, was from the start a political concept that politicized the meaning of 'Asia'.

ORIENTALISM AND SELF-ORIENTALIZATION

The study of Asianism, of course, centrally involves the study of 'Asia'. As the quotation from Tokutomi Sohō (above) from the mid-Meiji period reveals, the consciousness of 'Easterners' being instrumentalized objects of the 'West' existed in Japan almost a century before Edward Said's *Orientalism* (1978) popularized the critique of 'Western' discourse on 'Asia'.[29] The opening lines of Said's Introduction to *Orientalism*, in fact, echo Tokutomi's claim directly. 'The Orient', Said writes, 'was almost a European invention, and had been since antiquity a place of romance, exotic beings, haunting memories and landscapes, remarkable experiences'.[30] As Said continues:

> Orientalism can be discussed and analysed as the corporate institution for dealing with the Orient—dealing with it by making statements about it, authorizing views of it, describing it, by teaching it, settling it, ruling over it: in short, Orientalism as a Western style for dominating, restructuring, and having authority over the Orient. [...] In brief, because of Orientalism the Orient was not (and is not) a free subject of thought or action.[31]

Both Said's and Tokutomi's critiques of the unequal practical and epistemological relationship between the 'West' and the 'East' are based on the assumption of monolithic entities that are exclusively and fundamentally opposed to each other. In other words, they are premised on an 'East' *versus* 'West' or 'Orient' *versus* 'Occident' binary. As neither statement is a mere observation that criticizes Orientalist practice from a neutral viewpoint, another dichotomy emerges, namely that of the 'Self' *versus* 'Other'—the problem of identity and alterity. Said's critique of Orientalism—much as Tokutomi's critique of 'Western' instrumentalizations of the 'East'—is also an attempt to raise the ('Eastern' or 'Asian') 'Self' vis-à-vis the 'Other', to rescue and defend it from oppression and exploitation. Although Asianism does not mainly deal with questions of identity but rather formulates a political agenda on the basis of assumed commonality and similar interests, the 'Self'–'Other' dichotomy, in this sense, is nevertheless relevant to the study of Asianism. First, and almost unavoidably, given the terminological root of the concept, Asianism participates in the 'Othering' of non-'Asia' and therefore *ex negativo* contributes to the self-definition of 'Asia'. Second, in doing so it practises a form of 'self-Orientalization' as self-definition, in Arif Dirlik's words.[32] By this, Dirlik means tendencies of self-essentialization in Asian views of 'Asia' which partly result from the consumption of 'Western' Orientalist views and from an Asian Occidentalist reaction to Western Orientalism. Ultimately, however, as Dirlik argues, this self-Orientalization does not contribute to overcoming the foreign-imposed character of identification:

> In the long run self-orientalization serves to perpetuate, and even to consolidate, existing forms of power. [...] Self-essentialization may serve the cause of mobilization against 'Western' domination; but in the very

process it also consolidates 'Western' ideological hegemony by internalizing the historical assumptions of Orientalism. At the same time, it contributes to internal hegemony by suppressing differences within the nation.[33]

Affirmative Asianism discourse as a practice of self-Orientalization displays both facets observed by Dirlik. First, by establishing a counter-discourse to 'Western' Orientalism it reaffirms the validity of the stereotypical and discriminatory categories set up by Orientalist discourse in the first place. Second, by means of (conscious or unconscious) self-essentialization it not only confirms many of the prejudices and stereotypes advanced by Orientalist discourse but also rejects acknowledging internal diversity. Instead, it forcefully suppresses minorities, be they quantitative or regarding access to power or both, by subsuming them under larger categories. This can be observed in the case of the Chinese nation and the relations between the Han Chinese and its minorities in contemporary China[34] or between the Japanese and other Asians in the Japanese Empire. In the same context, Zhang Yiguo has criticized the 'Occidentalism of "Easterners"' (Dongfang ren de 'Xifang zhuyi') and 'Self-Orientalism' (ziwo Dongfang zhuyi) as falsifications that rely on 'pan-Western imaginations' (fan Xifang xiangxiang) and result in either 'demonization' (yaomo hua) or 'divinization' (shensheng hua) of the 'West'.[35] This predicament of two-dimensional oppositions, Zhang suggests, can only be overcome if, as Ge Zhaoguang proposes, the 'Self' becomes reflected through multi-sided mirrors instead of one-sided mirrors; by creating 'an age of multi-sided mirrors' (duomian jingzi de shidai), such as by adopting perspectives from the periphery, we can break through the two-dimensional knowledge pattern of 'old–new or Chinese–Western', Zhang argues.[36] Potentially, Asianism discourse in Japan offered the opportunity to discover a 'Self' that was more nuanced and multi-dimensional than just a negation of the 'Other', usually the 'West', because it provided the chance to discover in Asia a multitude of positively connoted 'Others'. At least for those who were sympathetic towards other Asians, their conceptions of Asianism therefore cannot simply be reduced to represent anti-Western Self-Orientalism. As Stefan Tanaka has argued, however, much of Japan's 'Asia' discourse was informed by attempts at applying the binominal 'Self'–'Other' scheme to 'Asia' in order to construct Japan's own, backward and mysterious 'Orient', vis-à-vis which Japan would appear superior, as the 'West' appeared superior to the 'East'.[37] According to this rationale, 'Asia' had to be a foreign-defined, foreign-authorized, foreign-taught, and foreign-managed object (Said) or, as Tanaka put it, a 'voiceless thing'.[38] Only the subject that spoke on behalf of the 'voiceless thing' (i.e. the object called Asia) changed and became a little less foreign: it was no longer the 'Euro-Americans' but the Japanese.

As the case studies in this book aim to demonstrate, however, Chinese and Japanese consciousness of 'Asia' and Chinese-Japanese Asianism discourse was much more complex than that. No one conception of Asianism within China or Japan gained dominance to a degree that all other conceptions could be rendered peripheral; nor were non-Japanese (or non-Chinese) voices from Asia absent from 'Asia' discourse in Japan (or China). In other words, Asianism discourse during the 1910s and 1920s cannot be reduced to a vertical discursive practice between a hegemonic subject and an oppressed object; instead of being a 'voiceless thing', 'Asia' itself in this discourse had many voices, no few of which publicly criticized and challenged the presumably hegemonic Japanese views of 'Asia'. In the framework of Orientalist 'Self'–'Other' dichotomy, Asianism therefore did in fact contribute to the self-definition of 'Asia' by Asians and to its reinterpretation—at the peak of Yellow Peril discourse in the 'West'—as a positively, not negatively, connoted concept. As a consequence, if, following Edward Said, 'Asia' discourse in the 'West' was above all 'a Western style for dominating, restructuring, and having authority over the Orient', Asianism could then functionally be defined as an 'Eastern' or 'Asian' style for reclaiming this authority over 'Asia'.

STATE OF THE FIELD

The study of Asianism at least in Japan is almost as old as the concept itself, if one excludes occasional early references to Asianism from the late nineteenth century that left no notable mark on the later debate.[39] In fact, some of the contributions to Asianism discourse examined in the following chapters could be classified primarily as studies of Asianism rather than political propagations or rejections of the concept. Ōyama Ikuo's essay on the 'Fate of Greater Asianism' of 1916 (see Chap. 3) could be counted as belonging to this category. Of course, his study—not surprisingly against the background of the times and given Ōyama's political engagement—displays explicit political dimensions and was neither written in an academic style nor directed at an academic audience. In part, these observations are also true for the most influential study of Asianism published to this day, 'The prospects of Asianism' (1963), by the Japanese Sinologist Takeuchi Yoshimi (1910–1977). Takeuchi's influence on subsequent scholarship and on our understanding of Asianism has been so strong that his major theses will be examined in more detail in the following chapter (Chap. 2). Here, it is sufficient to briefly summarize four major influences. First, Takeuchi's definition of Asianism as a relatively vague 'inclination' (keikōsei)[40] has led to a rather loose understanding of Asianism.[41] Takeuchi did not grasp Asianism as a well-defined or well-definable concept, and, as a consequence, no academic study in the following three decades attempted a vigorous study of the concept. Second, Takeuchi's focus on Asianism as 'thought' (shisō) has led subsequent scholarship to trace Asianism—or Asianist inclinations—in writings of 'great thinkers' of the time (see Chap. 2). Asianism articulated by less prominent Japanese or Chinese as well as more practically oriented Asianist activities, such as the holding of pan-Asian conferences or the work of many Asianist organizations, have remained relatively obscure until recently. Third, Takeuchi's neglect of Asianism during the Taishō period (1912–1926) in favour of the preceding Meiji and succeeding Shōwa periods[42] has led to a general preference in scholarship to portray Asianism as representing a dichotomous opposition of solidarity (rentai) *versus* invasion (shinryaku), with the Movement for Freedom and Civil Rights (Jiyū Minken Undō) of the 1880s representing the former and Japanese imperial policy as well as ideological collaborationists from the 1930s and 1940s representing the latter. Fourth, Takeuchi's focus on China as an object of Japanese Asianists has limited the spatial scope of investigations into Asianism during the following decades. Takeuchi disregarded the fact that Asianism was highly reactive to non-Japanese influences, in particular from the 'West' and China, and that it was initially rejected in Japan for exactly this reason. Instead, most scholarship followed his interpretation and traced the origins of Asianism to the *Jiyū Minken Undō*. In sum, Takeuchi's influence on the study of Asianism in postwar Japan may rightfully be characterized as 'absolute'[43] and most of his findings have remained the cornerstones of any research into Asianism until today.

As mentioned above, research into Asianism did not start with Takeuchi Yoshimi. Harada Katsumasa (1930–2008) was probably the first Japanese scholar who re-established Asianism as a study object in post-war Japan. Writing in the late 1950s, Harada's studies anticipated several of Takeuchi's later foci: Harada temporally focused (a) on the 1880s and 1890s as the formative period of Asianism, which Harada refers to as 'the principle of international solidarity' (kokusai rentaishugi) and (b) on the 1930s and 1940s as its use as a cover-up for 'invasionism' (shinryakushugi)[44]; Harada completely skipped the Taishō period. According to Harada, Asianism called for (I) the protection of Japan's independence and (II) the liberation of the oppressed peoples of Asia.[45] As such, it partially overlapped with nationalism and imperialism but also with liberalism and internationalism. Most of these early postwar insights into Asianism were adopted, refined, and popularized by Takeuchi in the following decades.

In the wake and aftermath of the normalization of relations with the People's Republic of China in 1972, studies of Asianism in Japan with a particular focus on China experienced a boom. While case studies emerged in large numbers, including special issues of journals,[46] the parameters of research did not change. Around the same time, in one of the first studies outside Japan that considered Asianism more than in passing, Wolfgang Seifert drew attention to the complex character of Asianism and to the emergence of the first challenges to Takeuchi's ambivalent interpretation. Referring to studies by the Japanese historians Inoue Kiyoshi (1913–2001) and Yamada Shōji (born 1930), Seifert highlighted the possibility of distinguishing 'real' from 'self-acclaimed' Asianism (Takeuchi) according to its different political agendas rather than by identifying 'real' and 'self-acclaimed' Asianists.[47] In this context, Seifert also suggested that Asianism should be defined in two different ways: first, in a wider sense, as Asianist tendencies or sentiments that only vaguely advanced the cooperation of Asian peoples based on the assumption of racial or cultural commonality; and, second, in a narrower sense, as a 'well-defined ideology and movement' with precise political aims that largely coincide with Japanese nationalism. Because of his focus on Japanese nationalism, Seifert omitted the existence of well-defined Asianist agendas that did *not* coincide with Japanese nationalism but instead coincided with Chinese or Indian nationalism, or with Japanese or other Asian internationalism. However, his reminder of practical aspects of Asianism beyond mere 'thought', as well as his focus on the relevance of Asianism for political discourse and activity beyond the 1945 divide, have later been taken up by scholarship in Japanese and English alike.

It was not until the 1990s, however, that the first studies began to enquire in more detail into contemporary views of Asianism and its functions as a concept in political discourse. Until then, one was led to believe that only in China—that is, in Li Dazhao's proposal of a 'New Asianism' to counter Japanese 'Greater Asianism' and in Sun Yat-sen's 'Greater Asianism' speech—had the term Asianism actually been employed historically. It is a merit of Itō Teruo's (1990) and Furuya Tetsuo's (1994) scholarship to have called attention to the fact that in Japan, too, the term 'Asianism' was widely in use from the 1910s onwards. Both closely examined the historical usage of Asianism and the surrounding dispute over its meaning, significance, and practicability. Itō defined Asianism as 'the union of Asia's weak to resist the invasion of Asia by the Euro-American powers' and suggested that Asianism became controversially debated in Japan during the early 1910s 'as the Japanese reaction to the "Yellow Peril" thesis (Kōka Ron) which was flourishing in Europe around that period'.[48] As the main representative of this Asianism as 'White Peril' thesis, Itō introduced Kodera Kenkichi's monograph *Dai Ajiashugi Ron* (On Greater Asianism) from 1916.[49] As will be examined in more detail later (Chap. 4), Kodera's anti-Westernist book was in fact one of the inspirations of Li Dazhao's formulation of a 'New Asianism' in 1919. A clear shift in the study of Asianism, however, only occurred with Furuya Tetsuo's path-breaking analysis of Asianism.[50] Furuya not only reaffirmed the significance of the World War One and interwar periods for the development of Asianism as a well-defined and politicized concept,[51] but also placed Asianism as a concept in its discursive context of competing conceptions, criticism, and rejection. To Furuya, this context naturally transcended the narrow boundaries of Japan to include the influence of and responses from China, India, and the 'West'. It is hardly an exaggeration to claim that Furuya has changed the way Asianism is studied almost to the same degree that Takeuchi had influenced the field three decades earlier. Furuya's re-examination of Asianism as an object of study started with his interest in the political usages of 'Asia', which he considered inappropriately absent from both Takeuchi's and subsequent scholarship:

> Without doubt, it can be said that this direction of research may have revealed one aspect of Asianism. However, if the core of the matter is developed within the framework of 'solidarity and invasion' (rentai to shinryaku), Asianism's aspect of 'Asia', that is to say, why and how 'Asia'

was advanced, is driven to the background. To put it extremely, even if the term 'Asia' was not used at all, as long as we can discover some sort of attention to solidarity with people in Asia, this would be treated as Asianism. Of course, I am not denying the relevance of such research. However, if we choose 'Asianism' as our object I would think that we must base our inquiry on the questions of what has been proposed through the term 'Asia' and which ideology was served thereby.[52]

Starting from this premise Furuya, unlike many preceding authors, was less interested in examining the consciousness of 'Asia' held by Japan's foremost intellectuals in the pre-war and wartime periods. Instead, he focused on the functions of 'Asia' in Japan's mainstream political discourse. Ultimately, Furuya concluded, it was the inability of Asianism to release 'Asia' from the limitations set by the reality of the nation state which contributed to its own absorption by the state against the civil society actors from Japan and colonized countries who had initially employed the concept against the state.[53]

Placing Asianism in the context of debates on international order, Hiraishi Naoaki has likewise directed attention to World War One as a turning point of 'Asia' discourse in Asia, from a pro-European to a pro-Asian perspective.[54] Hiraishi, too, emphasizes that different conceptions of Asianism—revealing different views of 'Asia'—competed in Japan's political discourse, ranging from Tokutomi Sohō's 'exclusive' (heisateki) Asianism to Ukita Kazutami's participatory internationalism, and Miyazaki Tōten's anti-colonial conception of Asianism.[55] Also Yamamuro Shin'ichi, in his *magnum opus* on Japan's Asia discourse, has largely followed Furuya's new direction of research into Asianism. His study defines 'Asia' as a transnational regional entity and distinguishes 'Asia' as 'conceived' (ninshiki sareta) space (Japanese learn from the 'West' about the 'existence' of Asia), 'linked' (tsunagatte ita) space (Japanese link 'Asia' to their own 'world', viewpoints), and 'projected' (keika sareta) space (Japanese utilize their Asia consciousness for their own purposes/projects). Yamamuro generally portrays Asianism as the opposite of *Datsu A* (Departing from Asia, dissociating from Asia)[56] and stresses (a) the functional aspect of 'Asia', (b) the disputed character of its content and significance, and (c) the transnational context of its negotiation. As Yamamuro concludes,

> Japanese Asianism may not have been more than an illusion about Asia but at the same time it is also a fact that there existed common actions with

other [Asian] peoples. [...] As for the treatment of the Asians who came to Japan for support, [Japan] had to respond to the demands of the Euro-American suzerains. This truly displayed Asianism's dilemma. At any rate, Asianism as a project developed from the basic feeling of national destiny, namely of bearing a special responsibility for the independence and liberation of the Asian peoples, which in Asia only the Japanese possessed.[57]

The basic dilemma of Asianism, according to this view, therefore, was not the ambivalent character of Asianist claims but rather the obstructive political reality which hampered even the most well-intended Asianist activities. This view does not aim at exculpating Japanese imperialist agency. Rather, it stresses the historical context of international politics within which Asianism as 'thought' and as 'practice' materialized—or failed to do so. This context, as Yamamuro emphasizes, includes the 'reality' of Japan's special position within Asia as the country that had 'modernized' or 'Westernized' more than any other country and which resulted in a 'feeling of destiny' (shimeikan).[58] At any rate, Yamamuro developed Takeuchi's more narrow definition of Asianism as 'Japanese thought' (Nihon shisō) in two new directions: first, by adopting an explicit transnational perspective ('Western' impact on Japan and impact on Asia, including responses from Asia), and second, by defining 'thought' widely as including Asianist activities ('Asia' as a joint Asianist and Japanese imperialist project).

In China, against the background of China's new proactive role within Asia since the late 1990s, the diversification of scholarly engagement with Asianism during the past decade has led to a remarkable interpretative shift in the evaluation of historical Asianism. First, regarding historical Asianism, within scholarly and political communities, Japanese Asianism has been revisited and has become interpreted in a more nuanced way. Second, as for Chinese Asianism, new political and cultural definitions of Asianism for today have emerged (I) in the context of regionalism and regional identity formation and (II) as a self-affirmative epistemology.[59] In the realm of scholarship, the Chinese historians of modern Japan Sheng Banghe and Wang Ping have contributed most to this shift. Given the Japan-centred view of Asianism in China, it appears logical that the revision of Asianism in China should start with a revision of Japanese Asianism. In 2000, Sheng Banghe argued that Japanese Asianism had historically undergone a process of development. In other words, it could not adequately be described as a Japanese invention for the justification or planning of the conquest of China, as most previous scholarship had done. Instead, early Asianism, Sheng proposed, was mainly an attempt at resisting the Western powers by adopting the 'thesis of an Asian alliance' (Yazhou tongmeng lun), which only later developed into a 'theory of invasionism' (qinlue zhuyi lilun) and became linked with Japan's mainland policy.[60] This view was immediately attacked by some Chinese scholars as apologetic.[61] Nevertheless, in the following years similar views emerged. In 2004, Wang Ping, a historian at the Chinese Academy of Social Sciences and a commentator on Sino-Japanese relations in the official national *People's Daily* newspaper (Renmin Ribao) argued:

> [M]odern Japanese 'Asianism' [...] took shape during a time of crisis due to intensified aggression by Western powers against the East and revolved around the question of how to understand concepts of 'East' and 'West'. As a result of the complicated and particular historical development process which modern Japanese Asianism underwent, it displays the three forms of Classical Asianism (Gudian Yaxiya zhuyi), emphasizing equal cooperation in Asia, of Greater Asianism (Da Yaxiya zhuyi), emphasizing expansion, and of the 'Greater East Asian Co-Prosperity Sphere', which implemented the invasion of Asia. In the course of its formation, development, and extinction, modern Japanese Asianism completed its historical process as a qualitative transformation from 'Reviving Asia' (Xing Ya) to 'Invading Asia'. (Qin Ya)[62]

Similar to Sheng, Wang—in the first Chinese monograph on Asianism ever published—emphasizes that Asianism cannot be studied detached from its historical context of a 'Western threat', which did not automatically lead to a Japanese formulation of a blueprint for military aggression. Rather, for Wang as for Sheng, in the early period 'Classical Asianism' stood for cooperation and representatively expressed itself in the Asian Solidarity thesis (Jp. Ajia Rentai Ron, Ch. Yaxiya Liandai Lun). This thought, Wang claims, was dominant in the last two decades of the nineteenth century, between the foundation of the *Shin A Sha* [Rouse Asia Society] in 1878, assumed to be the first Asianist organization,[63] and the foundation of the *Tōa Dōbunkai* [East Asia Common Culture Association] by Konoe Atsumaro in 1898.[64] Rescuing historical Asianist thought and activity from the indiscriminate conflation with Japanese imperialism and from the anachronistic attribution to constituting a grand scheme to occupy China may be seen as the most important achievement of both Sheng's and Wang's studies. Simultaneously, this also constitutes the most important development in post-war Chinese scholarship on Asianism. In addition, Wang Ping transcended the scope of her study to propose that her revision of Japanese Asianism might allow for a revival of Asianism throughout Asia today. Arguing for a 'New Classical Asianism' (Xin gudian Yaxiya zhuyi), which, according to Wang, rejects any particularistic claims for 'Asian values' and 'Asian thought', she positioned herself against the 'conservative "New Asianism"' advanced by Tokyo's former governor Ishihara Shintarō and the former Prime Minister of Malaysia, Mahathir Mohamad. She also rejects hegemonic hopes for an 'Asian century'.[65] Instead she argues for non-exclusive regional cooperation based on 'horizontal contacts' (hengxiang jiaowang)[66] both within and outside the region. However, her perception of Asian commonality draws explicitly on traditional Confucian concepts and the claimed singular characteristics of 'Chinese civilization' (Zhonghua wenming), such as its 'power of [cultural] absorption' (xi yin li) and 'tolerance' (bao rong xing) or its unique unbroken line among the ancient civilizations.[67] This interpretation facilitates two potential claims: first, China may function as the core of a regionalist 'New Classical Asianism', and second, the scope of this benevolent and highly civilized and tolerant idealism may also transcend the regional limits of Asia to be applied to the world. In other words, new Chinese Asianism can ideologically supplement diplomatic blueprints both regionally and internationally.[68] This persistence of Asianist conceptions in today's political discourse on regional leadership—both in Japan and China—will be addressed again in the Conclusion.

Apart from Wolfgang Seifert's early analysis of Asianism in relation to Japanese nationalism, scholarship in 'Western' languages on Asianism remained scarce until recently. Obviously unaware of the extent of historical Asianism discourse,[69] William Beasley made an important original contribution to the study of Asianism by placing the concept in a comparative context of pan-isms outside Asia.[70] As Beasley argued, pan-movements either propose 'action from weakness', that is 'to bring about cross-frontier cooperation among the disadvantaged' in order to facilitate 'resistance to the oppressor' (some anti-Ottoman Pan-Slavism; anti-colonial pan-Africanism) or 'action from strength', that is 'intervention by an outside power on behalf of subject peoples elsewhere', justified by claimed racial or cultural links. The latter, Beasley argued, often becomes 'an instrument of [...] expansion' (intra-Russian pan-Slavism; pan-Germanism).[71] Beasley concluded that Pan-Asianism in Japan 'seems to have elements of all these things',[72] suggesting that Asianism's rationale lay in its attitude of strength towards Asia, in particular China, and of weakness towards the 'West'. Later, this attempt at comparatively classifying Asianism was refined by Sven Saaler, who suggested distinguishing irredentist, regionalist, hegemonic, and anti-colonial pan-movements and identified Japanese Asianism as partly overlapping with any type.[73] While the direct insights gained from typological classifications may be limited, they serve as an important reminder of the international context within which pan-Asian ideas developed both in Japan and in China, and in other parts of Asia. As Saaler argued, 'the term Pan-Asianism was used consciously within the rhetoric of Japanese politics following the existence of such movements in Europe and other parts of the world'.[74] His observation indicates the actual transnational entanglement of historical Asianism discourse and of global pan-nationalist reality, to which Japanese and Chinese scholarship has paid relatively little attention.

As this brief discussion of the main tendencies and developments in Japanese, Chinese, and 'Western' scholarship on Asianism illustrates, Asianism as an object of study has attracted rather diverse scholarly attention. In Japan, although the framework set up by Takeuchi's study of 1963 has remained 'state of the art', from the 1990s onwards research into Asianism has become diversified to include lesser-known voices, Asianist activities, and transnational dimensions. In China, despite tense bilateral relations between China and Japan during the early 2000s, a partial reappreciation of Japanese Asianism has allowed for a more in-depth and critical inquiry into the diverse content and functions of Asianism beyond ideological appraisals and dismissals. In addition, both in Japan and in China, recent scholarship has started to link historical studies to the new political reality of increasing regional integration of East Asia. It is this contemporary context that has triggered a renewed interest in the study of Asianism within and outside Asia since the early 2000s.

THE STRUCTURE OF THIS BOOK

With the exception of Chap. 2, which discusses epistemological problems of studying Asianism, this book is largely organized chronologically. The temporal divisions are according to what could be called 'Asianist moments'.

These moments influenced mainstream political discourse on Asianism to a considerable degree, changed it, and sometimes even turned it upside down. The temporal boundaries also correspond to different topical foci. Obviously, they do not represent strict lines of demarcation but are indicative of new directions or of a shifting focus in Asianism discourse at a given time.

Chapter 2 takes up specific problematic aspects of the historiography of Asianism and addresses predominant patterns of dichotomies, definitions, and canons to assess the impact of Takeuchi Yoshimi on the study of Asianism. Chapter 3 traces the late nineteenth- and early twentieth-century origins of Asianism and analyses the inception of Asianism discourse in pre-World War One Japan and China. Chapter 4 discusses World War One as an 'Asianist moment' which, partly in reaction to the perceived 'decline of the "West"', triggered the first wide emergence of different conceptions of Asianism in mainstream Chinese and Japanese public discourse. Chapter 5 examines how after the Paris Peace Conference and the tightened immigration legislation in the United States, the Asianist moments of 1919 and 1924 promoted racialist conceptions of Asianism to the centre of debate and includes a study of Sun Yat-sen's famous Kobe speech on Greater Asianism. Chapter 6 focuses on practical and theoretical attempts to 'regionalize "Asia"' by concrete Asianist activities from below and on regionalist conceptions of Asianism inspired by pan-movements elsewhere. The Manchurian Incident of 1931, the founding of Manchukuo in 1932, and Japan's announcement in 1933 that it was leaving the League of Nations constitute the final Asianist moments of this study. The analysis of Chap. 7 discusses the appropriation of Asianism from above and the employment of the concept for the supposed realization of Asianist idealism in Manchuria and to justify pro-Japanese collaboration in China. The Conclusion summarizes the findings of this study and transcends the temporal scope by addressing the legacy of early twentieth-century Asianism discourse in today's political discourse in Japan and China, with a particular focus on the employment of Asianist rhetoric and concepts in the debate on the creation of an East Asian Community (Jp. Higashi Ajia Kyōdōtai, Ch. Dongya Gongtongti) and as part of the so-called history problems between China and Japan.

Notes

1. Tokutomi Iichirō [Sohō], *Shōrai no Nihon* [Future Japan], Tokyo: Keizai Zasshi Sha 1886, 51–52; for a complete translation of this book into English see Tokutomi Sohō, *The Future Japan*, transl. and ed. Vinh Sinh, Edmonton: University of Alberta Press 1989.

2. Okakura Tenshin, *The Awakening of the East*, unpublished manuscript handwritten by Okakura in 1901/02, first printed in its original English version in Okakura Kakuzō, *The Awakening of the East*, Tokyo: Seibunkaku 1940, 3.
3. Asianism after the Manchurian Incident of 1931 has been studied in greater detail. The best book-length study in English is Eri Hotta, *Pan-Asianism and Japan's war 1931–1945*, New York: Palgrave Macmillan 2007.
4. In this book, the terms 'transnational', 'civil society', and 'public (discourse)' are used as closely interlinked concepts. By 'transnational' I understand phenomena that occur in nationally defined spaces but consciously transcend the existing national borders. As opposed to 'international', *transnational* refers to phenomena that are not (mainly) informed and driven by nation states or their representatives. Rather, 'transnational' refers to activities by members of civil society from different nations. 'Civil society', here, refers to institutions and relationships that organize political life and debate 'at a level between the state and the family' (Calhoun). 'Public' discourse refers to political communication in the public sphere that addresses both state and civil society and seeks to influence state actions, civil society, and even private life by debate that is published and meant to be consumed by a wide audience. See Craig Calhoun, 'Civil Society/Public Sphere: History of the Concept', *International encyclopedia of the social & behavioral sciences*, ed. Neil J. Smelser/Paul B. Baltes, New York: Elsevier 2001, 1897–1903 (quotation from page 1897) and Jürgen Mittag/Berthold Unfried, 'Transnationale Netzwerke—Annäherungen an ein Medium des Transfers und der Machtausübung [Transnational Networks—Approaches to a medium of transfer and power], *Transnationale Netzwerke im 20. Jahrhundert* [Transnational Networks in the 20th Century], Leipzig: Akademische Verlagsanstalt 2008, 9–25. For definitions of 'discourse' and 'political discourse', see below.
5. In the field of Japanese history, the oppositional terminology 'from below' and 'from above' is frequently linked to Maruyama Masao's famous distinction of the characteristics of so-called Japanese fascism and fascism in Europe. Here and in the following discussion, however, 'from below' and 'from above' are not used as references to Maruyama but to distinguish mainly civil society activities from those that were initiated and promoted by state authorities, the government, and the military leadership. For Maruyama's classic distinction see Maruyama Masao, 'Nihon Fashizumu no shisō to undō' [The Thought and Movement of Japanese Fascism], *Maruyama Masao Shū* [Collected Writings of Maruyama Masao], Vol. 3, Tokyo: Iwanami Shoten 1995 (1948), 259–322 and, for an English translation, 'The Ideology and Dynamics of Japanese Fascism', *Thought*

and behavior in modern Japanese politics, ed. Ivan Morris, Oxford: Oxford University Press 1969, 25–83.
6. On the uses of Asianist rhetoric as 'strategies of legitimization by the political and military leadership' with particular reference to Manchuria see Wolfgang Seifert, 'Japans Systemtransformation in den 1930er Jahren und die 'Asiatisierung' Ostasiens' [Japan's system transformation in the 1930s and the 'Asiatization' of East Asia], *Ostasien im 20. Jahrhundert. Geschichte und Gesellschaft* [East Asia in the 20th Century. History and Society], ed. Sepp Linhart and Susanne Weigelin-Schwiedrzik, Wien: Promedia Verlag 2007, 45–61 (quotation from page 46).
7. Eri Hotta was, to the best of my knowledge, the first to propose using the metaphor 'embrace' to describe Japanese attitudes towards Asianism. I share her notion and extend her view that 'the Japanese embrace of Pan-Asianism ended up strangling Japan itself' to the—in my view—more significant Japanese strangling of other Asians, in particular Chinese. See Hotta, *Pan-Asianism and Japan's war 1931–1945*, 237.
8. I will refer to 'Asia' in inverted commas when it denotes a concept that intentionally contains political, culturalist, or racialist implications and to Asia without inverted commas when it refers to the commonly used geographic term; in other words, Asia is the continent of Asia as we know it whereas 'Asia' is the Orientalist or self-Orientalist political concept.
9. On the translation of 'shugi' as 'principle' see Chap. 3.
10. Although each of the three terms in question (Asianism, Greater Asianism, Pan-Asianism) carries slightly differing connotations, I regard all three terms as by and large synonymic. Most contemporary debaters have neglected the minor differences in meaning, and here I follow Takeuchi Yoshimi who subsumed all three terms under the general term Asianism (Ajiashugi); see Chap. 2.
11. On this aspect, see also Chap. 3.
12. On the different historical conceptions of nationalism in Japan see Kevin M. Doak, *A history of nationalism in modern Japan: placing the people*, Leiden/Boston: Brill 2007 and Yamanouchi Masayuki, 'Nēshon to wa nani ka?' [What is the nation?], *Minzoku, Kokka, Esunishiti* [Nation, State, Ethnicity], ed. Inoue Shun et al., Tokyo: Iwanami Shoten 1996. For China see *Imagining the People: Chinese Intellectuals and the Concept of Citizenship, 1890–1920*, ed. Joshua A. Fogel and Peter G. Zarrow, Armork, NY: M.E. Sharpe 1997.
13. This tendency is strongest in Chinese scholarship (see below). However, scholarship in the English language also continues to characterize Asianism more generally as an ideology; see, for example, Hotta, *Pan-Asianism and Japan's war 1931–1945*, passim, Sven Saaler, 'Pan-Asianism in modern Japanese history. Overcoming the nation,

creating a region, forging an empire', *Pan-Asianism in Modern Japanese History. Colonialism, regionalism and borders*, ed. Sven Saaler and J. Victor Koschmann, London: Routledge 2007, 1–18: 1, and J. Victor Koschmann, 'Asianism's Ambivalent Legacy', *Network Power. Japan and Asia*, ed. Peter J. Katzenstein and Takashi Shiraishi, Ithaca: Cornell University Press 1997, 83–110: 83.

14. For a distinction between concepts and different conceptions of a concept see Gerald F. Gaus, *Political Concepts and Political Theories*, Boulder: Westview Press 2000, 32.
15. For a critique of Koselleck's project see Melvin Richter, 'Pocock, Skinner, and the Geschichtliche Grundbegriffe', *History and Theory*, 19 (1990), 38–70 and *The Meaning of Historical Terms and Concepts. New Studies on Begriffsgeschichte*, ed. Hartmut Lehmann/Melvin Richter, Washington: German Historical Institute Washington 1996.
16. Reinhart Koselleck, 'Begriffsgeschichte' [Conceptual History], *Lexikon Geschichtswissenschaft. Hundert Grundbegriffe* [Encyclopaedia of History Science. One Hundred Key Concepts], ed. Stefan Jordan, Stuttgart: Reclam 2002, 40–44: 43.
17. Wafula defines political discourse as 'any text uttered or written that may have political implications or that may influence the outcome of a communicative procedure politically'; see Richard Wafula, 'Language and Politics in East African Swahili Prose: Intertextuality in Kezilahabi's Dunia Uwanja Wa Fujo 'The World, A Playground of Chaos', *Surviving through obliqueness: language of politics in emerging democracies*, ed. Samuel Gyasi Obeng and Beverly Hartford, Hauppauge: Nova 2002, 19–29: 20. Observing that 'politics and discourse are inextricably intertwined', Gastil stated that in some sense 'all discourse is political'. In a narrower definition, however, political discourse has been defined as communication about political matters, for political purposes by political actors, in and out of government, which includes 'every citizen who deliberates and creates messages about civic affairs'. See John Gastil, 'Undemocratic discourse: a review of theory and research on political discourse', *Discourse & Society* 3–4 (October 1992), 469–500: 469. In recent years this broader and more democratic definition of political discourse, which includes the participation of non-professional political agents, has become widely accepted. Terence Ball, too, dismisses the notion that agents of political discourse are 'speakers of specialized sublanguages' but links discourse to language shared 'in our common capacity as citizens'; see Terence Ball, 'Conceptual History and the History of Political Thought', *History of Concepts: Comparative Perspectives*, ed. Iain Hampsher-Monk et al., Amsterdam: Amsterdam University Press 1998, 75–86: 79.

18. See Michel Foucault, *The Archaeology of Knowledge and The Discourse on Language*, New York: Pantheon 1972 and his 'Politics and the study of discourse', *The Foucault Effect: Studies in Governmentality*, ed. Colin Gordon et al., Chicago: University of Chicago Press 1991, 53–72.
19. W. B. Gallie, 'Essentially Contested Concepts', *Proceedings of the Aristotelian Society, New Series*, Vol. 56 (1956), 167–198: 169. Note that Gallie distinguishes such contestable concepts, which he calls 'essentially contested concepts', from non-essentially contested concepts, which refer to more factual descriptions. From Gallie's classification it becomes evident, however, that *political* concepts belong to the former category. Interestingly, one of his primary examples of an essentially contested concept is democracy.
20. See Gaus, *Political Concepts and Political Theories*, 32 and also Gallie, 'Essentially Contested Concepts', 176.
21. Richard Bellamy and Andrew Mason, 'Introduction', *Political concepts*, ed. Richard Bellamy and Andrew Mason, Manchester: Manchester University Press 2003, 1–3: 2.
22. See Ball, 'Conceptual History and the History of Political Thought', 82.
23. Ball, 'Conceptual History and the History of Political Thought', 82.
24. Heywood, in fact, implicitly suggests this point himself when he writes that 'facts and values are invariably interlinked, even apparently descriptive concepts being "loaded" with a set of moral and ideological implications'. See Andrew Heywood, *Key concepts in politics*, Basingstoke: Palgrave Macmillan 2000, 5.
25. See Heywood, *Key concepts in politics*, 5.
26. See J. Victor Koschmann, 'Constructing Destiny: Rōyama Masamichi and Asian Regionalism in Wartime Japan', *Pan-Asianism in Modern Japanese History. Colonialism, regionalism and borders*, ed. Sven Saaler and J. Victor Koschmann, London: Routledge 2007, 185–199: 185.
27. See Melvin Richter, 'Begriffsgeschichte Today—An Overview', *The Finnish Yearbook of Political Thought*, Vol. 3 (1999), 11–27: 15.
28. The best-known example of academic 'Asia' discourse from the later Meiji through the wartime periods is Stefan Tanaka's study of 'Far Eastern History' (Tōyōshi); see Stefan Tanaka, *Japan's Orient*: Rendering Pasts into History, Berkeley: University of California Press 1993.
29. Takeuchi Yoshimi, in several of his writings and most explicitly in his comparison of Chinese and Japanese modernity (1948), had also anticipated the rationale of Said's later critique of 'Western' construction and hegemony of the 'East'. On this aspect see Wolfgang Seifert, 'Japan und seine Moderne nach dem Asiatisch-Pazifischen Krieg: Takeuchi Yoshimis Intervention 1948' [Japan and its modernity after the Asian-Pacific War: Takeuchi Yoshimi's Intervention in 1948], *Intervalle 11. Schriften*

zur Kulturforschung. Japanische Intellektuelle im Spannungsfeld von Okzidentalismus und Orientalismus [Intervals 11. Writings on Cultural Research. Japanese intellectuals between Occidentalism and Orientalism], ed. Takemitsu Morikawa, Kassel: Kassel University Press, 75–120. For a discussion of 'Asia' as a European invention and pre-World War Two Japanese criticism of this binary see Tessa Morris-Suzuki, 'Invisible countries: Japan and the Asian dream', *Asian Studies Review* 22-1 (1998), 5–22, in particular 5–8.
30. Edward W. Said, *Orientalism*, New York: Vintage 1978, 1. Interestingly, throughout his influential book Said makes very little of Yellow Peril discourse as a form of Orientalism. He only once in passing refers to the 'dogma [...] that the Orient is at bottom something either to be feared (the Yellow Peril, the Mongol hordes, the brown dominions) or to be controlled (by pacification, research and development, outright occupation whenever possible)'; see Said, *Orientalism*, 301.
31. Said, *Orientalism*, 3.
32. Arif Dirlik, 'Chinese History and the Question of Orientalism', *History and Theory*, 35-4 (December 1996), 96–118: 104. Said had already, although rather vaguely, pointed out the complicity of 'the modern Orient [...] in its own Orientalizing'; Said, 1978, 325.
33. Dirlik, 'Chinese History and the Question of Orientalism', 114. Instead of 'nation' one could also use 'Asia' or 'region'.
34. It is this example that Dirlik mainly refers to; see Dirlik, 'Chinese History and the Question of Orientalism', 96–118.
35. Zhang Yiguo, 'Yazhou kongjiangan de fangfa lun yiyi' [The significance of the methodology of a spatial sentiment of Asia], *Shanghai Caijing Daxue Xuebao* [Journal of Shanghai University of Finance and Economics], Vol. 10, No. 1 (February 2008), 15–21: 20.
36. Zhang, 'Yazhou kongjiangan de fangfa lun yiyi', 20.
37. See Tanaka, *Japan's Orient*.
38. Tanaka, *Japan's Orient*, 21. Tanaka borrows this expression from Mikhail Bakhtin's theory of 'dialogical imagination', which views any dialogue (or discourse) as a hegemonic process involving a powerful knowing subject and a voiceless known object.
39. See Chap. 3.
40. I have decided to translate *keikōsei* as 'inclination' (Neigung) rather than using the more frequently employed term 'tendency', in order to emphasize its opposition to 'risei' (reason, in the sense of *Vernunft*). Following Kant's ethics, 'risei' refers to the 'ability to think conceptually', whereas 'keikōsei' is defined as a 'sensual pleasure which has become a custom' that, despite displaying some degree of consistency, does not contain any moral value. I find that this opposition best represents Takeuchi's

dismissal of the conceptual quality of Asianism in favour of a mere inclination. His choice of case studies included in the Asianism volume appears to confirm this view. See 'keikōsei', *Kōjien* [Wide Garden of Words], Tokyo: Iwanami Shoten 2003, 5th edition (electronic version).
41. As a consequence, Asianism was not perceived and studied as a political concept in its own right but only as an aspect of other concepts such as imperialism, nationalism, or fascism and, albeit rarely, anarchism and socialism. This conflation was mutually reinforced by Takeuchi's selection of groups and individuals that were assumed to represent Asianism best: the imperialist *Genyōsha* and *Kokuryūkai*, the fascist-minded Kita Ikki and Ōkawa Shūmei, and the Sinophiles Miyazaki Tōten and Ozaki Hotsumi, who had strong socialist leanings. It is interesting, however, that, while an intensive debate existed about the meaning and usefulness of the concept, few contemporaries appear to have viewed any of the above-mentioned, nor Okakura Tenshin or Tarui Tōkichi—largely unknown in Japan at the time but today viewed as Japanese Asianists *par excellence*—as 'representatives' of Asianism.
42. By and large, Takeuchi ignores the significance of the Taishō period, which—as we will see below—in fact constitutes the beginning of broader public discourse on Asianism in Japan as well as in China and in Western countries. None of the major Japanese contributors to Asianism discourse during that period features in Takeuchi's study. Only one out of eleven works he chose as representative of historical Asianism originates in the Taishō period. See Chap. 1.
43. Lee Gyeongseog, 'Takeuchi Yoshimi no Ajiashugi Ron no kōzō oyobi sho mondai' [The structure and some problems of Takeuchi Yoshimi's discussion of Asianism], *Waseda Seiji Kōhō kenkyū* [Waseda Research into Politics and Public Law] 64 (August 2000), 227–257: 228.
44. See Harada Katsumasa, 'Ajia Rentaishugi ni tsuite no kenkyū nōto' [Research Note on the Principle of Asian Solidarity], *Rekishi Hyōron* [History Review], Vol. 102 (January 1959), 28–37: 28, 37.
45. See Harada, 'Ajia Rentaishugi ni tsuite no kenkyū nōto', 63.
46. See, for example, 'Kindai Nihon to Ajia' (Modern Japan and Asia) as a special issue of *Dentō to Gendai* [Tradition and Contemporary], Vol. 32 (March 1975), including case studies on Tōyama Mitsuru and the Genyōsha, Kōtoku Shūsui, Uchida Ryōhei, Kita Ikka, Ōkawa Shumei, Tachibana Shiraki; 'Kindai Ajia no naka no Chūgoku to Nihon' (China and Japan in modern Asia) as a special issue of *Rekishi Kōron* [History Review], 5–4 (April 1979), including studies on the *Tōa Dōbun Shoin*, Sun Yat-sen, Kita Ikki, Ōkawa Shūmei; Kawahara Hiroshi, *Kindai Nihon no Ajia Ninshiki* [Modern Japanese Consciousness of Asia], Tokyo: Daisan Bunmeisha 1976, including studies of Sakuma Shōzan, Fukuzawa

Yukichi, Tarui Tōkichi, Okakura Tenshin, Kita Ikki and Ishiwara Kanji; *Kindai Nihon to Chūgoku* [Modern Japan and China], ed. Takeuchi Yoshimi and Hashikawa Bunzō, Tokyo: Asahi Sensho 1974, 2 volumes.
47. Wolfgang Seifert, *Nationalismus im Nachkriegs-Japan. Ein Beitrag zur Ideologie der völkischen Nationalisten* [Nationalism in Post-war Japan. On the Ideology of Ethnic Nationalists], Hamburg: Institut für Asienkunde 1977 (Reihe Mitteilungen, Bd. 91), 232–233.
48. Itō Teruo, *Ajia to Kindai Nihon: han shinryaku no shisō to undō* [Asia and modern Japan: Anti-invasionist thought and Movement], Tokyo: Shakai Hyōronsha 1990, 286 and 304.
49. Kodera's treatise had long remained neglected although it was first introduced to scholarship by Hashikawa Bunzō (1922–1983), a student of Maruyama Masao and member of Takeuchi Yoshimi's Sinophile *Chūgoku no Kai* (China Study Society), as early as the 1970s. See Hashikawa Bunzō, *Kōka Monogatari* [Yellow Peril Story], Tokyo: Chikuma shobō 1976, 1–5.
50. See Furuya Tetsuo, 'Ajiashugi to sono shūhen' [Asianism and its environs], *Kindai Nihon no Ajia Ninshiki* [Modern Japanese Asia Consciousness], ed. Furuya Tetsuo, Tokyo: Ryokuin Shobō 1996, 47–102.
51. See Furuya, 'Ajiashugi to sono shūhen', 48. Furuya refers to the time around World War One as the starting point of 'ideologized "Asia"'.
52. Furuya, 'Ajiashugi to sono shūhen', 48.
53. See Furuya, 'Ajiashugi to sono shūhen', 98.
54. See Hiraishi Naoaki, 'Kindai Nihon no Kokusai chitsujokan to "Ajiashugi"' [Modern Japanese views of the international order and 'Asianism'], *20seiki shisutemu 1: Kōsō to keisei* [20th century system 1: Design and Formation], ed. Tokyo Daigaku Shakai Kagaku Kenkyūjo, Tokyo: Tokyo Daigaku Shuppankai 1998, 176–211.
55. See Hiraishi, 'Kindai Nihon no Kokusai chitsujokan to "Ajiashugi"', 191–197.
56. See Yamamuro Shin'ichi, *Shisō Kadai toshite no Ajia* [Asia as a matter of thought], Tokyo: Iwanami Shoten 2001, 23.
57. Yamamuro, *Shisō Kadai toshite no Ajia*, 24.
58. Yamamuro, *Shisō Kadai toshite no Ajia*, 24.
59. For this second aspect see the Conclusion.
60. See Sheng Banghe, '19 shiji yu 20 shiji zhi jiaode Riben Yazhou zhuyi' [Japanese Asianism in the Transitional Period from the nineteenth to the twentieth centuries], *Lishi Yanjiu* [History Research], March 2000, 125–135: 125.
61. See Wang Xiangyuan, 'Cong "he bang", "yi ti" dao "da yaxiya zhuyi": Jindai Riben qinhua lilun de yi zhong xingtai' [From 'merged states', 'an integral whole' to 'Greater Asianism': A theoretical form for Japanese

invasion of China in modern times], *Huaqiao Daxue Xuebao* [Bulletin of Huaqiao University], February 2005, 77–84 and Qi Qizhang, 'Riben Da Yaxiya zhuyi tanxi: Jianyu Sheng Banghe Xiansheng shangque' [Exploring Japanese Greater Asianism: A Discussion with Mr. Sheng Banghe], *Lishi Yanjiu* [History Research], March 2004, 132–145.
62. Wang Ping, *Jindai Riben de Yaxiya zhuyi* [Modern Japanese Asianism]. Beijing: Shangwu Yinshuguan 2004, 15.
63. There is no historical proof of the factual existence of this organization.
64. See Wang, *Jindai Riben de Yaxiya zhuyi*, 10–11.
65. See Wang, *Jindai Riben de Yaxiya zhuyi*, 362–369. On Ishihara's so-called Asianism see Klaus Antoni, '"Wir Asiaten" (ware-ware Ajiajin)—Ishihara Shintarō und die Ideologie des Asianismus' ['We Asians'. Ishihara Shintarō and the ideology of Asianism], *Selbstbehauptungsdiskurse in Asien: China—Japan—Korea* [Discourses of Self-Affirmation in Asia: China, Japan, Korea], ed. Iwo Amelung et al., München: Iudicium 2003, 159–180.
66. Wang, *Jindai Riben de Yaxiya zhuyi*, 367.
67. See Wang, *Jindai Riben de Yaxiya zhuyi*, 366.
68. On recent Chinese political proposals for an adoption of Asianism see my 'Remembering or overcoming the past? "History politics", Asian identity, and visions of an East Asian Community', *Asian Regional Integration Review*, ed. Tsuneo Akaha, Tokyo: Waseda University 2011, 39–55 and the Conclusion of this book.
69. On the Japanese term *han Ajiashugi* (Pan-Asianism) Beasley writes, 'I do not recall having come across it in Japanese books or pamphlets before 1945'; see William G. Beasley, 'Japan and Pan-Asianism: Problems of Definition,, *Aspects of Pan-Asianism*, ed. Janet Hunter, London: Suntory Toyota International Centre for Economics and Related Disciplines, London School of Economics and Political Science 1987 (International Studies 1987/II), 1–16: 1.
70. See Beasley, 'Japan and Pan-Asianism', 1–16.
71. See Beasley, 'Japan and Pan-Asianism', 1–2.
72. Beasley, 'Japan and Pan-Asianism', 2.
73. See Sven Saaler, *Pan-Asianism in Meiji and Taishō Japan: A Preliminary Framework*, Tokyo: Deutsches Institut fur Japanstudien 2004 (Working Paper 02/4): 9–10, 25–27.
74. Saaler, *Pan-Asianism in Meiji and Taishō Japan*, 10.

CHAPTER 2

Studying Asianism: The Impact and Legacy of Takeuchi Yoshimi

Asianism is multifaceted. No matter how many definitions one assembles and classifies, it cannot be grasped as thought that has the shape of functioning in reality. This is not limited to Asianism but, in a sense, applies to all thought. This characteristic, however, is particularly strong in Asianism.[1]
—Takeuchi Yoshimi (1963)

This chapter discusses epistemological problems of Asianism as an object of study. What does it mean to study Asianism; how can Asianism be studied; and how has the way Asianism has been studied in the past shaped our understanding of Asianism? In particular, it addresses problems of definitions, of canonization, and of the predominance of dichotomies that have formed our perception of Asianism.

Takeuchi Yoshimi's Asianism

Studying Asianism in the past half-century has become almost synonymous with studying Takeuchi Yoshimi's Asianism. Although Takeuchi's seminal essay of 1963 was by no means the first post-war study of Asianism (see Introduction), it certainly constituted the first detailed enquiry into Japanese Asianism from the Meiji period to the end of World War Two. In addition, as the editor of the volume on Asianism in the notable series on 'Contemporary Japanese Thought', Takeuchi was not only given an authoritative format that reinforced the impact of his

© The Author(s) 2018
T. Weber, *Embracing 'Asia' in China and Japan*,
Palgrave Macmillan Transnational History Series,
https://doi.org/10.1007/978-3-319-65154-5_2

analysis but he could also establish a canon of Asianist thought by selecting essays—and omitting others—as primary sources for that volume. To be sure, in addition to the brilliance of his critical discussion of Japanese Asianism, these aspects contributed to the lasting impact Takeuchi's work had on any study of Asianism in the following decades.

One of Takeuchi's main legacies for the study of Asianism is his quest for a definition of Asianism, both in the classical sense of providing an answer to the question 'what is Asianism?' and, more indirectly, by exploring 'who represents Asianist thought and activity?' and 'where is the location of Asianism in the history of Japanese thought or, more generally, in Japanese history?'. Although Takeuchi's introductory essay alone, which exceeds fifty pages, provides an abundance of leads to answer these questions, post-1963 scholarship on Asianism has predominantly focused on two aspects of Takeuchi's approach: Asianism as a dependent 'inclination' (keikōsei) and Asianism as an expression of 'solidarity' (rentai). Takeuchi's provisional definition reads:

> In my view, Asianism is no thought that possesses any real content (jissai naiyō) and that can objectively be qualified but it must rather be understood as one inclination (hitotsu no keikōsei). Both within the Right and the Left we can classify things as Asianist and non-Asianist. It is this vague definition that I want to use provisionally. [...] Because, as I have prescribed above, Asianism is something that adheres as an inclination to different individual 'thought' (shisō), it is nothing that exists independently. However, no matter how much we remove, we must acknowledge that as a point of commonality the intention of solidarity of the countries of Asia – be it as an instrument of invasion or not (Ajia shokoku no rentai – shin'ryaku o shudan suru to ina to o towazu – no shikō) – is involved.[2]

In this minimal definition, Takeuchi emphasizes his understanding of Asianism as constituting an 'inclination', but also addresses the limitation of his view to the category of 'thought'. In other words, according to Takeuchi, Asianism as *thought* did not possess any actual content and did not exist independently of other thought. Asianism as *thought*, to Takeuchi, was a mere inclination. Takeuchi's focus on the philosophical-intellectual dimension of Asianism was natural in an essay for the series 'Contemporary Japanese *Thought*'. This, however, does not preclude the notion that Asianism was indefinable or that Asianism did not exist independently as something other than 'thought', for example as a political concept.[3] Clearly, Takeuchi was also interested in terminological, conceptual, and definitional problems on a functional level. Since it is crucial for the understanding of Takeuchi's approach to Asianism (and of his impact on subsequent scholarship), the opening section of his essay is reproduced here in greater length:

> Any discussion of Asianism first of all requires a definition of 'Asianism'. If it were a universal concept (fuhen gainen) like democracy or socialism, which to some degree possess a common understanding, I could save going to all the trouble of starting with a definition. I could directly embark on the main essay. Asianism, however, is special and it is horribly multifaceted. Everyone assigns different content to it. For the time being, I therefore have to set limitations. This does not mean, however, that I want to give a final definition. I cannot do such a thing. Even with the submission of this entire volume, I will probably not be able to present a final definition. [...]
>
> I have consulted some dictionaries which I had at hand but the definitions of Asianism are extremely diverse. Some define it as reactionary thought, others as expansionism or invasionism. Others define Asianism as a form of regionalist bloc thinking. Yet others treat Japanese Asianism separately to Sun Yat-sen's and Nehru's Asianism. It is probably not an overstatement to say that there are as many definitions as there are dictionaries.
>
> Already the names for Asianism are diverse. Sometimes it is called 'Greater Asianism' (Dai Ajiashugi), sometimes 'Pan-Asianism' (Han Ajiashugi). In place of 'Asia', the [Chinese] characters for 'Far East' (Tōyō), 'Orient' (Tōhō), or 'East Asia' (Tōa) are used. The use of the abbreviation of Asia by [the Chinese character of] *A* (Ch. Ya) can be seen in the idiom Raise Asia (Kō A), and an organization that used this idiom and added 'society' as its name already existed during the 1880s. We could certainly view it [the *Kō A Kai*] as an Asianist organization. In China, Asia is also called the 'Asian continent' (Jp. Ashū, Ch. Yazhou) and in English we have the term *Asianism*. Then there is [the Chinese character of] *han* (Ch. fan) as a transliteration of Pan which was adapted from terms such as 'Pan-Slavism', 'Pan-Germanism', 'Pan-Islamism' and others. Because this Pan-ism was globally in fashion from the end of the nineteenth century into the twentieth, in Japan around the same time 'Pan-Asianism' (Han Ajiashugi) became fashionable too. Subsequently it became replaced by 'Greater Asianism' (Dai Ajiashugi). As it exceeds my abilities to trace the changes of words and the meanings of words and this has no direct relation to my present task, I shall skip this part. I do not see a difference between calling it 'Greater Asianism', 'Pan-Asianism' or otherwise. I shall collectively refer to all of them as Asianism (Ajiashugi).[4]

This opening passage of Takeuchi's essay—simultaneously the opening section of the Asianism volume in the above mentioned series—reveals the importance Takeuchi attached to defining his object of study. While he conceded the multifaceted character of Asianism, Takeuchi nonetheless engaged in approaching Asianism first and foremost by determining terminological and conceptual aspects and limitations. Most of his stipulations have become commonly accepted knowledge and are rarely discussed by scholarship any more; 'Asia' as *Ajia* may not entirely be the same as the Chinese term *Yazhou*, and the same may be true for the pair *Tōyō* (East) and *Tōa* (East Asia). In Asianism discourse, however, these terms have mostly been used indiscriminately. This also applies to Takeuchi's subsuming of different terms under the name *Ajiashugi*. As the case studies in the following chapters will show, the differences in meaning between Asianism as 'Greater Asianism' or 'Pan-Asianism' are minimal and the debate about their differences—as well as the critique thereof—is informed by the larger context of Asianism's contents and viability. The nominal distinction between Asianism and Greater Asianism, therefore, is of little importance historically and has also been abandoned as an instrument of historiographical analysis.[5] On a side note, it is noteworthy that Takeuchi in passing placed the conceptual origin of Asianism in Japan in relation to other pan-isms of the time. Although he—like almost all subsequent scholars[6]—did not take up this reference again at any point, it serves as an important reminder of one of the political and intellectual contexts within which Asianism discourse in Japan and China was located historically: conceptually, Asianism was seen as corresponding to the trend of the times and terminologically, it imitated similar thought and activity in other parts of the world.

The most controversial point in Takeuchi's opening section, however, constitutes his classification of Asianism as a concept of no universal character. Unlike other well-established *ism*s, Takeuchi argued, Asianism was not a 'universal concept' (fuhen gainen). Of course, Asianism was never as widespread and commonly used as socialism (shakai shugi) and democracy (minshu shugi), the two *ism*s that Takeuchi explicitly mentions. Combined with his characterization of Asianism as a non-independent inclination, his comparison invites the potential misinterpretation of Asianism as an ahistorical concept or, at least, a concept of only peripheral diffusion or significance in history.

Defining Asianism

Takeuchi's struggle to come to terms with defining Asianism is well reflected in his above-quoted *bon mot*: 'as many definitions as there are dictionaries'. It would not be a difficult task to demonstrate that Takeuchi's observation is true for most thought, doctrines, or *isms*, not only for Asianism. One only has to think of the heated disputes between historians on whether German National Socialism may rightfully be subsumed under the term fascism and whether or not Japanese or Chinese movements of the 1930s and 1940s may be called fascist.[7] Similarly, the Swiss political system defines (its direct) democracy differently from many other (e.g. representative) democracies, which are different again from monarchical or presidential democracies, not to mention self-acclaimed democracies such as the Democratic People's Republic of Korea or the former German Democratic Republic. But Takeuchi's comparison should not be dismissed easily on the grounds of these reservations. Rather, it indicates a fundamental difference between Asianism and other *isms*, at least in Takeuchi's view: while there are blueprints for socialism and democracy and both ideas have, to some degree at least, been put into practice at certain times and certain places in history, Asianism has remained a utopia. Takeuchi, to be sure, refused to acknowledge the so-called Greater East Asian Co-Prosperity Sphere as an instance of Asianism. Instead, he criticized the reality of this project as well as its Asianist propagation as 'the end of Asianism' (Ajiashugi no kiketsu), a 'deviation from Asianism' (Ajiashugi kara no itsudatsu), and 'pseudo thought' (giji shisō).[8] As a consequence, to Takeuchi the problem of defining Asianism remained a difficult and abstract undertaking. Eventually, Takeuchi selected as closest to his own understanding of Asianism Nohara Shirō's entry in the *Encyclopaedia of Asian History*, which summarized 'Greater Asianism' (Dai Ajiashugi) as follows:

> The claim that the peoples of Asia should unite, with Japan as their leader (meishu toshite), in order to resist the invasion of Asia by the Euro-American powers (Ōbei rekkyō).[9]

As we shall see below, this brief definition by Nohara summarizes the historical understanding of Asianism rather well. With regard to Japanese Asianism during the first decades of the twentieth century, Nohara writes:

> [...] Greater Asianism was, together with Tennōism, selected as the main slogan by many right-wing groups and served Japan's policy of planning the seizure of Manchuria and Mongolia. In 1926 in Shanghai and in 1927 in Nagasaki[10] Greater Asianists held assemblies of the Eastern peoples. Against this, continuous criticism was voiced by the Chinese revolutionary forces. The *Minbao* [People's Paper], organ of the Chinese Revolutionary Alliance (Tongmenghui), named a popular union of the two countries of China and Japan one of its six main principles, proposed a union of equal relations and severely attacked Japan's annexationism – that is Greater Asianism (Dai Ajiashugi). Soon after, Li Dazhao censured it as a code word for the invasion of China in his essay of 1919, 'Greater Asianism and New Asianism'. He contrasted this with a new Asianism (shin Ajiashugi) which envisioned the liberation of the Asian peoples, the formation of a Greater Republic of Asia by an equal union which should then join with the European Republic, and the American Republic to form a World Republic. In a speech given in 1924 in Kobe, Sun Yat-sen urged [the Japanese] to choose: 'starting with Asia, we want to ally all oppressed peoples of the world to resist the powers that adhere to the culture of the Rule of Might. Will Japan become the watchdog of Western Rule of Might or the bulwark of Eastern Rule of Right?' This constituted a frank criticism of Japan's imperialism adorned with Greater Asianism.[11]

While Takeuchi's critique of Nohara's definition focused on aspects of Meiji Asianism,[12] Nohara's treatment of the Taishō and interwar period are of particular relevance for this study. Basically, Asianism of that period is absent from Nohara's entry, at least as far as Japanese Asianism is concerned. Implicitly, Nohara conflates all Japanese Asianism after the turn of the nineteenth century with Japanese imperialism and attributes the concept to the vocabulary of right-wing groups. Even the Pan-Asian Conferences of 1926 in Nagasaki and 1927 in Shanghai appear as part of right-wing activities in support of Japan's expansionism. As the analysis of the Conferences later will demonstrate (see Chap. 6), this assessment could not be more distant from historical reality. Nohara underlines his implication by contrasting Japanese 'Greater Asianism' with Chinese criticism from the period under study here. In other words, Nohara suggests that during the 1910s and 1920s Japanese Asianism (Greater Asianism) was characterized by a pro-government policy of aggression towards China and the Asian mainland, whereas Chinese Asianism (New Asianism) opposed this view and envisioned a peaceful union based on equality. As will become clear below, this binary portrayal is too simplistic. But Nohara must be given credit for having enlarged the scope of discussing and defining Asianism by including Chinese voices.[13] As a Sinologist, Takeuchi did not need this reminder, but Nohara's—and subsequently Takeuchi's—early consideration of non-Japanese contributions to Asianism discourse helped to create an awareness of the relevance of Asianism in public political debate during the interwar years outside of Japan too.

Probably owing to the limited number of historical sources available to him, in his effort to define Asianism Takeuchi omitted an interesting body of materials that would have thrown additional light on the contemporary understanding of Asianism and that could also have helped to put Nohara's definition into perspective: definitions of Asianism from encyclopaedias of the 1910s, 1920s, and 1930s. Which definitions did contemporaries encounter when they searched for authoritative information and widespread knowledge on Asianism? And how has this knowledge changed from the 1910s to the 1960s and today? The first definition of Asianism in a Japanese dictionary of neologisms is believed to have appeared in 1919 under the entry 'Pan-Asianism' (Han Ajiashugi)[14]:

> The principle (shugi) that demands that – resting on the fact that the 3000-year-old history of the Asian peoples is based on common race, religion, history, and material civilization – these peoples of Asia must once rise in unity to rebel against the world of the Whites of Europe and America (Ōbei no hakujin no sekai) and eventually subdue them under the hegemony of the East (Tōyō no haken).[15]

This definition not only spelt out the underlying Asianist assumption of Asian commonality, that is, a common past and shared heritage, but also left no doubt about Asianism's anti-Western political ambition in the present and future. Based on a racialist understanding of world order, it aimed—according to this earliest entry—at reversing this order by replacing Western hegemony with Eastern hegemony. Interestingly, the term *haken* (hegemony) was employed, which included the term *ha* as used in *hadō* (Ch. badao). This term, denoting *tyrannis*, despotism, or the Rule of Might, was typically reserved in modern political discourse as a denunciatory term for Western imperialism and contrasted to the Asian Rule of Right, benevolent rule, or literally the Kingly Way (Jp. ōdō, Ch. wangdao). If we take this early definition as authoritative or representative of Asianism during the late 1910s, it not only reveals the strongly reactionary and revisionist character of Asianism, but also indicates a possibly negative interpretation of the concept. Precisely because of these revisionist ambitions, it was not likely to gain support in mainstream political discourse in Japan. In addition, the reference to the 'hegemony of the East' reveals that the oppositional pair of (Western) *hadō* versus (Eastern) *ōdō*, which would later—in particular after Sun's Kobe speech—become so central in Asianism discourse, had not been part of the mainstream understanding of Asianism in 1919.[16]

In 1923, one year before the so-called anti-Japanese immigration legislation shook Japan's public political discourse and catapulted Asianism right to its centre (see Chap. 4), a slightly altered dictionary definition of 'Han Ajiashugi' (Pan-Asianism) provided a number of additional interesting insights:

> In English called Pan-Asianism. National mass movements (minzokuteki dai undō) that claim that the Asian peoples (Ajia minzoku) because of their innate racial and historical commonality should unite these commonalities to prepare for the future rivalry between the races of the world. Needless to say, Japan must be its leader (meishu).[17]

Asianism here is portrayed in a less aggressive manner although it is even more strongly linked to racialist notions. This tendency is hardly surprising, given the generally racialized political discourse following the Paris Peace Conference, the extension of anti-Asian immigration legislation in the United States, and the revival of Yellow Peril discourse there that eventually led to the nationwide ban on Asian immigration to the United States in 1924. By providing the English term, the definition implicitly referred to this context and, more generally, to the foreign origin of Pan-Asianism as a term and political concept. As we shall see later (Chap. 3), Asianism entered the mainstream of political discourse in Japan in 1913, when Japanese newspapers reported a public dispute on Japanese assimilation that originally took place in the London *Times* and the *New York Times*. Another difference between the 1923 and the 1919 definitions was the characterization of Asianism as a 'large movement' or 'mass movement'. In 1919, by contrast, Asianism appeared as a 'principle' (shugi), which indicated its largely theoretical character. By the mid-1920s, however, Asianism had inspired—or was used as a slogan or banner of—activities such as the formation of political organizations with an Asian-minded agenda that, unlike the notorious and more extreme and subversive *Genyōsha* (Dark Ocean Society) or *Kokuryūkai* (Black Dragon Society), advanced concrete political plans that were to be realized without revising or reversing the existing political order. Lastly, this new definition explicitly named Japan as the leader.

From the 1930s onwards, with the now undeniable political relevance of Asianism also definitions became more extensive. In Japan's first major modern encyclopaedia, published as a 28-volume work by the Heibonsha publishing house from 1931 to 1934, the entry on 'Pan-Asianism' was authored by Gushima Kanesaburō (1905–2004), a left-leaning scholar of international politics.[18]

> The movement which – presuming that the peoples in Asia possess thought, religion, and interests that are fundamentally different from those of the Euro-American peoples – plans a great union of the Asian peoples and, through this force, aims at expelling the Euro-American powers from the lands of Asia in order to build an Asia for Asians. This movement displays itself in different forms today but among these the most powerful movement is that which advances the self-determination of peoples. Its main claim is to rely on the joint cooperation of all Asian peoples to liberate the yellow race, which accounts for more than half of Asia's population and is completely dominated by the white races of Euro-America, from this control. [...] With Japan at its centre, in Nagasaki in 1926 and in Shanghai in 1927 Pan-Asian Conferences were held, but due to confrontations of opinions between Japanese and other delegates in the end they could not achieve any notable results. Recently, taking the opportunity of [Japan's] departure from the League of Nations, the opinion has once more been proposed strongly that in this case an Asian League should be created. However, in light of the vast extent of the Asian mainland and the great number of people living there and, furthermore, considering the confrontations over economic and political interests that occur one after another, there are strong doubts about the possibility of creating such a league.[19]

Gushima offers two new insights. First, he presents the key Asianist slogan—Asia for Asians—as the main aim of any Asianist thought and activity. Different from the oft-quoted motto 'same script, same race' (Jp. dōbun dōshu, Ch. tongwen tongzhong), which more narrowly refers to assumed Japanese–Chinese cultural and racial commonality, 'Asia for (the) Asians' summarized the political claim of Asianism, that is, self-determination, and the larger geographical scope, that is, Asia as opposed to just China and Japan. Second, Gushima mentions the aim of creating an Asian League as an alternative to the Geneva-based League of Nations. This claim had surfaced on several occasions before—for example, after the rejection of Japan's racial equality proposal of 1919—but prominently resurfaced, as Gushima points out, in the context of the Manchuria problem and Japan's departure from the League. Neither Nohara nor Takeuchi include this practical aim in their discussions of Asianism. In addition, it is noteworthy that Gushima, as Nohara would do twenty-seven years later, also refers to the Pan-Asian Conferences of 1926 and 1927 as the only cases of Asianist practice during the 1920s. Gushima, more accurately, attributes their failure to a clash of opinions between the respective representatives rather than characterizing the whole undertaking as driven by the Japanese Right.

This brief review of entries on Pan-Asianism in historical Japanese dictionaries and encyclopaedias suggests that from 1919 onwards, definitions of Asianism were readily accessible, not only indirectly from the large amount of pro- and anti-Asianist writings published since the early 1910s, but also via separate entries in dictionaries and encyclopaedias. Their authoritativeness as a means of spreading and defining knowledge may not be underestimated, given their wide accessibility and the high number of reprints. In addition, we see that during the time period under research Asianism was a rather well-defined political concept whose core ideas were presented as consisting of (I) Asian commonality and (II) resistance against the 'West'. While race and racial discrimination took a prominent position in locating Asianism within historical political discourse, Sun's conception of Asianism and the opposition between pro-Asianist and anti-Asianist concepts (*Datsu A* vs *Kō A*) or what were claimed to be 'Western' and 'Eastern' ways of rule (*badao* vs *wangdao*) played no major role yet. They therefore attest to the ahistoricity of these dichotomous pairs in the historiography of Asianism.[20]

What would Takeuchi discover if he were to consult present-day academic encyclopaedias for definitions of Asianism? And how is Takeuchi's influence reflected there? Extending the time frame proposed by both Nohara and Takeuchi (early Meiji to 1945), the temporal scope has been considerably enlarged and now ranges from the late eighteenth century to the present. Horii Kōichirō, for example, argues that 'the shoots of Asianism can already be seen in the Edo period' and refers to the debate on anti-foreignism (Jōi ron) of the later Edo years.[21] Nakamura Shunsaku locates the intellectual source of Asianism in the dissolution of the traditional Chinese world view that distinguished the civilized centre (China) and barbarian periphery (Jp. Ka-I shisō, Ch. Hua-Yi sixiang). During this period, Nakamura states, Japanese consciousness of the world outside Japan was remodelled and Asianism emerged as one stream of thought.[22] Katsurajima Nobuhiro, on the other hand, stresses that the premodern Confucian world view of *Ka-I* formed the basis of Asianist thought, since it rested on the assumed civilizational commonality among peoples in Asia.[23] In a similar manner, Asianism is linked with pre-Meiji expansionist thought of the *Rangakusha* (scholars of Dutch or Western Learning) Honda Toshiaki (1743–1820), Satō Nobuhiro (1769–1850), and Hashimoto Sanai (1834–1859), or with Yoshida Shōin (1830–1859) and the *Movement to Revere the Emperor and Repel the Barbarians* (Sonnō Jōi Undō) of the 1850s and 1860s. Hirano Ken'ichirō has described their impact on later Asianist thought as having linked the Japanese 'consciousness of crisis' (kiki ishiki) with the claim to preserve independence not simply by defending oneself but by 'proactively developing and expanding abroad'.[24]

Transcending the temporal borderline of 1945, Nakamura states that 'most of this [pre-1945 Asianism] has become the object of criticism, but, on the other hand, in the vogue of civilizational discourse of the post-Cold War era there is also the tendency for a transformation and revival [of Asianism] within the new discourse of "Return to Asia" (Ajia kaiki)'.[25] The 'Return to Asia' debate of the 1990s was part of the Asian Values debates that recycled some of the pre-1945 assumptions of Asian cultural commonality with implications for a political reorientation against the 'West' and 'Western' values, such as democracy and freedom of speech.[26] Kagami Mitsuyuki has proposed a quite different extension of Asianist thought and activity beyond 1945. To him,

Takeuchi Yoshimi's refusal to completely dismiss Asianism but instead to engage in self-reflection (hansei) and re-evaluate historical Asianism in parts forms the vital link between wartime and post-war Asianism. Kagami views post-war activities by Japanese civil society groups such as the Society for the Support of Cambodian Refugees or the Society for the Cooperation of Ophthalmologists to support 'less developed' countries in East and Southeast Asia as instances of the realization of 'solidarity' (rentai) which Takeuchi had placed at the centre of his conception of Asianism.[27] As opposed to the rationale of previous Asianism, Kagami concludes, this post-war Asianism was not aiming at—or purporting to aim at—establishing equal relations of solidarity between *countries* but rather focused on 'establishing relations of co-existence and solidarity in the relations between human beings and [other] human beings as the ones who are "living" [ordinary lives] (seikatsusha toshite)'.[28]

Two more factors in the comparison of Nohara's and more recent definitions of Asianism are noteworthy: first, the opposition—rather than interdependence—of Japanese and Chinese Asianism which is inherited from Nohara and, second, the emergence of a variety of dichotomies as an instrument for defining Asianism. Following Nohara's definition of 1960, the sense of a monolithic opposition between Chinese and Japanese conceptions of Asianism has prevailed until today. Horii even suggests that, not only for the Chinese but also for most other non-Japanese Asians, Asianism represented 'nothing but an expedient of invasion'. However, like Nohara, Horii only refers to a very limited number of Chinese cases, namely Li Dazhao's critique of Japanese Greater Asianism and Sun Yat-sen's Kobe speech. Interestingly, however, he slightly breaks up this binary opposition by including—as a negative Chinese example—Wang Jingwei's use of 'Asianism in the broad sense of the term' to propagate his policy of Sino-Japanese alliance and collaboration (see Chap. 7).[29] Horii's definition therefore includes the possibility of cases of self-acclaimed Asianism not only by Japanese but also by Chinese. Nevertheless, the predominant comparative view of Japanese and Chinese Asianism has remained one of incompatibility, opposition, and rejection. The entry on 'Greater Asianism' (Dai Ajiashugi) in the *Encyclopaedia of the Nations of the World* is even subdivided into two parts: Japanese Asianism and Sun Yat-sen's Asianism. In the former part, Hatsuse Ryūhei claims that the Japanese understanding of Greater Asianism totally differed from Sun's argument of 'international equality' and explains this by highlighting the different 'international conditions of both [countries]'. In the latter part, Fujii Shōzō argues that Sun's conception of Asianism was first formed during his time as a refugee in Japan and originally shared many features with Japanese conceptions of Asianism. Eventually, however, according to Fujii, Sun's conception changed into one that conflated Japan's Asia policy with that of the Western powers and therefore stood in opposition to the Asianist essence of *wangdao* (Kingly Way).[30] In this way, Sun's historical distinction itself has become the rationale of historiographical analysis that distinguishes imperialist-leaning Japanese Asianism from benevolent Chinese Asianism, in particular Sun's Asianism.

The Chinese *Encyclopaedia of Isms*, interestingly, completely ignores any Chinese examples of Asianism. Instead, its entry on 'Greater Asianism' (Da Yaxiya zhuyi) traces the changes from its affiliation with the proposal for people's rights in the early 1890s (Tarui Tōkichi), when neither the intention of invasion nor Japan's leadership had been prominent, to its conflation with 'Japanese fascism' during World War Two (Greater East Asian Co-Prosperity Sphere, 1940 and Greater East Asia Joint Declaration, 1943). At an undefined moment in between, according to the entry, Asianism became the 'rationalization of Japan's invasive conduct' while purporting 'to protect Asia from the invasion by the Euro-American powers'.[31]

Another prominent pattern of defining Asianism is by means of dichotomies. The problems associated with this phenomenon will be addressed in the following section, but, here, it should already be noted that dichotomies dominant today seemed to have played a smaller role in the historical definitions of Asianism. Naturally, Asianism's 'Asia' has always been opposed to the 'West', 'Euro-America', or, in a racialist inflection, the 'Whites'. In present-day definitions, however, the range of oppositional pairs has considerably broadened. In addition to Sun's *wangdao* versus *badao* dichotomy, which Nohara had prominently employed, Takeuchi's distinction between solidarity (rentai) and invasion (shinryaku) has taken a prominent place in definitions of Asianism. Takeuchi had contradicted Nohara's view of a turn or conversion from Asianism (as solidarity) to Greater Asianism (as invasion) but argued for a co-habitual relation between both: solidarity and invasion were two co-existing sides of the same coin of historical Asianism. Nakamura follows this suggestion and argues that pre-1945 Asianism discourse is characterized by 'views of Asia held by modern Japanese intellectuals that have blended solidarity and invasion'. Asianism's basic goal and assumption, according to him, was the 'unity and solidarity of "Asia" ("Ajia" no ittai, rentai to iu koto)'.[32] Similarly, Katsurajima suggests that the 'dangerous balance between "invasion" and "solidarity"' was part of Asianism discourse from its earliest days.[33]

The most powerful—and ahistorical—dichotomy that serves to define Asianism today has become the *Datsu A* versus *Kō A* divide. This dichotomy, too, will be addressed in more detail below but here it should be noted that for definitions of Asianism this distinction provides a convenient tool to link Asianism to the now widely known political concept of *Datsu A* (Departing from Asia, dissociating from Asia) in order to define Asianism *ex negativo*. Nakamura, for example, defines Asianism as political thought that 'consisted of the genealogy of mainly advocates of *Kō A* [Raise Asia] within the bifurcated search for an image of the country of either "Datsu A" or "Kō A" which took place in the context of Japan's advanced Westernization and modernization compared to other countries within Asia'.[34] In other words, Asianism may be seen as representing the position of Raising Asia (Kō A), thus the opposite of *Datsu A*. Hatsuse confirms this view:

> Japan's choice was to either fight Euro-American imperialism together with the peoples of the neighbouring Asian countries or to become itself a Euro-American-style country (Ōbei ryū no kokka) and control the neighbouring countries as its colonies. To express this intellectually, the former [position] is Asianism (Ajiashugi) and the latter is *Datsu A*.[35]

However, Hatsuse admits that this view—albeit widely used today—represents a stereotype that does not fully correspond with historical reality.[36] 'In reality', Hatsuse continues, 'these two lines are entangled and there were people who idealistically advanced the former but in reality argued for the latter position.'[37] Takeuchi's impact and legacy on the study of Asianism could hardly be summarized more appropriately in just one sentence: Asianism was ambiguous, not least because many of those who claimed to be Asianists were in fact not Asianists. At this point, it becomes clear that Asianism historically and historiographically cannot be understood without an awareness of the political implications of Asianist self-references, the instrumentalization of Asianist concepts, the desire to be perceived as Asianist (or as non-Asianist), and the rehabilitation (or rejection) of Asianism after World War Two. All of these issues are—sometimes strongly, sometimes only implicitly—reflected in the way scholarship has engaged with the creation and revision of an Asianist canon.

Asianism and Canons

Definitions in encyclopaedias, of course, do more than define objects of study. They also set up canons and they reflect the existing canonization of thinkers and works on the object of study in a condensed form. Nohara's and Takeuchi's impact on the canonization of Asianist thinkers and works was particularly strong for two reasons: first, they belonged to the very first to have worked on Asianism after the concept had become dissolved from the so-called Asianist 'reality' of the Japanese empire in Asia. Nohara's entry of 1960 was probably the first on Asianism to appear in any post-war encyclopaedia or dictionary, save for the *Kōjien*[38]; second, as briefly addressed at the beginning of this chapter, Takeuchi's edited volume constituted the first book-length approach to studying Asianism after 1945 and included—as did all volumes of that series—reproductions of primary sources that would naturally form the core of an Asianist canon.

As much as canons provide orientation and facilitate debate by providing a joint basis of knowledge, they have also been identified as highly problematic, particularly in the field of the history of political thought. Siep Stuurman has summarized the criticisms of canons as consisting of (I) a democratic and (II) a methodological critique.[39] These criticisms are informed by the following self-reflective questions posed by historians to historians:

> 1. Whose history is this, and on what grounds are a limited number of authors awarded canonical status? This leads to the democratic critique.
>
> 2. How historical is such a history? Can it ever do full justice to the 'otherness' of times past? This leads to the methodological critique.[40]

As for the democratic critique, the focus of scholarship on 'great thinkers'—in a mixture of sarcasm and irony often referred to as 'Dead White European Males (DWEMs)'—according to critics, has led to the 'omission of "plebeian", non-Western, and female voices from the traditional canon'.[41] To counter this deficit, historians needed to undertake '[h]istorical rescue operations'[42] to save alternative voices from oblivion. The methodological critique, on the other hand, highlights the 'anachronistic' and 'Whiggish'[43] character of the construction of such canons. Referring to two of the most influential contemporary historians of political thought, Quentin Skinner and John Pocock, Stuurman explains:

As Quentin Skinner forcefully argued in 1969, the history of political thought is constructed *ex post*, by interpreting earlier authors as forerunners of later ones, thus replacing their original context with the anticipation of a future they could not possibly foresee. At this point, the methodological critique comes close to the democratic one: both reject the traditional canon as a form of *Whig history*. Skinner proposed to interpret texts in political theory as parts of specific debates, 'speech acts' wherein authors are making specific 'points' in a particular intellectual as well as political discursive space. Intellectual history is thus represented as a perpetual sequence of 'moves' and 'counter-moves', in which authors and texts compete for prominence and legitimacy: some succeed and others are marginalized. Canons are thus constructed, deconstructed, and reconstructed all the time. John Pocock, whose work has exerted an enormous influence, suggests that we ought to study not so much systematic and well-polished philosophies, still less isolated individual theorists, but rather political languages, modes of discourse available to people discussing political affairs in particular times and places.[44]

Certainly, one could easily dismiss both streams of criticism as a desperate search for a politically correct canon, which in itself is a 'Whiggish' enterprise, since it responds to the powerful demands of today's political correctness and would itself be subject to changing political climates. However, one must also acknowledge the constructive character of this critique, which, by means of proposed alternatives, has stimulated the field of intellectual history. As Stuurman has summarized, this critique has brought about a shift of focus 'from "thinkers" to "thinking", and from "theories" to "arguments"'.[45] The boom in studies of political thought that take a conceptual history approach—to which this book also subscribes—is conventionally seen as one constructive outcome of this critique.

What does this mean for the study of Asianism? As the review of the state of the field in the Introduction has revealed, 'great thinkers' have, until recently, dominated the historiography of Asianism. Also, definitions in encyclopaedias naturally include only a very limited number of thinkers and works. Still, the Asianist canon is relatively diverse. This is probably owing to Takeuchi's ambivalent definition of Asianism as an 'inclination'. This characterization allowed for the inclusion of a wide range of thought and thinkers to be identified as Asianist, ranging from early civil rights activists Ueki Emori (1857–1892) and Ōi Kentarō (1843–1922) to the art historian and idealist Okakura Tenshin

(1862–1913), and from Sun Yat-sen's friend Miyazaki Tōten (1870–1922) to wartime Socialist Ozaki Hotsumi (1901–1944) and fascist-inclined Ōkawa Shūmei (1886–1957), who was later persecuted as a A-class war criminal. In addition, as Takeuchi only hinted at, there is no 'bible' of Asianism that was regarded by contemporaries as the blueprint of Asianist thought or is regarded as such today by scholarship. Neither Okakura Tenshin—whose 'Asia is One' has been identified as a key Asianist slogan—nor Sugita Teiichi, the author of the *Kō A Saku* [Raise Asia Policy],[46] an early pamphlet advocating Japan's commitment to raising Asia, have gained the status of *the* representative work of Asianism. This lack of a model has surely encouraged the study of a wide range of materials as sources of Asianist thought. The situation is slightly different regarding Chinese Asianism. As mentioned above, the attention of scholarship clearly focuses on Sun Yat-sen, Li Dazhao, and Wang Jingwei. While Wang is discredited as a collaborator with the Japanese and Li is more well known as a Socialist and critic of Asianism, it is usually Sun's writings and speeches on Asianism that are portrayed as the most impactful, affirmative contribution to Asianism discourse. As has been discussed above (regarding definitions of Asianism) and will be discussed again later (Chap. 7), Sun's influence on Asianism discourse was unparalleled historically. Nevertheless, since Japan (not China) was the hub of debates about Asianism, and because of Sun's premature death (in 1925), his conception of Asianism ultimately failed to become *the* Asianist template.

The relatively wide range covered by the Asianist canon, however, has its blind spots too. One grave consequence of the focus on prominent and illustrious thinkers on the one hand and of the overwhelming influence of Nohara's and Takeuchi's early studies of Asianism on the other, is the almost complete absence of the 1910s and 1920s from the canon. As analysed above, Nohara did not include any writings from that period but focused on Meiji and early Shōwa Asianism and referred to the pan-Asian conferences of 1926 and 1927 only in passing. Takeuchi's canon, as established by his choice of primary sources, displays a similar focus: Okakura's *Tōyō no Risō* (Ideals of the East) from 1903 and Tarui Tōkichi's *Dai Tō Gappō Ron* (Great Union of the East) from 1893 as the two 'fundaments' (genri); Miyazaki Tōten's *Sanjūsan Nen no Yume* (Thirty-three Years' Dream) from 1902, and three essays dealing with Sun Yat-sen's early Japanese comrade Yamada Yoshimasa (1868–1900), Tōyama Mitsuru (1855–1944) of the *Genyōsha*, and the Indian revolutionary Rash Behari Bose (1886–1944) as 'sentiments' (shinjō); *Nikkan*

Gappō (Japan–Korea Union), dating from 1932, by Uchida Ryōhei (1874–1937) of the *Kokuryūkai*, and two essays each by Ōkawa Shūmei, dating from 1922 and 1951, and Ozaki Hotsumi, dating from 1939 and 1941, as 'logic' (ronri). Of all the selected writings, only Ōkawa's 'Kakumei Yōroppa to fukkō Ajia' (Revolutionary Europe and Asia in Revival), taken from his *Fukkō Ajia no sho mondai* (Various Problems of Asia in Revival),[47] was published in the Taishō period.[48] Although Takeuchi had more space to include a great variety of thinkers in his analytical essay (kaisetsu) and does in fact include occasional references to the 1910s and 1920s, his focus too lies on the Meiji and early Shōwa years: from Asianism's links with the *Movement for Freedom and Civil Rights* (Jiyū Minken Undō) of the 1880s to its monopolization by the Right at the end of the Meiji period[49] and its ideologization and deconstruction as thought during World War Two. The absence of a 'great' piece of writing by a 'great thinker' may have caused Takeuchi to skip the years in between, which, as this book hopes to demonstrate, however, belong to the most important and exciting periods of Asianism discourse in transnational Chinese–Japanese history—maybe exactly because of this absence of an undisputed template of Asianism.

A different kind of 'great thinkers' problem or, maybe more adequately, 'famous politicians' problem can be attested to the treatment of Chinese Asianism. Sun Yat-sen's and Li Dazhao's contributions temporally fill 'the Taishō gap in Japanese Asianism'. However, the inclusion of Chinese voices beyond the level of prominence of Li, Sun, and Wang Jingwei remains a *desideratum*. Stuurman's critique of the lack of inclusion of 'non-Western thinkers' in Western historiography of political thought could be transferred to non-Japanese thinkers in the case of Asianism. Apart from the above-mentioned prominent exceptions they are hardly, if ever, considered part of Asianist discourse. As outlined in the Introduction, it is one main aim of this book to enlarge and therefore 'democratize' the range of publications and writers hitherto studied as part of historical Asianism. Explicitly, this includes non-Japanese contributions, which account for one transnational dimension of this discourse. Many of the thinkers studied here, in fact, are not part of the existing canon of Asianism. To borrow Stuurman's phrasing, it is one aim of this book to participate in a 'historical rescue operation' that seeks to save lesser-known contributions to the formation of Asianist thought from oblivion.

Regarding the epistemological problems of studying Asianism, the methodological critique of studying canons of political thought appears even more relevant than the democratic critique. As will be addressed again later, Takeuchi's study of Asianism is obviously informed by his pro-Asianist political agenda; although he was by no means a historical revisionist (see Chap. 8), Takeuchi sought to rediscover positive aspects of Asianism[50] that would potentially encourage the Japanese to get interested again in 'Asia' and put into perspective both Asianism's conflation with Japanese imperialism and the dominant Western orientation of the Japanese after 1945. An additional problem is the partially anachronistic character of the canon of Asianism. What has been studied as Asianism or part of Asianism discourse in the past few decades may not necessarily have been regarded as part of that discourse contemporarily, or may not even have been widely known at all: for example, Fukuzawa Yukichi's 'Datsu A Ron' of 1885—the assumed antithesis of Asianism—or Okakura Tenshin's *The Ideals of the East*, originally written and published in English in 1903. Okakura's book includes the famous Asianist line 'Asia is One', but was not translated into Japanese until the 1930s.[51] From the mid-1990s, however, the study of Asianism in Japan as a concept or as discourse, as discussed in the Introduction, has contributed to a gradual historicization of the Asianist canon. As a consequence, '"moves" and "counter-moves", in which authors and texts compete for prominence and legitimacy' (Stuurman on Skinner) have begun to become integrated into the existing canon of Asianism and, as a consequence, this canon has become even more diversified, nuanced, and historical.

ASIANISM AND DICHOTOMIES

Lastly, as the review of historical and contemporary definitions and canons of Asianism have revealed, studying Asianism centrally involves studying dichotomies. By and large, scholarship has designed or adopted a 'schema of binominal opposition of Asianism and *Datsu A*'[52] and interpreted Asianism as the 'antithesis' of *Datsu A*,[53] the famous concept attributed to Fukuzawa Yukichi (1834–1901), which argues for Japan's dissociation and difference from 'Asia' (see Chap. 3). Within this schema, Asianism is seen as representing the concept of *Kō A* or Raising Asia, the more obvious opposition of *Datsu A*. Historically, this polarity has been traced back to the 1880s, when Sugita Teiichi penned an essay called 'Kō A Saku' (Raising Asia Policy) and Sone Toshitora's *Kō A Kai*

(Raise Asia Society) was founded. Around the same time Fukuzawa published his 'Datsu A Ron' and—in reaction to the foundation of the *Kō A Kai*—people called for the establishment of *Datsu A Kai* (Dissociating from Asia Society).[54] Asianism as *Kō A* therefore highlights Japan's engagement with and interest in 'Asia', for whichever reasons, whereas *Datsu A* as anti-Asianism stands for Japan's disinterest in and disregard of 'Asia'. While the latter position openly answers the question of Japan's own Asianity and belonging to Asia in the negative, the former includes the option of engaging with 'Asia' as an essential part of Asia. Ultimately, however, both positions suggest that 'Asia' is one of Japan's 'Others', namely its neighbouring, backward 'Other', which either needs to be distanced discursively from Japan (Datsu A) or must be revived following the model—and leadership—of Japan (Kō A). The underlying assumptions of both positions are geographical and cultural-racialist proximity, which are considered to be potentially dangerous, either because Japan itself may become regarded as part of the backward 'East' (Datsu A) or because Japan may be negatively affected by political instability nearby (Kō A). In the case of Asianism, however, they include the possibility of shared interests between Japanese and other Asians and therefore put both essentialist and nation-centred arguments into perspective. In a similar manner, Okakura Tenshin's 'Asia is One'—suggesting Asian unity and commonality—has become employed as a variation of *Kō A* and another counterpart of Fukuzawa's *Datsu A*.[55]

This Asianist *Kō A*/'Asia is One' versus anti-Asianist *Datsu A* dichotomy is, of course, premised on a more fundamental opposition, namely between 'Asia' or the 'East' (Tōyō) and the 'West' (Seiyō). Historically this contrast was not—or not mainly—of a geographical nature. Rather, it indicated assumed substantial differences in culture and civilization as well as in race, political reality, and strategy. As politico-civilizational binaries, they became widely known as the above-mentioned Kingly Way (Jp. ōdō, Ch. wangdao) as the Confucian ideal of benevolent Rule of Right *versus* the despotic Rule of Might (Jp. hadō, Ch. badao), represented by the unjust rule by force of Western imperialism. *Kō A* in this culturalist sense epitomizes the ambition to resist discursive and practical discrimination against 'Asia' at the hands of the 'Whites' (hakujin) and 'Euro-Americans' (Ōbeijin), who had not only colonized most of Asia but also demonized its peoples as 'Yellow Peril'.[56] The real danger, however, not only Asianists argued, was the 'Whites' themselves (Fig. 2.1) and early twentieth-century positions that resembled Asianism were

Fig. 2.1 White Peril cartoon. 'Doitsu Kōtei no manako ni eijitaru Kōjinshu Dōmei' [The Alliance of Yellow Peoples as reflected in the eyes of the German Emperor], *Yomiuri Shinbun*, 1 October 1900, p. 1. In a satirical allusion to the famous Knackfuss painting the cartoon shows armed Asian warriors, led by Confucius, in place of the assembly of Europeans led by Saint Michael. Confucius warns of Christian missionaries, represented by a large ship and a cross, and he is portrayed as saying: 'Peoples of Asia, protect your holiest Gods!'. Reproduced by kind permission of Yomiuri Shinbun, Tokyo

therefore also known as the 'White Peril Thesis' (Hakka Ron). *Datsu A*, on the other hand, is seen to represent the Japanese ambition to distinguish Japan from the 'other Asians'; in the politico-cultural realms it advances Western modernity to replace 'outdated' Confucianism,[57] while racially it refers to attempts to include the Japanese as 'honorary Whites' in the category of Caucasians.[58] Consequently, the departure from 'Asia' is envisioned as a complete leaving behind of (Chinese) traditions to enter the sphere of the 'West' (nyū Ō) as an equal partner. Placed in this context of dichotomies, Asianism as a political concept inevitably represents one polarity of a bipolar system whose extremities are relatively well defined, whereas the qualitative and quantitative range in between remains obscure. Unavoidably, Asianism, if seen within this framework, itself becomes a stereotype whose appropriateness and authenticity—or inappropriateness and inauthenticity—historical research cannot prove without leaving behind the 'arrangement of binominal antithesis'[59] it has proposed to study in the first place.

Another problem of studying Asianism within the *Datsu A* versus *Kō A* divide lies in the continuous political and politicized character of defining Japan's historical and contemporary relations with 'Asia' in a dualistic manner. *Datsu A*, rediscovered in post-war Japan to account for the new relations between the country and the United States forced upon Japan after World War Two, symbolizes pro-Americanism (or positive views of alliances with other 'Western' countries). Historically it represents the road not taken from the 1930s onwards and the road to which Japan was forced to return after 1945. Asianism, then, even after the normalization of Japanese–Chinese relations in 1972, was suspicious of anti-American, pro-Communist, or at least pro-Chinese inclinations. Ironically, in the highly politicized context of defining Japan's cramped position between 'Asia' and the 'West', Asianism could also symbolize the exact opposite, namely the glorification of Tennō-centrism, Japan's wartime imperialism, militarism, fascism—and anti-China*ism*.[60] Of course, the cases of Asianism that both types refer to are fundamentally different. Nevertheless both are informed by the either-or framework in which the Japanese 'Self' either poses as the leader of the Asian 'Other' or as a loyal—albeit grudging—follower of the Western 'Other'.

This picture is partly relieved, but also further complicated, by another binary set which does not aim at distinguishing Asianism from anti-Asianism but rather contrasts two streams *within* Asianism: solidarity (rentai) and invasion (shinryaku).[61] On the one hand, studying Asianism from this perspective, above all, distinguishes between the different kinds of visions and policies that were advanced in the name of Asianism. They could either emphasize (I) cooperation and like-mindedness as an expression of solidarity or (II) aggression and oppression as a means and result of invasion. Rather than being dichotomous, the solidarity *versus* invasion set may be seen as representing the ambiguous character inherent in Asianist proposals and practices within the given historical circumstances of nationalist antagonisms and grave political and economic imbalances within Asia. This distinction of Asianist intentions can—as the following chapters demonstrate—be traced back to historical Asianism discourse and has become a dominant pattern of interpretation following Takeuchi Yoshimi's famous minimal definition of Asianism as 'the intention of solidarity of the countries of Asia'[62] and a 'condition of a subtle separation and combination of invasionism and the consciousness of solidarity'.[63] This ambivalent character of Asianism, on the other hand, however, sets up an even more intricate and convoluted dichotomy of scholarly appraisal and political orientation by establishing a distinction between 'self-acclaimed' and 'real' Asianism which inevitably leads to a normative critique of Asianism that separates 'good' Asianism from 'bad' Asianism. It was Takeuchi who first introduced a distinction between 'self-acclaimed' Asianism, which he branded 'void of intellectual character' (jishō Ajiashugi no hi shisō sei), and 'real' (hon mono) Asianism.[64] The latter, according to Takeuchi, did 'not chase after the trend of the times' but openly confessed to its interest in Asia—as solidarity or invasion or a blend of both—when Asianism was still unpopular.[65] Although he provides examples for the former (Hirano Yoshitarō) and the latter types (Genyōsha, Sun Yat-sen), Takeuchi's definition of 'real' Asianism remains vague. How can we distinguish between real intentions and mere lip service in the field of political thought? Are only those who have a history of propagating Asianism before Asianism was appropriated from above 'real' Asianists? Where do we draw the line between substantial Asianism and self-acclaimed or empty Asianism? Who is to decide where this line should be drawn? Studying Asianism from the perspective of conceptual history, the following chapters propose to adopt a different approach that is less concerned with distinguishing 'real' from 'fake' Asianists. Instead, it focuses on the definition and functions of different conceptions of Asianism in the conceptual contest for authority, authenticity, and hegemony. At the same time, however, Takeuchi's *caveat* against overlooking the real intentions behind Asianist proposals or proposals in the name of Asianism must form the premise of any critical study of Asianism.

Conclusion

Rescuing Asianism from the cliché of binominal polarity comes at the price of vagueness. Takeuchi has addressed this ambivalence by coining the above-quoted minimal definition, which prioritizes solidarity as Asianism's core substance. The impact of Takeuchi's Asianist-inclined scholarship of Asianism has been so strong that some have started to use Asianism (Ajiashugi) as an equivalent of Asian Solidarity (Ajia Rentai).[66] As a consequence, Asianism is rescued from its conflation with aggression, invasion, and imperialism. But is Takeuchi's

Asianism not too positive and even apologetic at times?[67] Clearly, his pro-Asianist study of historical Asianism is also a product of his times. As Takeuchi's work *in toto* makes clear, he was highly critical of the predominant orientation in Japan and among the Japanese towards the 'West'. He not only criticized the Japanese lack of sense of resistance against the 'West' compared to that of China[68] but also encouraged young Japanese to discover alternatives to 'Western' modes of thought and of life within Asia.[69] Takeuchi's politico-intellectual agenda apparently informed his search for alternatives to dismissing Asianism in totality as either lacking intellectual content or having only functioned as a fig-leaf for Japanese imperialism.

At any rate, for Takeuchi Asianism was an 'inclination' that he shared. In order to rescue its history from the previous appropriation by the military and political leadership during the 1930s and 1940s, it almost had to be reduced to a multifaceted and dependent inclination. The war had demonstrated that Asianism could be used as a means to propagate aggression and invasion but Takeuchi refused to let this history monopolize the contemporary understanding of 'Asia' and of Asianism. As an inclination, it could also be part of other agendas and express itself, for example, in civil society or scholarly engagement with 'Asia' that was sympathetic to Asia and the Asians. Asianism as an expression of solidarity enabled the Japanese to speak affirmatively of 'Asia' again less than twenty years after the end of World War Two without dismissing the entire history of Japanese 'Asia' consciousness. In this sense, the ambiguity of Asianism, which stems only partly from its history but also partly from its historiography (with Takeuchi's influence being monumental) has nurtured the continuous scholarly interest in 'Asia'.

Notes

1. See Takeuchi Yoshimi, 'Ajiashugi no tenbō' [The prospect of Asianism], *Ajiashugi* [Asianism], ed. Takeuchi Yoshimi, Tokyo: Chikuma Shobō 1963, 7–63: 12. Compare Christian Uhl's German translation 'Der japanische Asianismus'(Japanese Asianism), *Japan in Asien. Geschichtsdenken und Kulturkritik nach 1945* [Japan in Asia. Historical Thought and Cultural Critique after 1945], ed. and translated by Wolfgang Seifert and Christian Uhl, München: Iudicium 2005, 121–189 and Uhl's 'Takeuchi Yoshimi: "Japan's Asianism", 1963', *Pan-Asianism: A Documentary History 1860–2010*, Vol. 2, ed. Sven Saaler and Christopher

W. A. Szpilman, Boulder: Rowman & Littlefield 2011, 317–326, which includes a partial English translation. Quote reproduced with kind permission of Takeuchi Hiroko.
2. Takeuchi, 'Ajiashugi no tenbō', 12, 14.
3. As briefly discussed in the Introduction, political concepts are means to express and negotiate political thought. They are therefore closely linked to *thought* but should not be viewed as identical with thought. *Cum grano salo*, concepts highlight the practical and functional dimensions, whereas thought refers more exclusively to the theoretical level and content. See Iain Hampsher-Monk, Karin Tilmans and Frank van Vree, 'A Comparative Perspective on Conceptual History—An Introduction' and Terence Ball, 'Conceptual History and the History of Political Thought', *History of Concepts: Comparative Perspectives*, ed. Iain Hampsher-Monk, Karin Tilmans, Frank van Vree, Amsterdam: University of Amsterdam Press 1998, 1–10, 75–86.
4. Takeuchi, 'Ajiashugi no tenbō', 7–8.
5. In fact, this was Takeuchi's achievement, too. While Takeuchi quoted extensively from Nohara Shirō's article on Asianism (see below), he criticized his distinction between Asianism and Greater Asianism. See Takeuchi, 'Ajiashugi no tenbō', 11.
6. As addressed above, interestingly, the most thorough discussions of Japanese Asianism that include its relation to other pan-isms were produced in English; see William G. Beasley, 'Japan and Pan-Asianism. Problems of Definition', *Aspects of Pan-Asianism*, ed. Janet Hunter, London: Suntory Toyota International Centre for Economics and Related Disciplines, London School of Economics and Political Science 1987 (International Studies 1987/II), 1–16: 1–2 and Sven Saaler, *Pan-Asianism in Meiji and Taishō Japan: A Preliminary Framework*, Tokyo: Deutsches Institut für Japanstudien 2004 (Working Paper 02/4), 9–10.
7. For a concise summary of the debates on definitions of fascism see Kevin Passmore, *Fascism: A Very Short Introduction*, Oxford: Oxford University Press 2002, especially Chap. 2. See also Stanley G. Payne, *A history of fascism, 1914–1945*, Madison: University of Wisconsin Press 1995, which includes chapters on China and Japan.
8. See Takeuchi, 'Ajiashugi no tenbō', 12–13. For an in-depth analysis of Takeuchi's critique of the ideology and reality of the so-called Greater East Asian War see Christian Uhl, *Wer war Takeuchi Yoshimis Lu Xun? Ein Annäherungsversuch an ein Monument der japanischen Sinologie* [Who was Takeuchi Yoshimi's Lu Xun? An Attempt at Approaching a Monument of Japanese Sinology], München: Iudicum 2003, particularly Chap. 2.

9. Nohara Shirō, 'Dai Ajiashugi' [Greater Asianism], *Ajia Rekishi Jiten* [Encyclopaedia of Asian History], Tokyo: Heibonsha 1960, 6–7: 6 quoted in Takeuchi Yoshimi, 'Ajiashugi no tenbō', 9.
10. Nohara confuses the dates and locations of these conferences.
11. Nohara, 'Dai Ajiashugi', 6–7.
12. For example, Takeuchi rejected Nohara's distinction between early Meiji Asianism, which centred on freedom and popular rights (*minken*), on the one hand and later Meiji Greater Asianism, which advanced militarism and the power of the state (*kokken*). Takeuchi also rejected Nohara's view that Asianist organizations such as the *Genyōsha* and the *Kokuryūkai* had turned from earlier opposition to the Asia policy of the Japanese government to later support or a 'cover up' of Japan's expansive policy. See Takeuchi Yoshimi, 'Ajiashugi no tenbō', 10–12.
13. Still, considering that Nohara composed his entry for an encyclopaedia of *Asian* history, his references to non-Japanese Asian impact on and responses to Asianism in Japan appear relatively scarce.
14. For a more detailed discussion of this definition in its temporal context of the post-World War One era see Chap. 3 of this book.
15. 'Han Ajiashugi' [Pan-Asianism], *Atarashii Kotoba no Jibiki* [Dictionary of New Words], ed. Hattori Yoshika and Uehara Rorō, Tokyo: Jitsugyō no Nihonsha 1919 quoted in 'Han Ajiashugi' [Pan-Asianism], *Nihon Kokugo Dai Jiten* [Encyclopaedia of the Japanese Language], Vol. 11, Tokyo: Shōgakkan 1972, 5. The same entry and definition appeared in a revised edition of the dictionary in 1925; see 'Han Ajiashugi' [Pan-Asianism], *Atarashii Kotoba no Jibiki* [Dictionary of New Words], ed. Hattori Yoshika and Uehara Rorō, Tokyo: Jitsugyō no Nihonsha 1925, 591–592.
16. This fact further attests to the paramount role for the understanding of Asianism since the 1930s played by Sun Yat-sen's Greater Asianism speech of 1924 (see below, Chaps. 4 and 6 and Conclusion).
17. 'Han Ajiashugi' [Pan-Asianism], *Atarashiki Yōgo no Izumi* [Fountain of New Terminology], ed. Kobayashi Kamin, Tokyo: Teikoku Jitsugyō Gakkai 1923, 1075. The same entry and definition later appeared in as 'Han Ajiashugi' [Pan-Asianism], *Atarashii Kotoba no Izumi* [Fountain of New Words], ed. Takatani Takashi, Tokyo: Sōzōsha 1928, 564–565.
18. Gushima is best known for his early research into fascism. See Kumano Naoki, 'Gushima Fashizumu Ron no sai kentō' [Re-examining Gushima's analysis of fascism], *Hōsei Kenkyū* [Law and Politics Research] 71–4 (March 2005), 423–461. In 1942, as a member of the Manchurian Railway Research Office (Mantetsu Chōsabu), Gushima was imprisoned for his criticism of the tripartite alliance between Japan, Germany, and Italy. After the war, Gushima held professorships at Kyūshū University and Nagasaki University and continued his research into fascism and international politics with a particular focus on Asia.

19. Gushima Kanesaburō, 'Han Ajiashugi' [Pan-Asianism], *Dai Hyakka Jiten* [Great Encyclopaedia], Vol. 21, ed. Shimonaka Yasaburō, Tokyo: Heibonsha 1933, 291–292.
20. See Horii Kōichirō, 'Ajiashugi' [Asianism], *Gendai Ajia Jiten* [Encyclopaedia of Contemporary Asia], ed. Hasegawa Hiroyuki et al., Tokyo: Bunshindō 2009, 21–22: 21.
21. See Nakamura Shunsaku, 'Ajiashugi' [Asianism], *Nihon Shisōshi Jiten* [Encyclopaedia of the History of Japanese Thought], ed. Koyasu Nobukuni, Tokyo: Perikan sha 2001, 7–8: 7.
22. See Katsurajima Nobuhiro, 'Ajiashugi' [Asianism], *Iwanami Tetsugaku Shisō Jiten* [Iwanami Encyclopaedia of Philosophy and Thought], ed. Hiromatsu Wataru, Koyasu Nobukuni, Mishima Ken'ichi et al., Tokyo: Iwanami Shoten 1998, 15–16: 15.
23. See Hirano Ken'ichirō, 'Ajiashugi' [Asianism], *Kokushi Dai Jiten* [Great Encyclopaedia of National History], ed. Kokushi Dai Jiten Henshū I'inkai, Tokyo: Yoshikawa Kōbunkan 1979, Vol. 1, 154.
24. Nakamura, 'Ajiashugi', 8.
25. See Sebastian Conrad, 'Remembering Asia: History and Memory in Post-Cold War Japan', *Memory in a Global Age. Discourses, Practices and Trajectories*, ed. Aleida Assmann and Sebastian Conrad, Houndsmill: Palgrave Macmillan 2010, 163–177, Eun-Jeung Lee, '"Asien" als Projekt. Der Asiendiskurs in China, Japan und Korea' ['Asia' as project. Asia discourse in China, Japan, and Korea], *Leviathan* 31–33, 2003, 382–400, particularly 396–398, and the Conclusion of this book.
26. See Kagami Mitsuyuki, 'Ajiashugi' [Asianism], *Sengoshi Dai Jiten* [Great Encyclopaedia of Post-War History], ed. Sasaki Takeshi, Tsurumi Shunsuke et al., Tokyo: Sanseidō 1991, 9.
27. Kagami, 'Ajiashugi', 9. On the different meanings of *seikatsusha* and the difficulties in translating the word into English see Wolfgang Seifert, 'seikatsu/seikatsusha', *The Blackwell Encyclopedia of Sociology*, ed. G. Ritzer, Malden & Oxford: Blackwell Publishing 2007, 4150–4154. Here, the connotation of 'ordinary people' in the sense of civil society actors as opposed to official representatives of a country appears most appropriate.
28. See Horii Kōichirō, 'Ajiashugi' [Asianism], *Gendai Ajia Jiten* [Encyclopaedia of Contemporary Asia], ed. Hasegawa Hiroyuki et al., Tokyo: Bunshindō 2009, 21–22: 22.
29. See Hatsuse/Fujii, 'Dai Ajiashugi', 623.
30. See 'Da Yaxiya zhuyi' [Greater Asianism], *Zhuyi Dacidian* [Encyclopaedia of Isms], ed. Liu Jianguo, Beijing: Renmin Chubanshe 1995, 19.
31. See Nakamura, 'Ajiashugi', 7.
32. See Katsurajima, 'Ajiashugi', 16.
33. See Nakamura, 'Ajiashugi', 7.

34. Hatsuse/Fujii, 'Dai Ajiashugi', 623.
35. Despite this *caveat*, Hatsuse too fails to address the fact that this dichotomous view cannot represent mainstream historical Asianist consciousness as these opposing concepts were not in wide use until the post-World War Two era.
36. Hatsuse/Fujii, 'Dai Ajiashugi', 623.
37. The definition of 'Pan Asianism' in the latest version of the *Kōjien* dictionary (see above) is—with the exception of a change of one *kana* from the historic *ya* to the current *a* in 'Aji*ya*'/'Aji*a*'—exactly the same as in the first edition of the post-war *Kōjien*, published in 1955. See 'Han Ajiyashugi' [Pan-Asianism], *Kōjien*, Tokyo: Iwanami Shoten 1955, 1772.
38. See Siep Stuurman, 'The Canon of the History of Political Thought: Its Critique and a Proposed Alternative', *History and Theory* 39 (May 2000), 147–166.
39. Stuurman, 'The Canon of the History of Political Thought', 152.
40. See Stuurman, 'The Canon of the History of Political Thought', 147, 152.
41. Stuurman, 'The Canon of the History of Political Thought', 153.
42. 'Whiggish' refers to the intentional (mis-)interpretation of the past as history for the present-day political purposes of those who write or commission these histories. The term was introduced by Herbert Butterfield's classical study *The Whig interpretation of history*, London: G. Bell 1931.
43. Stuurman, 'The Canon of the History of Political Thought', 157; footnotes in the original are omitted.
44. Stuurman, 'The Canon of the History of Political Thought', 161.
45. Although Takeuchi concedes that Okakura's position among Asianists was 'isolated', he nevertheless presents Okakura (together with Tarui) as the 'fundaments' of Asianism. Okakura's *Ideals of the East* was first published in English in 1903 and written for an American audience. Translations into other Western languages appeared in the 1920s but it was not translated into Japanese until the early 1930s. Choi has drawn attention to the fact that Okakura's portrayal of the unity of the 'East' was inspired by 'Western' Orientalist views of a monolithic 'East'. See Choi Won-shik, 'Non-Western Colonial Experience and the Specter of Pan-Asianism', http://www.changbi.com/english/related/related11.asp (last accessed 16 October 2016), originally published in the Korean quarterly *Changjak-kwa-Bipyong* [Creation and Criticism], No. 94, Winter 1996. For Okakura see also below and for Sugita see Chap. 3.
46. See Christopher W.A. Szpilman, 'Ōkawa Shūmei: "Various Problems of Asia in Revival", 1922', *Pan-Asianism: A Documentary History 1860–2010*, Vol. 2, ed. Sven Saaler and Christopher W.A. Szpilman, Boulder: Rowman & Littlefield 2011, 69–74.

47. On Ōkawa's Asianism see Christopher W.A. Szpilman, 'Ōkawa Shūmei', 69–74, Go Kaichū, *Ōkawa Shūmei to Kindai Chūgoku: Nitchū kankei no arikata o meguru ninshiki to kōdō* [Ōkawa Shūmei and Modern China. Consciousness and Behaviour pertaining to the state of Japanese–Chinese relations], Tokyo: Nihon kyōhōsha 2007, in particular 64–88, Cemil Aydin, *The politics of anti-Westernism in Asia: visions of world order in pan-Islamic and pan-Asian thought*, New York: Columbia University Press 2007, and Takeuchi Yoshimi, 'Profile of Asian Minded Man X: Ōkawa Shūmei', *The Developing Economies*, 7–3 (September 1969), 367–379.
48. See Takeuchi, 'Ajiashugi no tenbō', 52.
49. Even without an explicit confession to this task, this tendency is quite obvious throughout Takeuchi's essay if seen in the context of his other writings. In 1971, on the occasion of his discovery of Ishibashi Tanzan's work, Takeuchi revealed that he had been searching for a 'Liberalist *cum* Asianist for many years' for inclusion in the Asianism volume of 1963 but had failed to identify 'a thinker who opposed colonialism from the perspective of liberalism'. See Takeuchi Yoshimi, 'Waga Ishibashi hakken' [My discovery of Ishibashi], *Takeuchi Yoshimi Zenshū* [Complete Works of Takeuchi Yoshimi], Vol. 8, ed. Nunokawa Kakuzaemon, Tokyo: Chikuma Shobō 1980, 199–203: 202.
50. See Urs Matthias Zachmann, 'Blowing Up a Double Portrait in Black and White: The Concept of Asia in the Writings of Fukuzawa Yukichi and Okakura Tenshin', *Positions: East Asia Cultures Critique*, 15–2 (Fall 2007), 345–368. On Okakura see also Jing He, *China in Okakura Kakuzo with special reference to his first Chinese trip in 1893* (unpublished PhD dissertation, University of California, Los Angeles, 2006) and Ikimatsu Keizō, 'Profile of Asian Minded Man IV: Okakura Tenshin', *The Developing Economies*, 4–4 (December 1966), 639–653.
51. See Sakai Tetsuya, *Kindai Nihon no Kokusai Chitsujo Ron* [The Debate on Modern Japan's International Order], Tokyo: Iwanami Shoten 2007, 239.
52. See Yamamuro Shin'ichi, *Shisō Kadai toshite no Ajia* [Asia as a matter of thought], Tokyo: Iwanami Shoten 2001, 23.
53. This initiative is not only little known today but also historically appears to have had little, if any, impact. None of the materials studied in this book ever makes any reference to it. On the initiative see Urs Matthias Zachmann, *China and Japan in the Late Meiji Period. China Policy and the Japanese Discourse on National Identity, 1895–1904*, London: Routledge 2009, 28.
54. See Hashikawa Bunzō, 'Fukuzawa Yukichi to Okakura Tenshin" [Fukuzawa Yukichi and Okakura Tenshin], *Kindai Nihon to Chūgoku* [Modern Japan and China], ed. Takeuchi Yoshimi and Hashikawa

Bunzō,, Vol. 1, Tokyo: Asahi Sensho 1974, 17–35. Hashikawa uses the same term as Yamamuro, 'taikyokuteki' (antithetical), to refer to their views vis-à-vis Asia. Quite revealingly, this essay was chosen as the opening text of this two-volume collection, which studies the Asia consciousness of seventy Japanese thinkers. For a critique of the dichotomous portrayals of Fukuzawa and Okakura see Zachmann, 'Blowing Up a Double Portrait in Black and White', 345–368.

55. See Heinz Gollwitzer, *Die gelbe Gefahr: Geschichte eines Schlagworts* [The Yellow Danger: History of a Catchphrase], Göttingen: Vandenhoeck & Ruprecht 1962, Hashikawa Bunzō, *Kōka Monogatari* [Yellow Peril Story], Tokyo: Chikuma shobō 1976 and Iikura Akira, *Ierō Periru no Shinwa: Teikoku Nihon to Kōka no Gyakusetsu* [The Myth of the Yellow Peril: Imperial Japan and the Paradox of the Yellow Danger], Tokyo: Sairyūsha 2004 and below (Chap. 3).

56. For Takeuchi Yoshimi's critique of Japan's striving for Westernization and modernization in comparison to China see Wolfgang Seifert, 'Japan und seine Moderne nach dem Asiatisch-Pazifischen Krieg: Takeuchi Yoshimis Intervention 1948' [Japan and its modernity after the Asian-Pacific War: Takeuchi Yoshimi's Intervention in 1948], *Intervalle 11. Schriften zur Kulturforschung. Japanische Intellektuelle im Spannungsfeld von Okzidentalismus und Orientalismus* [Intervals 11. Writings on Cultural Research. Japanese intellectuals between Occidentalism and Orientalism], ed. Takemitsu Morikawa, Kassel: Kassel University Press, 75–120.

57. See, for example, the case 'Ozawa vs United States', as discussed in Chap. 5.

58. Yonetani Masafumi, *Ajia/Nihon* [Asia/Japan], Tokyo: Iwanami Shoten 2006, v.

59. Right-wing groups in Japan today often use Asianist concepts and terminology employed by militarist circles in the 1930s and 1940s, such as *Kō A* and *Dai Tōa* (and also prefer to refer to China by its historical Japanese name *Shina* which rejects claims of China's centrality as the Middle Kingdom). Revisionist writers in post-war Japan have also attempted to whitewash Japanese imperialism as pro-Asian Asianism. See Hayashi Fusao, *Dai Tōa Sensō Kōtei Ron* [Affirmation of the Greater East Asian War], Tokyo: Banchō Shobō 1964 and Ashizu Uzuhiko, *Dai Ajiashugi to Tōyama Mitsuru* [Greater Asianism and Tōyama Mitsuru], Tokyo: Nihon Kyōbunsha 1965. In particular, Hayashi's book has served as an inspiration for more recent Japanese nationalist revisions of assumed Asianist policies during the 1930s and 1940s. See Tomioka Kōichirō, *Shin Daitōa Sensō Kōteiron* [New Affirmation of the Greater East Asian War], Tokyo: Asuka Shinsha 2006. A critique of these attempts is Matsuzawa Tetsunari, *Ajiashugi to Fashizumu: Tennōtei kokuron hihan* [Asianism and

Fascism: A Critique of the Tennō Empire Thesis], Tokyo: Renga Shobō Shinsha 1979 and *'Ajiashugi' no Sensō Sekinin* ['Asianism' and War Responsibility], ed. Ajia ni taisuru Nihon no Sensō Sekinin o tou Minshū Hōtei Junbikai [Society for the Preparation of a Popular Court to investigate the Japanese War Responsibility towards Asia], Tokyo: Kinohana Sha 1996. An early critical analysis of Hayashi's treatise in a Western language can be found in Wolfgang Seifert, *Nationalismus im Nachkriegs-Japan. Ein Beitrag zur Ideologie der völkischen Nationalisten* [Nationalism in Postwar Japan. On the Ideology of Ethnic Nationalists], Hamburg: Institut für Asienkunde 1977 (Reihe Mitteilungen, Bd. 91).
60. See Furuya, 'Ajiashugi to sono shūhen', 47 and Yonetani, iii. Both refer to Takeuchi Yoshimi's use.
61. Takeuchi, 'Ajiashugi no tenbō', 14; see also above.
62. Takeuchi, 'Ajiashugi no tenbō', 22.
63. Takeuchi, 'Ajiashugi no tenbō', 13, 19.
64. Takeuchi, 'Ajiashugi no tenbō', 19.
65. See Yonetani, *Ajia/Nihon*, vii. A prominent and prolific advocate of a positive interpretation of Asianism is Matsumoto Ken'ichi. See, for example, his 'Ajiashugi wa shūen shita ka' [Is Asianism dead?], *Takeuchi Yoshimi 'Nihon no Ajiashugi' seidoku* [Close Reading of Takeuchi Yoshimi's 'Japanese Asianism'], ed. Matsumoto Ken'ichi, Tokyo: Iwanami Shoten 2000, 89–190 and, *Ajia wa kawaru no ka* [Will Asia change?], ed. Matsumoto Ken'ichi and Matsui Takafumi, Tokyo: Wedge 2009.
66. For this criticism see Suzuki Masahisa, 'Hajime ni' [Introduction], *Takeuchi Yoshimi Serekushon* [Takeuchi Yoshimi Selection], Vol. 2, ed. Marukawa Tetsushi and Suzuki Masahisa, Tokyo: Nihon Keizai Hyōronsha 2006, 7–16.
67. See in particular Takeuchi Yoshimi, 'Chūgoku no Kindai to Nihon no Kindai' [China's Modernity and Japan's Modernity], *Nihon to Ajia* [Japan and Asia], Tokyo: Chikuma Shobō 1993 (1948), 11–57, translated into German by Wolfgang Seifert as 'Was bedeutet die Moderne? Der Fall Japan und der Fall China' [What is modernity? The case of China and the case of Japan], *Japan in Asien. Geschichtsdenken und Kulturkritik nach 1945* [Japan in Asia. Historical Thought and Cultural Critique after 1945], ed. and translated by Wolfgang Seifert and Christian Uhl, München: Iudicium 2005, 9–54.
68. See, for example, Takeuchi Yoshimi, 'Hōhō toshite no Ajia' [Asia as method], *Nihon to Ajia* [Japan and Asia], Tokyo: Chikuma Shobō 1993 (1961), 442–470.

CHAPTER 3

Asia Becomes an *ism*: Early Chinese and Japanese Asianism

> *The surest sign that a society has entered into possession of a new concept is that a new vocabulary will be developed, in terms of which the concept can then be publicly articulated and discussed.*[1]
> —Quentin Skinner (1978)

Conceptually, Asianism discourse during the Taishō period could draw on a multifaceted, albeit marginalized and mostly negative, heritage of Asia discourse from the preceding decades. Throughout most of its history in Japan and China, 'Asia' had been a rather insignificant and peripheral concept in public political discourse. This gradually changed with the inception of Asianism in mainstream discourse from the early 1910s onwards, which triggered an intensive debate about the meaning and relevance of 'Asia' for Japan and China as nation states, as peoples and societies, and as empire of the past or empire-in-the-making. This chapter reviews the legacy of pre-1912 Asia discourse and analyses early Chinese and Japanese affirmations of Asianism as a newly established political concept in the pre-World War One period.

'Asia' Before Asianism

The inception of Asianism as an omnipresent and powerful political concept in mainstream discourse during the early 1910s was preceded by some decades of discourse—mostly dismissive or marginalized—on 'Asia' in Japan and China. Until the mid-nineteenth century, the term 'Asia', which had been introduced to the region by Jesuit missionaries in the early seventeenth century,[2] under the influence of the Western-oriented 'Dutch Studies' (rangaku) remained a rather neutral term of geographical convenience that was mostly employed without political or cultural implications.[3] The pro-Western *rangakusha* (Japanese scholars of Dutch or Western Studies) had not attributed any Eurocentric or discriminatory dimensions to the concept.

Since Asianist self-affirmations, however, did not only include the emphasis on an assumed difference from the *outside*, namely from the 'West' as 'Asia's' 'Other', but also rested on Asian commonality *within*, 'Asia' and Asian commonality were not popular themes in Japan's mainstream political discourse even among anti-Western forces. The few exceptions initially focused on China rather than 'Asia', such as the Nativist scholar Hirano Kuniomi (1828–1864) and Katsu Kaishū (1823–1899), who both advocated an anti-foreign—meaning anti-Western—cooperation between Japan and the Chinese Qing Empire (Nisshin Teikei Ron) during the 1850s and 1860s. However, when 'Asia' became politicized for the first time in Japan, it was mainly dismissed as a negative and discriminatory concept. Pursuing the emancipation of Japanese traditions vis-à-vis both the pre-modern dominance of Chinese studies and the turn towards Western studies in the late pre-Meiji period, most scholars of the school of National Learning (kokugaku), unlike Hirano, criticized the proto-Orientalist and Western-centric understanding of 'Asia'. Aiming at a re-evaluation of Japan's relationship with China, Aizawa Seishisai (1782–1863), the most famous representative of the anti-Western and China-critical later Mito School, rejected the subsuming of Japan under the general term 'Asia'. In his view, 'Asia' as a collective term, which included both Japan and other Asian countries, would stress Asian commonality at the expense of Japanese uniqueness and superiority. 'Asia' therefore obstructed the dissemination of the later Mito School's worldview. Predating Edward Said's famous critique of Western Orientalism by almost 150 years, Aizawa, therefore, dismissed 'Asia' as a concept that the 'Western barbarians' (seii) employed without authorization to justify their self-assumed superiority.[4]

Japanese opposition to a foreign-imposed concept of 'Asia' intensified after the Chinese defeat in the Opium Wars (1839–1842). 'Asia' stood in the way of the Japanese process of self-definition that stressed difference from, not commonality with, China. Most importantly, this difference had to be manifested in a different reaction to the Western threat. In addition, however, it was to be supplemented by a discourse that emphasized Japan's political and civilizational difference from the rest of Asia. Naturally, Asianist conceptions were perceived as harmful to this end. As a consequence, from the mid-nineteenth century onwards, Japanese consciousness of 'Asia' was closely linked with a 'consciousness of crisis' (kiki ishiki).[5] That is, the fear of being identified with 'Asia', of being relegated to the same level of backwardness as China and other parts of Asia, and of being treated accordingly. For at least half a century, this 'sense of threat' or, as Matsuda Kōichirō put it, 'the danger of being "Asia"',[6] dominated political thinking and diplomatic strategies in Japan and even increased when 'Yellow Peril' discourse started to boom in Europe and America from the late nineteenth century onwards.

In China, the introduction of the concept of 'Asia' in the seventeenth century initially had as little impact as in Japan and until the late nineteenth century remained in limited use for geographical purposes only. As Rebecca Karl writes, 'Asia' 'was simply not relevant' to the Chinese and 'had little autonomous significance as a meaningful category in Chinese conceptualizations of the world and China'.[7] This changed a little later than in Japan but still before the turn of the century, when ' "Asia" did not solely and simply designate a geographical area or concept; rather it incorporated quite an abundant colouring of politics'.[8] As in Japan, this new politicized meaning responded to the needs of the time, above all to the changing discursive and political context in which China found itself in the 1890s. Naturally, China's relationship with Japan, by which it had been defeated in 1895, was an important element of this context, as was domestic instability following the decline of the weakened Qing dynasty. Resembling Japan's above-mentioned 'sense of threat', some Chinese thinkers conceived of their home as being a 'lost country' (wang guo),[9] which could refer to many different notions of losses: the enduring loss of the Han majority by being ruled by the Manchu minority under the Qing dynasty (since 1644); the subjugation under Western imperialist powers since the loss of the Opium Wars since the mid-nineteenth century, and the defeat by the Japanese in the First Sino-Japanese War of 1894/95. Reform-minded Chinese intellectuals suffered an additional blow when their Reform Movement of 1898, which had partly been inspired by the Meiji Restoration, had failed. In this context, 'Asia' entered Chinese political discourse as a political concept denoting sameness with Japan and the Japanese regarding race, civilization, and geopolitical interests. As opposed to the Japanese notion of a 'danger of being "Asia"', Chinese reformers such as Zhang Zhidong,

Kang Youwei, Liang Qichao, and Zhang Binglin used 'Asia' affirmatively in the sense of Japanese-Chinese sameness as expressing an opportunity and potential rescue from being a 'lost country'. Nevertheless, as Kawashima Shin has pointed out, against the background of China's search for its place and identity among modern nation states, until the second decade of the twentieth century '"Asia" was hardly ever discussed'.[10] This was quite different in Japan, where, after the integration of Hokkaidō and the Ryūkyū Islands as Okinawa, 'Asia' served as a geographical and discursive map on which Japan's place and status among the modern nation states was to be defined.

'Asia' in Meiji Japan

Japanese efforts at dissociating the country from 'Asia' are probably best captured in Fukuzawa Yukichi's famous 'Datsu A Ron', published in 1885.[11] He concluded his essay by advising that,

> my country does not have time to wait for the enlightenment of our neighbours so that we can together revive Asia. On the contrary, we must leave their company and proceed together with the civilized nations of the West, without treating China and Korea in a special way because they are our neighbours but only approach them in the same way as the Westerners do. Because those who are intimate with bad friends are also regarded as bad, I will from my heart decline the bad friends of East Asia (Ajia tōhō no akuyū).

Fukuzawa's request for Japan's 'De-Asianization' in itself offers a multifaceted view of 'Asia' and has continued to this day to inspire controversies about his authorship, intention, and Asia consciousness in general.[12] But Fukuzawa's view of 'Asia' cannot simply be summarized as anti-Asianist. Instead, he refers to pressure from outside (the 'West') that compelled Japan to dissociate from 'Asia' in order to be treated as a civilized country by Western nations rather than having innate contempt for Japan's Asian neighbours as his prime argument. Fukuzawa's argumentation demonstrates particularly well the Japanese *kiki ishiki* (consciousness of crisis) that Matsumoto had diagnosed as the underlying motif in much of Japanese 'Asia' discourse since the Meiji period. At any rate, Japan's escape or turn away from 'Asia' (Datsu A) to enter the civilizational ranks of Europe (Nyū Ō) was the leading rationale during the 1880s in Japan, a period that has consequently become known as the 'era of Europeanizationism' (Ōkashugi no jidai).

Though certainly dominant then, Asia-critical positions did not remain unchallenged. Possibly in direct reaction to Fukuzawa's 'Datsu A Ron', the aforementioned Tarui Tōkichi (1850–1922) had authored a 'Treatise on the Great Union of the East' (Dai Tō Gappō Ron).[13] Tarui was an activist in the civil rights movement of the 1880s and founder of the *Tōyō Shakaitō* (Eastern Social Party). He advocated the formation of 'a great union of the countries of the yellow peoples of Asia', initially consisting of Japan and Korea and later to be joined by China. Tarui argued that,

> there is notable proof that these white people wish to exterminate us yellow people. If we yellow people cannot prevail we will become the white people's fodder. But in order to prevail, there is no other way but to raise a joint union of the peoples of the same race.[14]

Apart from these 'practical' reasons of mere survival, Tarui also referred to the assumed cultural proximity of the Japanese and the Koreans: 'our sentiments are like those of brothers and our morals are like among friends'.[15] Asian commonality, according to Tarui, therefore rested on a combination of inherent similarity regarding customs and thought on the one hand and practical considerations of a common fate due to the – real or imagined – threat from common enemies on the other. The fact that Tarui's writings were banned from publication reveals how little his arguments were acceptable to, let alone representative of, official or mainstream discourse in Japan.

Similar writings, such as Sugita Teiichi's 'Kō A Saku' (Raising Asia Policy) of 1883, probably the first Asianist treatise ever published, also remained marginalized in political discourse, but nevertheless paved the way intellectually for the wider embrace of Asianism from the 1910s onwards. Sugita (1851–1929), like Tarui a leading figure in the civil rights movement and co-founder of the Liberal Party (Jiyūtō), had employed similar concepts and arguments to Tarui. In fact, Sugita may be considered as Tarui's main Asianist inspiration, although most scholarship has overlooked Sugita's pre-Taishō Asianist writings and credited Tarui's text with being a prototype, if not *the* prototype, of Asianist writings.[16] In a familiar fashion, Sugita argued:

> The yellow race is about to be devoured by the white race. We have long heard that they love freedom and value equality. How then can these hands that love freedom and value equality deprive other people of their freedom and destroy equality? They may boast themselves as guarantors of freedom but I cannot but conclude that on the contrary they are the destroyers of freedom. Against this, although our countries in Asia are close and interdependent as lips and teeth, we are separated and our thoughts ten thousand miles apart. We lack mutual empathy and the spirit of mutual aid as members of the same race.[17]

To overcome these intra-Asian problems and form an opposition to the Western powers, Sugita called for the creation of a 'great union of Asia'.[18] During World War One and in the context of the heated Asianist debate in 1924 (see Chap. 5), Sugita reformulated his Asianist ideas and reiterated his proposal for a union of Asian peoples and countries. His proposal then was met with much more agreement than his original plan of 1883.

Nevertheless, Raising Asia (Kō A) as a counter position to Japan's official policy of accomodationism towards the Western powers remained on the agenda of Asiaphile thinkers and activists, with Asianist conceptions slowly starting to penetrate Japanese public discourse.[19] As seen above in the cases of Tarui and Sugita, racialist-culturalist notions, such as of shared culture and race, coexisted with regionalist conceptions as expressed in the formula 'shinshi hosha' (lips and teeth, cheekbones and gums), denoting close relations of interdependency. Both implied a political dimension of Asian commonality, namely a common destiny of Asian peoples in their struggle for survival and independence from the 'West'.

Simultaneously, from the early 1880s onwards, Asianist discourse was supplemented by the founding of the first Asianist organizations.[20] While some were co-initiated or joined by civil rights actors, such as Tarui, Sugita, Ōi Kentarō and others, the establishment of Asia-related business and research institutions must also be seen in the context of Japanese expansionist aspirations. Despite the 1871 Sino-Japanese Treaty of Amenity the territorial status of the Ryūkyū Islands (Okinawa) and of Taiwan remained issues of conflict between both countries. Some Asianist organizations, at least partly, became collaborators in the preparation and implementation of imperialist policies on these islands and later on the Chinese mainland. The first Asianist organization founded in Japan, the Raising Asia Society (Kō A Kai), which even bore the key Asianist motto of the day in its name, fully represents this ambivalence.[21] It was founded in Tokyo in 1880 by an illustrious assembly of mainly government officials and military representatives, and Watanabe Kōki (1848–1901), a participant in the Iwakura Mission, later governor of Tokyo, and a member of the Upper and Lower houses, became its leading figure. Both Fukuzawa Yukichi and Katsu Kaishū temporarily served as its councillors, while other associates included members of the imperial family, diplomats, and entrepreneurs. Interestingly, it was open to non-Japanese, and the Chinese journalist and reformer Wang Tao (1828–1897) as well as He Ruzhang (1838–1891), the first Chinese minister to Japan, participated in the organization. In his inaugural speech, Watanabe formulated the organization's aim as being the promotion of 'building friendships and exchanging information between the peoples of Asia'.[22] However, apart from the establishment of a school for Chinese language (Kō A Gakkō), it appears to have contributed little to the mutual exchange and understanding of Asian peoples. In 1883 it changed its name into *Ajia Kyōkai* and in 1900 merged with the *Tōa Dōbunkai*.[23] Founded by Konoe Atsumaro (1863–1904), the *Tōa Dōbunkai*, which also had close links with government and business circles, set up a language and research school in Shanghai (*Tōa Dōbun Shoin*) in 1900,[24] and—like its predecessors, the *Tōa Kai* and the *Dōbunkai*—focused almost exclusively on collecting information on China and training China experts. China was also the main focus of the *Tōyō Gakkan*, set up in 1884 in Shanghai in collaboration of mainland adventurers (Tairiku rōnin) and members of the *Jiyū Minken* faction, including Sugita Teiichi and Ueki Emori. But their school went bankrupt after only one year and was dissolved.[25] An equally short-lived but fundamentally different Asianist organization was the *Asiatic Humanitarian Brotherhood*, also known under its respective Chinese (Yazhou Heqinhui) or Japanese (Ashū Washinkai) names.[26] It grew out of the Chinese-led but Tokyo-based 'Socialism Study Group' (Jp. Shakaishugi Kenkyūkai, Ch. Shehuizhuyi Yanjiuhui).[27] Historical sources on the *Brotherhood* are scarce, but according to the recollections of one of its founders, the Japanese socialist Takeuchi Zensaku, it was initiated in 1907 by Chinese, Indian, and Japanese socialists and anarchists who lived or temporarily resided in Tokyo, including Zhang Binglin (1868–1936), Zhang Ji (1882–1947), Liu Shipei (1884–1919), Kōtoku Shūsui (1871–1911), Sakai Toshihiko (1870–1933), and Ōsugi Sakae (1885–1923).[28]

The society's agenda was outspokenly anti-imperialist but internal disputes on their stance towards nationalism and internationalism prevented it from growing into a formidable and lasting transnational political voice.[29] Eventually, it appears that its members gave highest priority to the independence of their respective national states and subordinated their Asianist claims.[30] Despite the Asianist tone of its founding manifesto,[31] the *Brotherhood*'s 'Asia' (*Ashū* or *Yazhou*) as a result denoted little more than the geographical origin of its participants.

As these brief examples reveal, the overall Asia-critical mood in Japan during most of the Meiji period did nevertheless prompt and allow for some notable objections that were characterized by Asianist inclinations. Asianist slogans such as 'same script, same race' and 'Raising Asia'—which, like so much of Asianist rhetoric and rationale, was later appropriated from above and even adopted as the name of a government policy institute, *Kō A In* (Asia Development Board), founded in 1938—established a rhetorical framework on which Asianism as a key concept in political discourse from the 1910s onwards could draw. Another legacy of early Asianist affirmations is the interdependent rationale of their arguments: to act as One Asia, in the Asianist view, was necessary not only because of assumed cultural-racial commonality but also because of geographic and consequently geopolitical interdependency as well as due to shared political interests. From the mid-1920s onwards, when Asianist discourse became dominated by racialist arguments, this non-essentialist branch re-emerged in the form of an alternative, geopolitical and regionalist discourse (see Chap. 6).

Although some of the pre-1912 Asianist activities appear to have been supported unofficially by Japanese government authorities, Asianist rhetoric remained notably absent from mainstream and official political discourse. A good case in point is Konoe Atsumaro's famous appeal to form an 'alliance of the same races' (dōjinshu dōmei), published in the *Taiyō* journal in January 1898, which caused tremendous uproar and prompted Konoe to withdraw his statement. As Matthias Zachmann has demonstrated, when the Japanese foreign ministry 'considered Konoe's article so damaging that it saw no other way than to publicly disown Konoe and portray him as an incompetent radical',[32] under such pressure Konoe immediately renounced his proposal. The Japanese public could openly discuss different strategies towards the Asian mainland, such as the preservation of China's integrity (Shina Hozen Ron) *versus* the China partition thesis (Shina Bunkatsu Ron). However, the danger of being viewed as a potential leader of Asia forbade any racialist or culturalist proposal of Asian commonality that would be prone to confirm Western fears of a 'Yellow Peril' under Japanese leadership.

Still during the Russo-Japanese War of 1904/05, the Japanese government had been careful to prevent the impression of the war being a clash between Europe and a Japanese-led 'Asia'. To this end, it had sent Count Suematsu Kenchō to Europe to dispel European fears of a future Asiatic alliance under Japanese leadership. Suematsu dismissed the 'talk about the Yellow Peril, or the possibility of a Pan-Asiatic combination' as 'nothing more than a [sic] senseless and mischievous agitation'.[33] In particular, he criticized the notion that Japan would strive for the position of Asian leadership on the grounds of the supposed peace-loving national character of the Japanese (note: Japan was at war with Russia!) and the fundamental difference between the Japanese and other Asians. Suematsu concluded:

> How, then, could it be expected for one moment that the various peoples of the East, with their varying degrees of intelligence, their conflicting interests, and their long-standing feuds and jealousies, could ever have cohesion enough to range themselves under one banner against the powers of the Occident? And if they could do so, is it to be imagined that Japan would enter upon so quixotic an enterprise as to place herself at the head of so unmanageable a mob?[34]

Feeling 'the danger of being "Asia"' greater than ever, at the beginning of the twentieth century Japan wanted to be perceived by the 'West' as a civilized and modernized country that fundamentally differed from the rest of Asia, the 'unmanageable mob'.

'Asia' Becomes a Principle

In the meantime, the neologism Asianism, literally the principle of Asia, had first appeared in Japanese media. The translation of *shugi* as 'principle' in fact represents a retranslation of the earliest noted translation of the English word 'principle', which the Japanese journalist Fukuchi Ōchi (Gen'ichirō) had rendered into Japanese as *shugi*.[35] From there it also entered the Chinese language around 1900.[36] Writing in 1900, the social scientist Endō Ryūkichi argued that *shugi* was different from a mere *setsu* (theory) or *ron* (argument). Endō regarded *shugi* as equivalent to 'ism'—which makes Asianism a particular suitable translation of *Ajiashugi*—and defined it as follows:

> first, 'shugi' has a unifying character. 'Shugi' is the psychological backbone and all activity is invoked by it. Therefore, it is the unifying element within a given range. Second, 'shugi' is the personal moving force because it provides motivation as the psychological backbone. In short, 'shugi' means giving subjectively an opinion from one's psychological backbone whereas 'ron' or 'setsu' denote an opinion from an objective elaboration.[37]

For obvious reasons, political leaders frequently emphasized this link between *shugi* as a mere opinion and as action derived from it as a means of political agitation. In his lectures on the 'Three People's Principles' (Sanmin Zhuyi), delivered in 1924, Sun Yat-sen stressed the requirement to proceed from contemplation to implementation. At the very beginning of his lectures, he therefore defined the meaning of *shugi* (Ch. zhuyi) as follows:

> 'zhuyi' is a kind of thought (sixiang), a kind of belief (xinyang), and a kind of force (liliang). Any human examination generally starts with thought. After thought has been realized, belief emerges. And belief brings about force. Therefore, 'zhuyi' is fully established when, after starting from thought and belief, it initiates force.[38]

The transition of 'Asia' as a principle from thought to power, from contemplation to implementation, is also reflected in the quotations from contemporary dictionaries (see Chap. 3), where Asianism had first been defined as a 'claim' (shuchō) in 1919 and later, in 1933, as a 'movement' (undō). More broadly, it corresponds to the general development of Asianism as a concept of which controversial debate initially generated different conceptions but that was later also linked to the practical implementation of Japan's Asia policy.

But *Ajiashugi*, which exultantly affirmed 'Asia' by elevating it to the status of a principle, could not only have a unifying or standardizing quality regarding the personal belief or behaviour of Asiaphile thinkers and activists. It could also precipitate a discursive unity of some sort by encompassing previous Asianist notions, such as 'same script, same race' or 'Raise Asia', under one concept—Asianism—exactly because it was rather vague and ambivalent. It could refer to racialist, culturalist, regionalist, or other aspects of assumed commonality and it could be part of political, cultural, or other agendas. Even Asianism's 'Asia'—Central? East? West? All?—was rarely strictly defined, although it often, if only implicitly, centred on East Asia, consisting of Japan, China, and Korea.

Not surprisingly, Asianism in Japan first appeared in negation, namely in reaction to the 'Imperial Rescript on Education' of 1890 (kyōiku chokugo), which had been issued under pressure from conservative circles aiming at strengthening traditional values. Together with a portrait of the Meiji Emperor, the Rescript was distributed to schools, and students were instructed to memorize the text, which emphasized the unique character of Japan's polity (kokutai) centring on the imperial throne. To pro-Western thinkers the Rescript signalled a nationalist upsurge and a step back into pre-modern times. In protest, in the early 1890s, a number of incidents occurred in which teachers refused the obligatory bow to the emperor's portrait.[39] Most famously, the Christian thinker Uchimura Kanzō (1861–1930) had to resign from his position as a teacher at the First Higher Middle School in 1891 after his bow had apparently been too lax. Objecting to the government's interference in issues of education and world views, other Christian and pro-Western educators followed Uchimura's example and publicly criticized the new policy. In his new year's inaugural speech, Okumura Teijirō, a Christian and teacher representative at the famous Kumamoto English School, defined the guiding principles of his school as follows:

> The educational policy of this school is neither Japanism (Nihonshugi), nor Asianism (Ajiashugi), nor Euro-Americanism (Ōbeishugi). Instead it is philanthropist worldism (hakuai sekaishugi) which prepares personalities for the wider world. Therefore, in our view, there are no countries and no foreigners.[40]

Only three days after his speech had been reprinted in a regional newspaper, Okumura was dismissed by the prefecture's governor on the grounds that Okumura's conception of 'philanthropism' was inconsistent with the nationalist orientation requested by the Rescript.[41]

Okumura's usage of *Ajiashugi*, the earliest ever usage known today, reveals two important characteristics that would remain valid in Asianism discourse, which only started two decades later. First, Asianism explicitly opposed 'Asia' to other geographical concepts and their respective cultural or political implications; this included 'Asia's' opposition not only to the 'West' as its most obvious 'Other' but also to Japan. 'Asia' as a principle (Ajiashugi) apparently signified something that was different from Japan as a principle (Nipponshugi/Nihonshugi). While this short reference leaves the question unanswered as to how Asianism differed from Japanism, the divergence of both concepts, rather than their convergence, became a prominent issue in early Asianism discourse, when affirmations of Asianism were frequently criticized from a nationalist perspective. Second, the oppositional listing of Japanism, Asianism, and Euro-Americanism highlighted the comprehensive character of either of those *isms* as principles that could not easily coexist with each other. As guiding principles or doctrines, 'Asia', 'Japan', and 'Euro-America' were mutually exclusive. Again, the precise meaning of these principles here must remain unclear but both their comprehensiveness and exclusiveness were features that would become focal points two decades later.

Only one month later the first affirmative political elaboration of Asianism appeared in the *Ajia* (Asia) journal of the Seikyōsha,[42] a political organization founded in 1888 by journalist-philosopher Miyake Setsurei (1860–1945), geographer and writer Shiga Shigetaka (1863–1927), and others in opposition to the government's pro-Westernism.[43] The anonymous author of the leading article placed Asianism alongside regionalist concepts such as 'Pan-Americanism', 'Australian Confederationism', and 'Europeanism', and criticized those Japanese—by far the majority—who dismissed Asianist thought:

> Obviously there is no doubt that there are people who claim that we must not use our energy to promote the revival and courage of burning ambition to compete against the invasive movement of the West towards the East to rival the European countries' colonial policy. Far from it, these people even control Asian Asianists. Japan is a beautiful island empire in the East Sea of Asia which, ahead of the Asian countries, is fully perfecting civilization. As pioneers among the Asian countries we have the great responsibility to lead the late developers and explain how this country was accomplished and to teach them science. We must know the divine mission, respect it and act accordingly. And we must quickly understand and learn from our mistakes. When today we hear the word Asianism (Ajiashigi) [sic], and feel frightened or strange and suspect its incoherence, then we behave like only idiots do who take a narrow view as their compass.[44]

Although this statement constitutes only a tentative affirmation of Asianism, which makes rather little of the concept as such, it permits revealing insights into contemporary 'Asia' discourse. Owing to its fierce criticism of the Japanese government's pro-Western attitude and policies, the *Seikyōsha* had become the object of public pressure right from its founding in 1888. Initially, it had called its journal *Nihonjin* (The Japanese) but in late June 1891 changed its name to *Ajia* (Asia), in itself an act of provocation in reaction to the ban its predecessor had received in early June that year. 'Asia' was exactly the opposite of everything the Japanese government wanted to be promoted publicly or associated with. In the eyes of the *Seikyōsha*, therefore, 'Asia' was the ideal signal of continued opposition and a perfect screen on which to project their criticism of the government and of its pursuit of 'modernization' and Westernization. The change of name, however, did not necessarily lead to a change of attitude towards the relationship between Japan and other Asians. Asian commonality, not unlike the government's official stance, was not a popular thesis among the *Seikyōsha* either. Instead, 'Asia' provided the spatial context in which Japan's uniqueness and perfection could be accentuated. Consequently, it viewed Japan as leader of Asia that might even flirt with the idea of challenging Western colonialism. But for the time being, it remained a flirt and neither the *Seikyōsha* itself nor any other group managed to bend Japan's 'Asia' discourse in a pro-Asianist direction.

The first known, unreserved affirmation of Asianism was proposed seven years later, in 1898, when the general political context had changed somewhat favourably regarding Asianist sentiments. Japan's victory in the first Sino-Japanese War (1894/95) was followed not only by the humiliating Russian-French-German Triple Intervention but also by a 'Golden Decade' of exchange in Sino-Japanese relations which brought people from both countries closer together than ever before. In parts, it had also triggered in China the so-called Hundred Days Reform movement led by the Chinese scholars Kang Youwei (1858–1927) and Liang Qichao (1873–1929).[45] In addition, the USA had expanded its influence into Southeast Asia by annexing the Philippines, Russia gained a long-term lease on the Liaodong Peninsula (which the Triple Intervention had denied to Japan), while Germany acquired the Kiautschou Bay concession in the same year. Japan's own imperial expansion to Taiwan from 1895 onwards may have provided another stimulus to this debate.

Against this background, Kubota Yoshirō (1863–1919), a lawyer from Nagano who later became a member of parliament for Inukai Tsuyoshi's *Rikken Kokumintō* (Constitutional People's Party), warned of the 'complete extinction of Asia' (Ajia no shōmetsu) at the hands of the Europeans and proposed Asianism (Ajiashugi) as Japan's counter-policy.[46] In his speech at Tokyo's *Kinkikan* Kubota emphasized that the 'political protagonists in Eurasia', Britain and Russia together with the other European powers, aimed at subjugating Asia in the same manner they had dealt with Africa.[47] As the only Asian protagonist in Eurasia, Japan should adopt Asianism as the guiding principle to repel the imperialist ambitions of Russia and Britain and to restore 'Asia'—which in his view had become void of any meaning beyond mere geography—politically.[48] In this enterprise, Kubota put special emphasis on the role of China:

> Asia's independence will not be brought about by China. Instead, people think that it will be brought about by Japanese enlightenment. If in this manner the Japanese army manages to awaken China and eventually at some point the Asian lands linked with China follow, it would surely mean the end to the power of Europeans in Asia. Ah! The sovereignty of Asia must now be restored to the Asians. [...] The birth of Asianism, my country's great plan and hope for the next hundred years, will finally cause the Europeans to acknowledge [us]. We will jump for joy and not forbid our hearts to secretly recollect Genghis Khan and Tamerlane [Timur] of the past. It is hard to bear the delight of thinking of the future ambition of the yellow races. I say that my Asianism means 'Asia is the Asia of Asia' or 'Asia is the Asia of the Asian race'. However, my friends, will this Asianism as we anticipate it ever be born, will it be delivered? And even after its birth, how will it grow and become a healthy child? Maybe it cannot stand on its own two feet as it will be feeble? Will it live or will it die? Or is its birth nothing but a onenight dream? When I think of this now, I really cannot endure the anger I feel.[49]

Kubota's likening of Asianism to an unborn child is a very fitting metaphor. In his time, although political discourse displayed some signs of an early Asianist pregnancy, it was more than doubtful whether Asianism would ever grow and mature to leave its footprints on Japanese political discourse. At the same time, Kubota's conception of Asianism foreshadowed many of the facets the concept would later become synonymous with. Kubota's reference to a Japanese military engagement in China for China's own good – in order to 'enlighten' it – anticipates Asianism's later role in the propagandistic justification of Japan's war against China. His remark is also noteworthy as it obviously rests on the same premise as Fukuzawa's 'Datsu A Ron': waiting for China's enlightenment is in vain. However, Kubota's conclusion is quite different from Fukuzawa's. Rather than proposing a Japanese turn away from 'Asia', Kubota argues for a forcible enlightenment of China and Asia by the Japanese military. This affirmative Asia position coincides with Kubota's regionalist understanding of Asia, from which Japan, due to its geographic location, could not escape. In fact, Kubota makes little of racialist-culturalist arguments, such as *dōbun dōshu* rhetoric, which had informed most Asianist writings of the mid-nineteenth century and earlier Meiji decades. Instead, he takes Western geopolitical thinking and action as a model for Japan to follow. As he puts it, Asia had to become the 'Asia of the Asians'. This key Asianist slogan was in fact an imitation of 'America for the Americans', the logic that underlay the declaration and implementation of the US-American Monroe Doctrine. Concerned over European interference in their colonies in the Americas, the Monroe Doctrine was first declared in 1823 and stated that European countries could not colonize in any of the Americas (North, Central, or South as well as the islands of the Caribbean), with the US deeming any attempt at colonization a threat to its national security. In return the US would only be involved in European affairs if America's rights were disturbed.[50] Technically, US President James Monroe had postulated two separate political spheres (America and Europe), which should deal with each other following the principles of mutual non-intervention and non-colonization. In effect, of course, while excluding European powers from interfering in their (former) colonies in Central and South America, it paved the way for US supremacy over the whole American continent, including the Caribbean. Until 1917, the doctrine was applied in more than two dozen cases in which the US intervened in Latin America or the Caribbean. There, the originally anti-European slogan 'America for the Americans' soon became known in its ironic Spanish version '*America para los Americanos*' (meaning America for the US-Americans). Propagating 'neighbourly altruism', American 'solidarity' and 'protection' had soon turned into a cover-up for US-American hegemonic interventionism and expansionism on the American continent, without further disturbance by other powers. Kubota envisioned exactly this kind of implementation of Asianism:

> Ah, my friends, how then can we realize the healthy Asianism that I have mentioned earlier? Alas, at present Asianism is on the brink of death.

> Asia has completely been encroached on by Europe and if Asia ceases to exist, what will happen to Korea, China, Vietnam, Burma, Persia, and Afghanistan? Japan should then know its fate. Ah, our country's life and death are really linked with the fate of Asianism! Our people must in national unity plan the growth and nourishment of Asianism. My Asianism is only meant as a policy in diplomatic relations, and not with regard to arts and culture. The only medicine renowned for its efficacy for the cultivation and promotion of this principle is the prescription called East Asian Monroe Doctrine (loud applause). [...] To transfer this principle to East Asia in order to make Asia the Asia of the Asians must be the mission of the Asians. If we transplant this principle to the lands of East Asia in a firm and determined manner, the independence of Asia will only be a matter of time. Asianism will certainly be the best medicine to save us from the danger of extinction! (loud applause).[51]

Kubota ended his speech with a triple *banzai* to East Asian Monroeism,[52] the main message of his geopolitical conception of Asianism, which he explicitly distinguished from culturalist conceptions or mere academic interest in Asia. Kubota's fervent appraisal and propagation notwithstanding, Asianism quickly disappeared from public discourse. His fear of the malnourishment and premature death of Asianism as a political concept appeared to be justified. Neither the *Asahi* nor *Yomiuri* daily newspapers, which had advertised Kubota's speech in a brief notice on the day before it was delivered, published a follow-up report on the assembly and his speech. In mainstream public discourse at least, Asianism remained neglected and even in the immediate aftermath of the victorious war against Russia Asianism did not resurface prominently. Apart from the absence of a prominent advocate—Kubota remained a marginal political figure throughout his career—Japan's striving for modernization and acknowledgement from the West seem to have obstructed a wider embrace of Asianist positions in the first decade of the twentieth century. In addition, Asianist perceptions, though to varying degrees, normally included a proactive interest in China which rested on the belief in the importance of China for Japan's future. However, after the failed reform movement of 1898 and the half-hearted government-implemented reforms there, this position was often looked down on as illusionary and China was treated as a hopeless case.

This suddenly changed with the Chinese Revolution, which came so unexpectedly that even its leader, Sun Yat-sen, was taken by surprise and had to hurry home from a trip abroad in order to actively participate in the post-revolutionary business. The Chinese Revolution of 1911 meant both an opportunity and a danger to Japan. While Japan was fearful of losing its foothold on the mainland, the political quarrel over power in the new setting opened up many opportunities for political repositioning. In addition, the annexation of Korea in the previous year had called for a revision of Japan's imperial policies. How would Japan navigate between accommodating the 'West' and its own empire-building project? Against the background of continued denigration from abroad—articles decrying the anti-Japanese immigration policy in the United States had appeared almost on a daily basis between 1906 and 1909—and the new situation in China, Japan's own need for an imperial agenda along with new political options became discussed in public discourse. It was in this context that 'Asia' re-emerged as a projection screen for the debate about the future of Japanese–Chinese relations on the one hand and about the question of racial assimilation on the other. Interestingly, it was through foreign—Chinese and British-American—mediation that Asianism re-entered Japanese political discourse in the early 1910s, this time to stay.

Asianism as a Chinese Trick?

In November 1912, the Chinese pro-Republican newspaper *Minli Bao*, which had been founded in 1910 to promote the 'people's spirit of self-reliance and independence',[53] published an article 'On Greater Asianism' (Da Yaxiya zhuyi lun) in its foreign opinion section.[54] The authorship of the text remains unclear but—although in its original version it was possibly written (or given as a speech in Japanese) by a Japanese person—it was regarded in Japan as a Chinese revolutionary pamphlet. The *Minli Bao* actually names the 'Japanese parliamentarian Ibuka Hikotarō' as its author, claiming that he had toured post-revolutionary China as part of a Japanese parliamentary delegation and, on that occasion, had advocated the adoption of 'Greater Asianism'. Japanese and Chinese newspaper coverage confirms the existence of such a Japanese observation tour of China, although neither Ibuka's participation could be verified nor did any report include references to the proposal of Asianism by a participant.[55] In any case, Ibuka's first name is most likely a misprint for Hikosaburō, who had been a member of parliament for the *Rikken Seiyūkai* (Friends of Constitutional Government) from 1912. Ibuka Hikosaburō (1866–1916), had served as an interpreter during the first Sino-Japanese War and later became an advisor to China's

Republican government.[56] He was married to the younger sister of Arao Sei (1859–1896), a well-known Japanese pioneer of Sino-Japanese exchange and founder of the *Nisshin bōeki kenkyūjo* (Japanese-Qing Trade Research Institute) in Shanghai in 1900.[57] It would therefore not be implausible that Ibuka had in fact authored the text. Xu Xue'er (1891–1915), an early supporter of Sun Yat-sen and the Chinese revolutionary cause who worked as a journalist for the *Minli Bao*, was named as the editor in charge. The text defined 'Greater Asianism' as follows:[58]

> Asians! Asia for the Asians! Asians must preside over the main issues of Asia. People from outside Asia must not be covetous of this. This is called Greater Asianism! It is the eternal and inextinguishable divine right of the Asian people. The number of all Asian countries is not small, their political systems differ, and they are not homogenous regarding race or religion either. However, this Greater Asianism is providing hope like an eternal ray of light.

Interestingly, here too, rather than suggesting Asian commonality, the author explicitly concedes Asia's heterogeneity and appeals to the right of political self-determination as the core of Asianism. Consequently, as both the *Seikyōsha*'s article and Kubota had done, it likened Greater Asianism to the American Monroe Doctrine:

> America has not at all given up Greater Americanism (Da Meizhou zhuyi) despite its policy of supporting national independence. If America can understand Greater Americanism in a way that allows for the support of the independence of countries, we should also be able to interpret Greater Asianism exactly in this way. [...] If we cannot take control as Asians of the matters of Asia, this will surely bring about Asia's death and extinction. If the peoples of the countries of this continent cannot protect their lands and the people cannot govern their lives, all countries will be burned to the ground and all people will become chopped fish.

As the quotation above reveals, the comparison to the American case was also meant to convince those critics of Asianism who feared that any supranational collaboration among Asian countries would undermine national sovereignty. This message was important both to the Chinese audience, where in the immediate aftermath of the Revolution national independence was one prominent goal, and the Japanese audience, where sceptics viewed close links with Asian countries and China in particular as a risk to national independence. The previously mentioned 'divine mission' here takes on a fatalistic determinism which foreshadows Asianism's usage as wartime propaganda. In his conclusion, however, the author sounded more reconciliatory, probably with a Western or pro-Western audience in mind:

> Greater Asianism means planning Asia's eternal peace. It does not mean oppressing other races and only wishing to become strong oneself. Racial struggle runs counter to morals and heavenly order and shall [therefore] not be pursued by the human race. Only, if we Asians do not act according to Greater Asianism, that is, if we cannot stand independently and cannot act by ourselves, aimlessly fight against people of other continents and cannot obtain control, we will not only become unhappy ourselves as Asians but bring great misfortune to the whole human race.

These concluding lines once again emphasize the non-essentialist character of this conception of Asianism. Neither culturalist nor racialist arguments play any prominent role in this affirmation of the principle of Greater Asia. Rather, it attempts to draw its legitimization from other pan-isms (Americanism, Monroe Doctrine) as a regionalist instrument to attain national self-determination and independence. It overlooked, however, the question of leadership that in the case of Americanism had clearly been taken by the United States and in the case of (East) Asia had already been claimed by Japan. Unsurprisingly, the article remained without notable influence in China.[59]

Japan is not mentioned once in the text, possibly to persuade Chinese of a pro-Asianist attitude that does not explicitly include Japanese participation or even Japanese leadership. In Japan, however, the text was indiscriminately treated as of Chinese origin. It probably first appeared as an appendix to Gotō Shinpei's *Nihon Shokumin Seisaku Ippan* (General Outline of Japan's Colonial Policy)[60] in 1914. Gotō, the former director of the Civil Administration Bureau of Taiwan (Minseibu) and of the South Manchurian Railway Company, had since 1912 been the director of the Colonization Bureau (Takushoku kyoku) and was known for his 'conception of Japan as a civilizing force in East Asia'.[61] In his book, he reviewed Japanese colonial policy on Taiwan with regard to its applicability to the growing Japanese Empire and Manchuria in particular. As Gotō would elaborate in more detail in later writings, Asianism appealed to him as a useful principle for the 'development'—that is, colonization—of parts of the Asian mainland.

Gotō introduced the text analysed above to his audience as a pamphlet he had recently received from China's south-western Sichuan province.[62] Affirming the principle of Greater Asia, he briefly referred to the 'pamphlet' and argued,

> if we do not pursue 'Pan-Asianism', that is, a Greater Asia policy (Dai Ajia seisaku) and a policy of racial unity, I believe that the debate about the policy towards Manchuria and Mongolia is incomplete.[63]

Interestingly, he used the non-culturalist and non-racialist arguments from the 'pamphlet' to demand a racialization of Japanese Asia policy. While this certainly misrepresented the argument of the 'Dayaxiya zhuyi lun', it reflected the influence of racialist debate in Japan in 1913, which will be analysed below. In the following years, Gotō combined both lines of argumentation—racialist-culturalist essentialism and regionalist pragmatism *cum* imperialist aspirations—to become the first prominent Japanese to openly advocate Greater Asianism as a political principle in the 1910s.[64] Gotō apparently found Asianism an appropriate doctrine to support and justify his colonial political visions. To this end, after Japan had gained new rights on the Asian mainland following the acquisition of the German possession in Shandong (1914) and after the acceptance of the Twenty-One Demands by the Chinese government (1915), he appealed to the Japanese to help colonize the new territory:

> Just having acquired new rights has no special worth. The rights must not stop on paper. Sentences a hundred miles long have no worth. The [Japanese] people must become active, attempt the great colonial development of Manchuria and Mongolia, and promote the future welfare of our two countries [Japan and China] by implementing the ideal of Greater Asianism, that is, putting 'Asia is the Asia of the Asians' into practice.[65]

Against those who rejected an active Japanese engagement on the Asian continent but insisted on a Western-oriented policy that would appease the Western powers, Gotō proposed close Sino-Japanese cooperation as a prerequisite to realize Asianism. In his search for a formula for the colonization of Manchuria and Mongolia, Gotō added a racialist dimension to refer to assumed cultural commonalities of the Chinese and the Japanese:

> It is needless to say that China is Japan's foremost defence line, and because we have in various points close relations, we cannot overlook

peace and war in China as affairs of another country. China and my country in the past have been close despite distance and this relationship has been uninterrupted. Consequently we have adopted many things from their civilization and we have preserved many commonalities regarding customs. Therefore they must rely on us as friends and teachers, and we must build friendly relations and ally with each other to help realize Greater Asianism (Dai Ajiashugi).[66]

Like most other Asianists (and non-Asianist Japanese) at the time, Gotō, too, held the view that China unilaterally had to learn from Japan and follow it as its student. While Gotō's Asianism was not based on contempt for China and Asia, it was ultimately informed and limited by its function as a leading principle for Japan's colonial policy. For Gotō, Sino-Japanese cooperation was not an end but only a means. Nevertheless, in the early 1910s, Gotō could use this conception of Asianism as a counter-policy to criticize the government's pro-Western and anti-Chinese political stance. Repeating the pamphlet's position that 'Asia must be the Asia of the Asians' he argued that,

> although the people of the East (Tōyōjin) must hold up Pan-Asianism to the last, the recommendation of our government [for a China policy] has invited the countries of Britain and France and consequently it has taken the form of their demands for rights in the Far East. Will this not certainly lead to their eventual demand to interfere in the politics of the East? Will such a thing not become the cause of misfortune in diplomatic relations? It feels as if there is still a long way to go to achieve the adoption of an Asian Monroe Doctrine as our country's national policy in order to bring about change to this colour-divided map.[67]

Asianism, therefore, in this period clearly functioned as a means of criticism of the pro-Western and anti-Asianist official policy of the Japanese government. The government, in response, rejected this position by downplaying not only racial but also geographical links with Japan's neighbour China. A Japanese cabinet resolution of 1917 accordingly rejected claims of 'a common destiny of the two countries of Japan and China on the grounds of racial and geographical interdependence' as 'an extremely dangerous argument' that would 'provoke even further the feeling of a Yellow Peril and fear of Japan'.[68]

Most likely by means of Gotō's introduction, a Japanese version of the *Minli Bao* essay was also reprinted in the *Daisan Teikoku* (The Third

Empire)[69] journal in 1915. The journal had been founded in 1913 by journalists Ishida Tomoji (1881–1942) and Kayahara Kazan (1870–1952). Both were activists in the constitutional democracy movement of the Taishō period and initially belonged to the supporters of an anti-imperialist policy of non-expansion. The *Daisan Teikoku* published the text as 'Sō Ajiashugi' (Comprehensive Asianism), without adding any commentary and only introduced it with the following brief passage:

> This essay has reached us originally written in Chinese (kanbun) by an unnamed person from the Chinese Republic. We had first placed it in a box for a while but as we now sense some interest, the translation of this essay follows.[70]

The growing interest, felt by the anonymous editor, reflected a general increase in debates about the so-called China Problem (Shina mondai) in Japanese political discourse in the post-revolutionary scenario and, in particular, after the Twenty-One Demands had been issued by Japan. Still, as Furuya has demonstrated, pro-Asianist affirmations of an Asian Monroe Doctrine remained scarce and instead, 'it seems that in this period criticism of Monroeist ideas became stronger'.[71] As Furuya argues, 'at this stage, it was generally thought that in a situation where not even China could be fully won over, it was out of touch with reality to provoke a confrontation with the West (Ōbei) by announcing an Asian Monroe Doctrine'.[72]

In this debate on how to deal with China, one author, writing on the China Problem in the *Daisan Teikoku*'s Thought and News column, advocated Greater Asianism as a 'wise policy to confuse and control Chinese public opinion'.[73] In the political mood of the day and given the Japanese perception of Asianism being of Chinese origin, however, the opposite explanation may have been more convincing: Asianism was a trick played on the Japanese by the Chinese and other 'weak' peoples of Asia. This at least was Ōyama Ikuo's interpretation of the 'pamphlet', who discussed it in a longer article in the *Shin Nihon* (New Japan) journal in the following year (1916). Ōyama (1880–1955), a professor at Tokyo's Waseda University, was a well-known leader of the Taishō democracy movement who later turned to Socialism and became chairman of the Japanese Workers' and Peasants' Party (Rōdō Nōmintō). In the early 1930s he left Japan for the United States and only returned to Japan after the end of the World War Two. Ōyama's critique, the first elaborated discussion of Asianism ever published in Japan, will be analysed in more detail in the following chapter. Here, his references to the 'pamphlet' are of particular interest. According to Ōyama, the essay appeared in a small monograph that was written by a Chinese person, secretly printed in China, and constituted 'in its entirety a propagation of Greater Asianism (Dai Ajiashugi no sengen)'.[74] Quoting from the paper, Ōyama argued:

> writing about endless transformation such as divine right theory ('to realize Greater Asianism is the eternal and inextinguishable divine right of the Asians') and evolutionary theory ('the strong win, the weak lose, that is the common law of nature') may be the special charm of Chinese logic and has no particular relevance here. The general argument, however, is that the Euro-Americans should be expelled from the political sphere of the Asians, peace and order in the Asian countries should be planned (implicitly including the preservation of the territorial integrity of China and the realization of India's independence), and despite the lack of viability as a country they should jointly share the benefits of this movement.
>
> This is the gospel of the many weak countries of Asia. As the champion of this movement, only Japan could shoulder this all at once. If the enterprise fails, Japan would surely find itself in serious straits while the weak countries that are after all bound to die would be right back where they had started. They have little to lose. And even if the enterprise ended successfully (if we fancy to think of the almost impossible becoming real), Japan would be like the leader of the Balkan allies, Bulgaria, which accomplished meritorious deeds in the subjugation of Turkey, but after the war faced the fate of a running dog after the death of the rabbit when Serbia joined with Greece. Who would guarantee that this case would not follow the same logic?[75]

As becomes clear, Ōyama's critique of 'Greater Asianism' is based on the assumption that Asianism is of Chinese origin. As such, he acknowledged its possible efficacy and validity in the Chinese struggle against the 'West'. As for Japan, however, he dismissed Asianism as extremely risky and, most likely, disadvantageous. Interestingly, Ōyama, despite his leftist leanings, gave preference to national security over solidarity with the colonized Asian countries. This attitude—Ōyama speaks of 'an undertaking with plenty of extreme dangers' and 'a gamble with an empty gun that surpasses all degrees of adventure'[76]—was indicative of contemporary political discourse in Japan. Certainly, in the pre-World War One years and partly also during the war, Asianism remained a cause that was alien to the Japanese 'success story' since the Meiji Restoration, which had relied on modernization along Western lines combined with a turn to nationalist symbols, rhetoric, and practices. It was therefore perceived as pernicious to national interests. 'Asia' was the symbol of weakness and backwardness and any cry for help from the side of (non-Japanese) Asians was to be viewed with suspicion and scepticism. Consequently, Asianism to Ōyama, as to many Japanese, contained little to gain and much to lose for Japan. It was nothing but a trap set by the Chinese in a renewed version of their ancient 'stratagem of using one barbarian against another',[77] in Ōyama's words.

It is not unlikely that the text also appeared in other Japanese journals during the 1910s. Although its distribution and authorship may ultimately remain unclear, it was not without influence on Japanese political discourse. In the still infant stage of Japanese Asianism discourse, it achieved two notable results. First, it terminologically and conceptually established Asianism as a—still minor—part of public political discourse. As a consequence, Asianism was first seriously discussed as a political key concept that could potentially both replace existing Japanese policies towards the 'West' and define its policy towards its Asian neighbours, in particular China. Japanese affirmations of Asianism, however, remained the rare exception, also owing to the assumption that Asianism was a concept of the weak. As such, it was perceived in Japan as a deceptive argument, not as a sincere appeal to Asian commonality.

Sun Yat-sen's and Dai Jitao's Appeals to Asianism

The assumption that Asianism was a concept of Chinese origin grew even stronger when prominent Chinese leaders first proposed its application. The most prominent of all was certainly Sun Yat-sen. Sun's Asianist convictions reach back to at least the late Qing period and Marius Jansen even goes as far as to claim that 'this aspect [Pan-Asianism] underlies the entire history of Japanese relations with Sun Yat-sen', which started when Sun first fled to Japan after a failed coup d'état in Canton in 1895.[78] In the following decades, according to Jansen, for Sun Pan-Asian ideas had become 'more than words; they were the integrating rationale that made possible his alliance with the Japanese'.[79] In March 1913, during his first post-revolutionary visit to Japan and as an official guest of the Japanese government, Sun Yat-sen for the first time publicly confessed to the principle of Greater Asia. Like his famous Asianism speech of 1924, it is a particularly influential example of transnational Chinese-Japanese Asianism discourse. The speech was given by a Chinese in the Chinese language in Japan, to a mostly Japanese audience. It was quickly translated into Japanese and circulated throughout Japan through Japanese newspaper reports. Sun's remarks, of course, must be viewed against the background of domestic power struggles within China, where Sun and his revolutionary followers were faced with the growing influence of Western-supported Yuan Shikai. Sun's turn to Japan and Asia, therefore, appeared a natural choice, although his friendship with Asian-minded Japanese may have led Sun to falsely assume a general pro-Asianist mood in Japan.[80] In his speech to members of the Christian Youth Association of Osaka (Seinenkai), Sun proposed 'cooperation between Japan and China' in order to secure peace in East Asia against 'Euro-American imperialism' and against the 'Euro-American barbarian civilizationism'.

> To promote the East (Tōyō) is the best method of defending the East. The progress of the East must be the progress of the world. For this aim, I should be greatly indebted to the members of the Christian Youth Association for their help with realizing Greater Asianism so that Asians can govern Asia.[81]

One month earlier (February 1913), at the invitation of the *Tōa Dōbunkai*, Sun had delivered a speech in which he enhanced his anti-colonial and anti-Western conception of Asianism through racialist arguments of commonality between China and Japan, 'China's befriended country of the same culture and same race'. Sun argued,

> Asia is the Asia of the Asians! Because the people of China and Japan are relatives and neighbours, they must not only abandon suspicion but also have trust in each other and give up the evil practice of attacking each other. [...] I wish that Japan will to the best of its ability plan the nurturing of China and cooperate with China. This is not only my individual hope but the enthusiastic desire of all Chinese people. Asia is our family and Japan and China are siblings within this family. If these twin-like siblings engage in infighting, the Asian family can never attain peace. Japan is Asia's strongest country and China is the largest country in the East. There is no doubt that if both countries can cooperate, we cannot only easily maintain peace in the East but also throughout the whole world.[82]

Even if we deduct the obvious lip service to his Japanese hosts, taken together these early appeals foreshadow Sun's later conception of Asianism which linked the quest for political autonomy to a view of 'Eastern' *versus* 'Western' civilization. This included a critique of Western racialist discourse. Like early Japanese Asianist proposals, Sun's conception of Asianism was also based on a demand for Sino-Japanese cooperation in order to attain political self-determination, above all in China. It was not surprising that Sun would appeal to the Japanese side, which had been supportive in various ways since his first exile there in the late 1890s, for help in his domestic struggle against Yuan Shikai and the warlords. As Sun's close follower and translator Dai Jitao (1890–1949) explained,[83] Sun had felt warmly welcomed by the Japanese in 1913, not only because of his eminent status but also because he openly expressed the political wish that many of his Japanese hosts also harboured: ever closer Sino-Japanese cooperation.

> On the occasion of Zhongshan's [Sun Yat-sen's] visit, all Japanese – in and out of power, high or low, old or young, male or female – expressed their attitude of welcoming him. This was not a welcome to Sun as a person but in fact because they deeply wished for Sino-Japanese cooperation to pacify the situation in East Asia. [...] In today's situation, if China wishes to develop it must cooperate with a foreign country. Japan is one of the countries that are reaching out for such cooperation. Why does Japan now wish to cooperate with our country and not before? It is because the politics of our country have become corrupted.[84]

Sino-Japanese cooperation, like Asianism, in this period was clearly an object of political and rhetorical games. It appears to have been Dai's worry that China only became an interesting partner once it was weak enough for Japan to dictate the conditions of this partnership. China's appeal to Asianism, on the other hand, was viewed in Japan as a trick to lure Japan into a trap. Attempts at constructing a discourse that would appeal to both sides failed. In the pre-war period, the perception of Asianism as a Chinese 'trick' nevertheless prevailed, since no person of a similar prominence to Sun had embraced Asianism on the Japanese side. And the more Chinese elaborations appeared, the more suspicious the Japanese became. Chinese writings that were not directed at a Japanese audience reveal that this suspicion was not quite unreasonable. In 1914, for example, Dai himself unmasked his Sinocentric understanding of Asianism as a political strategy:

Some Japanese politicians recently seem to think Japan could form an alliance with European countries to consolidate the status of the country. [...] But they don't realize that the reason the Europeans occupy China is not only China itself. The Chinese have suffered the European invasion but the damage is not only done to the Chinese. [...] In today's Asia, there is only one country that possesses the capability to act: Japan. But geographically, racially, culturally there is only one country that represents Asia: China. [...] China has already become part of the European sphere of influence and provides economic profits to the European powers as a consequence of their invasion. And Japan acts as an aide to them! It is for this reason that we see the danger and advocate Greater Asianism. In the coming years, Japanese public opinion must eventually awake to the situation in the world and Asia's status![85]

Dai's explanation above all reveals two aspects. First, regardless of all *dōbun dōshu* or common fate rhetoric, Asianism as a concept was receptive to ethnocentric arguments on a national(ist) level. To the Chinese, therefore, a positive concept of 'Asia' could denote Sinocentrism just as it could mean Japan-centrism to the Japanese (although in contemporary Japanese discourse at first a negative and non-self-referential understanding of 'Asia' prevailed). Second, from a Chinese perspective, Asianism was perceived as a potential tool to pull Japan to its side. In a way that foreshadows the final part of Sun's Greater Asianism speech delivered a decade later, Dai saw Europe and 'Asia' as being in opposition to one another and demanded the Japanese side with their geographic home—'Asia'. It becomes quite clear that already in the first years of Chinese-Japanese Asianism discourse the concept was above all employed for non-Asianist political agendas. There was little common ground between the two countries and the discursive battle for 'Asia' attested to the different perspectives and aspirations. Gotō's colonialist conception was, to be sure, miles apart from Sun's and Dai's appeal to support China's self-strengthening, independence, and its own development as a nation state within Asia, not as a part of the Japanese Empire.

The Mahan–Chirol Controversy about Japan's Asianity

In the meantime Asianism in Japan had also entered mainstream debate in a different political context which had little to do with Sino-Japanese relations but was also foreign in origin. In the early summer of 1913, the London *Times* newspaper reported on a political dispute about

Japan, although no Japanese participated directly in the debate. The protagonists in this dispute were the British journalist and diplomat Sir Valentine Chirol (1852–1929) and the American Admiral Alfred Thayer Mahan (1840–1914).[86] Interestingly, the subject of their debate was neither political-military deliberations about the coming war in Europe nor issues relating to the Middle East, about which both had published previously. Instead, they engaged in a discussion about Japan's Asianity. Against the background of the latest Californian land legislation, which in May 1913 had forbidden land acquisition by Asians ('California Alien Land Law'),[87] they discussed the Japanese ability to assimilate. Although the law was not explicitly directed at Japan or the Japanese the preceding debate there clearly revealed that it aimed at a restriction of Japanese economic influence in California. Consequently, in Japan it became known as 'anti-Japanese land law' (hai Nichi tochi hō).[88] Like many Americans outside (and possibly also within California), Chirol condemned the law as a 'bar of race' which unjustifiably discriminated against the Japanese.[89] Mahan, on the other hand, welcomed the law as a necessary consequence of the Japanese inability to assimilate. The Japanese, Mahan argued, were 'constituting a homogeneous foreign mass' that the Americans might not be able to digest:

> America doubts her power to digest and assimilate the strong national and racial characteristics which distinguish the Japanese, which are the secret of much of their success, and which, if I am not mistaken, would constitute them continually a solid homogeneous body, essentially and unchangingly foreign.[90]

As the *Times* commented in its moderation of the debate, 'the ultimate point in dispute does not affect the United States alone, still less the State of California; it is essentially a world-question'.[91] Chirol spoke of a 'grave international issue', that is, the question of whether Japan—unlike other Asian countries—was 'entitled to rank among the civilized nations'. He argued that 'other Asian peoples may more or less entirely lack the national energy and discipline and the many other peculiar qualities to which Japan owes her exaltation'.[92] Acknowledging the Japanese success in modernization and democratization, therefore, one should consider whether Japan 'has ceased to be an Asiatic nation'.[93] Mahan, however, raised doubts about the degree to which Japan's Westernization had influenced the 'racial characteristics' of the

Japanese.⁹⁴ The *Times*, too, viewed the dispute and the Japanese policy ambivalently. It reminded its readers of anti-Western tendencies in Japanese political circles and asked the crucial question:

> On the one hand, she [Japan] demands recognition because her people are not as other Asiatics. On the other hand, as our Tokyo Correspondent told us on Saturday, her publicists are now asserting that 'to Japan is assigned' the leadership in the claim of the 'coloured' races against the 'non-coloured'. These two sets of claims are mutually destructive. Japan cannot have it both ways. Before this problem becomes acute, she must make up her mind whether she wishes to present herself as aloof from other Asiatic races, or as the avowed champion of Pan-Asiatic ideals.⁹⁵

The response of published opinion in Japan to this choice was almost unanimous. The *Tokyo Nichi Nichi* daily newspaper affirmed that Japan was only aiming at fighting the injustice that Japanese were suffering as a consequence of the unfair Californian legislation. If other Asians viewed this complaint as an opportunity to decry their oppression by the 'Whites', Japan could not be held responsible. The editorial tried to conciliate:

> Not even in its dreams does [Japan] think of planning such a disadvantageous and risky undertaking as leading under the banner of Asianism (han Ajiashugi) other Asians to fight against the white countries of Euro-America.⁹⁶

While the author tried to distinguish Japan and the Japanese from 'other Asians', he conceded that Japan's 'progress and superiority' might inspire the awakening of all Asians. Also the *Osaka Asahi*, the leading Japanese newspaper of the day, rejected Japan's assumed pan-Asian ambitions as an unjustified accusation by the 'West'. Rather surprised about the Mahan–Chirol debate, it explained to its readers:

> Admiral Mahan argues that, because the Japanese and Americans historically differ regarding race, the Japanese people may rightfully be excluded for their health and strength. He views the modern development of the Japanese people only from the viewpoint of the Yellow Peril theory. When the *Times* asks that Japan must consider if it is embracing Asianist ideals or not and if the progress of the Japanese people should not awake all Asian people and should be the start of the outbreak of an All-Asian movement

in which Japan plays a central part, this idea is based on the viewpoint of a small group of debaters. [...] To claim that the Japanese would become active believing in All Asianism, reveals how he [Mahan] is caught in the supposition of a future philosophical or civilizational clash between the West and the East and reflects the fear of [Mahan's] own illusion. [...] To unify one people already demands great effort and there is no reason why the practically oriented Japanese would ever embrace a fantasy such as All Asianism. Among the Whites, the racial bond is stronger than the national but as for the Japanese, our national bond is stronger than our racial. This makes the existence of the ideal of All Asianism even more unlikely.[97]

While the author himself was not free of certain stereotypical thoughts about the 'West' and the 'Whites', he rightfully linked the debate about Japan's assimilability to 'Western' Yellow Peril theory, on which it was based. In fact, while Japan's empire had been growing, it had avoided everything that would portray Japan as a possible instigator or leader of 'Asia'. Nevertheless, the Mahan–Chirol controversy as 'Western' 'Asia' discourse *en miniature* reminded the Japanese of the almost inseparable link—in the eyes of non-Asians—between them and the 'other Asians', from which many Japanese tried to dissociate rather desperately. Therefore it was felt in Japan, as the editorial concluded, that 'a boycott out of fear of All Asianism (zen Ajiashugi) is an extremely unfair punishment of the Japanese'.[98]

With their comments, both Japanese newspapers fully conformed to the policy of the Japanese government in this case. It was still careful to avoid anything that could raise fear in the West of a joint Asianist agitation under Japanese leadership. To this end, it supported the collection and publication of essays written by thirty-five Japanese opinion leaders and translated into English in the following year (1914). *Japan's Message to America*[99] was an obvious propagandistic measure which appeared to be rather effective.[100] The *New York Times* praised the 'remarkable book' as 'Japan's friendly message to the United States' and as 'a reply to the sensationalists, jingoists, and yellow journalists of both countries', which fed the fear of 'yellow peril' here and of 'American aggression' there.[101] In detail, the paper quoted Premier Ōkuma Shigenobu's eulogies of East–West conciliation and pro-American contributions from prominent Japanese politicians and entrepreneurs such as Kaneko Kentarō, Ozaki Yukio and Kondō Renpei. Ōkuma's essay most directly reads like a reply to the Mahan–Chirol controversy. Ōkuma argued that the Japanese were different from other Asians, particularly apt to adapt to the outside world and to harmonize East and West. Therefore, in contrast to the Chinese, who were characterized by 'a narrow provincialism peculiar to them', Japan had already become part of the civilized world. He concluded:

> To brand us Japanese as inferior because we are a coloured race is a bigotry that we must combat and destroy through the fulfilment of our national mission.[102]

Japanese, English and American newspapers reported in detail about the dispute between Chirol, who had agreed with this differentiation between the Japanese and other Asians, and Mahan, who had remained sceptical. The controversy and its coverage had two important consequences for Japanese 'Asia' discourse. First, following the coverage of this issue in widely read Japanese media, the larger Japanese public learnt for the first time that Japanese Asianity and Japan's potential role as a leader of 'Asia' was controversially discussed abroad, that is, in the 'West'. This included the attribution of the leadership role to Japan. Second, the politico-cultural debate about Asia's meaning and significance for Japan terminologically and conceptually gained well-defined contours. In place of previous rather loosely employed concepts of Asian commonality, such as 'same culture, same race' (dōbun dōshu), 'Raising Asia' (kō A), or 'White Peril' (hakka), Asianism as the principle of 'Asia' now entered mainstream discourse as a comprehensive key concept.[103] The overwhelming reaction of published discourse in Japan, however, remained negative; the Japanese, it appeared, were not yet willing to embrace 'Asia'.

Among the few Japanese who, against the dominant official and public trend, immediately welcomed Asianism as 'new thought' in international politics was the Buddhist scholar Ōzumi Shōfū (Shun). Ōzumi (1881–1923) had been a journalist with the liberal *Yorozuchōhō* (Morning News) newspaper before he became a professor at Shinshū Ōtani University, a Buddhist university of the Pure Land Sect denomination. He died while he was studying abroad in Paris. In his view, All Asianism (zen Ajiashugi) represented an Asian version of ethnic nationalism (minzokushugi) which stood for the demand for the 'awakening of nations'. Drawing analogies from pan-Germanism and pan-Slavism, Ōzumi argued that the Japanese should follow suit and pursue the realization of a pan-nationalist agenda, namely Asianism. Interestingly, Ōzumi's conception of Asianism was not directly influenced by racialist arguments from the Mahan–Chirol controversy; nor did he refer to the Asian Monroe Doctrine as proposed in the *Minli Bao* article. Instead, Ōzumi viewed Asianism as the principle that Japan should adopt to prove its role as a vanguard of modern civilization, since pan-isms represented—to Ōzumi—the global political future for the twentieth century, just as the nation state had represented the paradigm of the nineteenth century. Consequently, he critically assessed the lack of Asianist consciousness both in Japan and in the rest of Asia:

> However, between most countries in Asia there are almost no ethnic bonds. [...] Therefore, it is extremely difficult to discover psychological linkages to unify Asia beyond its mere geographical relations. Consequently we could say that All Asianism is ultimately only an illusion and its realization is no more than a fantasy. But why do we only talk so negatively? It is Japan's responsibility to discover how All Asianism can be realized and confront All Slavism by searching for these psychological linkages, by connecting Asia, and by establishing a belief. In other words, it is we who must grasp the pivots of All Asianism and make them the foundation of our belief. The later we can establish All Asianism, the later we will be able to play a key role within global civilization. The real status of Japanese civilization in the world will be determined by its ability to grasp this belief. The destiny to establish All Asianism is on the shoulders of the Japanese people and this mission is quite enormous.[104]

Ōzumi's early affirmative contribution to Asianism discourse signals the beginning of the spread of a conception that views Asianism as a part of an unstoppable trend of the time. For this reason, his conception was less explicitly informed by racialist or culturalist than geopolitical considerations. Yet, to Ōzumi Asia constituted a community of fate that the Japanese had to lead, since the Japanese had, unlike the Chinese and Koreans, already grasped the need of the time correctly in the nineteenth century, when they replied to the Western challenge by adopting the framework of a 'modern' nation state. Now, the Japanese needed to accept their role as forerunners in Asia in order to participate in a perceived new global phenomenon: the geopolitical organization of peoples according to geographical proximity and psychological commonality. The emergence of Asianism on the surface of mainstream political debate in Japan equipped Ōzumi with a conceptual tool to place Japan's future policy in the context of global trends and, simultaneously, to formulate a specific agenda for his fellow Japanese. In the course of the following decade, Japan's Asianist 'mission' came to be increasingly taken for granted without further elaboration. In this sense Ōzumi's inclusion of All Asianism in his collection of 'new thought' in 1913 seems almost prophetic. Although Asianism continued to be received sceptically in Japan for some time it would not disappear from playing an important role in political debate in the following months, years, and indeed decades.

Conclusion

Japanese consciousness of 'Asia' before the inception of Asianism had already centred on defining Japan's own position vis-à-vis other countries, empires, and regions. 'Asia' discourse until the early twentieth century contained many of the arguments and references that would later become cornerstones in the debate about the meaning and importance of Asianism. As a principle that linked and sometimes unified geopolitical, racialist, and culturalist elements of previous discourse, Asianism facilitated and also required a new approach to 'Asia'. What are the implications of Japan's commitment or denial of 'Asia'? Are there alternatives to accepting its Asianity? By the early 1910s, Japanese society had come into possession of a new conceptual tool to analyse and debate these pressing questions. As a new concept Asianism became 'publicly articulated and discussed' (Skinner). To borrow Kubota's metaphor, by the beginning of the Taishō period Japan's political discourse was visibly pregnant with Asianism but at first it remained denied as an unwanted child. With few exceptions, Asianism was rejected, partly because of its assumed foreign—Chinese or 'Western'—provenance. Asianism before World War One was neither perceived as being of Japanese pedigree nor as advantageous for Japan. This view, however, would change rather rapidly with the beginning of World War One. In China, on the other hand, prominent public figures were quicker to embrace Asianism as a concept that might foster the nation- and state-building processes within and help to improve China's position in the region, above all vis-à-vis Japan. In China, too, however, a wider discussion of the new concept only started during World War One.

Notes

1. Quentin Skinner, *The Foundations of Modern Political Thought*, Cambridge: Cambridge University Press 1978, Vol. 2, 352. With kind permission of Quentin Skinner.

2. See Yamamuro, *Shisō Kadai toshite no Ajia*, 32.
3. For the following see Matsuda Kōichirō, '"Ajia" no "tashō"sei. Ajiashugi izen no Ajiaron' [The foreign-imposed character of 'Asia'. Asia discourse before Asianism], *Nihon Gaikō ni okeru Ajiashugi* [Asianism in Japan's foreign policy], ed. Nihon Seiji Gakkai, Tokyo: Iwanami Shoten 1999, 33–53: 41–45.
4. See Matsuda, ' "Ajia" no "tashō"sei', 42–43.
5. See Matsumoto Saburō, 'Shōwa shoki ni okeru Nihon no Chūgokukan' [The Japanese view of China in the early Showa period], *Nitchū kankei no sōgo imēji* [The mutual image of Japanese–Chinese relations], ed. Fujii Shōzō et al., Tokyo: Ajia Seikei Gakkai 1975, 32–65: 32–35 and Matsuda, '"Ajia" no "tashō"sei', 43–45.
6. Matsuda, ' "Ajia" no "tashō"sei', 43.
7. See Rebecca E. Karl, 'Creating Asia: China in the World at the Beginning of the Twentieth Century', *American Historical Review*, Vol. 103, No. 4 (October 1998), 1096–1118: 1100–1101.
8. Zhao Jun, *Xinhai geming yu dalu langren* [The Xinhai Revolution and Mainland Ronins], Beijing 1991, 17 quoted in Karl 1998, 1101.
9. See Karl, 'Creating Asia', 1102.
10. Kawashima, 'Kindai Chūgoku no Ajia kan to Nihon', 420.
11. Fukuzawa's original essay is reprinted in *Fukuzawa Yukichi Zenshū*, Vol. 10, Tokyo: Iwanami Shoten 1960, 238–240. Although hardly known until the 1930s, conceptually Fukuzawa's 'Datsu A Ron' may be regarded as representative of the dominant anti-Asianist political thinking of the time.
12. See Yasukawa Junosuke, *Fukuzawa Yukichi no Ajia ninshiki. Nihon kindai shizou o toraekaesu* [Fukuzawa Yukichi's Asia consciousness. Responding to the image of modern Japan's history], Tokyo: Kōbunken 2000 and for an English summary of a classical early post-war Japanese evaluation Sannosuke Matsumoto, 'Profile of Asian Minded Man V: Yukichi Fukuzawa', *The Developing Economies*, 5-1 (March 1967), 156–172.
13. Tarui is thought to have first written this treatise in the same year as Fukuzawa's 'Datsu A Ron' was published (1885). The original manuscript, however, got lost when Tarui was imprisoned for conspiracy in 1885 and was first published only in 1893, written in classical Chinese (kanbun). See Kawahara Hiroshi, *Kindai Nihon no Ajia Ninshiki* [Modern Japanese Consciousness of Asia], Tokyo: Daisan Bunmeisha 1976, 77–108 for a comparative study of the Asia consciousness of Fukuzawa and Tarui.
14. Quoted in Takeuchi Yoshimi's adaption of Tarui's 'Dai Tō Gappō Ron', *Ajiashugi* [Asianism], ed. Takeuchi Yoshimi, Tokyo: Chikuma Shobō 1963, 106–129: 129. On Tarui's treatise in English see Tadashi Suzuki,

'Profile of Asian Minded Man IX: Tōkichi Tarui', *The Developing Economies*, 6–1 (March 1968), 79–100.
15. Quoted in Takeuchi, *Ajiashugi*, 107.
16. See, for example, Takeuchi, 'Ajiashugi no tenbō', 7–63. A rare but notable exception is Bunzō Hashikawa, 'Japanese Perspectives on Asia: From Dissociation to Coprosperity', *The Chinese and the Japanese. Essays in Political and Cultural Interactions*, ed. Akira Iriye, Princeton: Princeton University Press 1980, 328–355. See pages 331–332 on Sugita's 'Kō A Saku'.
17. Amended translation of Sugita's text as reproduced in Hashikawa, 'Japanese Perspectives on Asia', 331–332. The original is reprinted in *Sugita Junzan-ō* [The honourable Mr. Sugita Junzan], ed. Saiga Hakuai, Tokyo: Junzan Kai 1928, 543–551.
18. *Sugita Junzan-ō* [The honourable Mr. Sugita Junzan], ed. Saiga Hakuai, Tokyo: Junzan Kai 1928, 548.
19. For pre-Taishō Asianist writings other than Sugita's and Tarui's, including Taoka Reiun's proposal of a 'Great Alliance of East Asia' (Tō-A no dai dōmei) from 1897, see Itō Teruo, *Ajia to Kindai Nihon. Han shinryaku no shisō to undō* [Asia and modern Japan. Anti-invasionist thought and movement], Tokyo: Shakai Hyōronsha 1990.
20. Hazama Naoki, 'Shoki Ajiashugi ni tsuite no shiteki kōsatsu. Sone Toshitora to Shin A Sha' [Historical observations on early Asianism. Sone Toshitora and the Raise Asia Society], *Tōa* [East Asia], 411 (September 2001), 88–98.
21. On the *Kō A Kai* see Morifumi Kuroki, 'Kō A Kai no Ajiashugi' [Asianism of the Kō A Kai], *Hōsei Kenkyū* [Journal of law and politics], 71–4 (March 2005), 615–655 and Urs Matthias Zachmann, 'The Foundation Manifesto of the Kōakai (Raising Asia Society) and the Ajia Kyōkai (Asia Association), 1880–1883', *Pan-Asianism: A Documentary History 1860–2010*, Vol. 1, ed. Sven Saaler and C.W.A. Szpilman, Boulder: Rowman & Littlefield, 2011, 53–60.
22. Watanabe Kōki, 'Kō A Kai sōritsu taikai ni okeru enzetsu' [Speech to the great founding assembly of the Kō A Kai] (1880) as quoted in Itō Teruo, *Ajia to Kindai Nihon. Han shinryaku no shisō to undō* [Asia and modern Japan. Anti-invasionist thought and movement], Tokyo: Shakai Hyōronsha 1990, 20–22: 21.
23. On the *Tōa Dōbunkai* see Aibara Shigeki, 'Konoe Atsumaro to Shina Hozen Ron' [Konoe Atsumaro and the preserving China debate], *Kindai Nihon no Ajiakan* [Modern Japanese views of Asia], ed. Okamoto Kōji, Kyoto: Mineruva Shobō 1998: 51–77 and Urs Matthias Zachmann, 'The Foundation Manifesto of the Tōa Dōbunkai (East Asian Common Culture Society), 1898', *Pan-Asianism: A Documentary*

History 1860–2010, Vol. 1, ed. Sven Saaler and C.W.A. Szpilman, Boulder: Rowman & Littlefield, 2011, 115–120. The organization was founded in 1898, when the *Tōa Kai* and *Dōbunkai*, two other Asianist associations founded in the same year, had merged.

24. See Douglas R. Reynolds, 'Chinese Area Studies in Prewar China: Japan's Toa Dobun Shoin in Shanghai, 1900–1945', *The Journal of Asian Studies*, 45–5 (November 1986), 945–970.
25. See Itō, *Ajia to Kindai Nihon*, 26–27.
26. On the *Brotherhood* see Lee Gyeongseog, 'Ajiashugi no kōyō to bunki. Ashū Washinkai no sōritsu o chūshin ni' [The Uplift and Divergence of Asianism. Focusing on the Asiatic Humanitarian Brotherhood], *Waseda Seiji Kōhō kenkyū* [Waseda Research into Politics and Public Law] 69 (May 2002), 167–199.
27. For this group and its links to the *Brotherhood* see Gotelind Müller, *China, Kropotkin und der Anarchismus: eine Kulturbewegung im China des frühen 20. Jahrhunderts unter dem Einfluss des Westens und japanischer Vorbilder* [China, Kropotkin and Anarchism. A Cultural Movement in China in the early twentieth century under the influence of the West and of Japanese Models], Wiesbaden: Harrassowitz 2001, 162–179.
28. See Takeuchi Zensaku, 'Meiji makki ni okeru Chū-Nichi kakumei undō no kōryū' [Exchanges of the Chinese and Japanese Revolutionary Movements in the late Meiji Period], *Chūgoku Kenkyū* [China Research], No. 5 (September 1948), 74–95.
29. See Müller, *China, Kropotkin und der Anarchismus*, 179.
30. See Lee Gyeongseog, 'Ajiashugi no kōyō to bunki. Ashū Washinkai no sōritsu o chūshin ni' [The Uplift and Divergence of Asianism. Focussing on the Asiatic Humanitarian Brotherhood], *Waseda Seiji Kōhō kenkyū* [Waseda Research into Politics and Public Law] 69 (May 2002), 167–199: 195.
31. For a reprint of its Japanese version see Takeuchi Zensaku, 'Meiji makki ni okeru Chū-Nichi kakumei undō no kōryū' [Exchanges of the Chinese and Japanese Revolutionary Movements in the late Meiji Period], *Chūgoku Kenkyū* [China Research], No. 5 (September 1948), 74–95: 77–78.
32. Zachmann, *China and Japan in the Late Meiji Period*, 72.
33. See Baron Suyematsu [Suematsu Kenchō], *The Risen Sun*, London: Archibald Constable 1905, 292.
34. Suyematsu, *The Risen Sun*, 294–295.
35. See 'shugi', *Kōjien*, Tokyo: Iwanami Shoten 2003, 5th edition (electronic version). Fukuchi (1841–1906) was a son of a Nagasaki physician who worked as a translator for the Tokugawa *bakufu* and belonged to the first Japanese who had travelled to Europe several times, initially

sent by the *bakufu* (1861, 1865) and later as a member of the Iwakura mission (1871). After 1874, Fukuchi became well-known and influential, first as an essayist and then as president of the *Tokyo Nichi Nichi Shinbun* newspaper company. Due to his prolific and influential spread of 'Western' knowledge in Japan, together with Fukuzawa Yukichi, he was referred to as one of 'the Country's twin fortunes', which alludes to the common character 'fuku' (fortune, blessing) in their family names. On Fukuchi's life and career see James L. Huffman, *Politics of the Meiji press: the life of Fukuchi Gen'ichirō*, Honolulu: University Press of Hawaii 1980.

36. For a detailed history of Chinese *isms*, see Ivo Spira, *A Conceptual History of Chinese -Isms. The Modernization of Ideological Discourse, 1895–1925*, Leiden: Brill 2015.
37. Endō Ryūkichi, 'Shugi o ronzu', *Shakai* [Society], 20 (1900), 37–38.
38. Sun Yat-sen, *Sanmin Zhuyi* [Three People's Principles], Taipei: Cheng Chung Books 1988, 1.
39. On the Rescript and its role in school education see Carol Gluck, *Japan's Modern Myth. Ideology in the Late Meiji Period*, Princeton: Princeton University Press 1985, 146–150.
40. 'Izureka ze, izureka hi' [Which is right and which is wrong], *Kyūshū Nichi Nichi Shinbun* [Kyūshū Daily Newspaper], 2831, 12 January 1892.
41. See Ono Masaaki, 'Kumamoto Eigakkō jiken no tenmatsu to kyōiku kai' [The circumstances of the Kumamoto English School incident and the education world], *Kyōikugaku Zasshi* [Pedagogy Journal] 28 (1994), 177.
42. On the Seikyōsha and their publications see Satō Yoshimaru, *Meiji Nashonarizumu no kenkyū. Seikyōsha no seiritsu to sono shūhen.* [Research into Meiji nationalism. The founding of the Seikyōsha and its environs] Tokyo: Fusō Shobō 1998 and Nakanome Tōru, *Seikyōsha no kenkyū* [Research into the Seikyōsha], Kyoto: Shibunkaku 1993 and pages 207–210 in particular for the group's view of Asia.
43. Miyake, Shiga, and other members of the *Seikyōsha* had been founding members of the *Tōhō Kyōkai*, an Asianist organization founded in 1891 which contemporary newspapers characterized as 'conservative' and 'academic' rather than political. See Hazama Naoki, 'Shoki Ajiashugi ni tsuite no shiteki kōsatsu. Tōhō Kyōkai ni tsuite' [Historical observations on early Asianism. On the Tōhō Kyōkai], *Tōa* [East Asia], 414 (December 2001), 66–74.
44. 'Ajiashigi to wa nan zo' [What is Asianism?], *Ajia* [Asia], 32 (1 February 1892), 2–3: 3. Asianism as 'Ajiashigi' conforms to the frequent use of 'shigi' instead of 'shugi' in publications of the *Seikyōsha*.

See Hiraishi Naoaki, 'Kindai Nihon no Ajiashugi. Meiji ki no sho rinen o chūshin ni' [Modern Japan's Asianism. Focusing on different ideals in the Meiji period], *Kindaikazō. Ajia kara kangaeru* [The image of modernization. Thinking from Asia], 5, ed. Mizoguchi Yūzō et al., Tokyo: Tokyo Daigaku Shuppankai 1994, 265–291: 286 (fn. 1).
45. See Douglas R. Reynolds, *China 1898–1912: The Xinzheng Revolution and Japan*, Cambridge, MA: Harvard University Press 1993.
46. Kubota Yoshirō, *Tōyō no kiki tsuku taigai kokuze* [Crisis in the East and national foreign policy], Tokyo: Fuzan bō 1898, 12.
47. The *Kinkikan* in Tokyo's Kanda district became famous as the place of a political scandal ('Red Flag Incident', Akahata Jiken) exactly one decade later. In June 1908, leading Japanese socialists including Ōsugi Sakae, Sakai Toshihiko, and Yamakawa Hitoshi were arrested by police when they tried to leave the hall carrying a red flag with the five white characters 'mu seifu kyōsan' on it, denoting anarchism (mu seifu shugi) and communism (kyōsan shugi).
48. Kubota Yoshirō, *Tōyō no kiki tsuku taigai kokuze* [Crisis in the East and national foreign policy], Tokyo: Fuzan bō 1898, 29.
49. Kubota, *Tōyō no kiki tsuku taigai kokuze*, 31–32.
50. For details of the Monroe Doctrine and a discussion of Pan-Americanism in the context of Pan-Nationalisms see Louis L. Snyder, *Macro-Nationalisms. A History of the Pan-Movements*, Westport: Greenwood Press 1984, 225–246.
51. Kubota, *Tōyō no kiki tsuku taigai kokuze*, 185–187.
52. See Kubota, *Tōyō no kiki tsuku taigai kokuze*, 198.
53. On the *Minli Bao* see Zhang Yufa, *Qingji de geming tuanti* [Revolutionary groups in the Qing period], Taibei: Zhongyang Yanjiuyuan Jindaishi Yanjiusuo 1992 (2nd ed.), 406–415: 407.
54. 'Da Yaxiya zhuyi lun' [On Greater Asianism], *Minli Bao* [Independent People's Paper] 15 November 1912, 2. On this article and other Asianist writings in the *Minli Bao* see Craig A. Smith, *Constructing Chinese Asianism:Intellectual Writings on East Asian Regionalism (1896–1924)*, PhD dissertation (University of British Columbia), 2014, Chap. 4.
55. Although Ibuka's name initially appears on the list of potential participants from the *Seiyūkai* (see 'Seiyūkai no Shina yuki giin' [Members of parliament from the Seiyūkai going to China], *Asahi Shinbun*, 27 September 1912, 3), two days later his name is not mentioned on a final list of nine participants from different political parties ('Shina yuki daigishi kettei' [Decision on members of parliament going to China], *Asahi Shinbun*, 29 September 1912, 2). Later reports, however, suggest that more than the previously mentioned nine members of the Lower House participated in the tour. See 'Giindan' [Group of Parliamentarians],

Asahi Shinbun, 25 October 1912, 2. In October and November 1912, the *Minli Bao* carried several short articles that mentioned (and welcomed) the inspection tour. According to these reports, members of the Japanese group also met with Sun Yat-sen.
56. See *Gikai seido hyakunenshi* [One hundred years of parliamentary system], Vol. 12, ed. Shugiin/Sangiin [Lower and Upper Houses], Tokyo: Ōkura shō insatsukyoku 1990, 39–40.
57. I am grateful to Professor Kawashima Shin for this information.
58. 'Da Yaxiya zhuyi lun' [On Greater Asianism], *Minli Bao* [Independent People's Paper] 15 November 1912, 2.
59. I have been unable to identify even a single reaction to this article in any Chinese publication. In March 1913, the *Minli Bao* published a series of articles by Ye Chucang (1887–1946), one of the paper's editors, titled '*Da Yazhou zhuyi*' (Greater Asianism). Ye defined the cornerstones of his conception of Asianism as (1) 'concluding contracts to protect or promote the common interests of Asia', (2) 'morally supporting the independence of the countries of Asia', (3) 'jointly planning Asia's expansion abroad', and (4) 'containing the international confrontation of Asia from abroad'. See Ye Chucang, 'Da Yazhou zhuyi', *Minli Bao*, 15 March 1913, 3. However, Ye makes no reference to the 1912 article and it is doubtful whether his articles were indeed inspired by the piece published in the same journal four months earlier. A potential different and maybe more likely source of inspiration are Sun Yat-sen's first references to Asianism in public speeches in February and March 1913 (see below). I am grateful to Craig Smith for the reference to Ye's articles. For a discussion of Ye's and other Asianist writing in the *Minli Bao* see Smith, *Constructing Chinese Asianism*, Chap. 6.
60. The book was based on a speech Gotō had delivered in May 1914 on the same topic at the *Saiwai Kurabu* (Happiness Club), an association of members of the Upper House based in Tokyo's Kōjimachi. His book was republished by the *Takushoku Shinpōsha* in 1921. Apart from a new preface, however, the content of both books was identical.
61. Chang Han-Yu and Ramon H. Myers, 'Japanese Colonial Development Policy in Taiwan, 1895–1906: A Case of Bureaucratic Entrepreneurship', *Journal of Asian Studies*, 22-4 (August 1963), 433–449: 437.
62. Gotō Shinpei, *Nihon Shokumin seisaku ippan* [General outline of Japanese Colonial Policy], Tokyo: Takushoku Shinpōsha 1921 [1914], 113.
63. Gotō, *Nihon Shokumin seisaku ippan*, 114.
64. Gotō later claimed that he had proposed Greater Asianism as a colonial policy to Itō Hirobumi as early as 1907. In fact, the 'Itsukushima

Yawa' [Evening talks on Itsukushima], a recollection of their conversation, includes such references. However, these recollections were only written in the 1920s and it would appear strange that, when Gotō first publicly advocated Greater Asianism as being of Chinese origin in 1914, he would not have referred to his own previous proposal had he indeed made one. It appears more likely that Gotō anachronistically rephrased his conversation with Itō and adopted the concept, just as he later adopted the authorship of the 'pamphlet' (1924) which he had initially introduced as being from Sichuan. For the Gotō–Itō talk in 1907 see Komatsu Midori, *Meiji Gaikō Hiwa* [Unknown episodes of Meiji foreign policy], Tokyo: Chikura Shobō 1936, 414–417 and Tsurumi Yūsuke, *Seiden Gotō Shinpei. Mantetsu jidai 1906–1908 nen* [Real Biography of Gotō Shinpei, the times at the Manchurian Railway Company, 1906–1908], Tokyo: Fujiwara Shoten 2005, 487–526.
65. Gotō Shinpei, *Nihon Shokumin Ron* [On Japanese colonization], Tokyo: Kōmindōmei 1915, 98–99.
66. Gotō, *Nihon Shokumin Ron*, 99–100.
67. 'Gotō dan no sokumenkan" [Baron Goto's point of view], *Asahi Shinbun*, 10 November 1915, 9.
68. See 'Kakugi Kettei' [Cabinet resolution], 9 January 1917, quoted in Nohara Shirō, *Ajia no Rekishi to shisō* [Asian history and thought], Tokyo: Kōbundō 1966, 105 (fn. 7).
69. On the journal see Matsuo Takayoshi, 'Kaisetsu', *Daisan teikoku. Kaisetsu, sōmokuji, sakuin* [The Third Empire. Commentary, general table of contents, index], Tokyo: Fuji Shuppan 1984, 5–22.
70. 'Sō Ajiashugi' [Comprehensive Asianism], *Daisan Teikoku* [The Third Empire], 5 May 1915, 27.
71. Furuya, 'Ajiashugi to sono shūhen', 72.
72. Furuya, 'Ajiashugi to sono shūhen', 73.
73. 'Shina Mondai Ikan' [How to deal with the China Problem], *Daisan Teikoku* [The Third Empire], 5 May 1915, 26.
74. Ōyama Ikuo, 'Dai Ajiashugi no unmei' [The fate of Greater Asianism], *Shin Nihon* [New Japan], 6–3 (1 March 1916), 18–30: 22.
75. Ōyama, 'Dai Ajiashugi no unmei', 22–23.
76. Ōyama, 'Dai Ajiashugi no unmei', 24.
77. Ōyama, 'Dai Ajiashugi no unmei', 30.
78. Marius B. Jansen, *The Japanese and Sun Yat-sen*, Stanford: Stanford University Press 1954, 201.
79. Jansen, *The Japanese and Sun Yat-sen*, 2.
80. On Sun's view of Japan and his reception in Japan in 1913 see Jansen, *The Japanese and Sun Yat-sen*, Chap. 7.

81. 'Sai Zaka no Son Issen shi' [Sun Yat-sen in Osaka], *Osaka Asahi* (12 March 1913), quoted in *Son Bun Kōen 'Dai Ajiashugi' shiryōshū* [Collection of materials of Sun Yat-sen's 'Greater Asianism' speech], ed. Chin Tokujin and Yasui Sankichi, Kyoto: Hōritsu Bunkasha 1989, 294–295: 295.
82. Sun Yat-sen, 'Chū-Nichi wa tagai ni teikei subeshi' [China and Japan must cooperate] (15 February 1913), quoted in *Chūgokujin no Nihonjinkan 100nen shi* [A History of one hundred years of Chinese views of the Japanese], ed. Kojima Shinji et al., Tokyo: Jiyū Kokuminsha 1974, 151. A slightly diverging Chinese version is reprinted in *Sun Zhongshan ji wai ji* [Writings by Sun Yat-sen not included in his collected writings], ed. Chen Xulu and Hao Shengchao, Shanghai: Renmin Chubanshe 1990, 76–81.
83. On Dai and his Asia consciousness see Kubo Juntarō, *Dai Jitao ni okeru 'Chūgoku Kakumei' to sono shisō. Chūgoku, Nihon, Ajia o megutte.* [Dai Jitao's 'Chinese Revolution' and its thought: China, Japan, Asia] (PhD Dissertation Kobe University 2005), accessible online: http://www.lib.kobe-u.ac.jp/repository/thesis/d1/D1003482.pdf (last accessed 16 September 2017).
84. Dai Jitao, 'Qiangquan yinmou zhi heimu' [The mastermind of intrigues by state power] (3 April 1913), *Dai Jitao Xinhai Wenji* [Collection Dai Jitao's Xinhai Writings], Vol. 2, 1401–1403, quoted in Dong Shikui, 'Dai Jitao minzokushugi no myakuraku. Han-Nichi to kyō-Nichi ni yureta jikohozonshugi' [The context of Dai Jitao's nationalism. The principle of self-preservation unsettled by Anti-Japanism and the fear of Japan], *Kotoba to Bunka* [Word and Culture], Vol. 6 (2005), 121–140: 127.
85. Dai Jitao, 'Ouluoba Datongmeng lun' [On a great union of Europe] (10 July 1914), *Dai Jitao Ji* [Collected Writings of Dai Jitao], ed. Tang Wenquan and Sang Bing, Wuhan: Huazhong Shifan Daxue Chubanshe 1990, 730–753: 731.
86. I have introduced this dispute as an origin of mainstream Japanese Asianism discourse in my '"Unter dem Banner des Asianismus": Transnationale Dimensionen des japanischen Asianismus-Diskurses der Taishō-Zeit (1912–26)' [Under the banner of Asianism: transnational dimensions of Japanese Asianism discourse in the Taishō period, 1912–26], *Comparativ*, 18–6 (2008), 34–52: 40–42.
87. On the background and the reception of the 'California Alien Land Law' of 1913 see Minohara Toshihiro, *Kariforunia shū no hai Nichi undō to Nichi–Bei kankei. Imin mondai o meguru Nichi–Bei masatsu, 1906–1921 nen* [The anti-Japanese movement in California and Japanese–American relations. Japanese–American friction in the immigration

problem], Tokyo: Yūhikaku 2006, Chap. 2 and Roger Daniels, *The Politics of Prejudice. The Anti-Japanese Movement in California and the Struggle for Japanese Exclusion*, New York: Atheneum 1974, Chap. 4. The law was the result (and 'success') of the continuous lobbying by racist groups such as the 'Oriental Exclusion League' or the 'Japanese Exclusion League of California', which—despite the 'Gentlemen's Agreement'" of 1907 between Japan and the United States that obstructed Japanese immigration to California considerably anyway— fought for even stricter measures against Asians and Japanese in particular, under the slogan 'Keep California white!'.
88. Today, in Japan the name 'First anti-Japanese land law' (Daiichiji hai Nichi tochi hō) has become common as California passed a second law of similar content in 1920 ('California Alien Land Act of 1920'). See Minohara, *Kariforunia shū no hai Nichi undō to Nichi–Bei kankei*, 35 and 91.
89. Valentine Chirol, 'Japan Among the Nations. The Bar of Race', *The Times*, 19 May 1913.
90. Alfred Thayer Mahan, 'Japan Among the Nations. Admiral Mahan's Views', *The Times*, 23 June 1913.
91. 'Leading Article: Japan's Place in the World', *The Times*, 19 May 1913, 7.
92. Chirol, 'Japan Among the Nations'.
93. Chirol, 'Japan Among the Nations'.
94. See Mahan, 'Japan Among the Nations'.
95. 'The American Attitude towards Japan', *The Times*, 23 June 1913.
96. See 'Nihonjin to hoka no Ajiajin' [Japanese and other Asians], *Tokyo Nichi Nichi Shinbun*, 26 June 1913.
97. See 'Nihon minzoku no dōkasei' [The assimilability of the Japanese people], *Osaka Asahi Shinbun*, 28 June 1913. When Mahan died only one year later, the memory of his anti-Japanese stance was still fresh and the *Asahi* reported the news under the headline 'Anti-Japanese Shogun dies' (Hai-Nichi shōgun chōsei), see *Tokyo Asahi Shinbun*, 4 December 1914, 2.
98. 'Nihon minzoku no dōkasei' [The assimilability of the Japanese people], *Osaka Asahi Shinbun*, 28 June 1913.
99. *Japan's Message to America*, ed. Naoichi Masaoka, Tokyo: [s.n.] 1914. In the same year an 'authorized American version' was published under the title *Japan to America. A Symposium of Papers by Political Leaders and Representative Citizens of Japan on Conditions in Japan and on the Relations between Japan and the United States*, ed. Naoichi Masaoka, New York/London: G.P. Putnam's Sons 1914.

100. The positive reception of the book in the East of the United States is not very surprising, as this part of the country was affected by Asian immigration far less than the Western part. In addition, the Californian legislation had from the beginning been criticized by the federal government. On the dispute in this question between Washington and Sacramento see Minohara, *Kariforunia shū no hai Nichi undō to Nichi–Bei kankei*, Chap. 2 and Thomas A. Bailey, 'California, Japan, and the Alien Land Legislation of 1913', *Pacific Historical Review*, No.1 (1932), 36–59. *Japan to America* was probably less well received in California as anti-Japanese groups continued their agitation and achieved a further tightening of land and immigration legislation in 1920.

101. See 'Japan's friendly message to the United States', *New York Times*, 4 October 1914.

102. See Shigenobu Okuma [Ōkuma Shigenobu], 'Our National Mission', *Japan to America. A Symposium of Papers by Political Leaders and Representative Citizens of Japan on Conditions in Japan and on the Relations between Japan and the United States*, ed. Naoichi Masaoka, New York/London: G.P. Putnam's Sons 1914, 1–5: 4.

103. On this aspect see also Sven Saaler, 'The Construction of Regionalism in Modern Japan: Kodera Kenkichi and his "Treatise on Greater Asianism" (1916)', *Modern Asian Studies* 41 (2007), 1261–1294: 1281–1282.

104. Ōzumi Shōfū, *Shin Shisō Ron* [On New Thought], Tokyo: Rikutō Shuppansha 1913, 353–354.

CHAPTER 4

Asianism During World War One: Macro-Nationalism or Micro-Worldism?

> *If one says Greater Asianism is ambivalent, we shall insist it is extremely ambivalent. Its core part is yet undefined, and its point of departure is undecided. However, this ambivalence and vagueness is not at all the disease of our Greater Asianism. Isn't it a characteristic of human thought that any claim becomes ambivalent if its range is enlarged? Indeed, any principle (shugi) in the initial phase of its movement inevitably rests in a stage of vagueness.*[1]
> —Wakamiya Unosuke (1917)

After the inception of Asianism in Japanese and Chinese political discourse in the early 1910s, World War One triggered its immediate and extensive spread. To many, the war served as proof of a decline of the West. The war also provided a practical opportunity for less self-restrictive actions in the region during the relative absence of the European powers. Both factors facilitated a wider acceptance of Asianist views and the birth of a variety of conceptions of Asianism. Ranging from worldist conceptions influenced by socialist internationalism to nation-centred imperialism, Asianism's agenda became multifaceted and diverse as never again. Consequently, different conceptions competed to represent the 'true meaning' of Asianism. On the eve of the Paris Peace Conference, its role as a rationale for the political utopia of 'one worldism' or internationalism was not necessarily secondary to its rhetorical link with imperialism. This chapter analyses Asianism discourse during World War One as a heated political debate involving a variety of Japanese and Chinese

© The Author(s) 2018
T. Weber, *Embracing 'Asia' in China and Japan*,
Palgrave Macmillan Transnational History Series,
https://doi.org/10.1007/978-3-319-65154-5_4

thinkers in search of a new formula for the post-war political order. While many of these new conceptions were either Japan- or China-centred and therefore became tools in the political arena of Japanese–Chinese rivalry, other conceptions proposed less self-centred and non-hegemonic versions of Asianism.

The Significance of World War One

Conventionally, World War One has not been regarded as a major watershed in East Asian history. Different historiographic traditions (dynasties or imperial reigns as eras) and other historic events have shaped historical narratives more strongly than the 'European War', as it was appropriately called throughout East Asia. The war was, above all, a European affair and its consequences for East Asia were far less significant than those for Europe or those of the subsequent World War Two for East Asia. Nevertheless, World War One did have an immense impact on political debate and the development of political thought. As the Japanese historian Yamamuro Shin'ichi has argued, the war facilitated the wide embrace of modern thought and culture while simultaneously giving birth to scepticism about modernity and to attempts to 'overcome modernity'. Therefore, Yamamuro argues, 'it is necessary to become aware again of the importance [of World War One] as the origin of various incidents and trends of thought' in East Asian history that occurred and became influential in the following decades.[2]

The epochal significance that Yamamuro attributes to the 'Great War' was well grasped by many contemporaries. Lenin's early judgement of the war as a 'tremendous historical crisis, the beginning of a new epoch',[3] formulated in December 1914, may have been wishful thinking on his part, yet after the war his notion was shared by some prominent and less revolutionary-inclined intellectuals. Writing in the early 1920s, historian Arnold J. Toynbee argued that the 'changes in the distribution of territory which had so greatly transformed the map of the world between 1914 and 1920 implied an even more important change in the invisible map of international relationships. Not only had the fortunes of particular states risen or fallen, but the former order of international society had disappeared.'[4] Political geographer Isaiah Bowman (1878–1950), a founding director of the Council on Foreign Relations (1921), even spoke of a post-war 'New World'. As a member of Wilson's Inquiry Committee Bowman had been present at Versailles and upon his return to the United States he penned the following opening lines of his new book, which bore the revealing title *New World: Problems in Political Geography*.

> The effects of the Great War are so far-reaching that we shall have henceforth a new world. Shaken violently out of their former routine, people everywhere have created or adopted new ideas and new material arrangements. [...] Everywhere men have been stirred by new ideas.[5]

On a global level, the principle of national self-determination—be it Lenin's or Wilson's conception thereof[6]—and that of international cooperation may belong to the most influential 'new ideas' of the time. Of course, they were not entirely new ideas. Rather, the degree to which they managed to influence contemporary political debate and reality was unprecedented. In East Asia, and many other parts of the 'non-West', however, disillusionment with 'Western' modernity and civilization triggered by World War One gave birth to alternative visions of a different, and maybe a fairer, decentralized world order.[7] Some four years before Oswald Spengler's famous *Untergang des Abendlandes* [transl. as *Decline of the West*] (1918) was first published, Japanese writers started to proclaim the 'downfall of European civilization' as a result of the 'European War', which was rendered 'the largest event of global scale [...] since the beginning of the world'.[8] Tokutomi Sohō (1863–1957), a prolific Japanese liberal-turned-imperialist writer, perceived the war as the product of the 'weakness and deficits of European civilization'.[9] The Japanese fascist-inclined socialist Kita Ikki (1883–1937) even likened the 'war between the European countries' to 'Noah's flood'; it was 'heaven's punishment for their [the Europeans'] arrogance and immorality'.[10] For anti-Western critics of Japan's 'idiotic' pursuit of Westernization and 'worship of the West',[11] the World War provided an unparalleled welcome opportunity for voicing scepticism, criticism, and denunciation. The Paris Peace Conference further reinforced this anti-Western attitude, which, in the case of Japan, became inseparably linked with opposition to the pro-Western orientation of the Japanese government.[12] Against this background, Asian-minded Japanese during the war took the lead in proposing alternative—Asianist—plans for the post-war order. Although these proposals displayed a remarkable diversity, their envisioned new order commonly rested on two key demands: first, the demand for political self-determination ('Asia for the Asians', Asian Monroe Doctrine), and, second, the creation of an Asian League or Asian Union. In these respects, wartime Asianism represented an extension of similar pre-war conceptions. Now, however, they were discussed as serious political alternatives. As a consequence, a greater number of debaters than before, including many prominent public opinion leaders, participated in Asianism discourse.

Importantly, the appeal of Asianist conceptions was by no means limited to Japan.[13] Chinese Republicans and Socialists, most prominently Sun Yat-sen (1866–1925), his disciple Dai Jitao (1890–1949), and the Socialist Li Dazhao (1889–1927), embraced at least temporarily (China-centred) conceptions of Asianism as useful supplements to their political agendas from the mid-1910s onwards.[14] Similarly, a number of Indians, including the Bengali and Hindu revolutionaries Taraknath Das (1884–1958) and Rash Behari Bose (1886–1945), found value in the political programme of Asianism for Indian independence and in recruiting Japanese help to this end.[15] As a result, on the eve of the Paris Peace Conference, Asianism had become a widespread political concept in public discourse throughout many parts of Asia, particularly in East Asia and India. Interestingly, around the same time in Europe and the United States too, a large number of works appeared that discussed Asian unity and Asian commonality, partly in a derogatory tone reminiscent of Yellow Peril literature, but sometimes also as research into world and Asian affairs.[16] Asianism had developed into an issue of global political concern; to be sure, it had become one of the 'new ideas' that, according to Bowman's contemporary observation, had started to stir up people everywhere. And it had emerged as one of the new 'trends of thought' (Yamamuro) in Asia which would strongly influence political debate and reality in the following decades.

In addition, World War One—although mostly in an indirect way—changed the political and diplomatic conditions in which Asianists proposals were discussed. Japan's 'China Problem' had become ever more pressing when the Japanese government issued the Twenty-One Demands in 1915 after Japan's acquisition of German possessions in Shandong. Yuan Shikai's death in 1916 opened the door for yet another 'fresh start' in Sino-Japanese relations, and the Russian Revolution of 1917 inspired Socialist internationalist thinkers, some of whom temporarily welcomed Asianist conceptions. Moreover, the Lansing–Ishii Agreement of 1917 left the impression on the Japanese that the United States had acknowledged Japanese 'special rights' on the Asian mainland in the form of an Eastern or Asian Monroe Doctrine, as the flood of publications on this topic from 1917 onwards demonstrates. All in all, the new situation during the war not only made discussions of Japanese Asia policy appear to have become a political issue of more urgency but also created a general public mood that was more receptive to Asianist thinking.

In this environment, the Japanese public from left to right, including politicians, scholars, journalists, members of the military, artists, and others, embarked on various discussions about Asianism, and, as a result, Asianist affirmations emerged in growing numbers. Consequently, Asianism as a political key concept, in its various and diverging conceptions, started to penetrate mainstream political discourse, above all in Japan, and a dense net of closely interlinked debates unfolded. During the war, Asianism discourse became a political debate within which the meaning and significance of the concept for the future of Japan, China, Asia, and the world was negotiated. At least with regard to its new place in published political discourse World War One helped to facilitate Asianism's rise from a marginal topic to one of central concern, which it remained during the following decade. To a lesser degree this also applies to China, where the increase in Japanese affirmations of Asianism was observed very carefully.

Among the first to re-embark on the quest of spreading Asianist proposals during World War One was Sugita Teiichi. In the midst of the war, he renewed his earlier call for the creation of an Asian League (Ajia Renmei) based on a Sino-Japanese alliance that would ultimately link the Buddhist countries of East Asia with the Muslims of Central and Western Asia, including Afghanistan and Turkey. Although Sugita, who had become a member of the Upper House in the meantime, considered Japan's alliance with Great Britain as disadvantageous, he emphasized that his conception of Asianism would neither run counter to any of Japan's existing alliances nor promote any exclusionist thought based on racialist notions.[17] Racialist dimensions only re-emerged as part of his agenda in the context of the racial equality proposal at Versailles and the subsequent immigration legislation in the United States.[18] As with his pioneering essay of 1883, Sugita's proposal yet again proved almost prophetic. Anticipating later debates about supranational leagues that were triggered by the proposal of the creation of a League of Nations in 1919, in early 1916 Sugita proposed organizing an East Asian or Asian League (Tōa Renmei, Ajia Renmei). In the aftermath of the Paris Peace Conference, similar suggestions for regional leagues to balance the perceived European predominance in the League of Nations quickly emerged. However, Sugita's understanding of Greater Asianism as a principle for practical political collaboration among Asian countries was rather unique in its time. As Sugita argued, the policy that Japan should adopt right now is first planning friendly relations between Japan and China, and through this force it must work for the creation of an Asian League (Ajia Renmei). If through the combined force of Japan and China the cause of India's independence can be helped, the three hundred million Muslims of East and West will certainly awake and support this movement. Luckily, Japan as a Buddhist country already possesses a psychological link [with them]. [...] I hope that this Greater Asianism will not run counter to the Anglo-Japanese Alliance or to Japanese–Russian friendship. And that it will not inspire exclusionist thought or racialist feelings. [...] Greater Asianism is not at all something exclusionist or protectionist of the yellow race. Instead, it is the nature of human feelings that surpasses the logic of speech and one important condition of the heavenly ordered existence as a nation.[19]

Sugita's emphasis on what Asianism should *not* be, in fact points towards the most direct and common sense understanding of the concept, namely exclusionism and rac(ial)ism. As an advocate of Asianism, therefore, he was cautious not to confirm these existing suspicions. This was most easily achieved by affirming Japan's considerate and accommodating attitude towards the 'West' on the one hand and its adherence to the diplomatic *status quo* (treatises with Britain and Russia) on the other hand. At the same time as Sugita affirmed a politically conservative attitude, however, he also argued for a fundamental revision of the *status quo* and for the adoption of a self-affirmative attitude of Asians as Asians. These inherent contradictions hampered the emergence of a widely accepted definition of Asianism (certainly, at least, the wider acceptance of Sugita's conception) and, simultaneously, provoked criticism from nationalists and internationalists, conservatives and progressives alike.

Liberal Critique of Asianism

Sugita's affirmation was immediately rejected by Ōyama Ikuo, who, as we have seen above (Chap. 3), had most immediately focused on dismissing Asianist claims made in the Chinese 'pamphlet' of 1912. But he also rejected Sugita's vision of pan-Asian solidarity as 'pretty extensively arrogant'. Ōyama argued that—unlike Sugita's claim—there was no obvious link between Buddhism and Islam that would naturally expand the scope of Asianism from Japan and China further westwards. In a manner that almost ridiculed Sugita's argumentation, Ōyama continued:

> He [Sugita] is declaring that Greater Asianism is not inconsistent with the Anglo-Japanese Alliance and Japanese–Russian friendship! I shall refrain from calling his argument sloppy. But if he has made these remarks seriously I must say that his and my views of national psychology are fundamentally incompatible.[20]

Indirectly, Ōyama's critique addresses the larger dilemma that Japanese views of the world had been trapped in for decades: either Japan joined, accommodated, pleased the 'West' or it became part of an Asian enterprise to raise or revive Asia. Japan, it appeared, could not have it both ways. But why not? To some, Asianism in its early years possessed exactly this potential function of reconciling Japan with Asia without seeking colonial hegemony and challenging the vested interests of 'Western' countries there. Ōyama, however, did not see such prospects. Instead, he embarked on a full-scale deconstruction of Sugita's conception of Asianism, which proved a rather easy task for someone possessing Ōyama's political and scholarly background. Ōyama questioned the soundness of Asianist arguments at this early stage, and, as expected, Sugita's elaborations appeared immature and unrealistic in the context of the time. After Ōyama had worked through a list of 'at least seven obstacles in the way of the prospect of an implementation of Greater Asianism', which included the 'vested footing of the powers' in Asia, the 'weakness of a common practical foundation' of the Asian countries, the lack of common institutions, of mutual trust, of a common goal, and of a common belief, he continued:

> However, the shortcomings of Greater Asianism regarding its thought do not stop here. There is an even more profound point. In the contemporary world, there are two main currents of political thought. One is nationalism (kokuminshugi) and the other is supranational worldism (chō kokkashugi-teki sekaishugi). Nationalism is the movement for self-government of the races. As is plain to see, it is under way in all corners of this world. In Japan there is a tacit conflation with Japanism. In Euro-America, there are the extremely active movements of Pan-Slavism, Pan-Germanism, and Pan-Serbism. As far as worldism is concerned, there are religious, capitalist, and workers' movements which are noticeably active but usually incomplete. Among these two kinds of political thought, the most powerful is without doubt not the latter but the former. [...] It is plain to see that Greater Asianism is not based on nationalism. Although we could say that its base

is supranational worldism, it is obviously not worldism but equally obviously it is not supranationalism either. In that it is not worldism but antiforeignism it will provoke the antipathy of other parts of the world and because it lacks the morals of nationalism, its unifying force will be too feeble.[21]

Ōyama's critique can be summarized in two points. First, in his view, Asianism was against the tides of the times, whose political thought was dominated by nationalism and internationalism. Despite Asianism's internationalist aspirations and its possible function as a tool of supranationalism, to Ōyama, Asianism was neither one nor the other. It lacked the self-centredness of nationalism but also the cosmopolitan and open spirit of internationalism. While to others, this in-between dimension of Asianism constituted its political appeal as a regional mediator between the level of the nation and of the world, Ōyama simply dismissed Asianism as immature. Second, Ōyama rejected the exclusionist dimension of Asianism. 'Asia', by definition, if it was to denote anything at all, needed an 'Other' to confirm its 'Self'. To Ōyama this 'Self'–'Other' distinction could only be realized as an irreconcilable dichotomy. Despite the fact that, by early 1916, only fairly moderate proposals of Asianism had been brought forward that did not yet display an aggressive tone towards other Asians or to the 'West', Ōyama insisted that Asianism was holding up the 'signboard of xenophobia'.[22] This he even likened to Japan's pre-Meiji policy of seclusionism (sakoku shugi).[23] Partly, at least, Ōyama's indiscriminately negative view of Asianism seems to have rested on his conviction of Asianism's Chinese origin—and Ōyama's negative view of China. 'Young Japan', he contrasted his country to its neighbour, 'must be full of vigour and by no means learn from the attitude of a country that calls itself the central country of blossom and prides itself as an old decaying country.'[24] As we have already seen above, many Japanese—including liberals such as Ōyama—perceived closer relations of friendship with China at the (potential) expense of friendly relations with 'Western' countries as perilous and unfavourable.

In the following months and years, as Japanese affirmations of Asianism appeared in increasing numbers, critics of Asianism referred less and less to its assumed foreign origin than to either its hypocritical attitude towards 'Asia' or its disadvantageous agenda for Japan. Independent of its alleged role as the country of Asianism's origin, China remained central to any discussion of the concept. China expert Yoshino

Sakuzō (1878–1933),[25] a Sinophile commentator on Chinese affairs and leading figure of the Taishō democracy movement, did not for a moment consider Asianism as being of Chinese origin. On the contrary, he was sure that Japanese conceptions of Asianism would not be able to appeal to the Chinese because of Japan's ignorance of Chinese affairs. In addition, he dismissed Asianist rhetoric for its lack of realism.

> It is not necessary to say that the two peoples of Japan and China must absolutely live in harmony eternally. Indeed, from a political point of view, the national characteristics cannot be harmonized. Conventionally, both peoples have only negotiated in political relations which, in reality, have frequently been far from peaceful. If we really plan the friendship of the two peoples of Japan and China, we must first negotiate in a direction that overcomes political relations that seek national benefit. [...] In relations of fierce enmity for political benefit, inciting empty phrases such as same script, same race, lips and teeth, and Pan-Asianism will not enable relations of heartfelt friendship.[26]

According to Yoshino, Asianist rhetoric was only 'empty phrases' as long as political reality rested on maximizing national interests. In other words, the predominance of the national posed the major obstacle to the realization of Asianism, understood by Yoshino as a transnational concept that implied cultural, racial, and geographic proximity, commonality, and shared interests. Importantly, this proximity and commonality did not exist *a priori* as a result of historical influence and territorial aspects. On the contrary, they had to be initiated and established from scratch and by respective actions, not merely by friendly words. Only a few months later, a leading article in the same journal, the liberal *Shinjin* [New Man],[27] took Yoshino's critique even further. Japanese Asianism, it insinuated, did not pursue sincere supranational intentions but aimed at imitating hegemonic versions of pan-nationalism:

> It appears as if the age of cure-all nationalism has come to an end quickly. Recently, there is a thing called Asianism that extends nationalism. Its meaning is pretty obscure but we can suppose it aims at forming an Asian League (Ajia Renmei) of which Japan should become the leader (meishu). [...] In a sense, Asianism denotes the union of Japan and China. To put it boldly, one could say that Asianism aims at implementing All Germanism (Zen Doitsushugi) in the East.[28]

This definition reflected and rejected the ambitions of some, such as Gotō Shinpei (Chap. 3), Tokutomi Sohō, and Ōtani Kōzui (below), to employ Asianism as a nationalist-driven means to legitimize the expansion of Japan's empire in the name of Asian commonality. Focusing on China and Japan, the editorial not only dismissed assumed common cultural features of both countries—although it conceded racial identity—but also reminded the Japanese of their historical indebtedness to the Chinese.

> If the Japanese should have the mission to guide the Chinese, this would not inspire Asianism but Euro-Americanism. As the Japanese have before everyone's eyes adopted and applied Euro-American civilization, they do not possess any more of Asian civilization than the Chinese and there is no reason why the Chinese should take the Japanese as their [Asianist] teacher.[29]

Strictly applying Asianist logic, including its reference to historical roots of Asian commonality, the author revealed the implausibility of essentialist conceptions of Asianism that envisioned a central role for Japan. Japan could only claim, as Tokutomi had argued, the Asianist model role for practical reasons; there was simply no other country that was able to initiate and implement meaningful and functional Asianist policies apart from Japan. Culturally, however, Japan continued to be indebted to China. This was particularly true with regard to Japan's Asianity, given the country's rapid Westernization during the past half century. Therefore, the editorial continued, in many spheres such as poetry, philosophy, logic, and arts, the Chinese were *senpai* (elders) to the Japanese, and not vice versa. The home of 'the civilization of the East', it emphatically concluded, lies in China and 'Japan is no more than a branch office'.[30] The author, however, did not imply that Japan should take China as its model or advocate an Asian union guided by China. Instead, he used his identification of 'Asia' with China as an argument to dismiss Asianism altogether. Reviewing Japan's victory over Russia a decade earlier, he rejected the view that the war had been 'a war between Europeanism and Asianism'. If Japan had indeed professed to Asianism, it would not have achieved victory, he claimed. Instead, because it adopted a 'worldly civilizationalism', it succeeded and gained the sympathy of Britain and the United States. It was this quality of not being 'caught in regional sentiments' that was characteristic of the Japanese.

Asianism, on the other hand, symbolized backwardness that the Japanese would be ridiculed for if they subscribed to its rationale.[31] Japan, the editorial finally advised, should therefore neither confine itself to narrow and exclusionist nationalism nor to an enlarged regionalist version. Either would lead Japan into international isolation. Only 'worldly humanitarianism' and 'progressivism of an open country' could save Japan from the fear and potential reality of isolation. It concluded,

> this is the way to nourish Japanese of great personalities and to make Japan a grand nation. Things like Asianism that resemble anti-Westernism of the time of the [Meiji] Restoration will not contribute to the aggrandizement of our imperial country and it will not win honour for the Japanese people.[32]

It is important to note here that the article's pro-Chinese and anti-Asianist stance did not preclude a Japan-centred and rather nationalistic reasoning. At this point in history, at least, to the anonymous author Japan appeared to have more to lose if it abandoned its pro-Western attitude than it could gain by adopting a pro-Chinese or pro-Asian policy. Explicitly, as quoted above, he also criticized Japan's ignorance of China's role in Japanese civilization. However, his fear of an appropriation of Asianism by anti-Western circles that might eventually also reject the 'Western' values of democracy and Christianity—two main principles of Ebina Danjō and his *Shinjin* journal—as un-Japanese or 'Western' decadence seems to have been stronger. 'Asia', and consequently also Asianism, to them meant backwardness and regression. Like Ōyama they believed that Japan's success and future lay with continuous emancipation from China and its turn away from 'Asia'—not in its embrace.

Nationalist Critique of Asianism

This rationale bore a remarkable resemblance to that of nationalist anti-Asianist critics who otherwise had little in common with leftist liberals such as Yoshino and the *Shinjin* affiliates. While the latter, despite a high degree of Sinophilism, refused to turn away from the 'West' because it had been the source of their political (democracy) and religious (Christianity) convictions, the former appeared more concerned with practical disadvantages should Japan declare itself participant in or even leader of an Asianist enterprise. As we have seen above, Asianism was viewed by many as irreconcilable with Japan's focus on developing into a first-rate nation pursuing political and economic autarky. Most nationalists, therefore, still by the mid-1910s found limited value in a concept that would link Japan's fate to that of Asia. Probably the most persistent critic of Asianism from an anti-Asian and nationalist point of view was Ninagawa Arata (1873–1959). From the early 1910s through the late 1930s,[33] when Asianism had long been adopted by the Japanese military and government as semi-official rhetoric and rationale, Ninagawa continuously dismissed various conceptions of Asianism as irrational, disadvantageous, and absurd. Ninagawa was a Western-trained graduate of Tokyo Imperial University from Shizuoka and a former advisor to the Korean Imperial Government (1907–1913). He studied in Paris (1913–1914) and after World War One returned to Europe as an advisor to the Red Cross in Geneva (1918–1920). In 1922, he visited Europe again and also went to the United States for the first time. He was a professor of international law at Kyoto's Dōshisha University (1914–1917) and then at Komazawa University (1929–1947). Because of his nationalist—but nevertheless outspokenly anti-Asianist—writings he was purged from office after World War Two (Fig. 4.1).

This latter aspect makes Ninagawa a particularly interesting critic of Asianism. His critique helps to understand the fine line that existed, no matter how fine, between nationalism and Asianism and that irreconcilably separated some Japanese nationalists from Japanese Asianists. Only a few months after the publication of Gotō Shinpei's *Japan's Colonial Policy* (1915), Ninagawa harshly criticized Asianism as a Japanese attempt to imitate American Monroeism.[34] Comparing the situation in America at the time of the declaration of Monroeism to contemporary Japan, he argued that the former European colonies in America had already been independent and US-Monroeism therefore meant to maintain the *status quo*. By contrast, the declaration of an Asian Monroe Doctrine at this point in history was a revisionist position that would only be disadvantageous for Japan, since Asian countries such as Turkey, Persia, Afghanistan, India, and Vietnam had long been controlled by other powers. China, the most immediate object of Japanese Asianism, was also under the control and influence of different powers. According to Ninagawa, Asian Monroeism could only be realized in two ways, both of which he strongly rejected: first, Asian Monroeism could mean that Asians relied on the Japanese to drive the non-Asians out of Asia. Japan would then rightfully be seen as 'an outlaw' by the 'West'. Alternatively,

Fig. 4.1 Ninagawa Arata, the fiercest and most persistent critic of Asianism, during his mission for the Japanese Red Cross in Europe, 1918 (Harris & Ewing collection, Library of Congress)

Japan's role could be more passive in that it would 'only' incite Asians to break away from their colonial masters. Then too, the Japanese would become outlaws, making all European countries their enemies as the Japanese would be seen as instigators.

Moreover, Ninagawa was sceptical of the explicit anti-Westernism inherent in Asianism. Displaying a pragmatic attitude, he demanded that Japan should 'befriend those who wish to befriend us and take as enemies those who cause damage to us'. The 'community of interests' should be more decisive for Japan's international and diplomatic behaviour, not geopolitical aspects or assumed cultural and racial commonality. In conclusion, he dismissed Asian Monroeism as 'a fool's dream', 'absurd argument', and 'not worthy of notice'.[35] Ninagawa's anti-Asianist position exemplified the pro-Western nationalist attitude and sentiment that sought to appease the Western powers for the sake of Japan's national development. This stream of thought and attitude was still dominant in

Japanese foreign political thought at the time, even more so after the international trouble the Twenty-One Demands (1915) had caused.

However, against the background of increasing numbers of publications on Asianism—including some prominent affirmations—in the following years, Ninagawa's attitude of simply dismissing Asianism by disparaging its logic or its advocates soon became insufficient. By 1917, Asianism could no longer be repudiated in a superficial tone. Ninagawa's general position of rejection, however, remained unaltered. Now in the opening article, which stretched over eight pages in the September issue of the same journal, Ninagawa systematically criticized the shortcomings of the new political concept and, in addition, provided a surprising— given his nationalist inclinations—alternative to Asianism: 'Worldism for worldists.'[36] This title was an obvious allusion to the key Asianist slogan 'Asia for Asians' and it constituted a dubious attempt at taking advantage of the internationalist mood in order to counter Asianist claims. 'Today's world', Ninagawa postulated, 'is neither the world of the Whites, nor the world of the yellow people, and Asia does not belong to the Asians. We should rather view the world as cooperating on the basis of the interests of different nations; a world of worldist people.'[37] As this passage reveals, Ninagawa's 'worldism' was an internationalist view that was based on nationalist assumptions. Ninagawa's main concern was 'national interests' and the nation remained his key unit of 'worldist' cooperation. In his emphasis on the nation, Ninagawa differed notably from the internationalist or worldist conceptions of Asianism that Li Dazhao or Ukita Kazutami advocated around the same time. Both envisioned the nation as well as the region (Asia) as non-essentialist but rather pragmatic units that would facilitate exchange and cooperation on different levels. To them, both the nation and the region functioned as means not ends. For Ninagawa, however, the nation remained the undisputable key unit of social life and political organization. Consequently, he tried to discredit Asianist claims as inconsistent, vague, and dangerous:

> first, is 'Asia for the Asians' supposed to apply to all of Asia or only a part thereof? This point remains extremely obscure [...]; second, if it only means to claim that Japan and China should form a league, then it is no more than a Japanese–Chinese alliance thesis. [...] Holding up a huge signboard claiming 'Asia for the Asians' is deceiving the public; third, if it means to incite the Asians to drive out the Whites from Asia, it would be an extremely dangerous theory and it would inevitably invite the hatred of all Europeans.[38]

Ninagawa, too, employs the widespread concern over a possible self-inflicted isolation of Japan as a consequence of a potential confrontation with the 'West' as an anti-Asianist argument. It implied that all efforts at 'modernization' along 'Western' standards would be in vain if they resulted in a confrontation with the original model of this process, that is, Europe or the 'Whites'.

But Ninagawa's rejection of Asianist claims also attests to the significance Asianism had achieved by the late 1910s. He appeared almost annoyed by the omnipresence and sudden popularity of the new concept. At some point, he even took issue with the foreignness of the name 'Asian Monroeism'. 'If Asia should really be in need of a principle (shugi), we should at least expect that Asians themselves think out a name for it.'[39] Ninagawa tried to omit no opportunity to invalidate Asianist conceptions, even terminologically. To him 'Asia' remained a foreign concept which had little to offer to Japan. While he greeted the attempted improvement of bilateral relations, for example, with China,[40] 'Asia' as a means of self-affirmation against the 'West' held little attraction for him. Similarly to Ōyama, Ninagawa emphasized the danger of such an enterprise and confirmed his adherence to Western accomodationism. Japan's priority, according to him, was to remain on friendly terms with Europe. To him, the 'European War' had not changed the political map decisively enough to risk any Asianist adventures. Ninagawa continued to argue against Asianism and Asianist positions in the following years, with his criticism peaking during a heated debate with Asianist thinker and activist Imazato Juntarō before the Pan-Asian Conference of Nagasaki in 1926 (see Chap. 6). Ninagawa's example therefore highlights that well into the later 1920s a distinction between contemporary understandings of Asianism on the one hand and nationalism on the other is necessary to understand who was supportive of which conceptions of Asianism and why—and who was not and for which reasons.

Tokutomi Sohō's Asian Monroe Doctrine

Ninagawa's example notwithstanding, nationalist convictions did not necessarily preclude an embrace of Asianism, if paired with imperialist ambitions. Here, Asianism could at least become a supplementary political doctrine. Like Gotō Shinpei, who was one of the first to advocate Asianism as a guiding principle for colonial development and the expansion of Japan's empire, a number of thinkers and writers saw

Asianism during World War One as an opportunity for imperial expansion. Tokutomi Sohō was the most prominent nationalist spokesman of this conception of Asianism during the late 1910s and early 1920s.[41] His expansionist conception of Asianism was directly influenced by Gotō's.[42] As quoted above, Tokutomi had viewed the World War as a proof of the 'weakness and deficits of European civilization', a civilization that the Japanese had idealized for too long. The revelation of the true character of European civilization, Tokutomi argued, was a 'most delightful lesson for us Japanese', as it liberated Japan from the European standard that had obviously not been lived up to and proved hypocritical.[43] Tokutomi's Asianism therefore can be seen as 'an expression of growing self-confidence of Japan in the international arena'.[44]

Tokutomi started openly advocating Asianist conceptions in 1916, when his influential *Taishō no Seinen to Teikoku no Zento* (The Young Generation of Taishō and the Future of the Empire) was published. In it, he proposed the adoption of an Asian Monroe Doctrine and demanded that, in the absence of other qualified Asians, the Japanese people should take the lead and deal with Asian matters. As we have seen above, Tokutomi was by no means the first Japanese to propose 'Asia for the Asians' or an 'Asian Monroe Doctrine'. However, his prominence surely helped to gain attention for the Asianist cause, and for his particular, expansionist-imperialist, conception of Asianism. Remarkably, in his definition, Tokutomi was anxious not to sound too anti-Western either.

> Asian Monroeism is the doctrine according to which Asian matters are dealt with by Asians. If we say Asians, that means, if except for the Japanese people, no one else has the qualification to shoulder this work, Asian Monroeism is the doctrine according to which Asian matters are to be dealt with by Japanese. To avoid misunderstandings, we do not hold any narrow-minded views such as to drive out the Whites from Asia. It only goes as far as not depending on the Whites and to fight the spread of the Whites.[45]

Tokutomi's position combined a comparatively conservative stance towards the 'West' with an unreserved request for Japan to become Asia's manager. His position was conservative in the literal sense as it adhered to the *status quo* rather than demanding the liberation of Asia from its Western oppressors. Nevertheless, his conception of Asianism could not conceal anti-Western sentiments. As recently as

1913, although not explicitly referring to Asia, Tokutomi had rejected Monroeism as a 'hegemonic principle' which the United States hypocritically only applied domestically while demanding an Open Door Policy abroad.[46] In his 'Theory for self-governance of the East' (Tōyō Jichi Ron), Tokutomi demanded equal relations with the 'Whites' as the precondition to any further dealings with the 'West', but did not suggest adopting an Asian version of Monroeism. Three years later, however, while his frustration with the 'Whites' remained ('their comradeship is the comradeship between Whites, their principle of equality is only a principle between the Whites, their principle of philanthropy is only a principle between Whites'[47]), Tokutomi had come to believe that a similar policy might successfully be applied by Japan in Asia. Racial discrimination and tendencies of geopolitical bloc formations in other parts of the world, real or perceived, served as the best justification for an Asian Monroe Doctrine:

> Today the Europeans deal with European problems, the Americans with American problems, and the Australians with Australian problems. Only in the problems of the East, the Easterners generally with folded arms simply leave things to the Euro-Americans.[48]

For Tokutomi, it was clear that, just as the United States had declared and implemented the American Monroe Doctrine in its hemisphere, it was the fate of the Japanese empire to implement an Asian Monroe Doctrine in its own hemisphere. In practice, however, the Asian Monroe Doctrine to Tokutomi meant 'Asia for the Japanese', not 'Asia for the Asians'. As seen above, Tokutomi justified this position by claiming that Japan's leadership was the only practical way of implementing Asian Monroeism, since Japan was the only economic and military power in Asia. Asianism, therefore, in Tokutomi's conception rested on practical deliberations of power politics, not cultural aspects or solidarity. As a consequence, in Tokutomi's proposal for an Asian Monroe Doctrine, the binary of solidarity and invasion that has been identified by scholarship as the immanent contradiction inherent in most conceptions of Asianism moved to the background. Asianism in Tokutomi's conception was never meant as an act of transnational solidarity. Rather, as Lee Gyeongseog has argued, although originating as an 'antithesis of the invasion of Asia by the European powers', Tokutomi's conception turned out as 'propaganda for the justification of imperialism'.[49]

Military Conceptions and the Persistence of a Consciousness of Crisis

Although Tokutomi's political conception of Asianism was not necessarily representative in its time, it became a template for affirmative Asianist conceptions that appeared in the following months. In a sense Tokutomi had taken the lid off a pot of boiling water by suggesting that Japan's openly declared turn to a proactive Asia policy would solve many of the country's problems and fears, not by suppressing the traditional *kiki ishiki* (consciousness of crisis) but by attempting to take the initiative as a self-determined actor on the regional, if not global, political stage. In his and other thinkers' views, World War One provided the unprecedented opportunity for Japan's Asianist coming out.

This opportunity to formulate a proactive mainland policy was also welcomed by members of the military, who appeared more than pleased by the prospect of Japan taking the role of the leader of Asia. Unsurprisingly, they tended to advocate a declaration of an Asian Monroe Doctrine which would further increase the status and power of the Japanese army and navy. For the Japanese army, lieutenant general Horiuchi Bunjirō (1863–1942), who had served in the brief battle that led to the surrender of the German troops in Qingdao (1914), proposed Asianism as the most appropriate post-war policy to be adopted by Japan. To him, Asianism was identical with an Asian Monroe Doctrine, which he suggested applying to the whole Asian continent east of the Suez Canal in the South and East of the Ural Mountains in the North. Naturally, to Horiuchi, Japan—'my Yamato people'—was to be the leader in the implementation of Asianism[50]:

> During the present war and in its aftermath, my Japan must proceed to make Greater Asianism or – by learning from the advanced nation of the United States – an Asian Monroe Doctrine the grand strategy of our foreign policy. The seventy million Japanese (Yamato minzoku) must first profoundly awake to this point. If we direct our united efforts at this aim we will surely be able to secure the peace, independence, and prosperity of the entire East, and consequently of a vast part of the whole world.[51]

Horiuchi's reference to the American Monroe Doctrine fulfils a similar function to Tokutomi's: if the United States continued to justify their quasi-imperialist foreign policy by Monroeism, Japan need not hesitate to apply a similar policy. Just as the American model had long ceased to be a passive policy in defence of the Americas but had changed into 'something entirely active and imperialist', Horiuchi argued that Japan needed to abandon its half-hearted Asia policy in favour of a grand strategy: Greater Asianism or an Asian Monroe Doctrine.[52]

A slightly different interpretation of Asianism, which resembled Gotō's developmental policy more than Tokutomi's conception, was proposed by Vice Admiral Kamiizumi Tokuya (1865–1946). Kamiizumi openly equated Greater Japanism (Dai Nihonshugi) with Greater Asianism (Dai Ajiashugi) and suggested the latter's propagation for the solution of Japan's 'population problem'. To him, Asianism was not a doctrine that needed to be declared in imitation of the foreign policy of other countries (such as Monroeism). Instead, and above all, it needed to be implemented in the Japanese colonial possessions in order to ease Japan's 'excessive population'.[53] Consequently, Kamiizumi's Asianism was not mainly directed at China—which had been the centre of most other Asianist conceptions—but at less populated areas in Siberia and Central Asia. Apparently, Kamiizumi was inspired and encouraged by the Siberian Expedition, which had started in early 1918 in reaction to the Russian Revolution but eventually ended in failure. The ultimate aim of Kamiizumi's conception of Asianism was the colonial development of Asian territories by the Japanese, as he openly admitted. 'It is extremely pleasant to realize', he wrote, 'that the pursuit of the fate of Greater Japanism results in the development of Asia. Greater Asianism, in my interpretation, is exactly indicating this.'[54] To Kamiizumi, Asianism was not about racial or cultural commonality. Japan had already exceeded the point of cooperation solely with its Asian compatriots, he claimed. Instead of sticking to peoples of the 'same race and same roots' (dōshu dōkon), it was Japan's mission to proceed to planning 'the harmonization and friendship with people of different races'.[55] In this respect, Kamiizumi had outpaced Gotō's earlier proposal for the development of Manchuria and Mongolia and he anticipated later justifications of Japanese military engagement in more remote parts of Asia.

Despite their different foci, Horiuchi's and Kamiizumi's conceptions shared a prioritized consideration of practical aspects of diplomacy and colonial development over culturalist and racialist rhetoric. In this sense, thriving Asianism discourse during the war offered them an opportunity to formulate programmes of imperialist expansion without sounding too provocative in terms of racialism. Since Asianism had been set on the agenda of public political discourse anyway by other debaters, why should members of the military not participate in its definition and discussion? Of course, their conceptions envisioned a prominent role to be played by the Japanese military in the practical implementation of Asianism.

Within a similar politico-intellectual framework, Ōtani Kōzui (1876–1948) discussed Asianism as a counter policy to a two-fold foreign threat Japan was facing. Ōtani, the former abbot of Kyoto's *Nishi Honganji*, the head temple of the Buddhist *Jōdō Shinshu* sect (True Pure Land), viewed the United States as the number one threat to Japan, since they not only barred Japanese from immigration but also extended their de facto empire into South East Asia (the Philippines). This constituted an indirect threat to Japan's security and, according to Ōtani, was only a first step of the United States' preparation to intimidate Japan's own empire. Eventually, this would lead to the invasion of Japan by American diplomacy, if not by its military. A second threat, related to the first, was posed to Japan, in Ōtani's view, by China. As an independent country, China would pose no threat to Japan, Ōtani argued; however, as a country that was virtually controlled by foreign countries and unstable, China could not be trusted by Japan. Ōtani had precise ideas as to how to relieve Japan of these 'internal and external troubles' (naiyū gaikan):

> Now there are two wonder drugs that may heal the serious illnesses our country has fallen to. One is militarism, and the other is Asianism. The former will heal our internal problems, the latter our external problems. However, they may also become poisonous drugs. If applied by a mediocre doctor, they will accelerate death. What our country needs to find most urgently is a master hand to save our country. The good medicine we have is difficult to use if we lack an expert.[56]

Although Ōtani remained less explicit than Tokutomi in his elaborations on how Asianism could provide a remedy for Japan's perceived sufferings, they clearly agreed on two major points. First, Asianism as a diplomatic instrument meant regional self-determination à la Monroeism. Therefore, its self-declared aim was 'the complete independence of China',[57] implicitly denoting its independence from 'Western' interference, while Japan would seek ever closer relations of 'friendship'. As a consequence, Japan would de facto become the sole power to be present in China. Second, Japan was to be the leader of the implementation of Asianism; Asianism was Japan's fate. In Ōtani's own words:

[Asianism means] to promote peace and welfare among Asians by guarding them against the invasion and violence of people who come from other countries to Asia. This is the divine mission of the Japanese people, its destiny. If we cannot achieve this our people will cease to exist.[58]

It is noteworthy to remember that Ōtani wrote this passage in early 1917, not the 1930s or 1940s, when Japan faced (partially self-inflicted) national isolation, war, and severe crises. Ōtani's rhetoric fits all too well into the later propagandistic appropriation of Asianism for the justification of imperial policies of invasion and aggression, both against the 'West' and against its Asian neighbours, in particular from the late 1930s onwards. The 'threats' that Japan was supposedly confronted with in 1917 appear, at least in retrospective, more than slightly exaggerated.

Interestingly, Ōtani apparently felt the urge to explain to his readers how Asianism could be rationalized as a supplement to militarism, the other remedy he prescribed. The Confucian ideal of the Kingly Way (Jp. ōdō, Ch. wangdao), or rule of right, which he explicitly linked to Asianism, would not *per definitionem* rule out resorting to military means, he argued. Historically, many righteous rulers had applied military force as a means to a justified end and in a virtuous way. Therefore, not militarism per se but the way and goal of militarism decided whether rulers fell into the category of unjust rule of might (Jp. hadō, Ch. badao) or benevolent rule of right.[59] 'Whether medicine is poison, or poison is medicine, only depends on the doctor', Ōtani concluded.[60]

The binary concepts of ōdō (rule of right) versus hadō (rule of might) would become central in later attempts to justify Japanese authority over Manchuria after the founding of Manchukuo (Chap. 7) and they had also underlain Sun Yat-sen's conception of Asianism (Chap. 5). Their inception in Asianism discourse in the late 1910s opened up a civilizational branch of Asianist conceptions that came to supplement the hitherto dominant political-diplomatic affirmative interpretation of Asianism as Asian Monroeism.

Asianism as Civilizational Critique

In direct response to Ōtani's proposal, sociologist and journalist Wakamiya Unosuke (1872–1938) took up the dichotomous view of civilization to contrast 'Asia' or the 'East' (Tōyō) with Euro-America or the 'West' (Seiyō). In other words, Wakamiya transferred the Confucian classification of virtuous *versus* despotic rule to characterize 'Eastern' civilization in opposition to 'Western' civilization. Wakamiya, who had lived and studied in the United States and England for almost ten years at the beginning of the twentieth century, took his inspiration not only from Ōtani's essay but also from his obvious disillusionment with the 'West' due to World War One—'Europe's suicide, the pinnacle of extreme foolishness'.[61] Wakamiya's 'analysis' of 'Western civilization' took the form of an attack on the 'West' which, according to Wakamiya, fully disclosed its present 'character of greed and principle of plunder'.[62] Economically, Wakamiya argued, 'the spirit of Western civilization is plundering. It plunders nature and humans. [...] Just as it applies the principle of unfair profits to plunder foreign countries, it uses concentrated capitalism to plunder its working classes. This will be the downfall of Western civilization.'[63] These internal problems of the 'West' led Wakamiya to a different conclusion from Ōtani, who had feared that Japan's security was threatened by Western countries. Instead, Wakamiya prophesied that the 'West' had already fallen into such a state of decline that it would probably not be able to constitute a threat to Japan in the near future. Nevertheless, Wakamiya interpreted 'Greater Asianism' as the 'rightful defence of Asia' and defined it as 'the claim that aims at sweeping out those non-Asian powers that plunder or seek to plunder Asia. In other words, it is the new ideal that advocates the construction of an Asia for the Asians and rejects the Euro-American powers from Asia.'[64] While Wakamiya named the 'unlawful siege of and attack on Asia by the Western powers'[65] as the immediate cause that justified the realization of Greater Asianism, his conception was more strongly influenced by cultural and civilizational considerations, such as 'Asia's cultural independence' and the 'striving for an Asian New Man (Ajia shinjin) that surpasses Western civilization'.[66] Political sovereignty, therefore, to Wakamiya was no more than a means to create the conditions to realize cultural autonomy and overcome the despotic civilization of the 'West'. As a consequence, Wakamiya was concerned with Japan as a country to a much lesser extent than Ōtani, who had seen the United States as Japan's main 'Western' enemy. Instead, his Asianism was more genuinely about 'Asia' and his political consideration did not focus on Japan's main rival in the region but on Britain, as India's colonizer. This concern revealed Wakamiya's relatively denationalized understanding of 'Asia'. While the United States may indeed have been Japan's main rival in South East Asia, Britain was widely perceived as a friendly nation to Japan, but simultaneously as the main obstacle in the way of pan-Asian activities and the formation of an Asian League, since it blocked India's participation in this enterprise. The 'change of control of India', therefore, was one major aim of Wakamiya's vision of Greater Asia.[67]

As an early advocate of Asianism, Wakamiya also addressed definitional problems, possibly to preclude crude dismissals of Asianism preemptively. He admitted that Asianism as a principle, or as Wakamiya put it, as a 'claim' or a 'new ideal', was 'vague' and 'ambivalent'. This was not only because Asianism was still—as Kubota had argued almost two decades earlier—in its embryonic stage but also a natural and common feature of similar claims and principles, Wakamiya argued:

> If one says Greater Asianism is ambivalent, we shall insist it is extremely ambivalent. Its core part is yet undefined, and its point of departure is undecided. However, this ambivalence and vagueness is not at all the disease of our Greater Asianism. Isn't it a characteristic of human thought that any claim becomes ambivalent if its range is enlarged? Indeed, any principle (shugi) in the initial phase of its movement inevitably rests in a stage of vagueness.[68]

It was precisely this vagueness and ambivalence, together with the acceptance of Asianism as a new principle, claim, or stream of thought by a great variety of writers that facilitated the widespread debate in mainstream journals and newspapers and that triggered the emergence of ever-new conceptions of Asianism. Obviously, a wide range of thinkers and activists found value in Asianism to express different political agendas. At any rate, despite a number of profoundly elaborated rejections and critiques, the growing number of Asianist affirmations that emerged during the war constitutes a notable change in Asianism discourse. In particular, Asianism was no longer considered of non-Japanese origin, although a majority of debaters still insisted it was opposed to Japanese interests.

In the meantime, Asianism, at least for some, had also become a selling point, for example, in individual election campaigns. Miyazaki Tōten, otherwise known for his dedication to Sino-Japanese friendship, was not the only but arguably the most prominent candidate running for the Lower House who listed 'Greater Asianism' explicitly as one of his key political principles. 'The main point of my candidacy is simple and clear', Miyazaki wrote in February 1915, 'I will use my limited power to fundamentally solve the contemporary policy towards China, to contribute to the establishment of Greater Asianism and thereby return my favour to my country.'[69] Although Miyazaki had no space to elaborate on his conception of Asianism in his brief candidacy declaration, he made clear elsewhere—and his Sinophilism would imply nothing different—that he envisioned a shift in Japan's diplomacy towards Sinophile and Asiaphile positions which would allow for China's and Asia's cooperation on equal terms with Japan, if not prioritize China and Asia.[70] As Szpilman writes, 'for Miyazaki, China almost always took priority over Japan'.[71] Miyazaki failed to get elected, but apparently this did not discourage other candidates in subsequent elections from taking an equally affirmative stance towards Asianism. In March 1917, for example, Hara Fujirō (1875–1953), an independent candidate from Shimane, where he later became the first post-World War Two governor, as well as Isobe Hisashi (1875–1935), running for the Tokyo branch of the *Seiyūkai* party, declared their support for Asianism in interviews on their candidacies with the *Asahi* newspaper.[72] If neither of them appeared to have held any specifically elaborated conception of Asianism, their public confessions to Asianism, even if somewhat superficial, may serve as a further indication that the concept had arrived at the centre stage of public political debate. If nothing else, it was fashionable to mention and discuss Asianism and increasingly it also became fashionable to take an affirmative stance towards the new political principle.

Liberal and Cosmopolitan Asianism

Probably the most remarkable examples that attest to the new popularity of Asianist conceptions from the mid-1910s onwards stem from a niche area of political discourse: literature.[73] In the early 1910s, when a number of left-leaning thinkers and activists still flirted with Asianism as a potential political alternative to existing agendas, Kodama Kagai (1874–1943) began to fill the poetry columns of widely read journals such as *Taiyō* (The Sun) with songs of Asianist unity and solidarity. Kodama was a well-known and widely published socialist poet who had become famous when his 'Collected Poems of Socialism' (Shakaishugi jishū) were banned from publication in 1903. In today's Japan he is remembered as the author of Meiji University's official school song. Kodama's conception of Asianism remarkably resembled Miyazaki Tōten's 'sentimental' Asianism,[74] whose main feature was genuine sympathy with the Chinese people and the Chinese Republican cause.[75] In a number of poems, Kodama praised the dedication of Sun Yat-sen and of his followers to the pursuit of China's pacification and independence, which he viewed as an important step towards the pacification and independence of all of Asia. In fact, Kodama must be counted among the pioneers of pro-Chinese Asianist thought in the early 1910s, who, at a time when Asianism was neither widely accepted nor well known, had started to propagate Asianist aims such as Asian self-governance and an alliance of 'Yellow people'.[76] But, like Miyazaki, Kodama combined his hope for political change in China (where Sun and his followers were struggling against Yuan Shikai's regime and regional warlords) with demands for reform in Japan too. To him, the Meiji Restoration and 'Taishō democracy' had not brought true 'freedom', which was Kodama's key political ideal, to Japanese society. Any appeal to Asian commonality through political and social change in China and, to a lesser degree, also India therefore included the desire for domestic reforms in Japan, too. Asianism, consequently, as is very visible in Kodama's poems, could function as a tool for demanding political change, not only from a nationalist or imperialist point of view but also from a socialist and liberalist position.

Probably Kodama's most representative Asianist poem, '*Sake* cup to the Asian alliance' from 1917, revealed his sentimental conception of Asianism as solidarity and also included outspoken anti-Western notions:

> The *sake* cup, overflowing with the waves and the passion of the Pacific,
> A toast to the pledge of the comrades and brothers of the East.
> Ah, my Asia, bring back memories of the pioneering cradle of ancient civilization,
> Revive in the twentieth century and add your tide to our great force. [...]
> If we leave egoism and suspicion behind and unite as some hundred millions,
> Then New Asia's rebirth will come
> And the wind and waves of Pan-Asianism will stretch out. [...]
> Oh, India, China, Japan, this century is the time,
> To awake East Asia by an exalted chime.
> While the small countries of Europe one after another collapse and are buried in pity,
> Will we not sound the giant bell of the sympathetic peoples of Asia?[77]

Against the background of World War One, Kodama explicitly contrasted the decline of the 'West' to the revival of the 'East'. However, his optimism was limited by the lack of Asianist enthusiasm in Japan and other parts of Asia. 'Egoism and suspicion' posed the main obstacle to Asianist enterprises, not only in the late 1910s but also in the following decades. The 'comrades and brothers' that vowed their dedication to the Asianist cause remained only a few, and even those leaders that Kodama refers to as representatives of the Asianist cause, such as Sun Yat-sen and Rabindranath Tagore, despite general pan-Asianist inclinations remained sceptical of the possibility to realize Asianism.[78] Kodama, at any rate, cultivated the hope that 'China and Japan will under the sky of Asia clasp their hands' to form a union on the basis of 'heartfelt sympathy'.[79] To be sure, the frequent publications of Kodama's Asianist poetry in popular journals in Japan contributed to the dissemination of Asianism in general and of his own conception of Asian solidarity in particular. It possibly also reached a different audience from that which was following more theoretical political debate in the front sections of *Taiyō* (The Sun) or *Chūō Kōron* (Central Review), where Ōtani's and Wakamiya's essays had appeared. Kodama's poems were certainly not the adequate genre to critique imperialist-hegemonic conceptions of Asianism propagated by others around the same time. However, it is rather obvious that his sentimental yearning for Sino-Japanese friendship and pan-Asian sympathy were diametrically opposed to Tokutomi Sohō's or Gotō Shinpei's colonial and Japan-centred Asianisms.

Remarkably, in this relatively pro-Asianist mood even critics of certain conceptions of Asianism did not necessarily reject Asianism altogether, but instead formulated their own conceptions of Asianism. Yoshino Sakuzō, as we have seen above, who had taken a sceptical and dismissive stance early on, partially modified his position in the following years. The resulting ambivalence—what exactly is Asianism?—was effectively a result of the still undefined content of Asianism or, at least, of the absence of a widely agreeable definition of the new concept. As Wakamiya had argued, ambivalence and vagueness are inherent in any claim or principle that refers to more than a precise policy, and this applies even more to a concept that has only recently become part of mainstream political discourse. In response to new Asianist proposals, Yoshino considered revising his dismissive position, although he ultimately remained critical of the concept:

> Recently, many people have started to advocate Greater Asianism. If its meaning is that Japan must adopt as its national policy the aim of making Japan the cultural authority of all Eastern countries, then it is identical with my points about the cultural mission of the Japanese people. There is no objection against making this the future national policy. Although Japan must eventually wake up to its mission of contributing to the civilization of the entire world, there is no other way for the time being than to limit the scope of its cultural mission and activities to the East. If it cannot succeed here, Japan's worldly mission will end in failure. [...] However, with regard to Greater Asianism we must pay attention to the fact that conventionally, the letters of Greater Asianism have not been employed in such a noble spiritual meaning. The reason why the peoples of the East and the Chinese in particular have developed antipathy to the Japanese and will not easily cooperate with us is that we Japanese have evoked a future racial suppression by the Whites and proposed to forcefully form a union with the Eastern peoples for this reason. In this sense, Greater Asianism represents xenophobic thought. To aim at uniting the yellow people compulsorily as the joint enemy of the Whites is a rather desperate plan.[80]

Here, Yoshino reveals his general receptivity to Asianist proposals, even with Japan at their centre, as long as they include a prominent cultural aspect. By this Yoshino refers to the nurturing of an interest in and promotion of the study of Asia among Japanese, who, for the past decades, had almost exclusively turned to 'Western' knowledge. Any negative political definitions of Asianism, such as anti-Westernism or White Peril theories, however, were bound to fail, according to Yoshino, as they could not win trust in Japanese Asianism among other Asians. Stegewerns therefore refers to Yoshino's Asianism as 'cultural Asianism' and contrasts this form with 'political Asianism', which 'Yoshino invariably took heed to keep away from'.[81] Although Yoshino affirmed the existence and significance of the 'East' or 'Asia', he rejected its oppositional and dichotomous application as the enemy of the 'West'. In particular, Yoshino dismissed the fraternization of Asianist claims with racism. While in 1918, his criticism of such conceptions—which were still few in number—remained soft and reconciliatory, in the aftermath of the Versailles Conference he began to voice his disapproval more outspokenly (see Chap. 5). For the time being, Yoshino focused his comments on criticizing the lack of knowledge about 'Asia' that most Japanese Asianist proposals revealed to him:

> In reality, these prejudices [of a clash between the peoples of the East and the West] are held by the Japanese, whereas they can hardly be found among the Chinese and Indians. Compared to us, they are much more cosmopolitan. And from my personal exchange, I would say they feel closer to the British and Americans than to us Japanese. Therefore, in this sense Greater Asianism will not easily be accepted by the Chinese and the Indians. In addition, it will provoke the jealousy of the [non-Asian] foreigners and as a result the Japanese will become isolated not only psychologically. The tenet of Greater Asianism that aims at uniting the peoples of the East must argue from a position that also includes cooperation with the Euro-Americans.[82]

Yoshino addresses two crucial points. First, many Japanese, including many of those who advocated Asianism, lacked a profound understanding or experience of 'Asia' and Asians. This shortage of knowledge of Asia posed a formidable obstacle to Japanese dealings with the 'East' and consequently also to the realization of Asianist policies—although it must not be forgotten that the yet larger obstacle at this stage constituted the unwillingness of the Japanese government to implement any of these Asianist policies under debate. Yoshino's call for a 'cultural Asianism' resembled an earlier proposal by writer Uchida Rōan (1868–1929) who had criticized the lack of research institutes in Japan that concerned themselves with 'Asia'. While some organizations, such as the *Tōa Dōbunkai* (East Asia Common Culture Society) and the *Nichi–In Kyōkai* (Japanese–Indian Association) promoted knowledge about China or India respectively, apart from the *Tōyō Kyōkai* (Oriental Association)[83] no organization concerned itself with a wider range of Asian issues. Uchida called his proposal 'academic Pan-Asianism'.[84] Both Uchida's and Yoshino's rationale was that Japan, especially after its turn to the 'West' following the Meiji Restoration and the subsequent focus on itself (Japanism, *kokutai*, Tennōism),[85] had to re-learn about 'Asia' and Asians before it could make claims on behalf of 'Asia' and Asians. Second, Yoshino's qualified embrace of Asianism was based on what could be called 'open Asianism', that is, a focus on intra-Asian cooperation without excluding non-Asians. This focus on 'Asia' was less due to assumed racial and cultural commonality or an inevitable necessity because of an assumed shared fate but strictly for practical reasons only. 'Asia' was nothing more but a practical stepping stone to the world and, as Yoshino and Uchida would argue, an interesting and rewarding object of study and inspiration too.

Sawayanagi Masatarō's Cultural Asianism

It was this potential interpretation of Asianism based on an open and rather pragmatic view of 'Asia' that underlay Yoshino's conception of 'cultural Asianism' and that appealed to a number of more liberal and cosmopolitan Japanese thinkers and activists during the later 1910s. These conceptions of Asianist thought, together with sentimental conceptions à la Miyazaki and Kodama, constituted the non-hegemonic branch of Asianist views that challenged hegemonic views for the 'true' or authentic meaning of Asianism. While Yoshino's suspicion of Asianism and his assumption that it might never appeal to non-Japanese Asians impeded his full-blown affirmation of the concept, other thinkers, including Sawayanagi Masatarō and Ukita Kazutami, embraced Asianism more emphatically. Sawayanagi (1865–1927), a noted liberal educator and former vice minister of education,[86] had started to advocate Asianism in direct response to World War One, which, as Sawayanagi stated, had called for the establishment of 'thought of devoted public service towards the state'.[87] This service, to Sawayanagi, was not limited to Japan but, in Japan's interest, was to be extended to Asia—the geographic scope of implementation of 'philanthropism', 'humanitarianism', and 'world pacifisms'. Rather obviously, this rhetoric easily lent itself to imperialist convictions. In fact, several of Sawayanagi's writings on foreign affairs in the first decades of the twentieth century display a tendency to 'full support for the diplomacy of the Japanese Empire' that may be 'inexplicable or unexpected' of a leading figure of the Taishō democracy movement.[88] However, Sawayanagi's proposal of Asianism, above all, was meant as a wake-up call to the majority of anti-Asianist Japanese. 'The government and people of Japan', Sawayanagi demanded, 'must fundamentally change their attitudes towards China'. Otherwise, he continued, no cooperation between the two countries and peoples was realizable.[89] In other words, the most important task to pave the way for realizing Asianism for the Japanese was not to convince or persuade the Chinese to follow or trust Japan but to start with changing Japan's own behaviour towards its neighbour. Complying with this logic, Sawayanagi emphasized that any 'cooperation between Japan and China, needless to say, must be mutually beneficial'.[90]

His conception of Asianism, Sawayanagi was convinced, would also appeal to the Chinese. To this end, he had a collection of his writings translated into Chinese and published under the title *Ri–Hua Gongcun lun* (On Japanese–Chinese Coexistence).[91] A more nationalist or imperialist inclined audience in Japan certainly found Sawayanagi's Sino- and Asiaphilism difficult to digest. His affirmation of Japan's Asianity—even though it claimed for the Japanese the status of 'pioneers of the Asian peoples'[92] and despite attempts to reconcile Asianism with nationalism (kokkashugi)[93]—was far from common sense in 1917. Sawayanagi's affirmative definition of Asianism as 'thought that proposes we are Asians'[94] was hardly compatible with the efforts of others to legitimize a proactive 'Asia' policy by separating the identity of supposedly advanced Japanese and 'other', supposedly backwards, Asians. 'We are Asians' blurred this line of distinction and, as the essence of Sawayanagi's conception of Asianism, underlined his relatively Sinophile attitude.[95] At the same time, however, and in a sense as a response to Yoshino's suspicion, Sawayanagi emphasized that Asianism was neither 'seclusionist' nor necessarily directed against the 'West'. Asianism only claimed a 'status of equality with the European peoples'.[96] In 1917—five months before the publication of Yoshino's influential article—Sawayanagi had included the liberation of 'the seven to eight hundred million Asians' subjugated by 'the Europeans' as 'serving a great ideal for the sake of the human race' as a central part of his Asianist agenda, which he had explicitly defined in preparation for the post-war order.[97] In an obvious attempt to appeal to both anti-Asianist nationalists and anti-Asianist internationalists, he portrayed his 'worldist' conception of Asianism as contradicting neither nationalism nor internationalism. Instead, he concluded that Asianism provided the link between the former and the latter.[98] In other words, its mid-position, which Ōyama had diagnosed as Asianism's shortcoming, functioned as a point of legitimization in Sawayanagi's conception, as it sought to reconcile nationalists with internationalists.

Ukita Kazutami's New Asianism

The most remarkable and influential affirmation of Asianism proposed by a liberal-minded intellectual, however, was Ukita Kazutami's conception of 'New Asianism' (Shin Ajiashugi). A Kumamoto-born son of a *hanshi* (servant of a daimyō), Ukita (1859–1946) had studied Western learning at the *Kumamoto Yōgaku* (Kumamoto School for Western Studies). From 1886 until his death he taught history and politics, first at Dōshisha University in Kyoto and later at Waseda University in Tokyo.

Ukita is probably best known as the chief editorial writer of the influential *Taiyō* (The Sun) journal, in which—as we have seen above—much of Asianism discourse took place. Ukita held this post from 1909 to 1917.

In fact, Ukita combines several characteristics of the debate as analysed above. First, he clearly identified Asianism with the claim for an 'Asia of the Asians'; second, he rejected previous versions of Asianism without dismissing the concept altogether. Rather, he defined his own conception of Asianism in opposition to that of others. Third, Ukita formed one of the strongest links between Asianism discourse in Japan and China, not only because he had been the teacher of Li Dazhao, the most active Chinese contributor to Asianism discourse in the latter half of the 1910s (see below), but also because Ukita's famous 'New Asianism' essay[99] belongs to only a limited number of Japanese articles on Asianism that were published in full-length translation in China during the 1910s. Only weeks after it had first appeared as an editorial in his *Taiyō* journal, a Chinese version was published by one of the most important contemporary publications for political debate in China, the Shanghai-based *Dongfang Zazhi* (Eastern Miscellany).[100]

Reviewing the history of Asianist conceptions in Japan, Ukita distinguished between (a) seclusionist 'old Asianism' of the pre-Meiji period, (b) contemporary Asianism as represented by Tokutomi Sohō's Asian Monroeism, and (c) his own proposal for a 'new Asianism'. 'The gist of old Asianism', Ukita defined, 'was the assumption that since Asia is the home of the Asians, the Euro-Americans cannot be permitted to come and plunder the natives'.[101] According to Ukita, the seclusionist policy which characterized foreign relations during most of the Tokugawa reign (1603–1868) was not only pernicious to Japan but also to world peace. 'Ultimately', Ukita concluded, 'it was an irrational argument that lagged behind the times and brought misfortune to our own country'.[102] Moving to Tokutomi's *Taishō no Seinen to Teikoku no Zento* (1916) and his proposal of an Asian Monroe Doctrine, Ukita largely agreed with Tokutomi on the 'conservative' confirmation of the *status quo* but insisted his own 'new Asianism' would 'principally acknowledge the possibility of a change of the present condition'.[103] Very carefully, Ukita tried to balance his dismissal of confrontational views that demanded an immediate liberation of Asia from the 'Western' powers with his own advocacy of decolonization.[104] If in the future there was an opportunity for the exchange of territory, then there was 'no necessity for us to insist on the preservation of the *status quo*', Ukita argued. Interestingly, Ukita did not speak of a 'return' but 'exchange' of territory, although this could include financial compensation, as his example of the purchase of Alaska by the United States demonstrates.[105] On the other hand, however he insisted that the 'West' could not expect any further gains in Asia that exceeded its current sphere of influence there:

> Our new Asianism does not mean to expel the influence of the Euro-Americans from Asia so that the Japanese manage Asia in their place. But we do oppose ambitions of the Euro-American powers to realize their spheres of influence here in Asia as they did in Africa in the way prior to the Russo-Japanese War [1904/05].

In other words, while Ukita's Asianism rejected Tokutomi's explicit claim that Japan take over the management of Asian affairs from the Western powers, he objected to any further political and territorial ambitions of the 'West' in Asia beyond the current *status quo*. Like the above-mentioned Sinophiles, Ukita also displayed a higher degree of consideration of other Asians, who would 'turn pale' and strongly protest when they heard of Tokutomi's Japan-centred conception of Asianism, he feared.[106] Instead of simply replacing 'Western' by Japanese rule, Asianism, to Ukita as to Yoshino, Miyazaki, or Sawayanagi, could not simply be a Japanese project. It also needed to obtain the consent of other Asians. This 'new interpretation of the Monroe Doctrine for the East', as Ukita had subtitled his essay, formed the core of his new Asianism, which attempted to reconcile Japanese, Asian, and Western interests in a more pragmatic way. This was best revealed in his rejection of Tokutomi's racialist definition of 'Asia'. By contrast, Ukita proposed a more voluntaristic interpretation of 'Asia' and Asians as the basis of his conception of Asianism:

> In reality, the backbone of an Asian Monroe Doctrine will be Japan and without Japan this doctrine cannot be established. However, it is a grave mistake to place its foundation on a racial basis. First of all, because the distinction between Whites and Asians is not clear this definition cannot be employed in diplomacy and politics. [...] It is our principle, too, that Asia must be managed by Asians. This is the principle of Eastern self-governance or the principle that the affairs of the East must be handled by the peoples of the East. However, we deny that the so-called peoples of Asia or peoples of the East are simply those that are Asians, excluding the Whites. Our interpretation of Asia regards all people that have settled down in Asia

irrespective of their race as Asians. It therefore also views the Russians in Siberia, the British in India, the French in Tonkin [North Vietnam], and the Americans in the Philippines as Asians or Eastern peoples.[107]

Ukita's conception of 'Asia' and Asians that informed his 'conservative' view of Asianism was highly idealistic. At a high time of racialist and nationalist discourse and practice, his pragmatic view of treating people indiscriminately of race and nation but rather according to their place of residence was almost Utopian. More importantly, it was inadequate as a political principle that was meant to appeal to both Japanese and Asians alike. Its inclusive bias towards the 'West' would eventually prevent immediate revisions of the political and territorial order, even if it might have helped to ease tensions in the short term. It was another middle-of-the-road approach that could neither provide common ground for imperialist-inclined (mostly Japanese) Asianists nor appeal to revolutionary- and reformist-minded (mostly Chinese or other Asian) Asianists.

Taken even one step further, Ukita's non-racial, non-national, non-civilizational but strictly geographical interpretation of the Asian Monroe Doctrine culminated in his redefinition of Asianism as one side of a New Worldism (shin sekaishugi). This idea was closely linked to geopolitical ideas of the time, not least as a result of Monroeism: just as the United States had declared a de facto Pan-American bloc in the new world via Monroeism, it was expected that an alliance of the powers in Europe (after the War) would emerge. Ukita, like many of his contemporaries, envisioned 'establishing a sort of alliance that can ensure peace and justice in all of Asia', too.[108] As its core and as a first step towards such an alliance in the East, he envisioned Japanese–Chinese cooperation. Eventually, however, as Ukita did not hold any essentialist views of Asia, all these regional blocs were to merge into a 'world peace union', which should be established in the aftermath of the World War. In this sense, Ukita's Asianism can rightfully be described as an 'ideal of regional union that mediated between a Wilsonian world union and the modern Western national system of sovereign states'.[109] Like many of his generation at the time, Ukita, too, had high hopes for the establishment of a new world order after the end of World War One. According to Ukita and other Japanese it was—strictly for pragmatic reasons, not because of any supposedly innate qualification—Japan's mission to take its role as 'protector of the East'.[110] In fact, Ukita had a history of dismissing a conventional Monroe Doctrine for Asia that placed Japan at its centre and confronted the 'West'. Already in his writings before and after the Russo-Japanese War, Ukita had rejected talk of an Asian or Japanese Monroe Doctrine as 'lagging behind the times'.[111] Ukita only approved of measures that would accord with international law.[112] Therefore, considering the current *status quo*, any unilateral Japanese declaration of an Asian Monroe Doctrine must have appeared to Ukita as an unlawful and provocative act.

ASIANISM AS THE 'WHITE PERIL' THEORY

Before 1919, when during the Paris Peace Conference Asianism became prominently linked with racialist notions (see Chap. 5), race played only a relatively marginal role in conceptions of Asianism and racialist vocabulary, such as 'hakujin' (Whites) or 'hakubatsu' (White clique), was rarely linked to the new key concept. A remarkable exception is the first book-length affirmation of Asianism ever published, Kodera Kenkichi's *Dai Ajiashugi Ron* (On Greater Asianism), which was almost exclusively based on racial notions. Kodera presented an elaborated study of racial confrontation, but its influence remained limited as his conception was not only too radical but also too Sinophile and too anti-Western at the same time. Consequently, it also failed to become the authoritative view of Asianism or even a key reference in Asianism discourse, despite the fact that its early publication date and extensiveness would have theoretically qualified the text as such. In fact, its impact was dwarfed by Tokutomi's *Taishō no Seinen to Teikoku no Zento*, which had been published six months earlier. Nevertheless, it deserves attention as the most detailed proposal of Asianism ever published and because it anticipated the central role race would come to play in the following decades in Asianist and other political discourse. It is also noteworthy that Kodera's *Dai Ajiashugi Ron* was the only affirmation of Asianism as a new key political principle proposed as Japan's guiding national policy by an active Japanese parliamentarian in the 1910s. Kodera, a Western-trained politician and member of the Lower House from 1908 to 1930,[113] defined his conception of Asianism as the antithesis of Western Yellow Peril discourse, namely the White Peril thesis (Hakka ron):

> Isn't it strange? In Europe, which controls Asia and has completely subdued it, these days the yellow peril theory makes a considerable noise. However, among the coloured races, which are subjugated and threatened

by the white race, very little can be heard of a white peril. Moreover, while a yellow peril is nothing more than a bad dream, the white peril is a reality.[114]

As defined in this opening passage of the book's preface, the race question (jinshu mondai) was 'one of the predominant themes, if not the main theme, of Kodera's 1916 opus'.[115] Concretely, Kodera envisioned expelling the 'Whites' from Asia and declared that 'the time has come for Japan to become the leader of China, raise a second army of Attila, raise a second army of Genghis Khan, and engage in revenge against the Whites'.[116] Unlike Ukita, Kodera did not for a moment consider the preservation of the *status quo* a feasible option and response to the double denigration by the 'Whites': the physical domination and economic exploitation, on the one hand, and the rhetorical demonization on the other. As practical countermeasures, Kodera proposed a step-by-step unification of the Asian peoples on the base of a Sino-Japanese union. Clearly, China was Kodera's major concern and his argumentation was based on assumed cultural and racial kinship:

> Our Japan [...] has the highest mission to relieve East Asia from the oppression of the white race. Naturally, it must become the leader (meishu) of the yellow race and the guide to preserve the territorial integrity of China, and to qualify its nation [Chinese] as a people of rich culture. Following the politics of same culture and same race (dōbun dōshu) and of the relationship between lips and teeth (shinshi hosha), we must trust each other and cooperate, together resist the general situation in the world, and create the new civilization of mighty Asia. Then we must gradually expand this and revive under this principle (shugi) all yellow races that live in Asia, really attain political freedom and sovereignty, and eventually pursue the ultimate ideal of uniting the whole yellow race all over the world. It is the main point of my conclusion to say that Asianism means 'Asia is the Asia of the Asians'.[117]

Although Kodera does not directly mention the Asian Monroe Doctrine here, his summary of Asianism as 'Asia is the Asia of the Asians' essentially affirms the key position of Asian Monroeism: non-interference of non-Asians in Asian matters. Like Tokutomi, he sees Japan as the only possible leader of 'Asia', but unlike Tokutomi, Kodera links Japan's fate to that of China using the well-known metaphor of lips and teeth. If China (lips) falls, Japan (teeth) will remain unprotected. This metaphor had been used as early as in the *Bakumatsu* (late Edo) period to describe the fateful connection between China and Japan and was strongly rejected by anti-Asianists.[118]

Kodera was well read in Western literature on 'Asia' and world affairs, a fact which—together with his studies abroad at a high time of Yellow Peril discourse in Europe and the United States—may have strongly influenced the development of his Asianist consciousness. To be sure, Kodera who had first travelled to the 'West' shortly after the first Sino-Japanese War (1894/95) must have been surprised if not shocked to find that popular Western discourse indiscriminately treated Japanese and Chinese as the 'Yellow Peril'. At any rate, it is striking that some of the most fervent advocates of Asianism, including Gotō Shinpei, Tokutomi Sohō, Kodera Kenkichi, and others had lived in Europe or the United States for several years around the turn of the century.[119] This *Fremdheitserlebnis*[120] (feeling of being foreign) of foreign-imposed Orientalization by being subsumed under a category of 'Asians' may have largely contributed to the fact that some of those who travelled to the 'West' as 'Japanese' returned back to Japan as 'Asians'. Clearly, Kodera knew no Asian country nearly as well as he knew Germany, Austria, Switzerland, and the United States, and the bibliography of his *Dai Ajiashugi Ron* reveals his intellectual indebtedness to 'Western' thought; only nine Chinese books are listed while books and journals in English and German amount to more than 150. Unsurprisingly, therefore, Kodera's plan for the realization of Asianism was strongly influenced by his studies of 'Western' political discourse on 'Asia' and studies of Pan-isms. The main elements of Asianism, Kodera argued, were to be defined according to the nine categories that Roland G. Usher had proposed in his study of Pan-Americanism[121]: geography, race, language, political system, jurisdiction, religion, mixed marriages, and popular culture.[122] The 'geography' factor was self-evident and was an important factor for close military and economic cooperation between the naval power Japan and the continental power (to be) China. Racially, Kodera viewed the Chinese and Japanese as belonging to the yellow race. As for language, Kodera stressed the potential of Chinese characters as a common medium of written communication and thus a common bond uniting all nations of East Asia. The political system and jurisdiction, Kodera admitted, differed greatly in the two countries, but just as Japan had learnt from China in the past, he expressed optimism in the Chinese willingness to learn from Japan now. Also in terms of popular customs and religions, Kodera emphasized the legacy of centuries of commonalities, while he had to concede that the number of mixed marriages was low due to Chinese xenophobia and Japan's policy of seclusion during the Tokugawa period. In sum, however, Kodera stressed the mutual influences and overall commonalities that by far outweighed the differences between the Japanese and the Chinese. This could serve as the basis for future cooperation between both peoples, he argued.

Kodera's approach to Asianism differed from Ukita's pro-Western considerations in another important aspect. While the latter had checked Asianist conceptions against their potential feasibility as diplomatic tools—and had consequently dismissed 'emotional' (kanjōteki) arguments[123]—Kodera was concerned with its appeal on the popular, not diplomatic, level. Sharing the fears of Yoshino and Ukita that the Chinese might dismiss Japan-centred conceptions, Kodera paid particular attention to accommodating Chinese interests (although he, too, claimed Japanese leadership). To this end, he not only blamed the imperialistic policy of the 'Whites' for the tumultuous political state in China but also did not spare the Japanese from criticism. Providing the example of Chinese students in Japan, Kodera diagnosed that the 'materialistic attitude of the Japanese towards [Chinese] exchange students' was a major factor in the 'ill feeling' and 'anti-Japanese' propaganda against Japan by the Chinese.[124] While he stressed the particular importance of economic cooperation for a Chinese–Japanese alliance, Kodera harshly criticized Japanese businesses for not fairly sharing the benefits of their ventures on the mainland with the Chinese. 'It is natural to aim at high profits when engaging in business' he conceded, 'but one must have an attitude of sharing not monopolizing the benefits.'[125] For Kodera, Japan, not China, was the cause of ongoing disputes between both countries which ultimately, he lamented, would only benefit the 'Whites'.

To add credibility to his cause, Kodera aimed at demonstrating how reform-oriented Chinese thinkers such as Liang Qichao, Huang Xing, and Sun Yat-sen also demanded Sino-Japanese cooperation, which Kodera too saw as the base of his conception of Asianism. Already in 1905, Kodera explained, the *Minbao* (People's Paper), the public organ of Sun Yat-sen's Revolutionary Party (Tongmenghui), had adopted 'the demand for an alliance of the Japanese and Chinese people' as one of their six principles.[126] Kodera also extensively quoted from Liang

Qichao's speech given in early 1913, in which he referred to Japan as China's 'close ally of same culture and same race'. In the best Asianist manner, Liang had postulated that 'Asia is the Asia of the Asians' and that the Chinese and Japanese peoples must give up their mutual suspicion. 'Asia', Liang had claimed, 'is our family and in this family Japan and China are brothers.'[127] Although Liang had not directly proposed the adoption of an Asian Monroe Doctrine or of Asianism, Kodera happily summarized Liang's positions as 'a pure thesis of Greater Asianism' based on a Sino-Japanese alliance.[128] Similarly, Kodera quoted Sun's close follower Huang Xing advocating that 'Japan and China must to the utmost understand and ally each with other'.[129]

As a Japan-critical Asianist, Kodera was stuck in the middle. It was difficult, if not impossible, to find a wider audience in Japan that was receptive to his conception of Asianism. At the same time, his appeal to the Chinese was limited, not only by causing suspicion of playing a Sinophobe trick using a Sinophile cover. More importantly, as a member of the Japanese Imperial Diet he could not avoid being mistaken as a representative of Japan's policy towards 'Asia', even though domestically he was well known as an oppositional voice.[130] Kodera apparently saw himself as a bridge between the Chinese and Japanese, on the one hand, and between anti-Chinese Japanese and pro-Chinese Japanese on the other. Kodera's treatise aimed at functioning in both directions: despite its 1300 pages, his book was fully translated into Chinese and published in Shanghai less than two years after it had been published in Japan.[131] His work may have managed to impress Chinese readers who were not necessarily used to Japanese politicians paying much attention to Chinese public opinion. At the same time, his extensive references to pro-Japanese Chinese voices aroused questions among those Japanese who held deeply felt anti-Chinese sentiments. Kodera's message was that many Chinese were in fact pro-Japanese and those who were anti-Japanese often had good reasons for their attitude. For this reason, Kodera did not pay too much attention to why Sun or Huang or Liang were proposing close cooperation between China and Japan. Both before and after the Xinhai Revolution, reformists (Liang, Kang) and revolutionaries (Sun, Huang) alike were strongly dependent on Japanese aid, be it financial aid or shelter from persecution. Eventually, Kodera's balancing act between Chinese and Japanese interests proved too ambitious and he failed to reach either side.[132]

Japanese and Chinese Asianism in China

As we have seen in Chap. 3, the history of Asianism discourse in Japan from its earliest times is closely interlinked with China, not only regarding its content but also concerning the actual participation of Chinese thinkers and activists in the formation and development of Asianist conceptions. In addition to Sun Yat-sen and Dai Jitao, who had been among the earliest proponents of Asianism during the early 1910s (see Chap. 3) and who continued to influence Asianism in the following years and decades, World War One saw the emergence of new Chinese voices whose impact on Asianism discourse is second only to Sun Yat-sen's: Li Dazhao (1889–1927)[133] and the Shanghai-based journal *Dongfang Zazhi* (Eastern Miscellany),[134] which was published between 1904 and 1948. They became the two most important channels through which Asianism discourse in Japan transcended national borders and reached China. While individual publications, such as Sawayanagi's *Ri–Hua Gongcun lun* (On Japanese–Chinese Coexistence) and the Chinese translation of Kodera's book have left little traceable evidence of reception in China, Li's writings usually appeared in widely read newspapers, and the *Dongfang Zazhi* belonged to the most influential political journals. It is sometimes compared to the Japanese *Taiyō* (The Sun) journal.[135]

Li Dazhao is well known as a leading Marxist thinker and a founder of the Chinese Communist Party (CCP). As a student he spent three years in Japan (1913–1916), at the very time of the inception of Asianism into mainstream public discourse. Li had spent most of his time in Japan at Waseda University in Tokyo, where he met and studied under Ukita Kazutami. Upon his return to Beijing, Li first became head of Peking University's library and, after the May Fourth Movement of 1919, he was promoted to professor at the same university. After the failure of the first collaboration between the CCP and Chiang Kai-shek's *Guomindang* (GMD), Li was persecuted, arrested, and killed by warlord Zhang Zuolin in 1927.

Similarly to Sun's conception of Asianism, which is often reduced to his Kobe speech (or even only the last sentence thereof), Li's critical contributions to Asianism discourse are often shortened to his dismissal of Japanese Asianism as a 'different name for Greater Japanism' (Da Riben zhuyi de bianming), a 'principle of invasion' (qinlue de zhuyi), and of 'Japanese militarism' (Riben de junguo zhuyi), as expressed in his most famous essay on Asianism, 'Greater Asianism and New Asianism'.[136] Li's concern with the concept, however, was much deeper, more multifaceted, and underwent a significant change.

Between the Twenty-One Demands (January 1915) and the Russian Revolution (October 1917), Li's writings are dominated by strong Chinese nationalist sentiments. Quite contrary to his later well-known rejection of Pan-ideologies as 'argot for autocracy' (zhuanzhi zhi yinyu),[137] in 1917 Li still held the conviction that the positive driving force behind Pan-movements were national ambitions. Asianism, therefore, Li contested, could facilitate the awakening and revival of a new Chinese nationalism (xin Zhonghua minzu zhuyi), for without Chinese nationalism one could hardly speak of Asian nationalism. But Li's 'new Chinese nationalism' was not only meant as a tool for the unification of China. 'Certainly', Li stated, 'new Chinese Nationalism can develop East Asia and afterwards, Asianism can start to enlighten the world.'[138] In Li's view, Asianism was to become a tool for extending new Chinese nationalism to East Asia, similar to the way that Tokutomi and Gotō had envisioned Asianism as a means for extending Japanese imperial policy to the Chinese mainland. Li's 'pan-Asian nationalism'[139] was nothing more than Chinese nationalism applied to (East) Asia.

Li's nationalist claims remained dominant in his first essay fully dedicated to Asianism, published two months later, and he continued to argue that China, with its huge territory, its multitude of ethnicities, and its civilization, would best represent all of 'Asia'.[140] But a second dominant theme emerged: the rejection of the assumed clash between the 'Western' and 'Eastern' civilizations that was prevailing in many Japanese Asianist writings. Li directly reacted to Wakamiya Unosuke's essay (see above), in which he had called for Greater Asianism as an expression of resistance against the flawed and plundering civilization of the 'West'. Li, possibly under the influence of Ukita Kazutami, strongly rejected such claims of a confrontation between 'East' and 'West'. An Asianism that was not open to include other, even non-Asian, peoples was not compatible with the Asianism that Li envisioned. But Li also became more sensitive to the possibility that Asianist rhetoric might fall into a Japanese-led Asian version of imperialism. Although at this stage he did not charge the Japanese directly with such intentions, it is clear that only the Japanese could be meant when he warned of a replacement of 'Western' force in Asia by an Asian power, a fear that Ukita later tried to dispel. Li was sceptical but in principle still supportive of Asianism:

The Japanese acknowledge that our China is an important pillar for the general situation in Asia. If a foreign power unruly encroaches on us, not only must they [the Japanese] not assist the tyrant, but also out of 'same continent, same race' friendship (tongzhou tongzhong zhi yi) must we mutually assist each other, protect the righteousness of the world and guarantee the real peace of the world. If, for the time being, the banner of Greater Asianism aims at dressing up imperialism and grasping the rule of might in the Far East, prohibit others from plundering but plunder themselves, forbid others from bullying but bully themselves, this would only invite the jealousy of the Whites, and end in putting all our fellow Asians in disaster.[141]

By 1918, however, possibly under the influence of the Russian Revolution and the ongoing World War,[142] Li had started to reject Pan-isms in general and Greater Asianism in particular as the autocratic opposite of democracy. As mentioned above, Li's famous call for a 'New Asianism' (1919) is usually explained as a full-blown rejection of Japanese imperialism.[143] While Li outspokenly dismissed Japanese Asianism as proclaimed by Takebe Tongo,[144] Ōtani Kōzui, Tokutomi Sohō, and Kodera Kenkichi as 'Japanism' and a 'principle to annex China', interestingly, however, he did not dismiss Asianism altogether but rather argued for his own version of Asianism. Again, like many Japanese propagators of Asianism, he found the principle useful for his own political agenda although he had not yet encountered any existing interpretation he could approve of.

Li's criticism was based on his interpretation of Japanese Asianism as an 'Asian Monroe Doctrine' (Yaxiya Mengluo zhuyi): Japan as 'commanding' (zhihui) the Asian people, Japan as 'Asia's leader' (mengzhu), and Asia as 'the stage of the Japanese' (Ribenren de wutai). Implementing such an Asian Monroeism, Li concluded, would not mean that Asia would become the 'Asia of the Asians' but the 'Asia of the Japanese' (Ribenren de Yaxiya). Li's pun is reminiscent of the rejection of American Monroeism in Latin America ('America for the US-Americans'), as quoted above. Asianism, Li continued, would not represent 'Asian democracy' but 'Japanese militarism' and, most importantly, instead of being a seed for a world organization, Asianism would destroy the envisioned unity of the world, because one Pan-ism would always provoke the emergence of another, oppositional Pan-ism. Like many progressives of his generation, Li held high hopes for the post-war peace conference and its aim of creating an international organization for the promotion of peace and national self-determination.[145] For Li, as we have seen above and as he claimed again in 1919, Asianism was to be a first step towards a larger union not only of Asians but of all (likeminded) people throughout the world.

> We demand to take the liberation of the peoples as our basis and to bring about fundamental change. All Asian peoples, all annexed peoples must be liberated and the principle of self-determination of the peoples must be put into practice. Afterwards we will form a big alliance, together with the European and American unions to complete together a world federation and to promote the happiness of the human race.[146]

It is partly for these rather radical ambitions that Li also rejected Ukita Kazutami's more conservative 'New Asianism' and proposed his own version. As outlined above, in his 'New Asianism', Ukita had rejected Tokutomi's exclusive and Japan-centred Asian Monroe Doctrine in favour of a more inclusive and non-racial version. But Ukita's Asianism, which proposed to maintain the *status quo*, ran counter to Li's plan to liberate China, the oppressed peoples of Asia and in other parts of the world. In this respect, Li was much closer to Kodera's demand 'to raise a second army of Attila' than Ukita's focus on reconciliatory diplomacy. A second reason for Li's critique of Ukita's Asianism may be anti-Japanese sentiments, which had grown rapidly between 1918 and 1919. Early in 1919, but even more so in his renewed call for a 'New Asianism' published in November of the same year, Li was no longer open to seeing different nuances in Japanese Asianism but, instead, he dismissed all proposals coming out of Japan indiscriminately as 'Japanese Greater Asianism'.[147]

Yet it is remarkable that Li's rejection of Japanese Asianism had not led him to completely dismiss Asianism by 1919. Li mainly kept clinging to the principle as a solution both for domestic and external problems for two reasons. First, rather than constituting a contradiction to contemporary Chinese internationalism, as Hoston suggests,[148] Li's 'panAsian nationalism' in 1919 no longer possessed any inherent value. It functioned as a practical tool and a first step to internationalism. To Li the direct realization of internationalism in the form of a world federation, which he saw as his ultimate goal, was not possible for practical reasons.[149] Second, Li kept on advocating his own conception of Asianism because he felt the urgency to counter and check Japanese Asianism. Because the principle as such—implying Asian unity, self-determination, peace, and co-prosperity—was positive, it was necessary to create a conception that actually represented this potentially positive meaning of Asianism. In this way it could expose the failings and hypocrisy of Japanese versions of Asianism. Li's critique of Japanese Asianism reveals the originality of his own conception:

> Because we are under pressure from Japan's Asianism, we just have to raise the great banner of New Asianism (Xin Yaxiya zhuyi de daqi) as the movement for the liberation of the Asian peoples. The first step of an Asian peoples' liberation movement is not directed against the outside but against the inside. It is against Japanese Asianism, not against European and American anti-Asianism (Ou, Mei pai Ya zhuyi). [...] My opinion is: if we don't remove the force that is used within Asia against Asians by Asians, we certainly cannot have hope for the retreat of non-Asians from Asia. After we have smashed the force applied by Asians to Asians in Asia, the force used by others will naturally be extinguished.[150]

Li's conviction that other powers would retreat once the Japanese stopped oppressing the Chinese (and Taiwanese and Koreans), was, of course, highly idealistic. After all, even before Japan obtained its first colony in 1895, the 'Western' powers had oppressed and colonized vast parts of Asia. Li's deeply rooted Chinese nationalism and Japan's anti-Asianist foreign policy, it appears, obstructed a more nuanced evaluation of different streams of Japanese Asianism. Kodera's appeal to the Chinese and his radical proposal to raise an army to liberate Asia might have received a different reception from Li (and other Chinese) if it had not been trumped by official Japanese policy, which suggested rather different Japanese strategies towards China. Li's political and intellectual struggle found a premature end when he was captured in Beijing and, together with 19 others, was executed on the orders of the warlord Zhang Zuolin on 28 April 1927.

Asianism Discourse in the Dongfang Zazhi

In addition to Li Dazhao's writings, a number of Japanese Asianist writings, including Ōyama Ikuo's anti-Asianist essay of 1916 and Ukita Kazutami's 'New Asianism' essay of 1918, were introduced to a wider

Chinese audience through the *Dongfang Zazhi* (Eastern Miscellany) journal.[151] This popular Chinese journal was an 'important channel for the introduction of civilizational discourse'; its editor, Du Yaquan (1873–1933), was 'a tireless promoter of the idea of the superiority [...] of the East'.[152] His journal regularly carried translated Japanese essays and, apart from Li Dazhao's writings, it was this journal that introduced Asianism discourse to a larger Chinese audience. The publication of Ukita Kazutami's 'New Asianism' in the *Dongfang Zazhi*, in fact, triggered a debate between Li Dazhao and Gao Yuan, both of whom rejected Ukita's conception.[153] Gao was a student of the progressive political thinker Zhang Shizhao (1881–1973) and a friend of Li Dazhao's. After graduation from Beijing's National School of Law and Politics (Beijing Guoli Fazheng Xuexiao), he published several articles on Japanese Asianism in the school's quarterly, *Fazheng Xuebao* (Studies in Law and Politics), some of which were reprinted in the *Dongfang Zazhi*.

Gao's criticism of Japanese Asianism was influenced by Li's earlier writings but it was much sharper. Gao did not see any value in Asianism at all and therefore, unlike Li, dismissed not only Japanese Asianism but the concept *in toto*, with one of his essays being expressively titled 'Ugh! Asianism!'[154] Without discrimination, Gao rejected Tokutomi's and Ukita's Asianism in one blow. 'We know Asian Monroeism and New Asianism', Gao claimed, 'it wants to establish Japan as the East Asian protagonist. All the other countries will be their slaves.'[155] While he cynically gave Tokutomi credit for openly admitting that his Asianism envisioned an Asia controlled by the Japanese, he despised Ukita, who 'put it more craftily', Gao contended. But ultimately, according to Gao, Ukita's 'New Asianism' was only a 'mask for Greater Asianism of the Japanese, the enemy of democracy, and a good friend of German militarism'.[156]

Dai Jitao's Criticism and Sun Yat-Sen's Affirmations

In the meantime, Dai Jitao had also developed a more critical attitude towards Asianism. His Sinocentric conception of 1914 (see Chap. 3), which had contained his hope for a Chinese Asianism that could overshadow Japanese Asianism, had turned out illusionary against the recent political developments. Not only had the domestic power struggle in China intensified, but, more significantly, Japan's territorial, political, and economic pressure on China had also increased. Dai now identified

Asianism with 'the desire of the Japanese people to expand their national power' and with 'Greater Japanese Imperialism'. His own 'Greater Asianism', which he still upheld, in contrast envisioned a 'union based on noble thought' that leaves behind 'temporary feelings and interests'.[157] In 1918, towards the end of World War One, Dai concluded that his ideal of Asianism was the exact opposite of the way the Japanese acted and participated in the War. Instead of opposing the European powers and pushing them out of Asia, Japan itself had turned to militarism, he criticized.[158]

Sun Yat-sen, as the more prominent and politically aspiring figure, could not make similarly critical statements, at least not publicly, if he wanted to continue to appeal to the Japanese. Remarkably, even in Chinese and only directed at a Chinese audience, Sun reiterated his conception of Asianism as the principle of Sino-Japanese cooperation for the development of Asia in general, and of China in particular. At the same time, his Asianism was not (yet) openly opposed to the 'West' but merely worked as a line of demarcation of interests:

> Realizing Asianism, Japan and China can together exploit the natural resources in the West of the Pacific, while the United States, in application of its Monroe Doctrine can unify authority in the East of the Pacific. If each pursues growth in its own sphere, there will not be any conflict for a hundred years. In the future, if these three countries cooperate, disarmament and détente can be achieved and permanent peace in the world secured. This will not only be to China's fortune. If China employs this way as its diplomacy, we can be sure not to invite any causes for national extinction.[159]

Also for Sun, Asianism contained the geopolitical logic of Monroeism. Naturally, his main concern was China—this section is taken from an essay on the question of China's survival—and it is noteworthy that Sun, not unlike Li Dazhao in 1917, affirmed Asianism as a potential tool for the improvement of China's international status. Sun appeared much less concerned than Li or Gao about Japan's potential role as China's hegemonic power. Instead, in a fashion that resembles his earliest references to Asianism in the early 1910s (see Chap. 3), Sun supplemented his practical deliberations with racialist and culturalist appeals to Sino-Japanese commonality:

> In the relationship between China and Japan, both are interlinked in matters of life or death, peace or threat. Without Japan, there is no China and without China, there is no Japan. [...] Because Japan is of the same race and same culture (tongzhong tongwen) it can assist us even more in developing [than America]. China's fortune, the stability of both countries, and the prosperity of the cultures of the whole world depend on harmonious relations between both countries. From the racial point of view, China and Japan are brother countries.[160]

Sun therefore not only based his argument for Sino-Japanese friendship and cooperation under the banner of Asianism on the assumed interdependent relations of both countries. He also tried to evoke feelings of commonality that reached beyond pragmatic considerations such as the common political interests that China, for example, also shared with the United States. The relationship between the East Asian siblings of China and Japan, however, was special regarding their essentialist commonality. In this respect, Sun's 'Asia' hardly reached beyond Japan and China. Of course, this focus on Japan had a pragmatic side, too. At home, Sun attempted to calm down domestic anti-Japanese sentiments which never really relaxed between Japan's Twenty-One Demands (1915) and the reactions to the results of the Paris Peace Conference (1919) that triggered the May Fourth Movement. On the other side, towards the Japanese public and officials, Sun would employ no less Asianist rhetoric than domestically, although—knowing that Japanese officials had remained hesitant towards racialist and culturalist arguments of commonality—he focused more explicitly on pragmatic arguments. Only after 1919, when Asianism discourse became strongly racialized in Japan, too, did Sun refer more openly to essentialist arguments (see Chap. 5). Against the background of the War and in expectation of a renewed focus on 'Asia' by the European powers after its end, Sino-Japanese cooperation had become an urgent matter, Sun argued, for example, in a conversation with Japanese Consulate General Ariyoshi Akira in Shanghai.[161] Hoping for Japanese aid for his unfinished revolutionary project, Sun wasted no opportunity to propagate his 'ideal of an East Asian League', suggesting that it was also in Japan's best interest to act quickly and jointly before the War ended and a subsequent peace conference perhaps created disadvantageous *faits accomplis*. Genuinely Asianist or not, it was this position of mediator between the Chinese and the Japanese that had made Sun Yat-sen a major proponent of Asianism in the realm of politics by the late 1910s.

Conclusion

Studying examples from politics, culture, journalism, academia, and the military this chapter has examined the changes and continuities in the use of Asianism as a key concept in Japanese and Chinese political discourse from the mid- to the late-1910s. It has demonstrated how World War One functioned as a catalyst for the spread and diversification of Asianist conceptions, many of which were encouraged by the perceived 'decline of the West' and the hope for a greater degree of self-determination in Asia. The majority of Asianist conceptions were explicitly formulated in opposition to the 'West' in general and as political alternatives to existing 'Western' blueprints of the world order. While proposals ranged from military actions to repel the 'Euro-American' powers to more reconciliatory plans for harmonious 'East–West co-existence', Asianism took on an undisputed key meaning of Asian self-determination: 'Asia' is the home of the Asians and as such should be controlled by Asians. During the wartime years, this Asianist core message often became conflated with the propagation of an Asian Monroe Doctrine.

The new prominence Asianism had gained as a political concept during the mid-1910s prompted many public opinion leaders to suggest their own interpretations of Asianism. While many of them remained sceptical or dismissed Asianism as anachronistic or unrealistic, a large number of debaters generally agreed with the concept as such, although they disagreed with most of the existing conceptions. Criticism of Asianism therefore became an essential part of the densely interlinked debate on the definition and applicability of Asianism. Through this debate Asianist conceptions during the war not only became more refined but they also facilitated the establishment of 'Asia' as an affirmative and significant category that transcended its mere geographical meaning. As a consequence, by the end of World War One Japanese and Chinese thinkers had gained a noticeable degree of discursive self-determination over the content of 'Asia' and its role in political debate. The output and intensity of Asianism discourse in East Asia rendered it impossible for 'Western' media and experts to ignore this self-affirmative 'Asia' discourse centring on the concept of Asianism. Although the war facilitated such debate to an unparalleled degree of plurality and diversity, resulting political activities remained scarce. Asianism, during World War One, remained above all a theoretical enterprise; the concept represented a 'claim' and a stream of 'thought' but not yet a movement.

Notes

1. Wakamiya Unosuke, 'Dai Ajiashugi wa nan zo ya' [What is Greater Asianism?], *Chūō Kōron* [Central Review], 32-4 (April 1917), 1–14: 4–5.
2. See Yamamuro Shin'ichi, 'Daiichiji Sekai Taisen: Shiten toshite no jūdaisei' [The First World War: Its significance as a starting point], *Asahi Shinbun*, 24 March 2008, 13.
3. W.I. Lenin, 'Der tote Chauvinismus und der lebendige Sozialismus' [Dead Chauvinism and living Socialism], *Werke* [Works], Vol. 21, Berlin: Dietz 1970 (December 1914), 83–90: 87.
4. Arnold J. Toynbee, *The World After the Peace Conference*, London: Oxford University Press 1925 (1920), 44.
5. Isaiah Bowman, *The New World: Problems in Political Geography*, New York: World Book Company 1921, 1–2.
6. See Erez Manela, 'Imagining Woodrow Wilson in Asia: Dreams of East–West Harmony and the Revolt against Empire in 1919', *American Historical Review*, 111-5 (December 2006), 1327–1351: 1331.
7. See, for China, Dominic Sachsenmaier, 'Alternative Visions of World Order in the Aftermath of World War I: Global Perspectives on Chinese Approaches' and, for Japan and Islamic Western Asia, Cemil Aydin, 'A Global Anti-Western Moment? The Russo-Japanese War, Decolonization, and Asian Modernity', *Competing Visions of world order: global moments and movements, 1880s–1930s*, ed. Sebastian Conrad/Dominic Sachsenmaier, New York: Palgrave Macmillan 2007, 151–178 and 213–236.
8. Endō Kichisaburō, *Ōshū bunmei no botsuraku* [The downfall of Europe's civilization], Tokyo: Fuzan bō 1914, 1.
9. Tokutomi Sohō, *Sekai no henkyoku* [The World in emergency], Tokyo: Min'yūsha 1915, 480.
10. Kita Ikki, 'Nihon Kaizō Hōan Taikō' [An Outline Plan for the Reorganization of Japan], *Kita Ikki Shisōshūsei* [Compilation of Kita Ikki's Thought], Tokyo: Shoshi shinsui, 2005 (1919), 680–767: 688.
11. Endō Kichisaburō, *Ōshū bunmei no botsuraku* [The downfall of Europe's civilization], Tokyo: Fuzan bō 1914, 108.
12. See Nakano Seigō's popular *Kōwa Kaigi o mokugeki shite* [Having witnessed the Peace Conference], Tokyo: Tōhō Jironsha 1919, and, for a later account which reveals the lasting impact of the Conference on Asian-minded Japanese, Naruse Masao, 'Ajia Minzoku Kaigi ni tsuite' [On the Asian Peoples Congress], *Ajia Minzoku Kaigi ni tsuite, Jiyū Byōdō Hakuai no hongi, gekken shōrei no yōshi* [On the Asian Peoples' Congress, the true meaning of freedom, equality' and philanthropy, and

an outline for the promotion of Japanese fencing], Tokyo: Chijin Yūsha 1927, 2–14. Naruse strongly criticizes the decision of the Japanese 'worshippers of Euro-America' (Ōbei sūhaika) to participate in the League of Nations, which he blames for destroying the 'ancient virtues of the East' (Tōyō korai no dōtoku o hakai seru); quotations from page 4.

13. Nonetheless, Japan played a crucial role both as a cradle for ever-new Asianist visions and activities as well as a hub for the exchange of ideas among Asian-minded Asians. Most of the non-Japanese Asians mentioned in this chapter had lived in Japan for some time as students (Dai, Li) or refugees (Sun, Bose) and formulated their own Asianist visions in relation to different Japanese conceptions of Asianism. See in particular Li Dazhao's 'New Asianism' as a rejection of, among others, Kodera Kenkichi's and Tokutomi Sohō's 'Greater Asianism' and as a modification of Ukita Kazutami's own 'New Asianism'. For Li see below and Marc Andre Matten, 'Li Dazhao: "Greater Asianism and New Asianism", 1919', *Pan-Asianism: A Documentary History 1860–2010*, Vol. 1, ed. Sven Saaler and C.W.A. Szpilman, Boulder: Rowman & Littlefield, 2011, 217–222.

14. On the appropriation of Asianism by Chinese thinkers in the 1920s and 1930s see Kawashima, 'Kindai Chūgoku no Ajia kan to Nihon', 415–441 and Smith, *Constructing Chinese Asianism*, Chap. 5 and 6.

15. See Taraknath Das, *Is Japan A Menace to Asia?* Shanghai (without publisher) 1917 and for Bose's Asianism Nakajima Takeshi, *Nakamuraya no Bōsu. Indo dokuritsu undō to kindai Nihon no Ajiashugi* [Bose of Nakamura's. India's independence movement and modern Japanese Asianism], Tokyo: Hakusuisha 2005 and Eri Hotta, 'Rash Behari Bose: The Indian Independence Movement and Japan', *Pan-Asianism: A Documentary History 1860–2010*, Vol. 1, ed. Sven Saaler and C.W.A. Szpilman, Boulder: Rowman & Littlefield, 2011, 231–240.

16. See James Francis Abbott, *Japanese Expansion and American Policies*, New York: Macmillan 1916, G. Lowes Dickinson, *An Essay on the Civilization of India*, China and Japan, London: J.M. Dent & Sons 1914, Sidney L. Gulick, *The American Japanese Problem*, New York: Charles Scribner's 1914, Roland G. Usher, *Pan-Americanism*, New York: The Century 1915. While only a few contemporary Western writers displayed an awareness of the diversity of 'Asia' discourse in Asia, Japanese and Chinese Asianists frequently formulated their own conceptions of Asian unity through explicit affirmation or rejection of Western notions of Asian commonality, for example, as expressed in the works mentioned above.

17. See Sugita Teiichi, 'Waga Gaikō to Tōa Renmei' [Our foreign policy and an East Asian League], *Nihon oyobi Nihonjin* [Japan and the Japanese], 674 (February 1916), 25–30.
18. See Sugita Teiichi, 'Dai Ajia Gasshō Ron' [On the United States of Greater Asia], *Tōyō Bunka* [Eastern Culture], 8 (September 1924), 7–13 for a racialist-culturalist version of his more moderate 1916 essay. On this essay see also Sven Saaler, 'Pan-Asianism during and after World War I', *Pan-Asianism: A Documentary History 1860–2010*, Vol. 1, ed. Sven Saaler and C.W.A. Szpilman, Boulder: Rowman & Littlefield, 2011, 255–269: 257–258.
19. Sugita, 'Waga Gaikō to Tōa Renmei', 30.
20. Ōyama Ikuo, 'Dai Ajiashugi no unmei' [The fate of Greater Asianism], *Shin Nihon* [New Japan], 6-3 (1 March 1916), 18–30: 23.
21. Ōyama, 'Dai Ajiashugi no unmei', 27–28.
22. Ōyama, 'Dai Ajiashugi no unmei', 29.
23. Ōyama, 'Dai Ajiashugi no unmei', 30.
24. Ōyama, 'Dai Ajiashugi no unmei', 30.
25. On Yoshino see Matsumoto Sannosuke, *Yoshino Sakuzō*, Tokyo: Tokyo Daigaku Shuppankai 2008, Mitani Taichirō, *Taishō Demokurashī ron: Yoshino Sakuzō no jidai* [On Taishō Democracy: The times of Yoshino Sakuzō], Tokyo: Tokyo Daigaku Shuppankai 1995 and, in English, Jung-Sun N. Han, 'Envisioning a Liberal Empire in East Asia: Yoshino Sakuzō in Taishō Japan', *Journal of Japanese Studies* 33:2 (2007), 357–382, Dick Stegewerns, *Adjusting to the New World. Japanese Opinion Leaders of the Taishō Generation and the Outside World, 1918–1932* (Unpublished Ph.D. dissertation, Leiden University, 2007), and Takayoshi Matsuo, 'Profile of Asian Minded Man VII: Sakuzō Yoshino', *The Developing Economies*, 5-2 (June 1967), 388–404.
26. Yoshino Sakuzō, 'Nichi-Ro kyōyaku to Shina no saigi' [Japanese-Russo Agreement and Chinese suspicions], *Shinjin* [New Man], 17-8 (1 August 1916), 5–7: 6.
27. The *shasetsu* (editorial) was probably authored by the journal's editor-in-chief, the famous educator and Christian minister Ebina Danjō (1856–1937).
28. Anonymous, 'Ajiashugi o bakusu' [Repelling Asianism], *Shinjin* [New Man], 18-12 (1 December 1917), 11–16: 12.
29. Anonymous, 'Ajiashugi o bakusu', 13–14.
30. See Anonymous, 'Ajiashugi o bakusu', 14.
31. See Anonymous, 'Ajiashugi o bakusu', 15.
32. Anonymous, 'Ajiashugi o bakusu', 16.
33. The last article by Ninagawa dismissing Asianism I have been able to identify dates from September 1939, in which he argues against the subsuming of Buddhism under 'so-called Asianism', a doctrine he decries

as 'bragging bluster'. See Ninagawa Arata, 'Bukkyō to iwayuru Dai Ajiashugi' [Buddhism and so-called Greater Asianism], *Chūō Bukkyō* [Central Buddhism], 23-9 (September 1939), 2–6. It is interesting to note that by 1939, Ninagawa's fierce criticism of Asianism was no longer published in prominent journals such as the semi-official *Gaikō Jihō*, where many of his anti-Asianist writings had been published in the 1910s. They now appeared in journals of special interest and of much lower circulation.

34. See Ninagawa Arata, 'Monrōshugi no mohō' [An imitation of Monroeism], *Gaikō Jihō* [Diplomatic Review], 267 (December 1915), 16–20.
35. Ninagawa, 'Monrōshugi no mohō', 18.
36. Ninagawa Arata, 'Sekaijin no Sekaishugi' [Worldism for worldist people], *Gaikō Jihō* [Diplomatic Review], 309 (15 September 1917), 1–8.
37. Ninagawa, 'Sekaijin no Sekaishugi', 4.
38. Ninagawa, 'Sekaijin no Sekaishugi', 2–3.
39. Ninagawa Arata, 'Ugu o kiwametaru Ajia Monrōshugi' [Extremely arrogant Asian Monroeism], *Dai Nihon* [Greater Japan], 4-7 (1 July 1917), 96–97: 96.
40. See his 'Nisshi shinzen no issaku' [A policy towards Japanese–Chinese friendship], *Gaikō* [Diplomacy], 3-6 (20 May 1917), 7–10 or his 'Nisshi shin dōmei no seiritsu' [The establishment of a new alliance between Japan and China], *Chūgai* [Home and Abroad], 2-8 (1 July 1918), 14–20.
41. On Tokutomi's Asianist convictions see Lee Gyeongseog, 'Tokutomi Sohō no Ajia Monrōshugi' [Tokutomi Sohō's Asian Monroeism], *Waseda Seiji Kōhō kenkyū* 73, 201–235, Yonehara Ken, *Tokutomi Sohō. Nihon Nashonarizumu no Kiseki* [Tokutomi Sohō. Tracks of Japanese Nationalism], Tokyo: Chūō Kōron Shinsha 2003, in particular Chap. 5, and, in English, Alistair Swale, 'Tokutomi Sohō and the "Asiatic Monroe Doctrine", 1917', *Pan-Asianism: A Documentary History 1860–2010*, Vol. 1, ed. Sven Saaler and C.W.A. Szpilman, Boulder: Rowman & Littlefield, 2011, 279–286.
42. See Tokutomi's preface to Gotō Shinpei's *Nihon Bōchō Ron* [On Japan's Expansion], Tokyo: Dai Nihon Yūbenkai 1913, 'Jo' [Preface], 1–9. Tokutomi's Japan-centric understanding of Asianism becomes obvious in his summary of Gotō's text as 'Greater Japanism' (Dai Nihonshugi). To Tokutomi, even more than Gotō, there was not only no contradiction between Asianism and Japanism. Effectively, to him, they could be used as synonyms.
43. See Tokutomi Sohō, *Sekai no henkyoku* [The World in emergency], Tokyo: Min'yūsha 1915, 580.
44. Swale, 'Tokutomi Sohō and the "Asiatic Monroe Doctrine", 1917', 280.

45. Tokutomi Sohō, *Taishō no Seinen to Teikoku no Zento* [The Young Generation of Taishō and the Future of the Empire], Tokyo: Min'yūsha 1916, 230; see also Hiraishi Naoaki, 'Kindai Nihon no Kokusai chitsujokan to "Ajiashugi"' [Modern Japanese views of the international order and 'Asianism'], *20 seiki shisutemu 1: Kōsō to keisei* [20th century system 1: Design and Formation], ed. Tokyo Daigaku Shakai Kagaku Kenkyūjo, Tokyo: Tokyo Daigaku Shuppankai 1998, 176–211: 192.
46. See Lee, 'Tokutomi Sōho no Ajia Monrōshugi', 216.
47. Tokutomi Sohō, *Taishō no Seinen to Teikoku no Zento*, 231.
48. Tokutomi Sohō, *Taishō no Seinen to Teikoku no Zento*, 230.
49. Lee, 'Tokutomi Sōho no Ajia Monrōshugi', 204, 230.
50. See Horiuchi Bunjirō, 'Dai Ajiashugi to ga kokumin no shimei' [Greater Asianism and the fate of my people], *Taiyō* [The Sun], 24-9 (September 1918), 120–121: 121.
51. Horiuchi, 'Dai Ajiashugi to ga kokumin no shimei', 121.
52. See Horiuchi, 'Dai Ajiashugi to ga kokumin no shimei', 120.
53. See Kamiizumi, *Dai Nihonshugi* [Greater Japanism], Tokyo: Kōbundō Shoten 1918: 180.
54. See Kamiizumi, *Dai Nihonshugi*, 181.
55. See Kamiizumi, *Dai Nihonshugi*, 176.
56. Ōtani Kōzui, 'Teikoku no kiki' [Crisis of the Empire], *Chūō Kōron* [Central Review], 32-3 (March 1917), 1–30: 20.
57. Ōtani, 'Teikoku no kiki', 29.
58. Ōtani, 'Teikoku no kiki', 23.
59. See Ōtani, 'Teikoku no kiki', 23.
60. See Ōtani, 'Teikoku no kiki', 23.
61. Wakamiya Unosuke, 'Dai Ajiashugi wa nan zo ya' [What is Greater Asianism?], *Chūō Kōron* [Central Review], 32-4 (April 1917), 1–14; see also Furuya, 'Ajiashugi to sono shūhen', 89–90.
62. Wakamiya, 'Dai Ajiashugi wa nan zo ya', 5.
63. Wakamiya, 'Dai Ajiashugi wa nan zo ya', 4.
64. Wakamiya, 'Dai Ajiashugi wa nan zo ya', 3.
65. Wakamiya, 'Dai Ajiashugi wa nan zo ya', 8.
66. See Wakamiya, 'Dai Ajiashugi wa nan zo ya', 4.
67. See Wakamiya, 'Dai Ajiashugi wa nan zo ya' [What is Greater Asianism?], *Chūō Kōron* [Central Review], 32-4 (April 1917), 1–14: 13 and Furuya, 'Ajiashugi to sono shūhen', 90.
68. Wakamiya, 'Dai Ajiashugi wa nan zo ya', 4-5.
69. Miyazaki Tōten, 'Rikkōho sengen' [Declaration of Candidacy], *Miyazaki Tōten Zenshū* [Complete Writings of Miyazaki Tōten], vol. 2, ed. Miyazaki Ryūsuke and Onogawa Hidemi, Tokyo: Heibonsha 1971, without page number; see Hiraishi Naoaki, 'Kindai Nihon no Kokusai

chitsujokan to "Ajiashugi"' [Modern Japanese views of the international order and 'Asianism'], *20seiki shisutemu 1: Kōsō to keisei* [Twentieth century system 1: Design and Formation], ed. Tokyo Daigaku Shakai Kagaku Kenkyūjo, Tokyo: Tokyo Daigaku Shuppankai 1998, 176–211: 196. See also Christopher W.A. Szpilman, 'Miyazaki Tōten's Pan-Asianism, 1915–1919', *Pan-Asianism: A Documentary History 1860–2010*, Vol. 1, ed. Sven Saaler and C.W.A. Szpilman, Boulder: Rowman & Littlefield, 2011, 133–139, which also contains a full translation of his candidacy declaration.
70. See Hiraishi, 'Kindai Nihon no Kokusai chitsujokan to "Ajiashugi"', 197.
71. Szpilman, 'Miyazaki Tōten's Pan-Asianism, 1915–1919', 136.
72. See 'Senkyokai no shin jinbutsu: Hara Fujirō-kun' [New Faces of the election: Mr. Hara Fujirō], *Asahi Shinbun*, 18 March 1917, 3 and 'Senkyokai no shin jinbutsu: Isobe Hisashi-kun' [New Faces of the election: Mr. Isobe Hisashi], *Asahi Shinbun*, 17 March 1917, 3.
73. Asianism in general has hardly been studied as a phenomenon in popular culture or arts. Focusing on the early 1930s, Kawano has studied the propagation of Asianist conceptions in youth literature; see Kawano Takashi, 'Ajiashugi no rinen to roman, denki shōnen shōsetsu' [The ideal of Asianism and romantic juvenile novels], *Nihon Jidō Bungaku* [Japanese Children's Literature], 38-3 (March 1992), 48–55.
74. Takeuchi Yoshimi has coined this characterization of Miyazaki's Asianism. See Takeuchi, 'Ajiashugi no tenbō', 49. On this stream of Asianism see also Kawahara Hiroshi, 'Ajiashugi no shinjōteki kiso' [The sentimental base of Asianism], *Jinbun Shakaikagaku Kenkyū* [Humanities and Social Science Research], 33 (March 1993), 1–15.
75. See Satō Kazuki, 'Yohakuran no Ajiashugi. Taishō ki 'Taiyō' no shibunran to Kodama Kagai' [Asianism of the open columns. The poetry columns of Taiyō in the Taishō period and Kodama Kagai], *Zasshi Taiyō to kokumin bunka no keisei* [The journal Taiyo and the formation of popular culture], ed. Suzuki Sadami, Kyoto: Shibunkaku 2001, 324–348 and Nakamura Tadashi, 'Chūgoku kindai o yonda shijin. Kodama Kagai to Son Bun, Chin Kibi, Kō Kō' [Poets who sang China's modernity: Sun Yat-sen, Chen Qimei, Huang Xing], *Nishō Gakusha Daigaku Tōyōgaku kenkyūjoshūkan* [Collected Publication of the Oriental Research Institute of Nishō Gakusha University], 31 (2001), 111–151.
76. Kodama's first Asianist poem was actually published before World War One, in March 1913: 'Son Issen ni ataeru shi' [Poem dedicated to Sun Yat-sen], *Taiyō* [The Sun], 19-3 (March 1913), 152; see Nakamura Tadashi, 'Chūgoku kindai o yonda shijin. Kodama Kagai to Son Bun, Chin Kibi, Kō Kō' [Poets who sang China's modernity: Sun

Yat-sen, Chen Qimei, Huang Xing], *Nishō Gakusha Daigaku Tōyōgaku kenkyūjoshūkan* [Collected Publication of the Oriental Research Institute of Nishō Gakusha University], 31 (2001), 111–151: 121–122.
77. Kodama Kagai, 'Ajia no meihai' [Sake cup to the Asian alliance], *Taiyō* [The Sun], 23-14 (1 December 1917), 62–64.
78. For Sun see Chapter 4. For Tagore's ambivalent position towards Asianist conceptions see Stephen N. Hay, *Asian ideas of East and West: Tagore and his critics in Japan, China, and India*. Cambridge, MA: Harvard University Press 1970.
79. See Kodama Kagai, 'Gekka Kinsonkyō' [Poem on a golden barrel under the moonlight], *Tōhō Jiron* [Eastern Review], 3-6 (June 1918), 104–105: 104.
80. Yoshino Sakuzō, 'Wagakuni no Tōhō keiei ni kansuru sandai mondai' [Three paramount problems our country is facing regarding the management of the East], *Tōhō Jiron* [Eastern Review], 3-1 (January 1918), 42–68: 66–67.
81. See Dick Stegewerns, *Adjusting to the New World. Japanese Opinion Leaders of the Taishō Generation and the Outside World, 1918–1932* (Unpublished PhD dissertation, Leiden University, 2007), 228.
82. Yoshino, 'Wagakuni no Tōhō keiei ni kansuru sandai mondai', 67.
83. The *Tōyō Kyōkai* referred to by Uchida was the *Tōyō Kyōkai Senmon Gakkō* (Vocational School of the Oriental Association), founded in 1907 as the successor school of the *Taiwan Kyōkai Gakkō* (Taiwan Association School), which had been established in 1900 by Katsura Tarō, the former governor general of Taiwan and future Prime Minister, to educate future Japanese colonists of Japan's recently acquired colony of Taiwan. In 1918, the School was given its present name, Takushoku University. Through its bulletin, the *Tōyō Kyōkai* spread a quite unique conception of Asianism: it rejected confrontational views such as White Peril versus Yellow Peril theory and instead defined 'Greater Asianism' affirmatively as 'promoting the fortune of Asia by fusing yellow and white thought (ōhaku shisō) and harmonizing the civilizations of East and West, and to share with the Powers these delights'. See 'Dai Ajiashugi o hyō su' [Commenting on Greater Asianism], *Taiwan Jihō* [Taiwan Times], Vol. 89 (15 February 1917), 1.
84. See Uchida Rōan, 'Gakujutsuteki Han Ajiashugi' [Academic Pan-Asianism], *Taiyō* [The Sun], 23-14 (1 December 1917), 65–75.
85. For this aspect in the late Meiji period see Gluck, *Japan's Modern Myth*, passim.
86. On Sawayanagi and his Asianism see also Sven Saaler, 'Pan-Asianism during and after World War I', *Pan-Asianism: A Documentary History 1860–2010*, Vol. 1, ed. Sven Saaler and C.W.A. Szpilman, Boulder:

Rowman & Littlefield, 2011, 255–269. Saaler suspects that Sawayanagi started writing about Asianism in 1917 as 'a chance to gain popularity by jumping on the pan-Asianist bandwagon' (256).
87. Sawayanagi Masatarō, 'Ajiashugi' [Asianism], *Teikoku Kyōiku* [Education for the Empire], 422 (1 Sept 1917), quoted in *Sawayanagi Masatarō Zenshū* [Complete Writings of Sawayanagi Masatarō], Vol. 9, ed. Sawayanagi Masatarō Zenshū kankōkai, Tokyo: Kokudosha 1977, 269–275: 269.
88. See Nakano Akira, 'Kaisetsu' [Explanation], *Sawayanagi Masatarō Zenshū* [Complete Writings of Sawayanagi Masatarō], Vol. 9, ed. Sawayanagi Masatarō Zenshū kankōkai, Tokyo: Kokudosha 1977, 542–554: 542.
89. See Sawayanagi Masatarō, 'Ikan ni shite kyokoku itchi no jitsu o agubeki ka' [How can we realize national unity?], *Kokuron* [On our country] 3-1 (1917), quoted in Nakano Akira, 'Kaisetsu' [Explanation], *Sawayanagi Masatarō Zenshū* [Complete Writings of Sawayanagi Masatarō], Vol. 9, ed. Sawayanagi Masatarō Zenshū kankōkai, Tokyo: Kokudosha 1977, 542–554: 548.
90. Sawayanagi Masatarō, 'Bunkateki han Ajiashugi o teishō su' [Proposing Cultural Pan-Asianism], *Shin Nihon* [New Japan], 7-3 (1 March 1917), quoted in *Sawayanagi Masatarō Zenshū* [Complete Writings of Sawayanagi Masatarō], Vol. 9, ed. Sawayanagi Masatarō Zenshū kankōkai, Tokyo: Kokudosha 1977, 213–226: 222.
91. Sawayanagi Masatarō/Ebi Saikichi, *Ri–Hua Gongcun lun* [On Japanese–Chinese Coexistence], Tokyo (without publisher) 1919.
92. Sawayanagi, 'Ajiashugi', 274. Note Sawayanagi's choice of vocabulary: as opposed to the more dominant *meishu* (leader of a league) he uses the more neutral *sendatsu* which denotes 'a senior in a certain field' (*Kōjien*, 5th ed., electronic version, Tokyo: Iwanami Shoten 2003).
93. See Sawayanagi, 'Ajiashugi', 274–275. At the end of his essay, Sawayanagi goes to great lengths to argue the compatibility of the leading principle of the day, *kokkashugi*, with his conception of Asianism. His main argument in this brief section is that Asianism supplements nationalism where nationalism alone cannot account for Japan's mission to plan the 'rise of Asia'.
94. Sawayanagi, 'Ajiashugi', 274.
95. Although Sawayanagi continued to refer to 'Asia' (Ajia) and 'the East' (Tōyō), he clarified that he found the range of Asia understood as consisting of India, Persia, the South Sea, Burma, Thailand, and Vietnam too large. Ultimately, he argued, 'only China possesses close relations with Japan historically, geographically, racially, and culturally'. See Sawayanagi, 'Bunkateki han Ajiashugi o teishō su', 222.

96. Sawayanagi Masatarō, 'Ajiashugi to Nihon no shimei' [Asianism and Japan's fate], *Taiyō* [The Sun], 24-8 (15 June 1918), 41–48: 43.
97. See Sawayanagi Masatarō, 'Sengo junbi no kontei' [Foundation of post-war preparations], paper from Sawayanagi's estate, 24 July 1917, quoted in *Sawayanagi Masatarō Zenshū* [Complete Writings of Sawayanagi Masatarō], Vol. 9, ed. Sawayanagi Masatarō Zenshū kankōkai, Tokyo: Kokudosha 1977, 258–269: 268.
98. Sawayanagi, 'Ajiashugi to Nihon no shimei', 48.
99. Ukita Kazutami, 'Shin Ajiashugi. Tōyō Monrōshugi no shin kaishaku' [New Asianism. A new interpretation of Asian Monroeism], *Taiyō* [The Sun], 24-9 (September 1918), 2–17.
100. Ukita Kazutami, 'Xin Yaxiya zhuyi' [New Asianism], *Dongfang Zazhi* [Eastern Miscellany], 15-11 (15 November 1918), 9–21 (translated by Gao Lao).
101. Ukita, 'Shin Ajiashugi', 2.
102. Ukita, 'Shin Ajiashugi', 3.
103. Ukita, 'Shin Ajiashugi', 11.
104. Ukita's hesitant position, which always displayed careful consideration of the 'West', led Matsuda Yoshio to conclude that 'despite the word "New Asianism" Ukita was, in the tradition of Fukuzawa Yukichi, a proponent of "Datsu A" and not an Asianist'. In as far as Ukita acknowledged the established international order and its protagonists, this claim seems justified. However, here it is more revealing to see how Ukita renegotiates the applicability of Asianism in a positive way' as a political concept within the given order. For Matsuda's judgement see Matsuda Yoshio, *Ukita Kazutami Kenkyū. Jiyūshugi seiji shisō no tenkai* [Research on Ukita Kazutami. The development of Liberalism as political thought], Kurashiki: Matsuda Yoshio 1996, 121.
105. See Ukita, 'Shin Ajiashugi', 11–12.
106. See Ukita, 'Shin Ajiashugi', 4.
107. Ukita, 'Shin Ajiashugi', 7–8. See Hiraishi, 'Kindai Nihon no Kokusai chitsujokan to "Ajiashugi"', 194.
108. See Ukita, 'Shin Ajiashugi', 13.
109. Hiraishi, 'Kindai Nihon no Kokusai chitsujokan to "Ajiashugi"', 195.
110. Ukita Kazutami, 'Shin Ajiashugi', 13.
111. Ukita Kazutami, *Teikoku to Kyōiku* [Empire and Education], Tokyo: Min'yūsha 1901, 35–36, quoted in Furuya, 'Ajiashugi to sono shūhen', 52.
112. Ukita, *Teikoku to Kyōiku*, 35–36, quoted in Furuya, 'Ajiashugi to sono shūhen', 52.
113. On Kodera's life see Sven Saaler, 'The Construction of Regionalism in Modern Japan: Kodera Kenkichi and his "Treatise on Greater Asianism" (1916)', *Modern Asian Studies*, 41-6, 1261–1294: 1265–1268.

114. Kodera Kenkichi, *Dai Ajiashugi Ron* [Treatise on Greater Asianism], Tokyo: Hōbunkan 1916, 1; amended translation in Saaler, 'The Construction of Regionalism in Modern Japan', 1271. On Kodera's Asianism see also Noriko Kamachi, 'Asianism in Prewar, Postwar and Post-Cold-War Japan', *Asia-Pacific Forum* 29 (September 2005), 136–161, particularly 144–147.
115. Saaler, 'The Construction of Regionalism in Modern Japan', 1279.
116. Kodera, *Dai Ajiashugi Ron*, 1267.
117. Kodera, *Dai Ajiashugi Ron*, 13 (my translation).
118. The first use of this phrase is traced back to Yokoi Shonan's *Kokuze Sanron* [Three Theses on State Policy], dating from 1860; see Yamamuro Shin'ichi, *Shisō Kadai toshite no Ajia* [Asia as a matter of thought], Tokyo: Iwanami Shoten 2001, 585–586. For a rejection of such a relationship in the contemporary political debate see Ninagawa Arata. 1926. 'Ajiajin hon'i ka Nihon kokumin hon'i ka' [The Standard of the Asians or the standard of the Japanese people?], *Tōhō Kōron* [Oriental Review], 1-1 (January 1926), 37–43: 42.
119. Gotō Shinpei had lived in Germany from 1890 to 1892, Tokutomi Sohō had lived in Europe and the United States between 1896 and 1897, and Kodera Kenkichi, with the brief interruption of 1904/05 had spent ten years in Germany, Austria, Switzerland, and the United States from 1897 onwards. Konoe Atsumaro, the founder of the *Tōa Dōbunkai* (East Asia Common Culture Society), too had lived in Germany from 1885 to 1890, while Ukita Kazutami had studied at Yale University (1892–1894). Nagai Ryūtarō, whose essay 'Hakka Ron' (published in *Shin Nihon* [New Japan], 2-3, 1 March 1912) had first popularized the term 'White Peril' in Japan, had studied in England from 1906 to 1909, where, according to Duus, 'for the first time he encountered both antioriental prejudice and the color line'; see Peter Duus, 'Nagai Ryūtarō and the "White Peril" 1905–1944', *Journal of Asian Studies*, 31-1 (November 1971), 41–48: 44.
120. Duus, 'Nagai Ryūtarō and the "White Peril" 1905–1944', 44.
121. Roland G. Usher, *Pan-Americanism. A Forecast of the inevitable clash between the United States and Europe* Victor, New York: The Century 1915.
122. See Kodera, *Dai Ajiashugi Ron*, 275–282.
123. Ukita, 'Shin Ajiashugi', 4.
124. Kodera Kenkichi, 'Jinshu mondai yori mitaru Nisshi kyōzon' [Japanese–Chinese coexistence as seen from the race problem], *Jitsugyō no Nihon* [Business Japan], 22-13 (June 1919), 84–87: 86.
125. Kodera, 'Jinshu mondai yori mitaru Nisshi kyōzon', 87.
126. See the inaugural issue of *Minbao* [People's Paper], October 1905; quoted in Kodera, *Dai Ajiashugi Ron*, 1017. For the background to the

Tongmenghui's 'Six Principles' see *Chūgokujin no Nihonkan 100 nenshi* [100 years of Chinese views of Japan], ed. Kojima Shinji et al., Tokyo: Jiyū Kokuminsha 1974, 57.
127. Liang Qichao (original text unknown), quoted in Kodera, *Dai Ajiashugi Ron*, 1017–1018.
128. Kodera, *Dai Ajiashugi Ron*, 1018.
129. Huang Xing (original text unknown), quoted in Kodera Kenkichi, *Dai Ajiashugi Ron* [Treatise on Greater Asianism], Tokyo: Hōbunkan 1916, 1023.
130. See Saaler, 'The Construction of Regionalism in Modern Japan', 1281.
131. Kodera Kenkichi, *Dai Ajiashugi Ron: kan'yaku* [Treatise on Greater Asianism: Chinese Translation]. Shanghai: Hyakujō Shosha 1918. Already in 1917 an abridged version in Chinese had been published under the title On Annexing China: Originally Called On Greater Asianism. See Smith, *Constructing Chinese Asianism*, 205–206.
132. The only Chinese reaction to Kodera's Asianism known today is Li Dazhao's severe but very brief criticism (see below). In Japan, Kodera remained a relatively minor figure not only regarding Asia discourse but also regarding public political discourse in general.
133. On Li's life and thought see Maurice J. Meisner, *Li Ta-chao and the origins of Chinese Marxism*, Cambridge, MA: Harvard University Press 1967 and Mori Masao, *Ri Taishō* [Li Dazhao], Tokyo: Jinbutsu Ōraisha 1967.
134. For the *Dongfang Zazhi* see Kō Shin Hō (Kou Zhenfeng), 'Chūgoku no "Dongfang Zazhi" to Nihon no "Taiyō"' [China's 'Dongfang Zazhi' and Japan's 'Taiyō'], *Media to Shakai* [Media and Society], ed. Nagoya Daigaku Daigakuin Kokusai Gengo Bunka Kenkyūka, Vol. 1 (March 2009), 7–22 and Prasenjit Duara, 'The discourse of civilization and pan-Asianism', *Journal of World History* 12-1 (2001), 99–130.
135. See Kō Shin Hō (Kou Zhenfeng), 'Chūgoku no "Dongfang Zazhi" to Nihon no "Taiyō"' [China's 'Dongfang Zazhi' and Japan's 'Taiyō'], *Media to Shakai* [Media and Society], ed. Nagoya Daigaku Daigakuin Kokusai Gengo Bunka Kenkyūka, Vol. 1 (March 2009), 7–22.
136. See Li Dazhao, 'Da Yaxiya zhuyi yu xin Yaxiya zhuyi' [Greater Asianism and New Asianism], *Guomin Zazhi*, 1-2 (1 February 1919), quoted in *Li Dazhao Xuanji* [Selected Writings of Li Dazhao], Beijing: Renmin Chubanshe 1959, 119–121. This is the only one of Li's texts on Asianism that to date has been published in full Japanese translation; see for example, *Chūgokujin no Nihonkan 100 nenshi* [100 years of Chinese views of Japan], ed. Kojima Shinji et alii, Tokyo: Jiyū Kokuminsha 1974, 137–140. A more recent example of the contraction of Li's Asianism is Yamamuro, *Shisō Kadai toshite no Ajia*, 141, 632.

137. Li Dazhao, 'Pan...ism zhi shibai yu Democracy zhi shengli' [The defeat of Pan-isms and the victory of democracy], *Taipingyang* [Pacific Ocean], 1-10 (15 July 1918), quoted in *Li Dazhao Xuanji* [Selected Writings of Li Dazhao], Beijing: Renmin Chubanshe 1959, 105–108: 105.
138. Li Dazhao, 'Xin Zhong Hua minzu zhuyi' [New Chinese Nationalism], *Jiayin* [Year 1914], volume and pages unknown (19 February 1917), quoted after *Li Dazhao Wenji* [Collection of Li Dazhao's Writings], Vol. 1, Beijing: Renmin Chubanshe 1984, 301–303: 303.
139. Germaine A. Hoston, *The state, identity, and the national question in China and Japan*, Princeton: Princeton University Press 1994, 203.
140. See Li Dazhao, 'Da Yaxiya zhuyi' [Greater Asianism], *Jiayin* [Year 1914], volume and pages unknown (18 April 1917), quoted in *Li Dazhao Wenji*, 449–450.
141. Li, 'Da Yaxiya zhuyi'(18 April 1917), 450.
142. See Hoston, *The state, identity, and the national question in China and Japan*, 181 and 190 and I Ko, *1919nen zengo ni okeru Ni-Chū 'Ajiashugi' bunkyoku no shosō* [Various aspects of polarizations in Japanese-Chinese 'Asianism' around the year 1919], (Unpublished MA thesis, Hōsei University Tokyo, 2006), 13 for influences on Li's changed attitude towards Pan-ism.
143. See for example Yamamuro, *Shisō Kadai toshite no Ajia*, 141–142.
144. Takebe (1871–1945) was a Niigata-born sociologist, professor at Tokyo Imperial University, and member of the Upper House. While all other of Li's references are obvious and have been discussed in this chapter, I have failed to identify which of Takebe's writings Li is referring to. Takebe was, however, a member of the Asianist *Zen Ajia Kyōkai* (All Asia Association), founded in 1924 (see Chap. 5); see 'Zen Ajia Kyōkai setsuritsu shushi' [Purpose for the establishment of the All Asia Association], *Zen Ajia Kyōkai Kaihō* [Bulletin of the All Asia Association], April 1926, 1.
145. See Erez Manela, 'Imagining Woodrow Wilson in Asia: Dreams of East–West Harmony and the Revolt against Empire in 1919', *American Historical Review*, 111-5 (December 2006), 1327–1351, Frederick R. Dickinson, *War and national reinvention: Japan in the Great War, 1914–1919*, Cambridge, MA: Harvard University Press 1999, and Furuya, 'Ajiashugi to sono shūhen', 47–102.
146. Li, 'Da Yaxiya zhuyi yu xin Yaxiya zhuyi', 121.
147. See Li Dazhao, 'Zai lun Xin Yaxiya zhuyi' [Discussing New Asianism again], *Guomin Zazhi* [Citizen Magazine], 2-1 (12 December 1919), quoted in *Li Dazhao Xuanji* [Selected Writings of Li Dazhao], Beijing: Renmin Chubanshe 1959, 278–282.

148. See Hoston, *The state, identity, and the national question in China and Japan*, 203.
149. See Li's reply to Gao Yuan's critique in Li, 'Zai lun Xin Yaxiya zhuyi', 278–282.
150. Li, 'Zai lun Xin Yaxiya zhuyi', 279.
151. See 'Da Yaxiya zhuyi zhi yunming' [The Fate of Greater Asianism], *Dongfang Zazhi* [Eastern Miscellany], 13-5 (May 1913), 16–19 and 'Xin Yaxiya zhuyi' [New Asianism], *Dongfang Zazhi* [Eastern Miscellany], 15-11 (November 1918), 9–20.
152. See Duara, 'The discourse of civilization and pan-Asianism', 114.
153. See Gao Yuan, 'Duoduo Yaxiya zhuyi. Duoduo Futian Hemin de Xin Yaxiya zhuyi' [Ugh, Asianism! Ugh, Ukita Kazutami's New Asianism!], *Dongfang Zazhi* [Eastern Miscellany], 16-5 (May 1919), 197–199.
154. See Gao, 'Duoduo Yaxiya zhuyi', 197–199.
155. Gao, 'Duoduo Yaxiya zhuyi', 198.
156. Gao, 'Duoduo Yaxiya zhuyi', 198.
157. See Dai Jitao, 'Shina ni okeru Kyōwa seitai' [The Republican System in China], *Koyū* [Shanghai Friend], Vol. 4 (March 1918), based on Dai's speech given on 11 January 1918 at Shanghai's *Tōa Dōbunkai*, quoted in Kubo Juntarō, *Dai Jitao ni okeru 'Chūgoku Kakumei' to sono shisō. Chūgoku, Nihon, Ajia o megutte*. [Dai Jitao's 'Chinese Revolution' and its thought: China, Japan, Asia], Ph.D. Dissertation Kobe University 2005, accessible online: http://www.lib.kobe-u.ac.jp/repository/thesis/d1/D1003482.pdf (last accessed 16 October 2016), 55–56.
158. See Dai Jitao, 'Shijie Zhanzheng yu Zhongguo. Wei Taipingyangshe yi "Shijie zhanzheng yu Zhongguo" zuo de xu' [The World War and China. Preface to the translation of 'The World War and China' for the Taipingyang Society], *Jianshe* [Construction], 2-1 (February 1920), quoted in Kubo, *Dai Jitao ni okeru 'Chūgoku Kakumei' to sono shisō*, 56.
159. Sun Yat-sen, *Zhongguo Cunwang Wenti* [The Question of China's Life or Death], without place or publisher, May 1917, quoted in *Sun Zhongshan Quanji* [Complete Writings of Sun Yat-sen], ed. Zhongguo Shehui Kexueyuan Jindaishi yanjiusuo Zhonghua minguoshi yanjiushi [Research Unit for Chinese Republican History at the Modern History Department of the Chinese Academy for Social Sciences] et al., Vol. 4, Beijing: Zhonghua Shuju Chuban 1985, 39–99: 95. On the question of the essay's authorship and origin see page 39 of that reprint.
160. Sun, *Zhongguo Cunwang Wenti*, 94–95.
161. See Fujii Shōzō, 'Son Bun no minzokushugi sairon. Ajiashugi o chūshin ni' [Again on Sun Yat-sen's nationalism. Focusing on Asianism], *Rekishi Hyōron* [History Review], 549 (January 1996), 16–27: 20.

CHAPTER 5

The Racialization of 'Asia' in the Post-Versailles Period

> *As has become obvious in the attitude of Great Britain and the United States regarding the race issue, they completely ignore the people of the East. On this occasion, the people of Japan and China must wake up and call for the establishment of Greater Asianism. The people of the East must never forget how the issue of racial discrimination was smothered at the Paris Conference.*[1]
> — Ōishi Masami (May 1919)

As we have seen in Chap. 3, racialist notions had already played a central role in the inception of Asianism as a new concept in political discourse during the early 1910s. However, its link to race was also a reason why Asianism was rejected as a feasible political concept in Japan when it was first introduced to the mainstream of public discourse there in 1913. Possibly also in order to be able to appeal to a wider public, therefore, Asianist conceptions during World War One rarely focused on racial aspects, which later became so prominently linked with wartime propaganda during the Pacific War. In 1919, however, the tide began to turn. The Paris Peace Conference, which sought to end all wars and establish peace and justice throughout the world, to Japan and China alike, instead brought a strong sense of humiliation and discrimination. Dissatisfied with the pro-Japanese decision regarding the Shandong question, the Chinese delegation refused to sign the peace treaty and returned home to a China where the 'Versailles humiliation' had caused massive anti-Japanese boycotts and anti-imperialist demonstrations.[2] The Japanese

© The Author(s) 2018
T. Weber, *Embracing 'Asia' in China and Japan*,
Palgrave Macmillan Transnational History Series,
https://doi.org/10.1007/978-3-319-65154-5_5

public, however, was not satisfied either. Not only had Japan failed to be acknowledged as equal by the leading powers at Versailles, but it was also subjected to national embarrassment when its proposal (supported by the Chinese delegation) for the abolition of racial discrimination was rejected. To Asianists this was the last bit of proof of the civilizational corruption and hypocrisy of the 'West' that they had already sensed earlier and openly started to proclaim during the war. From then onwards, racialist aspects became closely linked with Japanese views of 'Asia' and they eventually became central to Asianism discourse after the adoption of the immigration exclusion legislation by US federal law in 1924.

If it had not been for Japanese–Chinese and Japanese–Korean tensions following the anti-Japanese uproar in spring 1919, the rejection of the racial equality clause might have caused much stronger anti-Western reactions (and maybe joint Asianist activities) throughout East Asia than it did. But, as Naoko Shimazu has observed, the racial issue in Japan itself (including its empire) was far too complex to allow for a united outcry against obvious 'Western' anti-Asian racism. Shimazu has called the contradiction between conceptions of universal racial equality and views of Japanese superiority versus other Asian races a Japanese 'two-tiered conception of "race"'.[3] This view, she argues,

> allowed the Japanese, especially those of pan-Asian persuasion, to reconcile the seemingly contradictory position of, on the one hand, appealing to the pan-Asian racial alliance with the Chinese and Koreans against the West, while on the other, placing Japan clearly in the position of leadership in Asia (Ajia no meishu). In other words, 'race' meant two things: the more Gobineaurian conceptualisation of the world according to three races of white, yellow, and black, which the Japanese utilised to pitch themselves together with China and Korea against the white race; and the more 'nation' based concept of differentiating the Japanese from the Chinese and Koreans within the yellow race, in order to stake out their special position of leadership.[4]

It is debatable whether the second version, 'nation based' racialism, belongs to the category of racialism at all or must instead be seen as a force of (mutually exclusive) nationalism which contested and contradicted racism instead of being a sub-category thereof. It is important, however, to be reminded of the fact that racialist claims made by the Japanese were always checked by Japan's own treatment of non-Japanese Asians in its empire. In a sense, this problem is well represented in the oft-quoted dichotomy of solidarity and invasion ascribed to Asianism: claims for racial solidarity *versus* claims for national superiority which allegedly legitimized the Japanese invasion of other Asian countries as measures of 'protection'. Contemporary commentators on Asianism discourse, in particular (but not exclusively) non-Japanese, were extremely sensitive to this question and openly addressed its inherent contradiction.[5] Against the background of a growing racialization of political discourse and of political reality in the post-1919 era, this chapter explores how and why racialist conceptions of Asianism became dominant after Versailles and how Asianism gradually changed from a theoretical enterprise into a movement.

The Asianist Moment at Versailles

At first sight, the Paris Peace Conference is not particularly conspicuous as a catalyst of Asianist thought and action. Instead, it is more frequently perceived as having promoted, both theoretically and practically, nationalism and internationalism.[6] In fact, the second half of the 1910s in East Asia illustrates particularly well the impact of competing nationalist agendas. During the war, Japan had issued the infamous Twenty-One Demands (1915) to the Chinese government, and amidst the Peace Conference in Versailles the anti-Japanese March First Movement for independence in Korea broke out. Only a few weeks later anti-Japanese demonstrations triggered the May Fourth Movement in China, the origin of popular Chinese nationalism. Nonetheless, as historian Akira Iriye has noted, as a result of China's decision to enter the war on the side of the Allies, at Versailles 'for the first time, China and Japan sat on the side of the victors'[7] together. In spite of bitter rivalry, the Chinese delegation also supported Japan's proposal for the inclusion of a racial equality clause in the covenant of the League of Nations. According to Iriye this was 'as striking an example of Asian self-consciousness as any, for it was the first time in modern history that non-European states got together to insist on equal treatment'.[8] However, neither the two countries' participation on the same side at Versailles nor Chinese support for Japan's racial equality proposal was intentional Asianist behaviour. In fact, neither side linked its actions to the cause of 'Asia'. Revealingly, apart from the racial equality proposal there was little that the representatives of the Chinese and Japanese governments at Versailles could agree on. Not even the Japanese delegation, which had proposed the racial equality clause in the first place, had intended to speak or act on behalf of 'Asia'. The proposal itself, as presented to the League of Nations Commission by the Japanese delegation in February 1919, did not contain a single reference to the cause of 'Asia', the 'East', or the Coloured peoples. As has been argued, it is probably best understood as a rather symbolic expression of Japan's claim for world power status and as a bargaining chip.[9] Indeed, the racial equality proposal was all about Japan and its pursuit of entry to the exclusive club of Western powers. In the realm of diplomacy, Japan remained as committed as ever to a policy that sought conciliation, not confrontation, with the 'West'. Therefore, when the proposal was officially rejected in Paris, the Japanese delegation protested only half-heartedly and the Japanese government decided to join the League of Nations as a founding member nonetheless.

The Asianist twist to the proposal was rather given 'from below'—by the popular outcry that followed its rejection at Versailles. On 5 February 1919, several hundred people had assembled in Tokyo's Ueno Park to adopt a resolution that urged the Japanese delegation to fight for the inclusion of the clause in the covenant of the League of Nations. 'The Japanese People', it read, 'resolve that at the Peace Conference the racially discriminatory treatment practised internationally up to now be abolished.'[10] To support and coordinate its activities the assembly, representing more than thirty organizations and political parties, decided to found a League for the Promotion of the Abolition of Racial Discrimination (Jinshuteki Sabetsu Teppai Kisei Taikai).[11] It claimed to 'wholeheartedly' support the creation of a future League of Nations if only the proposal to abolish racial discrimination were adopted. In the following months, under the leadership of the above-mentioned liberal writer and politician Sugita Teiichi (1851–1929)—the author of the proto-Asianist *Kō A Saku* (Raising Asia Policy, 1883) and early advocate of an East Asian League[12]—the *Taikai* organized several public gatherings, gave interviews, and distributed articles and speeches. Its aims were to influence Japan's public opinion in the direction of a positive attitude towards the proposal in general and, eventually, towards an outspokenly pro-Asianist attitude.

From February to April 1919, the *Taikai* convened three major assemblies that were attended by several hundred members and sympathizers. With few exceptions, such as Sugita and the future ministers of law Ōki Enkichi (1871–1926) and Ogawa Heikichi (1870–1942), all participants were activists, academics, or journalists of relatively little prominence or mid- and low-ranking politicians and military staff.[13] Interestingly, the *Taikai* also welcomed non-Asian members, and the French journalist-researcher Paul Richard (1874–1967) soon became its most fervent spokesman and 'a celebrity in Japan'.[14] Richard was an illustrious writer and traveller in Asia with personal contacts to a number of well-known Asian-minded thinkers, including Okakura Tenshin, Ōkawa Shūmei, and Miyazaki Tōten. In fact, it was Richard who most explicitly linked the debate about racial equality to 'the revival of Asia'. In particular, Richard called on the Japanese to embark on the task of 'awakening Asia' and of forming an Asian League:

> Awaken her in two ways. For your work must be double: at once material and spiritual. Awaken Asia by organising her, by uniting her. And to that end, be not masters, but allies of her peoples. Cease you also to cherish against them prejudices of race. Treat them as brothers, not as slaves. Those who are slaves liberate that they may become your brothers. Form with them all one single family. Organise the League of Nations of Asia – the United States of Asia.[15]

The anti-colonial notion in Richard's conception of an Asian League of Nations, as expressed above, formed the crux in any proposal for a united Asia. From a Chinese and Indian perspective, 'Asia for the Asians' always contained the precondition of national liberation: 'India for the Indians' and 'China for the Chinese'. In other words, an Asian League had to consist of free and decolonized nations. While Japan's assistance and even leadership towards this end was warmly welcomed, any Japanese ambitions to replace 'White' rule by Japanese rule was strongly rejected. Richard's speech directly confronted the Japanese with this ambivalence. On the one hand, he ascribed to the Japanese the role of the organizer and 'saviour' of Asia. On the other hand, however, he criticized the Japanese for their racial prejudice against other Asians. Japan's own racism and its imperialist ambitions also formed the main objections from Chinese and Koreans, whereas, in general, Asianists from India—geographically out of immediate reach of Japanese imperialism—appeared more tolerant of Japan.[16] Chen Duxiu (1879–1942), a co-founder of the Chinese Communist Party, had identified the abolition of racial prejudice and the establishment of 'equality among the human race' as 'the most urgent demand of all Eastern people', which the delegates of the Asian countries at Versailles should insist on unanimously.[17]

Later, however, Chen warned that 'we yellow people ourselves must first demand equal treatment by yellow people'. Without naming the obvious culprit, Chen asked rhetorically: 'If we yellow people claim towards other yellow people to have something like a special position in China or a suzerain relation with Korea, then how can we face the Whites and demand equal treatment from them?'[18] For similar reasons, Li Dazhao had started to advance an anti-colonial 'New Asianism' to replace Japanese 'Greater Asianism', which he characterized as imperialist and militaristic (see Chap. 4). Importantly, 'Asia' and Asianism as valuable and significant concepts remained central to their political agendas, and Li also argued that the rejection of racial equality at Paris constituted 'a common problem for the Asian peoples and must be solved by uniting the power of our Asian peoples'.[19] This Asian union, however, was to be only the first step towards a 'world federation to promote the happiness of mankind'.[20] Few Asians appeared to trust that a Geneva-based League of Nations that rejected racial equality would be able to achieve this task. Although 'Asia' had indeed become a matter of shared concern throughout Asia by 1919, the role that Imperial Japan and the Japanese would play in the Asianist project was far from clear.

Asianism and Self-determination

In his vision for post-war China and Japan, Takeuchi Masashi (1854–1920),[21] a former journalist with Osaka's *Mainichi Shinbun*, co-founder of Itagaki Taisuke's Liberal Party (Jiyūtō), and member of the Upper House from 1894, proposed 'Greater Asianism' as the central political principle for the cooperation of both countries. Takeuchi's conception of Asianism was clearly inspired by the dominant political rhetoric of the day: it was an expression of 'ethnic self-determination' (minzoku jiketsu shugi). To him, as to many other pro-Asianist thinkers, the example set by the American Monroe Doctrine served as a legitimizing argument.[22] In indirect response to previous objections to the applicability of Asianism in view of the current *status quo*, Takeuchi admitted the existence of a number of obstacles, including the presence of 'Western' powers in vast parts of Asian territory. However, in the context of an increased importance attached internationally to ethnic coherence and homogeneity, he welcomed the prospects of a 'spiritual union of peoples of the same race' as an opportunity for renewed Sino-Japanese cooperation, despite the fact that both peoples still lacked the consciousness of racial sameness:

Between both countries there exist close relations regarding trade and commerce but although they have been deepened in the past few years, we lack a heartfelt ethnic self-awareness and a sincere understanding. Friendly feelings as countries or peoples of siblings are still missing.[23]

Therefore, Asianism to Takeuchi was to serve as a concept that could appeal to both the Chinese and Japanese in order to overcome this lack of common identity. In this effort, race was to play the decisive role. Similarly to Kodera—a friend of Takeuchi's who contributed the afterword to his book[24]—Takeuchi's focus on race stemmed from his rejection of 'Western' Yellow Peril theory; above all, his Asianism was meant as a counter discourse to the Yellow Peril debate. It explicitly built on the possibility of a future clash of the White *versus* Yellow races and criticized the current discrimination against the Asians by the 'Whites'. To the Chinese, Takeuchi hoped, Asianism would appeal as 'a policy of self-defence for the sake of humanity and peace by preventing the threat imposed by other races'.[25] In order to awaken the Chinese to this situation, Takeuchi argued, Japan needed to propagate 'Greater Asianism'. In addition, Takeuchi's focus on racialist arguments was informed by the predominant role of ethnicity in the discourse of national self-determination. Ethnicity was portrayed as assembling more than just people of the same race; commonality in other regards, such as culture, history, and customs, was at least implied. The reason why the Japanese should first propagate Asianism with a focus on China and Japan, according to Takeuchi, lay exactly in this link between racial and other commonality. 'The two countries of Japan and China', he argued, 'belong to the same race that shares commonality regarding history, religion, customs and other features.'[26] This, however, in Takeuchi's conception did not serve as an imperative for common Asianist behaviour but only constituted a precondition to the successful implementation of Asianism. To Takeuchi, Asianism was not about 'equal benefits or sharing joy and sorrow'. Rather, it was in Japan's interest to support and lead China in their joint struggle against the 'White Peril' (hakka) because China shared with Japan geographical and racial commonality (dōshū dōshu).[27] Consequently, Takeuchi was rather outspoken about the envisioned hierarchy in the joint Asianist project: Japan as leader and saviour, China as follower.[28] Interestingly, Takeuchi appeared to be less fearful of a possible Chinese rejection of this plan but worried about Japanese reluctance. If the Japanese did not accept this task, Takeuchi warned, the prospects for the future of all of Asia—including Japan—were grim:

> Then, the construction of Greater Asianism, which corresponds so well to the present situation in the world and as thought conforms to the tides of the time, will, no matter how much we emphasize the ideal, ultimately end as an empty debate on our tables. In this way, because we will not even be able to exert passive self-defence for us and for the peoples of the same race, we must eventually surrender to the force of the Whites and we must resign ourselves to swallowing their contempt.[29]

Takeuchi's interpretation of Asianism reflects two characteristics of post-war Asianist affirmations. First, he explicitly combines regionalist arguments of self-determination with racialist arguments whose language reveals their indebtedness to Wilsonian idealism. Second, Takeuchi affirms Asianism as a political concept of the present and for the future. To an increasing number of thinkers and activists, Asianism no longer mainly denoted the seclusionism of the pre-Meiji period or other outdated and backwards-oriented thought. Instead, in the aftermath of the war it provided an alternative plan for the post-war order that corresponded to the dominant streams of political thought globally. Now was the opportunity to realize Asianism as a part of the global trend towards 'national self-determination'. While 'national self-determination' and racialist regionalism at first glance appear to be contradictory concepts, the translation of the concept into Japanese and Chinese may account for their convenient conflation: *minzoku* in Japanese or *minzu* in Chinese could refer to the nation but more frequently it was employed as denoting ethnicity, similar to *jinshu* in Japanese or *renzhong* in Chinese. When 'national' referred to the independence of a country, *koku/kuni* (Ch. guo) was employed as the corresponding Chinese character, such as in nation state (Jp. kokka, Ch. guojia) or national citizen (Jp. kokumin, Ch. guomin). In compounds, however, *minzoku* frequently referred to larger groupings, such as 'people of East Asian ethnicity/origin' (Jp. Tōa minzoku, Ch. Dongya minzu), and not to the nation. Therefore, as the Wilsonian principle of self-determination was rendered in Japanese and Chinese as *minzoku jiketsu shugi* and *minzu zijue zhuyi*, it could easily be employed as an Asianist (or regionalist, for that matter), not nationalist slogan.[30]

Asianism's Penetration of Political Discourse

Reflecting Asianism's increasing penetration of mainstream discourse, in 1919 it first appeared—as Pan-Asianism (han Ajiashugi)—in a separate entry in a Japanese dictionary of neologisms. Here, too, race (jinshu) played an important role. First, as the most immediate and significant trait that unified the 'peoples of Asia' (Ajia minzoku), and second, as the most distinctive characteristic unifying Asia's opponent—the Whites (hakujin). The dictionary's definition (see also Chap. 2) read:

> Pan-Asianism. The principle (shugi) that demands that – resting on the fact that the 3000 year-old history of the Asian peoples is based on common race, religion, history, and material civilization – these peoples of Asia must once rise in unity to rebel against the world of the Whites of Europe and America and eventually subdue them under the hegemony of the East (Tōyō no haken).[31]

This definition is remarkable in that it displays a strong sense of active resistance against the 'West' that even includes the option of revenge; mere liberation of the oppressed peoples of Asia was not enough. Instead, according to this definition, the peoples of Asia themselves envisioned a hegemonic order that would establish Asian rule over the 'West'. Obviously, this conception of Asianism was much closer to Kodera Kenkichi's call to raise a 'second army of Genghis Khan' than to Ukita Kazutami's inclusive and passive interpretation of Asianism. In the post-World War One period, liberal conceptions, such as Ukita's, almost completely disappeared while proponents of Asianism who had previously advocated non-racialist conceptions now added racialist notions to their agenda. Kodama Kagai, for example, the Asianist champion of 'freedom' and Sino-Japanese solidarity, demanded the creation of an 'Asian League' (Ashū no renmei)—similar to Richard—as a step towards the establishment of a 'World League'.[32] This, he argued, could facilitate the abolishment of racial discrimination and eventually realize the long-awaited freedom.

It is important to remember here that, while contemporary publications reveal a remarkable Asianist shift and a pro-Asianist trend emerged in mainstream Japanese public opinion, Asianist discourse continued to be accompanied by scepticism and rejections in Japan too. Was it in Japan's national interest to support the independence of India and China? Were efforts at Asia's decolonization, however morally justified they appeared, worth risking Japan's *status quo*? Was Asianism not merely a selfish trick played on Japan by Asia's weak? In the early postwar years, with the increase of racialist notions, leftist and liberal conceptions of Asianism largely disappeared from public discourse. Yoshino Sakuzō and Miyazaki Tōten now argued along similar lines to Chen

Duxiu and Li Dazhao. While Yoshino dismissed Japanese Asianists' claims in the context of racial equality as hypocritical and preferred to see the Japanese as perpetrators rather than victims regarding racial discrimination,[33] Miyazaki criticized Japan's China policy as the major obstacle in the realization of Asianism: Sun Yat-sen, who remained receptive to Japanese Asianist claims and himself continued to propagate Asianism to the Chinese and Japanese alike, would probably 'end as a victim of the principle of Japanese–Chinese friendship and a martyr to the cause of Asianism (Ajiashugi no jundōsha)', Miyazaki prophesied in 1918.[34] He rejected Japanese behaviour towards China but did not abandon his support for Asianism. On the contrary, against the background of the negotiations for a new post-war order, his Asianism gained a practical aspect which supplemented his previous sentimentalism. Discussing Japan's political options in 1919, he wrote:

> should we unfailingly insist on nationalism (kokkashugi) and are we prepared to fight until death? Or should we preserve conciliation with the [Western] powers or even take a higher position and – as Dr Richard has been proposing – propagate an Asian League based on radical humanism, liberate Korea and Taiwan, fundamentally change our China policy towards friendship, help other weak countries and set up a league as an organization of equality to resist the Whites? Or should we cooperate with the Bolsheviks and fight Euro-American nationalism (Ōbei no kokkashugi)? Of all possible policies, my country and people will probably have to choose between these three.[35]

Out of the three choices—extreme and isolationist nationalism, conciliatory and anti-imperialist Asianism, or radical anti-Westernism—Miyazaki's writings clearly suggest he favoured the second choice, which could both appeal to the 'West', due to its modesty, and to 'Asia', due to its anti-imperialist stance, alike. This sequence once again demonstrates that to Miyazaki, Asianism was not the extreme opposite of 'Western' accommodationism but that both positions could in fact be reconciled.[36] To him at least, conceptions of Asianism that envisioned a Japanese contribution to the realization of freedom and equality—Japan's surrender of its own colonies—as a prerequisite to demands for a renegotiation of the *status quo* with the 'Western' powers were, at any rate, more realistic than openly fighting 'Western' imperialism in the Bolshevik sense. In this respect, Asianism could be both pro-Asian and pro-Western, although pro-Westernism was limited by the fact that eventually the 'Western' powers too would be forced to give up their privileges and colonial possessions, at least in Asia. But could his conception be reconciled with Japanese national interests at all? In the light of Japan's search for world power status, it was more than unlikely that its politicians, military, and business leaders would agree to give up Japan's growing empire. The problem with Miyazaki's political vision, therefore, was that the price for reconciling the perceived irreconcilable divide between Japan by either joining the 'West' or joining 'Asia' was too high. In Japan's political discourse in general, not only among Asianists, Japanese positions that demanded the abandonment of Japan's colonies remained scarce and marginal.[37] More representative of published opinion were views that blamed China and the Chinese for the strained Sino-Japanese relations. In reaction to anti-Japanese demonstrations and boycotts in China after May Fourth, the *Osaka Mainichi*, for example, simply ordered the Chinese to 'calm down' (reisei nare). Asianism, the editorial suggested, was the right policy for China, Japan, and other Asian countries in the light of increasing discrimination at the hands of the 'Western' powers. The Chinese delegates at Versailles should have 'strengthened cooperation with Japan, adopted the attitude of an ally and united under the banner of All Asianism', it claimed. Instead, however, as the anonymous author complains,

> the Chinese, as ever, employed their traditional strategies of 'using one barbarian to check another' and 'befriending the far away to attack the nearby'. They have prompted the British and the Americans to restrain Japan. They have behaved flirtatiously towards the American Monroe Doctrine, which is nothing but an instrument of American selfishness, while betraying the idea of All Asianism, which must be the foundation of Japanese–Chinese friendship. [...] They must understand that there is no other way but to adopt Greater Asianism as a pro-Japanese policy as the spiritual base for the foundation of their country. Anger and riots are pointlessly causing trouble at home and abroad. This behaviour resembles the hysterical madness of women who set their house on fire and then throw themselves into a well.[38]

As Nohara Shirō has pointed out, Asianism understood in this sense and advocated in this context symbolized the complete lack of mutual understanding between pro-Asianist Japanese and anti-Japanese Chinese.[39] For the latter, as Li Dazhao's critique revealed, Japanese Asianism was an essential part of the problem, not its solution. Asianism to them aggravated the tensions between both peoples, since it appeared to rationalize Japanese imperialist policy towards China. As the excerpt from the article quoted above from one of Japan's most widely read newspaper reveals, this fear was by no means far-fetched. Japanese demands for unconditional Chinese trust and loyalty were far more representative of published opinion than Miyazaki's proposal to abandon imperialism to realize 'humanism'. Asianism, in principle, lent itself to either position.

In the midst of this heated and controversial political debate, the *Taikai*—probably owing to Sugita's prominent participation—not only managed to receive extensive media coverage in Japan but also gained support from various organizations, including Japan's National Federation of Employers' Association (Dai Nippon Jitsugyō Kumiai Rengō). In line with the *Taikai*'s own resolution, the Federation demanded that the Japanese peace conference delegation 'insist to the utmost on the abolition of racial discrimination'. If the proposal was rejected, Japan should not join the League of Nations, even if this would be disadvantageous for Japan's commerce and industry.[40] Representatives of the Japanese government, however, avoided the *Taikai*, and the only prominent politician who agreed to support it, Ōkuma Shigenobu, preferred to send a letter rather than appearing in person. Contrary to the *Taikai*'s resolution, Ōkuma refused to link the racial equality proposal to Japan's participation in the League of Nations. Instead he limited his criticism to the Australian Prime Minister Hughes' 'extreme racial prejudice' and the Powers' lack of support at Versailles for Japan's efforts at establishing 'common happiness and peace for all mankind' and 'eternal peace in the world'.[41]

Ōkuma's commitment to the *Taikai*'s cause was as half-hearted as the Japanese delegation's stance in Versailles regarding the racial equality clause. Although the proposal received the majority of votes in April 1919, upon Wilson's intervention the clause was eventually dropped and the case at Paris was closed. The case was not closed, however, for Asianists in Japan and elsewhere in Asia. While there is no evidence that the *Taikai* institutionally continued its campaigns after the rejection of the racial equality clause in Versailles, its rhetoric and political rationale survived the whole interwar period and blended rather well with Japan's later official wartime propaganda.

Asianist Reactions to the American Immigration Legislation of 1924

Despite the *Taikai*'s short-lived fate, the topic of racial discrimination remained on the agenda of mainstream political discourse throughout the 1920s. Further legal restrictions on Asian land ownership, first in California (1920), then in other states (1920–1924), and eventually on a national level in the United States (1924), continued to fuel Asianist discourse.

In 1924 the US infamously 'shut the door'[42] to Japanese immigration to the United States when President Coolidge signed the so-called 'Johnson–Reed Act' on 26 May 1924. The bill consisted of the National Origins Act and the Ineligibility to Citizenship Act. While the former introduced a system of immigration quotas based on nationality, the latter excluded non-Caucasians from eligibility for citizenship. Unsurprisingly, Japanese and Chinese published opinion harshly criticized this legislation. It was widely seen as a final step of the government-approved racism by the United States that had begun in 1882 with the Chinese Exclusion Act (euphemistically named 'An act to execute certain treaty stipulations relating to Chinese') and that had intensified after the formation of the Asian Exclusion League in 1905, the California Alien Land Law of 1913, and the 'barred Asiatic zone' created by Congress in 1917.[43] In fact, according to some calculations, the Immigration Act of 1924 'barred half the world's population from entering the United States'.[44] The near-exclusive focus on Japan in Japanese debate which was reflected in the terminology chosen ('anti-Japanese immigration law') may not appear inadequate, since other Asian immigration had already been excluded by previous Acts. However, the cleavage between claims made by Japanese Asianists for leadership and representation of Asia on the one hand and an almost exclusive focus on Japanese concerns symbolizes the contradiction inherent in Japanese Asianist rhetoric. It revealed that 'Asia' only seemed to matter when Japanese interests were at stake.

In Japan the reaction to the Johnson–Reed Act was particularly strong also because it confronted even the most tolerant and pro-Western Japanese with the foreign-imposed relegation of the Japanese to the rather unpopular category of 'Asians'. The 1924 Act, therefore, appeared to prove that Asianists had been right from the beginning in criticizing the hypocrisy of 'the Whites', who had coined justice and righteousness, peace and equality as key phrases at Versailles but refused to extend these values and rights to non-Whites. Reported acts of protest against the law ranged from the theft of the Star-Spangled Banner from the grounds of the American Embassy in Tokyo to a public ritual suicide in protest against the bill.[45] The first day of July, the day the law went into effect, quickly became known as the 'Day of National Humiliation' in Japan. Tsurumi Yūsuke (1885–1973), a liberal and originally pro-Western politician, provides an interesting insight into how deeply Japanese felt betrayed by America's policy.[46]

> The Immigration Act of the United States [...] swept the whole country like a hurricane. All the papers were unanimous in protesting against it. At first it seemed as though it were going to affect only the political sphere. It gradually began to go deeper. It made a tremendous impression on the thinking part of the nation. The disappointment with the West drove them to turn to their old schools of thought for enlightenment. Orientalism[47] received a new stimulus. [...] What kind of new thought will emerge, nobody is yet in a position to predict.

As Tsurumi put it, after the United States had 'slammed the door in the face of the Japanese nation',[48] Japanese sentiments that resistance against the 'West', rather than a imitation of it based on (open or secret) admiration, was the most adequate policy for Asian countries to pursue could no longer simply be dismissed as xenophobic anti-Westernism. Despite its military victories and colonial gains from 1895 onwards and 'Western' talk of the equality of nations, Japan—at least in the mainstream self-perception—remained only a slightly more privileged country among the underprivileged nations. Both the Paris Peace Conference and the Washington Conference had left the Japanese delegations and the Japanese public in great disappointment. Already in Paris, it had become clear that Japanese interpretations of the Lansing–Ishii Agreement of 1917 had been faulty. Neither the US, nor any other power was willing to concede political and economic privileges to Japan to a degree similar to that which the 'Western' powers had *nolens volens* conceded to each other. The Washington Conference of 1921 and 1922 confirmed this assumption and increased the antagonism between Japan and the powers, in particular the United States. As a result, the Lansing–Ishii Agreement was cancelled and Japan had to cede the Shandong peninsula, gained from Germany in 1914, back to China.

To understand just how strongly the Act of 1924 affected Japanese national consciousness, the recollections of the Shōwa Emperor Hirohito may serve as an indicator. The Tennō even suggested 1924 as a turning point in Japanese history and a 'remote cause for the Greater East Asian War' (Dai Tōa Sensō no en'in):

> If we examine its reason, we have in the distance the content of the peace treaty after World War One. The racial equality proposal, advanced by the Japanese, was not accepted by the Powers and the refusal of immigration in California which left the sentiment of discrimination between yellow and white as ever fuelled the anger of the Japanese people.[49]

In fact, the thirteenth year of Taishō (1924), when public anger over the racial discrimination imposed on the Japanese by American immigration legislation peaked, also shook political discourse on 'Asia' in Japan. The legislation served as proof that Japan's denial of its own 'Asianity' and its efforts to join the 'West', which had dominated political discourse and reality ever since the Meiji Restoration had failed. While racial discrimination by Western countries against the Japanese had been nothing new, the *de iure* abolishment of the Gentlemen's Agreement of 1907/08 and adoption of exclusionist clauses that had originally only applied to California by federal law turned the tide. Asianists rejoiced.

The Special Edition on Greater Asianism of the Nihon Oyobi Nihonjin (October 1924)

In reaction to the Immigration Act, the *Nihon oyobi Nihonjin* journal (Fig. 5.1)[50] was among the first to renew the call for joint Asian solidarity and resistance under the banner of 'Greater Asianism' (Dai Ajiashugi) to oppose discrimination against Asians. A special *Dai Ajiashugi* volume published in October 1924, which contained no fewer than 50 (pro- and anti-Asianism) essays, reaffirmed the concept's significance for public discourse in Japan. Here, it should be noted that, contrary to what one might expect from this right-leaning political journal, Asianism was not simply propagated as an orthodox political ideology to be adopted by Japan and other Asian countries. Rather, Japanese and foreign (exclusively Asian) public opinion leaders, regardless of their political inclinations, were invited to present their views and interpretations of Asianism. In addition to foreign voices, the journal's editors also included critical

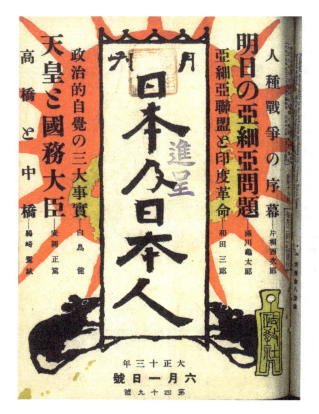

Fig. 5.1 Cover of the Japanese journal *Nihon oyobi Nihonjin* (1 June 1924) in which many contributions to Asianism discourse were published during the 1920s; this cover reflects the impact of the anti-Japanese racial immigration legislation on political debate in this journal after May 1924. Articles announced on the cover include 'Prelude to Race War', 'Tomorrow's Asia Problem', and 'Asian League and India's Revolution'. In October 1924, the same journal published the special issue on 'Greater Asianism' discussed in this chapter. Reproduced with kind permission from the collection of Waseda University Library

and dismissive contributions by some Japanese. Interestingly, the opening essay by the Chinese Japanophile Yin Rugeng constituted a full-scale deconstruction of Asianism that the editors apparently felt had to be balanced by a pro-Asianist foreword authored by Ōishi Masami (1855–1935).[51]

One of the principal proponents of Asianism, Ōishi[52] had participated in the People's Rights Movement of the 1880s, during which time he translated Spencer's *Representative Government* into Japanese (1883). Alongside Ōkuma Shigenobu and Inukai Tsuyoshi, he had also been a leader of the Progressive Party (Shinpotō, 1896–1898). He was elected as a member of the Lower House in 1898 and consecutively re-elected six times (until 1914). Later he also helped to organize the *Rikken Dōshikai* (Association of Comrades for Constitutional Government) but retired from politics in 1915. As early as 1892, Ōishi had proposed an 'Asian alliance' (*Ajia dōmei*) between Japan, China, and Great Britain (!) to counter the perceived threat posed to Japan by Russia. Some three decades later—when Russia had been defeated by Japan on its own and Japan's alliance with Great Britain had already been abandoned—Ōishi again proposed a tripartite alliance in which, ironically, (a yet to be freed) India was to take Britain's place alongside China and Japan. As with most of Japanese Asianist writings in reaction to the racial exclusion legislation of 1924, Ōishi's contributions revealed less a concern over Japan's security but instead conveyed a strong sense of having been insulted. Rather than seeing the exclusion act as a sad and unfair event which, however, did not constitute a grave practical problem as far as Japan's agendas in domestic and foreign policy were concerned, many Japanese fell into the racial trap that the United States had seemingly prepared for them. The racialist and, not rarely, racist outcry against the United States legislation, including Asian claims of superiority and plans for an Asian union against the 'West', in turn only appeared to confirm those in the United States who had proposed a ban on Asian immigration in the first place: Asians were unassimilable aliens whose entry to America needed to be prohibited.

Ōishi, 'a "liberal" chauvinist', in Jansen's words,[53] was one of the first voices to demand an alliance of the 'Eastern peoples' (Tōyō minzoku) in reaction to the discussion of the bill draft in Congress. In an article published ten days prior to Congress' approval of the bill, Ōishi called the draft 'really outrageous' and 'an insult to all Asian peoples'.[54] Borrowing a phrase from the times of the Freedom and People's Rights Movement of the 1880s, *daidō danketsu* (great union of common interests), Ōishi postulated unity among the peoples of the East, or, even broader, of the 'coloured peoples'. To realize such a union, Japan would have to start internally by implementing national unity, in preparation for the creation of an 'alliance of the peoples of East Asia'.[55] Ōishi, like most contributors to early 1910s Asianism discourse, left no doubt as to who should lead such an alliance:

> If we say the peoples of the East, today there is no other country that exerts authority apart from Japan. Very sadly, China has become a country of decrepitude. And the internal troubles are continuous all year through. [...] Whatever you can say, it must be Japan as the centre and as the leader (meishu) that must preserve authority and peace in the East. To this end, at any cost, a great union of common interests of the peoples of the East is necessary and the Japanese people must plan the realization of strong national unity.[56]

Although Ōishi pays some attention to public opinion in China and India, where, according to him, anger about the US has led to favourable views of Japan that provide a good chance for the rapprochement of Japan and other Asian nations, he is more concerned with domestic issues. In particular, he criticizes the Japanese for not grasping the significance of this grave situation of 'combined internal and external difficulty', which he likens to the times of the Meiji Restoration. Back then, Ōishi claims, Japan had heroes such as Saigō Takamori and Katsu Kaishū, who, although opposed to each other, had selflessly committed themselves to the higher cause of 'justice and righteousness'. Now, faced with the task of completing the 'Taishō Restoration' (Taishō Ishin), the people had to be brave and discerning to overcome private ambitions and self-centredness to accomplish justice and righteousness in their struggle against 'the Whites'. This struggle, according to Ōishi, was no less than the fight for the protection of the 'divine right of the East' (Tōyō no tenken), in which the union of Eastern peoples was either to preserve or to lose its assumed cultural heritage comprising Confucianism, Buddhism, and Shintoism. Here, the recurrent theme in Asianist thought, namely that of a divine mission, displays itself explicitly: Japan as the leader of Asia must protect the divine right of the East and 'complete the great mission of the magnificent East'.[57] To Ōishi, not only Japan but Asia *in toto*—at least theoretically and rhetorically—constitutes a place of splendour and grandeur, not backwardness and decay. This was the Asianist answer to the question that had arisen in the aftermath of the Paris and Washington conferences and the new US immigration legislation:

will Japan continue to strive for the status of a political global player or will it withdraw to the regional sphere? Tsurumi, in his 1926 lectures at Columbia University, had highlighted this bifurcated interpretation of the continuous rejection of Japanese ambitions on the global stage. As he explained to his American audience, 'the issue in Japan was whether the Japanese nation was to stand on an equal footing with Western powers, or to be cut off from the fellowship and be driven back upon a purely Oriental policy and theatre of operation'.[58] The Immigration Act of 1924, which deprived the Japanese of the privileged position compared to other Asian nations and forced upon them a status equal with that of other Asians, was therefore seen, by Japanese Asianists, as proof of their assumption that Japan's accommodationism towards the 'West' had failed: not only politically but also culturally and, most obviously racially. Ultimately, Japan could 'modernize' along 'Western' lines as much as it wanted, but the Japanese would never become Caucasians as the *Ozawa v. United States* case had shown. In 1922, two years before racial exclusion became federal law, the US Supreme Court ruled that the Japanese Ozawa Takao was ineligible for naturalization under the Naturalization Act of 1906, which only allowed white persons and persons of African descent or African nativity to naturalize. Ozawa had indeed attempted to have himself and the Japanese in general classified as 'white'. This view, however, was rejected by the Court, which argued that only Caucasians were white, and therefore the Japanese, not being Caucasian, were not white.[59] The 1924 Act gave even more ground for such rulings,[60] which, prior to the Ineligibility Law, had not been too far from circular reason.[61] This racial ostracism encouraged many Japanese to (re-)discover their 'Asianity'—an idea that had only gradually gained currency after 1919 in Asianism discourse. At least the assumption that within Asia Japan was the unchallenged powerhouse provided consolation for the unsuccessful pursuit of membership in the exclusive club of 'Western' powers. In much of public discourse, the impression was created that Japan's application to this club, which dated from the early Meiji days and had been on hold for some decades, was ultimately declined in 1924.

Nevertheless, Ōishi's call for a 'general alliance of Asian peoples'[62] in July 1924 in the widely read and moderate *Taiyō* (The Sun) showed signs of possible reconciliation. Unlike the lurid title of his essay, Ōishi did not immediately demand to set up a league of Asian nations or peoples to counter 'Western' hegemony. Instead, he proposed three steps to solve the issue which he now, more accurately, called 'problems between Japan and America' (Nichi–Bei mondai). As a first step, the present Japanese government, which he held responsible for diplomatic failure, had to be replaced by a new and stronger cabinet. Second, both domestically and abroad (above all in China and India) public opinion was to be influenced in the direction of regarding the problem not as between Japan and America but as relating to 'the entirety of coloured peoples'.[63] Third, Japan was to call on the League of Nations to file a suit against the United States. Ōishi acknowledged that the US was not a member of the League; however, if it condemned the actions taken by the US, Ōishi argued, the public opinion of the whole world would turn against the United States. This pressure would surely be enough to cause the US to reverse its legislation, he contested. It is highly interesting that Ōishi would put so much trust in an organization that had grown out of Anglo-American interests and had previously failed to acknowledge racial equality.

Only three months later, however, Ōishi was less trusting in anything 'Western'. His contribution to the Asianism special edition of the *Nihon oyobi Nihonjin* journal appears to mark a shift from a view that adhered to international cooperation to one that now sought confrontation. Instead of trusting the League of Nations, he now advocated the establishment of an alternative, regionalist union made up of the three nations of Japan, China, and India. Greater Asianism, a term Ōishi had not yet proposed in his July contribution to the *Taiyō*, in October 1924 became the key principle that he proposed to put into practice 'in self-defence of Japan's empire and protection of the peoples of Asia'.[64] Ōishi's rhetoric was no longer conciliatory:

> The adoption of the Japanese exclusion act by the US Congress is a great proclamation of war towards all peoples of Asia. It insults the sovereignty of Japan, tramples down justice and humanity, and is the precondition [for the US] themselves to control the Pacific and strengthen their evil attentions on the mainland. If we have a government that knows shame and have people who love their country, it is only natural to punish the US. We must, for the self-defence of the Empire and the preservation of the Asian peoples, wholeheartedly put our efforts into raising the people's spirit and realizing our material capability. This calls us to establish Greater Asianism to rouse the public opinion at home and abroad. It is the aim of Greater Asia to promote the civilization of Japan, China, and India, and to

preserve the independence and freedom of this territory and the peoples there.⁶⁵

As this excerpt reveals, the discussion of Asianism in the context of racial discrimination was not simply limited to the practical problems caused by the so-called anti-Japanese immigration legislation. Instead, Asianism was easily linked to a wider range of more fundamental issues of bilateral relations and regional politics. The Law stimulated this debate and linked the discussion of the denigrating attitude of 'the Whites' towards Asians with that of 'Western' power politics in Asia. Consequently, Ōishi now openly focused on American ambitions in Asia and the Pacific and, implicitly, on the clash of those interests with Japan's own ambitions on the Asian mainland and in the Pacific region. Shifting from dealing with the Law as such to designing a grand Asianist strategy, Ōishi quickly abandoned his original proposal to protest against discrimination via the League of Nations. Instead, he now demanded the punishment of the US at the hands of the Asians themselves. Simultaneously, his critique reflected the opinion held by many Japanese, not only Asianists, that Japan deserved better treatment by the 'West' than other Asians. Although many Japanese had failed to show solidarity with weaker Asian nations on several occasions—for example, when the US had gradually excluded the Chinese from immigration to the US decades before this policy was applied to Japan—Japanese Asianists now demanded solidarity with Japan from other Asians. But why would the Chinese feel that the new regulation of 1924 constituted a major turning point for 'Asia' and the Asians when only the Japanese had eventually been subjected to the same treatment the Chinese had been experiencing for many years? Why had Japan shown little sympathy then? And how seriously were Koreans or Indians to take Asianist claims when demands for the 'preservation' of their 'independence and freedom' only showed how detached its Japanese propagators were from reality?

As public debate continued, Ōishi's plan for the unity of Japan, China, and India based on the 'two religions of Confucianism and Buddhism',⁶⁶ also gained a more practical outlook that acknowledged the importance of cooperation with other Asians. As precise steps towards the propagation and implementation of Asianism, Ōishi envisioned the establishment of universities in China and India to foster human capital. In addition, newspapers, journals, and other popular writings in both countries were to be targeted in order to influence public opinion towards a pro-Asianist position.

Despite the unprecedented pro-Asianist mood and an almost unanimous outcry against the Immigration Act in 1924, 'national unity' (Ōishi) against the exclusionist policy of the US did not automatically mean 'national unity' regarding an affirmative stance towards Asianism. First, on the government level the new coalition also kept its distance from Asianist activities and debate. The unpopular Kiyoura cabinet, which had been held responsible by some for not having prevented the US immigration legislation, had been brought down by the so-called Second Movement for the Protection of the Constitution, and, in the May 1924 elections, the joint faction of *Seiyūkai*, *Kenseikai*, *Kakushin* Club (Goken sanpa) had dramatically won almost two-thirds of the total seats to form the first party coalition government in Japanese history under the premiership of Katō Takaaki (1860–1926)—the same Katō who had issued the notorious Twenty-One Demands to China in 1915. Second, voices of dissent also remained prominent in mainstream discourse and attest to the controversial nature of the issue and to the relatively liberal intellectual atmosphere of the time. In fact, many contributors to the *Nihon oyobi Nihonjin* special volume remained critical of Asianism as a political concept and many dismissed it altogether, be it for practical or for idealistic reasons. Interestingly, it was not only liberals and socialists (the fact they had been invited to contribute to this issue being remarkable in itself), such as Ozaki Yukio and Fuse Tatsuji, who either dismissed the concept as 'a daydream' (kūsō)[67] or objected to its confrontational and destructive character.[68] Rather, and in continuation of the political discourse of the early 1910s, Asianism continued to be criticized from both 'the left' and 'the right'.

Shiga Shigetaka's Repudiation of Asianism

Among the most prominent Japanist critics was the founder of the *Seikyōsha* (Society for Politics and Education), Shiga Shigetaka (1863–1927). He dismissed Asianism out of nationalistic concerns, but, simultaneously, did not spare the Japanese from harsh criticism. Shiga's essay was titled 'Hopeless Asian League' (Mikomi naki Ajia renmei) and the subtitle left no doubt about Shiga's deprecation of Greater Asianism or an Asian League: 'If Japan was the first to advocate an Asian League it would be Japan's suicide'.[69] Shiga, a geographer and the author of the famous *Nihon Fūkei Ron* (On the Landscape of Japan, 1894),[70] had just returned to Japan from a trip around the world in 1924 and based his dismissal of an Asian League on his experience with and observations of other Asians, save only for the Chinese. 'Initially I had great hopes for an Asian League and travelled to many Asian countries, but I have returned to Japan in the greatest disappointment', Shiga admitted:

> Through many trips around the world I have come to believe that, regrettably, except for Japan and China, Asians have been reduced to beggars. I know that the peoples of Eastern Europe are rude but they have not yet turned to evil spirits. [...] We propagate Greater Asianism and the Asian League but for Japan there is no other country that can be trusted apart from China.[71]

To unite with such 'evil-spirited' peoples in an Asian League under the banner of 'Greater Asianism', Shiga continued, would only invite the contempt of other nations, notably America and Britain:

> For the sake of declaring an Alliance with beggars to turn away from the two great Anglo-Saxon peoples and eventually be pushed as far as going to war with them is the same as preparing for one's suicide. For the fundamental existence of the Japanese people, I am opposed to this declaration of an Asian League, and I announce my determination to strongly oppose it.[72]

Claims for an Asian League, Shiga concluded, are like 'observations of a blind man'.[73] While Shiga's dismissal of Asianism seems to stem from his contempt for his fellow Asians (except for Chinese), his comments do not fall short of criticism of the Japanese, in particular regarding Japanese treatment of China and of the Chinese. In fact, Shiga revealed himself to be a Sinophile and, in a manner reminiscent of Kodera's 1919 essay, Shiga criticized Japanese behaviour towards the Chinese as 'extremely rude'. The Japanese, he criticized, had always been interested in obtaining rights in and profits from China while speaking of 'same culture, same race' (dōbun dōshu) or proposing an 'Asian alliance' (Ashū no teikei).[74] In this respect, the 'Euro-Americans' were to be given credit for honestly admitting their mere interest in profits without resorting to *dōbun dōshu* rhetoric, which characterized the 'disgusting' attitude of his fellow Japanese.[75] Like Kodera, Shiga provided the example of Chinese exchange students in Japan to illustrate his frustration with Japanese treatment of the Chinese:

> Chinese students study abroad in the US in great numbers and they praise the people there and those who go to Britain mention the favourable traits

of the [British] people. Also many go to study abroad in France and upon their return a 'praising France fever' is in real fashion. However, without exception, those who studied in Japan start to hate Japan. They actually become the main agitators of the anti-Japanese movement in China. What on earth is the reason that things have come that far?[76]

To Shiga the answer lay in the Japanese lack of virtue, which he held responsible for the hypocritical behaviour of claiming one thing (same culture, same race) and doing the other (exploiting fellow Asians for their own profit). 'If we Japanese', Shiga demanded, 'do not awaken thoroughly to this point and do not ourselves repent and improve ourselves, we cannot even plan for a real alliance with the only country in all of Asia that we can trust, China.'[77] Importantly though, despite some notable similarities, Kodera and Shiga arrive at different conclusions. Whereas Kodera had advocated retaining Asianism as the banner under which first the Japanese and Chinese, later also other Asians, should befriend each other and unite, Shiga dismissed the concept and was opposed to anything that exceeded a Sino-Japanese alliance. In this respect, Shiga's negative view of Asianism represents a combination of Kodera's Sinophilism and Ninagawa's Japan-centred and pro-Western anti-Asianism. More generally, Shiga's intervention exemplifies the complexity of the intellectual structure of Asianism discourse. Asiaphobia (Shiga, Ninagawa) did not necessarily pre-empt Sinophilia (Kodera, Shiga), which in turn could lead to the confession to either pro- (Kodera) or anti-Asianist (Shiga) positions. This complexity was further complicated by non-Japanese nationalistic agendas. As we have already seen in the writings of Li Dazhao and in Sun Yat-sen's appropriation of Asianism—and as we will see in the subsequent claims to its authoritative interpretation by various Chinese leaders after Sun's death (see Chap. 7)—Asianism was not consentaneously dismissed as a propagandistic tool of Japanese imperialism. Instead it was proposed in a positive way as far as it suited the nationalistic or other ideological purposes of the proponent—regardless of nationality. This tension between a general approval of the concept and the dismissal of precise conceptions on the one hand and an approval of details but a general dismissal of the concept on the other became apparent in the two[78] foreign contributions to the *Nihon oyobi Nihonjin* special volume.

Rash Behari Bose and Yin Rugeng's Deconstruction of Asianism

Rash Behari Bose (1886–1944), the famous Indian independence fighter who had fled from British persecution to Japan in 1915, used his contribution to discuss Asianism as a means for the cause of Indian independence. Avoiding a clear-cut position towards the significance and suitability of 'Asia' as the main political point of reference, he instead elaborated on the details of the revolutionary situation in India. Only in his conclusion did Bose eventually address the 'common cause of the Asian peoples'. Unsurprisingly, in his conception India's independence constituted the precondition to any Asianist undertakings. Japan and China, which stood at the centre of Japanese and Chinese (and most of 'Western') 'Asia' discourse, were of marginal interest. 'Asia' only mattered as far as it supported the national agenda of India. As Bose concluded,

> Because India would be lost as the foothold for the Whites' suppression of Asia I believe that only if India becomes independent surely the expulsion of the Whites will be accomplished. Yes, let's first secure India's independence and then plan the unity of all of Asia.[79]

Similarly to Li Dazhao and other Chinese, Bose gave priority to national independence, followed by an Asian union of independent states. Despite his open pro-Japanese inclinations, Bose also appeared to fear the interference of a strong Japan (or of a unified and revived China) in Indian matters if either country should get too directly involved in the liberation of India. At that time, roughly through the 1920s, he was still confident that India's primary national mission—liberation from British rule—could be achieved from 'within India'. Bose had subscribed to Gandhi's conviction that 'India must gain its lost freedom and independence through its own power', a line which Bose quoted at the end of his *Nihon oyobi Nihonjin* essay.[80] At the same time, as we have seen above, Bose had begun to flirt with Asianist rhetoric in as far as it appeared useful to India's national mission. Later, particularly after Japan's first military successes against European colonial powers at the beginning of World War Two, Bose embraced Asianism much more willingly, thus acknowledging India's need for a strong partner.[81]

A quite different stance was taken by the Chinese politician Yin Rugeng (1885–1947)[82] in his contribution to the journal, which was selected as the opening essay. An early anti-Qing revolutionary activist and graduate of Tokyo's Waseda University, Yin was not only married to a Japanese but also politically kept very close relations with the Japanese. In 1927, Yin became the Guomindang government's special envoy to Japan and, after 1935, collaborated with the Japanese in North East China. He later supported Wang Jingwei's regime and was arrested and executed as a traitor (hanjian) by the Guomindang troops in Nanjing in 1947. Far from being one of the Chinese exchange students that Shiga had mentioned who engaged in anti-Japanese propaganda or activities, Yin was no yes-man who would simply contribute a eulogy of Asianism either. Rather, he critically engaged in a detailed discussion of the meaning of the concept. In fact, Yin provided one of the most sophisticated analyses of the possible prospects of Asianism and, more generally, the significance of Asianism as a political concept during the 1920s. His essay is simply but aptly titled 'What is Greater Asianism?'

> The question of what Greater Asianism is has conventionally been discussed in assemblies such as Asia societies or Asia problem research groups that have been held quite often. One could see here and there different directions of writings discussing what Asia is; however, I feel that after the problem of the American exclusion of the Japanese occurred recently [this question] has become even more discussed. Speaking of Greater Asianism, if it encompasses the meaning of an advancement of the international status of the Asian peoples and the increase of economic profit, then, we, being an element of the same Asian peoples, should not be opposed to it. Instead, as a greatly hopeful plan we must support it as much as we can. However, when we think carefully about what Greater Asianism is and what content fills the literal meaning of the term, [...] then I must confess that, as much as I myself am concerned, I cannot unconditionally approve of it.[83]

In other words, while Yin affirmed the new significance of Asianism as a political concept beyond specialist and academic debate and also felt compelled to support 'Asia' as an Asian—Yin clearly displayed an Asian self-consciousness—he remained critical of the attitude that self-declared Asianists displayed under the banner of Asianism. Yin subsequently divided Asianist claims into two groups: first, Asianism as 'thought' or as a cultural viewpoint and second, Asianism as 'expediency'. The former, according to Yin, combined Confucian and Buddhist ideals of 'perfect virtue' and impartial equality of all people and things in this universe. But instead of internalizing and following these ideals, Yin argued, Asianism seemed to advocate the employment of this 'particular culture as a weapon against the culture of the West'.[84] Therefore, rather than being propagators of 'Eastern' thought and culture, Asianists were in fact betraying this very thought.[85] Put differently, as the first dictionary definition of Asianism from 1919 had revealed, Asianism, in some prominent conceptions at least, aimed less at an universal spread of 'Eastern' values than a confrontation of 'East' and 'West' in the struggle for dominance and hegemony. Such Asianism, Yin continued, was in fact not 'Asian' at all but merely an imitation of a 'Western' idea.

> Many Westerners advocate Pan-Germanism or Pan-Europeanism. In recent years, in America some very vehemently propose Americanism or Pan-Americanism, Anglo-Saxonism, and things like 'we must turn the entire world into an Anglophone people'. [...] To the people who claim Greater Asianism I say the following: Does not Greater Asianism resemble something Western? If you really want to be sincere to the cause of Asia, you must awake from the illusion of confining yourself to one local corner and being at enmity with others, based on Western teachings. [...] By all means, we must discover ourselves from within ourselves.[86]

Many prevalent conceptions of Asianism, therefore, to Yin did not represent 'the true cause of Asia'. Yin agreed with the aim of spreading mutual knowledge of 'Asia' among Asians and approved of the aim to arouse a consciousness of being Asian among Asians. Yet he insisted that this process must be the result of self-discovery, not political propaganda or political instrumentalization. Asianism, therefore, to Yin, was acceptable only as a slogan for self-cultivation. Consequently, Yin criticized those who were less idealistic but more practically minded in their propagation of Asianism. To this end he embarked on a full-scale deconstruction of the term 'Greater Asianism' (Dai Ajiashugi). First, he opposed the use of *shugi*, which should be reserved for more significant and lasting phenomena in history. Second, he rendered *Ajia* as inappropriate because the unequal treatment by 'the Whites' was not restricted to Asians but also affected the Africans and American Indians. 'If their [Asianists'] aim was to exterminate this inequality', Yin argued, 'it must be as a great league that includes all coloured people. If we call it a principle (shugi), it goes without saying that it has to be exactly like this'.[87] Only for the sake of convenience, he conceded, one may start by thinking about how to realize a union of Asian peoples, and, if this proves to be impractical, one that at least includes East Asia, India, and Vietnam. If even this should prove impossible, Yin continued, the term Asianism, let alone *Greater* Asianism, was improper and had to be abandoned. This, his third point, completed the de(con)struction of the very concept of Asianism into its apparently corrupt and incompatible components. To summarize Yin's words: if Asianists meant what they said, their demands were not about 'Asia' but about the coloured and oppressed peoples; if it was to be a principle (shugi), it had to have a master plan which included a way of realizing the liberation of the oppressed peoples in the world; and if it meant to be 'great', either geographically or idealistically or both,[88] it had to include more than just China and Japan. As none of the three conditions seemed to be even close to being realizable but, instead, 'a union [...] under the banner of Greater Asianism was a troublesome matter, there is no need to put up a sheep's head in order to sell dog's meat'.[89] If anything, only a union of Japan and China appeared to be within the range of practical achievement and, therefore, Yin proposed replacing Greater Asianism with a discussion of Sino-Japanese cooperation, although he admitted that even the realization of such a bi-national alignment seemed difficult at this moment. As a major obstacle, unsurprisingly, he identified Japanese behaviour. This Yin characterized as arrogant as a result of Japan's international successes, which had lifted Japan to the position of the leading nation among the coloured people. Before long, he complained, the Japanese copied the Western powers and Sino-Japanese relations deteriorated. In particular, Yin took offence at Japanese pride that had led them to overuse the word 'great' (dai).

> You [Japanese] seem to have become extremely pleased with the [Chinese] character 'great' (dai). This had already been so earlier but it has become extreme after the Russo-Japanese War. Say Great Japanese Empire, say Five Great Powers. You are so proud to have become one of the three great powers after the European War. Even every ordinary Japanese who travels within China calls himself a subject of the Great Japanese Empire. There can be no doubt that Japan has become one of the Three Greats but you don't have to call yourself that. If you are not really 'great' but only claim to be 'great', others will certainly not think of you as 'great'. But if you are really 'great', you don't call yourself so but you will be treated as such.[90]

In a similarly sharp-witted manner, Yin criticized Japan's self-designated position as leader (meishu) of a future Asian league. This 'premature announcement' alone he deemed so arrogant that he predicted its defeat; in history, he argued, 'self-recommending has usually led to failure'. Furthermore, Yin rejected the Japanese claim to solely possess the qualifications to lead and command other Asians when he reminded the Japanese of their support for the British in their oppression of India and of Japanese diplomacy towards China. 'Where is this qualification to speak of an Asian League? Still more, is it not true that there is no qualification at all to declare yourself the leader?'[91]

Although Yin showed some signs of reconciliation and optimism by appealing to Japan's 'well-informed people' to push the Japanese people towards a benevolent and real partnership of China and Japan, he nevertheless concluded that neither an essential nor an expedient version of Asianism could be realized. Instead, if there had to be a principle (shugi), he proposed the adoption of a Great Union of the World principle (Sekai Daidō shugi) as an intellectual basis, to be realized by an alliance of Japan and China as a first step.

> No matter what happens, Greater Asianism will not materialize. If we only research the Asia problem, this is nothing close to a principle (shugi). And if we teach the Asians that they are Asians, I will object and say, let's teach them straight away that they are members of the human race.[92]

Yin's unmasking rhetoric constitutes a compelling array of arguments against Asianism. It is striking that such an outspoken and foreign critic of Asianism was given the first ten pages of the *Nihon oyobi Nihonjin*'s special Asianism volume, which, if we take Ōishi's introduction as a mission statement, meant to propagate exactly the opposite of everything that Yin had to say about Asianism and about prevailing Japanese conceptions of 'Asia'. It is a fascinating document that displays much of the character of Asianism discourse in the early 1920s. The concept itself, increasingly embraced by many but still harshly criticized by others, facilitated a sort of criticism of Japanese consciousness of China and of 'Asia' by non-Japanese and Japanese alike. It appears as if criticizing 'Asia' as an imagined 'Other' enabled an exchange of arguments in a more direct and outspoken manner than criticizing Japan. In this sense, Asianism discourse had become an arena of political debate among Asians on diverse matters of concern that transcended the rather well-defined political agenda (Asian unity, resistance against white powers) that Asianism had started to represent in the aftermath of World War One. As many contributions to the debate reveal, national and nationalist concerns remained prominent and Asianist rhetoric often possessed an outspoken nationalist dimension. Due to this tension between regionalist and nationalist outlooks and the diversity of political agendas held by the participants, Asianism discourse remained a relatively multifaceted and rather controversial public discussion. At any rate, as the *Nihon oyobi Nihonjin* special edition clearly reveals, rather than being an ideology, through the 1920s the concept of Asianism functioned as a catalyst for mainstream political debate centring on Japanese and other Asian views of Asia in relation to national, regional, and global politics. While Yin transcended this nation-centred view, others, such as Bose and Ōishi, reinforced self-centred nationalistic positions. As a prominent political concept of the time Asianism facilitated the transnational political communication between these different actors and standpoints.

Tagore's Japanophilism as Asianism

The year 1924 takes a special place in the history of transnational Asianism discourse also because it saw two eminent Asians leaders visiting Japan and reaffirming the message of Asian unity and resistance against Western hegemonism and racism. In June, the Nobel laureate Rabindranath Tagore (1861–1941) visited Japan for a second time, and in November Sun Yat-sen paid a final visit to Japan, four months before his death in March 1925. Both had extraordinary charisma and were widely respected throughout Asia. Their relationships with Japan were not without difficulty but there is a general consensus that both were sympathetic to, if also critical about, the Japanese.[93] In 1924, both men, different as they were—the spiritualist poet and the nationalist politician—had a similar message for Japan: that in the conflict between 'the spiritual East' and 'the materialistic West', Japan would be best advised to side with the 'superior civilization of the East'. Tagore's visit came only days after the US Congress had passed the Immigration Act and it should not be surprising that he sympathized with Japanese outrage.[94]

> Japan has now been severely insulted by another country. Not I alone, but all people of India think that this is an insult to all Asian peoples. The materialistic civilization of the West, working hand in hand with its strong nationalism, has reached the height of unreasonableness. But the West will suffocate [from greed] after a short time, and will bow to the great and natural thought of the East.[95]

Quite different from his first visit to Japan in 1916, when Tagore's criticism of Japan's 'Westernization' and 'modernization' had caused mutual estrangement,[96] 1924 brought about a rapprochement between Japan and Tagore. Reacting to the racial exclusion legislation Tagore included Japan again in the list of Asian victims of 'Western' oppression. He did not stop at merely expressing his sympathy with Japan. In an obvious act of reconciliation, Tagore declared the Japanese his 'dear friends' and referred to himself as 'someone who greatly loves Japan'.[97] Tagore's remarks did not fail to receive a warm welcome in Japan and they obviously confirmed the Japanese sense of having been gravely insulted by the United States. But Tagore's potential appeal to Japanese Asianists was limited: his spiritual and civilizational Asianism was difficult to reconcile with the political outlook of many Japanese Asianists. His focus on criticizing materialism and nationalism and his insisting on friendship between 'East' and 'West' based on 'humanistic and virtuous'[98] relations contradicted the logic of more pro-actively and practically minded Asianists to a considerable degree. While calls for resorting to 'Eastern natural thought' may still have appealed to Asianists who discussed 'Asia' theoretically during the 1910s, they missed the overwhelming mood of Asianist conceptions in the mid-1920s, when perceived political provocations from the 'West' had nourished demands for more practical countermeasures. Tagore's warning to the Japanese not to lose their commitment to enhancing 'Eastern spirituality' foreshadowed Sun Yat-sen's message to the Japanese in his Greater Asianism speech in Kobe later that year.

Yet while Tagore remained open to a possible reconciliation between 'East' and 'West', Sun's 'Asia' discourse had by 1924 taken a different direction. More explicitly than anyone else had done, Sun presented the Japanese with an either–or choice which left little space for compromises: either remaining faithful to its original Asian character or joining the despotic 'Western' powers. Of course, this dichotomous choice—reminiscent of the historic *datsu A* (leaving Asia) versus *kō A* (raising Asia) divide from the Meiji period—never corresponded to political reality. As the post-World War One order clearly proved, the decades of Japan's 'modernization' and 'Westernization' after the Meiji Restoration had in fact not led to the hoped-for degree of acknowledgement and the admission to equal status with the 'Western' powers. On the contrary: when—after Japan's war victories and its 'modernization'—arguments of supposed backwardness were difficult to uphold, the 'West' resorted to the ultimate essentialist argument that would indisputably draw a line of separation between Japan and the 'West': race. Despite all the pragmatic deliberations that informed Sun Yat-sen's Kobe speech of 1924, this feeling of discrimination on grounds of race was shared by Sun, as by Tagore, and by many other Asianists (and by non-Asianists too). It is for this reason that Sun's conception of Asianism, which—as we have seen in previous chapters—had always drawn on racialist arguments, in the 1920s centred on race even more prominently.

Sun Yat-Sen's Kobe Speech on Greater Asianism

On 13 November, one day after his fifty-eighth birthday, Sun had boarded a ship in Canton heading for Northern China via Hong Kong and Shanghai. The purpose of his trip was to attend a national convention and to negotiate about national unity with warlord Feng Yuxiang, who had seized Beijing and ejected Wu Peifu's government a month earlier.[99] While his mind must have been absorbed with thoughts of the vicissitudes of the north–south dialogue and the prospects of support from his Soviet and Communist allies ('a marriage of convenience'[100]), he accepted a Japanese invitation to pause in Kobe for several days before moving on to Tianjin. In Tianjin he fell so sick that three weeks later he had to be taken to a hospital in Beijing, where he spent the last ten weeks of his life until he died on 12 March 1925. Sun's cold reception in Shanghai, where he stopped between 17 and 21 November before setting off for Kobe, may have been an important factor in his decision to return to the topic of Asianism during his stay in Japan. After 1919, which is usually seen as the turning point in Sun's perception of Japan from a favourable view to disappointment, Sun had rarely made use of Asianist remarks and, instead, had approached the Soviet Union—a less obvious object of Asianism—as a strategic partner in his struggle for national unity and independence. However, in Shanghai the foreign press declared Sun an 'undesirable person' who should be barred from the city. Sun is reported to have replied that 'as a Chinese citizen I have every right to reside in my own territory' and reminded his 'Western' 'hosts' that actually the Chinese were hosts in Shanghai and that the 'Western' foreigners were the guests.[101] Jansen stresses the sharp contrast of Sun's reception in foreign-controlled Shanghai with that in Japan a few days later, where 'his treatment was that of an honoured guest'.[102]

It should also be noted, however, that Sun did not receive exclusively favourable headlines in the Japanese press prior to his visit to Kobe.[103]

Of course, Sun's visit to Kobe was more than a reunion with old friends. It was highly political in nature and in order to achieve the desired effect—to receive Japanese support for his scheduled negotiations over national unity in Beijing—Sun had taken precautions for his stay. He had sent ahead to Japan a former *Guomindang* general from Jiangxi, Li Liejun (1882–1946), who in October was advised by Sun per telegram to propose an Asian Alliance (Yazhou Datongmeng) and Asianism (Yazhou zhuyi) to the Japanese.[104] In fact, in the following weeks Li repeatedly spoke in interviews with Japanese newspapers about an 'Eastern Union or Asian League' (Dongyang Tongmeng huo Yaxiya lianmeng).[105] But Li obviously failed to inform Sun that, even without his preparatory work, the anti-Western political and intellectual climate in Japan had already turned relatively favourable towards Asianism as a result of the US Immigration Act—although, as we have seen above, this did not necessarily coincide with general approval for proposals for an Asian League. To be sure, the controversy over an adequate reaction to the Immigration Act in general and the usefulness of the concept of Asianism in particular was by no means confined to elevated intellectual circles in Tokyo and highbrow publications there. In fact, it was in Kobe, the port city that had become the permanent or transitory home of a large Chinese community in Japan, where the implications of the law were debated fiercely, too. On 15 June, two and a half weeks after the US Congress had adopted the bill and five and a half months before Sun's historic speech there, the Kobe Newspaper sponsored a 'Great Lecture on Current Events' on the topic of an Asian League (Ajiajin Dōmei).[106] The main speaker was Zhang Youshen (1876–1946),[107] the doyen of overseas Chinese in the Kansai region of Western Japan and leader of various Chinese overseas and business groups since the 1910s. Zhang was courageous enough to explicitly link the recent American exclusion of Japanese to the exclusion of Chinese workers from entry to Japan, a regulation which varied regionally but in general had become stricter in the aftermath of the Great Kantō Earthquake of 1923.[108] According to a newspaper report, Zhang asked his audience:

> Because [Japan] is now suffering from the American exclusion of the coloured people, it promotes the idea that an Alliance of Asians (Ajiajin

dōmei) is necessary, but is it not equally important for Japan to consider the matter concerning the immigration of the Chinese [into Japan]?[109]

In its editorial, the *Kōbe Shinbun* dismissed Zhang's criticism based on the comparison of Japanese and American behaviour. Japan, it argued, suffered from a 'demographic surplus', whereas America had plenty of 'spare capacity' to accommodate foreigners.[110] Therefore, following the paper's rationale, the exclusion of foreigners from Japan and simultaneous Japanese complaints about the exclusion of Japanese abroad did not constitute a logical contradiction. While such arguments for Japanese *Lebensraum* (living space) abroad were not entirely new in their support of Asianist rhetoric—Gotō Shinpei had used a similar logic in his early proposals for the adoption of Asianism as a policy for the cultivation of the Asian mainland by Japanese immigrants (see Chap. 4)—their link with racialist discourse in the aftermath of the Immigration Act of 1924 is rather rare. More frequently, such arguments surfaced and gained prominence in the 1930s and 1940s. Particularly in the case of Manchuria, in combination with the so-called lifeline metaphor, the argument of overpopulation was employed to support proposals for Japanese 'expansion' into the Asian mainland, and, later, into other regions of the Pacific.[111]

At any rate, the controversy that had unfolded prior to Sun's arrival in Japan must have contributed to the fact that the interest in Sun's talk was immense, and hours before its scheduled beginning, thousands were already waiting to be admitted to the auditorium of the Prefectural Secondary School for Girls in Kobe. Sun gave his speech in Chinese, and Dai Jitao, his pupil and follower, translated. The chaotic circumstances of his speech—the room was extremely crowded and hundreds more were waiting in adjacent rooms of the school to listen to or catch a glimpse of the Chinese leader—the fact that his speech was translated, and above all, the fact that Sun did not use a written draft but spoke without notes may have contributed considerably to the diverging reproductions and interpretations of the speech (Fig. 5.2).

Throughout most of his speech[112] Sun in fact praised Japan's achievements vis-à-vis the 'West' and explicitly commended them as models for other Asians. Comparing the present political situation in Asia with that of before the turn of the century (1899), he expressed admiration for Japan's success in its attempt to achieve equal relations with the 'Western' powers by abolishing the so-called Unequal Treaties. 'The very

5 THE RACIALIZATION OF 'ASIA' IN THE POST-VERSAILLES PERIOD

◀ **Fig. 5.2** Sun Yat-sen (front) and his interpreter Dai Jitao during Sun's famous speech on Greater Asianism in Kobe on 28 November 1924. Both photos show the great public interest in his speech. Dai Jitao later became one of the contenders in the contest between different *Guomindang* politicians for representing Sun's Asianism in the most truthful way. Reproduced with kind permission of Hyogo Prefectural Kobe High School

day Japan abolished the Unequal Treaties', Sun claimed, 'was the day of the revival of all our Asian peoples. From this time onwards, Asia's front was formed by an independent country.' Sun continued:

> Since Japan has become an independent country in the East, great hopes have been born among all countries and nations of all of Asia to achieve the same as Japan. Many independence movements have started to escape the oppression and colonization by the Europeans. The thought of becoming the protagonist of Asia has really only emerged within the past thirty years and is extremely optimistic.[113]

Sun went on to compare this present 'optimistic thought' with that of the late nineteenth century, when, according to Sun, Asians had agreed with disappointment that only the European civilization was progressive and therefore the model to follow. This, Sun claimed, had led to the 'extremely pessimistic thought' that 'Asia' always had to follow and imitate the 'West' but could never shake off the European oppression of the Asians. This changed, however, with Japan's 'independence' and even more so after Japan's victory over Russia in 1905. This victory not only gave new hope to each Asian country but also strengthened the sense of Asian brotherhood, as Sun added in a personal anecdote:

> In the year of the outbreak of the Russo-Japanese War, I was in Europe. One day news came that Admiral Togo [Tōgō Heihachirō][114] had defeated the Russian navy, annihilating in the Japan Sea the fleet newly dispatched from Europe to Vladivostok. The population of the whole continent was taken aback. Britain was Japan's Ally, yet most of the British people were painfully surprised. 'Japan's great victory was certainly not for the Whites', they assumed, a belief that comes from the concept of 'Blood is thicker than water', as they say in English. Later on I sailed for Asia. When the steamer passed the Suez Canal a number of natives came to see me. All of them wore smiling faces, and asked me whether I was Japanese. I replied that I was Chinese and inquired what was in their minds, and why they

were so happy. They said they had just heard the news that Japan had completely destroyed the Russian fleet recently dispatched from Europe, and were wondering how true the story was. Some of them, living on both banks of the Canal had witnessed Russian hospital ships, with wounded on board, passing through the Canal from time to time. That was surely proof of the Russian defeat, they added. [...] We [Asians] regarded that Russian defeat by Japan as the defeat of the West by the East. We regarded the Japanese victory as our own victory. It was indeed a happy event.[115]

While this episode certainly worked to flatter many Japanese, it is important to remember that historically Japan was most careful not to have its victory over Russia mistaken as an Asian victory over the 'West'. If the episode was indeed based on facts, it represented a wilful appropriation of Japan's success by peoples in Western Asia that most Japanese would not even have thought of as Asians. By the mid-1920s, at the latest, however, many Japanese would probably have subscribed to the slogan 'blood is thicker than water' in the light of the US immigration legislation. Sun's moderate references to racialist conceptions here became more outspoken during his speech. It was in fact in Kobe that Sun most explicitly defined his conception of Greater Asianism as a combination of (I) the political claim for autonomy, (II) the rejection of 'Western' claims to White supremacy, and (III) the Asian claim to civilizational superiority over the 'West'. In other words, Sun linked Japan's past success (autonomy) with the present dilemma (race) and its future orientation (civilization). To this end, he illustrated the supposed decay of 'Western' civilization by references to 'Western'—above all American—racism. Similarly to the way Asianists in the early 1910s had unmasked the Yellow Peril debate as White Peril reality, Sun now aimed at correcting the supposed revolt of Asian peoples 'against civilization' as the rightful resurrection of (Asian) civilization against (Western) barbarianism. This view, Sun argued, only represented a minority and an extremist opinion in the 'West' but seemed to have borne fruit in the massive and eventually successful campaign that lobbied for the immigration legislation in the US. Referring to the two books by the notorious White supremacist Lothrop Stoddard,[116] Sun complained:

> One American scholar has written a book to discuss the rise of the coloured peoples, where he maintains that Japan's defeat of Russia amounts to a victory of the Yellow race over the White race, and that such a

tendency, if unchecked, will result in the unification of the entire Yellow race, which will be a calamity for the White peoples, and ways and means should therefore be devised to prevent it. Subsequently, he wrote another book in which he described all emancipation movements as revolts against civilization. [...] Now they wish to extend their evil practice to Asia, with a view to suppressing the nine hundred million people of Asia, and treating them as their slaves. This American scholar considers the awakening of the Asiatic peoples as a revolt against civilization. Thus, the Westerners consider themselves as the only ones possessed and worthy of true culture and civilization; other peoples with any culture or independent ideas are considered as barbarians in revolt against civilization. When comparing Occidental with Oriental civilization they only consider their own civilization logical and humanitarian.[117]

From this racialist reasoning, which was a sure-fire argument in Japan in the light of the Immigration Act, it was a short distance to contrasting the 'material Western civilization' that relied on 'aeroplanes, bombs, and cannons' and that represented the rule of Might (Jp. hadō, Ch. badao) on the one hand with 'Eastern morality', 'benevolence, justice and morality' represented by the 'rule of Right' or 'the Kingly Way' (Jp. ōdō, Ch. wangdao).[118] Sun's definition of Asianism therefore relied on this framework set out by the dichotomy of 'East' versus 'West' or *ōdō* (wangdao) versus *hadō* (badao). Indeed, in Sun's conception Asianism *was* the Kingly Way. In other words, to Sun Asianism represented a method and a way of governance or of approaching life and the world. Thus, though not directly, Sun rejected those Japanese Asianists who had proposed the concept in imitation of Western conceptions of regional hegemony. At the same time, Sun's 'Asia' was—in transcendence of Ukita's voluntaristic interpretation—rather abstract and ultimately went beyond geographical or racial boundaries. 'Asia' was the cause of the suppressed peoples and therefore not bound to place or race. Rather, Asia as a geographical term was merely a case study—albeit a very pressing and significant one in 1924. In this sense, Greater Asianism was to restore the status of Asia in order to solve the problem of 'Asia'. In Sun's conclusion these meanings may be understood as overlapping: 'In a word, Asianism represents the cause of the oppressed Asian ['Asian'] peoples.'[119]

Of course, one needs to be careful not to attach too much idealism to Sun's conception of Asianism. In the light of Sun's latest political strategy of forging alliances for the unification of Northern and

Southern China under his leadership, this proposal of an open Asianism that included Russia may not be surprising. From the first contacts between Sun and Soviet Comintern leaders in the early 1920s onwards, Sun had (lacking alternatives) gradually developed closer links with the Comintern. During 1923 the collaboration became even firmer. Eventually, Sun and Adolf Joffe, the negotiator of the Soviet government for the normalization of diplomatic relations with China, agreed on a Joint Statement (Sun–Joffe Joint Statement of Shanghai).[120] However, in the absence of support from other nations, in 1924, when plans for a unification of China seemed to become more concrete, he obviously did not rely on Soviet support too much but instead proposed a tripartite alliance including Russia and Japan. It should be noted that the inclusion of Russia in plans for an Asian alliance sharply contrasts with his previous praise for Japan's victory over 'the European power' Russia, which Sun had elaborated on in so much detail in the anecdote at the beginning of his speech. To his Japanese audience the possibility of befriending Russia under the banner of Asianism was likely to be seen as using oil to extinguish a fire.

Whether Sun in 1924, or for that matter at any point in history, seriously believed in Asianism or only tried to please his Japanese supporters has become a matter of scholarly dispute. Even in the light of his 1924 speech, some scholars insist that Sun was not a supporter of Asianist ideals or policies but 'at best a willing listener'.[121] Indeed, Sun's views of Sino-Japanese cooperation, which were at the core of the concept of Asianism, were complex, contradictory at times, and underwent important changes. While, in 1917, he still continued to employ Asianist rhetoric to call for an alliance between the Chinese and Japanese, by 1919, he had turned his efforts to find support for his cause of national unification further away from Japan to the Soviet Union. However, to conclude that Sun's involvement with Asianism 'was only in response to the Japanese advocacy of it so that he himself might get what he wanted for his revolution in, or reconstruction of, China'[122] appears to be missing two important points. First, as we have seen above, Sun had publicly advocated close Sino-Japanese cooperation under the name of Asianism when 'Western' accommodationism was the political trend of the time in Japan. In fact, Sun had even proposed Asianism as a formula for Sino-Japanese and Asian cooperation some years before the concept had emerged in the Japanese public arena. It appears therefore doubtful that Sun's political agenda, including his advocacy of Asianism, was entirely in reaction to Japanese claims. Second, Sun's influence on the Japanese and Chinese understanding of the concept became so dominant that whether or not he truly held Asianist convictions almost seems to be a minor side note. Sun's 1924 speech alone prompted considerable reactions in Japan's published opinion and, later, became one of the central arguments in the fight over his political and intellectual succession in China (see Chap. 7). His affirmation of the concept as such was more important than his precise conception of Asianism, which left much space for dispute, speculation, and appropriation from various sides.

The controversy that evolved around the reception and interpretation of Sun's Asianism in general and of his Kobe speech in particular is mainly rooted in the existence of at least four different versions of the speech—if one only includes those versions that were published in the first few months after it was given. The first full text of the speech was published in a local Kobe newspaper and was almost identical with the version the *Osaka Mainichi* carried in early December.[123] Interestingly, neither version included what is claimed to be the closing section, as follows:

> The Japanese have already arrived at the Western culture of the Rule of Might (Ōbei no hadō no bunka). But they retain the substance of the Asian Rule of Right (Ajia ōdō). Will Japan from today onwards for the future of the culture of the world become the hunting dog of the Western Rule of Might (Seihō hadō no ryōken) or the bulwark of the Eastern Rule of Right (Tōhō ōdō no kanjō)? This, my Japanese friends, you must thoroughly consider and make one choice.[124]

Ironically, this last part has become best known and according to most scholarship constitutes the essence of Sun's speech. These final sentences were also omitted from the first English translation, which had appeared, in extracts, in the English-language version of the *Osaka Mainichi* on 29 November, two days before the Japanese publication in that newspaper started.[125] Despite the extraordinarily intensive engagement of multinational scholarship with Sun's speech, it is still unclear why the final part was not reproduced in the first reprints of the speech in Japan. Although the fact that this section did appear in the earliest Chinese version, published by the organ of Sun's party, seems to confirm suspicions of Japanese (self-)censorship, a different explanation appears reasonable too. Were the final sentences included by Sun's Chinese party friends, who edited the text to please a Chinese audience, since otherwise, due to Sun's overwhelmingly pro-Japanese references throughout his speech, it might have generated doubts about their leader's critical attitude towards Japan?

Given the fact that Sun's speech has often been condensed to the final part, and given the prominent position that Sun's Asianism speech inhabits in the study of Asianism in general, this question is more than just an interesting detail. Rather, as it will probably never be solved, it points to the blurred relation between historical fact and representation. The fact of whether or not Sun actually said those words and whether the Japanese or the Chinese falsified previous or later versions does not seem to matter any more. What really matters is what is acknowledged as a fact, and what has become 'authentic' through the process of repeated uncritical reproduction. In a different context, Paul Cohen has distinguished the specific uses of history as an event and as a myth to explain how (perceptions of) the past serve(s) the cause of the present, including the present of the past.[126] Marion Dönhoff summarized—and maybe slightly overstated—this phenomenon as 'facts don't play any role in history, decisive are the perceptions that people have of the facts'.[127]

The Reception of Sun's Kobe Speech

With regard to Sun's Asianism speech, the overwhelmingly accepted 'perception of the fact' includes the last section as 'authentic' and, as briefly addressed above, some even go as far as to rest their interpretation of Sun's Asianism solely on it. No matter whether Japanese or Chinese censorship, plain carelessness, or a mistake caused the exclusion of the final sentences in the early publications of the speech, the 'full' version, including Sun's choice for Japan—whether to be a 'Western hunting dog' or an 'Eastern bulwark'—was not withheld from the Japanese audience for long. In January 1925, the left-leaning journal *Kaizō* (Reconstruction) printed a complete translation of the speech, which was not based on the *Yūshin* or *Mainichi* texts but on that which had appeared in the Shanghai-based *Minguo Ribao* (Republican Daily).[128]

Due to the partially contradictory content of Sun's speech, Takatsuna has suggested analysing Sun's idea of Asianism divided into separate dimensions.[129] First, Sun's Asianism as a 'foreign policy strategy' which envisioned the creation of an Asian Union based on a tripartite cooperation between Japan, China, and Russia. Second, Sun's Asianism as a text, or more generally, the reception of his speech as reproduced in Japanese and Chinese media. The audience of his speech in Kobe, if we follow a report that appeared in the *Osaka Mainichi*, reacted euphorically and interrupted Sun's two-hour speech nineteen times for applause, when he either praised Japan (six times), praised Asia (five times), praised China (four times), or criticized the 'West' (four times).[130] Change in Japanese mainstream 'Asia' consciousness from the 1910s through the 1920s—from initial rejection to increasing affirmation—was also reflected in the immediate reception of Sun's speech in contemporary media. The major Japanese national newspapers the *Osaka Mainichi* and the *Tokyo Asahi* dedicated editorials to his speech. In fact, the editorial in the *Osaka Mainichi* was so euphoric about the speech that at first glance it appeared more like a reprint of Sun's speech than an actual journalistic article written on the speech. Under the headline 'The unification of the Asian peoples. The necessity of Japanese–Chinese cooperation' the editorial—in sharp contrast to its reaction a decade earlier in the context of the Mahan–Chirol debate (see Chap. 3)—now enthusiastically confessed to Japan's Asianist mission:

> Asia is the Asia of the Asian peoples. We cannot allow foreign peoples without any relation to Asia to interfere in matters of common interests of all of Asia or that touch issues pertaining to the development of its common civilization. We must insist that Asians themselves deal with the issues of Asia, just as the United States in the name of the Monroe Doctrine dominate the Northern hemisphere. We peoples [of Asia] must under the banner of Greater Asianism stand together and intervene whenever the wellbeing of our Asian comrades is even slightly at stake. [...] To escape from the oppression at the hands of the Euro-American countries, it is our duty towards the home of our Asian peoples to take this opportunity to initiate a serious movement for the unification of the peoples of same race.[131]

As opposed to 1913, Asianism was no longer rendered a dangerous or disadvantageous 'illusion' but represented the legitimate struggle of Asian peoples as against 'Western' imperialism and included Japan's participation.

Yet Sun's Greater Asianism as advanced by him in 1924 on the one hand and Asianism in Japan as it was increasingly embraced by Japanese in the 1920s on the other were not easily compatible. In one of the first essay-long elaborations on Sun's Kobe speech, Nakano Seigō (1886–1943)[132] noted this veritable obstacle in the way of 'Japanese–Chinese cooperation' or even a 'union of Asian peoples' as demanded by the *Osaka Mainichi* editorial: a gap in Asianist perceptions. Nakano, a Waseda graduate from Fukuoka who had studied under Ukita Kazutami, was a member of the Lower House after 1920 for the *Kenseikai* (Constitutional Party) and later for the *Rikken Minseitō* (Constitutional Democratic Party). Initially he was known for his liberal or left-leaning convictions, but today he is primarily remembered as a right-wing propagator or 'populist nationalist'[133] who advocated a strong Japanese stance towards China, the 'Western' powers, and the League of Nations after the Manchurian Incident of 1931. Later, Nakano opposed Tōjō Hideki's regime, was arrested under suspicion of toppling Tōjō's cabinet, and committed suicide after his release from prison. Not lacking a sense of sarcasm, Nakano characterized Sun as someone who was 'not interested in everyday small politics' but wished to dedicate himself to the 'heroic undertaking of fighting the two oppressors of the world, Britain and America'.[134] Referring to Sun's speech, Nakano attested a sharp divide between Japanese and Chinese Asianists:

> The basis of argumentation is completely different between Japanese Asianists and Sun. Japanese Asianists have a tendency to propose a different form of imperialism based on a unification of Asia, a fight of races against the Whites, and resistance against White imperialism with Japan at the centre. Against this, Sun and others aim at staging a liberation war based on internationalist thought and argue for resistance against the White imperialists of Britain and America by first uniting the Asian peoples as victims of White imperialism, and then joining with the victims on the side of the Whites, such as Russia and Germany. Among Japanese Asianists, there are many old-fashioned people. They religiously believe in Asia like a blind man and despise the Whites racially. To calculate things like being on good terms with Russia is what makes them shiver in disgust. Among Chinese anti-Westerners like Sun there are many people of the new type. They do not want to blindly follow Asia as our ultranationalists do but bitterly deplore Asia's unavailing efforts. They do not hate the Whites because they are white but take offence at the repressive system of the Whites. Because they are outraged by economic imperialism, they join as comrades with those who are oppressed among the Whites and aim at destroying White despotism.[135]

Nakano's analysis of Sun's distinctive conception of Asianism as an open and therefore potentially internationalist concept was rather sharp and accurate. Nakano overlooked, however, the fact that, no matter how inclusively Sun may have addressed non-Asians, his conception ultimately centred on Confucian ideals and affirmed essentialist views of Asianity. At the same time, Nakano neglected the fact that in the meantime—in addition to old-fashioned Asianist thinkers and activists of the late Meiji period—in Japan too 'people of the new type' had emerged who embraced a different kind of Asianism. His teacher Ukita Kazutami was but one of them. In this sense, of course, it was impossible to collectively subsume all Asianists of Japan and China under the same agenda. Asianism, as we have seen by now, was too diverse to subsume even Asianists from only one country under one conception. Nevertheless, the general affirmative attitude towards Asianism as a political concept that might challenge 'Western' hegemony and contribute to the decentralization of the world order was shared by an increasing number of thinkers and activists in both countries, including Nakano himself. Nakano in fact praised the practical and open attitude of Chinese Asianists in comparison to the 'old-fashioned' attitude of Japanese Asianists, who, like Tagore, believed in some spiritual essence of 'Asia'. This is why, according to Nakano, Tagore received a rather warm welcome in Japan but was turned away by progressive thinkers in China, who deplored Tagore's abstraction and lack of a practical sense. Curiously, Nakano's sympathetic view of Chinese Asianists and progressives did not lead him to take a favourable view of the Chinese cause for national unification and autonomy. Ultimately, Nakano advocated a proactive Japanese involvement in Chinese matters as part of an Asianist 'grand strategy for co-prosperity' to fight the realization of an 'Anglo-American China' (Ei-Bei no Shina).[136]

For different reasons the leftist Sinophile Tachibana Shiraki (1881–1945) also was critical of Sun's Asianism. Tachibana[137] was one of the *tairiku rōnin* (mainland adventurers) who had moved to Manchuria after the Russo-Japanese War and spent most of his life as a journalist-scholar on the Chinese mainland. He founded his own journal, *Manshū Hyōron* (Manchuria Review), which was simultaneously a platform for journalistic writings, scholarship, and political propagation. After the so-called Manchurian Incident of 1931, under the influence of General Ishiwara Kanji (1889–1949), Tachibana began to advocate Japanese military actions in China but never abandoned his socialist convictions and his

Marxist view of history. Quite different from Nakano, Tachibana mainly identified Sun's Asianism with cultural idealism, not practical flexibility or openness.

> [Sun's] Asianism is theoretically based on the so-called thought of the Kingly Way (ōdō shisō). [...] In short, Sun's Asianism has the meaning of resistance against the White force and as the first principle it emphasizes 'Eastern culture' as opposed to 'Western culture'.[138]

It was exactly Sun's focus on culture and 'benevolence and virtue', which Nakano had largely ignored, that Tachibana dismissed as vague and far from reality. 'In politics', Tachibana argued, 'benevolence and virtue had not only not worked in the West but also in the East there is no example in which it had been realized.' Society based on morality was nothing more than a 'utopia', and indeed a dream shared by all humans. 'Everyone, not only Easterners or Chinese, is therefore an advocate of the Kingly Way', Tachibana claimed. In general, he concluded, in the modern world, there are no prospects for politics based on moral values. Therefore, any form of Asianism based on morality or virtues was bound to fail.[139] Furthermore, Tachibana criticized the vagueness of Sun's cultural claims in connection with the geographical scope of Asianism:

> Does China's so-called Kingly Way have anything in common with Arabian Mohamedism [Islam]? If we look at the issue from this angle, firstly, this thing called Greater Asianism lacks a theoretical and practical foundation. Secondly, even if we regard the weak string that connects the different peoples of Asia geographically or due to the common circumstance of being suppressed, we cannot take the so-called Kingly Way, which is a peculiarity of Chinese culture, as a common factor and unite under this slogan. It is really desirable to eternally reconcile the relations between Japan and China on the basis of a deep motivation but this motivation must be found outside of Greater Asianism or the Kingly Way thought from a direction that is linked with a realistic inclination.[140]

Tachibana's interpretation of Sun's Asianism separated it from its racialist tone and strongly focused on its civilizational discourse. Moreover, Tachibana's view of China differed greatly from Nakano's. As we have seen above, Nakano did not conceal his support for Japanese claims for a stronger foothold in China. Tachibana, however, who had already spent twenty years of his life in China at that time, was much more critical of the attitude of the Japanese. In his critique of Sun's misperception of Japan's willingness to support China's fight for the abolition of the Unequal Treaties, Tachibana confessed:

> It is true that if the Japanese help China to raise her international status, as a result the friendship between both peoples will progress. However, in order to be able to provide such help to China, the Japanese themselves must first abolish their own unequal treaties that they have forced upon China. There are some Japanese who do in fact advocate such a policy but the great majority tend to say that for a frivolous and immoral China that is still tied in traditional and conservative thought we cannot sacrifice even one hair.[141]

It may not always be true that distance helps to see things more clearly, but Tachibana's long stay in China had certainly not reduced his grasp of the public mood in his home country of Japan. Equally appropriate was Tachibana's conclusion that 'from today's viewpoint, we must say that Sun's last attempt[142] at a speech in Japan has for the most part ended in failure'.[143] Indeed, Sun had failed to convince or persuade Japanese leaders of his political agenda. On the other hand, however, while Nakano and Tachibana remained sceptical, his Kobe speech was not only well received by parts of Japanese media but also reaffirmed the domestic significance and transnational character of Asianism discourse in late Taishō Japan. Not least, it attested to the remarkable variety of Asianist conceptions discussed in the mid-1920s, when racialist agendas prevailed. The impact Sun's Greater Asianism would have on political discourse in the following decades (and to this day), at any rate, was still unpredictable when Sun passed away in March 1925.

Conclusion

'Asia' after Versailles was not the same as before. Through heated debate rather than consensus and often as expediency or a mere rhetorical tool rather than principle, 'Asia' as an already established key concept in political discourse in Japan, China, other parts of Asia had taken on racialist dimensions that it would retain through the following two decades. Different from the early 1910s, a greater number of activists and thinkers were now willing to take seriously, discuss, and affirm the concept. During and after the epoch-making World War One Asians increasingly started to embrace 'Asia' as a potentially positive concept which would allow them to self-affirmatively confront their 'Other', 'the Whites of Euro-America' who had dominated vast parts of 'Asia' politically, economically, militarily, and discursively for decades and centuries. After World War One had revealed the deficiencies of the self-declared superior 'Western' civilization—a model that many Japanese in particular had followed and believed in—the Paris Peace Conference once more brought to light the contradictions of rhetoric of peace, equality, and righteousness on the one hand and the power-based and interest-led *Realpolitik* on the other. As expressed in the initial quotation by Ōishi Masami, the rejection of the racial equality proposal at Versailles therefore functioned as a catalyst for the smouldering dissatisfaction with the new, yet in many ways old, post-war *status quo* that continued to relegate 'non-Whites' in general to an inferior position. To the same degree that World War One and the Paris Peace Conference had failed in the eyes of many Asians to mark a new beginning in world affairs, it nourished visions of alternative world and regional orders: 'Asia for the Asians', the key Asianist slogan, combined the two major political ideas of the post-war era—self-determination and internationalism—in an Asianist inflection with the abolition of racial discrimination and the formation of an Asian League as its pursued instantiations. This discourse became even more intense in 1924, when 'Asia' as a racial category became forced upon the Japanese more dramatically even than in 1913. The immigration legislation of 1924, therefore, was a powerful symbolic act that left the Japanese with few alternatives but to accept the foreign-imposed identity as Asians. It is remarkable that, despite this heated climate of Asianist discourse, not a few Japanese repudiated Asianism as a suitable political concept to be adopted by Japan. While some rejected the 'bad company' of other Asians, others were simply sceptical of the strong racialist tendencies that had become part of the Asianist rationale in reply to the double humiliation of Versailles in 1919 and the exclusionist clause of 1924. Together with Sun Yat-sen's appeal to the Japanese to side with 'Asia' (not with the 'West') they remained the most powerful Asianist legacies of the Taishō period for the following decade of Chinese-Japanese Asianism discourse.

Notes

1. 'Shakkin dan kanyū wa fuka' [It's wrong to join the loan group], *Osaka Mainichi* (28 May 1919) and 'Kanyū furi narazu' [Joining the loan group is not disadvantageous], *Tokyo Nichi Nichi* (29 May 1919). Ōishi (1855–1935) had been a participant in the Japanese Movement for Freedom and Civil Rights (Jiyū Minken Undō) of the 1880s and had proclaimed visions of Asian unity since the 1890s. He was a member of the Lower House until 1914 and in the interwar period became a major proponent of Asianism in Japan. Ōishi was also listed as a Counsellor of the All Asia Association, which co-hosted the two All Asian Peoples Conferences in 1926 and 1927 (see below and Chap. 6).
2. See Rana Mitter, *A bitter revolution: China's struggle with the modern world*, Oxford & New York: Oxford University Press 2004 (quotation from page 37).
3. See Naoko Shimazu, *Japan, race*, and equality: the racial equality *proposal of 1919*, New York: Routledge 1998, 183 and Naoko Shimazu, 'The Japanese attempt to secure racial equality in 1919', *Japan Forum* 1-1 (April 1989), 93–100: 93.
4. Shimazu, *Japan, race*, and equality, 183–184.
5. See below. For a more recent discussion of Asianism and the solidarity–invasion dichotomy see Yonetani, *Ajia/Nihon*.
6. See Dick Stegewerns, 'The dilemma of nationalism and internationalism in modern Japan: national interest, Asian brotherhood, international cooperation or world citizenship?', *Nationalism and Internationalism in Imperial Japan: Autonomy, Asian Brotherhood, or World Citizenship?*, ed. Dick Stegewerns, London: Routledge 2003, 3–16.
7. Akira Iriye, 'East Asia and the Emergence of Japan, 1900–1945', *The Oxford History of the Twentieth Century*, ed. Michael Howard and Wm. Roger Louis, Oxford/New York: Oxford University Press, 139–150: 143.
8. Iriye, 'East Asia and the Emergence of Japan, 1900–1945', 143.
9. See Shimazu, *Japan, race*, and equality, 115–116 and Thomas W. Burkman, *Japan and the League of Nations: Empire and world order, 1914–1938*, Honolulu: University of Hawaii Press 2008, 80–86.
10. 'Sabetsu Teppai Sengen' [Declaration of the Abolishment of Discrimination], *Yomiuri Shinbun* (6 February 1919), 3.
11. The *Taikai* and other 'pressure groups' are briefly discussed in Shimazu, *Japan, race, and equality*, 51–52. For an English version of the *Taikai*'s manifesto see Sven Saaler, 'The Kokuryūkai, 1901–1920', *Pan-Asianism: A Documentary History 1860–2010*, Vol. 1, ed. Sven Saaler and C.W.A. Szpilman, Boulder: Rowman & Littlefield, 2011, 121–132:

130–132. Saaler maintains that the *Taikai* was 'one of the many smaller offshoots of the Kokuryūkai' and elsewhere claims that the latter even 'organized' the rally of the *Taikai* on 5 February 1919. See Saaler, 'The Kokuryūkai (Black Dragon Society)', 142. This author has been unable to find any proof for these claims.
12. On Sugita and his earlier Asianist writings see Chap. 3 and the relevant footnotes.
13. They included Soejima Giichi (1866–1947), Ōtake Kan'ichi (1860–1944), Okabe Jirō (1864–1925), Shiba Teikichi (1869–1939), Tanaka Zenryū (1874–1955), Shimada Saburō (1852–1923), Nishimura Tanjirō (1866–1937), Itō Tomoya (1873–1921), and Andō Masazumi (1876–1955).
14. On Paul Richard see Christopher W. A. Szpilman, 'Paul Richard: *To Japan*, 1917, and *The Dawn Over Asia*, 1920', *Pan-Asianism: A Documentary History 1860–2010*, Vol. 1, ed. Sven Saaler and C.W.A. Szpilman, Boulder: Rowman & Littlefield, 2011, 287–295. Quotation from page 289.
15. Paul Richard's speech to the assembly on 22 March 1919, quoted in his 'The Unity of Asia', *The Dawn of Asia*, Madras: Ganesh & Co. 1920, 1–10: 6.
16. See Taraknath Das, *Is Japan a Menace to Asia?* Shanghai (without publisher) 1917 and Benoy Kumar Sarkar, 'The Futurism of Young Asia', *International Journal of Ethics*, 28-4 (July 1918), 521–541. On Indian Asianism see Carolien Stolte and Harald Fischer-Tiné, 'Imagining Asia in India: Nationalism and Internationalism (ca. 1905–1940)', *Comparative Studies in Society and History*, 2012, 54(1), 65–92 and Carolien Stolte, '"Enough of the Great Napoleons!" Raja Mahendra Pratap's Pan-Asian projects (1929–1939)', *Modern Asian Studies*, 2012, 46–2, 403–423.
17. See Chen Duxiu, 'Ouzhan hou Dongyang minzu zhi juewu ji yaoqiu' [The resolution and demands of the Eastern peoples after the European War], *Duxiu Wencun* [Collected Writings of Duxiu], Hongkong: Yuandong tushu gongsi 1965 (1918), 585–588: 586.
18. Chen Duxiu, 'Renzhong chabie daiyu wenti' [The problem of racial discriminatory treatment], *Duxiu Wencun* [Collected Writings of Duxiu], Hongkong: Yuandong tushu gongsi 1965 (1919), 599–600: 600.
19. Li, 'Da Yaxiya zhuyi yu xin Yaxiya zhuyi', 120.
20. Li, 'Da Yaxiya zhuyi yu xin Yaxiya zhuyi', 121.
21. On Takeuchi see *Keiō Gijuku Shusshin Meiryū Redden* [The Lives of Distinguished Graduates of Keiō University], ed. Mita Shōgyō Kenkyūkai [Mita Business Research Society], Tokyo: Jitsugyō no Sekaisha 1910, 375–376. Although Takeuchi contributed a brief essay

(afterword/preface) to Kodera's Asianism book of 1916, Takeuchi's contributions to Asianism discourse have thus far been overlooked by scholarship on Asianism.
22. See Takeuchi Masashi, *Sengo no Nihon oyobi Shina* [Postwar Japan and China], Tokyo: Hakubunkan 1919, 39.
23. Takeuchi, *Sengo no Nihon oyobi Shina*, 40.
24. In his afterword (actually a second preface, before the main text but after a first foreword by Ōkuma Shigenobu), besides his usual rhetoric of 'same script, same race' and a reference to Chinese visions of Sino-Japanese cooperation (Sun Yat-sen), Kodera mentions two interesting points. First, he traces Takeuchi's Asianization to his stay in Europe, where he first realized the 'rampant tyranny of the White race'. Second, Kodera attacks the hypocrisy of the 'Euro-American powers' who claimed 'racial equality' and 'non-discriminatory treatment' but adopted an 'attitude of cold ignorance' when confronted with the demands of the non-Whites for the implementation of these rights in Asia. It appears as if the *Fremdheitserfahrung* abroad, as mentioned above, together with the actual political practice in Asia indeed form the main base for both Kodera's and Takeuchi's embrace of Asianism. Quotations from pages 1–2 of Kodera's afterword ('batsu').
25. Takeuchi, *Sengo no Nihon oyobi Shina*, 42.
26. See Takeuchi, *Sengo no Nihon oyobi Shina*, 42.
27. See Takeuchi, *Sengo no Nihon oyobi Shina*, 51.
28. Takeuchi refers to Dostoyevsky's Russo-centric conception of Pan-Slavism to draw an analogy between the relationship between Japan and China on the one hand and Russia and other Slavs on the other. See Takeuchi, *Sengo no Nihon oyobi Shina*, 49.
29. Takeuchi, *Sengo no Nihon oyobi Shina*, 52.
30. On terminological and conceptual issues regarding the nation in Japan and China see, for Japan, Kevin M. Doak, *A History of Nationalism in Modern Japan*, Leiden: Brill 2007, passim and, for China, Frank Dikötter, 'Culture, "race" and nation: the formation of national identity in twentieth century China', *Journal of International Affairs* 49-2 (1996), 590–605 and, with particular reference to the concept of race, Gotelind Müller, 'Are We "Yellow"? And Who is "Us"?— China's Problems with Glocalising the Concept of "Race" (around 1900)', *Bochumer Jahrbuch zur Ostasienforschung* 32, 2008, 153–180 and Gotelind Müller, 'Glocalizing "Race" in China: Concepts and Contingencies at the Turn of the Twentieth Century', *Racism in the Modern World. Historical Perspectives on Cultural Transfer and Adaptation*, ed. Manfred Berg and Simon Wendt, New York/Oxford: Berghahn 2011, 236–254.

31. 'Han Ajiashugi' [Pan-Asianism], *Atarashii Kotoba no Jibiki* [Dictionary of New Words], ed. Hattori Yoshika and Uehara Rorō, Tokyo: Jitsugyō no Nihonsha 1919, quoted in 'Han Ajiashugi' [Pan-Asianism], *Nihon Kokugo Dai Jiten* [Encyclopaedia of the Japanese Language], Vol. 11, Tokyo: Shōgakkan 1972, 5.
32. See Kodama Kagai, 'Ajia no wakaki koe' [The young voice of Asia], *Taiyō* [The Sun] 25-3 (March 1919), 207.
33. See Yoshino Sakuzō, 'Jinshuteki sabetsu teppai undōsha ni atau' [To the activists for the abolition of racial discrimination], *Chūō Kōron* [Central Review], March 1919.
34. See 'Shōka Manroku' [Essay on Enduring Summer], *Shanghai Nichi Nichi Shinbun*, 24 July 1918, reprinted in *Miyazaki Tōten Zenshū* [Complete Writings of Miyazaki Tōten], vol. 4, ed. Miyazaki Ryūsuke/Onogawa Hidemi, Tokyo: Heibonsha 1973, 330–337: 335 and Yabuta Kenichirō, 'Kenkyū nōto: Miyazaki Tōten no "Ajiashugi" to Daiichiji Sekai Taisen go no Sekai shichō' [Research note: Miyazaki Tōten's 'Asianism' and ideas of a new world order after the First World War], *Dōshisha hōgaku* [Doshisha law review], 48-1 (1996), 277–377.
35. Miyazaki Tōten, 'Tōkyō dayori' [Letter from Tokyo], 1 May 1919, quoted in *Miyazaki Tōten Zenshū* [Complete Writings of Miyazaki Tōten], vol. 2, ed. Miyazaki Ryūsuke/Onogawa Hidemi, Tokyo: Heibonsha 1971, 126–128: 128.
36. This position resembles the thesis of a harmonious coexistence of Eastern and Western civilizations (or 'Harmony of Eastern and Western Civilizations'), which is usually believed to have been particularly influential from the end of the Russo-Japanese War until World War One. For obvious reasons, liberals such as Miyazaki Tōten and Ukita Kazutami (see Chap. 4), who had been attracted by this thesis, proposed Asianist conceptions that were based on the co-existence, not confrontation, of East and West. On this thesis see Kamiya Masashi, '"Tōzai bunmei chōwaron" no mittsu no kata' [Three patterns of the 'Thesis on the Harmony of Eastern and Western Civilization'], *Daitō Hōsei Ronshū*, No. 9 (March 2001), 159–180 and Stegewerns, 2007: 38.
37. Miura Tetsutarō (1874–1972) and Ishibashi Tanzan (1884–1973), both journalists with the liberal *Tōyō Keizai Shinpō* [Far Eastern Economist], belong to the most prominent proponents of 'Small Japanism' (Shō Nihonshugi), a position which called for the (partial) renunciation of Japan's colonial policy. Miura had already proposed this policy in 1913, although Ishibashi is today viewed as the main representative of this position. The terminology 'Small Japanism' may be somewhat misleading but is to be understood as the principle of a small Japan as opposed to that of an expansive imperial Japan ('Greater Japanism'). See Miura

Tetsutarō, 'Dai Nihonshugi ka Shō Nihonshugi ka' [Greater Japanism or Small Japanism], *Tōyō Keizai Shinpō* [Far Eastern Economist], 631–636 (15 April–15 June 1913), reprinted in *Taishō Shisō shū* [Collection of Taishō Thought], Vol. 1, ed. Imai Seiichi, Tokyo: Chikuma Shobō 1978, 65–87 and Ishibashi Tanzan, 'Dai Nihonshugi no gensō' [The illusion of Greater Japanism], *Tōyō keizai shinpō* [Far Eastern Economist], 959–961 (July–August 1926), reprinted in *Taishō Shisō shū* [Collection of Taishō Thought], Vol. 2, ed. Kano Masanao, Tokyo: Chikuma Shobō 1977, 395–406. A similar position was advocated around the same time by the economist and professor at Tokyo Imperial University Yanaihara Tadao (1893–1961). For Yanaihara see Susan C. Townsend, *Yanaihara Tadao and Japanese colonial policy: redeeming empire*, London: Routledge 2000.
38. Anonymous, 'Reisei nare Shinajin' [Calm down, Chinese], *Osaka Mainichi Shinbun*, 6 May 1919, 1. On this editorial see also Nohara Shirō, *Ajia no rekishi to shisō* [Asian history and thought], Tokyo: Kōbundō 1966, 97–98.
39. See Nohara, *Ajia no rekishi to shisō*, 98.
40. See 'Jitsugyō kumiai ketsugi. Jinshu sabetsu teppai' [Resolution of the employers' association. Abolition of racial discrimination], *Osaka Shinpō*, 18 March 1919.
41. See the editorial 'Hai Sabetsu Ron. Shubetsu teppai taikai ni okeru ryō enzetsu' [On Anti-Discrimination. Two speeches at the Assembly for the abolition of racial discrimination], *Tokyo Nichi Nichi*, 26 April 1919.
42. Title of speech by Senator Ellison DuRant Smith before Congress on 9 April 1924, in which he argued that 'we now have sufficient population in our country for us to *shut the door* and to breed up a pure, unadulterated American citizenship'. See *Congressional Record*, 68th Congress, 1st Session (Washington DC: Government Printing Office, 1924), vol. 65, 5961–5962. (http://historymatters.gmu.edu/d/5080).
43. For an account of restrictions on Japanese immigration into the United States and racial discrimination against Asians in the US see Shimazu, *Japan, race, and equality*, 74–78, Mae M. Ngai, 'The Architecture of Race in American Immigration Law: A Reexamination of the Immigration Act of 1924', *The Journal of American History*, 86-1 (1999), 67–92, and, with special reference to California, Roger Daniels, *The Politics of Prejudice. The Anti-Japanese Movement in California and the Struggle for Japanese Exclusion*, New York: Atheneum 1974, in particular 65–105.
44. See Chap. 3 and Mae M. Ngai, 'The Architecture of Race in American Immigration Law: A Reexamination of the Immigration Act of 1924', *The Journal of American History*, 86-1 (1999), 67–92: 80.

45. See Nancy Stalker, 'Suicide, Boycotts and Embracing Tagore: The Japanese Popular Response to the 1924 US Immigration Exclusion Law', *Japanese Studies*, 26-2 (September 2006), 153–170: 153, 167.
46. Yusuke Tsurumi [Tsurumi Yūsuke], *Present Day Japan*. New York: Columbia University Press 1926, 47–48. The following quotation is from a series of lectures Tsurumi gave at Columbia University, New York, in 1926. For further reactions, including Nitobe Inazō's pledge never to set foot in the US again, see also Izumi Hirobe, *Japanese pride, American prejudice: modifying the exclusion clause of the 1924 Immigration Act*. Stanford: Stanford University Press 2001, 1.
47. As the original of his speech was in English, it is difficult to determine which Japanese word Tsurumi may have thought of. While he probably meant Asianism (Ajiashugi), Orientalism (in the pre-Said sense of the word) would more precisely be translated as *Tōyōshugi*. The latter term had occasionally been used in the late 1910s as a synonym of Asianism but had almost disappeared in the following decade.
48. Tsurumi, *Present Day Japan*, 104.
49. Terasaki Hidenari, 'Shōwa Tennō no dokuhaku hachi jikan: Taiheiyō Sensō no zenbō o kataru' [The Shōwa Emperor's eight-hour monologue: Telling the full story of the Pacific War], *Bungei Shunjū*, Vol. 12 (1990), 94–144: 100. This passage constitutes the opening of a monologue by the Emperor as recorded by his close adviser, Terasaki Hidenari, in March 1946. Terasaki's papers were only published after Hirohito's death.
50. On the *Seikyōsha*, the political organization that published the *Nihon oyobi Nihonjin* journal, see Nakanome Tōru, *Seikyōsha no kenkyū* [Research into the Seikyōsha], Kyoto: Shibunkaku 1993 and Satō Yoshimaru, *Meiji Nashonarizumu no kenkyū. Seikyōsha no seiritsu to sono shūhen* [Research into Meiji nationalism. The founding of the Seikyōsha and its environs], Tokyo: Fuyō Shobō 1998.
51. Another notable affirmation of Asianism that—together with Ōishi's essay—physically framed Yin's article and put his criticism in perspective was Gotō Shinpei's 'Ajiashū kisū no ha'aku' [Grasping the pivots of the Asian Continent], *Nihon oyobi Nihonjin* [Japan and the Japanese] 58-5 (October 1924), 17–18, a reprint of an essay that had previously appeared in the Chinese *Minli Bao* in 1912 and in Gotō Shinpei's *Nihon Shokumin Seisaku Ippan* [General Outline of Japan's Colonial Policy] in 1914. See Chap. 4.
52. Ōishi also belongs to those Asianists who have thus far largely been overlooked by scholarship. A notable exception is Furuya, 'Ajiashugi to sono shūhen', 47–102.
53. See Jansen, *The Japanese and Sun Yat-sen*, 84.

54. See Ōishi Masami, 'Tōyō minzoku no tenken' [The divine right of Eastern peoples], *Tōyō Bunka* [Eastern Culture], No. 5 (May 1924), 11–14: 11, 13.
55. See Ōishi, 'Tōyō minzoku no tenken', 12.
56. Ōishi, 'Tōyō minzoku no tenken', 12.
57. Ōishi, 'Tōyō minzoku no tenken', 14.
58. Tsurumi, *Present Day Japan*, 103.
59. See Mae M. Ngai, 'The Architecture of Race in American Immigration Law: A Reexamination of the Immigration Act of 1924', *The Journal of American History*, 86-1 (1999), 67–92: 84 and 'Ozawa v. United States', *The American Journal of International Law*, 17-1 (January 1923), 151–157 for details.
60. Ozawa was not the only person who sued the US for its racial immigration policy. A better known case, turned down with the same argument, is that of the Indian Thind versus United States in the following year (1923). For Thind see Raymond Leslie Buell, 'Some Legal Aspects of the Japanese Question', *The American Journal of International Law*, 17-1 (January 1923), 29–49.
61. The Supreme Court had acknowledged that colour as an indicator of race was insufficient, yet the result of this ruling was that, although all Whites were considered Caucasian, Caucasians were not necessarily considered white. See Ngai, 'The Architecture of Race in American Immigration Law', 67–92.
62. See Ōishi Masami, 'Ajia minzoku no sōdōmei o saku seyo' [Let's plan a general alliance of the Asian peoples], *Taiyō* 30-7 (July 1924), 106–109.
63. See Ōishi, 'Ajia minzoku no sōdōmei o saku seyo', 109. Note the contradiction with his previous terming of the problem as 'Japanese-American'.
64. Ōishi Masami, 'Dai Ajiashugi no kakuritsu' [Establishing Greater Asianism], *Nihon oyobi Nihonjin* [Japan and the Japanese] 58-5 (October 1924), 4.
65. Ōishi, 'Dai Ajiashugi no kakuritsu', 4.
66. Note that Ōishi dropped Shintō from his list, which he had previously included (see above). This reduction was probably intended as an emphasis on the supranational influence of Confucianism and Buddhism and therefore of its potential pan-Asian significance. The previous inclusion of Shintō as a religion with no influence outside of Japan, however, may simply have been a concession to please the nativist-nationalist Hiranuma, in whose journal, *Tōyō Bunka*, Ōishi's first article (May 1924) had appeared.

67. Ozaki Yukio, 'Ajia Renmei ni tsuite. Mazu mizukara naka ni yashinae' [On an Asian League. Let's first cultivate it ourselves], *Nihon oyobi Nihonjin* [Japan and the Japanese] 58-5 (October 1924), 20–22: 22.
68. Fuse Tatsuji, 'Dai Ajiashugi ni tsuite no kansō' [Thoughts on Greater Asianism], *Nihon oyobi Nihonjin* [Japan and the Japanese] 58-5 (October 1924), 139–141: 140. While Ozaki was openly dismissive of Asianism, Fuse, in an almost ironic manner, presented an intentionally naive interpretation of Asianism as meaning that the East had produced important, cosmopolitan figures such as Confucius and Mencius. He felt compelled 'to agree from the heart' with such an interpretation. However, in the form of short additions, he warned that, if Asianism was in fact advocating the use of force against other peoples, he would have to object.
69. Shiga Shigetaka, 'Mikomi naki Ajia Renmei' [Hopeless Asian League], *Nihon oyobi Nihonjin* [Japan and the Japanese] 58-5 (October 1924), 26–30: 26.
70. For Shiga's founding of Japanese nationalism on its geographical characteristics in his masterpiece see Asaba Michiaki, *Nashonarizumu. Meicho de tadoru Nihon shisō nyūmon* [Introduction to Japanese Thought by Masterpieces], Tokyo: Chikuma Shobō 2004, 92–117. For an intellectual evaluation of Shiga in the context of the immigration law of 1924 see Miwa Kimitada, 'Crossroads of Patriotism in Imperial Japan: Shiga Shigetaka, Uchimura Kanzō, and Nitobe Inazō' (PhD dissertation, Princeton University 1967), 385–393.
71. Shiga, 'Mikomi naki Ajia Renmei', 29.
72. Shiga, 'Mikomi naki Ajia Renmei', 29–30. Shiga's beggars are reminiscent of Fukuzawa Yukichi's famous phrasing 'bad friends of East Asia' (Ajia Tōhō no akuyū), in which he, however, counted the Chinese, too.
73. Shiga, 'Mikomi naki Ajia Renmei', 26.
74. See Shiga, 'Mikomi naki Ajia Renmei', 26, 28.
75. See Shiga, 'Mikomi naki Ajia Renmei', 28.
76. Shiga, 'Mikomi naki Ajia Renmei', 28.
77. Shiga, 'Mikomi naki Ajia Renmei', 29.
78. In a stricter sense there are three, not two, foreign contributions. The Korean-born proletarian writer Jeong Yeon-kyu (Tei Zenkei), who contributed the longest of the fifty essays (thirteen pages), had immigrated to Japan in the early 1920s, where he had participated in the Proletarian Literature Movement.
79. Rash Behari Bose, 'Kakumei tojō no Indo' [India at the stage of revolution], *Nihon oyobi Nihonjin* [Japan and the Japanese] 58–5 (October 1924), 190–203: 201.
80. Bose, 'Kakumei tojō no Indo', 201.

81. On Bose in general and his collaboration with Japan in particular, see Nakajima Takeshi, *Nakamuraya no Bōsu. Indo dokuritsu undō to kindai Nihon no Ajiashugi* [Bose of Nakamura's. India's independence movement and modern Japanese Asianism], Tokyo: Hakusuisha 2005 and Eri Hotta, 'Rash Behari Bose and his Japanese Supporters: An Insight into Anti-Colonial Nationalism and Pan-Asianism', *Interventions* 8-2 (2006), 116–32.
82. On Yin's activities in relation to Japan see Kindai Nitchū Kankeishi Nenpyō Henshū Iinkai [Editorial Committee of the Chronological Table of the History of Modern Japanese–Chinese Relations], ed., *Kindai Nitchū Kankeishi Nenpyō 1799–1949* [Chronological Table of the History of Modern Japanese–Chinese Relations 1799–1949], Tokyo: Iwanami 2006, passim.
83. Yin Rugeng, 'Dai Ajiashugi wa nan zo ya' [What is Greater Asianism?], *Nihon oyobi Nihonjin* [Japan and the Japanese] 58-5 (October 1924), 5–16: 5.
84. Yin, 'Dai Ajiashugi wa nan zo ya', 5.
85. Yin, 'Dai Ajiashugi wa nan zo ya', 6.
86. Yin, 'Dai Ajiashugi wa nan zo ya', 6.
87. Yin, 'Dai Ajiashugi wa nan zo ya', 8.
88. Great, here, may either refer to a 'great principle of Asia' or a 'principle of Greater Asia'.
89. Yin, 'Dai Ajiashugi wa nan zo ya', 8.
90. Yin, 'Dai Ajiashugi wa nan zo ya', 13.
91. Yin, 'Dai Ajiashugi wa nan zo ya', 14.
92. Yin, 'Dai Ajiashugi wa nan zo ya', 13.
93. After his third and last visit to Japan, Tagore stated in 1929 that 'my love for Japan is deepening more and more. At the same time, I sincerely hope that Japan will continue to develop the spiritual side of her life' (see Stephen N. Hay, *Asian Ideas of East and West: Tagore and his Critics in Japan, China, and India*, Cambridge, MA: Harvard University Press 1970, 317).
94. While Tagore's anti-Westernism—combined with the fact that he was angered by difficulties in obtaining permission to enter the US prior to his trip to Japan—suggests that he was sincerely sympathetic to Japan, Stalker claims that he had kept his reservations about the Japanese and only paid lip service to them in 1924 because he was fundraising for a school he had newly set up in India. See Stalker, 'Suicide, Boycotts and Embracing Tagore', 165.
95. Tagore in the Tokyo's *Nichi-Nichi Shinbun* (11 June 1924), quoted in Hay, *Asian Ideas of East and West*, 316.

96. After his first visit to Japan in 1916, Tagore is said to have been frustrated by the cold reception he had received. On the different reception of his 1916 and 1924 visits see Hay, *Asian Ideas of East and West* and Stalker, 'Suicide, Boycotts and Embracing Tagore', 153–170.
97. See 'Jūteki na ban kōi. Zen Ajia e no dai bujoku' [Bestial behaviour of barbarians. Great insult to all of Asia], *Tokyo Asahi Shinbun*, 26 April 1924, 2.
98. 'Jūteki na ban kōi. Zen Ajia e no dai bujoku', 2.
99. For the domestic development leading up to Sun's trip to Kobe see Marie-Claire Bergere, *Sun Yat-sen*, translated from the French by Janet Lloyd, Stanford: Stanford University Press 1998, 395–398. The most important work to consult on Sun's Asianism with a particular focus on his Kobe speech is *Son Bun Kōen 'Dai Ajiashugi' shiryōshū* [Collection of materials of Sun Yat-sen's 'Greater Asianism' speech], ed. Chin Tokujin and Yasui Sankichi, Kyoto: Hōritsu Bunkasha 1989.
100. Roger H. Brown, 'Sun Yat-sen: "Pan-Asianism", 1924', *Pan-Asianism: A Documentary History 1860–2010*, Vol. 2, ed. Sven Saaler and Christopher W.A. Szpilman, Boulder: Rowman & Littlefield 2011, 75–85.
101. See Bergere, *Sun Yat-sen*, 402.
102. Jansen, *The Japanese and Sun Yat-sen*, 210.
103. The *Osaka Mainichi*, for example, called Sun a radicalist and one Kobe newspaper named him an extreme opportunist and an untrustworthy, careless politician. See *Son Bun Kōen 'Dai Ajiashugi' shiryōshū*, 11.
104. See Sun Yat-sen, 'Dao Li Liejun dian' [Telegram to Li Liejun] (13 October 1924), *Sun Zhongshan Quanji* [Complete Writings of Sun Yat-sen], ed. Guangdong sheng Shehui Kexueyuan Lishi Yanjiusuo et al., Beijing: Zhonghua Shuju 1986, Vol. 11, 180 and Bergere, *Sun Yat-sen*, 403.
105. See Li Liejun 'Yu Riben "Mensi Bao" jizhe de tanhua' [Conversation with journalists from the Japanese 'Mensi' (Moji Shinpō) newspaper] (11 November 1924), *Li Liejun Ji. Shang* [Collected Writings of Li Liejun, Vol. 1], ed. Zhou Yuangao et al., Beijing: Zhonghua Shuju 1996, 550–551: 551.
106. See *Son Bun Kōen 'Dai Ajiashugi' shiryōshū*, 8–9.
107. For Zhang see Jiang Haibo, 'Ōsaka Kakyō Zhang Youshen ni kan suru kisoteki kenkyū' [Basic research on the overseas Chinese Zhang Youshen], presentation at the 6th Seminar at the Mukogawa Kansai Culture Research Center, November 2004; see http://mkcr.jp/archive/041111.html (last accessed 16 October 2016).
108. See *Son Bun Kōen 'Dai Ajiashugi' shiryōshū*, 9.
109. See *Son Bun Kōen 'Dai Ajiashugi' shiryōshū*, 9.

110. See *Son Bun Kōen 'Dai Ajiashugi' shiryōshū*, 9.
111. For the development of the *Lebensraum* concept in interwar Japan, see Li Narangoa, 'Japanese Geopolitics and the Mongol Lands, 1915–1945', *European Journal of East Asian Studies*, Vol. 3, No. 1 (2004), 45–68.
112. In the following discussion, for the sake of convenience, I will – with one exception – use the most widely circulated English translation provided in the semi-official English version published as 'Pan-Asianism', *China and Japan: Natural Friends, Unnatural Enemies*, ed. Tang Liangli, Shanghai: China United Press 1941, 141–151. Where references to the Japanese version appear appropriate, I will refer to that published in *Kaizō* in 1925. This version was probably most widely known in contemporary Japan as it was reprinted several times, for example, in the *Nihon Hyōron* in 1939. It also appeared, with marginal alterations, in several Japanese versions of Sun Yat-sen's collected writings published in pre-war, wartime, and post-war Japan; see Son Bun, 'Dai Ajiashugi no igi to Nisshi shinzen no yui'itsu saku' [The significance of Greater Asianism and the singular policy of Japanese–Chinese friendship], *Kaizō* [Reconstruction] (January 1925), 213–228. It should be noted that *China and Japan: Natural Friends, Unnatural Enemies* was a collaborationist publication intended to support Wang Jingwei's pro-Japanese regime and that its selection of articles and speeches is to be read with this political context in mind.
113. Sun Yat-sen, 'Pan-Asianism', *China and Japan*, 142 and Son Bun, 'Dai Ajiashugi no igi to Nisshi shinzen no yui'itsu saku' [The significance of Greater Asianism and the singular policy of Japanese–Chinese friendship], *Kaizō* [Reconstruction] (January 1925), 213–228: 215.
114. According to Esenbel, in honour of Admiral Tōgō Heihachirō's contribution to Japan's victory, the Turkish nationalist feminist, Halide Edip, 'like many other women, named her son Togo'; for this and more references to the jubilant reception of Japan's defeat of Russia among Muslims see Selcuk Esenbel, 'Japan's Global Claim to Asia and the World of Islam: Transnational Nationalism and World Power, 1900–1945', *The American Historical Review*, 109-4 (2004), 1140–1170: 1140.
115. 'Pan-Asianism', *China and Japan*, 143.
116. Sun referred to Lothrop Stoddard's *The Rising Tide of Color*, New York: Charles Scribner's Sons 1920 and his *The Revolt against Civilization*, New York: Charles Scribner's Sons 1922.
117. See 'Pan-Asianism', *China and Japan*, 144–145.
118. See 'Pan-Asianism', *China and Japan*, 145–146.

5 THE RACIALIZATION OF 'ASIA' IN THE POST-VERSAILLES PERIOD   225

119. In fact, Sun emphasized the inclusive view of 'Asia' as open to non-Asian 'oppressed peoples': 'even in Great Britain and America', the two Western countries Sun knew best, 'there are people who advocate the principles of benevolence and justice', he claimed. Sun maintained that only a minority there, 'the privileged classes in Europe and America', who oppressed the majority, viewed the independence movements of Asia as 'revolts against culture'. By Asianist standards, this concession of the existence of a non-monolithic, maybe even by majority friendly, 'West' constituted a rarity. See *China and Japan*.
120. See Bergere, *Sun Yat-sen*, 305–311.
121. See J. Y. Wong, 'Sun Yatsen and Pan-Asianism', *Aspects of Pan-Asianism*, ed. Janet Hunter, London: Suntory Toyota International Centre for Economics and Related Disciplines, London School of Economics and Political Science 1987, 17–32: 19.
122. Wong, 'Sun Yatsen and Pan-Asianism', 27.
123. It was first serialized from 29 November to 1 December in the daily *Kōbe Yūshin Nippō* under the title 'Dai Ajiashugi. Son Bun shi kōen' [Greater Asianism. Speech by Mr. Sun Yat-sen]; for the *Osaka Mainichi* text and an explanation of the different versions see *Son Bun Kōen 'Dai Ajiashugi' shiryōshū*, 42–54.
124. Son Bun, 'Dai Ajiashugi no igi to Nisshi shinzen no yui'itsu saku', 223. In the earliest Chinese version the oppositions are rendered as 'Ouzhou badao de wenhua' (European culture of Rule of Might) *versus* 'Yazhou wangdao' (Asian Rule of Right) and 'Xifang badao de yingquan' (hunting dog of Western Rule of Might) *versus* 'Dongfang wangdao de gancheng' (bulwark of the Eastern Rule of Right); see 'Sun xiansheng "Da Yazhou zhuyi" yanshuo ci' [Text of Dr. Sun's speech on Greater Asianism], *Minguo Ribao* [Republican Daily] (Shanghai), 8 December 1924 as reprinted in *Son Bun Kōen 'Dai Ajiashugi' shiryōshū*, 65.
125. See Jansen, *The Japanese and Sun Yat-sen*, 211 and 264.
126. See Paul A. Cohen, *History in Three Keys. The Boxers as Event, Experience, and Myth*. New York: Columbia University Press 1997, xii. Cohen's 'keys' comprise of event, myth, and experience, the last of which seems of less relevance in this context here.
127. Marion Gräfin Dönhoff, 'Wandel der Wahrheit. Wie Nationen sich ihre Geschichte schreiben' [Changes of Truth. How nations write their histories], *Die Zeit*, No. 45 (31 October 1997), http://www.zeit.de/1997/45/Wandel_der_Wahrheit (last accessed 16 October 2016).
128. Both pairs, the *Kaizō/Minguo Ribao* versions and the *Yūshin/Mainichi* versions, contained further but minor differences which were mostly of a factual nature. See *Son Bun Kōen 'Dai Ajiashugi' shiryōshū*, 42–54.

129. See Takatsuna Hirofumi, 'Nitchū kankeishi ni okeru Son Bun no Dai Ajiashugi. Senzen hen' [Sun Yat-sen's Greater Asianism within the history of Japanese–Chinese relations. Pre-war section], *Chikaki ni arite* [Being Nearby], 32 (November 1997), 58–78: 58–60. Takatsuna suggests three dimensions: foreign strategy, speech, and text. As the speech as such did not have an impact nearly as far-reaching as the published text, the second dimension is neglected here and rather incorporated into the third (text), that is, the reception of the speech.
130. See *Son Bun Kōen 'Dai Ajiashugi' shiryōshū*, 10. For the reprint of Sun's speech in the *Osaka Mainichi* see *Son Bun Kōen 'Dai Ajiashugi' shiryōshū*, 44–53.
131. 'Ajia minzoku no danketsu. Nisshi teikei no hitsuyō' [The unification of the Asian peoples. The necessity of Japanese–Chinese cooperation], *Osaka Mainichi* (2 December 1924), reprinted in *Son Bun Kōen 'Dai Ajiashugi' shiryōshū*, 139–141.
132. For a political biography of Nakano see Leslie Russell Oates, *Populist nationalism in prewar Japan: a biography of Nakano Seigo*, Sydney & London: Allen & Unwin 1985.
133. Aydin, *The politics of anti-Westernism in Asia*, 243.
134. Nakano Seigō, 'Son Bun-kun no kyorai to Ajia undō' [Mr. Sun Yat-sen's passing through and the Asia movement], *Gakan* [My View], 7 (January 1925), 112–117: 112. The text was published under Nakano's pen name Nijūrokuhō Gaishi (Unofficial History of twenty-six mountains).
135. Nakano, 'Son Bun-kun no kyorai to Ajia undō', 112–113.
136. Nakano, 'Son Bun-kun no kyorai to Ajia undō', 117.
137. For a political biography of Tachibana see Yamamoto Hideo, *Tachibana Shiraki to Chūgoku* [Tachibana Shiraki and China], Tokyo: Keisō Shobō 1990; in English see Hideo Yamamoto, 'Profile of Asian Minded Man III: Shiraki Tachibana', *The Developing Economies*, 4–3 (September 1966), 381–383. For Tachibana's view on Asianism see Nomura Kōichi, 'Tachibana Shiraki. Ajiashugi no hōkō' [Tachibana Shiraki. Roamings of Asianism], *Rikkyō Hōgaku* 19 (1980), 36–116 and Ri Saika, 'Tachibana Shiraki no Ajiashugi. Manshū Jihen ikō no gensetsu o chūshin ni' [Tachibana Shiraki's Asianism. Focusing on the discourse after the Manchurian Incident], *Nenpō Nihon Shisōshi* [Annual of Japanese intellectual history], 9 (March 2010), 1–13. Lincoln Li's judgement, according to which Tachibana was a 'fascist', is difficult to uphold, while Louise Young's characterization of Tachibana as a 'Sinologist' and a 'genuine *tenkōsha*' appears misleading. In fact, as Tanaka rightly points out, Tachibana's views were closer to that of the socialist Sinophile Ozaki Hotsumi, even after Tachibana's 'hōkō tenkan' (conversion as

regards the political course, not cause). See Louise Young, *Japan's total empire: Manchuria and the culture of wartime imperialism*, Berkeley: University of California Press 1998, 276, Lincoln Li, *The China Factor in Modern Japanese Thought: The Case of Tachibana Shiraki, 1881–1945*, Albany: State University of New York Press 1996, and Tanaka, *Japan's Orient*, 191 and 219–225.

138. Tachibana Shiraki, 'Son Bun no Tōyō bunka kan oyobi Nihonkan' [Sun Yat-sen's views of Eastern culture and of Japan], *Gekkan Shina Kenkyū* [China Research Monthly], 1–4 (March 1925), reprinted in and quoted in *Tachibana Shiraki Chosakushū*, ed. Tachibana Shiraki Chosakushū kankō iinkai, Tokyo: Keisō Shobō 1966, Vol. 1, 360–399: 381.
139. See Tachibana, 'Son Bun no Tōyō bunka kan oyobi Nihonkan', 383–384.
140. Tachibana, 'Son Bun no Tōyō bunka kan oyobi Nihonkan', 391.
141. Tachibana, 'Son Bun no Tōyō bunka kan oyobi Nihonkan', 394.
142. Sun was still alive for another month when Tachibana finished this essay (10 February 1925) but he correctly predicted that Sun would die from his incurable disease before he had a chance to return to Japan again.
143. Tachibana, 'Son Bun no Tōyō bunka kan oyobi Nihonkan', 399.

CHAPTER 6

The Regionalization of 'Asia': Asianism from Below and Its Failure

> *Because the question of whether in the future a Pan-Asia consisting of Japan and China will be established and of whether the League of Nations can be reorganized are critical, research into Pan-Asia has now been separated from the scope of documentary studies and has become a matter of real politics.*[1]
> —Nagatomi Morinosuke (March 1925)

While the regionalization of 'Asia' in Japan and China in the sense of defining the geographical location of Asia and linking this location with political claims has a longer tradition,[2] from the mid-1920s a different kind of regionalization of 'Asia' started. Through pan-Asian conferences (1926 and 1927) that assembled activists from various parts of Asia attempts were made to regionalize Asianist ideas. This regionalization was a two-fold enterprise. On the one hand, through various practical projects it aimed at spreading a sense of Asian commonality throughout different parts of the Asian continent and the East Asian maritime regions: regionalizing 'Asia' meant that ideas of 'Asia' were sent to its regions. On the other hand, the conferences aimed at institutionalizing a common body that (more or less) represented Asia, both vis-à-vis other world regions and vis-à-vis the nation states within Asia: regionalizing 'Asia' here meant constituting Asia as a tangible and institutionally definable region. As regards the content and main rationale behind Asianist conceptions articulated during the conferences, racialist ideas remained forceful, since the racialist debates that had prominently resurfaced after the so-called

© The Author(s) 2018
T. Weber, *Embracing 'Asia' in China and Japan*,
Palgrave Macmillan Transnational History Series,
https://doi.org/10.1007/978-3-319-65154-5_6

anti-Japanese immigration legislation of 1924 provided the main stimulus to the organizers of the conferences. Yet in response to and rejection of the racialist seizure of Asianism in the first half of the 1920s, alternative conceptions of Asianism emerged in growing numbers. Most of these conceptions emphasized pragmatic aspects of Asian commonality and frequently envisioned a non-racialist regional order based on geopolitical views. Regionalizing 'Asia' for these proponents meant a simultaneous deracialization and rationalizing of (the idea of) 'Asia' as (a region called) Asia. Asianism as a political concept managed to appeal to both extremes of conceptualizations, which—in Terence Ball's historical analysis of the general functions of political concepts—may be seen as representing the opposition of appealing to the 'heart' (essentialist, racialist conceptions) and to the 'mind' (existentialist, geopolitical conceptions).[3] Or, according to Victor Koschmann's distinction, they may be seen as representing 'the rationalist extreme of Pan-Asianism' as opposed to 'highly intuitive, naturalistic, or culturalist visions of Asia'.[4] While such rationalist conceptions of Asianism are most prominently linked with the debate on an 'East Asian Community' (Tōa Kyōdōtai ron) and, in particular, with Rōyama Masamichi's writings of the early 1930s, this geopolitical focus was anticipated by Nagatomi Morinosuke and others in the context of the emergence and spread of pan-movements in the mid- and late 1920s.

Apart from triggering a new stream of pro-Asianist discourse that countered the predominant racialist trend, the Asianist moment of 1926/1927 is also noteworthy for its practical supplementation—in continuation of the *Taikai*'s short-lived activities—of the hitherto rather theoretical elaborations on 'Asia'. The Pan-Asian Conferences of 1926 and 1927 marked the peak of non-governmental, transnational Asianist activity in the twentieth century—and simultaneously signalled its premature end. These abortive efforts represent a unique transnational search for a way of implementing regional institutions in Asia to promote a decentralized non- (and mostly anti-) Western world order. The frustrated outcome of the Nagasaki conference of 1926, the collapse of the Shanghai conference in 1927, and the failure to continue the series of conferences after 1927 marked the defeat of civil society attempts to employ Asianism as a common denominator for peoples in Asia against the tides of nationalist and imperialist antagonisms. This failure of Asianism from below paved the way for the gradual appropriation of Asianism from above which openly emerged step by step in the early 1930s, first in Japan and later in collaborationist China.

This chapter analyses how and why Asianism in the second half of the 1920s was linked with attempts at practical implementation of an alternative regional order against the Western-centric and nationalist domination of global affairs and how rationalist conceptions of Asianism responded to the predominance of racialist conceptions during the 1920s.

THE PAN-ASIAN CONFERENCES

The Formation of the Zen Ajia Kyōkai

Unlike the infamous 'Greater East Asia Conference' (Dai Tōa Kaigi) held in 1943 in Tokyo at the invitation of the Japanese government together with collaborative governments in East Asia,[5] its non-governmental predecessors, the Pan-Asian Conferences of 1926 and 1927, have not become a lasting part of Asian consciousness of 'Asia'. Whereas the 1943 Assembly is relatively easy to unmask as quasi-Asianist political theatre staged to distract from un-Asianist political reality in the so-called Greater East Asian Co-Prosperity Sphere, the Nagasaki and Shanghai Conferences are complex and difficult to appraise. They could easily be dismissed as representing Japanese imperialist ambitions dressed in the garb of transnational cooperation and solidarity, not too differently from the Tokyo Assembly of 1943. But how then can we account for the controversial debates during the gatherings, the willingness to accept and include dissonances, and the official state efforts at preventing and even closing the conferences? How do we account for the fact that, despite police and government repression and despite the limited achievements of the first conference, participants from several countries made the effort to convene a second conference?

In the aftermath of the so-called anti-Japanese immigration legislation racialist conceptions triggered a new phase of intense Asianism discourse. On the surface this debate was about race. The underlying rationale, however, for many debaters transcended matters of racial discrimination and racial equality. Instead, race was only an instance of the imbalance of political, economic, and epistemological power between the 'Whites' and 'Yellow', between the 'West' and 'Asia', and more generally between the privileged and the underprivileged. As many contributors to the *Nihon oyobi Nihonjin* special issue of 1924 had made clear, they expected

Asianism to represent more than just a political or economic alliance between Japan and China. Tagore and Sun Yat-sen, too, had revealed an understanding of 'Asia' that only started from reacting to the 'tyrannical behaviour of the Whites' but moved on to encourage the Japanese to abandon their pro-Western stance to fight for the liberation of oppressed peoples in general.[6] The envisioned 'Great Alliance of the Asian Peoples' was not to be limited to people of yellow skin. On the contrary, it included all people who suffered from discrimination and inequality. 'Western' ideals of humanism, virtue, and civilization were not rejected per se but, on the contrary, also appealed to Asianist Asians. Therefore, Asianist anti-Westernism based on an irreconcilable 'East' versus 'West' dichotomy remained but one facet of Asianism. Rather than assuming or even promoting a strict and eternal 'West'–'East' dichotomy, many Asianists in the interwar period in fact attempted to overcome this polarity by combining an affirmative stance towards 'Western' ideals and a self-affirmative stance as Asians. It was 'Asia', however defined, that had to remind the 'West' of the universality of its own values[7]; irrespective of its substantive or regional definition, 'Asia' now mattered as a concept representing the righteous demand for equality, freedom, and peace. According to Asianist logic, the task of improving the general conditions in the world, put on the agenda under Wilson's leadership at Versailles, had now fallen to the Asians—as Asian peoples, not governments. But how could this transformation be initiated?

Against the given political background, there was little need to agitate public opinion any further and Asianists found it easier than ever to channel public outrage into Asianist straits. As their argumentation had increasingly become self-explanatory in the light of continuous racial discrimination, Asianists in Japan now turned from theoretical and propagandistic work to more practical steps towards the creation of a common forum for discussing and implementing Asianist policies with the eventual aim of creating an Asian League of Nations. In 1924, at the height of public anger over the American racial exclusion legislation, the *Zen Ajia Kyōkai* (All Asia Association) was founded in Tokyo.[8] Its self-declared aims were 'to strive for the development of freedom based on the equality of all human beings'. Asia's particular role in this project was explained as follows:

> We have founded the All Asia Association to promote the awakening of the Asians of our generation who are the grandchildren of the Asian race that

possessed a high civilization already some thousand years ago and which constitutes the basis of modern culture. We must nourish the capability to act as one in order to prevent a future clash of races. Moreover, we must plan the reconciliation of the Oriental and Occidental civilizations and work towards the establishment of a new global civilization.[9]

The functions ascribed to 'Asia' reveal the Association's concern with more than just racial or regional matters. It saw itself not only as a platform for the awakening of Asians but also aimed at reconciling 'East' and 'West' to establish 'a new global civilization'. The mission statement skipped elaborations of the substance of 'Asia' in favour of its potential functions for the improvement of the contemporary world *in toto*. Also, the reminder of Asia's past civilizational status may be viewed as an indirect acknowledgement of the achievements of modern 'Western' civilization—the scale against which achievements were to be measured. The rhetorical construction of a confrontational opposition of 'West' and 'East' therefore hardly fell into the range of the Association's aims. On the contrary, it affirmed 'modernity' in general while criticizing the gap between universal values created in the 'West' and hailed in Paris on the one hand and the exclusion of non-Whites from these values on the other. Therefore, the Association did not reject 'modernity' as such but rather aimed at replacing its perceived corruptness by a 'new global civilization'. According to Asianist logic, this task fell to 'Asia' because of the civilizational achievements of Asians in the past and the deficiency of 'Western' civilization in the present, which World War One and subsequent racial exclusionism had brought to light. Different from earlier (and later) conceptions of Asianism that displayed more aggressive and revanchist stances,[10] 'Asia' as envisioned by the Association was not to conquer and colonize the 'West' in revenge by force. Its self-declared aim was rather to improve the general conditions of the entire world within a framework of decolonization and decentralization. To this end, naturally, the tone of its founding manifesto was not outspokenly anti-Western. Although anti-colonial Asianist rhetoric generally drew much on anti-Westernism, the Association as well as its transnational activities put emphasis on reconciliation and harmony between 'East' and 'West' rather than on confrontation. The difference between their and the Japanese government's conciliatory position towards the 'West', however, lay in the Association's affirmative and inclusive view of 'Asia'; it affirmed Asia's existence and significance and, according to its conception of 'Asia', the imperial power Japan was to be an important and active part of this 'Asia'.

Similar to the *Taikai*, the Association's membership consisted of politicians, entrepreneurs, academics, and writers of limited prom inence. Some members of the defunct *Taikai* in fact later became members of the All Asia Association.[11] Initially it was led by Iwasaki Isao (1878–1927), a lawyer from Shizuoka who had been a member of the Lower House since 1912 and later became the secretary general of the centre-right *Rikken Seiyūkai* (Friends of Constitutional Government) party. Imazato Juntarō,[12] a minor political figure from the same party and member of the Lower House from 1924 to 1928, functioned as the Association's main spokesman and managing director. Both in parliament and in the press, Imazato was known as a pro-Chinese Asianist who was highly critical of Japanese government policies towards China. In July 1924, he had enquired about the government's position in the racial equality matter and linked this question with the reform of Sino-Japanese treaties and the formation of a Japanese-Chinese alliance (Nisshi dōmei) 'as a precise policy towards Japanese–Chinese friendship'. In his reply, foreign minister Shidehara Kijūrō (1872–1951), himself a dove rather than a hawk in questions of Japan's policy towards China, rejected Imazato's Asianist views. Shidehara explained that, although the government believed that China and Japan were tied by 'special relations', it believed it was necessary to keep the policy of 'conciliation with the great powers' and did 'not intend to reform or abolish any parts of Sino-Japanese treaties or pursue a Sino-Japanese alliance'.[13] Despite the notably pro-Asianist shift in published opinion, official Japanese policy, even after the Washington Conference of 1921/1922 and the termination of the Anglo-Japanese Alliance in 1922, remained carefully distant from Asianist positions and continued to prefer a pro-Western stance.

Different from the somewhat Japan-centred *Taikai* and contrary to later pan-Asian organizations active in the 1930s,[14] the Association actively sought cooperation with existing Asianist groups and activists outside Japan. To this end, it sent Imazato to Beijing, where a Great Alliance of Asian Peoples (Yaxiya Minzu Da Tongmeng) had been established in August 1925.[15] The Alliance had been founded in response to the May Thirtieth Movement of 1925, which itself was a reaction to the British-led crushing of anti-imperialist Chinese demonstrations in Shanghai. Originally these demonstrations had been caused by the killing of a Chinese worker by Japanese guards and therefore not only bore an anti-imperialist but also an anti-Japanese dimension. Under the leadership of some low-ranking officials[16] of the Nationalist Party (Guomindang) of Sun Yat-sen, who had died in March, academics, journalists, and entrepreneurs from China, Japan, Korea, and India had organized this transnational organization 'to resist the countries that practise imperialism in Asia and to attain the aim of freedom and equality of all peoples'.[17] The Japanese members gave a special declaration in which they explained their motivation for participating. 'The Japanese government', it read, 'is imperialist but we oppose imperialists and completely agree with the aims of this organization'.[18] The declaration and the transnational character of the organization obviously aimed at breaking away from the national(ist) paradigm which ran counter to the Asianist and anti-imperialist agenda of the Alliance.

The First Pan-Asian Conference in Nagasaki (1926)

After several meetings in China and Japan, the Japanese Association and the Chinese Alliance joined hands to prepare an All Asian Peoples' Congress (Jp. Zen Ajia Minzoku Kaigi, Ch. Quan Yaxiya Minzu Huiyi), also known as the Pan-Asiatic or Pan-Asian Conference, originally planned to be held in Shanghai or Tokyo in the spring of 1926. Its aims were to establish 'true international everlasting peace based on equality and righteousness', the 'promotion of freedom and happiness by abolishing class, racial, and religious discrimination', and the 'organization of an All Asian League' (Zen Ajia Renmei).[19]

Despite the Association's moderate and reconciliatory tone, which sometimes even resembled official Japanese diplomatic rhetoric of 'international accomodationism',[20] the Japanese Interior Ministry as well as several diplomatic missions of Japan abroad closely watched the activities of the Association and the preparations for the Congress.[21] Fearing that the assembly might be dissolved prematurely by the authorities, the originally planned locations of Shanghai or Tokyo were abandoned and replaced by Nagasaki, a port city far away from the capital in southern Japan. Contemporary press reports mention interference from foreign authorities, which were presumably concerned about the prospect of anti-foreign agitation by Indian revolutionaries and others at the site of recent violent protests (Shanghai) or in the Japanese capital, if the conference were hosted there. At any rate, this oppositional attitude was shared by Japanese officials.[22] While the foreign ministry cabled dismissive comments on the gathering to foreign diplomatic missions abroad and delayed the issuing of visas for participants in the Congress who it preferred not to enter Japan, the Interior ministry sent surveillance staff to Nagasaki, who reported in detail about the assembly.[23]

The delegates for the largest pan-Asian political gathering in history thus far had been recruited through the Japanese and Chinese host organizations and included fifteen Japanese, eleven Chinese, four Indians, four Filipinos, three Koreans,[24] one Afghani, and one Vietnamese. The most prominent of them, the Indian revolutionary Rash Behari Bose, who had lived in exile in Japan for more than a decade, was to play a significant role as mediator between conflicting interests, above all between Japanese and Chinese participants. In his opening address, Bose explained why the assembly was aiming at the creation of an Asian League.

> Some people may ask why we should create an Asian League as there already is an International League [of Nations]. But those two differ profoundly. The League of Nations was created for 500 million people, however, the Asian League will be made for 1500 million coloured people. [...] We must not only unite to give birth to a new Asian civilization but also to give birth to a new civilization. Ultimately, this is not only for the good of the Asian peoples but to save the unfortunate human race globally.[25]

Both points raised by Bose reveal the lasting impact of 1919 on Asianist political discourse. While agreeing in principle to the organization of an international league—as planned in Versailles and established in Geneva—it criticized the neglect of Asian concerns. Similarly, it agreed to the high-flying ideals of eternal peace and happiness of the human race enunciated at Paris but attributed the task of their realization to 'Asia', not the 'West'. The legacy of Versailles was also prominently reflected in the Provisional Constitution adopted by the Congress. Article One defined the object of the proposed Asian League as bringing 'permanent peace to the world, based on the principle of equality and justice, eliminating all discrimination, whether social, religious, or racial, and thus to assure liberty and happiness to all the races of the world'.[26] In other words, the Asian League was to accomplish more or less the same goals as the League of Nations in Geneva. Of course, this included rather prominently the abolition of racial discrimination, the demand that the Japanese and Chinese government delegations at Versailles had failed to insist on.[27] Despite its critique of the League, the assembly recommended that Asians should neither ignore the League of Nations nor lobby for Japan's withdrawal. Instead, it adopted the resolution to keep working towards the inclusion of a racial equality clause in the near future.[28]

The Congress also discussed a number of more practical issues which on the surface appeared to be instruments enforcing inter-Asian activities, such as the construction of a trans-Asian railway, and the establishment of Asian Cultural and Study Centres, an Asian Bank, and an institute for the promotion of trans-Asian business and industry. As all of these plans were proposed by Japanese delegates, they were met with immediate suspicion from Chinese delegates, who criticized them as a means of further Japanese economic penetration and subjugation of China: a trans-Asian railway could facilitate cheaper and easier travel but it could potentially also serve economic and military penetration; an Asian Bank could provide money without relying on the Western powers but it could potentially also enforce financial and therefore political dependency on Japan; the encouragement to use goods produced in Asia could promote indigenous industry but potentially it could also undermine anti-Japanese boycotts. In this manner, the strained political relations between Japan and other Asian countries hampered the constructive debate of pan-Asian projects to such a degree that the mere fact that the Congress lasted for three days at all may be taken as an indicator of the urgency and prevalence of some common issues over bitter rivalry. In the end, only less controversial proposals, such as the establishment of a joint inter-Asian publication and the establishment of an Asian College were passed, while others, such as the railway and monetary projects issues were deferred at the demand of the Chinese.[29] In fact, right from the start, political tensions between Japan and China—partially a legacy of Versailles, too—had impacted the mood and agenda at Nagasaki. Unsurprisingly, it was Japan's infamous Twenty-One Demands that led to the first controversy between Japanese and Chinese delegates before the Congress had even convened. Chinese delegates had urged the Conference to repudiate the Demands as a precondition to their participation, while the Japanese insisted that this matter should first be discussed at the Conference before any resolution could be taken.[30] Eventually, a compromise was reached in that the Japanese delegates agreed to lobby their government to abandon all unequal treaties between Japan and Asian countries. Acknowledging the special significance of Sino-Japanese relations for the project of Asian unity, the Congress also adopted a resolution to appoint a special committee to undertake research into the problems between the two countries. Chinese observers of the conference, however, were difficult to placate and reiterated the judgement of Asianism that Li Dazhao had first introduced a decade earlier (see Chap. 4): Asianism in principle was agreeable and useful but reality rendered it impossible to trust any Japanese Asianist proposal. As the following excerpt from an editorial from the Chinese journal *Xiandai Pinglun* (Contemporary Review), published shortly after the Nagasaki conference, reveals, even moderate liberals found it hard to distinguish different Japanese conceptions of Asianism and, more generally, official state policy on the one hand and transnational civil society activities on the other:

> Asia is the Asia of the Asians, it is not the Asia of the Euro-Americans! Of course, this kind of Greater Asianism (Da Yazhou zhuyi) is a very good instrument for the Asians with which to oppose the Euro-American invasion. However, in view of the current situation, as long as the Japanese do not abandon their imperialist thinking they cannot gain the consent of other Asian peoples. Therefore, this Asian-style national movement cannot succeed. Towards China, Japan as ever pursues the principle and policy of invasion and to Korea it refuses to grant independence. How can it possibly speak of Greater Asianism? […] As for now, Greater Asianism is Japan's Greater Asianism, not the Greater Asianism of the peoples of Asia.[31]

In general, the practical implications of assumed Asian commonality which underlay each of the individual proposals as well as the general framework of the Congress proved rather difficult. The language question was a case in point. By the mid-1920s Chinese was no longer, if it ever was, the *lingua franca* for most Asians and certainly not for those assembled in Nagasaki. Refugees from British- and French-colonized countries were usually Japanophiles and had a better command of Japanese than of Chinese. Nevertheless, the Chinese were suspicious of Japanese as the official language, since Japan was the only Asian country that had itself become an imperialist power. Japanese, therefore, was regarded as a rather unfitting representative of the Asianist cause. But English, perceived as the main language of the imperialist 'West', of course, was not acceptable either. Esperanto as an alternative was briefly discussed but likewise rejected as a language originating in the 'West'.

According to contemporary sources, communication during the sessions at the Congress was mainly conducted in Japanese, Chinese, and English, with translations provided. As a future goal, however, the Congress decided to undertake research into the invention of an Asian version of Esperanto as a neutral language.[32]

The language problem reflected well the artificial and forced character of the concept of 'Asia' in general. Where it implied cultural homogeneity (Confucian legacy, Chinese characters), it excluded vast areas such as India and Western parts of Asia and neglected the contemporary reality of 'modernity' in which Chinese traditions only played a minor role. Where it openly embraced its diversity, 'Asia' became void of any definable content—it needed to reinvent itself artificially. The assumed common history and heritage that so many Asianists appealed to faded once confronted with the challenge of practical implementation. However, as the Congress also symbolized rather well, by the mid-1920s Asians did not leave this definitional task to others, especially the 'West'. 'Asia' increasingly became a self-defined concept with positive connotations. As discussed in the Introduction, if, following Edward Said, 'Asia' discourse in the 'West' was above all 'a Western style for dominating, restructuring, and having authority over the Orient',[33] Asianism as represented by the delegates of the Congress could be defined as an Eastern or Asian style for reclaiming this authority over 'Asia'. Within this process, the self-affirmative embrace of 'Asia'—although not necessarily accompanied by accepting Asianity as the main source of cultural or regional identity—joined hands with the inherent and unavoidable 'Othering' of the 'West'. Importantly, as opposed to Asianism discourse that was limited to the relatively homogenous Sino-Japanese sphere, Asianist discourse that included wider parts of South and West Asia acknowledged the diversity of 'Asia' and avoided falling into the trap of extreme forms of culturalist self-essentialization. Instead, it embarked on the project of reviving 'Asia' as a 'modern' and, if necessary, consciously artificial concept that could appeal to Asians and, potentially, also to the wider world.

The Second Pan-Asian Conference in Shanghai (1927)

Despite the rather limited success of the Nagasaki Conference, the pan-Asian Congress reconvened in November of the following year in Shanghai for its second annual meeting. With only eleven delegates, the conference was much smaller than its predecessor. However, continuity regarding participants testifies to the significance attributed by the Chinese Alliance, led by Huang Gongsu, the Japanese Association, led by Imazato, and other returning delegates, including Bose (India) and Pratap (Afghanistan)[34] to the Asianist undertaking. Yet, against the background of China's national unification process under General Chiang Kai-shek (Jiang Jieshi) from 1926 onwards ('Northern Expedition') and attempts by the new Japanese government under the new Prime Minister Tanaka Giichi to secure what it defined as Japanese interests in China ('Tanaka Memorandum'), delegates at the Shanghai Conference found it ever more difficult to see in their counterparts more than representatives of national or even governmental interests.

Again, the conference almost failed before its opening. Only after Pratap's mediation did the Chinese and Japanese agree to alter their respective proposals so that they did not offend each other too blatantly. Instead of the original Chinese demand to end the 'Japanese invasion' of Manchuria and Mongolia, the final version of the resolution merely urged Japan to 'strive towards a reform of its policy in Manchuria and Mongolia in full acknowledgement that the current Japanese policy towards China hurts the feelings of the Chinese people'.[35] In turn, the Japanese dropped their plans for an Asian Central Monetary Institution and the inter-Asian railway project, which had both caused too much suspicion on the Chinese side. While these examples may serve as proof of the difficulties of any practical joint Asian enterprise beyond Asianist rhetoric, it also demonstrates the possibilities of inter-Asian—and more specifically Sino-Japanese—dialogue and compromise at a time of fierce nationalist agitation within both countries.

The Shanghai Conference had been watched with suspicion by both Chiang's ruling *Guomindang* (GMD) party and foreign authorities.[36] The premature end to the official part of the Conference after only one day, however, was caused by the GMD itself. It had forbidden any political gatherings on the tenth anniversary of the Russian Revolution, which unintentionally coincided with the day the Conference opened.[37] The assembly hurriedly adopted a ten-point 'common proposal' including the desire to 'help China by sincere cooperation with Japan', elected a standing executive committee consisting of Huang, Imazato, Bose, Pratap, and four others, and departed for Nanjing to continue informally as a private gathering.[38] Upon Pratap's suggestion, a third Pan-Asian Conference was announced for the following year in Kabul but historians have been unable to uncover any proof of its actual convention.[39] Similarly little is known about the host organizations after 1927.[40]

THE NINAGAWA–IMAZATO DISPUTE

Debate about the Asianist project, its significance, desirability, and practicality in the mid-1920s was not limited to Asianist organizations and the Pan-Asian Conferences. Instead, the degree of 'Asianization' of public political discourse after 1924 guaranteed a wide reception of any discussion of Asianism. A particularly noteworthy and almost perplexing series of documents that testifies to the controversial nature of Asianism in political debate in Japan was the dispute between Imazato Juntarō, the main activist of the Japanese All Asia Association, which co-organized the two Pan-Asian Conferences, and Ninagawa Arata, the most persistent nationalist and pro-Western critic of Asianism. Ninagawa had belonged to the first opponents of Asianism in the early 1910s (see Chap. 4) and continued to dismiss Asianist activities and thought well into the 1930s. It is quite astonishing that the Imazato–Ninagawa dispute, which comprised ten essays, was published between January 1926 and October 1927 in the *Tōhō Kōron* (Eastern Review), an openly pro-Asianist journal. After Ninagawa's first full-blown dismissal of plans for an 'Asian League' the journal felt compelled to publish an apologetic explanation for the inclusion of this anti-Asianist essay in its February 1926 edition. While the editorial board mainly disagreed with Ninagawa's view, it aimed to clarify, the journal had been founded as a 'public medium of all Eastern peoples' and therefore would not limit itself to opinions that exclusively conformed to the views of the editors.[41] Here again, rather than being propagated as an ideology, Asianism must be understood as a political concept that facilitated the debate about Japan's (or China's) 'Asia' policy and about the significance and possibility of 'Asia'—however defined—as an alternative to the predominance of nationalist and 'Western' modes of thought and action.

Ninagawa never ascribed to 'Asia' any theoretical or abstract qualities in the sense that Sun's 'Greater Asianism' or Bose's approval of the Pan-Asian Conferences transcended issues of racial or geographical belonging. On the contrary, Ninagawa exclusively focused on the narrowest meanings of 'Asia'. First of all, he argued, Asianist political agendas were unrealistic and impractical:

> In our country, the propagation of an 'Asia for the Asians' as the claim of Greater Asianism has become a reality for many years and is advocated by not a few people. These supporters loudly claim 'Asia is the Asia of the Asians'. [...] However, this aim cannot be achieved unless the Russians are driven out of Siberia, the British expelled from India and Hong Kong, and the French, Portuguese, and Dutch from the territories that they occupy. Mere rhetoric will not be sufficient to achieve this chauvinistic aim. One has to resort to force and a war of tens or hundreds of years will be necessary. This is the horrible and deplorable prospect.[42]

Although Ninagawa's description of Asianist aims is by no means completely incorrect, his portrayal of war as the only way to achieve the liberation of Asian peoples from 'Western' rule misrepresents the mainstream of Asianist proposals, which did not envision or propose immediate, military action against the 'West'. Instead—as the Pan-Asian Conferences had shown—above all they tried to focus on fostering inter-Asian commonality and reconciliation among Asians, for which anti-Western rhetoric often only served as a tool. Even as the ultimate goal few conceptions of Asianism actually advocated the expulsion of non-Asians from Asia but rather demanded that the territory of Asia should be ruled by Asians, not Europeans or Americans—just as, for example, Americans had gained independence from the British and no Asian country had ever ruled Germany, Britain, or France. Yet Ninagawa indicates no sympathy with this part of the Asianist agenda either. Above all, his awareness of the implications for Japan may have made it difficult for him to support the anti-colonial content of the main Asianist slogan 'Asia for the Asians'. How could Japan justify its imperialist policies towards Korea, Taiwan, and parts of mainland China if it adopted Asianism, including its anti-colonial demands, as its policy?

If Asia was indeed to unite politically, a second practical problem would arise, Ninagawa continued, namely of the character of the political body. Out of 'loyalty' the Japanese would find it hard to agree to a 'Greater Asia Republic' (Dai Ajia Kyōwakoku), Ninagawa argued, while most Asians would certainly object to a 'Greater Asian Empire' (Dai Ajia Teikoku) as a continuation of imperialism.[43] This brief excursus reveals Ninagawa's Japan-centred premise of his critique of Asianism. Arguing that Japanese and 'Asian' perspectives and interests were fundamentally and monolithically opposed to each other, he implied that other 'Asians' would have to abandon their traditional form of political organization since the Japanese would not voluntarily renounce their eternal loyalty to the empire, despite the fact that the 'Great Japanese Empire'—as an invention of the Meiji Constitution of 1889—had only existed for less than thirty seven years at the time Ninagawa penned his essay. The basis for his perspective was the general attitude towards Japan's recent past: while Ninagawa praised Japan's development after the Meiji Restoration as a success story which separated Japan from the rest of Asia, Asianists had harboured doubts about the viability of this pro-Western orientation for the future of Japan. After the experiences of 1913, 1919, and 1924, for a growing number of Japanese, 'Asia' and Asianism appeared as feasible alternatives, even though the precise content of these alternatives was difficult to define.

Apart from a lack of practicability of Asianist proposals, Ninagawa also rejected their racialist-culturalist arguments. Neither did the Japanese share a racial identity with all other Asians, nor did the proto-Asianist formula *shinshi hosha* (lips and teeth, cheekbones and gums), denoting close intimacy and interdependence, hold true for Japan's relations with other Asians, in particular the Chinese, he claimed. 'The Japanese people', he argued, 'are no poor and feeble people whose existence depends on another country; even if China ceases to exist, Japan will never perish'.[44] But Ninagawa did not stop here. He also rejected claims for racial equality that had become part of the Asianist agenda in reaction to continuous restrictions regarding Asian immigration to the United States and in 1919 had prominently surfaced at Versailles. In this context, too—representing the general mood of 1913 more than of the mid-1920s—Ninagawa continued to insist on a distinction between Japan and 'other Asians'.

> It is not only true according to international law but also in accordance with reality that we Japanese must insist on equality with the Whites since, after all, we are civilized peoples. However, we cannot agree to the claim of 'equality of human rights'. What then are races? There are not only differences between white and yellow races but regarding colour there are also red and black. In fact, from the perspective of historical anthropology, there are innumerable races. If the 'Wild' in Taiwan continue to live as cannibal races, we as civilized people do not wish to be perceived as equal to them. Just as the dull-witted Malayan people and the intelligent Dutch cannot be treated equally an identical treatment of uncivilized and civilized people (yabanjin to bunmeijin) would be as unfair as treating capable and incapable people alike.[45]

The Asianist project, therefore, according to one of its fiercest and most prolific critics, was neither justifiable as advantageous to Japan nor as a favour to the human race. Instead, as Ninagawa concluded, it was 'empty theory', the 'greatest nuisance to the [Japanese] people', and 'a calamity like the Bolsheviks'.[46] This passage particularly well illustrates that a general conflation of Asianism and racism or ultra-nationalist ideology fails to account for anti-Asianist rejections, of which some, on the contrary, were explicitly based on racism and Japanist chauvinist views, whereas Asianism, in some cases at least, represented the opposite claims.

Imazato's reply, subtitled 'correcting Dr. Ninagawa's erroneous views',[47] reads like a summary of the latest state of Asianist debate. First of all, as the concept of Asianism was—a highly obvious fact that Ninagawa had conveniently overlooked—extremely diverse in its political manifestations, Imazato emphasized that diverse conceptions of Asian unity and of the creation of an Asian League co-existed. Moving beyond this disclaimer, Imazato explained the gist of his own conception:

> In my understanding, All Asianism (Zen Ajiashugi) represents the effort, initiated by the Japanese people, to plan a harmonious league of all Asian peoples, to jointly develop the revival of the culture of Asia and the great resources of all of Asia which certainly are not inferior to those of Euro-America, to first and foremost use these resources of Asia for the survival and the prosperity of the Asian peoples and from there move on to political reconciliation and economic progress.[48]

Imazato's definition of Asianism displayed a practically oriented and regionalist understanding of the concept, which rested on neither anti-Westernism nor racialism. Instead, Imazato saw—as Bose would explain in his opening statement at Nagasaki three months later—the League of Nations as an imperfect model which the envisioned Asian League could improve, first within Asia and later maybe even on a global scale. An Asian League as a regional version of the League of Nations could be 'even faster and more practical' and 'freer' than its model.[49] Since this League would not aim at replacing the League of Nations, neither the 'West' nor the Japanese government should be opposed to its creation, Imazato hoped. The establishment of 'co-existence and co-prosperity in all of Asia' was to be only a stepping stone to the establishment of the same principles for the 'whole human race', and thereby conformed to the same—vague and idealistic—vocabulary employed in Versailles and

Geneva.⁵⁰ Lastly, Imazato insisted that one topic that the League in Geneva had thus far failed to deal with sufficiently needed to remain on the agenda of any Asianist enterprise: racial equality. Emphasizing that both Asians and Euro–Americans needed to review their attitudes and behaviour regarding racial discrimination Imazato could not reveal his astonishment about Ninagawa's blatant racism:

> As regards racial equality, I cannot conceal that I am really shocked to hear directly from Dr. Ninagawa's mouth that he is absolutely opposed to it. [...] As individuals we acknowledge human rights without discrimination of old and young, strong and weak. The same goes for race. We must not distinguish between superior and inferior, strong and weak in our esteem of human rights. [...] I demand that Dr. Ninagawa engages in self-reflection on this point.⁵¹

Ninagawa's sharp but sometimes simplistic and racist criticism of Asianism enabled Imazato to portray his Asianist convictions in an overly reconciliatory and enlightened manner. He and his fellow Asianists—who were in the middle of preparations for the Nagasaki conference—could easily dismiss anti-Asianism à la Ninagawa as a misinterpretation of Asianism and as flagrant chauvinism. In his reply, however, Ninagawa displayed no trace of self-reflection. Instead, he moved the discussion to a sidetrack in order to deconstruct Imazato's key term 'Asian peoples' (Ajia minzoku). If it referred to those people who currently lived in Asia, it needed to encompass Whites and Blacks as well, Ninagawa argued. If it referred to independent countries in Asia it would exclude the Indians, Indo-Chinese, Malayans, Burmese, and others. But if it referred to those people who had lived as groups in Asia from ancient times it needed to clarify the historical dimensions, which might actually exclude the Japanese, since they themselves had a history of no more than 2600 years.⁵² 'If one does not clearly explain what Asian peoples means', Ninagawa concluded, 'calling for a "League of Asian Peoples" is just like carrying an empty shrine on one's shoulders'.⁵³ Ninagawa obviously showed no willingness to acknowledge that 'Asian Peoples' right from the start did not refer to a well-defined group of people—and did not need to. To Imazato, as to some other Asianists, including Sun Yat-sen, racial origins or geographical locations mattered much less than shared interests and a common agenda. Compared to the difficulties the Pan-Asian Conferences would later face in their attempts at overcoming the lack of mutual knowledge and trust, Ninagawa's criticism was hardly more than a distraction—albeit a persistent one. Imazato did not conceal his pride when he terminated his participation in the dispute with Ninagawa in September 1926 by declaring in a *fait accompli* manner that the 'All Asian League has now been born'.[54] As the analysis of the conference above has demonstrated, in fact there was little else that could be celebrated as accomplishments of the Nagasaki conference. In the light of Ninagawa's fierce opposition and of grave dissonances among the delegates at the conference itself, however, the fact that the assembly had agreed on any resolutions at all and an awareness of Asian matters through personal exchange had been stimulated was not an achievement that could easily be neglected.

The Imazato–Ninagawa dispute of 1926/1927, which stretched from the months prior to the Nagasaki conference to the preparatory phase of the Shanghai conference, exemplifies the wide range of political views represented in Asianism discourse during the 1920s. As we have seen in the previous chapter, racialism had strongly influenced post-Versailles Asianism discourse. However, racial arguments informed not only Asianist but also anti-Asianist agendas. To be sure, anti-White sentiments functioned to a certain degree to generate transnational cooperation among Asianists from different countries, particularly in the context of the racial exclusion legislation of 1924 and the subsequent racialist debate. Nevertheless, positively defined racial commonality was difficult to employ as a common denominator in multi-racial Asia. Therefore, arguments for regional cooperation as an expression of practical Asianist agency started to gain influence and also helped to convince less racialist-inclined writers to find value in the concept of Asianism. In addition, the Imazato–Ninagawa dispute revealed the continuous problems of integrating Japan into Asianist conceptions in such a way that they would appear neither as disadvantageous for the Japanese nor as empty of any significant pro-Asian content. Imazato's careful phrasing of the Japanese special role in the creation of an Asian League as 'initiated by the Japanese people' (rather than openly claiming Japanese leadership) reflected the delicate balancing act performed by moderate Asianists when trying to appeal to both Japanese and non-Japanese Asian audiences. On the one hand, any interpretation of Asianism that would not acknowledge a special, meaning privileged, position for Japan was unlikely to become popular at home. On the other hand, any interpretation of Asianism that privileged Japan too much was unlikely to become accepted outside Japan. Ninagawa and other Japanese who refused to link Japan's fate to that of its Asian neighbours, of course, showed no interest in an enterprise that would 'relegate' the Japanese to equal or near equal staus with other Asians. This problem of balancing 'Japanese' and 'Asian' interests terminologically too became all the more pressing when, from the mid-1920s onwards, Asianism gradually developed into a transnational undertaking and Japanese started to directly discuss their ideas with other Asians to an increasing extent. The difficulty of reconciling the givens of Japanese political discourse, which for decades had been oriented towards 'Western' standards, with the interests of colonized and less 'Westernized' peoples in Asia had permanently overshadowed the conferences and continued to impede an easy and swift synthesis of Japanese and non-Japanese Asianist conceptions.

THE TRANSNATIONAL *YAZHOU MINZU XIEHUI* AND ITS ACTIVITIES IN SHANGHAI

Attempts to overcome this dilemma usually brought about incoherence or triviality, which can be observed in the activities of another pan-Asian group. The *Yazhou Minzu Xiehui* (Asian Peoples' Association) or, in its official English name, the Asiatic Association had been founded as a transnational organization by Japanese, Chinese, Philippine, and Indian activists in Shanghai in 1922.[55] Its self-declared aims were '(a) to connect the feelings among the different Asian peoples, (b) to mediate the opinions of the different peoples of Asia, (c) to interpret and spread the cultures of the different Asian peoples and (d) to advocate peace among the different peoples of Asia'.[56] The Association's main activity was the publication of a bilingual (Chinese/English) monthly journal which in its English section mainly focused on India and Western Asia while its Chinese language section almost exclusively dealt with Chinese affairs and, among other things, serialized Sun Yat-sen's six lectures on nationalism.[57] The director of the Association was Tongū Yutaka (1884–1974), a Japanese medical doctor based in Shanghai.[58] Like the Pan-Asian Conferences, the Association's activities were closely watched by the authorities and the Japanese consulate in Shanghai sent its observations and records to the Foreign Ministry in Tokyo. One of the reports described the journal's comments on Japanese–Chinese relations as 'extremely impartial' and praised its efforts at 'averting misunderstandings between people of different nationalities'.[59] The reasons for this evaluation probably lay in the heterogeneous character of the journal. On its front page it stated it was 'devoted to the Asiatic causes' but published hardly anything that would have caused the authorities of any country represented in the international settlement of Shanghai to intervene. In fact, it was more observing than demanding; it was careful not to antagonize the interests of either the 'West' or of any Asian country.

Like many Japanese Asianists, Tongū himself mainly focused on Japan and China as the nucleus of 'Asia', with occasional references to India. Above all, he rejected racialist conceptions of Asianism and instead proposed an alliance based on like-mindedness:

> The term 'Asian League' can be interpreted in different ways. To some it probably takes the meaning of a political and economic core against the Whites; to others it may mean a group based on a spiritual union which takes culture at its centre.[60]

Tongū clearly favoured the latter and argued that in order to avoid economic or ethnic revolutions or warfare that would surely arise from existing imbalances 'we must strive towards a cultural alliance and spiritual union between peoples'.[61] In this sense, Asians would not only save 'Asia' but also rescue 'European culture' from its current decline. In order to achieve both, 'the movement of Pan-Asianism as we expect it is philosophical and worldly'.[62] Writing in Japanese but in a journal published in Shanghai that, potentially at least, reached an audience that transcended Japanese readers, Tongū obviously aimed at pleasing a variety of readers: dismissing racialist conceptions, he placated the 'Whites'; paying attention to the situation of the 'oppressed peoples', calling China 'the protagonist of Asia' (Ajia no shuyaku), and referring to India and China as the 'father and mother of Asia's culture', he pleased Chinese and Indian readers alike.[63] It was probably the Japanese who—unless Asianists in the first place—found least to convince them of the cause of Tongū's Asianism. Through its organization and publications, however, the Association contributed to spreading a consciousness of shared interests and of belonging together. It approached 'Asia' as an Asia of regions (or countries/peoples) that shared many interests but that were also separated from each other through different customs and languages. In order to bridge these gaps, above all, gaps of mutual knowledge, the Association—on its rather small scale of activities in Shanghai—probably stayed more loyal to its self-declared aims than most other organizations that pursued or purported to pursue Asianist aims. As much as it appeared to be too uncritical of the *status quo* its moderate stance allowed the members of the Association in particular and Asians in general to cultivate their ethnic, religious, or linguistic distinctiveness under the roof of 'One Asia', rather than policing Asian peoples for Asian uniformity by force.

THE EMERGENCE OF GEOPOLITICAL VISIONS OF ASIA

Nagatomi Morinosuke's Vision of a Pan-Asian Movement

Among the distant observers of the Nagasaki conference was a low-ranking Japanese diplomat in Europe who had followed the Asianist initiatives that had evolved in Japan and China after 1924 with particular interest. Around the same time the All Asia Association had been founded in Tokyo in reaction to the US immigration legislation, Nagatomi Morinosuke (1896–1975) started to advocate the creation of a 'Far East Asian Republic'. The motivation for his support of Asianism, however, was completely different from that which triggered the actions of the Association. Nagatomi was one of the earliest Asianists in Japan who based his conception of Asianism on geopolitical regionalism that prioritized political-economic factors and aimed at a complete divorcing of Asianism from racialism. In this sense, as Hirawaka Hitoshi has pointed out, Nagatomi was a 'unique Asianist' who would continue to strive towards the realization of 'Pan-Asia' for the rest of his lifetime (Fig. 6.1).[64]

Originally from Hyōgo prefecture, Nagatomi had entered the Foreign Ministry after graduating with a degree in Politics from the Law Faculty of Tokyo Imperial University (1920). He briefly served in the Ministry's Commerce Office but was soon transferred to the Japanese Embassy in Berlin and later to Rome.[65] During his postings in Europe, he first encountered pan-European thought and movements, which initiated his embrace of pan-Asian ideals. In order to start a pan-Asian movement in Japan, he resigned from the Foreign Ministry and returned to Japan. When his campaign to get elected to the House of Representatives failed, he first turned to freelance writing and, in 1936, entered the Kajima Construction Company, which belonged to his father in law, Kajima Seiichi.[66] In the 1950s, he restarted his political career as a member of the Liberal Party, became elected to the House of Representatives, and served on several mid-ranking sub-Cabinet level offices. He is the author

Fig. 6.1 A rare photo of Nagatomi Morinosuke taken during his stay in Europe in the mid-1920s when he started to propose his own conception of Asianism, inspired by Coudenhove-Kalergi's Pan-European movement. Reproduced with kind permission from the collection of Kajima Corporation

and translator of more than one hundred books and, in 1967, initiated the Kajima Peace Prize (Kajima Heiwashō), whose first recipient was Count Richard Coudenhove-Kalergi, the founder of the pan-European movement and his main politico-intellectual inspiration.[67]

Nagatomi's approach to Asianism was unique in that it did not originate from a—real or pretended—sense of humiliation as a result of Asia's physical or discursive subjugation under European or American hegemony; neither did he envision a spiritual revival of 'Asia' nor advocate a quasi-imperialist and Japan-centred version of an Asian Monroe Doctrine. Instead, Nagatomi can be described as a 'realist'[68] who viewed the creation of supranational regional blocs as corresponding to the trends of the time and as the only guarantee of 'freedom, equality, and philanthropy/fraternity' (jiyū, byōdō, hakuai)—the ideals of the French Revolution he admired. Arguing that Europe (Pan-Europe), the United Kingdom (British Empire), Russia (Soviet Union), and the United States (Monroe Doctrine/Pan-Americanism) had already embarked on the formation or even succeeded in the realization of regional blocs, he urged East Asia to supplement these four supranational groups by a 'Far East Asian Republic' (Kyokutō Ajia Renpō).[69] Obviously, Nagatomi was either not aware of the popularity of similar calls in the aftermath of the Immigration Legislation of 1924 or did not recognize any of these proposals as related to his own regionalist conception of Asianism. At any rate, he argued that in East Asia alone no initiatives existed to push public discourse and political reality towards the creation of a Pan-Asia. 'Only Far East Asia', he claimed, 'as ever is trapped in old traditions, does not advance and develop politically, economically, culturally, but as before lives in the idleness of maintaining the status quo.'[70]

In sharp contrast to other Japanese Asianists, from the perspective of an observer based in Europe Nagatomi did not perceive the 'West' as being in decline. On the contrary, according to his assessment, the European powers and 'Europe' in general had already recovered from World War One and had learnt their lessons, while 'Asia' continued to be in a state of degeneration. In fact, here and throughout much of his writings, Nagatomi seems to attach too much weight and representativeness to Coudenhove-Kalergi's pan-European movement. While that movement had gained some influence in the first decade after its foundation in 1923, it was hardly comparable to the degree of influence that the American Monroe Doctrine or the British Empire had already and the extent to which the Soviet Union would organize and control regions in the pre-World War Two era. Not even the *idea* of pan-Europe as a geopolitical concept was very popular in Europe in the 1920s.[71] Nagatomi shared, however, with many Asianists his discontent with the League of Nations. According to Nagatomi it failed to take into account the interconnectedness of peoples and countries beyond national borders, and, in particular, it failed to grasp the special relationship between China and Japan and the special relevance of both countries for peace in East Asia. For these reasons, he argued, the League—imperfect as it was anyway—continued to be unsuccessful in its dealings with East Asia.[72]

> Despite the extent of intimacy between Japan and China, Japan and Serbia or Japan and Paraguay are treated in the same manner. Proximity and distance between countries that results from geographical, economic, and cultural relations is not taken into consideration at all. In addition, the matters treated by the League of Nations are almost exclusively European matters. And from the perspective of the Far East, its greatest deficit is the absence of the two neighbouring menaces in Far Eastern affairs, the United States and Russia. Therefore, the League of Nations cannot achieve its aims of becoming the court of peace that solves the conflicts in East Asia. Japan and China must, as the US has done, create a Monroe Doctrine in the Far East and refuse the requests and wishes of any third country to interfere.[73]

Nagatomi's criticism, however, remained closely related to practical matters and largely refrained from appealing to essentialist claims of racialist or spiritual commonality. An Asian League was necessary mainly for pragmatic reasons in order to modify the practical shortcomings of the League in Geneva, Nagatomi contended. He was careful not to fall into the anti-Westernist rhetoric that characterized much of Asianist discourse after 1924 and focused instead—probably under the influence of Coudenhove-Kalergi's strong anti-Bolshevism—explicitly on Russia as Asia's main opponent. The first and foremost aim of the Japanese–Chinese union as the core of the 'Far East Asian Republic' was the 'defence against the political and military oppression by Russia', he insisted.[74] Simultaneously, he attempted to be impartial towards China. Nagatomi neither attributed the role of leader to Japan nor denigrated the role or state of China in any way. Instead of referring to the current conditions in China as chaotic or disorganized, as many other contemporary observers did, Nagatomi only referred to the East Asian situation *in toto* as 'disorderly'. In addition, as the quotation above outlines, he viewed both Japan *and* China as the architects of an Asian Monroe

Doctrine and he also insisted that two central offices of a to-be-created Pan-Asian Assembly should be established in Tokyo and Beijing.[75] His sense of equality and unbiased attitude towards China was also reflected in his concluding summary: 'The aim [of the Japanese–Chinese union]', Nagatomi stressed, 'is not to abolish the individuality of the peoples of both countries but to combine their individualities to form one political and economic body in order to adapt to the demands of the times.'[76]

In this first of a series of writings on Pan-Asia and Asian unity dating from 1924, Nagatomi not only revealed his intellectual indebtedness to Coudenhove-Kalergi, whose geopolitical concept of five regional blocs *cum* anti-Sovietism he borrowed without much modification. More importantly, he established—amidst the heated racialized debate on Asian revival, 'Western' hypocrisy, and Japanocentrism—a new thread of rationalist-regionalist Asianism that he sought to distance from essentialist conceptions of Asian commonality. As Hirakawa has argued, 'Kajima [Nagatomi] as his principal position did not allow colonial control. However, in the eyes of an expert on diplomacy the main trend of Asianism within Japan that proposed to resist the imperial powers as the leader of Asia (Ajia no meishu) did reflect only dangerous thought which was unable to differentiate between ideals and reality.'[77] Nagatomi paid more attention than others to the prospects of a possible implementation of his plan. At the same time, of course, this non-confrontational position neglected the actual condition of vast parts of Asia that, unlike Japan, were not satisfied with the territorial *status quo*. Against more far-reaching conceptions of Asianism's 'Asia', represented for example by Imazato's All Asia Association, which also covered India and Western parts of Asia, Nagatomi made every effort to dismiss the subsuming of 'Western' colonies under the idea of a 'pan-Asian movement'. While he believed a regional Asian organization was necessary as an 'intermediate national body' on the level between the nation state and League of Nations, he insisted that the pan-Asian movement should eventually be established within the sphere of the League of Nations.[78] 'Under the same name of pan-Asian movement', he made the distinction, '[…] there are movements for the unification of peoples that have already achieved independence and freedom and there are independence movements that aim at liberating peoples'.[79] Revealing his conservative view of Asianism, which supported the cornerstones of sustaining the territorial *status quo*, Nagatomi rendered both types incompatible. He called the former type 'Far Eastern pan-Asian movement' and subsumed the Chinese—and also

Koreans—under the range of peoples that were apparently satisfied with the current *status quo* and did not need to strive for liberation.

Nagatomi Morinosuke's Proposal of an 'East Asian League'

It is no surprise, therefore, that the organizers of the Pan-Asian Conferences in Nagasaki and Shanghai had little interest in Nagatomi's ideas—and vice versa. Slightly revising his previous terminology and clarifying his own conception of Asianism, in 1926 Nagatomi reviewed the Nagasaki conference only days after its conclusion. As the conference blended demands from both types of pan-Asianism that Nagatomi had previously characterized as incompatible, he was highly sceptical of the entire enterprise. 'The deadlock of this alliance', he predicted, 'will not be caused by pressure from outside but rather results from the collision and schism of the different streams of thought'.[80] These two streams of thought represented at Nagasaki were, according to Nagatomi, (a) nationalist movements, that is, movements for the independence and liberation of peoples and (b) movements for supranational unions.[81] Against the Asianism represented by Indians and Filipinos who propagated 'liberation, independence, revolution, and war', he reiterated his own proposal for a pan-Asian movement modelled on the pan-European and pan-American examples. These alliances were based, Nagatomi stated, on 'shared profits and the promotion of welfare'.[82] Now referring to an 'East Asian League', he again subsumed China under the countries that did not strive for liberation because they 'have already completely achieved independence'.[83] Although he changed his regional vocabulary from 'Far East Asian Republic' to 'East Asian League' his message remained clear: both geographically and regarding political aspirations 'Asia' was not one but must be viewed as consisting of disparate parts (East and Central/West). In Nagatomi's words: 'Asia is nothing more but a geographical concept. One must not think of lumping it together politically.'[84]

Of course, Nagatomi's distinction was as inconsistent as other attempts at defining 'Asia' homogeneously. Were the 'political conditions' in India and Western Asian countries really considerably more disparate than those of China and Japan? Was it really easier to define Asian commonality based on geopolitical rather than racialist-culturalist factors? In addition, Nagatomi's somewhat careless remarks about

China contributed little to promoting an 'East Asian' pan-Asian movement in China or among Sinophile Japanese. Apparently, his targeted audience above all were pro-Western and Asia-critical Japanese who—in the mood of the times—Nagatomi expected to be more inclined to reconsider their attitude towards Asianism if the concept appeared more rational, regional, and realist than racialist and anti-Western. Nagatomi's emphasis on the compatibility of his Asianist conception with the *status quo* and pro-Western policies on the one hand and his rejection of the anti-colonial demands of the Pan-Asian Conference at Nagasaki on the other, certainly may have offered a more rationalist variant of Asianism to the debate. But if the scope of Nagatomi's Asianism was nothing more than a Japanese–Chinese alliance, why should it be called Asianism, which invited suspicion from anti-Asianist Japanese and 'Westerners' alike? And if this alliance was not meant to be confrontational towards any third party,[85] as Nagatomi stressed, which aims would it be able to achieve anyway apart from consolidating the *status quo*? How realistic were visions of a supranational unity between the Chinese and Japanese peoples that turned a blind eye to the anti-colonial mood in China? It is probably not overstated to conclude that Nagatomi's attempt at transferring Coudenhove-Kalergi's blueprint to East Asia and at balancing and rationalizing existing conceptions of Asianism by all means was rather immature and naïve. Nevertheless, his proposal for a non-essentialist, strictly regionalist, and 'functional union' (yūkiteki ketsugō)[86] foreshadowed a stream of Asianist thought that gained wider prominence in the early 1930s and is frequently linked to either Rōyama Masamichi's proposal of an 'East Asian Community' (Tōa Kyōdōtai)[87] or to the geopolitical justification of Japan's imperialist Asia policy. It was Nagatomi himself, however, who contributed to the conflation of his early Asianist regionalism and the expansionist policy of the Japanese Empire after 1932. While, after the founding of Manchukuo (Jp. Manshūkoku, Ch. Manzhouguo), he still insisted on a solution based on 'small Asianism' (shō Ajiashugi) which only comprised Japan, Manchukuo, and China as the scope of 'Pan-Asia',[88] in 1941—after the declaration of the 'Greater East Asian Co-Prosperity Sphere' (Dai Tōa Kyōeiken) by the Japanese government in the previous year—he no longer drew a line between different scopes. Nagatomi now demanded that 'adding further the Southern territories that lie within the range of our East Asian Co-Prosperity Sphere, the East

Asian League (Tōa Renmei) must then form an Asian League (Ajia Renmei)'.[89] By 1943, Nagatomi had fully embraced the official Asianist rhetoric of the Japanese government and appeared almost eager to confess that his original vision of 'Pan-Asia' had in fact anticipated Japan's wartime Asia rhetoric and policy.

> The creation of the Greater East Asian Co-Prosperity Sphere is the same as the theory and ideal that I have been proposing for twenty years. [...] Unless all of Asia unites it will lose its independence. Against the separate nationalist movements we must form a united co-prosperity sphere movement. The pursuit of this policy of a united co-prosperity sphere is the great mission of the only powerful country in Greater East Asia, the Japanese Empire.[90]

As the quotation above demonstrates, by the early 1940s Nagatomi had betrayed his own ideals and basically abandoned all the features of his conception of Asianism which had previously characterized it as unique. Not only did he retrospectively portray his previous political convictions as conforming to contemporary official rhetoric, but in view of the changed political reality Nagatomi also renounced his distinction between different parts of Asia and gave up his refusal to elevate Japan to the status of a fate-commissioned leader; by the early 1940s, to Nagatomi 'ultimately Pan-Asia and the Greater East Asian Co-Prosperity Sphere indicated one and the same'.[91]

Conclusion

The Pan-Asian Conferences of 1926/1927, Tongū's Asian Peoples' Association in Shanghai, and Nagatomi Morinosuke's geopolitical Asianism reveal the necessity of grasping Asianism discourse during the 1920s in consideration of its transnational, regionalist dimensions. Discursively, Asianism had always been receptive of and reactive to political discourse and reality outside of Japan. By the late 1920s, however, both in content and form Asianism had become a trans-Asian project that was defined and promoted by non-governmental activists from different countries and that also displayed a keen (although incomplete) awareness of political developments and political discourse outside Asia. Drawing on the internationalist mood of the early interwar years, Asian transnationalism was envisioned as an alternative or supplement to global internationalism. At the same time these transnational dimensions were checked by the spectre of a drift towards (Japan-led) Asian imperialism. This spectre was not only informed by openly confessed Japanese political and economic ambitions but also by its hegemonic 'Western' models: the British pan-Anglo movement, Russian Sovietism, and pan-Americanism. In practical terms, the aim was to create an Asian League of Nations. While Asianism and 'pan-Asian thought continued as potential alternatives for expressing discontent with the interwar-era world order',[92] Asianist plans were not generally based on confrontational or irreconcilable views. The 'West' was still 'Asia's' 'Other' but one that had become internalized as a part of the scope of Asianist ambitions to revise the world order. As more moderate and pragmatic conceptions of Asianism emerged, the concept facilitated more than before a serious discussion of national and regional concerns in an Asianist inflection. As the initial quotation by Nagatomi suggests, Asianism had turned from an object of study and theoretical debate into a matter of real politics.

The attempts at linking Asianist debate to pan-Asianist practice through transnational organizations and assemblies were overshadowed from the beginning by nationalist and imperialist reality and aspirations. The Nagasaki and Shanghai Conferences did not fail because their 'Asia' discourse was meaningless or could be unmasked as flowery phrases; instead, they failed because 'Asia' was seriously discussed as a concept that signified more than superficial talk of 'Yellow peoples' or the mere opposite of the 'West'. As opposed to the staged political theatre of the so-called Greater East Asia Conference in 1943, the Pan-Asian Conferences represented a transnational enterprise from below that not only grappled to discover the commonalities among Asians it had naturally—and maybe prematurely—presumed but also struggled against the antagonistic political reality in an age of nationalism, imperialism, and rivalling political ideologies. Similar to Tongū's journal, the Conferences revealed that the more concrete Asianist plans and blueprints became, the less uniform Asianist interests appeared. As the Asianist moments of 1926 and 1927 revealed, regionalizing 'Asia' was not the same as uniting Asia. More often than not it resulted in the exact opposite therof.

Notes

1. Nagatomi Morinosuke, 'Han Ajia undō ni tsuite' [On the pan-Asian movement], *Gaikō Jihō* [Diplomatic Review] 487 (March 1925), 34–40: 35. Reproduced with kind permission of Kajima Corporation.
2. See Yamamuro, *Shisō Kadai toshite no Ajia*, 1–3 and 31–34 for various Japanese attempts to deal with the foreign-imposed geographical category 'Asia' in the eighteenth and early nineteenth centuries. The discussion of an Asian Monroe Doctrine at the beginning of Asianism discourse in Japan and in China constitutes another instance of a regionalist understanding of 'Asia' (see Chap. 3). For China see also Karl, 'Creating Asia', 1096–1118.
3. See Ball, 'Conceptual History and the History of Political Thought', 82.
4. See J. Victor Koschmann, 'Constructing Destiny: Rōyama Masamichi and Asian Regionalism in Wartime Japan', *Pan-Asianism in Modern Japanese History. Colonialism, regionalism and borders*, ed. Sven Saaler and J. Victor Koschmann, London: Routledge 2007, 185–199: 185.
5. On the *Dai Tōa Kaigi* see Aydin, *The politics of anti-Westernism in Asia*, 185–186, Hotta *Pan-Asianism and Japan's war 1931–1945*, 213–216 and Ian Nish, *Japanese foreign policy in the interwar period*, Westport: Praeger 2002, 172–174.
6. Sun quoted in 'Ajia minzoku no Daidō danketsu o hakare' [Let's plan a great union of Asian Peoples], *Tokyo Asahi*, 25 April 1924, 2.
7. On this aspect see Takeuchi, 'Hōhō toshite no Ajia', 442–470.
8. On the *Zen Ajia Kyōkai* and its activities, including the Pan-Asian Conferences, see Mizuno Naoki, '1920 nendai Nihon, Chōsen, Chūgoku ni okeru Ajia ninshiki no ichidanmen: Ajia minzoku kaigi o meguru sankoku no ronchō' [One section of Asia consciousness in Japan, Korea, and China in the 1920s: Debates Concerning the Pan-Asian Conferences], *Kindai Nihon no Ajia Ninshiki* [Modern Japanese Asia Consciousness], ed. Furuya Tetsuo, Tokyo: Ryokuin Shobō 1996, 509–548, Aydin, *The politics of anti-Westernism in Asia*, 154–155, Sven Saaler, 'The Pan-Asiatic Society and the "Conference of Asian Peoples" in Nagasaki, 1926', *Pan-Asianism: A Documentary History 1860–2010*, Vol. 2, ed. Sven Saaler and Christopher W.A. Szpilman, Boulder: Rowman & Littlefield 2011, 97–105. Saaler emphasizes that the organization's 'supporters included influential politicians' but in fact no prominent 'supporter' listed in its founding manifesto appeared to have ever spoken publicly on its behalf or participated in the conferences (quotation from p. 98).
9. 'Zen Ajia Kyōkai setsuritsu shushi' [Purpose for the establishment of the All Asia Association], *Zen Ajia Kyōkai Kaihō* [Bulletin of the All Asia Association], April 1926, 1.

10. See Kodera's *Dai Ajiashugi Ron* (1916), which called for Asian revenge on 'the Whites' (see Chap. 4) and wartime propaganda as published by Asianist journals of the Japanese *Dai Ajia Kyōkai* (Greater Asia Association; see Chap. 7) and *Tōa Renmei* (East Asian League) and by the Chinese branch of the latter, the *Dongya Lianmeng*.
11. Members of both organizations include Ogawa Heikichi, Tanaka Zenryū (1874–1955), Kokubo Kishichi (1865–1939), and Furuhata Mototarō (1864–1931).
12. Imazato originates from Ōmura, a city in Nagasaki prefecture, and graduated from the politics and economy department of Tokyo's Waseda University. He became a member of parliament in May 1924, when the debate over racial discrimination and pan-Asian solidarity in the context of the US immigration law reached its climax in Japan.
13. For Imazato's questions and Shidehara's reply see 'Gaikō hōshin ni kansuru shitsumon shuisho' and 'Shūgigiin Imazato Juntarō shi teishutsu Gaikō hōshin ni kansuru shitsumon ni taishi besshi tōbensho', *Kanbō gōgai: Dai 49 kai Teikoku gikai, shūgiin giji sokkiroku, dai 11 gō* [Official Gazette, extra edition: 49th Diet, Record of the Minutes of the House of Representatives, 11th edition], 16 July 1924, 196, and 'Nihon Teikokubō narabi Gaikō ni kansuru shitsumon shuisho' and 'Shūgigiin Imazato Juntarō shi teishutsu Nihon Teikokubō narabi Gaikō ni kansuru shitsumon ni taishi besshi tōbensho', *Kanbō gōgai: Dai 50 kai Teikoku gikai, shūgiin giji sokkiroku, dai 15 gō* [Official Gazette, extra edition: 50th Diet, Record of the Minutes of the House of Representatives, 15th edition], 18 February 1925, 291–292.
14. The Greater Asia Association (Dai Ajia Kyōkai), founded in 1933, was the major Asianist organization during the Fifteen Years War and, often via members of the military, set up branches throughout Japanese-occupied Asia. For the Association's thought and activities see Chap. 7.
15. On the Alliance's origins see Huang Gongsu, *Yaxiya Minzu Di Yici Dahui Shimo Ji* [Complete Record of the first conference of the Asian Peoples], Beijing: Yaxiya Minzu Datongmeng 1926, 3–4 and Zhou Bin, 'Yaxiya Minzu Huiyi yu Zhongguo de fandui yundong' [The Asian Peoples' Congress and the Chinese opposition movement], *Kang-Ri Zhanzheng Yanjiu* [Studies of China's War of Resistance against Japan], 2006 (3), 128–159.
16. For details on the participants see Zhou, 'Yaxiya Minzu Huiyi yu Zhongguo de fandui yundong', 129–133. The leading initiators were Huang Gongsu and Li Zhaofu (1887–1950), both members of the dissolved parliament of the Chinese Republic.
17. Quoted in Zhou, 'Yaxiya Minzu Huiyi yu Zhongguo de fandui yundong', 130.

18. Quoted in Zhou, 'Yaxiya Minzu Huiyi yu Zhongguo de fandui yundong', 130.
19. 'Zen Ajia Kyōkai setsuritsu shushi', 2–3.
20. Thomas W. Burkman, 'Nitobe Inazō: From World Order to Regional Order', *Culture and Identity: Japanese Intellectuals During the Interwar Years*, ed. Thomas J. Rimer, Princeton: Princeton University Press 1990, 191–216: 196.
21. An impressive collection of official reports on the host organizations and the Nagasaki Conference is available online via the Japan Center for Asian Historical Records (http://www.jacar.go.jp/), including reports by the Japanese consular representations from China, Australia, France, Argentina, by Japanese prefectural authorities on foreigners planning to enter Japan as participants of the Conference, and by the Asia Department of Japan's Foreign Office on the meetings of the All Asia Association in Japan. These detailed reports suggest that the Japanese government was extremely concerned about the potential damage the Association's activities and the Conference might inflict on Japan's image as a cooperationist partner of the West. Both Japan's Home and Foreign Offices also closely watched foreign press reporting on the Conference. See *Zen Ajia Minzoku Kaigi tenmatsu* [Details of the All Asian Peoples Conference], ed. Naimushō Keihōkyoku Hoan Ka [Home Ministry, Special Observation Office, Public Security Division], October 1926. In fact, the fear that these pan-Asian activities would raise suspicion abroad was not completely ungrounded. Some foreign news reports before and during the Conference cynically argued that in the light of current pan-Asian activities Kaiser Wilhelm's warning of the Yellow Peril (1890) and the recent exclusionist legislation in the US might not have been exaggerated after all; see 'Again the "Pan-Asia" Bogy', *New York Times*, 17 July 1926, 12. There were also reports, however, that took the various dissonances at the Conference as proof of the implausibility of any joint Asian enterprise in the near future; see 'Pan-Asiatic Conference. An assembly of no importance', *The Observer* (Manchester), 1 August 1926, 9.
22. See Naruse Masao, 'Ajia Minzoku Kaigi ni tsuite' [On Asian Peoples' Congress], *Ajia Minzoku Kaigi ni tsuite, Jiyū Byōdō Hakuai no hongi, gekken shōrei no yōshi* [On the Asian Peoples' Congress, the true meaning of freedom, equality, and philanthropy, and an outline for the promotion of Japanese fencing], Tokyo: Chijin Yūsha 1927, 1–42: 1–2 and 20–21, Grant K. Goodman, 'The Pan-Asiatic Conference of 1926 at Nagasaki', *Proceedings of the 3rd Kyushu International Cultural Conference*, ed. The Fukuoka Unesco Association, Fukuoka: Yunesuko [Unesco] 1973, 21–29: 22–23, 'Ajiya [sic] Minzoku Kaigi ni hatashite appaku no mashu' [As expected, fiendish oppression of Asian Peoples' Congress], *Yamato*

Shinbun, 15 July 1926, and 'Asiatic Congress. Foreign Office on the Alert', *Japan Weekly Chronicle*, 22 July 1926, 113.
23. See 'Pan-Asiatics meet in Old Nippon', *Daily Guardian* (Sydney), 9 August 1926. For intelligence reports on the Nagasaki Conference, see above.
24. Unsurprisingly, the Korean 'delegates' were denounced as collaborators in the Korean media, where the hypocritical character of the assembly was condemned. In a censored editorial, the Congress was denounced as 'obstructing the liberation of the oppressed peoples in Asia and the world' rather than promoting it; see 'A minzoku taikai hantai ketsugi' [Resolution to oppose the Asian Peoples Conference], *Choson Ilbo*, 20 July 1926, as reproduced (in Japanese) in *Kesareta Genron. Seiji hen* [Deleted speech. Politics edition], Tokyo: Koria Kenkyūjo 1990, 371. See also 'A Korean Denunciation', *Japan Weekly Chronicle*, 5 August 1926, 157.
25. 'Imazato Juntarō o gichō ni kaigi hajimaru' [The Conference starts with Imazato as chairman], *Osaka Mainichi*, 2 August 1926 and 'Ajia Minzoku Taikai' [Asian Peoples Conference], *Osaka Asahi*, 1 August 1926.
26. 'Ajia Minzoku Taikai'.
27. See 'Ajia Minzoku Taikai'.
28. See 'Ajia Minzoku Taikai'.
29. See 'Ajia Minzoku Taikai'.
30. See Naruse, 'Ajia Minzoku Kaigi ni tsuite', 39–40. Naruse criticized this Chinese demand as 'irresponsible' and withdrew as observer from the Conference, as did three Japanese delegates.
31. 'Da Yazhou Minzu Huiyi' [Greater Asian Peoples' Conference], *Xiandai Pinglun* [Contemporary Review], 14 August 1926; quoted in Zhou Bin, 'Yaxiya Minzu Huiyi yu Zhongguo de fandui yundong', 147–148. The *Xiandai Pinglun* was a moderate journal of Northern Chinese liberals.
32. On the language problem see Asada Hajime, 'Ajia minzoku kaigi ni nan kokugo o tsukau ka' [What language is to be used at the Asian Peoples Conference?], *Osaka Asahi*, 29–30 July 1926, 'Ajia Minzoku Taikai', *Osaka Asahi*, 1 August 1926 and 'Pan-Asiatic Congress', *Japan Weekly Chronicle*, 12 August 1926, 191.
33. Said, *Orientalism*, 3.
34. Mahendra Pratap had been a delegate for the 1926 conference but ultimately could not participate because the Japanese authorities delayed the issuing of his visa. When he eventually received his visa the conference had already closed. Pratap met with participants of the conference in Osaka instead. On Pratap's background, activities, and involvement in both conferences see Stolte, '"Enough of the Great Napoleons!"'.
35. Zhou, 'Yaxiya Minzu Huiyi yu Zhongguo de fandui yundong', 151–152.

36. See Zhou, 'Yaxiya Minzu Huiyi yu Zhongguo de fandui yundong', 150–153 and 'Asiatic Congress', *Japan Weekly Chronicle*, 10 November 1927, 497.
37. See Zhou, 'Yaxiya Minzu Huiyi yu Zhongguo de fandui yundong', 152.
38. See Zhou, 'Yaxiya Minzu Huiyi yu Zhongguo de fandui yundong', 152.
39. In August and September 1928, newspapers reported that at the invitation of King Amanullah a Pan-Asian Conference was scheduled to be held in Kabul in November that year and that T. E. Lawrence ('Lawrence of Arabia') was returning to Arabia to persuade Arabs not to participate in such a gathering. No follow-up reports in any newspapers could be found and there is no information on a third Pan-Asian Conference in Japanese intelligence documents or sources from the host organizations of the previous conferences. It appears likely that the conference was cancelled due to continuing Sino-Japanese disputes, official opposition from both countries, and in the light of the unstable domestic situation in Afghanistan in the late 1920s. See 'Lawrence Goes Back to Arabia', *Atlanta Constitution*, 26 August 1928, 8 and 'Pan-Asiatic Congress', *Manchester Guardian*, 27 September 1928, 12. Stolte writes that a third Pan-Asian Conference planned 'in either Tehran or Kabul fell through for lack of interest there'. See Stolte, '"Enough of the Great Napoleons!"', 413.
40. Matsuura writes that the *Zen Ajia Kyōkai* was involved in organizing a Pan-Asian Congress, convened in Dalian on 11 February 1934. While the organization's former leader Imazato is in fact reported to have been involved in that gathering, there is no proof that the organization itself continued to exist after 1927. Imazato had moved to Manchukuo in the meantime and the fact that the Congress was held on the mythical founding day of Japan—a highly symbolic day used to celebrate Japan's empire—highlights how little it shared with the Asianist spirit of the two previous meetings convened in 1926 and 1927. See Matsuura Masataka, *Daitōa sensō wa naze okita no ka: han Ajiashugi no seiji keizaishi* [Why did the 'Greater East Asian War' happen? A political and economic history of Pan-Asianism], Nagoya: Nagoya Daigaku Shuppankai 2010: 181, 212.
41. See untitled editorial postscript to Ninagawa Arata, 'Ajia Renmei no kūron' [Empty theory of an Asian League], *Tōhō Kōron* [Eastern Review], February 1926, 12–17: 17.
42. Ninagawa Arata, 'Ajiajin hon'i ka Nihon kokumin hon'i ka' [The standard of the Asians or the standard of the Japanese people?], *Tōhō Kōron* [Eastern Review], January 1926, 37–43: 37.
43. See Ninagawa, 'Ajiajin hon'i ka Nihon kokumin hon'i ka', 38.
44. See Ninagawa, 'Ajiajin hon'i ka Nihon kokumin hon'i ka', 41–42.

45. Ninagawa Arata, 'Ajia Renmei no kūron' [Empty theory of an Asian League], *Tōhō Kōron* [Eastern Review], February 1926, 12–17: 16.
46. See Ninagawa, 'Ajia Renmei no kūron', 17 and his 'Kiken naru jinshu byōdō no seikō' [Dangerous political plan of racial equality], *Tōhō Kōron* [Eastern Review], July 1927, 20–22: 21–22.
47. Imazato Juntarō, 'Ajia Renmei no Daishimei. Ninagawa hakushi no byūken o tadasu' [The great mission of an Asian League. Correcting Dr. Ninagawa's erroneous views], *Tōhō Kōron* [Eastern Review], May 1926, 50–55: 50.
48. Imazato, 'Ajia Renmei no Daishimei', 51.
49. See Imazato, 'Ajia Renmei no Daishimei', 51. While the former advantages were based on its regional character, the latter rested on the fact that not only nation states but also ethnic groups could become members. The Asian League thereby would contribute to the overcoming of the dominant Western-centric form of group organization as nation states.
50. See Imazato, 'Ajia Renmei no Daishimei', 52.
51. Imazato, 'Ajia Renmei no Daishimei', 54.
52. See Ninagawa Arata, 'Ajia Minzoku to wa nan zo' [What on earth does Asian Peoples mean?], *Tōhō Kōron* [Eastern Review], June 1926, 47–49: 47–48.
53. See Ninagawa, 'Ajia Minzoku to wa nan zo', 48.
54. See Imazato Juntarō, 'Zen Ajia Renmei wa umaretari' [The All Asian League has been born], *Tōhō Kōron* [Eastern Review], September 1926, 41–44: 41.
55. The members included the Chinese Cai Xiaobai, director of an English school who had been a delegate at the Pan-Asian Conference in Nagasaki, Qiu Shui, former director of the Chinese Student Association in Shanghai, Jin Kemin, director of the Chinese *Shenzhou Ribao* newspaper, the Filipino doctor Kalambakal, a colleague of Tongū's, and the Indian H. P. Shastri.
56. 'Yazhou Minzu Xiehui Xuanyan' [Declaration of the Asian Peoples' Association], *Da Ya Zazhi* [Greater Asia Journal], No. 35 (April 1925), 1.
57. Sun's lectures on nationalism are part of his lectures on the Three People's Principles (Sanmin Zhuyi) delivered between January and August 1924 and seen as his main political legacy. For a reprint of his lectures see Sun Yat-sen, *Sanmin Zhuyi* [Three People's Principles], Taipei: Cheng Chung Books 1988.
58. On Tongū's life and activities see Minamihori Eiji, *Kiseki no ishi: Tōyōichi no kojin sōgō byōin Shanhai Fukumin byōin o tsukutta jiai no igyō* [The doctor of miracles: The medical work of kindness by the Shanghai Fumin Hospital, the best private general hospital in the East], Tokyo: Kōjinsha 2010.

59. See for example the report from the Japanese General Consulate in Shanghai to the Foreign Ministry in Tokyo 'Shanghai Dai Ajia Kyōkai' [Shanghai Greater Asia Association], *Gaimushō kiroku, Ajia kyoku* [Records of the Foreign Ministry, Asia Office], 22 May 1924 (JACAR B03041003600).
60. Tongū Yutaka, 'Iwayuru Ajia Renmei zehi' [The Pros and Cons of an Asian League], *Shanghai Jiron* [Shanghai Times] 1–8, August 1926, 2–6: 3.
61. Tongū, 'Iwayuru Ajia Renmei zehi', 6.
62. Tongū, 'Iwayuru Ajia Renmei zehi', 6.
63. Tongū, 'Iwayuru Ajia Renmei zehi', 4–5.
64. See Hirakawa Hitoshi, 'Kajima Morinosuke to Pan Ajiashugi' [Kajima Morinosuke and Pan-Asianism], *Keizai Kagaku* [Economy Science], 55–4 (2008), 1–24: 1. For the only in-depth study of Nagatomi's Asianism in English see Hitoshi Hirakawa, 'Dr. Morinosuke Kajima and Pan-Asianism', *Sekiguchi Gurōbaru Kenkyūkai (SGRA) Repōto* 58, ed. SGRA, Tokyo: SGRA 2011, 37–76.
65. For biographical information see Hirakawa, 'Kajima Morinosuke to Pan Ajiashugi', 1–3 and Kajima Morinosuke, *Waga kaisōroku: shisō to kōdō* [My Memoirs: Thought and Action], Tokyo: Kajima Kenkyūjo Shuppankai 1965.
66. Nagatomi had adopted Kajima's family name upon his marriage in 1927. For the sake of convenience I will refer to Nagatomi consistently by his original name rather than switching to Kajima for his writings after 1927, except for bibliographical data, which is reproduced as in the original publications.
67. Interestingly, Nagatomi did not refer to Coudenhove-Kalergi's Japanese mother as an additional sales point of his pan-Asian views to the Japanese.
68. Matsuura, *Daitōa sensō wa naze okitanoka*, 548.
69. See Nagatomi Morinosuke, 'Kyokutō Ajia Renpō no kensetsu' [The establishment of a Far East Asian Republic], *Gaikō Jihō* [Diplomatic Review] 481 (December 1924), 99–107.
70. See Nagatomi, 'Kyokutō Ajia Renpō no kensetsu', 100.
71. See Katiana Orluc, 'Decline or Renaissance: The Transformation of European Consciousness after the First World War', *Europe and the Other and Europe as the Other*, ed. Bo Strath, Brussels: Peter Lang 2000, 123–156 and on Coudenhove-Kalergi see Vanessa Conze, 'Leitbild Paneuropa? Zum Europagedanken und seiner Wirkung in der Zwischenkriegszeit am Beispiel der Konzepte Richard Coudenhove-Kalergis' [Pan-Europe as Model? On Europe as thought and its impact in the interwar period, taking the example of Richard Coudenhove-Kalergi's concepts], *Leitbild Europa? Europabilder und ihre Wirkungen in der*

Neuzeit [Europe as Model? Views of Europe and their impact in modern times], ed. Jürgen Elvert and Jürgen Nielsen-Sikora, Wien: Franz Steiner 2009, 119–125.
72. See Nagatomi, 'Kyokutō Ajia Renpō no kensetsu', 99–101.
73. Nagatomi, 'Kyokutō Ajia Renpō no kensetsu', 101.
74. See Nagatomi, 'Kyokutō Ajia Renpō no kensetsu', 104.
75. See Nagatomi, 'Kyokutō Ajia Renpō no kensetsu', 106.
76. See Nagatomi, 'Kyokutō Ajia Renpō no kensetsu', 107.
77. Hirakawa, 'Kajima Morinosuke to Pan Ajiashugi', 6.
78. See Nagatomi Morinosuke, 'Han Ajia undō ni tsuite' [On the pan-Asian movement], *Gaikō Jihō* [Diplomatic Review] 487 (March 1925), 34–40: 35, 39.
79. Nagatomi, 'Han Ajia undō ni tsuite', 35.
80. See Nagatomi Morinosuke, 'Gendai no chōkokkateki rengō undō no ichi shimyaku toshite no han Ajia undō' [The contemporary movement for supranational unions as one branch of the pan-Asian movement], *Kokusai Chishiki* [International Knowledge], October 1926, 2–13: 3.
81. See Nagatomi, 'Gendai no chōkokkateki rengō undō no ichi shimyaku toshite no han Ajia undō', 2.
82. See Nagatomi, 'Gendai no chōkokkateki rengō undō no ichi shimyaku toshite no han Ajia undō', 4.
83. See Nagatomi, 'Gendai no chōkokkateki rengō undō no ichi shimyaku toshite no han Ajia undō', 5.
84. See Nagatomi, 'Gendai no chōkokkateki rengō undō no ichi shimyaku toshite no han Ajia undō', 4.
85. See Nagatomi, 'Gendai no chōkokkateki rengō undō no ichi shimyaku toshite no han Ajia undō', 12.
86. See Nagatomi, 'Gendai no chōkokkateki rengō undō no ichi shimyaku toshite no han Ajia undō', 12.
87. A collection of Rōyama Masamichi's early essays on the East Asian Community can be found in Rōyama Masamichi, *Nichi-Man kankei no kenkyū* [Research on Japanese–Manchurian Relations], Tokyo: Shibun Shoin 1933. See also Han Jung-Sun, 'Rationalizing the Orient: The "East Asia Cooperative Community" in Prewar Japan', *Monumenta Nipponica*, 60–4 (Winter 2005), 481–514 and J. Victor Koschmann, 'Constructing Destiny: Rōyama Masamichi and Asian Regionalism in Wartime Japan', *Pan-Asianism in Modern Japanese History. Colonialism, regionalism and borders*, ed. Sven Saaler and J. Victor Koschmann, London: Routledge 2007, 185–199.
88. See Kajima [Nagatomi] Morinosuke, 'Kokusai Renmei yori Han Ajia Renmei e' [From the League of Nations to a Pan-Asian League], *Keizai Ōrai* [Economic Traffic] 8-4 (April 1933), 184–192: 187.

89. Kajima [Nagatomi] Morinosuke, 'Nisshi Shin Jōyaku to Dai Tōa Renmei' [The new contract between Japan and China and a Greater East Asian League], *Gaikō Jihō* [Diplomatic Review] 866 (January 1941), 55–65: 62.
90. Kajima [Nagatomi] Morinosuke, *Teikoku no gaikō to Dai Tōa Kyōeiken* [The diplomacy of the Empire and the Greater East Asian Co-Prosperity Sphere], Tokyo: Yokusantosho Kankōkai 1943, 2–5, quoted in Hirakawa Hitoshi, 'Kajima Morinosuke to Pan Ajiashugi' [Kajima Morinosuke and Pan-Asianism], *Keizai Kagaku* [Economy Science], 55–4 (2008), 1–24: 11.
91. Hirakawa, 'Kajima Morinosuke to Pan Ajiashugi', 11.
92. Aydin, *The politics of anti-Westernism in Asia*, 160.

CHAPTER 7

Asianism From Above: The Realization of 'Asia' in Manchuria

Presupposing the founding of the Kingly Way's Manchuria, the opportunity for the realization of our ideal of the creation of a Greater Asia which we have been holding in our hearts for so many years has eventually been bestowed upon us. A 'Greater Asia League' is no longer a mere concept but a precise policy that has emerged in front of the eyes of the Japanese people.[1]
—Matsui Iwane (1933)

The anti-Asianist political reality that had cast dark clouds over many activities and proposals for Asian commonality and solidarity deteriorated further during the late 1920s. In May 1928, a second dispatch of Japanese troops to the north-eastern Chinese province of Shandong to 'protect' Japanese citizens there led to the Jinan Incident, a violent military conflict with more than five thousand casualties. This caused a massive growth in anti-Japanese popular sentiments throughout China and, as a consequence, the tense relations between China and Japan worsened further. In June of the same year, the Japanese Kwantung (Guandong) Army stationed in Manchuria plotted and executed the murder of Chinese warlord Zhang Zuolin (1875–1928) in Fengtian (today's Shenyang). In the following months and years leading up to the Manchurian Incident of September 1931 Japanese military and politics repeatedly took action, including a third military dispatch to Shandong, to prevent a potential unification of Manchuria with the newly united Chinese Republic in Nanjing under the leadership of Chiang Kai-shek (Jiang Jieshi). In Korea, anti-Japanese student strikes in Kwangju in 1929 were violently suppressed and in Taiwan in 1930 a rising of the indigenous population, the biggest rebellion against Japanese colonial forces on the island (the 'Wushe Incident'), led to massacres on both sides and was eventually suppressed by force. The tensions and conflicts between Japanese and 'other Asians' were to deteriorate further when the Kwantung Army invaded and seized Manchuria in 1931 and the Japanese government, faced with an undesired *fait accompli*, responded by establishing the puppet state of Manchukuo in March 1932.[2] Visions of Asian commonality and co-prosperity faded in the light of these events, and rivalry along national lines of demarcation rendered Asianist conceptions unrealistic and absurd. Ironically, however, at the end of two decades of intense Asianism discourse in the mainstream public political sphere, its content and rhetoric were eventually appropriated by the military and political leadership in Japan and employed as official ideology of pan-Asian racial harmony and later for legitimization of Japan's expansive policies in Asia.

Within Japan, the conditions of controversial public political debate had worsened, too. A reform in 1928 of the so-called Peace Preservation Law (literally Public Security Preservation Law; Jp. Chian Iji Hō) of 1925 and the establishment of the Special Higher Police (Tokubetsu Kōtō Keisatsu) as a kind of thought police further limited freedom of speech and, as a consequence, changed the parameters of public political discourse.[3] In 1928 and 1929, more than two thousand members of the Japanese Communist Party and of other Socialist and leftist groups were arrested (March 15th Incident 1928, April 16th Incident 1929). In 1932, the political atmosphere in Japan changed drastically when rightwing groups such as the *Ketsumeidan* (Blood Pledge Corps) started to resort to terrorism and assassinations. With the murder of Prime Minister Inukai Tsuyoshi (1855–1932) during the military-initiated coup d'état in May 1932 (May 15th Incident), the political system of party cabinets came to an end and the military took centre stage in Japanese politics.

In this political and social turmoil from the late 1920s to the early 1930s, Asianist debate in Japan receded from the headlines of published opinion, only to reappear forcefully again after the founding of Manchukuo in 1932 and Japan's announcement of its departure from the League of Nations in 1933.[4] In China, however, the consolidation process after the partial pacification and unification ('Nanjing Decade') intensified the struggle for political authority both between the *Guomindang* and the Communists and within Chiang Kai-shek's party itself. In this context, Asianism resurfaced prominently in Chinese political discourse from the early 1930s onwards as a claim to the legacy of Sun Yat-sen within the GMD leadership.

This final chapter examines how and why, after the failure of civil society-led and initiated transnational Asianist projects and the establishment of geopolitical conceptions of Asianism, Asianist rhetoric, and activity became increasingly diverted to government and military circles and was employed in justification—not rejection or critique, as previously—of official Japanese 'Asia' policy. In order to analyse this shift in agency and quality, from controversial debate to quasi-ideology, this chapter focuses on the 'hijacking' of Asianism (Duara), mainly by and for military propaganda, to justify Japan's actions in Manchuria, including the founding and controlling of the puppet state of Manchukuo in 1932. A second focus of this chapter is on parallel attempts among different *Guomindang* factions in China to claim the heritage of Sun Yat-sen's Greater Asianism in order to justify either anti-Japanese resistance or pro-Japanese collaboration. The ambiguity of Sun Yat-sen's conception of Asianism, as this chapter shows, meant it could be appropriated for either policy. Interestingly, the Japanese Greater Asia Association (founded 1933) also tried to base its legitimacy on references to Sun Yat-sen's proposals for a joint Asianist enterprise. Their propaganda activities—and later attempts by the Japanese government to use Sun's Asianism further attest to the necessity of studying Asianism in its historically transnational discursive space, where it continued to be used as an instrument to claim hegemony, be it within a party, nationally, regionally or even globally.

Claiming Sun's Legacy in Nanjing China

The so-called Nanjing Decade in modern Chinese history, from the end of the Northern Expedition (Beifa) and the anti-Communist coup d'état in 1927 to the outbreak of the Sino-Japanese War in 1937, was only on the surface an era of peace, stability, and unity. As Rana Mitter has pointed out, 'behind the façade of national unity, Chiang's government was an uneasy affair, desperately balancing rivals for power against each other: provincial warlords, the Communists, and the Japanese'.[5] In addition, within Chiang's party, the *Guomindang* (GMD), too, factions competed for authority and influence.[6] Ideologically, the rivals outside the GMD had defined the political agenda of Chiang's party's *ex negativo*, although neither anti-Communism nor anti-Japanism could be maintained consistently. A fixed point of reference, however, was Sun Yat-sen, the founder of the Republic of China in 1912[7] and Chiang's brother-in-law. In 1923 Sun had appointed Chiang as superintendent of the influential Whampoa (Huang Pu) Military Academy. Wang Jingwei (1883–1944), one of the earliest pre-revolutionary collaborators with Sun, who had drafted Sun's will in 1925, later became Chiang's fiercest inner-party rival. Hu Hanmin (1879–1936), like Wang, one of Sun's early comrades, who had edited the Revolutionary Alliance's *Minbao* and had also authored its guiding principles in 1905, first supported Chiang but during the 1930s became a leading anti-Chiang voice. Another, already familiar follower of Sun, Dai Jitao, managed to establish himself as a leading figure of the rightist faction within the GMD and became a loyal supporter of Chiang. Against pro-Soviet and pro-Communist ideological tendencies within the GMD, and more generally against competing interpretations of Sun's legacy, Dai had already begun in 1925 to canonize Sun's political views. It is rather astonishing and testifies to the significance of Asianism as a political concept that either of the leading contestants for Sun's succession was prominently involved in the debate on defining 'the true meaning' of Sun's Greater Asianism. In fact, together with references to Sun's *Sanmin Zhuyi* (Three People's Principles), the claim to Sun's Asianist conceptions was a major way of legitimizing political action and thought in public political discourse in China during the 1930s and 1940s, at least outside the CCP.

Dai Jitao's Claim to Sun's Asianism

Not unexpectedly, Dai Jitao played an important role in the definition of Sun's political thought, including his conception of Greater Asianism. After all, Dai had accompanied Sun on his trips to Japan, where Sun had frequently appealed to notions of Sino-Japanese friendship as the core of Asian commonality and Asian unity.[8] Most prominently, Dai had been the interpreter from Chinese to Japanese of Sun's famous Greater Asianism speech of 1924 in Kobe. Dai's interpretation of Sun's political thought is usually seen as conservative and traditionalist.[9] Certainly, his tracing back of Sun's thought to Confucian orthodoxy, ethical values, and humanism constituted no falsification of Sun's own words. As we have seen earlier (Chap. 5), in his Kobe speech too, Sun had centrally referred to Confucian values such as the principle of the 'Kingly Way' (wangdao), benevolence, and morality. However, apart from his focus on traditional sources Dai paid close attention to locating Sun in the context of contemporary political affairs; domestically, this was mainly intended to divorce Sun from potential appropriation by Communists by emphasizing anti-internationalist and anti-Communist conceptions of his principles of nationalism (minzu zhuyi) and livelihood (minsheng zhuyi); to the outside, he focused on portraying China as the core of 'Asia' in Sun's understanding and denouncing Japan as a morally non-Eastern country.[10] Referring to Sun's conception of Asianism, Dai explained:

> [Sun] was not an Asianist in the general sense. If we look at his complete works, we can understand that he was a patriot with the final aim of a 'world union and evolution of human community'. His Three People's Principles therefore are neither a negation of Greater Asianism nor do they denote a Greater China-ism (Da Zhongguo zhuyi). Instead, he postulated an alliance of the oppressed peoples that, theoretically, was not limited to Asia but comprised all weak and small peoples of the world. [...] For him Asia did not denote a clod of earth but it symbolized the bitter reality of pain and suffering of eight hundred million oppressed people.[11]

Dai's interpretation of Sun's Asianism was hardly misrepresenting the abstract and theoretical dimension inherent in Sun's conception of 'Asia'. It is important, however, to note that Dai had already in 1925 explicitly attempted to reconcile Sun's Asianism with his *Sanmin Zhuyi*, a matter that Sun himself had never addressed. Dai's attention to this aspect foreshadows later efforts by Hu Hanmin and Wang Jingwei to demonstrate the compatibility of both principles (see below). Their political messages, of course, were diametrically opposed to each other. While Hu and Dai in the 1930s tried to save Sun's Asianism from conflation with Japanese conceptions, in the 1940s Wang attempted to identify similarities between Sun's Asianism and the assumed Asianist reality in Japan's empire.

Unfortunately, Dai's critique of Japan does not help to answer the question of whether or not the famous final section of Sun's Kobe speech was historical. Neither did he quote from that speech, nor did he employ the same terminology. At any rate, if Sun had indeed pinned down the Japanese to answer the uncomfortable question of their adherence to their 'Eastern' origins, Dai was no longer posing that question but simply provided the answer:

> Regrettably, it [Japan] has abandoned the virtues of the Eastern peoples and completely adopted European imperialism. After Japan became strong, it first subdued Liuqiu [Ryūkyū, Okinawa], next Korea, and thereby acted against a unification of the Eastern peoples. If Japan had, after its becoming powerful and prosperous, continued to hold in high esteem the morals of the small Eastern peoples and of the nation, and shouldered the responsibility of relieving troubles, without doubt the history of the past thirty years not only in the East but also worldwide would have developed in completely different ways.[12]

Dai continued to promote Asianism and 'Asia' discourse in China in the following years and in 1932 was elected Chairman of the *Xin Yaxiya Xuehui* (New Asia Study Society). As its main activity this Society published a journal called *Xin Yaxiya* (New Asia). Despite its secondary English title 'New Asia'and in contrast to a different journal by the same name published in Tokyo and to Tongū's bilingual journal in Shanghai[13]—it exclusively carried articles in Chinese, mostly written by Chinese with only a few essays translated from foreign languages into Chinese. The journal was first published in Shanghai, moved to Nanjing in 1932, and stopped publication in April 1937. In 1944, it was briefly revived for only two issues, which were published in Chiang's refuge city of Chongqing.[14] Until his premature death, Zhang Zhenzhi (1906–1931) served as the core editorial figure of the journal. Originally from Jiangsu province and a graduate of Shanghai's *Zhonghua Fazheng Daxue* (Chinese Law and Politics University), from 1928 Zhang had worked in the government's Examination Yuan, of which Dai Jitao was president. After Zhang's death, Dai became the central figure of the journal and usually contributed several articles to each volume. Its first issue was like a homage to Sun Yat-sen. The opening article was a full reprint of Sun's Greater Asianism speech of 1924 under the headline 'Greater Asianism' (Da Yaxiya zhuyi), introduced as 'Sun's legacy to the Eastern peoples'.[15] The subsequent article, the founding declaration of the journal, constituted an Asianist plea *par excellence*. The anonymous author, however, was not entirely faithful to Sun's deterritorialized understanding of 'Asia', which he simply identified as 'one of the five continents'. After a comparison of size and population of different continents, the author turned to Asia's 'miserable present condition':

> Who comes to rescue Asia? Which principle (zhuyi) can save the peoples of Asia? The person who can save the peoples of Asia is the revolutionary leader of our *Guomindang*, Dr. Sun Yat-sen. The principle that can save the Asian peoples is the highest revolutionary principle of our *Guomindang*, the Three People's Principles.[16]

The author, of course, hastened to explain that the Three People's Principles needed to be applied to all of Asia in order to unite and liberate the peoples of Asia.

> The *zongli* [Sun] has frequently lectured on Greater Asianism. Is Greater Asianism an independent principle? No, Asianism surely is no independent principle. The *zongli* said Greater Asianism is the application of *Sanmin Zhuyi* to peoples internationally. [...] Greater Asianism is a method of applying *Sanmin Zhuyi*. There are many people who talk about Greater Asianism. In the East (Dongfang), there is even a country that has already attained a powerful and prosperous status and employs Greater Asianism as a slogan for the wild dream of uniting Asia. And there are some military people and politicians who offer imperialism in a charming way as Greater Asianism. [...] Because *Sanmin Zhuyi* as invented by the *zongli* will save China, *Sanmin Zhuyi* is the principle of saving the nation (jiuguo zhuyi). Because *Sanmin Zhuyi* will save the peoples of Asia, without doubt *Sanmin Zhuyi* is Greater Asianism.[17]

As this excerpt reveals, the *Xin Yaxiya* in a first step defined its own conception of Asianism against the official appropriation of Asianism that was beginning in Japan (and the assumed Asianist reality in Japan's empire). Once it had divorced Sun's Greater Asianism from possible conflation or confusion with Japanese Asianism it aimed at demonstrating that Asia's future, as the article concluded, was an 'Asia' of the Three People's Principles (Sanmin Zhuyi de Yaxiya). As a consequence, although Asianism in principle seemed to be about 'Asia', from a Japanese perspective this definition of Asianism was just as Sinocentric as from a Chinese perspective most Japanese conceptions of Asianism were too Japan-centric; Asianism therefore facilitated and accelerated the discursive contest between Japan's 'Asia' and China's 'Asia'.

Already in its mission statement, the journal had stated as 'the mission of new Asia/New Asia'—which could be read both ways: either the mission of the journal New Asia or more generally the mission of a new 'Asia'—to 'establish a China of the Three People's Principles and an Asia of the Three Peoples Principles' by liberating the Chinese people (Zhonghua minzu) and the Eastern peoples (Dongfang minzu).[18] The national and international aims were intertwined and the journal's adoption of Asianism was obviously not merely meant to challenge Japanese conceptions. Rather, the study group had developed its own hegemonic version of 'Asia' in which the Chinese project of 'Asia' was to be closely linked, and indeed dependent on, the question of territorial hegemony or border control. The 'frontier question' (bianjiang wenti) was in fact named as the second mission of the society, next to the 'liberation of the Eastern peoples'.[19] It therefore related the formation of China as a nation state to the development of China's border areas and the liberation of oppressed peoples in other parts of Asia. As a result, the adherence to Asianist vocabulary for Asianist aims was put into perspective; 'Asia'—not only for Japan but also for China—was useful as a tool in stabilizing ongoing projects of nation- or empire-building. As Prasenjit Duara has observed, 'Dai's pan-Asianism [...] could provide an alternative basis for solidarity with the non-Han. By emphasizing a strongly culturalist and weakly racialist (coloured peoples versus whites) basis for solidarity, ironically, pan-Asianism could be mobilized to secure national solidarity. This is, I believe, the only way to understand the journal's mission of deliberately juxtaposing the liberation of the minorities with that of Eastern nationalities'.[20] In other words, rather than being an abstract or ideology-driven concept, Asianism here was closely linked to the concrete and practical project of state building and nation formation. The frontier regions functioned as China's own domestic Asianist project that could, but did not necessarily have to, be linked to Asianist claims elsewhere. Duara has argued that these tensions between nationalist and trans- or inter-nationalist agendas represent an instance of the 'two-part strategy of "domesticating" transnationality whether by enlisting pan-Asianism to incorporate peripheral peoples into the geobody and colonized peoples into the empire, or by employing Han racialism and Confucian culturalism among Chinese transnationals'.[21] At the same time as the transnational was nationalized, the national was transnationalized. The New Asia journal, in any case, made no effort to conceal its outspokenly Sinocentric perspective and Sinocentric conception of 'Asia'. Apart from the fact that it saw China in a privileged position, since both Sun and his *Sanmin Zhuyi* were of Chinese origin, China was also quantitatively and qualitatively superior to any other country in Asia, its essayists argued.

From our point of view, among the peoples in Asia there are only the Chinese people (Zhonghua minzu) that can shoulder this heavy burden [of uniting and liberating Asia]! This is not an illusion but based on reality: first, the Chinese people have the largest population and can therefore fight against the Whites. Second, the Chinese people possess a thoroughly superior national character: national virtue, national thought, and national ability.[22]

Kawashima Shin's research has revealed that even more hegemonic and chauvinistic views of Asia existed among Chinese nationalists and that from the 1930s onwards this 'emphasis on China's superiority and former tributary relations' was characteristic not only of a certain stream of public political discourse on 'Asia' in China but also of school textbooks and official publications.[23]

Hu Hanmin's Claim to Sun's Asianism

Another prominent contestant in the fight over Sun's intellectual and political legacy was Hu Hanmin. From Guangdong province, like Sun, Hu belonged to the inner circle of the GMD leadership. Soon after Sun's death, however, Hu became opposed to Chiang and left China for almost two years to study in Moscow. Upon his return, he successfully negotiated between conflicting factions within the GMD and joined Chiang's Nanjing Government as president of the Legislative Yuan. Nevertheless, Hu remained in opposition to Chiang even after the Manchurian Incident had briefly unified all factions against the Japanese. In the early years of the twentieth century, Hu had twice studied in Japan but his link with that country never became as deep as Sun's, Dai's, or Wang Jingwei's.

From the founding days of the journal, Hu had been involved as a contributor to Zhang's *Xin Yaxiya*. However, after a few issues no more writings were published under his name, probably owing to the continuous tense relationship between Hu and Chiang, which also affected Hu's otherwise good relationship with Dai. Dissatisfied with the way that Chiang and Dai interpreted Sun's politico-intellectual legacy and used it as political propaganda, Hu founded his own political journal in 1933. Its title was simply *Sanmin Zhuyi* (Three People's Principles) and its most obvious mission was to provide a different interpretation of Sun's major political agenda. The journal had initially been founded as the organ of Hu's new political party, the *Xin Guomindang* (New Guomindang).[24] This new party opposed Chiang's Nanjing government in general and its appeasing attitude towards the Japanese after 1931 in particular. Hu's discussion of Greater Asianism in his journal consequently became a tool in criticizing both Japanese Asianism as imperialism and the existing versions of Asianism within the GMD as misinterpretations of Sun's Greater Asianism. Quoting extensively from Sun's Kobe speech, Hu argued that Sun's Asianism mainly consisted of two characteristics:

> first, the aims of Greater Asianism are to destroy the oppression of the Asian peoples by the hegemonic peoples of Europe and to restore the original status of the Asian peoples; second, the methods of Greater Asianism are to unite the peoples of Asia on the basis of their original culture of the Kingly Way in order to strive for the common profit of the Asian peoples.[25]

Sun's Asianism, Hu emphasized, was completely different from Japanese foreign policy that—in the name of Greater Asianism—practised imperialism. While this criticism of Japanese Asianism was by no means new, Hu's explicit link to his dismissal of Nanjing's diplomacy was rather remarkable. Rejecting both the 'use one barbarian to check another' strategy of the pro-Western faction and Wang Jingwei's 'stupid and frantic pro-Japanese claims', Hu openly attacked his party rivals. 'We have only one way', Hu concluded, 'and that is to save ourselves by fighting the Japanese, and by saving ourselves to establish Greater Asianism as proclaimed by Dr. Sun Yat-sen'.[26]

Hu's political engagement with Sun's Asianism continued over the following years. Only a few months after his first essay, Hu again elaborated on the meaning of Greater Asianism—and repeated his attacks on Japan and the Nanjing government. But Hu also attempted to develop a more abstract and visionary conception of Asianism. Sun's political philosophy, Hu argued, consisted of a four-step plan that proceeded from familial to group unification, from group unification to national unification and national independence, from there to the union of the Asian peoples—the realization of Greater Asianism—and finally from there to a 'worldist world union' (shijie zhuyi zhi shijie datong) to achieve 'equality and friendship' among all peoples.[27] By insisting on the importance of nationalism in general and by stressing the function of Asianism as a 'link' between nationalism and worldism,[28] Hu indirectly also reiterated his well-known anti-Communist stance and rejected Socialist internationalist ideas regarding both content and terminology. At the same time, he avoided both culturalist or racialist essentializations of Asianism and an aggrandizement of China's role in the Asianist project. Asia's revival, as envisioned by Hu, was not an end in itself: rather it was a means to gain political freedom and to resist—not collaborate with—the Japanese whose Asianism he unmasked as 'Greater Yamato nationalism'.[29] Therefore, Hu never failed to associate Japan's Asianism with that of the Chinese government in Nanjing. Referring to Wang's policy of 'resisting while negotiating', Hu asked rhetorically:

> Is this Greater Asianism? Or is this the Nanjing government's principle of treachery? Or is this the Japanese principle of controlling all of Asia centring on the Imperial Household? There should be no need for us to explain [further].[30]

Despite his strong anti-Japanism, Hu did not shun exchanging views directly with Japanese military leaders. In March 1935, Hu met with Major General Doihara Kenji (1883–1948)[31] of the Manchuria-based Kwantung (Guandong) Army in Hong Kong, and in February 1936, only three months before Hu's death, General Matsui Iwane visited Hu in Guangzhou. Inevitably their talks at some point turned to the matter of Asianism. According to Takatsuna Hirofumi, the aim of Doihara's and Matsui's visits may have been to check the 'conciliatory' diplomacy of the Japanese foreign minister Hirota and to search for a way to use Hu as an opponent of the Nanjing government for the purposes of the Japanese army.[32] According to Hu, in his conversation with Doihara he extensively explained his own conception of Asianism based on his understanding of Sun's Greater Asianism.

> Regarding a Sino-Japanese alliance, in principle I absolutely agree with you. But an alliance with someone else [Japan] must by all means be based on the teachings of Dr. Sun Yat-sen. That is, 'we must fight jointly with those peoples in the world that treat us as equals'. Because in the past there have been many reasons why we have not been able to form an alliance, we must first clear these obstacles to realize a proper alliance. For me, it was Japan which complicated the relations between both countries because it does not abandon its policy of invading China. In addition,

declarations such as that of April 7th (1934) [Amō Declaration][33] that place Japan itself as the leader of Asia similarly pose a grave obstacle to a Sino-Japanese alliance.[34]

Japanese Asianism, as Hu had already argued in his writings published in the *Sanmin Zhuyi* journal, could not serve the aims of rapprochement and alliance unless Japan abandoned its imperialist policies towards China. At the same time, however, Hu adhered to the concept of Greater Asianism as significant and rightful. 'I am an Asianist and simultaneously I am a follower of the principle of "resisting Japan"', he wrote. 'For me, the claim to resist Japan means nothing but fully practising Greater Asianism and realizing the last wish of Dr. Sun.'[35]

This statement, which underlined his critique of Japan and his ambition to represent Sun's legacy, also summed up his conversation with Matsui Iwane, according to Hu. In 1927, Matsui had already proposed to Hu 'implement[ing] Greater Asianism as the teaching of Dr. Sun Yat-sen in order to preserve peace in the Far East and seek Sino-Japanese co-existence and co-prosperity'.[36] In the meantime, however, little had happened to improve the relations between the two countries whereas much had occurred to worsen them. Hu expressed his hope that Matsui would contribute to correcting the past mistakes and 'to educate the state of mind of the Japanese people to lead them to the path of righteousness'.[37] Matsui, however, appeared to have a different impression of Hu's Asianism. 'Regarding our Greater Asianism', Matsui claimed, 'they [the Chinese] explained that ever since the time of Sun Yat-sen they had their own Greater Asianism; however, this by and large coincides with ours.'[38] A commonality that Matsui may have alluded to, as Takatsuna suggests, certainly lay in the fact that both Matsui—as we will see in more detail below—and Hu employed Asianism as weapons of persuasion or propaganda in the political struggle for power and authority.[39] In addition, in both cases Asianism was directed against the Chinese central government in Nanjing. Apart from this, however, Hu's Asianism and Matsui's were strongly opposed to each other. Sun's (Hu's) anti-colonial Asianism had just as little to offer Matsui as had Matsui's request to China to submit to Japanese leadership. Hu's untimely death helped Matsui to spread the impression that Chinese leaders had affirmed his own conception of Asianism. Reporting from Shanghai, the *Straits Times* of Singapore, at any rate, had confidence in the authenticity of Matsui's portrayal and published the following brief note:

Air defence preparations in Nanking are more intense than in any city in Japan, stated Gen. Matsui, founder of the Great Asia doctrine, on his return to Shanghai yesterday. Continuing, the General claimed that his idea of Great Asianism is supported by 'a certain section of Chinese officialdom'.[40]

In this way, conceptions of Asianism held by Japanese officials and their impact on transnational 'Asia' discourse gained disproportionate authority. Despite the newspaper's slightly distancing wording ('claimed'), it asserted in its headline that Asianism was seen favourably by the Chinese and even elevated Matsui to the rank of 'founder of the Great Asia doctrine', that is, of Greater Asianism. This is, of course, a stark misrepresentation of Hu's talk with Matsui and of the inspiration of Asianism which, even in the case of Matsui, in fact stemmed from Sun. Sun, however, had long been dead and with Hu's death in May 1936 a fearless, influential, critical and yet affirmative voice in transnational Asianism discourse of the 1930s was muted.

Wang Jingwei's Claim to Sun's Asianism

Hardly surprisingly, after the Xi'an Incident of 1936[41] and the Marco Polo Bridge Incident of 1937 had brought the rival groups within China closer together than ever, Asianism was no longer a topic of pressing political concern. Its potential to generate and advance political controversy had faded in the light of political reality. Only after Wang Jingwei's defection from Chiang's government in 1940 did Asianism resurface prominently—and in a rather familiar way.[42] Importantly, conceptions of Asianism as proposed by the main Chinese collaborators—Wang Jingwei and his followers—were neither a mere invention for propaganda reasons nor a wholesale and uncritical adoption of Japanese wartime rhetoric. Instead, similar to Dai's and Hu's Asianisms, they were part of an integrated attempt at seeking political legitimacy by claiming the intellectual heritage of Sun Yat-sen. As Rana Mitter has pointed out, '[f]or Wang, it was Sun's attachment to pan-Asianism that was most critical, since it provided the basis for an argument that collaboration with Japan was in fact a version of the nationalist project that Sun had pursued'.[43] Wang's Asianism, therefore, was essentially a 'restoration of Sun Yat-sen's Asianism',[44] particularly as expressed in his famous Kobe lecture of 1924. In Marius Jansen's words, it was 'primarily in this speech that

Wang Ching-wei [Wang Jingwei] claimed to find the justification for his cooperation with Japan'.[45] By adopting Sun's Asianism, Wang managed to combine his claim to Sun's legacy with appeasing the Japanese, on the one hand, and offering a political alternative in the domestic arena to the united front of Mao Zedong's Chinese Communist Party (CCP) and Chiang Kai-shek's *Guomindang*, on the other. Eventually, Wang's balancing act between pleasing the Japanese and appealing to the war-torn Chinese failed under the combined pressure of Chinese anti-Japanese resistance and the military success of the Allied forces.

Wang Jingwei was born in 1883 in Guangdong and first visited Japan in 1904 as an exchange student at Tokyo's Hōsei University, sponsored by the Qing court. In 1905, when Sun Yat-sen founded the *Tongmenghui* (Revolutionary Alliance) in Tokyo, Wang became an editor of its party bulletin, the *Minbao* (People's Paper).[46] For the revolutionary cause, Wang returned to China to assassinate the regent and father of the child-emperor Puyi in 1910. However, the plot was discovered and Wang was arrested and sentenced to death. Following the Republican Revolution of 1911, Wang was freed and became one of Sun's closest followers. In the 1920s, he held several posts in Sun's Revolutionary Government in Guangdong. Wang's rivalry with Chiang Kai-shek had begun after Sun's death, when Wang, as the most likely and legitimate candidate as Sun's successor, was quickly outstripped by Chiang. Although Wang was eventually reconciled with Chiang after the Manchurian Incident (1931) and became Premier of the Nationalist Government (1932–1935), his rivalry with Chiang continued. When Chiang was again forced to cooperate with the Communists and to actively resist the Japanese after the Xi'an Incident, Wang's anti-Communist and pro-Japanese stance estranged him further from the GMD leadership. Although Wang, together with Chiang and his GMD government, fled the Japanese invasion of Southern China (Shanghai, Nanjing) to Chongqing in 1938, his turning away from Chiang and toward the Japanese soon took on particular forms.

The Japanese *aite to sezu* declaration (no dealings with the Nationalist Government) of January 1938 had already expressed Japan's willingness to work with a new Chinese regime. In this context, Premier Konoe Fumimaro's announcement of a new China policy ('New Order in East Asia') in November was interpreted—both in Japan and in China—as an implicit invitation to Wang to become the head of a pro-Japanese government in occupied China. Just one month later Wang and his group left Chongqing. After a period of refuge in Hanoi and Hong Kong (December 1938–April 1939), where the group launched a 'peace movement' to settle the conflict with Japan, Wang decided to directly negotiate the conditions of his collaboration with Japan in Shanghai.[47] It is important to note that almost a year and a half passed between Wang's defection and his assuming the leadership of the Japanese-sponsored government in Nanjing in March 1940. Treatments of this period that portray Wang as a plain traitor (Jp. kankan, Ch. hanjian) overlook the fact that an appropriate political response to the situation was hotly debated within the Wang group in exile. Once the decision to collaborate had been taken, Wang negotiated intensively with the Japanese over the exact terms of his cooperation, which included the demand for a Japanese troop withdrawal.[48] Seen in this light, Wang appears to have been much less of a passive toy in the hands of his Japanese masters than the frequent characterizations of his government as a 'puppet regime' imply.

In order to legitimize his government in Nanjing, to appear to the Chinese as an attractive alternative to Chiang, and simultaneously to please the Japanese, Wang employed a number of striking political symbols and slogans.[49] He adopted the same name and structure as Chiang's Chongqing government, and built his political programme around the cornerstones of peace (heping), anti-communism (fangong), and national reconstruction (jianguo). These three slogans were usually displayed together with the national flag, the same one that had been adopted by the unified Nationalist government in 1928 ('blue sky – white sun – red earth'). Wang also insisted that his assumption of the leadership of the government in Nanjing would be publicized not as the creation of a new regime, but as a 'return to the capital' (huan du). Equally important, Wang linked the legitimacy of his government largely to the person of Sun Yat-sen. Together with Zhou Fohai (1897–1948), a close follower of Wang and senior minister in his government,[50] he visited Sun's tomb in Nanjing prior to the official inauguration of his new government. Sun's birthday (12 November) was also used as a powerful symbol of Wang's self-acclaimed succession to Sun's leadership.[51] While Wang openly embraced Japan's pan-Asian rhetoric, he explicitly linked his pro-Japanese and anti-resistance positions not to Japanese Asianism, but exclusively to Sun Yat-sen's. References to Sun soon became ubiquitous in Wang's speeches and articles (Figs. 7.1 and 7.2). In the foreword to a collection of Sun's writings which were published in 1941 and which included the

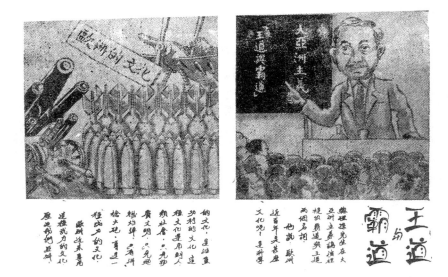

Fig. 7.1 In this cartoon 'Wangdao yu badao' [Rule of Right and Rule of Might], published in the Chinese journal *Dongya lianmeng huabao* [East Asian League Pictorial] by Wang Jingwei's collaborationist regime in February 1941, Sun Yat-sen is portrayed when delivering his famous speech on Greater Asianism in Kobe in 1924 (see Chap. 5). The Chinese text under the illustrations reproduces parts of Sun's speech, explaining the differences between Eastern rule of virtue and Western rule of might and culture of war. Note the ahistorical absence of Wang's rival Dai Jitao who interpreted Sun's speech (cf. Fig. 5.2). Reproduced with kind permission from the collection of Waseda University Library

text of Sun's Greater Asianism speech, Wang used Sun to argue for Sino-Japanese friendship:

> Racially, geographically, and historically, as well as in respect of environment, culture and material development, it is natural for China and Japan to be friends, unnatural for them to be enemies. Any dispute which arises between the two nations should be regarded as a transitory, unnatural phenomenon, and should be settled in an appropriate manner so that the natural relationship may resume its permanent and natural course of peace and friendship. This point has been expounded most clearly and most thoroughly in the teachings bequeathed us by our late leader, Dr. Sun Yat-sen. There are occasional passages to be found in those teachings in which

7 ASIANISM FROM ABOVE: THE REALIZATION OF 'ASIA' IN MANCHURIA   283

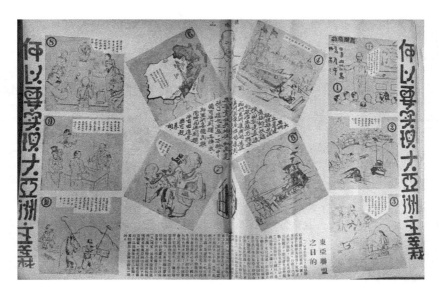

Fig. 7.2 Two-page illustration of Sun Yat-sen's Greater Asianism ('Heyi yao shixian Da Yazhou zhuyi?' [How can Greater Asianism be realized?]), published in the Chinese journal *Dongya lianmeng huabao* [East Asian League Pictorial] by Wang Jingwei's collaborationist regime in March 1941. Sun's Asianism is portrayed as consistent with the Japan-centred project of an East Asian League. Note the strong anti-Western visual elements in the cartoons, which dominate over direct appeals to Japanese-Chinese cooperation. Reproduced with kind permission from the collection of Waseda University Library

he blames China for her errors; there are others in which he takes Japan to task for her mistakes; but at no time and in no place did he ever suggest that the two countries should be or remain enemies. Rather it was his constantly proclaimed hope that they would become friends, joining wholeheartedly in a united effort to promote the glorious cause of Greater Asianism.[52]

In order to spread and solidify his claim to Sun's legacy and to justify his collaboration with Japan, a number of journals were published in Chinese which promoted Wang's adoption of Sun's Asianism, including the three monthlies *Da Yazhou Zhuyi* (Greater Asianism), *Da Yazhou Zhuyi yu Dongya Lianmeng* (Greater Asianism and an East Asian

League), and *Da Dongya* (Greater East Asia). While these publications clearly functioned as instruments of propaganda, it should not be overlooked that Wang himself and many of his followers held sincere pro-Japanese sentiments. In addition, humanitarian and idealistic motives, such as putting an end to the ongoing slaughter on the battlefield and his well-known anti-Communism, have been identified as being among the reasons that led Wang to his betrayal of Chiang and to his cooperation with the Japanese. To be sure, 'the nature of the differences between Jiang [Chiang Kai-shek] and Wang were not merely political factionalism, but ideological'.[53]

Wang's strategy was not too dissimilar from those of Dai and Hu, with the important and crucial difference of an outspoken—but not uncritical—pro-Japanese attitude. To this end, Wang attempted to construct as many parallels and commonalities between China and Japan as possible. In a widely distributed speech, Wang contended that the fate of both countries was linked and that the Japanese were ready to acknowledge Chinese efforts towards realizing Asianism throughout East Asia:

> After the Opium War, the imperialist invasion did not stop at China, but Japan was also threatened at the same time. However, Japan escaped this threat of invasion and thus achieved freedom and equality some decades before China. However, unless the aggressive forces of imperialism are extinguished, there is the danger that Japan will one day be subjected to invasion again. This is the very point that makes the destinies of the two countries of China and Japan identical. It is a great pity that we have neglected this fact of our identical destinies, but rather antagonized each other. After a process of reflection, we are now working hard to face our common destiny together. Fifteen years after the death of Dr. Sun, the ideals of Greater Asianism gleam with new splendour and illuminate the future path of two great peoples who are going forward together. When, in the past, the destinies of China and Japan were in conflict, it appeared that nationalism and Greater Asianism were incompatible ideals. Now, in the age of a joint Sino-Japanese future, they are not only intertwined but one could say they have even melded into one. If China fails to acquire its independence and freedom it will not be qualified to share responsibility for East Asia, and if East Asia is not liberated China's independence and freedom cannot be achieved or guaranteed. This is what every Chinese must bear in mind. Since Japan expects China to shoulder its share of responsibility for East Asia, it will naturally treat us on the basis of equality. Ever since the Konoe Declaration [of a 'New Order in East Asia',

November 1938], this has been Japan's unyielding national policy and the expression of unified public opinion.[54]

In addition to Sun's Greater Asianism, Wang and his supporters also adopted Sun's *Sanmin Zhuyi* as theoretical underpinnings of the new Nanjing regime—and took considerable pains to convince the Japanese of their compatibility with Asianism. Reportedly, the principles of nationalism (minzu zhuyi), democracy (minquan zhuyi), and livelihood (minsheng zhuyi), on which Sun had extensively lectured in the summer of 1924, were viewed as 'a menace' in Japan.[55] In order to achieve a more favourable view of *Sanmin Zhuyi*-blended Asianism, Wang and his followers produced a remarkable quantity of journalistic output directed at both Chinese and Japanese audiences. The main intention of these texts was to assuage Japanese concerns over the Three People's Principles, in particular, nationalism. The following excerpt, written by Wang's most prolific propagandist, Zhou Huaren,[56] reveals the gist of this enterprise:

> Greater Asianism and the Three People's Principles are essentially identical. President Sun said: 'The Three People's Principles are the principles of the salvation of the nation'. Mr Wang [Jingwei] says: 'If we can realize the Three People's Principles, we will naturally achieve the status of freedom and equality and at the same time we will increase our strength and share with Japan the responsibility for creating a stable East Asia. Thus, speaking from the perspective of China, the Three People's Principles relate to saving the nation and from the perspective of East Asia, the Three People's Principles are equivalent to Greater Asianism'. [...] To be sure, Japan is the strongest country in Asia and China is the largest country in Asia. If we cannot direct the power of both countries to become the driving forces behind a revival movement, Asia cannot possibly be saved. Japan has already gathered its strength. As China is currently in the process of building a modern nation state, China's present ambitions are twofold—to save China itself but also at the same time to save Asia. It is for precisely this reason that we can say that the Three People's Principles are equivalent to Greater Asianism.[57]

The rationale of this passage resembled remarkably Dai's attempts at conflating the cause of Chinese liberation and unification with that of the liberation and unification of Asian peoples—with the notable difference of Zhou's continuing trust in Sino-Japanese cooperation.

Although Zhou paid great attention to showing the conformity of the Principles with the ideals of Greater Asianism, the text had to be edited to fit the Japanese rhetoric before it appeared in translation in Japan. For example, the Japanese version explicitly affirms Konoe's declaration of a New Order ('to share the responsibility for establishing a New Order in East Asia'), whereas Zhou's original text in Chinese does not mention the 'New Order' but speaks only of 'the responsibility for building a stabilized East Asia'.[58] Wang's writings published in Japan were similarly altered to remove any references to Chinese nationalist aspirations which ran counter to the official Japanese political rhetoric. The fact that such editing was necessary further demonstrates that condemnations of Wang as a Chinese quisling who 'perverted Sun's Greater Asianism [...] in search of a theoretical basis for his own disgraceful behaviour or treason'[59] are, at best, greatly exaggerated.[60]

By the 1940s, however, Wang's systematic attempt at claiming Sun's Asianist legacy could no longer trigger any notable public political debate. It was too obvious that Asianist rhetoric that centred on Sino-Japanese commonality and friendship between both peoples was detached from reality. Asianism in China, unless it was very narrowly defined as in Li Dazhao's or Sun Yat-sen's conceptions, would be discredited for many decades.

Japanese Appropriations of Asianism from Above

Censorship and Confessions

In Japan, the Manchurian Incident of September 1931 and the subsequent dispute with the League of Nations created for the first time a situation in which the Japanese government had to take Asianist claims seriously. Previously, ideas of practical implementations of Asianism after 1924 that culminated in the two pan-Asian conferences were rather easily sidelined and suppressed (see Chap. 5). The new political reality after the manoeuvres of the Kwantung Army in Manchuria, however, was more difficult to deal with. Still aiming at a solution within the traditionally preferred framework of Japanese diplomacy—that is, cooperation with the 'Western' powers and the League of Nations—the Japanese government did not immediately proclaim the beginning of a new, Asianist, era. Rather, as has often been pointed out, the Japanese government in fact never officially declared Asianism its political strategy and the first

7 ASIANISM FROM ABOVE: THE REALIZATION OF 'ASIA' IN MANCHURIA

minister of the Greater East Asia Ministry (Dai Tōa Shō, 1942), Aoki Kazuo (1889–1982) later insisted that 'Greater Asianism was a civilian slogan (minkan no surōgan) and was not even once turned into an official policy by the government'.[61] It lies beyond the scope of this book to trace whether or not any Japanese minister ever used the term Asianism or Greater Asianism in justification of Japan's policy. To be sure, there are numerous instances of references made by high-level politicians and even more by representatives of the Japanese military (from where the political leadership, including most of Japan's Prime Ministers, were recruited after 1932) that advocated Asianism. For example, after the Amō Declaration of 1934, the Japanese Vice Foreign Minister Taki Masao (1884–1969) publicly advanced 'Asianism and the Far Eastern Monroe Doctrine' as the 'central thought of Japan's foreign policy'.[62] In addition, whereas pan-Asianist activities in the mid-1920s had been subjected to police surveillance and worldwide Japanese consular observation, from the 1930s onwards leading military and political figures such as Matsui Iwane, Konoe Fumimaro, and Hirota Kōki were less cautious in their socializing with Asianists, as we will see below. The changed political climate, in particular after the founding of Manchukuo in 1932 and the announcement of Japan's departure from the League of Nations in 1933, encouraged the Asianist coming out of many who had earlier harboured Asianist sentiments but had not been courageous enough to speak out against the (pro-Western) trend of times. Also, the *fait accompli* of Japan's seizure of Manchuria pushed Japanese officials and intellectuals alike to search for a new framework of political affiliation. In this context, the Japanese government's reactions to the Manchurian Incident in the following years constituted a point of no return. With a strong foothold in China proper rather than territorially limited control over Korea, Taiwan, and isolated parts of the Chinese mainland, Japan's empire demanded a more refined strategic orientation. Imperialist-minded Japanese Asianists must have rejoiced when the early 1930s offered the long-awaited chance to prove the significance of previous debates on Asianist policies. But due to this new link between Asianist theory and political practice, Asianism discourse also lost much of its variety and dynamism. Anti-Asianist voices gradually disappeared from mainstream public discourse, and, instead, Japanese criticism of Japanese Asianism started to become censored, for example Hasegawa Nyozekan's critique of Rōyama Masamichi's geopolitical Asianism[63] and Tadokoro Teruaki's socialist vision of an internationalist 'United States of Asia' as an Asianist alternative.[64] Kawai Eijirō's well-known critique of the May 15th Incident (1932), which included an attack on Asianism,[65] was also subjected to partial deletion. Fortunately—for research into Asianism—other sections gave more reason for censorship so that his rejection of Japanese Asianism remained readable.

> If Greater Asianism does not include evil territorial intentions but only aims at achieving equality regarding commerce and trade between Japan and foreign countries, there is no need to call it Greater Asianism. Instead, it is more likely to realize these aims by directly advocating freedom of commerce. In sum, it's a different matter if Greater Asianism is only a pretext for covering the pursuit of Japanese profits, but if it really means to liberate the Asian peoples, Japan must first implement the so-called Kingly Way (iwayuru Ōdō) within Japan itself.[66]

Although Kawai's criticism was certainly clear enough for everyone to understand it was indirect enough to escape censorship. The contradiction between claiming one thing (Asianism) and doing another (imperialism) that had limited the reception and success of transnational Asianist thought and activities in the 1920s had of course become even clearer by the early 1930s, both domestically and internationally. Eventually, this rendered the transnational cooperation of Asianists close to impossible. As an interesting side note, Kawai attributed Asianist aims to the coup d'étatists who had assassinated Prime Minister Inukai Tsuyoshi (1855–1932), whereas Hu Hanmin had referred to their victim—Inukai—as one of the few true Japanese Asianists.[67] For Hu, with Inukai's death the chances of a joint Sino-Japanese realization of Asianism had also died. For Kawai, the coup d'état signalled the predominance of action in the name of Asianism over true Asianist action, that is, action according to the principles of benevolence and virtue (Kingly Way). Both shared the notion of Asianism being, at least potentially, a positive concept that in theory could promote the rightful cause of 'Asia'.

The new, quasi-official role of Asianism in Japan was even more clearly revealed when confessing to Asianist ideals (rather than rejecting them) became a tool in proving one's conformity with government policy and state doctrine. In June 1933 Sano Manabu (1892–1953) and Nabeyama Sadachika (1901–1979), who had been imprisoned as leading Communist thinkers and activists in 1929, in a series of letters of conversion both openly pressed Japan to adopt an actively pan-Asian policy and to put Japan in the place of leadership in the project of pursuing Asian unity in preparation for a war against 'Western capitalism'.[68] Although their anti-capitalist conception of Asianism certainly differed from those Asianist proposals that came closest to Japanese government policies, it is astounding to see their embrace of Asianism as part of their political conversion (tenkō).

> Between the peoples of Asia there are common characteristics regarding language, culture, race and religion. Against Western capitalism there is a spiritual solidarity. [...] Pan-Asianism demands something higher than what could be called a popular union or fusion of various peoples. The struggle against Western capitalism will probably develop into war. This kind of war will be a progressive war for the Asian peoples. In this event, the Japanese people (Nihon minzoku) must be the leader of Pan-Asianism (han Ajiashugi no shidōsha).[69]

Whether Sano and Nabeyama displayed sincere Asianist inclinations or not is less important than their—correct—assessment that affirmations of Asianism together with appeals to Japanese leadership in this project would reduce the distance between their original Communist convictions and contemporary political orthodoxy in Japan during the early 1930s. The Sano/Nabeyama defection of 1933 not only constitutes the most famous case of political apostasy from Communism in Japan but, placed in the context of Asianism discourse in Japan, also sheds light on shifts in the hegemony regarding the embrace or rejection of the concept in public debate in Japan from the 1910s to the 1930s.

The Greater Asia Association and the Propagation of Asianism in Asia

Another proof of the changing quality and direction of Asianism discourse from the early 1930s onwards was the emergence of a high-profile organization that promoted Japan's expansive policies as Greater Asianism both in Japan and abroad. The Greater Asia Association (Dai Ajia Kyōkai) was probably the single most influential and active organization to propagate Pan-Asianism between 1933 and 1945. The *Dai Ajia Kyōkai* was the successor organization to the 'Pan-Asia Study Society' (Han Ajia Gakkai), which was founded in April 1932 by the Japanese publisher and entrepreneur Shimonaka Yasaburō (1878–1961), the writers and activists Nakatani Takeyo (1898–1990) and Mitsukawa Kametarō (1888–1936), the Indian revolutionary Rash Behari Bose (1886–1945), the Vietnamese Prince Cuong De (1882–1951), and others.[70] The society's self-declared aim was to study the political, economic, and cultural problems of Asia. Unlike most other pan-Asian organizations, its focus was not limited to East Asia but explicitly included southern, southeast, and central Asia. As a consequence, as Cemil Aydin has pointed out, the Greater Asia Association 'made an important contribution to Asianist thought with its introduction of news and information about the political, economic, and social trends of the entire Asian world, from China and India to Iran and Turkey'.[71] According to Nakatani, who later became the chief disseminator of Pan-Asianism within the Greater Asia Association, the *Gakkai*'s name was inspired by existing pan-movements in other parts of the world.[72] Shortly after the society had been founded, Lieutenant General Matsui Iwane of the Army General Staff Office proposed that the original study group be expanded into a larger organization. Initially, the members of the *Gakkai* declined Matsui's request even to join their group, for fear that their study and research group might be mistaken for a military-political organization. Shortly afterwards, however, the society changed its mind and permitted Matsui to join—though only as a private individual, not as a representative of the military. Eventually, however, most of its members also agreed to Matsui's proposal to develop a more practically oriented organization out of the original study group with a view to initiating a popular Asianist movement. It is unclear what caused this change of heart, or whether Nakatani's recollections of events incorrectly attributed the initiative for the society's transformation to Matsui. In any case, the new organization, named the Greater Asia Association (Dai Ajia Kyōkai), was founded in Tokyo on 1 March 1933, the 'auspicious day of the first anniversary of the founding of Manchukuo', with the aim of promoting 'the unification, liberation, and independence of the Asian peoples'.[73]

The Greater Asia Association managed to attract as members leading representatives from the political, cultural, academic, and military worlds—figures such as Prince Konoe Fumimaro (President of the House of Peers, later Prime Minister), Hirota Kōki (later Foreign and Prime Minister), the writer Tokutomi Sohō, Yano Jin'ichi (professor of Sinology at Kyoto University), Murakawa Kengo (professor of history at Tokyo University), and Admiral Suetsugu Nobumasa. Shimonaka

Yasaburō, founder of the publishing house Heibonsha (1914) and general editor of Japan's first multi-volume encyclopaedia (*Dai Hyakka Jiten*, 1931–1935), became the organization's official chairman. Nakatani Takeyo functioned as acting chairman, while Tanaka Masaaki (1911–2006), who would become notorious as a revisionist publicist in post-war Japan, became the editor-in-chief of the organization's publications.[74]

Nakatani, a 'professional nationalist'[75] who was also a professor at Tokyo's Hōsei University, had been a member of various nationalistic societies. Later he described his time with the Greater Asia Association as characterized by the closest intimacy in thought, trust, and human relationships, and named Shimonaka, Tanaka, and Matsui as the 'central axis' of the organization.[76] If we are to judge from his own productivity, Nakatani himself must certainly be included in the core of the group. In 1947, when Matsui was tried for war crimes at the International Military Tribunal for the Far East in Tokyo, both Shimonaka and Nakatani appeared at court to testify for him and emphasized the self-proclaimed philanthropic character of their organization.[77] Whereas Matsui was sentenced to death and executed in 1948, Shimonaka, following a three-year ban from public office under the American occupation, launched the movement for the World Federation of Nations (1951) and reassumed his post as president of the Heibonsha publishing house. Nakatani dedicated himself to the cause of Afro-Arab-Asian solidarity. In the late 1950s, he accompanied Prime Minister Kishi Nobusuke and the future Prime Minister Nakasone Yasuhiro on their trips to Southeast Asia and the Middle East. In 1958, Nakatani founded the Japan Arab Association.

The Dai Ajia Kyōkai and Manchuria

Apparently following the suggestion of Suzuki Teiichi (1888–1989), an army officer and later acting director of the Asia Development Board (Kō A In), both the organization *Dai Ajia Kyōkai* and its bulletin *Dai Ajiashugi* (Greater Asianism) were named after Sun Yat-sen's famous speech on 'Greater Asianism' in 1924 (Fig. 7.3). 'As we advocate the unification and liberation of all of Asia, resting on the firm cooperation of the peoples of Japan and China, based on Sun Yat-sen's Greater Asianism', Suzuki claimed, 'we should call our organization the "Greater Asia Association" and our organ "Greater Asianism"'. In his memoirs, Nakatani insisted that the partial change of the organization's

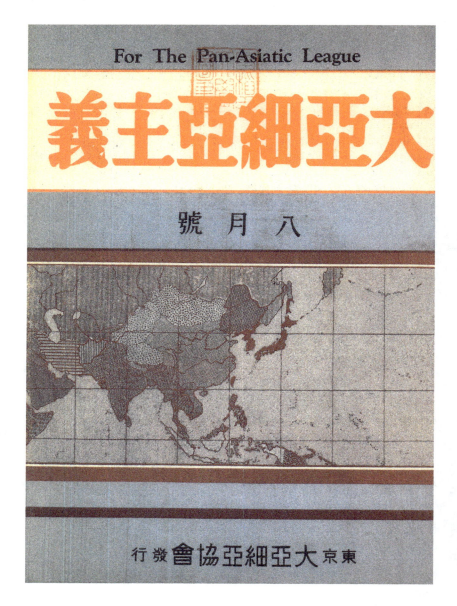

◀ **Fig. 7.3** Cover of the Japanese journal *Dai Ajiashugi* [Greater Asianism], published by the Greater Asia Association from 1933 to 1945. Note that the cover portrays Asia with national, and in the case of China also with regional borders. 'Greater Asia' to this organization meant an alliance of Asian nations with pro-Japanese regimes that would, at least in name, remain independent. The map on the cover also works as an obvious political instrument, implying that Japan despite its small size and peripheral location together with its colonial possessions in the South (Taiwan), to the West (Korea) and to the North (Sakhalin) was still the centre of a 'Greater Asia', even if Asia stretched as far west as the Caspian Sea. This issue from August 1933 is the only one with the English header 'For the Pan-Asiatic League'. Reproduced with kind permission from the collection of Waseda University Library

name from the initial *Han Ajia* to *Dai Ajia* was done for this reason only and should not be mistaken for the adoption of an expansionist or imperialist agenda.[78] In fact, the Greater Asia Association did appropriate some of Sun's key terminology, in particular when referring to the assumed distinctive features of the 'West' and the 'East', and the 'rule of might' (badao), based on force and aggression, versus the 'rule of right' or 'Kingly Way' (wangdao), based on benevolence and virtue. The Association interpreted the founding of Manchukuo as the first step in the revival of the Kingly Way on the Asian mainland. It declared that its aim was 'to mediate communal and cultural cooperation between Japan and Manchuria and to promote the Greater Asianism movement on the continent'.[79] The Association's founding manifesto left no doubt about the central role Manchuria would play as the place of realization of Asianism:

> In the wake of the Manchurian Incident, world politics are about to undergo an epoch-making transformation and conversion. The independence of Manchukuo, the world's youngest state, has already achieved the status of a major miracle in the post-war history of international affairs. Yet the emergence of an independent Manchukuo is merely a prelude to the historical transformation which is set to rapidly succeed it on the world stage. Following the independence of Manchuria, the autonomy of East Asia must be secured. The freedom and glory of Asia, the Mother of Civilization, must be revived, hard on the heels of the founding of the new state of the Kingly Way (Ōdō shin kokka). Once Manchuria was East Asia's final bulwark against the European conquest of the world. Now Manchuria itself has been strengthened and established as a country in its own right.

With this new situation in the Far East as a model, we must begin working for the unity and reorganization of all of Asia.[80]

But Manchuria was to be only the beginning of a complete reshuffle of the international order. The Association's journal *Dai Ajiashugi*, which was published continuously for exactly nine years, from May 1933 through April 1942, therefore initially focused on Manchuria but eventually covered a wide spatial and topical range. It included 'A history of the Republican movement in India' (Subhas Chandra Bose, September 1936) and 'Pan-Slavism and the Third Reich' (Imaoka Jūichirō, February 1935), 'The New Order in East Asia and in Europe' (Sugimori Kōjirō, September 1940), and 'The structure of Greater East Asian history and Japan's historical mission' (Yano Jin'ichi, April 1942). In its earlier volumes it also published translations of writings by Hans Kohn and Oswald Spengler, but contributions by non-Asians in general remained scarce. On its first anniversary, the Greater Asia Association declared that, despite the fact that only the preparatory stages had been achieved in terms of the 'great hundred-year plan for Greater Asia', the organization had already 'caused a remarkable stir both at home and abroad' and had sounded 'an incredible echo throughout the world'.[81] As proof, in its first annual report it reprinted articles about the Association and its activities that had appeared in English, German, Russian, Turkish, Indonesian, and Chinese newspapers. Interestingly, the leaders of the Association seemed to care little about the negative responses it had received—some of which were included in the annual report—but appeared to be pleased that, unlike previous Asianist organizations, its existence had been widely noted both at home and abroad. The organization's illustrious membership, its broad agenda, and the new political situation that developed following the Manchurian Incident and Japan's withdrawal from the League of Nations may have helped attract such wide attention. Tachibana Shiraki (1881–1945), the self-employed scholar-journalist based in Manchuria, where he published the 'Manchurian Review' (Manshū Hyōron), conceded that the Greater Asia Association commanded the greatest authority among the existing pan-Asian organizations—but went on to emphasize that, because of its theoretical immaturity and dullness, it was not worth listening to its claims.[82] The French journalist Marc Chadourne (1895–1975) was rather shocked by what he called a 'quasi-official, detailed imperialistic programme' when he read of the organization's aims during his travels in

East Asia in 1934. However, he expressed little concern over the potential damage Japanese pan-Asian ambitions might inflict on other Asians. Instead, he criticized Nakatani's outspoken anti-Westernism, which threatened British and French possessions in Asia.[83] In the context of Chadourne's comments, it appears less surprising that many of the members of the Greater Asia Association seemed to have taken seriously the rightfulness of their pan-Asian project. As a step towards achieving their aims they attempted to convince fellow Asians, initially mostly Chinese, of their undertaking by publishing pamphlets in the Chinese language. They were mostly authored by Nakatani or Matsui and were given titles such as 'The necessity and significance of an Asian League' (Matsui, in Chinese, 1933) or 'Greater Asianism and Japanese–Chinese relations' (Nakatani, Japanese and Chinese texts, 1933). Later, between 1941 and 1943 the Association also issued an English-language version of its journal, called *Asiatic Asia*. It was published by the Shanghai Greater Asianism Research Institute, a branch of the Association set up by Nakatani in Shanghai in 1940. *Asiatic Asia* mostly carried articles from the *Dai Ajiashugi* journal in English translation.

Tachibana's criticism of the Association partly rested on its 'right-wing' membership and its unspecific agenda that combined several Asianist factors and argued that 'Asia' constituted a 'community of fate' (unmei kyōdōtai).[84] The Association's agenda claimed to be informed by regionalist views that proposed territorial demarcations, yet it maintained that it was open and directed at the whole world. Simultaneously, its rhetoric was racially and culturally essentialist. Indeed, the founding manifesto explicitly reflected this incoherence—or variety, at best.

> We certainly believe that Asia constitutes a community of the same fate – culturally, politically, geographically and also racially. Real peace, welfare, and the development of the various peoples of Asia is only possible given Asia's self-awakening to its unity and its systematic unification. [...] In order to eliminate this mutual rivalry among the countries of Asia and to halt foreign interventions and manipulation, it is vital to strive for the creation of an alliance of the currently scattered and disorganized peoples of Asia. Moreover, the present chaos and disorder in Asia is not only the cause of Asia's own misery but, as it habitually stimulates the evil intentions and greed of Europe and America, it must also be seen as the greatest obstacle to world peace. The insecurity and unrest of the East are directly connected with insecurity and unrest in the world in general. Reforming Asia according to the principles of autonomy and self-reliance for Asians

is in fact the first step to stabilizing world politics. Seen in this light, the heavy responsibility for Asia's reconstruction and reorganization rests on the shoulders of Imperial Japan. Once before, a quarter of a century ago, when our national destiny was at stake, we pushed back the angry waves of an invasion of East Asia by Imperial Russia, rescued all of Asia from defeat, and even began empowering the coloured peoples of the world to raise their heads again. Now, on the occasion of the Manchurian Incident, the human race is again facing a wave of great historical change. It is now time for Imperial Japan to capitalize on the historical significance of the Russo-Japanese War and concentrate its entire cultural, political, economic, and organizational power on planning the next step in the revival and unification of Asia. [...] Viewed from the perspective of the current evolutionary process in international politics, the formation of a Greater Asia Union is an extremely natural prospect. It is necessary for human societies to organize political and economic alliances based on geographical, cultural, and racial affinities. On the other hand, it is both unnatural and impossible to jump from a national state (minzoku kokka) to a world state (sekai kokka). Because the League of Nations was prematurely established as a pan-world union without waiting for important historical factors to mature – in fact, it was an unintended outcome of the European War – it is now undergoing fundamental revisions by pan-continental and pan-nationalist movements as a natural consequence.[85]

While this assembly of different reasons for the assumed necessity of an Asian League as the implementation of Asianism could certainly be seen as attesting to the immature and uninspired character of the Association's agenda, it also demonstrates how by the 1930s different Asianist conceptions or different components thereof from previous Asianism discourse could readily be drawn on to form 'new' conceptions of Asianism. Both conceptually and rhetorically, Asianism discourse in the 1910s and 1920s had established the tools the Association could easily make use of in 1933. As had frequently been argued during World War One, Asianism provided an opportunity for imperial expansion (see Chap. 4); it could also demand racial equality, as early Asianist activists in the post-Versailles period had done (see Chap. 5); and it could be seen as a rational global phenomenon of regionalism, as Nagatomi and others had argued from the mid-1920s onwards (see Chap. 6). Manchuria now provided the background for the establishment of a 'new' Asianism that constituted an eclectic synthesis of previous Asianisms.

In addition to its publication activities, immediately after its inauguration the Greater Asia Association began establishing branches inside and outside Japan.[86] As early as May 1933, the *Da Yaxiya Xiehui* (Greater Asia Organization) was set up in Sun Yat-sen's former base of Guangdong in Southern China. In 1934, it was followed by a Taiwan branch, the *Chōsen Dai Ajia Kyōkai* (Korean Greater Asia Association) in Seoul, and the Filipino Greater Asia Association in Manila. In December 1935, on a visit to Northern China, Matsui and Nakatani set up the Chinese Greater Asia Association in Tianjin. The main character of the Association, however, remained that of 'a group devoted to thought and culture'[87] more than political action, and it focused on publishing articles, pamphlets, booklets, and holding lectures and meetings of research groups. Like similar organizations, in 1941 the Greater Asia Association was absorbed into the Greater Japan Raise Asia Alliance (Dai Nihon Kōa Dōmei) under the banner of the Imperial Rule Assistance Association. The *Dai Ajiashugi* journal, however, continued to be published for another year.

Interestingly, some of its most prominent members, such as Konoe and Tokutomi, rarely associated themselves openly with the Greater Asia Association. Apart from his speech at the opening ceremony, Tokutomi does not appear to have made any notable contributions and none of his prolific writings appeared in the *Dai Ajiashugi* journal. In similar vein, Prime Minister Konoe remained connected with the Association as a councillor (hyōgi'in) but he nevertheless supported the formation of another study group that would function as his personal think tank, the Showa Research Association (Shōwa Kenkyūkai).[88]

Matsui Iwane's Conception of Asianism

The most prominent activist in the Greater Asia Association was Matsui Iwane (1878–1948), who is today remembered for his role in the Japanese campaign to occupy Southern China in 1937 and the subsequent massacre in Nanjing. Matsui was born in Nagoya as the sixth son of the impoverished family of a former samurai.[89] At the age of 12, he was sent to the Army Youth School (Yōnen Gakkō), from which he advanced to the Imperial Japanese Army Academy (Rikugun Shikan Gakkō), graduating in 1897. During his studies at the Army War College (Rikugun Daigakkō) he was selected to serve as a company commander in the Russo-Japanese War (1904/05). After the war, he graduated in 1906 and was immediately posted to the General Staff Office (Sanbō Honbu). Around this time he developed a strong interest in Asia, particularly China; he admired Arao Sei (1859–1896), a 'mainland adventurer' (tairiku rōnin) and pioneer of Japanese research on China. However, as was the case with most of the senior military staff, Matsui was sent to study in Europe (in his case France). On his return he requested to be stationed in China, where he served as a resident officer from 1907 to 1912 (Beijing, Shanghai), and again from 1915 to 1919 (Shanghai, Nanjing, Hankou, Beijing). During World War One he was again posted to France, but soon returned to China, where he met influential Chinese political and military leaders, including Sun Yat-sen. In the army, Matsui was rapidly promoted—to colonel in 1918, to major general in 1923, to lieutenant general in 1927, and to full general in 1933. In 1931, he was sent as a plenipotentiary to the Geneva Disarmament Conference. After the Aizawa Incident of 1935 (the assassination of Army Ministry official Major General Nagata Tetsuzan by Lieutenant General Aizawa Saburō), Matsui retired from the army.

From the mid-1920s onwards, Matsui commented frequently on foreign affairs in the influential journal *Gaikō Jihō* (Diplomatic Review). Matsui's proposal for an Asian League (Ajia Renmei) dates to that time and was triggered by debates over the reform of the League of Nations. In particular, Matsui was influenced by a detailed reform plan proposed by Count Richard Coudenhove-Kalergi, the Austrian-Japanese founder of the Pan-European movement, who had also stimulated Nagatomi's geopolitical understanding of Asianism (see Chap. 6). But it was only after Japan's withdrawal from the League of Nations in 1933 that Matsui's proposal gained greater attention, as an Asian League now appeared more practical and realistic. As in his earlier writings, in 1933 too Matsui remained true to his original geopolitical inspiration of Asianism:

> Needless to say, our Greater Asia movement is not advocating the annexation of Manchuria. And we would never insist on ruling China or expelling all Westerners from Asia. The primary object of our Association is to relieve the peoples of Asia from the political, economic, and spiritual suffering which the region is currently undergoing. I believe that this goal, pursued together with our Asian compatriots, is the supreme destiny of Japan as the only fully independent country in Asia. Consequently, everyone who lives in Asia and binds himself to the mission of Asia and makes efforts for the welfare of Asia – be he British or American – is our comrade.

It is precisely our hope that we will all strive together for the cause of Asia. Therefore we must first make sure that we have a firm foothold in Asia. Today, we must be like the European Federation in Europe or the Pan-American Movement in both American continents, where compatriots of the same stock band together and take a firm foothold in their respective homes. In this way, pan-unions of Asia, Europe, America, and the Soviets can harmonize their efforts and, beginning from there, proceed on the road to a genuinely just peace in this world. In this time of unprecedented difficulty for the Empire and observing the world in terrible disorder, I firmly believe that there is only one path to a solution and that nothing else will do. My friends! Let's first observe the wide world, and then turn our attention to Asia on our doorstep. Then, I hope, our nine hundred million compatriots will wake up to Japan's vital mission and rise up as one man. In other words, 'First return to Asia. Then return to Greater Asianism'.[90]

His open and regionalist understanding of Asianism, which in parts even resembled Ukita Kazutami's voluntaristic conception of Asia (see Chap. 4), changed drastically over the following years. Matsui continued to adhere to Greater Asianism but the previous open and regionalist character vanished. Instead, he began to advance Asianism as a concept that promoted the construction of a 'community of morality and a cultural community'. The Sino-Japanese War was not a war between the Chinese and Japanese, he claimed in 1939, but 'a holy war for the resurrection of Eastern culture and for the construction of an Asiatic Asia'.[91] Asianism as the political agenda of leading politicians and the military by the late 1930s had turned into a principle to justify war.

As a result of his extensive knowledge of China and his personal acquaintance with Chinese leaders, including Chiang Kai-shek, Matsui had been called back into service and appointed commander of the Japanese Central China Area Army in 1937. Despite the fact that Prince Asaka, an uncle of the Emperor, and not Matsui, was the commanding general of the Japanese troops that took Nanjing, the International Military Tribunal for the Far East held Matsui primarily responsible for the massacre.[92] He was convicted and hanged in Tokyo's Sugamo Prison on 23 December 1948. In 1978, together with other convicted class A war criminals, Matsui's soul was enshrined in Tokyo's controversial Yasukuni Shrine. While in China Matsui has become a symbol of Japanese wartime atrocities and Japan's war guilt, among rightist groups in Japan he is revered as a hero in Japan's 'just war' for the 'liberation of Asia' and an innocent victim of 'victor's justice' at the Tokyo Trial.[93]

In the city of Atami (Shizuoka Prefecture) a statue of the goddess of mercy (Kannon), which Matsui had erected in 1940 to commemorate the raising of Asia (Kō A), is still standing today. An issue of the English-language journal *Asiatic Asia* carried a photograph of the so-called *Kō A Kannon*, as 'enshrined by General Matsui, Ex-Commander-in-Chief of [sic] Japanese Army in Central China, for happiness and spiritual peace of the Asiatic peoples'.[94]

Like the founding manifesto of the Greater Asia Association, Matsui's earlier conception of Asianism quoted above arose out of the increasing international pressure on Japan following the Manchurian Incident of 1931. China had immediately appealed to the League of Nations, which eventually formed a commission that presented the results of its investigation to the League in February 1933. The so-called Lytton Report acknowledged Japan's special interests in Manchuria, but rejected Japan's claims that its military activities in Manchuria were based on self-defence and that Manchukuo had been founded as an autonomous country. It demanded the conclusion of a new Sino-Japanese treaty over Manchuria, which would officially become a self-governing region under Chinese sovereignty but placed under international administration. After Japan's refusal to discuss the report on the grounds that Manchukuo had already been established and its 'independence' had been acknowledged by Japan, the General Assembly of the League adopted the Lytton Report by 42 votes out of 44, with one rejection (Japan) and one abstention (Siam). Following the vote, the Japanese delegation immediately left the Assembly in protest. However, as Matsui noted, critically,[95] the solution to the crisis was hotly debated by the Japanese public. It was over a month before Japan officially announced its withdrawal from the League on 27 March 1933.

Manchuria as Asianism in Practice

Asianism discourse in Japan from the 1930s onwards was built on the premise of Japan-centrism, similar to positions that had already been advanced from the early 1910s onwards as *Nihon meishu ron* (Japan as leader thesis) by several authors, including Tokutomi Sohō and Gotō Shinpei. In view of the open hostilities between Japan and China that would soon develop into a full-scale war, to most contenders in the discursive competition for Asianism no alternative to its conflation with an affirmation of Japanese leadership appeared viable. This, on the other hand, facilitated the—sincere or pretended, voluntary or forced—embrace of Asianism by a wider spectrum of debaters. Nationalist circles that had previously rejected Asianism as disadvantageous for Japan found it relatively easy to turn nationalist anti-Asianism into 'Japan-centrist Asianism' (Nihon chūshin no Ajiashugi) in order to achieve the aim of 'autarky and self-strengthening of the Asian peoples' as the national ideal and mission of Japan.[96] In palpable contrast to the special Asianism edition of the *Nihon oyobi Nihonjin* journal in 1924, the same journal displayed an outspokenly pro-Asianist stance in the early 1930s, and particularly after March 1933. Asianism was reconciled with 'Japanism' (Nihonshugi) as its 'extension abroad'.[97] Simultaneously, the 'Kingly Way' (ōdō) that had indisputably come to represent the core of Asianist critique of the 'West' was harmonized with the 'Imperial Way' (kōdō).[98] These conflations enabled Japanists, some for the first time, to speak affirmatively of 'Asia' without excluding Japan. 'Asia' was not yet—and to some it never became—the 'Self', but at least, as Ogawa Reikō put it in 1935, Japanists found their position as 'Asia's proxy' (Ajia daibensha)[99] and therefore had moved one step closer towards embracing 'Asia'.

Tokyo's Asianism in Manchuria, Manchurian Asianism in Tokyo

In Manchuria itself, various organizations propagated Asianist ideals, of which the *Manshūkoku Kyōwakai* (Manchukuo Concordia Association) was probably the most influential.[100] It was founded in July 1932 and existed until the end of World War Two. It was based in the capital of Xinjing (Jp. Shinkyō, 'New Capital') and Puyi, the *de iure* ruler of Manchukuo, was its honorary president. The term *kyōwa* (harmony) in the organization's name, of course, referred to the aim of creating a country and society in which different races would live—in the 'paradise of the Kingly Way' (Jp. Ōdō rakudo, Ch. Wangdao letu)—in harmony, peace, and co-prosperity: the slogan propagating harmonious cooperation of the five races or peoples (Jp. Gozoku Kyōwa, Ch. Wuzu Xiehe) comprising the Japanese, Han, Manchurian, Mongolian, Korean. The Japanese had borrowed and adapted this term from Sun Yat-sen's revolutionary and early republican aim of a 'Republic of Five Races' (Ch. Wuzu Gonghe, Jp. Gozoku Kyōwa) consisting of the Han, Manchurian, Mongolian, Uighur, and Tibetan races.[101] As Prasenjit Duara's research has revealed, the Association was originally envisioned as a bottom-up party to empower the different peoples and nationalities within Manchukuo, but in reality it quickly turned into 'an instrument of the army and government' as the 'ideological mother of government', in the words of the leadership of the Kwantung Army.[102] Hardly surprisingly, Greater Asianism not only appeared compatible with these aims but was seen as a useful tool in promoting the ideology of the new state of Manchukuo. Yu Jingyuan (1898–1969), head of the Association's General Affairs Office and formerly a member of Zhang Zuolin's Fengtian faction, perceived Asianism as representing the goal of countering the 'oppression and invasion by Euro-America' by forming an alliance between China, Japan, Manchuria, India, the Philippines, and Siam (Thailand). In other words, while *Ōdō rakudo* and *Gozoku kyōwa* mainly represented Manchukuo's domestic doctrines, Asianism was seen as the guiding principle of Manchukuo's relations with its Asian neighbours, above all with Japan and China. The core of this pan-Asian alliance was to be Sino-Japanese friendship; however, as Yu conceded, Chinese reactions to Japanese Asianist proposals were lukewarm. Instead of enthusiastically hailing the birth of Manchukuo as the beginning of the implementation of Asianism—as the Greater Asia Association had done—Yu diagnosed the dissatisfactory state of Sino-Japanese friendship and consequently the incompletion of the practice of Asianism. Yu held the 'Westerners' interference' and China's 'domestic disorder' responsible for these difficulties but also stressed that China needed to participate in the Asianist project voluntarily. 'If China rejoins voluntarily [the Japanese-Manchurian project], this will lead to the realization of Greater Asianism', Yu contended.[103] In fact, this brief statement combined Yu's general affirmation of Asianism with his specific criticism of Asianist conceptions and political practice that were too Japan-centred. The members of the Association, particularly the Chinese, were fully aware of the contradiction between Asianist rhetoric and the practice of Japanese hegemony in Manchuria and throughout Japan's empire. In a summary of the problems the *Kyōwakai* faced in the implementation and propagation of their policies it therefore included a critical review of Greater Asianism:

> What is this Greater Asianism that has been *en vogue* for some time? Is it a Greater Asianism for the sake of Japan? Or is it a Greater Asianism for the mutual sake of the different parts of Asia? The coloured peoples of East Asia have not yet started to form a league to resist the oppression by the Whites. It is just like with Japanese-Chinese friendship: there is no one who objects but we cannot succeed by boastful talk only. What could be a good counter policy?[104]

As this excerpt clearly reveals, the leadership of the Association was aware of the necessity to find ways to overcome the contradiction between Asianist rhetoric and anti-Asianist practice. Unlike domestic Asianist discourse in Japan, which could afford an outspokenly Japan-centred attitude, the Association required a different version that could survive the reality check of a multiracial Japanese enclave in China. But the search for a 'good counter policy' as an attempt at implementing Asianism from above was bound to fail. It was not only political reality that increasingly questioned the viability of Asianism as a concept based on solidarity and aiming at common goals. The self-appraising conceptions of Asianism that came to dominate Asianism discourse in Japan after 1933 too could hardly help to mask Japan's imperial project in northeast China. As a result, rather than spreading Japanese Asianism in Manchuria, 'Manchurian' Asianism spread in Japan; that is, from the early 1930s onwards voices claiming to representing Manchuria reaffirmed to the domestic audience in Japan that Asianism had started to be put into practice in Manchukuo. A lecture series in Tokyo by the first envoy of Manchukuo to Japan, the Chinese diplomat Bao Guancheng (1898–1975), who, like Yu, had defected from the Fengtian faction, exemplified this trend. Speaking on various occasions and to different audiences in Japan's capital, Bao tried to reassure his Japanese listeners of the importance of Asianism as the guiding principle for Japanese–Manchurian cooperation, reconciliation between China and Japan, and the creation of an Asian League to guarantee freedom and peace in Asia.[105]

> The aim of the founding of Manchukuo was to defeat the military cliques that oppress the people and, simultaneously, to plan a fundamental strategy of Japanese–Manchurian cooperation in order to strive for the realization of Greater Asianism. The spirit of the founding of Manchukuo is the principle of the Kingly Way. [...] Manchukuo's principle of the Kingly Way and Japan's Imperial Way are one and the same. They are the spirit of the culture of the East, which differs from Western civilization. Because the Kingly and the Imperial Ways are the expressions of this spiritual civilization, they cannot only achieve the happiness of Asia but they can also relieve the human race from their suffering and bring about the happiness of the whole human race. Taking the spirit of the Kingly Way and the Imperial Way as our basis, we will cooperate with the entire world.[106]

Like Japanist conceptions of Asianism, Bao attempted to reconcile the Kingly Way with the Imperial Way in order to dissolve potential tensions between the two ideals. In this way, he confirmed the more recent notion that Asianism and Japanism, or Asianist and Japanese interests, were not necessarily contradictory. Also, Bao linked Japanese–Manchurian cooperation under the banner of Greater Asianism to the wider sphere of regional and global politics. Thereby he followed a tradition of previous Asianism discourse from the post-World War One era, when Wilsonian idealism had first been adopted by Japanese and Chinese Asianists to suggest an alternative, non-Western world order. With Manchuria, the message could be read, the long-discussed project of establishing an alternative order (first) in Asia and (later) in the world had eventually begun to proceed to the stage of implementation.

Asianism in Education

As much as Asianism's controversial nature had receded, its implementation moved to the foreground. In 1933, the educator Horinouchi Tsuneo, a prolific author of educational and curricular guidebooks and advocate of the Emperor-revering 'ethics education'[107] that was abolished in 1945, proposed that the propagation of Greater Asianism become part of the civics education curriculum in primary schools. Rather than the mere passive feeling of 'ethnic harmony', new education should now foster an 'active spirit' that would unite the Japanese people 'on the basis of Greater Asianism' to rise up for the cause of the oppressed Asian peoples.[108] The latter, naturally, did not refer to Japan's own imperialist policy towards Taiwan, Korean, and China but exclusively to the 'West' (Seiyō) and its imperialism in Asia. This proposed commitment to the cause of 'Asia' never seriously questioned the role of Japan and its Asianist or anti-Asianist attitude towards other Asians. Instead, Japan was glorified as 'our country centring on the Imperial Family'.[109]

Similar ideas were propagated in educational pamphlets issued by the Social Education Association (Shakai Kyōiku Kyōkai), which cooperated with the Ministry of Education's General Education Office (Monbushō futsū gakumukyoku) and was directed at a mature audience and adults. Their topics ranged widely from travel accounts and Mahayana Buddhism to kabuki and the British Labour Party. In April 1934, it first issued a pamphlet on the 'liberation movement of the Eastern peoples', which focused on the Indonesian independence movement. 'It is not overstated', it claimed, 'to say that Greater Asianism is the foundation of the national and independence movements in Indonesia'. Just as the Japanese victory over Russia at the beginning of the new century had inspired people throughout Asia, Japan's departure from the League of Nations now gave a new boost to the 'oppressed coloured peoples'. Japan as 'Asia's senior country' was the object of admiration, it claimed.[110] Two months later, in the same series, Kodaira Kunio supplemented this claim by a more theoretically based propagation of Asianism as 'Asia for the Asians'. In Kodaira's words, '"Asia" was born in Asia and belongs to the Asian peoples'.[111] His claim was representative of the shift from 'Asia' as a foreign-imposed and foreign-referential concept to a self-defined and self-referential one. Kodaira claimed that 'Asia' *in toto* belonged to the Asians, that is, Asia not only as a place of political and economic autonomy but also 'Asia' as a self-defined concept. To him, 'Asia' was the complete opposite of the 'West': 'Western' materialism, capitalism, Communism, imperialism, militarism, belief in the omnipotence of science, and social Darwinism *versus* 'Asian' intrinsic values, anti-materialism, and the ideal of co-existence and co-prosperity.[112] Because of this fundamental and innate difference between 'Euro-America' and 'Asia' alone, Japan's role as the 'leader of the East' (Tōyō no meishu) was different from Western imperialism, Kodaira claimed. Nevertheless, according to Kodaira, the scope of this 'divine Asianism' was the whole world and 'Asia' only constituted a link between Japan and the rest of the human race.[113]

Of central importance for this change of attitude was the omnipresent link of Asianism with Manchuria, the founding of Manchukuo, and Japan's departure from the League of Nations. Asianism became such an essential part of the Japanese imagination of Manchuria that an affirmation of Asianism no longer appeared as a negation of the assumed Japanese uniqueness represented by the Imperial Way. Instead, Asianist ideas could, for example, be adopted as a Chinese supplement to Japan's own political, racial, and cultural orientation. Now the foreignness of Asianism, however, no longer possessed a Chinese, Indian, or Western Asian voice that challenged Japanese policies and Japanese conceptions of Asianism. The Asian 'Other' now was Manchurian and therefore discursively and politically mainly under Japanese control itself. In other words, with the founding of Manchukuo it was possible to embrace the Asian 'Other' without embracing dissent. In this sense, much of Japanese Asianism discourse from the early 1930s onwards was based on complacency and self-deception.

Conclusion

As analysed above, the founding of Manchukuo together with Japan's departure from the League of Nations completely altered the context in which Asianism—including its meaning, significance, practicability, viability, and so on—could be discussed. To Japan, 'Asia' was no longer the hostile 'Other' on the Chinese mainland but the friendly neighbour by the name of Manchukuo—a Japanese puppet. The conflation of traditional Confucian ideals with traditional Japanese ideals facilitated the dissolution of assumed contradictions and strangeness; Japan could be part of 'Asia' and vice versa. Importantly, this new direction of Asianism discourse was strongly promoted and driven from above. It was military and political leaders who began to openly advocate political aims dressed in Asianist language and through Asianist concepts. This probably constitutes the most remarkable shift that Asianism discourse experienced in the twentieth century. To be sure, as Cemil Aydin has pointed out, the 'official endorsement of a pan-Asian vision of regional world order in Japan' was 'one of the most striking aspects of the international history of the 1930 s'.[114] In China, Asianism in the 1930s was at the centre of the struggle for political authority between different contestants for the party and state leadership. To them, Asianism was important for two reasons: first, as a claim to the politico-intellectual inheritance of Sun Yat-sen, whose 'Greater Asianism' remained the ultimate blueprint of any conception of Asianism in China; second, as a conceptual means to reject Japan's imperialist advance in China, which had increasingly become justified by Asianist propaganda. When Wang Jingwei started to use Asianism as a key concept in justification of his collaboration regime in 1940, he not only utilized Sun's concept but also copied a Japanese strategy employed to sell Asianism to the Japanese since the early 1930s. Just as the Japanese were made to believe that Asianism as the fusion of the Imperial and Kingly Ways was essentially Japanese (focus on the Japanese Imperial Way), Wang's regime used the same concepts to convince the Chinese of the essentially Chinese character of this new Asianism (focus on the Confucian Kingly Way). As a consequence, spatially and terminologically Chinese-Japanese Asianism discourse had become more integrated than ever. The official embrace and institutionalization of Asianism, above all in Japan, however, also deprived Asianism discourse of much of its controversial nature. Gradually, it degenerated into a quasi-ideology. Asianism was no longer attractive to thinkers and activists that sought to transcend the pattern of nationalist or racialist competition. Instead, as Tachibana Shiraki had already warned in 1933, it turned into 'an important guiding principle of right-wing forces in Japan'.[115] The contest for hegemony between China and Japan that had centred on Asianism discursively for two decades would now be fought out in a full-blown war between the two countries.

Notes

1. Matsui Iwane, 'Shina o sukufu no michi' [The road to save China], *Dai Ajiashugi* [Greater Asianism], 1-1, May 1933, 6–10: 6.
2. On Manchukuo in general see Yamamuro Shin'ichi, *Kimera: Manshūkoku no shōzō* [Chimera: A Portrait of Manchukuo], Tokyo: Chūō Kōronsha 1993, its English translation *Manchuria under Japanese dominion*, translated by Joshua A. Fogel, Philadelphia: University of Pennsylvania Press 2006, Young, *Japan's total empire*, Rana Mitter, *The Manchurian myth: nationalism*, resistance and collaboration in modern China, Berkeley: University of California Press 2000, and Prasenjit Duara, *Sovereignty and authenticity: Manchukuo and the East Asian modern*, Lanham: Rowman & Littlefield 2003.
3. See Elise K. Tipton, *The Japanese Police State: the Tokko in Interwar Japan*, Sydney and Honolulu: Allen and Unwin and University of Hawaii Press 1990 and Richard Mitchell, *Thought Control in Prewar Japan*, Ithaca: Cornell University Press 1976.
4. For an overview of more general aspects pertaining to the founding of Manchukuo and changes in Japanese Asia policy and consciousness see Hotta, *Pan-Asianism and Japan's war 1931–1945*, Chap. 4. Hotta describes Pan-Asianism as a *kenkoku* (state founding) ideology and Manchukuo as Japan's 'Pan-Asianist empire' (116–117).
5. Rana Mitter, *A bitter revolution: China's struggle with the modern world*, Oxford and New York: Oxford University Press 2004, 39.
6. For a classical account of the political history in China during this era see C. Martin Wilbur 'The Nationalist Revolution: from Canton to Nanking, 1923–28', *The Cambridge History of China, Vol. 12: Republican China, 1912–1949, Part 1*, ed. John K. Fairbank, Cambridge: Cambridge University Press 1983, 527–720.
7. The well-known and now common title 'father of the Republic of China' (guofu) was only given to Sun in 1940.
8. To illustrate Dai's role as Sun's trusted comrade and interpreter, the first edition of Dai's main work on Sun carried a photograph of Dai standing next to Sun taken in Kobe just before Sun delivered his famous speech on

Greater Asianism. See Dai Jitao, *Sun Wen Zhuyi zhi Zhexue de Jichu* [The philosophical base of Sun Yat-senism], Shanghai: Minzhi Shuju 1925.
9. See Dieter Kuhn, *Die Republik China von 1912 bis 1937: Entwurf für eine politische Ereignisgeschichte* [The Republic of China from 1912 to 1937: draft of a political history], Heidelberg: Edition Forum 2007, 332 and Audrey Wells, *The political thought of Sun Yat-Sen: development and impact*, New York: Palgrave 2001, 135. While both include references to Dai neither mentions Dai's interpretation of Sun's Asianism.
10. See Dai, *Sun Wen Zhuyi zhi Zhexue de Jichu*, 32–38. Note that the first edition displays great variations compared to later editions. For a detailed comparison of the differences see Kubo, *Dai Jitao ni okeru 'Chūgoku Kakumei' to sono shisō*, 109–122.
11. Dai, *Sun Wen Zhuyi zhi Zhexue de Jichu*, 32, 35.
12. Dai, *Sun Wen Zhuyi zhi Zhexue de Jichu*, 37–38.
13. For Tongū's journal see Chap. 6. From 1933 the Indian activist Rash Behari Bose published in Tokyo a journal called *Shin Ajia* (New Asia) as the joint organ of the Japan-based Indian Independence Association and the New Asia Association. The bilingual journal (English–Japanese) was dedicated to the 'complete independence of Asia', which was later changed to 'complete independence of India, Asia and Humanity'; compare *The New Asia/Shin Ajia*, No. 5 & 6 (September 1933), 1 and *The New Asia/Shin Ajia*, No. 9 & 10 (January 1934), 1. For the journal see also Nakajima, *Nakamuraya no Bōsu* and Hotta, 'Rash Behari Bose and his Japanese Supporters', 116–132.
14. For details of the history of the journal and a complete collection of its tables of contents see Kubo Juntarō, 'Zasshi "Xin Yaxiya" ronsetsu kiji mokuji' [Tables of Contents of editorial articles in the journal 'New Asia'], *Kōbe Daigaku Shigaku Nenpō* [Kobe University Annual Bulletin of Historiography] 17, 2002, 80–124.
15. See Sun Yat-sen, 'Da Yaxiya zhuyi' [Greater Asianism], *Xin Yaxiya* [New Asia], 1-1 (October 1930), 1–7: 1.
16. 'Yaxiya zhi Jianglai' [The Future of Asia], *Xin Yaxiya* [New Asia], 1-1 (October 1930), 9–13: 11.
17. 'Yaxiya zhi Jianglai', 12–13.
18. See 'Xin Yaxiya de shiming' [The Mission of New Asia], *Xin Yaxiya* [New Asia], 1-1 (October 1930).
19. On this aspect, on Dai's Asianization of Sun's Three People's Principles in the *Xin Yaxiya* journal, and on Dai's links with Gu Jiegang's *Yugong Xuehui* (Yugong Study Group) see Sabine Dabringhaus, *Territorialer Nationalismus in China: Historisch-geographisches Denken 1900–1949* [Territorial Nationalism in China: Historical-Geographical Thought 1900–1949], Köln: Böhlau Verlag 2006, 65–67.

20. Prasenjit Duara, 'Transnationalism in the Era of Nation-States: China, 1900–1945', *Development and Change*, 29-4 (October 1998), 647–670: 658–659.
21. Duara, 'Transnationalism in the Era of Nation-States: China, 1900–1945', 667.
22. Yin Weilian, 'Yaxiya Minzu yundong zhi jinzhan' [The progress of the Asian peoples' movement], *Xin Yaxiya* [New Asia], 1-1 (October 1930), 91–97: 97.
23. See Kawashima, 'Kindai Chūgoku no Ajia kan to Nihon', 432.
24. For Hu's activity in the 1930s and his interpretation of Sun's Asianism see Takatsuna Hirofumi, 'Nitchū kankeishi ni okeru Son Bun no Dai Ajiashugi. Senzen hen' [Sun Yat-sen's Greater Asianism within the history of Japanese–Chinese relations. Pre-war section], *Chikaki ni arite* [Being Nearby], 32 (November 1997), 58–78: 62–65 and Itō Teruo, '"Dai Ajiashugi" to "Sanmin shugi". Ō Seiei [Wang Jingwei] kairai seiken shita no sho mondai ni tsuite' ['Greater Asianism' and 'The Three People's Principles'. On some problems under Wang Jingwei's puppet government], *Yokohama Shiritsu Daigaku Ronsō* [Yokohama City University Essay Collection], 40-1 (1989), 225–247: 233–235.
25. Hu Hanmin, 'Da Yaxiya zhuyi yu guoji jishu hezuo' [Greater Asianism and international technological cooperation], *Sanmin Zhuyi* [Three People's Principles], 2-4 (September 1933), quoted in Hu Hanmin, *Yuandong Wenti yu Da Yaxiya Zhuyi* [The Far Eastern Question and Greater Asianism], Guangzhou: Minzhi Shuju 1935, 1–26: 4.
26. Hu, 'Da Yaxiya zhuyi yu guoji jishu hezuo', 26.
27. See Hu Hanmin, 'Zai Lun Da Yaxiya zhuyi' [On Greater Asianism Again], *Sanmin Zhuyi* [Three People's Principles], 4-3, quoted in Hu Hanmin, *Yuandong Wenti yu Da Yaxiya Zhuyi* [The Far Eastern Question and Greater Asianism], Guangzhou: Minzhi Shuju 1935, 27–43: 29–30.
28. Note Hu's terminology: 'shijie zhuyi' (worldism), not internationalism (guoji zhuyi).
29. Hu, 'Zai Lun Da Yaxiya zhuyi', 38.
30. Hu, 'Zai Lun Da Yaxiya zhuyi', 42–43.
31. Doihara was known as a China expert (Shina tsū) within the Army and belonged to the main plotters of the Japanese occupation of Northeast China after the Manchurian Incident of 1931. Doihara was convicted as an A-class war criminal at the International Military Tribunal for the Far East in Tokyo, sentenced to death, and hanged in December 1948. On Matsui see below.
32. See Takatsuna, 'Nitchū kankeishi ni okeru Son Bun no Dai Ajiashugi. Senzen hen', 64.

33. The so-called Amō Declaration (Amō Seimei) was issued by Amō Eiji, head of the Japanese Foreign Ministry's information department. Rejecting economic interference of Western powers and of the League of Nations in China, it announced Japan's intention to abandon its open door and equal opportunity policies. It was seen as Japan's announcement to officially adopt an East Asian Monroe Doctrine with Japan as its leader. On the Declaration see Inoue Toshikazu, 'Amō Seimei to Chūgoku Seisaku', *Hitotsubashi Ronsō* [Essay Collection of Hitotsubashi University], 97-5 (May 1987), 661–679.
34. Ko Kanmin [Hu Hanmin], 'Warera no Dai Ajiashugi' [Our Greater Asianism], *Nihon Hyōron* [Japan Review], 11-5 (May 1936), 172–179: 172.
35. Ko [Hu], 'Warera no Dai Ajiashugi', 174.
36. See Hu Hanmin, 'Da Yaxiya zhuyi yu kang Ri' [Greater Asianism and Resisting Japan], *Sanmin Zhuyi* [Three People's Principles], 7-3 (March 1936), 12–15: 12. The full text of Hu's report on his meeting with Matsui was also published as 'Hu Hanmin yu Songjing [Matsui] tan Da Yaxiya zhuyi' [Hu Hanmin and Matsui talk about Greater Asianism] in the widely circulated *Da Gong Bao* in Hongkong on 23 February 1936.
37. See Hu, 'Da Yaxiya zhuyi yu kang Ri', 15.
38. See Matsui Iwane, 'Seinan yūki: Showa 11, nigatsu futsuka kara sangatsu hatsuka made' [Notes from the journey to Xinan: 2 February to 20 March 1936], *Matsui Iwane Taishō no jinchū nisshi* [General Matsui Iwane's War Diary], ed. Tanaka Masaaki, Tokyo: Fuyō Shobō 1985; quoted in Takatsuna, 'Nitchū kankeishi ni okeru Son Bun no Dai Ajiashugi. Senzen hen', 65.
39. See Takatsuna, 'Nitchū kankeishi ni okeru Son Bun no Dai Ajiashugi. Senzen hen', 65.
40. 'Great Asianism Wins Favour', *The Straits Times* (Singapore), 18 March 1936, 13.
41. In December 1936, Chiang Kai-shek was arrested in the northern Chinese city of Xi'an by warlord Zhang Xueliang and subsequently forced to collaborate with the CCP. The incident is generally viewed as an event 'pushing Chiang to take a more active anti-Japanese stand'. See Peter Zarrow, *China in war and revolution, 1895–1949*, London and New York: Routledge 2005, 302.
42. See also my 'Nanjing's Greater Asianism: Wang Jingwei and Zhou Huaren, 1940', *Pan-Asianism: A Documentary History 1860–2010*, Vol. 2, ed. Sven Saaler and Christopher W.A. Szpilman, Boulder: Rowman & Littlefield 2011, 209–219.
43. Rana Mitter, *China's War with Japan, 1937–1945. The Struggle for Survival*, London: Penguin 2014, 229.

44. So Wai-Chor [Su Wei Chu/So I Sho], 'Ō Seiei [Wang Jingwei] to Dai Ajiashugi' [Wang Jingwei and Greater Asianism], *Shōwa Ajiashugi no jitsuzō. Teikoku Nihon to Taiwan,* 'Nan'yō', *'Minami Shina'* [The true picture of Asianism in the Shōwa era. Imperial Japan and Taiwan, the Southern Islands, and Southern China], ed. Matsuura Masataka, Kyoto: Mineruva Shobō 2007, 182–204: 189.
45. Jansen, *The Japanese and Sun Yat-sen*, 213.
46. For Wang's life see Cai Dejin, *Wang Jingwei ping zhuan* [Critical Biography of Wang Jingwei], Chengdu: Sichuan Renmin chubanshe 1988.
47. See Tsuchiya Mitsuyoshi, 'Ō Seiei [Wang Jingwei] no "Heiwa undō" to "Dai Ashū shugi"' [Wang Jingwei's 'Peace Movement' and 'Greater Asianism'], *Seikei Ronsō*, [Essay Collection in Politics and Economy], 61-2 (1992), 105–140.
48. See Dongyoun Hwang, 'Some Reflections on war-time collaboration in China: Wang Jingwei and his group in Hanoi' (Working Papers in Asian/Pacific Studies 98-02), ed. Anne Allison, Arif Dirlik, Tomiko Yoda, 1998 and Tsuchiya, 'Ō Seiei [Wang Jingwei] no "Heiwa undō" to "Dai Ashū shugi"', 105–140.
49. See Andrew Cheung, 'Slogans, Symbols, and Legitimacy: The Case of Wang Jingwei's Nanjing Regime' (Indiana East Asian Working Paper Series on Language and Politics in Modern China, No. 6), 1995.
50. On Zhou see Brian G. Martin, 'The Dilemmas of a civilian politician in time of war: Zhou Fohai and the first stage of the Sino-Japanese War, July–December 1937', *Twentieth-Century China*, 39-2, 2014, 144–165 and Brian G. Martin, 'Collaboration within Collaboration: Zhou Fohai's Relations with the Chongqing Government, 1942–1945', *Twentieth-Century China*, 34-2, 2009, 55–88.
51. For example, the opening of Nanjing's Central Bank in 1940 was delayed to coincide with 12 November, and Wang's speech, from which I quote below, explicitly noted Sun's birthday as the occasion on which it was written.
52. Wang Jingwei, 'Foreword', *China and Japan. Natural Friends, unnatural enemies*, ed. Tang Liangli, Shanghai: China United Press 1941, ix–x: ix.
53. Hwang, 'Some Reflections on war-time collaboration in China', 15.
54. Wang Jingwei, 'Minzu zhuyi yu Da Yazhou zhuyi' [Nationalism and Greater Asianism], *Da Yazhou zhuyi* [Greater Asianism], 1-4 (November 1940), 1–5: 4–5.
55. See John Hunter Boyle, *China and Japan at War, 1937–1945: The Politics of Collaboration*, Stanford: Stanford University Press 1972, 246.

56. Zhou Huaren (1902–76) was Vice-Minister of Transportation and a delegate representing Nanjing-China at the first of three Greater East Asian Writers' Conferences (Dai Tōa Bungakusha Taikai), which was held in Tokyo in November 1942 to obtain the support of writers for the so-called Greater East Asian War and 'to create a Greater East Asian Literature'. Zhou was also Vice-Chairman of the Propaganda Committee of the All-Chinese Society for an East Asian League (Dongya Lianmeng Zhongguo zonghui), and Chairman of the China branch of the *Tōa Renmei Kyōkai* (East Asian League Association), founded in February 1941. Unlike Chen Gongbo (1892–1946), Zhou Fohai (1897–1948), and Lin Bosheng (1902–1946), Zhou Huaren did not belong to the innermost circle of Wang's confidants. However, he quickly emerged as the regime's main propagandist, in particular with regard to propagating the concept of Greater Asianism as a means of justifying Sino-Japanese collaboration. Zhou contributed numerous articles to the *Da Yazhou Zhuyi* journal from 1940 onwards and authored a 168-page *Outline of Greater Asianism* (Da Yazhou zhuyi gangyao, 1940), which set out the guiding principles of Wang's collaborationist politics according to the template provided by Sun's theoretical heritage. Zhou's writings in Japanese translation mostly appeared in *Dai Ajiashugi* (Greater Asianism), published by the Greater Asia Association, while some were also reprinted in magazines such as *Kaizō* (Reconstruction) and *Nihon Hyōron* (Japan Review).
57. Zhou Huaren, 'Da Yazhou Zhuyi yu Sanmin Zhuyi' [Greater Asianism and the Three People's Principles], *Da Yazhou Zhuyi* [Greater Asianism], 1-2 (September 1940), 11–15: 11.
58. Compare the Chinese version Zhou Huaren, 'Da Yazhou Zhuyi yu Sanmin Zhuyi', 11 and the Japanese versions Zhou Huaren, 'Dai Ajiashugi to Sanmin shugi' [Greater Asianism and the Three People's Principles], *Dai Ajiashugi* [Greater Asianism], No. 92 (December 1940), 16–19: 16 and Zhou Huaren, 'Sanmin shugi to Dai Ajiashugi' [The Three People's Principles and Greater Asianism], *Kokusai Bunka Kyōkai Kaihō* [Bulletin of the International Culture Association], No. 126 (December 1940), 137–148: 137.
59. Shi Jiafang, *'Tongwen tongzu' de pianju. Ri wei Dongya Lianmeng Yundong de Xingwang* [The fraud of 'same culture, same race'. The rise and fall of Japan's fake East Asian League movement], Beijing: Shehui Kexue wenxian Chubanshe 2002, 217.
60. See Hwang, 'Some Reflections on war-time collaboration in China', 2–6.
61. Aoki expressed this view in an interview in 1981 as quoted in Suzuki Shizuo and Yokoyama Michiyoshi, *Shinsei kokka Nihon to Ajia: senryō ka no han'nichi no genzō* [Holy country Japan and Asia: The original image

of anti-Japanese resistance under occupation], Tokyo: Keisō Shobō 1984, 344. See also Yamamuro, *Shisō Kadai toshite no Ajia*, 573.

62. Taki quoted in the May 1934 issue of *Shina* (China), the journal of the *Tōa Dōbunkai* (Society for Same Culture in East Asia), as reproduced in Hu Hanmin, 'Da Yaxiya zhuyi yu guoji jishu hezuo' [Greater Asianism and international technological cooperation], *Sanmin Zhuyi* [Three People's Principles], 2-4, quoted in Hu Hanmin, *Yuandong Wenti yu Da Yaxiya Zhuyi* [The Far Eastern Question and Greater Asianism], Guangzhou: Minzhi Shuju 1935, 1–26: 6.

63. See Hasegawa Nyozekan, 'Dai Ajiashugi', *Tokyo Asahi*, 3 February 1932, 9 for a heavily censored criticism of Asianist conceptions by the liberal writer and journalist Hasegawa Nyozekan (1875–1932). Hasegawa denounced Rōyama Masamichi's (1895–1980) regionalist understanding of Asianism as 'purely a principle of XX Manchuria and Mongolia'. From the context it is likely that XX stood for 'annexing' (heigō).

64. See Tadokoro Teruaki, 'Ajia Gasshūkoku Ron' [On United States of Asia], *Nihon Kokumin* [Japanese People], June 1932, 219–234 for an almost illegibly censored essay by the Socialist activist Tadokoro (1900–1934), who envisioned an anti-bourgeois and anti-fascist union of the peoples of Asia.

65. Kawai (1891–1944), a well-known sociologist and liberalist, identified six streams of thought that informed the substantial agenda of the incident's instigators: nationalism (kokka shugi), political restoration of the Emperor (tennō seiji, literally emperor politics), anti-parliamentarianism (han gikai shugi), militarism (gunbi jūjitsu shugi, literally principle of building up armaments), Greater Asianism (Dai Ajiashugi), and anti-capitalism (han jihonshugi). See Kawai Eijirō, 'Go Ichigo Jiken no Hihan' [Critique of the May 15th Incident], *Bungei Shunju* [Literary Times], 11-11 (November 1932), 48–58. On Kawai's life and thought see Atsuko Hirai, Individualism and socialism: the life and thought of Kawai Eijirō (1891–1944), Cambridge, MA: Harvard University Press 1986.

66. Kawai, 'Go Ichigo Jiken no Hihan', 56.

67. See Hu, 'Da Yaxiya zhuyi yu kang Ri', 14.

68. See Sano Manabu and Nabeyama Sadachika, 'Han Ajiashugi no ippan keisō' [The general form of Pan-Asianism] as reproduced in Yamamoto Katsunosuke/Arita Mitsuo, *Nihon Kyōsanshugi undō shi* [History of the Japanese Communist Movement], Tokyo: Seiki Shobō 1950, 381. It was Koyama Sadatomo (1888–1968), a core member of the editorial team of Tachibana's *Manshū Hyōron*, who first discussed Asianist tendencies in the Sano-Nabeyama conversion and drew analogies between their apostasy declaration and the Japanese Prime Minister Matsuoka Yōsuke's speech at the League of Nations, in which he had announced Japan's departure. See Koyama Sadatomo, 'Sano no Tenkō to Dai

Ajiashugi' [Sano's apostasy and Greater Asianism], *Manshū Hyōron* [Manchurian Review] 5-2, 8 July 1933, 22–24.
69. Sano Manabu and Nabeyama Sadachika, 'Han Ajiashugi no ippan keisō' [The general form of Pan-Asianism] as reproduced in Yamamoto Katsunosuke and Arita Mitsuo, *Nihon Kyōsanshugi undō shi* [History of the Japanese Communist Movement], Tokyo: Seiki Shobō 1950, 381.
70. On the circumstances of the founding of the *Gakkai* and for an account of the founding and activities of the Association see 'Dai Ajia Kyōkai' [Greater Asia Association], Shimonaka Yasaburō Jiten [Shimonaka Yasaburō Dictionary], Vol. 1, ed. Shimonaka Yasaburō Denkankōkai [Society for the publication of a biography of Shimonaka Yasaburō], Tokyo: Heibonsha 1965, 242–282, my 'The Greater Asia Association and Matsui Iwane, 1933', *Pan-Asianism: A Documentary History 1860–2010*, Vol. 2, ed. Sven Saaler and Christopher W.A. Szpilman, Boulder: Rowman & Littlefield 2011, 137–147 and Part Three in Matsuura, *Daitōa sensō wa naze okita no ka*.
71. Aydin, *The politics of anti-Westernism in Asia*, 178.
72. See Nakatani Takeyo, *Shōwa dōranki no kaisō. Nakatani Takeyo kaikoroku* [Recollections of the upheavals of the Shōwa period. The Memoirs of Nakatani Takeyo], Tokyo: Tairyūsha 1989, 349. Nakatani's recollections, written in a tone of self-defence and self-aggrandizement, are not always reliable and must be treated with care. On Nakatani see also Szpilman, Kindai Nihon no Kakushin ron to Ajiashugi.
73. See Murakawa Kengo, 'Dai Ajia Kyōkai Sōritsu keika' [The progress of the founding of the Greater Asia Association], *Dai Ajiashugi* [Greater Asianism], 1-1 (May 1933), 62.
74. The members who signed the foundation manifesto as representatives of the Association were (in the original order): Konoe Fumimaro, Hirota Kōki, Matsui Iwane, Suetsugu Nobumasa, Yano Jin'ichi, Kikuchi Takeo, Murakawa Kengo, Ogasawara Naganari, Tokutomi Iichirō (Sohō), Fujimura Yoshirō, Katō Keizaburō, Kanokogi Kazunobu, Shiratori Toshio, Tsubogami Teiji, Negishi Tadashi, Shiraiwa Ryūhei, Tozuka Michitarō, Yamawaki Masataka, Nonami Shizuo, Hiraizumi Kiyoshi, Shimonaka Yasaburō, Sumioka Tomoyoshi, Honma Masaharu, Sakai Takeo, Higuchi Kiichirō, Suzuki Teiichi, Ōta Kōzō, Mitsukawa Kametarō, Ishikawa Shingo, Shibayama Kenshirō, Naitō Chishū, Tsutsui Kiyoshi, Nakahira Akira, Ujita Naoyoshi, Shimizu Tōzō, Imada Shintarō, Imaoka Jūichirō, Nakayama Masaru, Handa Toshiji, Nakatani Takeyo. See 'Dai Ajia Kyōkai Sōritsu Shushi' [The reasons for the founding of the Greater Asia Association], *Dai Ajiashugi* [Greater Asianism], 1-1, May 1933, 2–5: 5.
75. Richard Storry, *The Double Patriots. A Study of Japanese Nationalism*, London: Chatto and Windus 1957, 150.

76. Nakatani Takeyo, 'Matsui Taishō to Dai Ajiashugi. Jō ni kaete' [General Matsui and Greater Asianism: In place of a preface], *Matsui Iwane Taishō no jinchū nisshi* [General Matsui Iwane's War Diary], ed. Tanaka Masaaki, Tokyo: Fuyō Shobō 1985, 4–6: 5.
77. See Nakatani, *Shōwa dōranki no kaisō*, 736–738 and 'A kyū Kyokutō Kokusai Gunji Saiban Kiroku' [Records from the Class A Far Eastern International Military Tribunal], No. 122 (JACAR A08071264100) and 'A kyū Kyokutō Kokusai Gunji Saiban Kiroku' [Records from the Class A Far Eastern International Military Tribunal], No. 156-1 (JACAR A08071270900).
78. See Nakatani, *Shōwa dōranki no kaisō*, 349–353.
79. See 'Jo' [Preface], *Dai Ajia kyōkai nenpō* [Annual Report of the Greater Asia Association], March 1934, ed. Nakatani Takeyo, Tokyo: Dai Ajia Kyōkai 1934, without page numbers.
80. 'Dai Ajia Kyōkai Sōritsu Shushi', 2.
81. See 'Jo' [Preface], *Dai Ajia kyōkai nenpō* (March 1934), without page numbers.
82. See Tachibana Shiraki, 'Han Ajia Undō no shin riron' [The new theory of the Pan-Asian movement], *Manshū Hyōron* [Manchurian Review] 5-2, July 1933, 14–21: 14 and Tachibana Shiraki, 'Ajia Renmei to Nisshi Kankei' [An Asian League and Japanese–Chinese Relations], *Manshū Hyōron* [Manchurian Review] 4-14, April 1933, 2–5: 4.
83. See Marc Chadourne, *Ostasiatische Reise* [East Asian Travels], Berlin: Dietrich Reimer 1936, 238–239 and in the original French version Marc Chadourne, *Tour de la Terre. Extreme Orient* [Tour of the World. The Far East], Paris: Libraire Plon 1935, 220–223. In both versions, Nakatani's family name is wrongly transcribed as Nakaya.
84. See Tachibana Shiraki, 'Han Ajia Undō' [The Pan-Asian movement], *Manshū Hyōron* [Manchurian Review] 4-11, 18 March 1933, 9–10.
85. 'Dai Ajia Kyōkai Sōritsu Shushi', 3–5.
86. On this aspect see Matsuura, *Daitōa sensō wa naze okita no ka*, chapters 10 to 12.
87. Gotō Ken'ichi, 'Dai Ajia Kyōkai to Nanpō mondai. "Ajiashugi" dantai no Nanpō kan o meguru ichi kansatsu' [The Greater Asia Association and the South Seas problem], *Shakai Kagaku Tōkyū* [Social Sciences Review], 27-2 (April 1982), 305–326: 308.
88. The *Shōwa Kenkyūkai* was founded in 1936 and absorbed, as the Greater Asia Association, by the Imperial Rule Assistance Association. See Sakai Saburō, *Shōwa Kenkyūkai. Aru chishikijin dantai no kiseki* [Showa Research Association. The tracks of a group of intellectuals], Tokyo: Chūō Kōronsha 1992 and William Miles Fletcher, *The search for a new order: intellectuals and fascism in prewar Japan*, Chapel Hill: University of North Carolina Press 1982.

89. For biographical information on Matsui see the otherwise hagiographic book by Tanaka Masaaki, *Matsui Iwane Taishō no jinchū nisshi*. [General Matsui Iwane's War Diary] Tokyo: Fuyō Shobō 1985.
90. Matsui Iwane, 'Dai Ajiashugi' [Greater Asianism], *Kingu* [King], May 1933, 12–19: 18–19.
91. Matsui Iwane, 'Shina Jihen no igi to Dai Ajiashugi' [The meaning of the China Incident and Greater Asianism], *Dai Ajiashugi* [Greater Asianism], 7-1 (January 1939), 2–4: 3.
92. See Timothy Brook, 'The Tokyo Judgment and the Rape of Nanking', *Journal of Asian Studies*, 60-3 (August 2001), 673–700.
93. See Tanaka, *Matsui Iwane Taishō no jinchū nisshi*.
94. See *Asiatic Asia* 1-2, March 1941, without page number.
95. See Matsui, 'Dai Ajiashugi', 12. Matsui argued that the hesitant position of the Japanese public led the League to the false assumption of Japan's eventual readiness to compromise.
96. See Yamada Fuhō, 'Nihon chūshin no Ajiashugi' [Japan-centrist Asianism], *Nihon oyobi Nihonjin* [Japan and the Japanese], 258 (October 1932), 22–23: 22.
97. See Yamada Bukichi, 'Nihonshugi to Ajiashugi' [Japanism and Asianism], *Nihon oyobi Nihonjin* [Japan and the Japanese], May 1933, 11–16: 14.
98. See 'Kōdō to Ōdō' (daigen) [Imperial Way and Kingly Way, prefatory note], *Nihon oyobi Nihonjin* [Japan and the Japanese], October 1932, without page number and Yamada Fuhō, 'Kōdō to Ōdō no hikari o hanate' [Having set free the rays of the Imperial and Kingly Ways], *Nihon oyobi Nihonjin* [Japan and the Japanese], 259 (October 1932), 21–22.
99. See Ogawa Reikō, 'Ajia o daiben suru Nihon no warera' [We Japanese as Asia's Proxy], *Nihon oyobi Nihonjin* [Japan and the Japanese], 312 (January 1935), 55–58: 55.
100. See Yamamuro, *Kimera*, its English translation *Manchuria under Japanese dominion*, translated by Joshua A. Fogel, Philadelphia: University of Pennsylvania Press 2006, Young, *Japan's total empire*, 287–290, and Duara, *Sovereignty and authenticity*. On the role of Asianist concepts in Manchukuo see also Wolfgang Seifert, 'Japans Systemtransformation in den 1930er Jahren und die "Asiatisierung" Ostasiens' [Japan's system transformation in the 1930s and the 'Asiatization' of East Asia], *Ostasien im 20. Jahrhundert. Geschichte und Gesellschaft* [East Asia in the 20th Century. History and Society], ed. Sepp Linhart and Susanne Weigelin-Schwiedrzik, Wien: Promedia Verlag 2007, 45–61.
101. Note the use of different characters in both slogans which were pronounced identically in Japanese but differently in Chinese (see Glossary).

102. See Duara, *Sovereignty and authenticity*, 73.
103. See Yu Jingyuan, 'Dai Ajiashugi to sono jissen' [Greater Asianism and its practice], *Manshūkoku to Kyōwakai* [Manchukuo and the Concordia Association], ed. Koyama Sadatomo, Dalian: Manshū Hyōronsha 1935, 135–138: 137.
104. 'Nihon wa doko e yuku' [Where is Japan heading?], *Manshūkoku to Kyōwakai* [Manchukuo and the Concordia Association], ed. Koyama Sadatomo, Dalian: Manshū Hyōronsha 1935, 153–170: 154.
105. See Bao Guancheng, *Speeches and Statements on the Foundation of Manchukuo*, Tokyo: Kokusai Shuppan 1933. The compilation includes 12 essays and speeches in Chinese, Japanese, and English.
106. See Bao Guancheng, 'Manshūkoku to Dai Ajiashugi' [Manchukuo and Greater Asianism], *Speeches and Statements on the Foundation of Manchukuo*, Tokyo: Kokusai Shuppan 1933, 36–42: 38–40.
107. His numerous writings on this subject include *Gendai Shūshin Kyōiku no konponteki seisatsu* [A Fundamental Reflection on Contemporary Ethics Education], Tokyo: Kenbunkan 1934, *Shin Jinjō Shogakkō shūshin kyōiku sho* [Book of New Common Primary School Ethics Education], Tokyo: Tōyō tosho 1929–1931 (3 volumes), and *Kōmin Kyōiku to Shūshin Kyōiku* [Civic Education and Ethics Education], Tokyo: Meiji Tosho 1927.
108. See Horinouchi Tsuneo, *Shōgakkō o chūshin to seru Warera no Kōmin Kyōiku* [Our Civic Education with a focus on Primary Schools], Tokyo: Meguro Shoten 1933, 320.
109. See Horinouchi, *Shōgakkō o chūshin to seru Warera no Kōmin Kyōiku*, 325.
110. See Iwata Kazuo, *Tōhō minzoku no kaihō undō* [Liberation Movements of the Eastern Peoples], Tokyo: Shakai Kyōiku Kyōkai 1934 (Shakai Kyōiku Panfuretto, 195), 38–39.
111. See Kodaira Kunio, *Ajiajin no Ajia* [Asia of the Asians], Tokyo: Shakai Kyōiku Kyōkai 1934 (Shakai Kyōiku Panfuretto, 198), 33.
112. See Kodaira, *Ajiajin no Ajia*, 36–37.
113. See Kodaira, *Ajiajin no Ajia*, 36, 38.
114. See Aydin, *The politics of anti-Westernism in Asia*, 161.
115. Tachibana, 'Han Ajia Undō', 10.

CHAPTER 8

Conclusion: Continuing Antagonisms and Asianism Today

This book has studied Asianism discourse in Japan and China in the core period from 1912 to 1933 with a focus on the changing meaning and functions of Asianism as a key political concept in mainstream public discourse within and between both countries. Identifying important moments in this discourse that considerably influenced or changed the direction and contents of Asianism discourse, it has argued that the Asianist moments of 1913, of World War One, of 1924, of 1927, and of 1933 represent points of crystallization which established Asianism as a new concept (1913), promoted certain conceptions of Asianism to temporary discursive hegemony (anti-Western civilizationalist, culturalist-racialist, and rationalist-regionalist conceptions), or signalled the end of controversial discourse as a consequence of the concept's quasi-official appropriation (1933).

Apart from its focus on studying Asianism as a political concept in its own right in order to identify the contemporary understanding of Asianism as the 'principle of Asia', this book has adopted two other foci. First, it has emphasized the importance of the two decades from the early 1910s to the early 1930s. This period has been overlooked for a long time but, as this study has demonstrated, is in fact a key period for the development of Asianism discourse and of Chinese and Japanese consciousness of 'Asia' in general. This is particularly obvious in the boom in mainstream publications on Asianism, such as in widely read newspapers and journals. Second, it has stressed the transnational dimensions of Asianism discourse which consist of (a) the political agenda of Asianism

© The Author(s) 2018
T. Weber, *Embracing 'Asia' in China and Japan*,
Palgrave Macmillan Transnational History Series,
https://doi.org/10.1007/978-3-319-65154-5_8

that transcends the national (be it as imperialist ambition or an expression of solidarity) and (b) its physical transcendence of national borders in the sense of discursive and personal transnational dimensions; although, for various reasons addressed in this book, the driving force of Asianism discourse and its main arena was Japan, Chinese and Japanese alike participated in the contest for Asianist discursive hegemony and strongly influenced each other's conceptions. The quality and significance of Asianism as a rising political concept from the 1910s onwards therefore can hardly be grasped if Japanese (or Chinese) Asianism is reduced to denote exclusively writings in Japanese (or Chinese) and by Japanese (or Chinese), respectively.

Both foci automatically also highlight the need to comprehend Asianism as a concept that contributed to the intense and controversial negotiation of political agendas in Japan and China. Asianist positions were articulated and discussed vis-à-vis other influential politico-intellectual positions of the time, including different forms of nationalism, internationalism, and imperialism. In addition, they were also negotiated in opposition to other conceptions of Asianism. The dividing lines in this discourse, which, as a consequence, includes affirmations and negations of Asianism, ran less along the national borders of China and Japan than they were informed by political and ideological convictions that not always but often transcended national demarcations.

The first chapter introduces Asianism discourse in China and Japan as the topic of the book and explains the goals of the study. It defines its spatial and temporal scopes, lays out the theoretical framework of Orientalism and self-Orientalization as well as the methodological framework of discourse analysis based on conceptual history within which the embrace of 'Asia' is analysed. The second chapter has more generally discussed the epistemological framework of studying Asianism with a particular focus on the role of definitions, dichotomies, and canons. It has argued that Takeuchi Yoshimi's outstanding and lasting impact on scholarship on Asianism has facilitated the study of a relatively wide body of sources of Asianist thought. However, it has also led to neglecting (a) the discursive character of the conceptual contest for 'Asia', (b) World War One and the interwar years as the constitutive period of this contest, and (c) debates about Asianism beyond 'great thinkers' and Japan.

Chapter 3 has introduced 1913 as the first Asianist moment, when a wider audience in China and Japan for the first time learnt of the existence and meaning of Asianism as the 'principle of Asia', mediated (a)

8 CONCLUSION: CONTINUING ANTAGONISMS AND ASIANISM TODAY

by a debate in Europe and the US about Japanese Asianity and assimilability and (b) by the publication of an Asianist text (1912) in China. Encouraged by the perceived decline of the 'West', during World War One (Chap. 4) Asianist conceptions emerged in great quantity and diversity, both in China and in Japan. Intellectually, this period, maybe up to 1919, constitutes the peak of theoretical debate on the content, significance, and viability of Asianism. Leftist-liberal conceptions coexisted with imperialist-hegemonic conceptions, all of which were attacked by Japanese nationalists who found no way to reconcile 'Asia' with Japanese interests; not yet, that is. In addition, Japanese conceptions of Asianism met with great interest in China (more than vice versa). Against the background of World War One, which had created a generally receptive mood towards Asianism in China too, Japanese conceptions were discussed intensely but scepticism about Japan's ultimate intentions prevailed.

After the rejection of Japan's racial equality proposal at Versailles in 1919 and peaking in 1924—Asianism's *annus mirabilis*—when the United States shut the door on Japanese immigration, Asianism discourse became dominated by racialist notions (Chap. 5). While the public outcry against racial discrimination appeared unanimous, the Japanese and Chinese 'embrace' of racialized 'Asia' remained hesitant; Asianism remained controversially discussed in mainstream political debate about national, regional, and global politics—and Asianism was but one option in this political contest. As a widespread concept that had gained prominence in the meantime, also because of Sun Yat-sen's 'Greater Asianism' speech in 1924 in Kobe, Asianism facilitated the political communication between different viewpoints and actors, including affirmations of the concept and rejections of specific conceptions by Japanese, Chinese, and other debaters.

Partly in reaction to the racialization of 'Asia', attempts at practical implementations of Asianism coincided with less essentialist proposals of Asian unity and commonality (Chap. 6), mainly in the second half of the 1920s. As a consequence of 'Asia's' regionalization, Asianism was turned from an object of study and theoretical debate into a matter of action. At Nagasaki (1926) and Shanghai (1927) Japanese and Chinese Asianists for the first time directly debated with other Asian-minded Asians over issues of assumed common political Asian interest. While Asians jointly reclaimed authority over defining and managing 'Asia', against the background of nationalist and imperialist reality they failed to initiate a lasting Asianist organization and to implement an Asianist agenda from below. In the changed political setting of the early 1930s (Chap. 7), Asianism gradually became appropriated from above, particularly as a rhetorical and conceptual tool of legitimization of Japan's occupation of Manchuria. In contrast to Asianism discourse in the early 1910s, affirmations of Asianism were no longer suppressed or rejected by the Japanese government but adopted, while criticism of Asianism now became censored. In this way, Asianism was—as Duara put it—'hijacked by Japanese militarism'[1] and turned into a quasi-ideology that was promoted throughout Asia, for example, by the Greater Asia Association. Eclectically borrowing from various conceptions of Asianism that had been advanced and discussed during the 1910s and 1920s, Asianism became conflated with Japanism or emperor-centred ideologies. In China too, embracing 'Asia' had become a prominent political matter and manifested itself in the competition in the *Guomindang* leadership for political authority by claiming Sun's legacy, which prominently included the contest to maintain the true interpretation of his Asianism. Largely disconnected from the original claim of jointly planning an 'Asia for the Asians', Asianism now represented different and increasingly incompatible agendas of nation-building and state formation in China. By the mid-1930s, Asianism was no longer a conceptual tool of political exchange and contest but of propaganda and ideological conflict.

Asianism discourse differed from previous and other 'Asia' discourse as it left no room for ambiguous answers about one's commitment to 'Asia'. Asianism as *Ajiashugi* or *Yazhou zhuyi* had elevated 'Asia' to the ranks of a principle, an *ism*. While few Japanese and Chinese debaters would have rejected the general relevance of Asia as a place, Asianism asked how deeply one was committed to 'Asia' as a principle and to 'Asia' as Japan's or China's main future political orientation. Unsurprisingly, given the intense efforts at 'Westernization' and 'modernization' during the preceding Meiji era, many Japanese remained hesitant. Similarly, in China the political reality of internal instability and the foreign threat prompted a generally hesitant reaction which viewed Asianist proposals with suspicion: was Asianism not just an Asian (or even Japanese) variation of (Western) imperialism? Nevertheless, as a result of the heated transnational debate about Asianism, 'Asia' was no longer exclusively the foreign-defined 'Other' but increasingly became part of the self-defined 'Self'. Through processes of self-affirmation and self-Orientalization, by the early 1930s the concept of 'Asia' and its functions in political discourse had been revised. Asian voices had started to reclaim authority over 'Asia' and affirmations of Asianism represented this claim in its most explicit and forceful manner. Ironically, maybe, this debate on commonality did not contribute to a mutual understanding between the Japanese and Chinese and to their peaceful coexistence in the following years and decades. On the contrary, it eventually intensified antagonisms and became a rhetorical tool in the war between both countries.

Asianism Discourse in the Twenty-First Century

As mentioned in the Preface, Asianism as a concept has by no means disappeared after World War Two.[2] Instead, even in the twenty-first century it has remained on the political agenda of Sino-Japanese relations and interactions, both as a potential means of reconciliation and as a tool of a continued or renewed contest for hegemony. Some suggest that an embrace of solidarity-based conceptions of Asianism may become the formula for true historical reconciliation between the two countries (and East Asia at large). Others, however, use Asianism's historical significance for exactly the opposite purpose, namely for continuous public attacks on China and Japan, respectively; historical revisionists in Japan seek to reclaim Japanese regional leadership by reaffirming wartime conceptions of Asianism, whereas in Chinese public discourse Japan's militarist and imperialist past is frequently conflated with Japanese Asianism, which in turn is portrayed as symbolic for the perceived inability of Japan *in toto* to repent and to come to terms with its past. In similar vein, the rhetorical potential of Asianism has been rediscovered for inter-state diplomacy, mainly as a tool for promoting either China-centric or Japan-centric positions.

A different set of binary divides in which Asianism continues to play a role in contemporary political discourse in East Asia concerns Asianism in relation to regionalism and globalization. Miyadai Shinji's declaration of a new Asianism as an expression of anti-globalism and anti-Americanism adds an anti-neoliberal dimension to the concept. In Miyadai's words, 'the time has come for the true meaning of Asianism (Ajiashugi no hongi) as thought that allies the weak against the globalization of the American "winner takes all" mentality'.[3] This conception directly opposes the 'neoliberal circumstances under which regional formation is taking place' and which 'can easily develop the concept of Asia for the rich and their representatives who attend to financial flows, knowledge economies, and corporatization, while containing or displacing the poor and privatizing public goods', as Prasenjit Duara has observed.[4] Whereas Asianism, also in Duara's words, was hijacked by militarism in the 1930s, in the early twenty-first century some see the danger of Asianism—and by extension all appeals to Asian commonality and integration—being hijacked by neo-liberal capitalism. The underlying themes of much of contemporary Asianism discourse sound more than familiar: first, Asianism as an alternative to the dominance of the 'West', in particular America (historically: 'Euro-America'), and second, Asianism as resting on assumed 'cultural similarity' of East Asians.[5] In this context of globalization and regionalism, the re-emergence of Asianism in public political debate from the mid-2000s onwards as a tool for promoting regional integration and regional identity formation in East Asia has come to be viewed critically by a group of Asiaphile scholars and activitists who prefer to grasp Asianism as self-affirmative epistemology. This understanding of Asianism constitutes an extension of Said's (or Takeuchi's or Tokutomi's) critique of Orientalism by directing it not only at the 'Western' 'Other' but also at the so-called 'Other' within.[6]

Asianism in Twenty-First Century Diplomacy

The most elaborate proposal on the diplomatic level for adopting a new outlook on Asianism is Wang Yi's call for a 'Neo-Asianism for the twenty-first century', which largely follows Wang Ping's proposal for a 'new classical Asianism', as discussed in the Introduction.[7] Wang Yi, currently foreign minister of the People's Republic of China and a former Chinese ambassador to Japan (2004–2007) introduced his Neo-Asianism thesis with a partial re-evaluation of historical Asianism. Before 'early Asianism was increasingly diverted down a side road and gradually lost credibility as a tool of, and pretext for, the invasion and monopolization of Asia', Wang claimed,

> a group of Japanese intellectuals took the lead in proposing the idea of an Asian alliance. They argued that Japan, China, and Korea were all members of an Eastern civilization faced with increasing pressure from the advancing Western powers. Therefore, a Sino-Japanese alliance was desirable, and a triple alliance of Japan, China, and Korea also needed to be formed. At the same time, some important political figures and thinkers at the Qing court were making similar claims.[8]

Rehabilitating historical Asianism in parts and infusing Chinese agency and origin in an otherwise believed-to-be Japanese project forms Wang's point of departure. Unlike Wang Ping's 'New Classical Asianism', however, which envisioned a renaissance of classical, cooperative Asianism, Wang Yi's 'Neo-Asianism' is largely divorced from any concrete historical model. Instead it focuses on present-day China and is based on what President Hu Jintao (2003–2013) called 'a harmonious Asia'. Hu's vision of an 'Asia that works together in the political sphere, is economically even-handed and mutually beneficial, is marked by mutual trust and cooperation with regard to security, and cooperates freely in the areas of cultural exchanges and academic research' forms the core of Wang's idea of a new Asianism.[9] Consequently, this New Asianism should follow the principles of cooperation (hezuo), openness (kaifang), and harmony (hexie). Despite his repeated emphasis on equality, openness, and mutual benefits, however, 'Asia', as defined by Wang, is essentially an 'Asia' centred on China—with 'Chinese virtues' as its philosophical basis and China's rising economy as its engine of development. In particular, he stresses, as does Wang Ping, China's 'outstanding cultural and spiritual heritage' and refers to Confucianism as a value system on which to base the 'revival of Asia'.[10]

While Wang Yi is known and respected in Japan as an expert on Japan and his emphasis on Sino-Japanese reconciliation was particularly welcomed at the time of strained relations between the two countries during the premiership of Koizumi Jun'ichirō (2001–2006), his Sinocentric version of Asianism was received critically. In an immediate response and as a rejection of implicit Chinese claims to leadership, the former secretary general of Japan's Liberal Democratic Party (LDP), Nakagawa Hidenao, stressed that 'Asia in the twenty-first century does not require a leader' (meishu wa iranai).[11] In many ways, this Chinese proposal and the Japanese response is reminiscent of historical Asianism discourse—only with the tables turned.

In the meantime, Japanese politicians too have embarked on efforts to regain agency and authority in discourse on Asian commonality and regional integration which draws heavily on historical Asianist concepts.[12] Most famously, former Prime Minister Hatoyama Yukio (2009–2010) of the Democratic Party of Japan has advanced his vision of an East Asian Community (Higashi Ajia Kyōdōtai) in which he explicitly referred to Coudenhove-Kalergi's model role as a visionary of pan-European integration—the same model that had inspired Nagatomi

Morinosuke eighty years earlier (see Chap. 6).[13] In addition, in 2004 the LDP-led Japanese government under Prime Minister Koizumi Jun'ichirō promoted the establishment of a think tank called the Council on East Asian Community (Higashi Ajia Kyōdōtai Hyōgikai), which makes policy suggestions to the Japanese government and represents Japan's voice in semi-official 'Asia' discourse in Asia as institutionalized in various networks of think tanks.[14] In line with the LDP's political programme, however, the Japanese Council takes a distancing stance towards issues of reconciliation and integration in East Asia and is particularly critical of China. It therefore emphasizes in its mission statement that it does not seek to promote the creation of an East Asian Community but only to study different options.[15] Rather than being instrumental in the promotion of regional integration the Council may be more adequately described as a group that seeks to advise the Japanese government and other groups in Japan on how to best position Japan in the contest for hegemony with China in the region. Unsurprisingly, the Council therefore does not advance pro-Asianist conceptions but prefers to remind the Japanese of their 'successful' turn to the 'West' after World War Two.[16] Consequently, it views Japan's home and fate as lying with the 'West', not Asia. As in many historical instances, the promotion of national interests seems to be so central to the political agendas of Wang Yi, the Japanese Council, and others[17] that Asianism as a discourse, at least in the realm of (official and semi-official) diplomacy, may best be characterized as a contest for nation-centred regional hegemony, not for overcoming national rivalry.

New Asianisms and the History Problems

Similarly to its historical predecessors, Asianism is advanced in a less nation-centred meaning by civil society actors today too. Many of those are scholars or practitioners who are actively involved in projects that re-address the past in order to promote a transnational historical consciousness and to overcome history problems. History textbook initiatives that counter the official national or nation-state-centred accounts—'often the prime curricular vehicle for official programmes of political socialisation'[18]—have been one central and more practically oriented part of this stream.[19] Asianism here becomes an alternative to nation-centred approaches. Another central aspect of Asianist discourse driven by non-government organizations and civil society actors, often transnational networks that themselves form an East Asian Community *en miniature*, is the more theoretical rejection of thinking in national units which has been identified as a key problem in the prevailing history problems. Transnational exchange, for these networks, is a means to create a transnational consciousness, to realize historical reconciliation, and to start various processes of (bottom-up) regional integration. In this context, Asianism has been welcomed and re-evaluated as a challenge to the production and spread of knowledge by and in a Western-dominated environment. Inspired by Takeuchi Yoshimi, proponents have referred to this view of 'Asia' as a site and subject of knowledge production as 'Asia as a method'. Similar to Takeuchi's original proposal of the 1960s, in which he complained about the Japanese lack of interest in other Asian countries, cultures, and languages,[20] this Asianism above all is self-reflective and mainly directed at oneself, namely the Asian 'Self'—as an encouragement to acquire knowledge, to discover and embrace commonality among Asians. As the Taiwanese scholar Chen Kuan-Hsing argues, this kind of Asianism must be different from historical Asianism, which had either been dominated by nationalist agendas or focused too much on the 'West' as the imperial and racial Other (e.g. in Sun Yat-sen's 'Greater Asianism' and the Japanese 'Greater East Asian Co-Prosperity Sphere'). Instead, new Asianism must transcend national borders and nationalist stereotypes on the one hand and confront the imperial 'Other' within, that is, forces that reject overcoming nationalism and view regionalism as a mere tool to maximize economic profits, Chen argues.[21]

Ironically, Asianism also remains present in today's political sphere as a major obstacle in solving the so-called history problems or 'history wars' in East Asia.[22] Despite a notable tendency in Chinese scholarship to acknowledge different conceptions of Japanese Asianism (see Introduction), in more general public discourse the indiscriminate conflation of Japanese Asianism and Japanese militarism and fascism remains deeply rooted in China.[23] In addition, this oversimplified interpretation of historical Asianism is frequently reactivated to criticize historical revisionism in Japan and the dissatisfactory attitude of the Japanese government in addressing Japan's imperialist past.[24] Simplistic and political as this criticism may be, it is not without reason. In Japanese revisionist circles, some of which have close connections with members of the Japanese government, narratives of Japan's imperialist past prevail that seek to whitewash Japan's wartime aggression, in particular in East Asia. Revisionists therefore use Asianism literally in the sense in which it was used by Japanese wartime propaganda. Publications by the so-called Japan Conference (Nippon Kaigi),[25] for example, portray Asianism affirmatively as the positive ideational foundation of Japan's 'noble' and 'righteous' fight for 'self-defence' and the 'liberation of Asia' from Western imperialism. Consequently, they dismiss any links to aggression and invasion. Asianism, they argue, was reflected in the supposedly benevolent Japanese policies of the 'Greater East Asian Co-Prosperity Sphere', the principle of the harmonious cooperation of the five races (wuzu xiehe) in Manchukuo, and the aim of 'liberating Asia'.[26] One could be tempted to simply dismiss these reappreciations of wartime Asianism as misguided historical understanding if the group did not infer from these revisionist views recommendations for the field of contemporary politics and diplomacy—and if it were not as influential and closely interconnected with the Japanese government as it is. Moreover, the *Nippon Kaigi* is not the only group that spreads such views. In 2014, an organization called 'Dream—Greater Asia' was founded, which propagates 'the creation of a strong Japan to liberate Asia once more'.[27] It openly utilizes Japan's wartime rhetoric, such as 'hakkō ichiu' (imperial rule over the eight corners of the earth),[28] and sets as its aim to 'raise Asia' (kō A) in order to liberate Tibet, Xinjiang, and Inner Mongolia from the 'colonial control' of the Chinese Communist Party. In this way, this group too explicitly links its revisionist reappreciation of Asianism as wartime ideology to contemporary policy advice. While it criticizes the Asia policy of Chinese President Xi Jinping as being 'mere hegemonialism, not Greater Asianism',[29] it turns a blind eye to Japan's own historical abuse of Asianism for the imperialist cause of becoming the hegemonic power in East Asia.

At the same time, in most of the above-mentioned conceptions—as diverse as they may be—this new Asianism retains its anti-Western dimension. 'Asia' becomes a method to critique the 'West' (a) as the origin of imperialism and/or the capitalist world order and (b) as the dominant place of knowledge production through paradigms that force Asians to adapt, for example, the narration of their histories, to Western terms and concepts (such as modernization or Cold War paradigms).[30] In this context, the Chinese intellectual and Japan scholar Sun Ge has revisited Sun Yat-sen's Asianism as the major historical source of Chinese Asianist discourse. Interestingly, Sun Ge dissociates Sun Yat-sen's Asianism from both its racialist and Confucian biases. Instead, she argues, for Asians the Asia question is primarily a question of the sense of solidarity, a sense that arises in the midst of the aggression and expansion perpetrated by the West. Thus, the sense of solidarity is articulated with a sense of national crisis.[31]

According to her, Sun Yat-sen proposed 'Greater Asianism' as a formula for resolving national crisis and evoking solidarity among Asian peoples, by which he meant 'all the coloured races of the Asian region'. Thereby, the concept of 'Asia' could 'defend the oppressed peoples against injustices perpetrated on them'.[32] Sun Yat-sen's role, according to Sun Ge, was to remind the Japanese of their lacking concern for weaker peoples. It is this historical message of solidarity on which Sun Ge also builds her contemporary vision of Asianism. Through remembering Sun Yat-sen's conception of 'Asia' the debate on regional integration and identity formation can be moved away from Confucianism, Asian values, and self-congratulatory 'Asia as Number One' rhetoric towards advancing solidarity and concern for the oppressed. In her view, the context in which Sun Yat-sen had proposed fighting 'aggression and expansion' has shifted from a military threat to economic exploitation. As a consequence, 'the oppressed people' nowadays refers mainly to the economically oppressed. Figuratively and linked to Takeuchi's original thesis of 'Asia as method' as an epistemological critique, however, 'the oppressed people' also includes oppressed opinions and therefore indirectly highlights the continuous and world-wide hegemony of 'Western' knowledge.[33]

This aspect becomes even more explicit in Wang Hui's discussion of historical 'Asia' discourse.[34] A well-known Chinese intellectual and founder of the influential *Dushu* (Reading) magazine, Wang also takes inspiration from Sun Yat-sen's Kobe speech (see Chap. 5) as a blueprint for inter-Asian cooperation and integration today.[35] To him, Sun's key message was 'independence', for which the nation-state historically constitutes the point of departure. Sun's 'Asia' was a region that comprised all Asian nations as independent nations. Rather than being a promoter of Confucianism, Wang argues, Sun must be seen as a pioneer of a 'multicultural Asia' whose unity was 'based on the independence of sovereign states'. Sun's vision of 'Asia' was the result of anti-colonial movements and therefore 'not an awkward imitation of European nation-states'. In other words, Sun's Asianism postulated a specifically Asian way to sovereignty (and modernity) that could be achieved by adhering to its own cultures and principles. Today's project of Asia, he implies, can only succeed if, as Sun had formulated for his own times, it enables 'a political culture that accommodates different religions, beliefs, nations, and societies',[36] in short: East Asian commonality that rests on its cultural heterogeneity. A basic condition for both—promoting solidarity (Sun Ge) and embracing cultural heterogeneity (Wang Hui)—however, is an awareness of the 'Other' within and a mindset that is free from Orientalist stereotypes.

The urgency of Wang's criticism becomes obvious in Huang Chun-chieh's attempt to apply Sun's Asianism to today's regional and global political context. A Taiwanese scholar of Confucianism, Huang grasps Sun's historical *badao* vs. *wangdao* dichotomy as a warning to China not to take the same wrong path that Japan had taken in the 1930s. Huang asks, 'will China, in its politics, follow the hegemonic way (badao) or the kingly way (wangdao) of benevolent government?'[37] As Sun had done historically, Huang also links these alternatives from the regional to the global sphere because 'China's choice will not only determine the fate of the greater Chinese sphere, but will also influence the future of humankind'. Interestingly, Huang too uses this historical analogy to reach a conclusion that is not only self-centred but also self-Orientalizing and Occidentalist. To Huang, the 'spiritual resource for the rejuvenation of the people and a common resource for the future of East Asian civilization' is based on 'Taiwan's diverse cultural symphony' and its 'kingly way of benevolent government'. Taiwan's unique qualification, according to Huang, lies in its historical experience of having neither suffered from the 'chaotic devastation' of the Cultural Revolution, nor the 'spiritual pollution of Western capitalism'.[38] In the light of Huang's cultural essentialist views, Chen Kuan-hsing's encouragement to discover the 'Other' within could hardly be more relevant.

In fact, Sun Yat-sen's Asianism has become one main point of reference of new Asianism in Japan too. An active role in the enterprise of re-establishing Sun as an Asianist model of the past for the future is played by the International Academic Society for Asian Community, a Japan-based think tank that was created in 2006. Its self-declared purpose is the creation of an East Asian Community as 'symbiotic regionalization'. It views itself as an 'Asian-wide society of studies and policy proposals for Asian regionalization' and aims 'to mould an epistemological community networking with citizens across the national borders in the region, to nurture an Asian identity, and to be a forerunner of the evolving East Asian Community, the realization of which is our common dream'.[39] Writing in the *Asahi* newspaper, the society's leader, Shindō Eiichi, portrays Sun Yat-sen and Umeya Shōkichi[40] as examples of 'Japanese–Chinese civic diplomacy'.[41] Sun and Umeya, as opposed to the *Genyōsha* and *Kokuryūkai*, which are often linked to Japanese expansionism, are characterized as 'good Asianists' who aimed at establishing a new order of equality and reforms from below. In order to bring East Asia further together, Asians needed to embrace a 'New Asianism' in a globalized world, centring on civil society activities and common culture in East Asia. 'New Asianism' was neither Japanese 'Nihon meishu ron' (Japan as leader theory), nor Chinese-led 'Sino-Japanese guidance', nor Korean-initiated 'Japanese–Chinese–Korean alliance'. Instead, its centre must be the 'weaker and smaller countries of ASEAN' (Association of Southeast Asian Nations), Shindō argues. Shindō concedes that historically not only Japanese Asianism but also Japanese 'Asia' policy had failed to make the right choice when Japan was confronted with either becoming 'a tool of Western despotism' or 'the stronghold of Eastern benevolent rule'. This choice, of course, is taken from Sun Yat-sen's famous speech on 'Greater Asianism' in 1924, as studied in Chap. 5. The difference between *wangdao* and *badao*, despotic and rightful rule, can be transferred, Shindō concludes, to today's politics of either demonizing one's neighbour or seeking relations of cooperation and harmony. In other words, Japan's choice to accept its Asianity would not only constitute in essence the 'right' or Kingly Way but also embody a correction of the wrong path taken historically by Japan.

While the link between Sun and Umeya constitutes a rather recent feature in public discourse,[42] Sun's Greater Asianism speech of 1924 has been a permanent point of reference within discourse on East Asian integration and identity formation in particular.[43] Possibly in reaction to too much credit given to Sun and his conception of Asianism, Baik Young-seo, however, a major contributor to the Korean *Changbi* journal (Creation and Criticism Quarterly), reminded the debaters of a more realist view of Sun's.[44] While Sun's concepts of the 'Yellow Race' and emphasis on Confucian principles may indeed reveal a transnational concern not too dissimilar to today's Asianist projects, Sun was ultimately driven by 'strategic considerations', Baik argues: against the background of Sun's decreasing domestic political power, he attempted to gain Japanese support for China. Although Sun did—despite some flattering remarks—criticize Japan, he neglected to demand 'solidarity with weak and small nations such as colonized Korea', Baik emphasizes. According to Baik, it was therefore 'natural for Koreans to denounce Sun'. Sun's strategic and self-centred appeal to Asian commonality, which was a result of emergency rather than being an ideal in itself, Baik suggests, can hardly serve as a model for today's transnational projects of historical reconciliation and regional integration. If anything, it may rather serve as a warning that—once again—Asia's name may be abused for all kinds of agendas that do not promote solidarity and cooperation but self-interest alone.

Baik's warning leads us back to the pitfalls of historical Asianism discourse. Asia, in its most immediate meaning—representing the world's largest and most populous continent stretching over ten standard time zones and encompassing more than two hundred languages—is void of any distinctive unifying content that could inform just one principle of 'Asia'. In this sense, 'Asia' and Asianism are and must be ambiguous and 'multifaceted' (Takeuchi). Consequently, the search for this principle will lead to any place one seeks to find. However, if we take Takeuchi's 'Asia as method' to an even more abstract level, 'Asia' (just as 'Europe', 'America', 'Africa', etc.) may be seen as a concept that reflects one's own present conditions and ambitions, those of one's immediate and more distant surroundings, as well as all the inherent imaginations thereof. As such, just like almost any other concept, it lends itself to many different political agendas. At the same time, however, 'Asia' as a concept comes with a history. Much of today's historical 'baggage' or historical significance of 'Asia' has been attached to the concept in Asianism discourse during the two decades that have been studied as the main temporal focus of this book. Today's 'Asia' discourse may rightfully be characterized as a constant and continuing renegotiation of (I) *remembering* its history and simultaneously of (II) *emancipation from* its history in order to deal with the new challenges of the present. These challenges, after all, may not be too different from those of the past.

Notes

1. Prasenjit Duara, 'Asia Redux: Conceptualizing a Region for Our Times', *Journal of Asian Studies* 69-4 (November 2010), 963-983: 973.
2. For an excellent overview of different streams of early twenty-first century Asia discourse in Japan see Tessa Morris-Suzuki, 'Asia is One: Visions of Asian Community in Twenty First Century Japan', *Okakura Tenshin and Pan-Asianism. Shadows of the Past*, ed. Brij Tankha, Folkestone: Global Oriental 2009, 158-170.

8 CONCLUSION: CONTINUING ANTAGONISMS AND ASIANISM TODAY 333

3. Miyadai Shinji (in the *Asahi Shinbun*, 18 August 2003) quoted in Inoue Toshikazu, *Ajiashugi o toinaosu* [Revisiting Asianism], Tokyo: Chikuma Shobō 2006, 28. Miyadai intentionally uses Chinese characters for his proposal of Asianism to represent the notion of a shared script in East Asia. For Miyadai's conception of Asianism see Miyadai Shinji, *Ajiashugi no tenmatsu ni manabe: Miyadai Shinji no han Gurōbaraizēshon Gaidansu* [Learn from the details of Asianism: Miyadai Shinji's guidance to anti-globalization], Warabi: Jissensha 2004.
4. Duara, 'Asia Redux', 983.
5. Miyadai Shinji quoted in Inoue Toshikazu, *Ajiashugi o toinaosu* [Revisiting Asianism], Tokyo: Chikuma Shobō 2006, 28.
6. Chen Kuan-Hsing, *Asia as method: toward deimperialization*, Durham, NC: Duke University Press 2010, Chap. 5 and the original Chinese version: Chen Guangxing, *Qu Diguo. Yazhou zuowei fangfa* [De-imperialization. Asia as method], Taibei: Xingren 2006.
7. See Wang Yi, 'Sikao Ershiyi shiji de Xin Yazhou zhuyi' [Considering Neo-Asianism in the twenty-first century], *Waijiao Pinglun* [Foreign Affairs Review], June 2006, No. 89, 6–10. For the context of his proposal and an English translation see my 'Wang Yi: 'Neo-Asianism' in 21st Century China', *Pan-Asianism: A Documentary History 1860–2010*, Vol. 2, ed. Sven Saaler and C.W.A. Szpilman, Boulder: Rowman & Littlefield, 2011, 359–370.
8. Wang, 'Sikao Ershiyi shiji de Xin Yazhou zhuyi', 6.
9. See Wang, 'Sikao Ershiyi shiji de Xin Yazhou zhuyi', 8–9.
10. See Wang, 'Sikao Ershiyi shiji de Xin Yazhou zhuyi', 9–10.
11. See Nakagawa Hidenao, 'Atarashii Ajiashugi' [New Asianism], *Nitchū taiwa* [Japanese–Chinese Dialogue], Tokyo: Genron NPO 2006, 12–19: 12.
12. Zöllner has called attention to the fact that in Japan official or semi-official East Asia discourse is characterized by a 'short memory' and by attempts to 'remain silent about Japan's intellectual copyright on "new East Asia"'. See Reinhard Zöllner, 'Alternative Regionalkonzepte in Ostasien' [Alternative regional concepts in East Asia], *Leitbild Europa? Europabilder und ihre Wirkungen in der Neuzeit* [Model Pan-Europe? Views of Europe and their impact in modern times], ed. Jürgen Elvert and Jürgen Nielsen-Sikora, Wien: Franz Steiner 2009, 295–303 (quotations from 298).
13. See Hatoyama Yukio, 'Watakushi no seiji tetsugaku' [My political philosophy], *Voice* (September 2009), 132–141.
14. For the Council's activities, see their webpage www.ceac.jp and their white book on East Asian integration; *Higashi Ajia Kyōdōtai Hakusho 2010* [East Asian Community White Book 2010], ed. Higashi Ajia Kyōdōtai Hyōgikai [Council on East Asian Community], Tokyo: Tachibana Shuppan 2010.

15. See *Higashi Ajia Kyōdōtai Hakusho 2010*, 606 and the group's website.
16. See *Policy Report 'The State of the Concept of East Asian Community and Japan's Strategic Response Thereto'*, ed. Council on East Asian Community, Tokyo 2005, 3 and 'Higashi Ajia to wa: rekishi no naka kara wakugumi taidō' [What is East Asia? Indications of a framework from history] ed. Higashi Ajia Kyōdōtai Hyōgikai [Council on East Asian Community], No. 2, 2004, http://www.ceac.jp/j/survey/survey002.html (last accessed 16 October 2016).
17. In South Korea, the Northeast Asian History Foundation pursues a similar nation-centred agenda. It was founded in 2006 'with the goal of establishing a basis for peace and prosperity in Northeast Asia by confronting distortions of history that have caused considerable anguish in this region'. See *A Window to the Future of Northeast Asia*, ed. Northeast Asian History Foundation, Seoul 2009. http://english.historyfoundation.or.kr/?sub_num=9 (last accessed 16 October 2016). For its activities see also my 'Remembering or overcoming the past? "History politics", Asian identity, and visions of an East Asian Community', *Asian Regional Integration Review*, ed. Tsuneo Akaha, Tokyo: Waseda University 2011, 39–55: 48.
18. Gotelind Müller, 'Introduction', *Designing history in East Asian textbooks: identity politics and transnational aspirations*, ed. Gotelind Müller, London: Routledge 2011, 1–6: 1.
19. See *Designing history in East Asian textbooks*. Importantly, not only history textbooks but also civics and ethics textbooks remain predominantly a vehicle of national(ist) discourse. See Klaus Vollmer, 'The Construction of "Self" and Western and Asian "Others" in Contemporary Japanese Civic and Ethics Textbooks', *Designing history in East Asian textbooks*, 60–84.
20. See Takeuchi, 'Hōhō toshite no Ajia', 442–470.
21. See Chen, *Asia as method*, 211–257.
22. On historical revisionism and the history problems in East Asia see *Rekishi Mondai Handobukku* [Handbook of History Problems], ed. Tōgō Kazuhiko and Hatano Sumio, Tokyo: Iwanami 2015, Sven Saaler, *Politics, Memory and Public Opinion. The History Textbook Controversy and Japanese Society*, München: Iudicium 2005, Philip A. Seaton, *Japan's contested war memories: the 'memory rifts' in historical consciousness of World War II*, London/New York: Routledge 2007, and *Contested Views of a Common Past. Revisions of History in Contemporary East Asia*, ed. Steffi Richter, Frankfurt: Campus 2008.
23. See Yu Xingwei, 'Renqing Riben "Da Yazhou zhuyi" de Junguo zhuyi shizhi' [Recognizing the militaristic essence of Japan's 'Greater Asianism'], *Renmin Ribao*, 25 August 2015; Cao Pencheng, 'Hanwei "lishi zhengyi" caineng zouxiang jiefang' [Upholding 'historical righteousness' will lead to liberation], *Renmin Ribao*, 14 August 2015; Sun Chunri, 'Dongya guojia

gongtong dizhi cuowu shiguan' [East Asian countries jointly reject erroneous historical views], *Renmin Ribao*, 9 July 2014.
24. See footnote above and also Wang, *Jindai Riben de Yaxiya zhuyi*, 358–377.
25. On this organization see Aoki Osamu, *Nippon Kaigi no shōtai* [The True Character of the Japan Conference], Tokyo: Heibonsha 2016 and *Nippon Kaigi to Jinja Honchō* [The Japan Conference and the Association of Shinto Shrines], ed. Narusawa Muneo, Tokyo: Kinyōbi 2016.
26. See *Kore dake wa shitte okitai Dai Tōa Sensō* [That much one should know about the Greater East Asian War], ed. Nippon Kaigi Jigyō Sentā, Tokyo: Meiseisha 2006 and *Dai Tōa Sensō to Ajia no dokuritsu* [The Greater East Asian War and the Independence of Asia], ed. Nippon Kaigi Jigyō sentā, Tokyo: Meiseisha 2013.
27. Ishii Hidetoshi, 'Ajia wo futatabi kaihō suru' [Liberating Asia once more], *Yume Dai Ajia* [Dream—Greater Asia], 2014, No. 1, 4–5: 4.
28. On this concept and its use in the 1930s and 1940s see Walter Edwards, 'Forging Tradition for a Holy War: The "Hakkō Ichiu" Tower in Miyazaki and Japanese Wartime Ideology', *Journal of Japanese Studies*, Vol. 29, No. 2 (Summer 2003), 289–324.
29. Tōyama Kōsuke, 'Kikan "Yume Dai Ajia" no sōkan o iwatte' [Congratulating the start of the quarterly 'Dream—Greater Asia'], *Yume Dai Ajia* [Dream—Greater Asia], 2014, No. 1, 14–16: 16.
30. See Sun Ge, 'The predicament of compiling textbooks on the history of East Asia', *Designing history in East Asian textbooks*, 9–31.
31. Sun Ge, 'How does Asia mean?', *The Inter-Asia cultural studies reader*, ed. Kuan-Hsing Chen and Chua Beng Huat, London: Routledge 2007 (2000), 9–65: 23. Sun's discussion of the way 'Asia' means forms the intellectual manifesto of the transnational Inter-Asia Cultural Studies Movement, which mainly publishes in English to reach a wider audience, in particular within more Anglophone parts of Asia. I have quoted from this more widely accessible English version. A previous version in Chinese first appeared in Taiwan as Sun Ge, 'Yazhou yiwei zhe shenme' [What does Asia mean?], *Taiwan Shehui Yanjiu Jikan* [Taiwan: A Radical Quarterly in Social Studies], No. 33 (March 1999), 1–64. A revised Japanese version appeared later as Sun Ge, 'Ajia to wa nani o imi shite iru no ka' [What does Asia mean?], *Shisō* [Thought] 986 (June 2006), 48–74 and 987 (July 2006), 108–129. For the movement see Kuan-Hsing Chen and Chua Beng Huat, 'Introduction', *The Inter-Asia cultural studies reader*, ed. Kuan-Hsing Chen and Chua Beng Huat, London: Routledge 2007, 1–5.
32. See Sun, 'How does Asia mean?', 23.
33. See *Posuto 'Higashi Ajia'* [Post-'East Asia'], ed. Sun Ge/Baik Young-Seo/Chen Kuan-Hsing, Tokyo: Sakuhinsha 2006, 1–4.

34. On Wang Hui's Asia discourse see Susanne Weigelin-Schwiedrzik, 'Ist Ostasien eine europäische Erfindung? Anmerkungen zu einem Artikel von Wang Hui' [Is East Asia a European invention? Notes on an article by Wang Hui], *Ostasien im 20. Jahrhundert. Geschichte und Gesellschaft* [East Asia in the 20th Century. History and Society], ed. Sepp Linhart and Susanne Weigelin-Schwiedrzik, Wien: Promedia Verlag 2007, 9–21.
35. Wang Hui, 'The politics of imagining Asia. A genealogical analysis', *The Inter-Asia cultural studies reader*, ed. Kuan-Hsing Chen and Chua Beng Huat, London: Routledge 2007 (2005), 66–102: 78–80. A previous version of this widely distributed essay had appeared in Chinese as Wang Hui, 'Yazhou Xiangxiang de puxi' [The genealogy of Imagining Asia], *Shijie* [Horizons] (8) 2002.
36. Wang Hui, 'The politics of imagining Asia', 79.
37. Chun-chieh Huang, 'Dr. Sun Yat-sen's Pan-Asianism Revisited: Its Historical Context and Contemporary Relevance', *Journal of Cultural Interaction in East Asia*, Vol. 3, 2012, 69–74: 72.
38. See Huang, 'Dr. Sun Yat-sen's Pan-Asianism Revisited', 74.
39. See 'Setsuritsu Shushi' [Mission and Purposes], 2006; http://wwwsoc.nii.ac.jp/isac/index-e.html, last accessed 10 June 2011.
40. Umeya Shōkichi (1868–1934) was a Nagasaki-born entrepreneur, originally in the film industry, who had worked in Hong Kong and Singapore and supported Sun financially. For the Japanese debate about the actual extent of Umeya's financial support of Sun see Hazama Naoki, 'Umeya Shōkichi no Son Bun shien' [Umeya Shōkichi's support of Sun Yat-sen], *Asahi Shinbun*, 4 June 2011.
41. See Shindō Eiichi, 'Ajia haken ka kyōchō ka' [Asian hegemony or harmony], *Asahi Shinbun*, 14 October 2010, 8. For Shindō's argument in a more elaborate version see also his *Higashi Ajia Kyōdōtai o dō tsukuru ka* [How to build an East Asian Community?], Tokyo: Chikuma shobō 2007, particularly Chapter 8.
42. Japanese Prime Minister Kan Naoto (in office 2010–2011) referred to the Sun–Umeya connection as a positive historical model for Sino-Japanese cooperation; see Kan Naoto, 'Rekishi no bunsuirei ni tatsu Nihon Gaikō' [Japanese Diplomacy at a Historic Watershed], 20 January 2011, http://www.kantei.go.jp/jp/kan/statement/201101/20speech.html (last accessed 16 October 2016).
43. Wang Yi had added Sun's adherence to *wangdao* to the canon of his own Confucian values-centred conception of a 'New Asianism'; see Wang, 'Sikao Ershiyi shiji de Xin Yazhou zhuyi', 7.
44. Baik Young-seo, 'Conceptualizing "Asia" in modern Chinese mind: a Korean perspective', *Inter-Asia Cultural Studies*, 3-2 (2002), 277–286: 280–281.

Appendix

List of Asianist organizations studied in this book (in chronological order)

Yazhou Minzu Xiehui 亞洲民族協會 (Asian Peoples' Association)
Founded 1922 in Shanghai (no activities recorded after 1925)
Key members: Tongū Yutaka, H. P. Shastri
Notable activities: publication of bilingual (Chinese/English) monthly *Da Ya Zazhi/The Asiatic Review*

Zen Ajia Kyōkai 全亜細亜協會 (All Asia Association)
Founded 1924 in Tokyo (no activities recorded after 1927)
Key members: Iwasaki Isao, Imazato Juntarō
Notable activities: co-organization of Pan-Asian Conferences (1926, 1927)

Yaxiya Minzu Da Tongmeng 亞細亞民族大同盟 (Great Alliance of Asian Peoples)
Founded 1925 in Beijing (no activities recorded after 1927)
Key members: Huang Gongsu, Li Zhaofu
Notable activities: co-organization of Pan-Asian Conferences (1926, 1927)

Xin Yaxiya Xuehui 新亞細亞學會 (New Asia Study Society)
Founded 1931 in Nanjing, dissolved 1946
Key members: Zhang Zhenzhi, Dai Jitao
Notable activities: publication of monthly journal *Xin Yaxiya*

Han Ajia Gakkai 汎亜細亜學會 (Pan-Asia Study Society)
Founded 1932 in Tokyo (renamed Dai Ajia Kyōkai in 1933)
Key members: Shimonaka Yasaburō, Nakatani Takeyo
Notable activities: founding of successor organization Dai Ajia Kyōkai

Dai Ajia Kyōkai 大亜細亜協會 (Greater Asia Association)
Founded 1933 in Tokyo, dissolved 1945
Key members: Shimonaka Yasaburō, Matsui Iwane, Nakatani Takeyo
Notable activities: publication of pamphlets and monthly journal *Dai Ajiashugi*, founding of branches throughout (Japanese-occupied) East and Southeast Asia

Glossary

of Japanese, Chinese, Korean personal names and terms (personal names that appear in the bibliography as authors or editors are not listed)

Romanized/Pinyin	Japanese/Chinese	English
personal names		
a. Japanese		
Aizawa Saburō	相沢三郎	
Aizawa Seishisai	会沢正志斎	
Amō Eiji	天羽英二	
Aoki Kazuo	青木一男	
Arao Sei	荒尾精	
Doihara Kenji	土肥原賢二	
Ebina Danjō	海老名弾正	
Fukuchi Ōchi	福地櫻痴	
Furuhata Mototarō	降旗元太郎	
Hashimoto Sanai	橋本左内	
Hirano Kuniomi	平野国臣	
Hirano Yoshitarō	平野義太郎	
Hirota Kōki	広田弘毅	
Honda Toshiaki	本多利明	
Ibuka Hikosaburō	井深彦三郎	
Inoue Kiyoshi	井上清	
Inukai Tsuyoshi	犬養毅	
Ishida Tomoji	石田友治	
Ishihara Shintarō	石原慎太郎	
Ishiwara Kanji	石原莞爾	
Itō Hirobumi	伊藤博文	

(continued)

Romanized/Pinyin	Japanese/Chinese	English
Kajima Seiichi	鹿島精一	
Kaneko Kentarō	金子堅太郎	
Katsu Kaishū	勝海舟	
Kayahara Kazan	茅原華山	
Kishi Nobusuke	岸信介	
Koizumi Jun'ichirō	小泉純一郎	
Kokubo Kishichi	小久保喜七	
Kondō Renpei	近藤廉平	
Konoe Fumimaro	近衛文麿	
Kōtoku Shūsui	幸徳秋水	
Matsuoka Yōsuke	松岡洋右	
Mitsukawa Kametarō	満川亀太郎	
Miyake Setsurei	三宅雪嶺	
Nagata Tetsuzan	永田鉄山	
Nakasone Yasuhiro	中曽根康弘	
Ogawa Heikichi	小川平吉	
Ōi Kentarō	大井憲太郎	
Ōkawa Shūmei	大川周明	
Ōki Enkichi	大木遠吉	
Ōkuma Shigenobu	大隈重信	
Okumura Teijirō	奥村禎次郎	
Ōsugi Sakae	大杉栄	
Ozaki Hotsumi	尾崎秀実	
Sakai Toshihiko	堺利彦	
Sakuma Shōzan	佐久間象山	
Satō Nobuhiro	佐藤信淵	
Shidehara Kijūrō	幣原喜重郎	
Shimonaka Yasaburō	下中弥三郎	
Suematsu Kenchō	末松謙澄	
Suetsugu Nobumasa	末次信正	
Suzuki Teiichi	鈴木貞一	
Takebe Tongo	建部遯吾	
Taki Masao	滝正男	
Tanaka Giichi	田中義一	
Tanaka Zenryū	田中善立	
Uchida Ryōhei	内田良平	
Uchimura Kanzō	内村鑑三	
Ueki Emori	植木枝盛	
Umeya Shōkichi	梅屋庄吉	
Yamada Shōji	山田昭次	
Yano Jin'ichi	矢野仁一	
Yoshida Shōin	吉田松陰	
b. Chinese		
Cai Xiaobai	蔡曉白	
Chen Gongbo	陳公博	

(continued)

Romanized/Pinyin	Japanese/Chinese	English
Du Yaquan	杜亞泉	
Feng Yuxiang	馮玉祥	
Ge Zhaoguang	葛兆光	
He Ruzhang	何如璋	
Hu Jintao	胡錦濤	
Jiang Jieshi	蔣介石	
Jin Kemin	金殼民	
Kang Youwei	康有為	
Li Zhaofu	李肇甫	
Liang Qichao	梁启超	
Lin Bosheng	林柏生	
Liu Shipei	劉師培	
Puyi	溥儀	
Qiu Shui	秋税	
Tang Liangli	湯良禮	
Wang Tao	王韜	
Wu Peifu	吳佩孚	
Xi Jinping	习近平	
Xu Xue'er	徐血兒	
Yuan Shikai	袁世凱	
Zhang Binglin	章炳麟	
Zhang Ji	張繼	
Zhang Shizhao	章士釗	
Zhang Xueliang	張學良	
Zhang Youshen	張友深	
Zhang Zhenzhi	張振之	
Zhang Zuolin	張作霖	
Zhou Fohai	周佛海	

c. Korean

Jeong Yeon-kyu	鄭然圭	

others

a. Japanese

aite to sezu	相手とせず	no dealings with the Nationalist Government
Ajia kaiki	アジア回帰	return to Asia
Ajia Monrōshugi	アジアモンロー主義/亜細亜モンロー主義	Asian Monroe Doctrine
Ajiashigi	亜細亜旨義	Asianism
Ajiashugi	アジア主義/亜細亜主義	Asianism
Amō Seimei	天羽声明	Amō Declaration (1934)
Chi Nichi ha	知日派	(foreign) expert on Japan
Chian Iji Hō	治安維持法	Public Security Preservation Law (1925)
Dai Ajia Kyōkai	大亜細亜協會	Greater Asia Association

(continued)

Romanized/Pinyin	Japanese/Chinese	English
Dai Ajiashugi	大アジア主義/大亜細亜主義	Greater Asianism
Dai Nihon Kō A Dōmei	大日本興亜同盟	Greater Japan Raise Asia Alliance
Dai Tōa Kaigi	大東亜会議	Greater EastAsia Conference (1943)
Dai Tōa Kyōeiken	大東亜共栄圏	Greater East Asian Co-Prosperity Sphere
Dai Tōa Shō	大東亜省	Greater East Asia Ministry
Datsu A (ron)	脱亜(論)	(Thesis of) Leaving/Dissociating from Asia
dōbun dōshu	同文同種	same script/culture, same race
dōshu dōkon	同種同根	same race, same roots
dōshū dōshu	同州同種	same continent, same race
enkō kinkō	遠交近攻	'befriending the far away to attack the nearby'
Genyōsha	玄洋社	Lit. Dark Ocean Society; Japanese nationalist group founded 1881
Gozoku Kyōwa	五族共和	(Chinese) "Republic of the Five Races"
Gozoku Kyōwa	五族協和	harmonious cooperation of the five races or peoples
hadō	覇道	Rule of Might, Way of the Despot
hakka	白禍	White Peril
hakkō ichiu	八紘一宇	Imperial rule over the eight corners of the earth
hakuai	博愛	philanthropy/fraternity
hakubatsu	白閥	white clique
hakujin	白人	White (person/people)
Han Ajia Gakkai	汎亜細亜學會	Pan-Asia Study Society
Han Ajiashugi	汎アジア主義/汎亜細亜主義	Pan-Asianism
hansei	反省	self-reflection
Higashi Ajia Kyōdōtai	東アジア共同体	East Asian Community
i i kō i	以夷攻夷	'using one barbarian to attack another'
i i sei i	以夷制夷	'using one barbarian to check another'
jinshu	人種	race

(continued)

Romanized/Pinyin	Japanese/Chinese	English
Jinshuteki Sabetsu Teppai Kisei Taikai	人種的差別撤廃期成大會	League for the Promotion of the Abolishment of Racial Discrimination
Jiyū Minken Undō	自由民権運動	(Japanese) Movement for Freedom and Civil Rights during the 1870s and 1880s
Jōi Ron	攘夷論	thesis of anti-foreignism
Ka-I shisō	華夷思想	traditional Chinese thought that distinguishes China as the civilized centre from the barbarian periphery (lit. China-barbarian thought)
kankan	漢奸	traitor
keikōsei	傾向性	inclination
Ketsumeidan	血盟団	Blood Pledge Corps
kiki ishiki	危機意識	consciousness of crisis
Kō A	興亜	Raise Asia
Kō A In	興亜院	Asia Development Board
Kō A Kai	興亜會	Raising Asia Society
Kō A Kannon	興亜観音	goddess of mercy for the raising of Asia
kōka	黄禍	Yellow Peril
kokka	国家	nation state
kokugaku	国学	National Learning
kokumin	国民	national citizen
Kokuryūkai	黒龍會	Lit. Black Dragon Society (Amur Society); Japanese nationalist group founded 1901
kokutai	国体	(Japan's) national polity
kyōiku (ni kansuru) chokugo	教育(ニ関スル)勅語	Imperial Rescript on Education, 1890
Kyokutō Ajia Renpō	極東亜細亜連邦	Far East Asian Republic
Manshūkoku Kyōwakai	満州国協和會	Manchukuo Concordia Association
Meiji	明治	era name of the reign of Mutsuhito as Japanese Emperor, 1868–1912
minzoku	民族	(ethnic) nation, peoples
minzoku jiketsu shugi	民族自決主義	national (ethnic) self-determination

(continued)

Romanized/Pinyin	Japanese/Chinese	English
Mitogaku	水戸学	(Japanese) Mito School
Monbushō futsū gakumukyoku	文部省普通学務局	Ministry of Education's General Education Office
Nisshin Teikei Ron	日清提携論	Thesis of cooperation between Japan and (Qing) China
nyū Ō	入欧	enter Europe
Ōbei (shugi)	欧米(主義)	Euro-America (nism)
ōdō	王道	Kingly Way, Rule of Right (Confucian)
ōdō rakudo	王道楽土	paradise of the Kingly Way
Ōkashugi	欧化主義	principle of Europeanization
rangakusha	蘭学者	scholars of Dutch (or Western) learning
rentai	連帯	solidarity
Seiyō	西洋	West/Occident (lit. Western Seas)
Shin A Sha	振亜社	Rouse Asia Society; assumed to be proto-Asianist organization, founded 1878
Shina tsū	支那通	(Japanese) China expert
shinryaku	侵略	invasion
shinshi hosha	唇歯輔車	close relations of interdependency (lit. lips and teeth, cheekbones and gums)
Shōwa	昭和	era name of the reign of Hirohito as Japanese Emperor, 1926–1989
Sonnō Jōi Undō	尊王攘夷運動	Movement to Revere the Emperor and Repel the Barbarians
tairiku rōnin	大陸浪人	(Japanese) mainland adventurer
Taishō	大正	era name of the reign of Yoshihito as Japanese Emperor, 1912–1926
Taishō demokurashī	大正デモクラシー	Taishō Democracy
Taishō Ishin	大正維新	Taishō Restoration
Tōa Dōbunkai	東亜同文會	East Asia Common Culture Association; founded 1898

(continued)

Romanized/Pinyin	Japanese/Chinese	English
Tōa Dōbun Shoin	東亜同文書院	East Asia Common Culture Study Institute; founded 1900 in Nanjing
Tōa Renmei	東亜連盟	East Asia League
Tōhō	東方	East/Orient (lit. Eastern direction)
Tokubetsu Kōtō Keisatsu	特別高等警察	Special Higher Police
Tōyō	東洋	East/Orient (lit. Eastern Seas)
Zen Ajia Kyōkai	全亜細亜協會	All Asia Association
Zen Ajiashugi	全アジア主義/全亜細亜主義	All Asianism
b. Chinese		
Beifa	北伐	Northern Expedition
Da Yaxiya zhuyi	大亞細亞主義	Greater Asianism
Da Yazhou zhuyi	大亞洲主義	Greater Asianism
Dongfang	東方	East/Orient (lit. Eastern direction)
Dongfang wenming	東方文明	Eastern civilization
Dongfang zhuyi	東方主義	Orientalism
Dongya Gongtongti	東亞共同體	East Asian Community
Fan Yaxiya zhuyi	泛亞細亞主義	Pan-Asianism
Fan Yazhou zhuyi	泛亞洲主義	Pan-Asianism
Gudian Yaxiya zhuyi	古典亞細亞主義	Classical Asianism
guojia	國家	nation state
guomin	國民	national citizen
Guomindang	國民黨	National(ist) Party (GMD, Kuomintang, KMT)
hanjian	漢奸	traitor
hexie	和諧	harmony
hezuo	合作	cooperation
kaifang	開放	openness
kang Ri	抗日	resist the Japanese
Manzhouguo	滿洲國	Manchukuo
minzu	民族	(ethnic) nation, peoples
minzu zijue zhuyi	民族自決主義	national (ethnic) self-determination
qin Ya	侵亞	invading Asia
ren yi dao de	仁義道德	virtue and morality
renzhong	人種	race
Sanmin Zhuyi	三民主義	Three People's Principles
Tongmenghui	同盟会	Revolutionary Alliance
tongwen tongzhong	同文同種	same script/culture, same race
Wangdao letu	王道樂土	paradise of the Kingly Way

(continued)

Romanized/Pinyin	Japanese/Chinese	English
Wuzu Gonghe	五族共和	(Chinese) "Republic of Five Races"
Wuzu Xiehe	五族協和	harmonious cooperation of the five races or peoples
Xifang zhuyi	西方主義	Occidentalism
Xin Yaxiya Xuehui	新亞細亞學會	New Asia Study Society
Xin Yaxiya zhuyi	新亞細亞主義	New Asianism
xing Ya	興亞	reviving Asia
Yaxiya Mengluo zhuyi	亞細亞孟羅主義	Asian Monroe Doctrine
Yaxiya Minzu Da Tongmeng	亞細亞民族大同盟	Great Alliance of Asian Peoples
Yaxiya zhuyi	亞細亞主義	Asianism
Yazhou lianhe	亞洲聯合	Asian alliance
Yazhou Minzu Xiehui	亞洲民族協會	Asian Peoples' Association
Yazhou zhuyi	亞洲主義	Asianism
ziwo Dongfang zhuyi	自我東方主義	self-Orientalism

BIBLIOGRAPHY

Abbott, James Francis, *Japanese Expansion and American Policies*, New York: Macmillan 1916.
Ahn Yonson 安姸宣, "Kyōyū sareta Kōkuri no rekishi to bunka isan o meguru ronsō" 共有された高句麗の歴史と文化遺産をめぐる論争 [The dispute on the joint history and cultural legacy of Koguryo], *Higashi Ajia no Rekishi seisaku. Nitchūkan taiwa to rekishi ninshiki* 東アジアの歴史政策: 日中韓対話と歴史認識 [History Policy in East Asia. Historical Consciousness and Conversations between Japan, China, and Korea], ed. Kondō Takahiro 近藤孝弘, Tokyo: Akashi Shoten, 2008, 44–67.
Aibara Shigeki 相原茂樹, "Konoe Atsumaro to Shina Hozen Ron" 近衛篤麿と支那保全論 [Konoe Atsumaro and the preserving China debate], *Kindai Nihon no Ajiakan* 近代日本のアジア観 [Modern Japanese views of Asia], ed. Okamoto Kōji 岡本幸治, Kyoto: Mineruva Shobō 1998, 51–77.
Ajia ni taisuru Nihon no Sensō Sekinin o tou Minshū Hōtei Junbikai アジアに対する日本の戦争責任を問う民衆法廷準備会 [Society for the Preparation of a Popular Court to investigate the Japanese War Responsibility towards Asia], ed., *'Ajiashugi' no Sensō Sekinin* アジア主義の戦争責任 ['Asianism' and War Responsibility], Tokyo: Kinohana Sha 1996.
Anonymous, "A Korean Denunciation", *Japan Weekly Chronicle*, 5 August 1926, 157.
Anonymous, "A minzoku taikai hantai ketsugi" 亜民族大会反対決議 [Resolution to oppose the Asian Peoples' Conference], *Kesareta Genron. Seiji hen* 消された言論. 政治篇 [Deleted speech. Politics edition], Tokyo: Koria Kenkyūjo 1990, 371 (originally *Choson Ilbo* 朝鮮日報, 20 July 1926).
Anonymous, "Again the 'Pan-Asia' Bogy", *New York Times*, 17 July 1926, 12.

Anonymous, "Ajia minzoku no Daidō danketsu o hakare" 亜細亜民族の大同団結を測れ [Let's plan a great union of Asian Peoples], *Tokyo Asahi shinbun* 東京朝日新聞, 25 April 1924, 2.

Anonymous, "Ajia Minzoku Taikai" 亜細亜民族大会 [Asian Peoples' Conference], *Osaka Asahi Shinbun* 大阪朝日新聞, 1 August 1926.

Anonymous, "Ajiashigi to wa nan zo" 亜細亜旨義とは何ぞ [What is Asianism?], *Ajia* 亜細亜 [Asia], 32 (1 February 1892), 2–3.

Anonymous, "Ajiashugi o bakusu" 亜細亜主義を駁す [Repelling Asianism], *Shinjin* 新人 [New Man], 18-12 (1 December 1917), 11–16.

Anonymous, "Ajiya Minzoku Kaigi ni hatashite appaku no mashu" アジヤ民族会議にはたして圧迫の魔手 [As expected fiendish oppression of Asian Peoples' Congress], *Yamato Shinbun* 大和新聞, 15 July 1926.

Anonymous, "Asiatic Congress. Foreign Office on the Alert", *Japan Weekly Chronicle*, 22 July 1926, 113.

Anonymous, "Asiatic Congress", *Japan Weekly Chronicle*, 10 November 1927, 497.

Anonymous, "Da Yaxiya zhuyi" 大亚细亚主义 [Greater Asianism], *Zhuyi Dacidian* 主义大辞典 [Encyclopaedia of Isms], ed. Liu Jianguo, Beijing: Renmin Chubanshe 1995, 19.

Anonymous, "Da Yaxiya zhuyi lun" 大亞細亞主義論 [On Greater Asianism], *Minli Bao* 民立報 [Independent People's Paper] 15 November 1912, 2.

Anonymous, "Da Yaxiya zhuyi zhi yunming" 大亞細亞主義之運命 [The Fate of Greater Asianism], *Dongfang Zazhi* 東方雜誌 [Eastern Miscellany], 13-5 (May 1913), 16–19.

Anonymous, "Dai Ajia Kyōkai Sōritsu Shushi" 大亜細亜協会創立主旨 [The reasons for the founding of the Greater Asia Association], *Dai Ajiashugi* 大亜細亜主義 [Greater Asianism], 1-1, May 1933, 2–5.

Anonymous, "Dai Ajia Kyōkai" 大亜細亜協会 [Greater Asia Association], *Shimonaka Yasaburō Jiten* 下中弥三郎事典 [Shimonaka Yasaburō Dictionary], Vol. 1, ed. Shimonaka Yasaburō Denkankōkai 下中弥三郎伝刊行会 [Society for the publication of a biography of Shimonaka Yasaburō], Tokyo: Heibonsha 1965, 242–282.

Anonymous, "Dai Ajiashugi o hyō su" 大亜細亜主義を評す [Commenting on Greater Asianism], *Taiwan Jihō* 台湾時報 [Taiwan Times], Vol. 89 (15 February 1917), 1.

Anonymous, "Gaikō hōshin ni kansuru shitsumon shuisho" 外交方針に関する質問趣意書, "Shūgigiin Imazato Juntarō shi teishutsu Gaikō hōshin ni kansuru shitsumon ni taishi besshi tōbensho" 衆議院今里準太郎氏提出外交方針に関する質問に対し別紙答弁書, *Kanbō gōgai: Dai 49 kai Teikoku gikai, shūgiin giji sokkiroku, dai 11 gō* 官房号外、第49回帝国議会衆議院議事速記録、第

11号 [Official Gazette, extra edition: 49th Diet, Record of the Minutes of the House of Representatives, 11th edition], 16 July 1924.

Anonymous, "Giindan" 議員団 [Group of Parliamentarians], *Asahi Shinbun* 朝日新聞, 25 October 1912, 2.

Anonymous, "Gotō dan no sokumenkan" 後藤男の側面観 [Baron Goto's point of view], *Asahi Shinbun* 朝日新聞, 10 November 1915, 9.

Anonymous, "Great Asianism Wins Favour", *The Straits Times* (Singapore), 18 March 1936, 13.

Anonymous, "Hai Sabetsu Ron. Shubetsu teppai taikai ni okeru ryō enzetsu" 排差別論、種別撤廃大会における両演説 [On Anti-Discrimination. Two speeches at the Assembly for the abolition of racial discrimination], *Tokyo Nichi Nichi Shinbun* 東京日日新聞, 26 April 1919.

Anonymous, "Hai-Nichi shōgun chōsei" 排日將軍長逝 [Anti-Japanese Shogun dies], *Tokyo Asahi Shinbun* 東京朝日新聞, 4 December 1914, 2.

Anonymous, "Han Ajiashugi" はんアジアしゅぎ (汎アジア主義) [Pan-Asianism], *Kōjien* 広辞苑, Tokyo: Iwanami Shoten 2003, 5th edition (electronic version).

Anonymous, "Han Ajiashugi" 汎アジア主義 [Pan-Asianism], *Atarashii Kotoba no Izumi* 新しい言葉の泉 [Fountain of New Words], ed. Takatani Takashi 高谷隆, Tokyo: Sōzōsha 1928, 564–565.

Anonymous, "Han Ajiashugi" 汎アジア主義 [Pan-Asianism], *Atarashii Kotoba no Jibiki* 新らしい言葉の字引 [Dictionary of New Words], ed. Hattori Yoshika and Uehara Rorō 服部嘉香, 植原路郎, Tokyo: Jitsugyō no Nihonsha 1925, 591–592.

Anonymous, "Han Ajiashugi" 汎アジア主義 [Pan-Asianism], *Nihon Kokugo Dai Jiten* 日本国語大辞典 [Encyclopaedia of the Japanese Language], Vol. 11, Tokyo: Shōgakkan 1972, 5.

Anonymous, "Han Ajiashugi" 汎アジア主義 [Pan-Asianism], *Atarashiki Yōgo no Izumi* 新しき用語の泉 [Fountain of New Terminology], ed. Kobayashi Kamin 小林花眠, Tokyo: Teikoku Jitsugyō Gakkai 1923, 1075.

Anonymous, "Han Ajiyashugi" はんアジヤしゅぎ (汎亜細亜主義) [Pan-Asianism], *Kōjien* 広辞苑, Tokyo: Iwanami Shoten 1955, 1772.

Anonymous, "Hu Hanmin yu Songjing tan Da Yaxiya zhuyi" 胡漢民與松井談大亞細亞主義 [Hu Hanmin and Matsui talk about Greater Asianism], *Da Gong Bao* 大公報 (Hongkong), 23 February 1936.

Anonymous, "Imazato Juntarō o gichō ni kaigi hajimaru" 今里準太郎を議長に会議始まる [The Conference starts with Imazato as chairman], *Osaka Mainichi Shinbun* 大阪毎日新聞, 2 August 1926.

Anonymous, "Izureka ze, izureka hi" 何れか是何れか否 [Which is right and which is wrong], *Kyūshū Nichi Nichi Shinbun* 九州日日新聞 [Kyūshū Daily Newspaper], 2831, 12 January 1892.

Anonymous, "Japan's friendly message to the United States", *New York Times*, 4 October 1914.

Anonymous, "Jitsugyō kumiai ketsugi. Jinshu sabetsu teppai" 実業組合決議、人種差別撤廃 [Resolution of the employers' association. Abolition of racial discrimination], *Osaka Shinpō* 大阪新報, 18 March 1919.

Anonymous, "Jo" 序 [Preface], *Dai Ajia kyōkai nenpō* 大亜細亜協会年報 [Annual Report of the Greater Asia Association], March 1934, ed. Nakatani Takeyo 中谷武世, Tokyo: Dai Ajia Kyōkai 1934, without page numbers.

Anonymous, "Jūteki na ban kōi. Zen Ajia e no dai bujoku" 獣的な蛮行為全アジアへの大侮辱 [Bestial behaviour of barbarians. Great insult to all of Asia], *Tokyo Asahi Shinbun* 東京朝日新聞, 26 April 1924, 2.

Anonymous, "Kanyū furi narazu" 加入不利ならず [Joining the loan group is not disadvantageous], *Tokyo Nichi Nichi Shinbun* 東京日日新聞 (29 May 1919).

Anonymous, "keikōsei" 傾向性, *Kōjien* 広辞苑, Tokyo: Iwanami Shoten 2003, 5th edition (electronic version).

Anonymous, "Kōdō to Ōdō" 皇道と王道 [Imperial Way and Kingly Way], *Nihon oyobi Nihonjin* 日本及日本人 [Japan and the Japanese], October 1932, without page number.

Anonymous, "Lawrence Goes Back to Arabia", *Atlanta Constitution*, 26 August 1928, 8.

Anonymous, "Leading Article: Japan's Place in the World", *The Times*, 19 May 1913, 7.

Anonymous, "Nihon minzoku no dōkasei" 日本民族の同化性 [The assimilability of the Japanese people], *Osaka Asahi Shinbun* 大阪朝日新聞, 27–28 June 1913.

Anonymous, "Nihon Teikokubō narabi Gaikō ni kansuru shitsumon shuisho" 日本帝国防並び外交に関する質問趣意書, "Shūgigiin Imazato Juntarō shi teishutsu Nihon Teikokubō narabi Gaikō ni kansuru shitsumon ni taishi besshi tōbensho" 衆議院今里準太郎氏提出日本帝国防並び外交に関する質問に対支別紙答弁, *Kanbō gōgai: Dai 50 kai Teikoku gikai, shūgiin giji sokkiroku, dai 15 gō* 官報号外、第50回帝国議会、週銀議事速記録第15号 [Official Gazette, extra edition: 50th Diet, Record of the Minutes of the House of Representatives, 15th edition], 18 February 1925, 291–292.

Anonymous, "Nihon wa doko e yuku" 日本はどこへ行く [Where is Japan heading?], *Manshūkoku to Kyōwakai* 満洲国と協和会 [Manchukuo and the Concordia Association], ed. Koyama Sadatomo 小山貞知, Dalian: Manshū Hyōronsha 1935, 153–170.

Anonymous, "Nihonjin to hoka no Ajiajin" 日本人と他の亜細亜人 [Japanese and other Asians], *Tokyo Nichi Nichi Shinbun* 東京日日新聞, 26 June 1913.

Anonymous, "Pan-Asiatic Conference. An assembly of no importance", *The Observer* (Manchester), 1 August 1926, 9.

Anonymous, "Pan-Asiatic Congress", *Japan Weekly Chronicle*, 12 August 1926, 191.

Anonymous, "Pan-Asiatic Congress", *Manchester Guardian*, 27 September 1928, 12.

Anonymous, "Pan-Asiatics meet in Old Nippon", *Daily Guardian* (Sydney), 9 August 1926.

Anonymous, "Reisei nare Shinajin" 冷静なれ支那人 [Calm down, Chinese], *Osaka Mainichi Shinbun* 大阪毎日新聞, 6 May 1919, 1.

Anonymous, "Sabetsu Teppai Sengen" 差別撤廃宣言 [Declaration of the Abolishment of Discrimination], *Yomiuri Shinbun* 読売新聞, 6 February 1919, 3.

Anonymous, "Seiyūkai no Shina yuki giin"政友会の支那行き議員 [Members of parliament from the Seiyūkai going to China], *Asahi Shinbun* 朝日新聞, 27 September 1912, 3.

Anonymous, "sendatsu" 先達, *Kōjien* 広辞苑, Tokyo: Iwanami Shoten 2003, 5th edition (electronic version).

Anonymous, "Senkyokai no shin jinbutsu: Hara Fujirō-kun" 選挙会の新人物、原夫次郎君 [New Faces of the election: Mr. Hara Fujirō], *Asahi Shinbun* 朝日新聞, 18 March 1917, 3.

Anonymous, "Senkyokai no shin jinbutsu: Isobe Hisashi-kun" 選挙会の新人物、磯部尚君 [New Faces of the election: Mr. Isobe Hisashi], *Asahi Shinbun* 朝日新聞, 17 March 1917, 3.

Anonymous, "Shakkin dan kanyū wa fuka" 借金団加入は不可 [It's wrong to join the loan group], *Osaka Mainichi Shinbun* 大阪毎日新聞, 28 May 1919.

Anonymous, "Shanghai Dai Ajia Kyōkai" 上海大亜細亜協会 [Shanghai Greater Asia Association], *Gaimushō kiroku, Ajia kyoku* 外務省記録、アジア局 [Records of the Foreign Ministry, Asia Office], 22 May 1924 (JACAR B03041003600).

Anonymous, "Shina Mondai Ikan" 支那問題如何 [What will become of the China problem?], *Daisan Teikoku* 第三帝国 [The Third Empire], 5 May 1915, 26.

Anonymous, "Shina yuki daigishi kettei 支那行き代議士決定" [Decision on members of parliament going to China], *Asahi Shinbun* 朝日新聞, 29 September 1912, 2.

Anonymous, "shugi" 主義, *Kōjien* 広辞苑, Tokyo: Iwanami Shoten 2003, 5th edition (electronic version).

Anonymous, "Sō Ajiashugi" 総亜細亜主義 [Comprehensive Asianism], *Daisan Teikoku* 第三帝国 [The Third Empire], 5 May 1915, 27.

Anonymous, "The American Attitude towards Japan", *The Times*, 23 June 1913.

Anonymous, "Xin Yaxiya de shiming" 新亞細亞的使命 [The Mission of New Asia], *Xin Yaxiya* 新亞細亞 [New Asia], 1-1 (October 1930).

Anonymous, "Xin Yaxiya zhuyi" 新亞細亞主義 [New Asianism], *Dongfang Zazhi* 東方雜誌 [Eastern Miscellany], 15-11 (November 1918), 9–20.

Anonymous, "Yaxiya zhi Jianglai" 亞細亞之将来 [The Future of Asia], *Xin Yaxiya* 新亞細亞 [New Asia], 1-1 (October 1930), 9–13.

Anonymous, "Yazhou Minzu Xiehui Xuanyan" 亞洲民族協會宣言 [Declaration of the Asian Peoples' Association], *Da Ya Zazhi* 大亞雜誌 [Greater Asia Journal], No. 35 (April 1925), 1.

Anonymous, "Zen Ajia Kyōkai setsuritsu shushi" 全亜細亜協会設立趣旨 [Purpose for the establishment of the All Asia Association], *Zen Ajia Kyōkai Kaihō* 全亜細亜協会会報 [Bulletin of the All Asia Association], April 1926.

Anonymous, *Congressional Record*, 68th Congress, 1st Session (Washington DC: Government Printing Office, 1924), vol. 65, 5961–5962. (http://historymatters.gmu.edu/d/5080).

Anonymous, *Zen Ajia Minzoku Kaigi tenmatsu* 全亜細亜民族会議顛末 [Details of the All Asian Peoples Conference], ed. Naimushō Keihōkyoku Hoan Ka 内務省警保局保安課 [Home Ministry, Special Observation Office, Public Security Division], October 1926.

Antoni, Klaus, "'Wir Asiaten' (ware-ware Ajiajin) – Ishihara Shintarō und die Ideologie des Asianismus" ['We Asians'. Ishihara Shintarō and the ideology of Asianism], *Selbstbehauptungsdiskurse in Asien: China – Japan – Korea* [Discourses of Self-Affirmation in Asia: China, Japan, Korea], ed. Iwo Amelung et al., München: Iudicium 2003, 159–180.

Aoki Osamu 青木理, *Nippon Kaigi no shōtai* 日本会議の正体 [The True Character of the Japan Conference], Tokyo: Heibonsha 2016.

Asaba Michiaki 浅羽通明, *Nashonarizumu. Meicho de tadoru Nihon shisō nyūmon* ナショナリズム : 名著でたどる日本思想入門 [Introduction to Japanese Thought by Masterpieces], Tokyo: Chikuma Shobō 2004.

Asada Hajime 浅田一, "Ajia minzoku kaigi ni nan kokugo o tsukau ka" 亜細亜民族会議に何国語を使うか [What language is to be used at the Asian Peoples Conference?], *Osaka Asahi Shinbun* 大阪朝日新聞, 29–30 July 1926.

Ashizu Uzuhiko 葦津珍彦, *Dai Ajiashugi to Tōyama Mitsuru* 大アジア主義と頭山満 [Greater Asianism and Tōyama Mitsuru], Tokyo: Nihon Kyōbunsha 1965.

Aydin, Cemil, "A Global Anti-Western Moment? The Russo-Japanese War, Decolonization, and Asian Modernity", *Competing Visions of world order: global moments and movements, 1880s–1930s*, ed. Sebastian Conrad and Dominic Sachsenmaier, New York: Palgrave Macmillan 2007, 213–236.

Aydin, Cemil, *The politics of anti-Westernism in Asia: visions of world order in pan-Islamic and pan-Asian thought*, New York: Columbia University Press 2007.

Baik Young-seo, "Conceptualizing 'Asia' in modern Chinese mind: a Korean perspective", *Inter-Asia Cultural Studies*, 3-2 (2002), 277–286.

Bailey, Thomas A., "California, Japan, and the Alien Land Legislation of 1913", *Pacific Historical Review*, No. 1 (1932), 36–59.

Ball, Terence, "Conceptual History and the History of Political Thought", *History of Concepts: Comparative Perspectives*, ed. Iain Hampsher-Monk, Karin Tilmans, Frank van Vree, Amsterdam: University of Amsterdam Press 1998, 75–86.

Bao Guancheng 鮑觀澄, "Manshūkoku to Dai Ajiashugi" 満洲国と大亜細亜主義 [Manchukuo and Greater Asianism], *Speeches and Statements on the Foundation of Manchukuo*, Tokyo: Kokusai Shuppan 1933, 36–42.
Bao, Guancheng, *Speeches and Statements on the Foundation of Manchukuo*, Tokyo: Kokusai Shuppan 1933.
Beasley, William G., "Japan and Pan-Asianism. Problems of Definition", *Aspects of Pan-Asianism*, ed. Janet Hunter, London: Suntory Toyota International Centre for Economics and Related Disciplines, London School of Economics and Political Science 1987 (International Studies 1987/II), 1–16.
Bellamy, Richard and Mason, Andrew, "Introduction", *Political concepts*, ed. Richard Bellamy/Andrew Mason, Manchester: Manchester University Press 2003, 1–3.
Bergere, Marie-Claire, *Sun Yat-sen*, translated from the French by Janet Lloyd, Stanford: Stanford University Press 1998.
Bose, Rash Behari, "Kakumei tojō no Indo" 革命途上の印度 [India at the stage of revolution], *Nihon oyobi Nihonjin* 日本及日本人 [Japan and the Japanese] 58-5 (October 1924), 190–203.
Bowman, Isaiah, *The New World: Problems in Political Geography*, New York: World Book Company 1921.
Boyle, John Hunter, *China and Japan at War, 1937–1945: The Politics of Collaboration*, Stanford: Stanford University Press 1972.
Brook, Timothy, "The Tokyo Judgment and the Rape of Nanking", *Journal of Asian Studies*, 60-3 (August 2001), 673–700.
Brown, Roger H. "Sun Yat-sen: 'Pan-Asianism', 1924", *Pan-Asianism: A Documentary History 1860–2010*, Vol. 2, ed. Sven Saaler and Christopher W.A. Szpilman, Boulder: Rowman & Littlefield 2011, 75–85.
Buell, Raymond Leslie, "Some Legal Aspects of the Japanese Question", *The American Journal of International Law*, 17-1 (Jan. 1923), 29–49.
Burkman, Thomas W. "Nitobe Inazō: From World Order to Regional Order", *Culture and Identity: Japanese Intellectuals During the Interwar Years*, ed. Thomas J. Rimer, Princeton: Princeton University Press 1990, 191–216.
Burkman, Thomas W., *Japan and the League of Nations: Empire and world order, 1914–1938*, Honolulu: University of Hawaii Press 2008.
Butterfield, Herbert, *The Whig interpretation of history*, London: G. Bell 1931.
Cai Dejin 蔡德金, *Wang Jingwei ping zhuan* 汪精卫评传 [Critical Biography of Wang Jingwei], Chengdu: Sichuan Renmin chubanshe 1988.
Calhoun, Craig, "Civil Society/Public Sphere: History of the Concept", *International encyclopedia of the social & behavioral sciences*, ed. Neil J. Smelser and Paul B. Baltes, New York: Elsevier 2001, 1897–1903.
Cao Pencheng 曹鹏程, "Hanwei 'lishi zhengyi' caineng zouxiang jiefang" 捍卫"历史正义"才能走向解放 [Upholding 'Historical Righteousness' will lead to liberation], *Renmin Ribao*人民日报, 14 August 2015.

Chadourne, Marc, *Ostasiatische Reise* [East Asian Travels], Berlin: Dietrich Reimer 1936.
Chadourne, Marc, *Tour de la Terre. Extreme Orient* [Tour of the World. The Far East], Paris: Libraire Plon 1935.
Chang, Han-Yu and Ramon H. Myers, "Japanese Colonial Development Policy in Taiwan, 1895–1906: A Case of Bureaucratic Entrepreneurship", *Journal of Asian Studies*, 22-4 (August 1963), 433–449.
Chen Duxiu 陳獨秀, "Ouzhan hou Dongyang minzu zhi juewu ji yaoqiu" 欧战后东洋民族之觉悟及要求 [The resolution and demands of the Eastern peoples after the European War], *Duxiu Wencun* 獨秀文存 [Collected Writings of Duxiu], Hongkong: Yuandong tushu gongsi 1965 (1918), 585–588.
Chen Duxiu 陳獨秀, "Renzhong chabie daiyu wenti" 人种差别待遇问题 [The problem of racial discriminatory treatment], *Duxiu Wencun* 獨秀文存 [Collected Writings of Duxiu], Hongkong: Yuandong tushu gongsi 1965 (1919), 599–600.
Chen Guangxing 陳光興, *Qu Diguo. Yazhou zuowei fangfa* 去帝國: 亞洲作為方法 [De-imperialization. Asia as method], Taibei: Xingren 2006.
Chen, Kuan-Hsing [Chen Guangxing], *Asia as method: toward deimperialization*, Durham: Duke University Press 2010.
Chen, Kuan-Hsing [Chen Guangxing]/Chua Beng Huat, "Introduction", *The Inter-Asia cultural studies reader*, ed. Kuan-Hsing Chen and Chua Beng Huat, London: Routledge 2007, 1–5.
Cheung, Andrew, "Slogans, Symbols, and Legitimacy: The Case of Wang Jingwei's Nanjing Regime" (Indiana East Asian Working Paper Series on Language and Politics in Modern China, No. 6), 1995.
Chin Tokujin 陳德仁 and Yasui Sankichi 安井三吉, ed., *Son Bun Kōen 'Dai Ajiashugi' shiryōshū* 孫文・講演「大アジア主義」資料集 [Collection of materials of Sun Yat-sen's 'Greater Asianism' speech], Kyoto: Hōritsu Bunkasha 1989.
Chirol, Valentine, "Japan Among the Nations. The Bar of Race", *The Times*, 19 May 1913.
Chūō Kōronsha 中央公論社, ed., *Chūō kōron sō mokuji* 中央公論総目次 [General Table of Contents of the Central Review], ed., Tokyo: Chūō Kōronsha 1970.
Cohen, Paul A., *History in Three Keys. The Boxers as Event, Experience, and Myth*, New York: Columbia University Press 1997.
Conrad, Sebastian, "Remembering Asia: History and Memory in Post-Cold War Japan", *Memory in a Global Age. Discourses, Practices and Trajectories*, ed. Aleida Assmann and Sebastian Conrad, Houndsmill: Palgrave Macmillan 2010, 163–177.
Conze, Vanessa, "Leitbild Paneuropa? Zum Europagedanken und seiner Wirkung in der Zwischenkriegszeit am Beispiel der Konzepte Richard Coudenhove-Kalergis" [Pan-Europe as Model? On Europe as thought and its impact in

the interwar period, taking the example of Richard Coudenhove-Kalergi's concepts], *Leitbild Europa? Europabilder und ihre Wirkungen in der Neuzeit* [Europe as Model? Views of Europe and their impact in modern times], ed. Jürgen Elvert and Jürgen Nielsen-Sikora, Wien: Franz Steiner 2009, 119–125.

Dabringhaus, Sabine, *Territorialer Nationalismus in China: Historisch-geographisches Denken 1900–1949* [Territorial Nationalism in China: Historical-Geographical Thought 1900–1949], Köln: Böhlau Verlag 2006.

Dai Jitao 戴季陶, "Qiangquan yinmou zhi heimu" 强权阴谋之黑幕 [The mastermind of intrigues by the powers], 3 April 1913, *Dai Jitao Xinhai Wenji* 戴季陶文集 [Collection Dai Jitao's Xinhai Writings], Vol. 2, 1401–1403.

Dai Jitao 戴季陶, "Ouluoba Datongmeng lun" 歐羅巴大同盟論 [On a great union of Europe] (10 July 1914), *Dai Jitao Ji* 戴季陶集 [Collected Writings of Dai Jitao], ed. Tang Wenquan 唐文权 and Sang Bing 桑兵, Wuhan: Huazhong Shifan Daxue Chubanshe 1990, 730–753.

Dai Jitao 戴季陶, *Sun Wen Zhuyi zhi Zhexue de Jichu* 孫文主義之哲學的基礎 [The philosophical base of Sun Yat-senism], Shanghai: Minzhi Shuju 1927, 5th edition.

Daniels, Roger, *The Politics of Prejudice. The Anti-Japanese Movement in California and the Struggle for Japanese Exclusion*, New York: Atheneum 1974.

Das, Taraknath, *Is Japan A Menace to Asia?* Shanghai (without publisher) 1917.

Dickinson, Frederick R., *War and national reinvention: Japan in the Great War, 1914–1919*, Cambridge, Mass.: Harvard University Press 1999.

Dickinson, G. Lowes, *An Essay on the Civilization of India, China and Japan*, London: J.M. Dent & Sons 1914.

Dikötter, Frank, "Culture, 'race' and nation: the formation of national identity in twentieth century China", *Journal of International Affairs* 49-2 (1996), 590–605.

Dirlik, Arif, "Chinese History and the Question of Orientalism", *History and Theory*, 35- 4 (December 1996), 96–118.

Doak, Kevin M., *A history of nationalism in modern Japan: placing the people*, Leiden/Boston: Brill 2007.

Dong Shikui 董世奎, "Dai Jitao minzokushugi no myakuraku. Han-Nichi to kyō-Nichi ni yureta jikohozonshugi" 戴季陶民族主義の脈絡。反日と恐日に揺れた自己保存主義 [The context of Dai Jitao's nationalism. The principle of self-preservation unsettled by Anti-Japanism and the fear of Japan], *Kotoba to Bunka* 言葉と文化 [Word and Culture], Vol. 6 (2005), 121–140.

Dönhoff, Marion Gräfin, "Wandel der Wahrheit. Wie Nationen sich ihre Geschichte schreiben" [Changes of Truth. How nations write their histories], *Die Zeit*, No. 45 (31 October 1997), http://www.zeit.de/1997/45/Wandel_der_Wahrheit (last accessed 16 October 2016).

Duara, Prasenjit, "Asia Redux: Conceptualizing a Region for Our Times", *Journal of Asian Studies* 69-4 (November 2010), 963-983.

Duara, Prasenjit, "The discourse of civilization and pan-Asianism", *Journal of World History* 12-1 (2001), 99-130.

Duara, Prasenjit, "Transnationalism in the Era of Nation-States: China, 1900–1945", *Development and Change*, 29-4 (October 1998), 647–670.

Duara, Prasenjit, *Sovereignty and authenticity: Manchukuo and the East Asian modern*, Lanham: Rowman & Littlefield 2003.

Duus, Peter, "Nagai Ryūtarō and the 'White Peril' 1905–1944", *Journal of Asian Studies*, 31-1 (November 1971), 41–48.

Edwards, Walter, "Forging Tradition for a Holy War: The 'Hakkō Ichiu' Tower in Miyazaki and Japanese Wartime Ideology", *Journal of Japanese Studies*, Vol. 29, No. 2 (Summer 2003), 289–324.

Endō Kichisaburō 遠藤吉三郎, *Ōshū bunmei no botsuraku* 欧州文明の没落 [The downfall of Europe's civilization], Tokyo: Fuzan bō 1914.

Endō Ryūkichi 遠藤隆吉, "Shugi o ronzu" 主義を論ず, *Shakai* 社会 [Society], 20, 1900, 37–38.

Esenbel, Selcuk, "Japan's Global Claim to Asia and the World of Islam: Transnational Nationalism and World Power, 1900–1945", *American Historical Review*, 109-4 (2004), 1140–1170.

Fischer-Tiné, Harald, "'The Cult of Asianism': Asiendiskurse in Indien zwischen Nationalismus und Internationalismus (ca. 1885–1955)" [Asia discourse in India between Nationalism and Internationalism], *Comparativ* 18-6 (2008), 16–33.

Fletcher, William Miles, *The search for a new order: intellectuals and fascism in prewar Japan*, Chapel Hill: University of North Carolina Press 1982.

Fogel, Joshua A, and Peter G. Zarrow, eds., *Imagining the People: Chinese Intellectuals and the Concept of Citizenship, 1890–1920*. Armork, NY: M.E. Sharpe 1997.

Foucault, Michel, "Politics and the study of discourse", *The Foucault Effect. Studies in Governmentality*, ed. Colin Gordon et al., Chicago: University of Chicago Press 1991, 53–72.

Foucault, Michel, *The Archaeology of Knowledge and The Discourse on Language*, New York: Pantheon 1972.

Fujii Shōzō 藤井昇三, "Son Bun no minzokushugi sairon. Ajiashugi o chūshin ni" 孫文の民族主義再論、アジア主義を中心に [Again on Sun Yat-sen's nationalism. Focusing on Asianism], *Rekishi Hyōron* 歴史評論 [History Review], 549 (January 1996), 16–27.

Fukuzawa Yukichi 福沢諭吉, "Datsu A Ron" 脱亜論 [On Leaving Asia], *Fukuzawa Yukichi Zenshū* 福沢諭吉全集, Vol. 10, Tokyo: Iwanami Shoten 1960, 238–240.

Furuya Tetsuo 古屋哲夫, "Ajiashugi to sono shūhen" アジア主義とその周辺 [Asianism and its environs], *Kindai Nihon no Ajia Ninshiki* 近代日本のアジア認識 [Modern Japanese Asia Consciousness], ed. Furuya Tetsuo 古屋哲夫, Tokyo: Ryokuin Shobō 1996, 47–102.

Fuse Tatsuji 布施辰治, "Dai Ajiashugi ni tsuite no kansō" 大亜細亜主義についての感想 [Thoughts on Greater Asianism], *Nihon oyobi Nihonjin* 日本及日本人 [Japan and the Japanese] 58-5 (October 1924), 139–141.

Futian Hemin [Ukita Kazutami] 浮田和民, "Xin Yaxiya zhuyi" 新亞細亞主義 [New Asianism], *Dongfang Zazhi* 東方雜誌 [Eastern Miscellany], 15-11 (15 November 1918), 9–21 (translated by Gao Lao).

Gallie, W. B. "Essentially Contested Concepts", *Proceedings of the Aristotelian Society, New Series*, Vol. 56 (1956), 167–198.

Gao Yuan 高元, "Duoduo Yaxiya zhuyi. Duoduo Futian Hemin de Xin Yaxiya zhuyi" 咄咄亞細亞主義 咄咄浮田和民的新亞細亞主義 [Ugh, Asianism! Ugh, Ukita Kazutami's New Asianism!], *Dongfang Zazhi* 東方雜誌 [Eastern Miscellany], 16-5 (May 1919), 197–199.

Garon, Sheldon, "From Meiji to Heisei: The State and Civil Society in Japan", *The state of civil society in Japan*, ed. Frank J. Schwartz and Susan J. Pharr, Cambridge: Cambridge University Press 2003.

Gastil, John, "Undemocratic discourse: a review of theory and research on political discourse", *Discourse & Society* 3-4 (October 1992), 469–500.

Gaus, Gerald F., *Political Concepts and Political Theories*, Boulder: Westview Press 2000.

Gluck, Carol, *Japan's Modern Myth. Ideology in the Late Meiji Period*, Princeton: Princeton University Press 1985.

Go Kaichū 呉懐中, *Ōkawa Shūmei to Kindai Chūgoku: Nitchū kankei no arikata o meguru ninshiki to kōdō* 大川周明と近代中国:日中関係の在り方をめぐる認識と行動 [Ōkawa Shūmei and Modern China. Consciousness and Behaviour pertaining to the state of Japanese–Chinese relations], Tokyo: Nihon kyōhōsha 2007.

Gollwitzer, Heinz, *Die gelbe Gefahr: Geschichte eines Schlagworts* [The Yellow Danger: History of a Catchphrase], Göttingen: Vandenhoeck & Ruprecht, 1962.

Goodman, Grant K., "The Pan-Asiatic Conference of 1926 at Nagasaki", *Proceedings of the 3rd Kyushu International Cultural Conference*, ed. The Fukuoka Unesco Association, Fukuoka: Yunesuko [Unesco] 1973, 21–29.

Gordon, Andrew, *Labor and imperial democracy in prewar Japan*, Berkeley: University of California Press 1991.

Gotō Ken'ichi 後藤乾一, "Dai Ajia Kyōkai to Nanpō mondai. 'Ajiashugi' dantai no Nanpō kan o meguru ichi kansatsu" 大亜細亜協会と南方問題。アジア主義団体の南方観をめぐる一観察 [The Greater Asia Association and the South

Seas problem], *Shakai Kagaku Tōkyū* 社會科學討究 [Social Sciences Review], 27-2 (April 1982), 305–326.

Gotō Shinpei 後藤新平, "Ajiashū kisū no ha'aku" 亜細亜州機枢の把握 [Grasping the pivots of the Asian Continent], *Nihon oyobi Nihonjin* 日本及日本人 [Japan and the Japanese] 58-5 (October 1924), 17–18.

Gotō Shinpei 後藤新平, *Nihon Shokumin Ron* 日本植民論 [On Japanese colonization], Tokyo: Kōmindōmei 1915.

Gotō Shinpei 後藤新平, *Nihon Shokumin seisaku ippan* 日本植民政策一斑 [General outline of Japanese Colonial Policy], Tokyo: Takushoku Shinpōsha 1921 [1914].

Gulick, Sidney L., *The American Japanese Problem*, New York: Charles Scribner's 1914.

Gushima Kanesaburō 具島兼三郎, "Han Ajiashugi" [Pan-Asianism], *Dai Hyakka Jiten* 大百科事典 [Great Encyclopaedia], Vol. 21, ed. Shimonaka Yasaburō 下中弥三郎, Tokyo: Heibonsha 1933, 291–292.

Hampsher-Monk, Iain, Karin Tilmans and Frank van Vree, "A Comparative Perspective on Conceptual History - An Introduction", *History of Concepts: Comparative Perspectives*, ed. Iain Hampsher-Monk, Karin Tilmans, Frank van Vree, Amsterdam: University of Amsterdam Press 1998, 1–10.

Han, Jung-Sun N., "Envisioning a Liberal Empire in East Asia: Yoshino Sakuzō in Taishō Japan", *Journal of Japanese Studies* 33:2 (2007), 357–382.

Han, Jung-Sun, "Rationalizing the Orient: The 'East Asia Cooperative Community' in Prewar Japan", *Monumenta Nipponica*, 60-4 (Winter 2005), 481–514.

Harada Katsumasa 原田勝正, "Ajia Rentaishugi ni tsuite no kenkyū nōto" アジア連帯主義についての研究ノート [Research Note on the Principle of Asian Solidarity], *Rekishi Hyōron* 歴史評論 [History Review], Vol. 102 (January 1959), 28–37.

Harada Katsumasa 原田勝正, "Dai Ajiashugi shisō keisei e no tenbō" 大亜細亜主義思想形成への展望 [Outlook on the formation of the Thought of Greater Asianism], *Rekishigaku Kenkyū* 歴史学研究 [History Research], Vol. 229 (March 1959), 63–70.

Hasegawa Nyozekan 長谷川如是閑, "Dai Ajiashugi" 大亜細亜主義 [Greater Asianism], *Tokyo Asahi Shinbun* 東京朝日新聞, 3 February 1932, 9.

Hashikawa Bunzō 橋川文三, *Kōka Monogatari* 黄禍物語 [Yellow Peril Story], Tokyo: Chikuma shobō 1976.

Hashikawa Bunzō 橋川文三, "Fukuzawa Yukichi to Okakura Tenshin" 福沢諭吉と岡倉天心 [Fukuzawa Yukichi and Okakura Tenshin], *Kindai Nihon to Chūgoku* 近代日本と中国 [Modern Japan and China], ed. Takeuchi Yoshimi and Hashikawa Bunzō 竹内好, 橋川文三, Vol. 1, Tokyo: Asahi Sensho 1974, 17–35.

Hashikawa, Bunzō, "Japanese Perspectives on Asia: From Dissociation to Coprosperity", *The Chinese and the Japanese. Essays in Political and Cultural Interactions*, ed. Akira Iriye, Princeton: Princeton University Press 1980, 328–355.

Hatoyama Yukio 鳩山由紀夫, "Watakushi no seiji tetsugaku" 私の政治哲学 [My political philosophy], *Voice* (September 2009), 132–141.

Hatsuse Ryūhei 初瀬龍平 and Fujii Shōzō 藤井昇三, "Dai Ajiashugi" 大亜細亜主義 [Greater Asianism], *Sekai Minzoku Mondai Jiten* 世界民族問題事典 [Encyclopaedia of the Nations of the World], Tokyo: Heibonsha 1995, 622–623.

Hay, Stephen N., *Asian Ideas of East and West: Tagore and his Critics in Japan, China, and India*, Cambridge, MA: Harvard University Press 1970.

Hayashi Fusao 林房雄, *Dai Tōa Sensō Kōtei Ron* 大東亜戦争肯定論 [Affirmation of the Greater East Asian War], Tokyo: Banchō Shobō 1964.

Hazama Naoki 狭間直樹, "Shoki Ajiashugi ni tsuite no shiteki kōsatsu. Sone Toshitora to Shin A Sha" 初期アジア主義についての史的考察 曽根俊虎と振亜社 [Historical observations on early Asianism. Sone Toshitora and the Raise Asia Society], *Tō A* 東亜 [East Asia], 411 (September 2001), 88–98.

Hazama Naoki 狭間直樹, "Shoki Ajiashugi ni tsuite no shiteki kōsatsu. Tōhō Kyōkai ni tsuite" 初期アジア主義についての史的考察、東方協会について [Historical observations on early Asianism. On the Tōhō Kyōkai], *Tō A* 東亜 [East Asia], 414 (December 2001), 66–74.

Hazama Naoki 狭間直樹, "Umeya Shōkichi no Son Bun shien" 梅屋庄吉の孫文支援 [Umeya Shōkichi's support of Sun Yat-sen], *Asahi Shinbun* 朝日新聞, 4 June 2011.

He, Jing, *China in Okakura Kakuzo with special reference to his first Chinese trip in 1893* (unpublished Ph. D. dissertation, University of California, Los Angeles, 2006).

Heywood, Andrew, *Key concepts in politics*, Basingstoke: Palgrave Macmillan 2000.

Higashi Ajia Kyōdōtai Hyōgikai 東アジア共同体評議会 [Council on East Asian Community], ed., "Higashi Ajia to wa: rekishi no naka kara wakugumi taidō" 東アジアとは　歴史の中から枠組胎動 [What is East Asia? Indications of a framework from history] ed., No. 2, 2004, http://www.ceac.jp/j/survey/survey002.html (last accessed 16 October 2016).

Higashi Ajia Kyōdōtai Hyōgikai 東アジア共同体評議会 [Council on East Asian Community], ed., *Higashi Ajia Kyōdōtai hakusho 2010* 東アジア共同体白書 2010 [East Asian Community White Book 2010], Tokyo: Tachibana Shuppan 2010.

Hirai, Atsuko, *Individualism and socialism: the life and thought of Kawai Eijirō (1891–1944)*, Cambridge: Harvard University Press 1986.

Hiraishi Naoaki 平石直昭, "Kindai Nihon no Ajiashugi. Meiji ki no sho rinen o chūshin ni" 近代日本のアジア主義、明治期の諸理念を中心に [Modern Japan's Asianism. Focussing on different ideals in the Meiji period], *Kindaikazō. Ajia kara kangaeru* 近代化像、アジアから考える [The image of modernization. Thinking from Asia], 5, ed. Mizoguchi Yūzō 溝口雄三 et al., Tokyo: Tokyo Daigaku Shuppankai 1994, 265–291.

Hiraishi Naoaki 平石直昭, "Kindai Nihon no Kokusai chitsujokan to 'Ajiashugi'" 近代日本の国際秩序観とアジア主義 [Modern Japanese views of the international order and 'Asianism'], *20seiki shisutemu 1: Kōsō to keisei* 20世紀システム1、構想と形成 [20th century system 1: Design and Formation], ed. Tokyo Daigaku Shakai Kagaku Kenkyūjo 東京大学社会科学研究所, Tokyo: Tokyo Daigaku Shuppankai 1998, 176–211.

Hirakawa Hitoshi 平川均, "Kajima Morinosuke to Pan Ajiashugi" 鹿島守之助とパンアジア主義 [Kajima Morinosuke and Pan-Asianism], *Keizai Kagaku* 經濟科學 [Economy Science], 55-4 (2008), 1–24.

Hirakawa, Hitoshi, "Dr. Morinosuke Kajima and Pan-Asianism", *Sekiguchi Gurōbaru Kenkyūkai (SGRA) Repōto* 58, ed. SGRA, Tokyo: SGRA 2011, 37–76.

Hirano Ken'ichirō 平野健一郎, "Ajiashugi" アジア主義 [Asianism], *Kokushi Dai Jiten* 国史大辞典 [Great Encyclopaedia of National History], ed. Kokushi Dai Jiten Henshū I'inkai 国史大辞典編集委員会, Tokyo: Yoshikawa Kōbunkan 1979, Vol. 1, 154.

Hirobe, Izumi, *Japanese pride, American prejudice: modifying the exclusion clause of the 1924 Immigration Act.* Stanford: Stanford University Press 2001.

Horii Kōichirō 堀井弘一郎, "Ajiashugi" アジア主義 [Asianism], *Gendai Ajia Jiten* 現代アジア事典 [Encyclopaedia of Contemporary Asia], ed. Hasegawa Hiroyuki 長谷川啓之 et al., Tokyo: Bunshindō 2009, 21–22.

Horinouchi Tsuneo 堀之内恒夫, *Shōgakkō o chūshin toeru Warera no Kōmin Kyōiku* 小學校を中心とせる我等の公民教育 [Our Civic Education with a focus on Primary Schools], Tokyo: Meguro Shoten 1933.

Horinouchi Tsuneo 堀之内恒夫, *Gendai Shūshin Kyōiku no konponteki seisatsu* 現代修身教育の根本的省察 [A Fundamental Reflection on Contemporary Ethics Education], Tokyo: Kenbunkan 1934.

Horinouchi Tsuneo 堀之内恒夫, *Shin Jinjō Shogakkō shūshin kyōiku sho* 新尋常小学校修身教育書 [Book of New Common Primary School Ethics Education], Tokyo: Tōyō tosho 1929–1931 (3 volumes).

Horiuchi Bunjirō 堀内文次郎, "Dai Ajiashugi to waga kokumin no shimei" 大亜細亜主義と我国民の使命 [Greater Asianism and the fate of my people], *Taiyō* 太陽 [The Sun], 24-9 (September 1918), 120–121.

Hoston, Germaine A., *The state, identity, and the national question in China and Japan*, Princeton: Princeton University Press 1994.

Hotta, Eri "Rash Behari Bose and his Japanese Supporters: An Insight into Anti-Colonial Nationalism and Pan-Asianism," *Interventions* 8-2 (2006), 116–32.

Hotta, Eri, *Pan-Asianism and Japan's war 1931–1945*, New York: Palgrave Macmillan 2007.

Hotta, Eri, "Rash Behari Bose: The Indian Independence Movement and Japan", *Pan-Asianism: A Documentary History 1860–2010*, Vol. 1, ed. Sven Saaler and C.W.A. Szpilman, Boulder: Rowman & Littlefield, 2011, 231–240.

Hu Hanmin 胡漢民, "Da Yaxiya zhuyi yu guoji jishu hezuo" 大亞細亞主義與國際技術合作 [Greater Asianism and international technological cooperation], *Yuandong Wenti yu Da Yaxiya Zhuyi* 遠東問題與大亞細亞主義 [The Far Eastern Question and Greater Asianism], Guangzhou: Minzhi Shuju 1935, 1-26 (originally in *Sanmin Zhuyi* [Three People's Principles], 2-4, September 1933).

Hu Hanmin 胡漢民, "Da Yaxiya zhuyi yu kang Ri" 大亞細亞主義與抗日 [Greater Asianism and Resisting Japan], *Sanmin Zhuyi* 三民主义 [Three People's Principles], 7-3 (March 1936), 12–15.

Hu Hanmin 胡漢民, "Zai Lun Da Yaxiya zhuyi" 再論大亞細亞主義 [On Greater Asianism Again], *Yuandong Wenti yu Da Yaxiya Zhuyi* 遠東問題與大亞細亞主義 [The Far Eastern Question and Greater Asianism], Guangzhou: Minzhi Shuju 1935, 27–43 (originally in *Sanmin Zhuyi* [Three People's Principles], 4-3).

Huang, Chun-chieh, "Dr. Sun Yat-sen's Pan-Asianism Revisited: Its Historical Context and Contemporary Relevance", *Journal of Cultural Interaction in East Asia*, Vol.3, 2012, 69–74.

Huang Gongsu 黄攻素, *Yaxiya Minzu Di Yici Dahui Shimo Ji* 亚细亚民族第一次大会始末集 [Complete Record of the first conference of the Asian Peoples], Beijing: Yaxiya Minzu Datongmeng 1926.

Huffman, James L., *Politics of the Meiji press: the life of Fukuchi Gen'ichirō*, Honolulu: University Press of Hawaii 1980.

Hwang, Dongyoun, "Some Reflections on war-time collaboration in China: Wang Jingwei and his group in Hanoi" (Working Papers in Asian/Pacific Studies 98-02), ed. Anne Allison, Arif Dirlik, Tomiko Yoda, 1998.

I Ko 伟虎, *1919nen zengo ni okeru Ni-Chū 'Ajiashugi' bunkyoku no shosō* 1919年前後における日中アジア主義分局の諸相 [Various aspects of polarizations in Japanese-Chinese 'Asianism' around the year 1919], Unpublished MA thesis, Hōsei University Tokyo, 2006.

Iikura Akira 飯倉章, *Ierō Periru no Shinwa: Teikoku Nihon to Kōka no Gyakusetsu* イエロー・ペリルの神話: 帝国日本と「黄禍」の逆説 [The Myth of the Yellow Peril: Imperial Japan and the Paradox of the Yellow Danger], Tokyo: Sairyūsha 2004.

Ikimatsu, Keizō, "Profile of Asian Minded Man IV: Okakura Tenshin", *The Developing Economies*, 4-4 (December 1966), 639–653.

Imazato Juntarō 今里準太郎, "Ajia Renmei no Daishimei. Ninagawa hakushi no byūken o tadasu" アジア連盟の大使命、蜷川博士の謬見を正す [The great mission of an Asian League. Correcting Dr. Ninagawa's erroneous views], *Tōhō Kōron* 東方公論 [Eastern Review], May 1926, 50–55.

Imazato Juntarō 今里準太郎, "Zen Ajia Renmei wa umaretari" 全アジア連盟は生まれたり [The All Asian League has been born], *Tōhō Kōron* 東方公論 [Eastern Review], September 1926, 41–44.

Inoue Toshikazu 井上寿一, "Amō Seimei to Chūgoku Seisaku" 天羽声明と中国政策, *Hitotsubashi Ronsō* 一橋論叢 [Essay Collection of Hitotsubashi University], 97-5 (May 1987), 661–679.

Inoue Toshikazu 井上寿一, *Ajiashugi o toinaosu* アジア主義を問いなおす [Revisiting Asianism], Tokyo: Chikuma Shobō 2006.

Iriye, Akira, "East Asia and the Emergence of Japan, 1900–1945", *The Oxford History of the Twentieth Century*, ed. Michael Howard and Wm. Roger Louis, Oxford/New York: Oxford University Press, 139–150.

Ishibashi Tanzan 石橋湛山, "Dai Nihonshugi no gensō" 大日本主義の幻想 [The illusion of Greater Japanism], *Taishō Shisō shū* 大正思想集 [Collection of Taishō Thought], Vol. 2, ed. Kano Masanao.鹿野政直, Tokyo: Chikuma Shobō 1977, 395–406 (originally in *Tōyō Keizai Shinpō* 東洋經濟新報 [Far Eastern Economist], July-August 1926, 959–961).

Ishii Hidetoshi 石井英輔, "Ajia wo futatabi kaihō suru" アジアを再び解放する [Liberating Asia once more], *Yume Dai Ajia* 夢・大アジア [Dream – Greater Asia], 2014, No. 1, 4–5.

Itō Shinya 伊藤信哉, ed., *Gaikō Jihō Sōmokuji Shippitsusha Sakuin. Senzen* 外交時報総目次・執筆者索引. 戦前編 [General Index of the Table of Contents and Authors in the Diplomatic Review, pre-war], Tokyo: Nihon tosho sentā 2008.

Itō Teruo 伊東昭雄, "'Dai Ajiashugi' to 'Sanmin shugi'. Ō Seiei kairai seiken shita no sho mondai ni tsuite" 大亜細亜主義と三民主義、汪精衛傀儡政権下の諸問題について ['Greater Asianism' and 'The Three People's Principles'. On some problems under Wang Jingwei's puppet government], *Yokohama Shiritsu Daigaku Ronsō* 横浜市立大学論叢 [Yokohama City University Essay Collection], 40-1 (1989), 225–247.

Itō Teruo 伊東昭雄, *Ajia to Kindai Nihon: han shinryaku no shisō to undō* アジアと近代日本: 反侵略の思想と運動 [Asia and modern Japan: Anti-invasionist thought and Movement], Tokyo: Shakai Hyōronsha 1990.

Iwata Kazuo 岩田千雄, *Tōhō minzoku no kaihō undō* 東方民族の解放運動 [Liberation Movements of the Eastern Peoples], Tokyo: Shakai Kyōiku Kyōkai 1934 (Shakai Kyōiku Panfuretto, 195).

Jansen, Marius B., *The Japanese and Sun Yat-sen*, Stanford: Stanford University Press 1954.

Jenco, Leigh, "Revisiting Asian Values", *Journal of the History of Ideas*, Vol. 74, No. 2, April 2013, 237–258.

Jiang Haibo 蒋海波, "Ōsaka Kakyō Zhang Youshen ni kan suru kisoteki kenkyū" 大阪華僑張友深に関する基礎的研究 [Basic research on the overseas Chinese Zhang Youshen], presentation at the 6th Seminar at the Mukogawa Kansai Culture Research Center, November 2004; http://mkcr.jp/archive/041111.html (last accessed 16 October 2016).

Kagami Mitsuyuki 加々美光行, "Ajiashugi" アジア主義 [Asianism], *Sengoshi Dai Jiten* 戦後史大事典 [Great Encyclopaedia of Post-War History], ed. Sasaki Takeshi 佐々木毅, Tsurumi Shunsuke 鶴見俊輔 et al., Tokyo: Sanseidō 1991, 9.

Kajima Morinosuke 鹿島守之助, "Kokusai Renmei yori Han Ajia Renmei e" 国際連盟より汎アジア連盟へ [From the League of Nations to a Pan-Asian League], *Keizai Ōrai* 經濟往來 [Economic Traffic] 8-4 (April 1933), 184–192.

Kajima Morinosuke 鹿島守之助, "Nisshi Shin Jōyaku to Dai Tōa Renmei" 日支新条約と大東亜連盟 [The new contract between Japan and China and a Greater East Asian League], *Gaikō Jihō* 外交時報 [Diplomatic Review] 866 (January 1941), 55–65.

Kajima Morinosuke 鹿島守之助, *Waga kaisōroku: shisō to kōdō* わが回想録: 思想と行動 [My Memoirs: Thought and Action], Tokyo: Kajima Kenkyūjo Shuppankai 1965.

Kamachi, Noriko, "Asianism in Prewar, Postwar and Post-Cold-War Japan", *Asia-Pacific Forum* 29 (September 2005), 136–161.

Kamiizumi Tokuya 上泉徳弥, *Dai Nihonshugi* 大日本主義 [Greater Japanism], Tokyo: Kōbundō Shoten 1918.

Kamiya Masashi 神谷昌史, "'Tōzai bunmei chōwaron' no mittsu no kata" 東西文明調和論の三つの型 [Three patterns of the 'Thesis on the Harmony of Eastern and Western Civilization'], *Daitō Hōsei Ronshū* 大東法政論集, No. 9 (March 2001), 159–180.

Kan Naoto 菅直人, "Rekishi no bunsuirei ni tatsu Nihon Gaikō" 歴史の分水嶺に立つ日本外交 [Japanese Diplomacy at a Historic Watershed], 20 January 2011, http://www.kantei.go.jp/jp/kan/statement/201101/20speech.html. (last accessed 16 October 2016).

Karl, Rebecca E., "Creating Asia: China in the World at the Beginning of the Twentieth Century", *American Historical Review*, Vol. 103, No. 4 (October 1998), 1096–1118.

Katsurajima Nobuhiro 桂島宣弘, "Ajiashugi"アジア主義 [Asianism], *Iwanami Tetsugaku Shisō Jiten* 岩波哲学・思想事典 [Iwanami Encyclopaedia of Philosophy and Thought], ed. Hiromatsu Wataru 広松渉, Koyasu Nobukuni 子安宣邦, Mishima Ken'ichi 三島憲一et al., Tokyo: Iwanami Shoten 1998, 15–16.

Kawahara Hiroshi 河原宏, "Ajiashugi no shinjōteki kiso" アジア主義の心情的基礎 [The sentimental base of Asianism], *Jinbun Shakaikagaku Kenkyū* 人文社会学研究 [Humanities and Social Science Research], 33 (March 1993), 1–15.

Kawahara Hiroshi 河原宏, *Kindai Nihon no Ajia Ninshiki* 近代日本のアジア認識 [Modern Japanese Consciousness of Asia], Tokyo: Daisan Bunmeisha 1976.

Kawai Eijirō 河合栄治郎, "Go Ichigo Jiken no Hihan" 五・一五事件の批判 [Critique of the May 15th Incident], *Bungei Shunju* 文芸春秋 [Literary Times], 11-11 (November 1932), 48–58.

Kawano Takashi 河野孝之, "Ajiashugi no rinen to roman, denki shōnen shōsetsu" アジア主義の理念とロマン、伝奇少年小説 [The ideal of Asianism and romantic juvenile novels], *Nihon Jidō Bungaku* 日本児童文学 [Japanese Children's Literature], 38-3 (March 1992), 48–55.

Kawashima Shin 川島真, "Kindai Chūgoku no Ajia kan to Nihon. 'Dentōteki' taigai kankei to no kanren de" 近代中国のアジア観と日本、伝統的対外関係との関連で [Japan and Modern Chinese views on Asia. With reference to 'traditional' foreign relations], *Gendai Ajia Kenkyū 1. Ekkyō* 現代アジア研究 1.越境 [Contemporary Asia Research: Transcending Borders], ed. Takahara Akio 高原明生, Tamura Keiko 田村慶子, Satō Yukihito 佐藤幸人. Tokyo: Keiō Gijuku Daigaku Shuppan kai 2008, 415–441.

Kindai Nitchū Kankeishi Nenpyō Henshū Iinkai 近代日中関係史年表編集委員会 [Editorial Committee of the Chronological Table of the History of Modern Japanese-Chinese Relations], ed., *Kindai Nitchū Kankeishi Nenpyō 1799–1949* 近代日中関係史年表:1799-1949 [Chronological Table of the History of Modern Japanese-Chinese Relations 1799–1949], Tokyo: Iwanami 2006.

Kita Ikki 北一輝, "Nihon Kaizō Hōan Taikō" 日本改造法案大綱 [An Outline Plan for the Reorganization of Japan], *Kita Ikki Shisōshūsei* 北一輝思想集成 [Compilation of Kita Ikki's Thought], Tokyo: Shoshi shinsui, 2005 (1919), 680–767.

Ko Kanmin [Hu Hanmin] 胡漢民, "Warera no Dai Ajiashugi" われらの大亜細亜主義 [Our Greater Asianism], *Nihon Hyōron* 日本評論 [Japan Review], 11-5 (May 1936), 172–179.

Kō Shin Hō (Kou Zhenfeng) 寇振鋒, "Chūgoku no 'Dongfang Zazhi' to Nihon no 'Taiyō'" 中国の東方雜誌と日本の太陽 [China's 'Dongfang Zazhi' and Japan's 'Taiyō'], *Media to Shakai* メディアと社会 [Media and Society], ed. Nagoya Daigaku Daigakuin Kokusai Gengo Bunka Kenkyūka 名古屋大学大学院国際言語文化研究科, Vol. 1 (March 2009), 7–22.

Kodaira Kunio 小平国雄, *Ajiajin no Ajia* 亜細亜人の亜細亜 [Asia of the Asians], Tokyo: Shakai Kyōiku Kyōkai 1934 (Shakai Kyōiku Panfuretto, 198).

Kodama Kagai 児玉花外, "Ajia no meihai" 亜細亜の盟盃 [Sake cup to the Asian alliance], *Taiyō* 太陽 [The Sun], 23-14 (1 Dec 1917), 62–64.

Kodama Kagai 児玉花外, "Ajia no wakaki koe" 亜細亜の若き声 [The young voice of Asia], *Taiyō* 太陽 [The Sun] 25-3 (March 1919), 207.

Kodama Kagai 児玉花外, "Gekka Kinsonkyō" 月下金樽興 [Poem on a golden barrel under the moonlight], *Tōhō Jiron* 東方時論 [Eastern Review], 3-6 (June 1918), 104–105.
Kodama Kagai 児玉花外, "Son Issen ni ataeru shi" 孫逸仙に与える詩 [Poem dedicated to Sun Yat-sen], *Taiyō*太陽 [The Sun], 19-3 (March 1913), 152.
Kodera Kenkichi 小寺謙吉, *Dai Ajiashugi Ron* 大亜細亜主義論 [Treatise on Greater Asianism], Tokyo: Hōbunkan 1916.
Kodera Kenkichi 小寺謙吉, "Batsu" [Afterword], Takeuchi Masashi 竹内正志, *Sengo no Nihon oyobi Shina* 戦後の日本及支那 [Postwar Japan and China], Tokyo: Hakubunkan 1919 1-3.
Kodera Kenkichi 小寺謙吉, "Jinshu mondai yori mitaru Nisshi kyōzon" 人種問題より見たる日支共存 [Japanese-Chinese coexistence as seen from the race problem], *Jitsugyō no Nihon* 實業之日本 [Business Japan], 22-13 (June 1919), 84–87.
Kodera Kenkichi 小寺謙吉, *Dai Ajiashugi Ron: kan'yaku*大亜細亜主義論:漢訳 [Treatise on Greater Asianism: Chinese Translation]. Shanghai: Hyakujō Shosha 1918.
Kojima Shinji 小島晋治et. al., ed., *Chūgokujin no Nihonkan 100 nenshi* 中国人の日本観100年史 [100 years of Chinese views of Japan], Tokyo: Jiyū Kokuminsha 1974.
Komatsu Midori 小松緑, *Meiji Gaikō Hiwa* 明治外交秘話 [Unknown episodes of Meiji foreign policy], Tokyo: Chikura Shobō 1936.
Koschmann, J. Victor, "Asianism's Ambivalent Legacy", *Network Power. Japan and Asia*, ed. Peter J. Katzenstein and Takashi Shiraishi, Ithaca: Cornell University Press 1997, 83–110.
Koschmann, J. Victor, "Constructing Destiny: Rōyama Masamichi and Asian Regionalism in Wartime Japan", *Pan-Asianism in Modern Japanese History. Colonialism, regionalism and borders*, ed. Sven Saaler and J. Victor Koschmann, London: Routledge 2007, 185–199.
Koselleck, Reinhart, "Begriffsgeschichte" [Conceptual History], *Lexikon Geschichtswissenschaft. Hundert Grundbegriffe* [Encyclopaedia of History Science. One Hundred Key Concepts], ed. Stefan Jordan, Stuttgart: Reclam 2002, 40–44.
Koyama Sadatomo 小山貞知, "Sano no Tenkō to Dai Ajiashugi" 佐野の転向と大亜細亜主義 [Sano's apostasy and Greater Asianism], *Manshū Hyōron* 滿洲評論 [Manchurian Review] 5-2, 8 July 1933, 22–24.
Kubo Juntarō 久保純太郎, "Zasshi 'Xin Yaxiya' ronsetsu kiji mokuji" 雑誌新亜細亜論説記事目次 [Tables of Contents of editorial articles in the journal 'New Asia'], *Kōbe Daigaku Shigaku Nenpō* 神戸大学史学年報 [Kobe University Annual Bulletin of Historiography] 17, 2002, 80–124.
Kubo Juntarō 久保純太郎, *Dai Jitao ni okeru 'Chūgoku Kakumei' to sono shisō. Chūgoku, Nihon, Ajia o megutte.* 戴季陶における「中国革命」とその思

想: 中国・日本・アジアをめぐって [Dai Jitao's 'Chinese Revolution' and its thought: China, Japan, Asia], Ph. D. Dissertation Kobe University 2005, accessible online: http://www.lib.kobe-u.ac.jp/repository/thesis/d1/D1003482.pdf (last accessed 16 October 2016), 55–56.

Kubota Yoshirō 久保田與四郎, *Tōyō no kiki tsuku taigai kokuze* 東洋之危機附対外国是 [Crisis in the East and national foreign policy], Tokyo: Fuzan bō 1898.

Kuhn, Dieter, *Die Republik China von 1912 bis 1937: Entwurf für eine politische Ereignisgeschichte* [The Republic of China from 1912 to 1937: draft of a political history], Heidelberg: Edition Forum 2007.

Kumano Naoki 熊野直樹, "Gushima Fashizumu Ron no sai kentō" 具島ファシズム論の再検討 [Re-examining Gushima's analysis of fascism], *Hōsei Kenkyū* 法政研究 [Law and Politics Research] 71-4 (March 2005), 423–461.

Kuroki Morifumi 黒木彬文, "Kō A Kai no Ajiashugi 興亜会のアジア主義" [Asianism of the Kō A Kai], *Hōsei Kenkyū* 法政研究 [Journal of law and politics], 71-4 (March 2005), 615–655.

Lee, Eun-Jeung, "'Asien' als Projekt. Der Asiendiskurs in China, Japan und Korea" ['Asia' as project. Asia discourse in China, Japan, and Korea], *Leviathan* 31-3, 2003, 382–400.

Lee Gyeongseog 李京錫, "Ajiashugi no kōyō to bunki. Ashū Washinkai no sōritsu o chūshin ni" アジア主義論の昂揚と分岐-亜洲和親会の創立を中心に [The Uplift and Divergence of Asianism. Focussing on the Asiatic Humanitarian Brotherhood], *Waseda Seiji Kōhō kenkyū* 早稲田政治公法研究 [Waseda Research into Politics and Public Law] 69 (May 2002), 167–199.

Lee Gyeongseog 李京錫, "Tokutomi Sōho no Ajia Monrōshugi" 徳富蘇峰のアジアモンロー主義 [Tokutomi Sohō's Asian Monroeism], *Waseda Seiji Kōhō kenkyū* 早稲田政治公法研究 [Waseda Research into Politics and Public Law] 73 (2003), 201–235.

Lee Gyeongseog 李京錫, "Takeuchi Yoshimi no Ajiashugi Ron no kōzō oyobi sho mondai" 竹内好のアジア主義論の構造及び諸問題 [The Structure and some problems of Takeuchi Yoshimi's discussion of Asianism], *Waseda Seiji Kōhō kenkyū* 早稲田政治公法研究 [Waseda Research into Politics and Public Law] 64 (August 2000), 227–257.

Lenin, W.I., "Der tote Chauvinismus und der lebendige Sozialismus" [Dead Chauvinism and living Socialism], *Werke* [Works], Vol. 21, Berlin: Dietz 1970 (December 1914), 83–90.

Li Dazhao 李大釗, "Da Yaxiya zhuyi yu xin Yaxiya zhuyi" 大亞細亞主義與新亞細亞主義 [Greater Asianism and New Asianism], *Li Dazhao Xuanji* 李大釗選集 [Selected Writings of Li Dazhao], Beijing: Renmin Chubanshe 1959, 119–121 (originally in *Guomin Zazhi* [Citizen Magazine], 1-2, 1 February 1919).

Li Dazhao 李大釗, "Da Yaxiya zhuyi" 大亞細亞主義 [Greater Asianism], *Li Dazhao Wenji* 李大釗文集 [Collection of Li Dazhao's Writings], Vol. 1,

Beijing: Renmin Chubanshe 1984, 449–451 (originally in *Jiayin*. [Year 1914], volume and pages unknown, 18 April 1917).

Li Dazhao 李大釗, "Pan…ism zhi shibai yu Democracy zhi shengli" Pan…ism之失敗與Democracy之勝利 [The defeat of Pan-isms and the victory of democracy], *Li Dazhao Xuanji* 李大釗選集 [Selected Writings of Li Dazhao], Beijing: Renmin Chubanshe 1959, 105–108 (originally in *Taipingyang* [Pacific Ocean], 1-10, 15 July 1918).

Li Dazhao 李大釗, "Xin Zhong Hua minzu zhuyi" 新中華民族主義 [New Chinese Nationalism], *Li Dazhao Wenji* 李大釗文集 [Collection of Li Dazhao's Writings], Vol. 1, Beijing: Renmin Chubanshe 1984, 301–303 (originally in *Jiayin* [Year 1914], volume and pages unknown, 19 February 1917).

Li Dazhao 李大釗, "Zai lun Xin Yaxiya zhuyi" 再論大亞細亞主義 [Discussing New Asianism again], *Li Dazhao Xuanji* 李大釗選集 [Selected Writings of Li Dazhao], Beijing: Renmin Chubanshe 1959, 278–282 (originally in *Guomin Zazhi* [Citizen Magazine], 2-1, 12 December 1919).

Li Liejun 李烈鈞, "Yu Riben 'Mensi Bao' jizhe de tanhua" 與日本門司報記者的談話 [Conversation with journalists from the Japanese 'Mensi' (Moji Shinpō) newspaper] (11 November 1924), Li Liejun Ji. Shang 李烈鈞集, 上 [Collected Writings of Li Liejun, Vol. 1], ed. Zhou Yuangao 周元高et al., Beijing: Zhonghua Shuju 1996, 550–551.

Li, Lincoln, *The China Factor in Modern Japanese Thought: The Case of Tachibana Shiraki, 1881–1945*, Albany: State University of New York Press 1996.

Mahan, Alfred Thayer, "Japan Among the Nations. Admiral Mahan's Views", *The Times*, 23 June 1913.

Manela, Erez, "Imagining Woodrow Wilson in Asia: Dreams of East–West Harmony and the Revolt against Empire in 1919", *American Historical Review*, 111-5 (December 2006), 1327–1351.

Martin, Brian G., "The Dilemmas of a civilian Politician in time of war: Zhou Fohai and the first stage of the Sino-Japanese War, July–December 1937", *Twentieth-Century China*, 39-2, 2014, 144–165.

Martin, Brian G., "Collaboration within Collaboration: Zhou Fohai's Relations with the Chongqing Government, 1942–1945", *Twentieth-Century China*, 34-2, 2009, 55–88.

Maruyama Masao 丸山真男, "Nihon Fashizumu no shisō to undō" 日本ファシズムの思想と運動 [The Thought and Movement of Japanese Fascism], *Maruyama Masao Shū* 丸山真男集 [Collected Writings of Maruyama Masao], Vol. 3, Tokyo: Iwanami Shoten 1995 (1948), 259–322.

Maruyama, Masao, "The Ideology and Dynamics of Japanese Fascism", *Thought and behavior in modern Japanese politics*, ed. Ivan Morris, Oxford: Oxford University Press 1969, 25–83.

Masaoka, Naoichi, ed., *Japan to America. A Symposium of Papers by Political Leaders and Representative Citizens of Japan on Conditions in Japan and on the Relations between Japan and the United States*, New York/London: G.P. Putnam's sons 1914.

Masaoka, Naoichi, ed., *Japan's Message to America*, ed., Tokyo: [s.n.] 1914.

Matsuda Kōichirō 松田宏一郎, "'Ajia' no 'tashō'sei. Ajiashugi izen no Ajiaron" 「亜細亜」の「他称」性-アジア主義以前のアジア論 [The foreign-imposed character of 'Asia'. Asia discourse before Asianism], *Nihon Gaikō ni okeru Ajiashugi* 日本外交におけるアジア主義 [Asianism in Japan's foreign policy], ed. Nihon Seiji Gakkai 日本政治学会, Tokyo: Iwanami Shoten 1999, 33–53.

Matsuda Yoshio 松田義男, *Ukita Kazutami Kenkyū. Jiyūshugi seiji shisō no tenkai* 浮田和民研究: 自由主義政治思想の展開 [Research on Ukita Kazutami. The development of Liberalism as political thought], Kurashiki: Matsuda Yoshio 1996.

Matsui Iwane 松井石根, "Shina o sukufu no michi" 支那を救ふの道 [The road to save China], *Dai Ajiashugi* 大亜細亜主義 [Greater Asianism], 1-1, May 1933, 6–10.

Matsui Iwane 松井石根, "Dai Ajiashugi" 大亜細亜主義 [Greater Asianism], *Kingu* キング [King], May 1933, 12–19.

Matsui Iwane 松井石根, "Shina Jihen no igi to Dai Ajiashugi" 支那事変の意義と大亜細亜主義 [The meaning of the China Incident and Greater Asianism], *Dai Ajiashugi* 大亜細亜主義 [Greater Asianism], 7-1 (January 1939), 2–4.

Matsumoto Ken'ichi 松本健一 and Matsui Takafumi 松井孝典, ed., *Ajia wa kawaru no ka* アジアは変わるのか [Will Asia change?], Tokyo: Wedge 2009.

Matsumoto Ken'ichi 松本健一, "Ajiashugi wa shūen shita ka" アジア主義は終焉したか [Is Asianism dead?], *Takeuchi Yoshimi 'Nihon no Ajiashugi' seidoku* 竹内好日本のアジア主義精読 [Close Reading of Takeuchi Yoshimi's 'Japanese Asianism'], ed. Matsumoto Ken'ichi 松本健一, Tokyo: Iwanami 2000, 89–190.

Matsumoto Saburō 松本三郎, "Shōwa shoki ni okeru Nihon no Chūgokukan" 昭和初期における日本の中国観 [The Japanese view of China in the early Showa period], *Nitchū kankei no sōgo imēji* 日中関係の相互イメージ [The mutual image of Japanese–Chinese relations], ed. Fujii Shōzō 藤井昇三 et al., Tokyo: Ajia Seikei Gakkai 1975, 32–65.

Matsumoto Sannosuke 松本三之介, *Yoshino Sakuzō* 吉野作造 [Yoshino Sakuzō], Tokyo: Tokyo Daigaku Shuppankai 2008.

Matsumoto, Sannosuke, "Profile of Asian Minded Man V: Yukichi Fukuzawa", *The Developing Economies*, 5-1 (March 1967), 156–172.

Matsuo Takayoshi 松尾尊兊, "Kaisetsu" 解説 [Commentary], *Daisan Teikoku. Kaisetsu, sōmokuji, sakuin* 第三帝国、解説、総目次、索引 [The Third Empire. Commentary, general table of contents, index], Tokyo: Fuji Shuppan 1984, 5–22.

Matsuo Takayoshi 松尾尊兌, *Taishō demokurashī* 大正デモクラシー [Taishō Democracy], Tokyo: Iwanami Shoten 2001.

Matsuo, Takayoshi, "Profile of Asian Minded Man VII: Sakuzō Yoshino", *The Developing Economies*, 5-2 (June 1967), 388–404.

Matsuura Masataka 松浦正孝, *Daitōa sensō wa naze okitanoka: han Ajiashugi no seiji keizaishi* 「大東亜戦争」はなぜ起きたのか:汎アジア主義の政治経済史 [Why did the 'Greater East Asian War' happen? A political and economic history of Pan-Asianism], Nagoya: Nagoya Daigaku Shuppankai 2010.

Matsuzawa Tetsunari 松沢哲成, *Ajiashugi to Fashizumu: Tennō teikokuron hihan* アジア主義とファシズム:天皇帝国論批判 [Asianism and Fascism: A Critique of the Tennō Empire Thesis], Tokyo: Renga Shobō Shinsha 1979.

Matten, Marc Andre, "Li Dazhao: 'Greater Asianism and New Asianism', 1919", *Pan-Asianism: A Documentary History 1860-2010*, Vol. 1, ed. Sven Saaler and C.W.A. Szpilman, Boulder: Rowman & Littlefield, 2011, 217–222.

Meiji shinbun zasshi bunko shozō zasshi mokuji sōran, Tōkyō Daigaku Hōgakubu fuzoku 明治新聞雑誌文庫所蔵雑誌目次総覧:東京大学法学部附属 [Compendium of Table of Contents of Journals stored in the Library for Meiji newspapers and journals, attached to the Law Faculty of Tokyo University], Tokyo: Ōzorasha 1993–1998 (150 volumes).

Meisner, Maurice J., *Li Ta-chao and the origins of Chinese Marxism*, Cambridge: Harvard University Press 1967 and Mori Masao, *Ri Taishō* [Li Dazhao], Tokyo : Jinbutsu Ōraisha 1967.

Minamihori Eiji 南堀英二, *Kiseki no ishi: Tōyōichi no kojin sōgō byōin Shanhai Fukumin byōin o tsukutta jiai no igyō* 奇跡の医師:東洋一の個人総合病院・上海福民病院を造った慈愛の医業 [The doctor of miracles: The medical work of kindness by the Shanghai Fumin Hospital, the best private general hospital in the East], Tokyo: Kōjinsha 2010.

Minohara Toshihiro 簑原俊洋, *Kariforunia shū no hai Nichi undō to Nichi-Bei kankei. Imin mondai o meguru Nichi-Bei masatsu, 1906–1921 nen* カリフォルニア州の排日運動と日米関係: 移民問題をめぐる日米摩擦1906–1921年 [The anti-Japanese movement in California and the Japanese-American relations. The Japanese-American friction in the immigration problem], Tokyo: Yūhikaku 2006.

Mita Shōgyō Kenkyūkai 三田商業研究会 [Mita Business Research Society], ed., *Keiō Gijuku Shusshin Meiryū Redden* 慶應義塾出身名流列伝 [The Lives of Distinguished Graduates of Keiō University], Tokyo: Jitsugyō no Sekaisha 1910, 375–376.

Mitani Taichirō 三谷太一郎, *Taishō Demokurashī ron: Yoshino Sakuzō no jidai* 大正デモクラシー論,吉野作造の時代 [On Taishō Democracy: The times of Yoshino Sakuzō], Tokyo: Tokyo Daigaku Shuppankai 1995.

Mitchell, Richard, *Thought Control in Prewar Japan*, Ithaca: Cornell University Press 1976.

Mittag, Jürgen /Berthold Unfried, "Transnationale Netzwerke – Annäherungen an ein Medium des Transfers und der Machtausübung [Transnational Networks – Approaches to a medium of transfer and power], *Transnationale Netzwerke im 20. Jahrhundert* [Transnational Networks in the 20th Century], Leipzig: Akademische Verlagsanstalt 2008, 9–25.

Mitter, Rana, *The Manchurian myth: nationalism, resistance and collaboration in modern China*, Berkeley: Univeristy of California Press 2000.

Mitter, Rana, *A bitter revolution: China's struggle with the modern world*, Oxford & New York: Oxford University Press 2004.

Mitter, Rana, *China's War With Japan, 1937–1945. The Struggle for Survival*, London: Penguin 2014.

Miura Tetsutarō 三浦鉄太郎, "Dai Nihonshugi ka Shō Nihonshugi ka" 大日本主義か小日本主義か [Greater Japanism or Small Japanism], *Taishō Shisō shū* 大正思想集 [Collection of Taishō Thought], Vol. 1, ed. Imai Seiichi 今井清一, Tokyo: Chikuma Shobō 1978, 65–87 (originally in *Tōyō Keizai Shinpō* 東洋經濟新報 [Far Eastern Economist], 631-636, 15 April–15 June 1913).

Miwa, Kimitada, "Crossroads of Patriotism in Imperial Japan: Shiga Shigetaka, Uchimura Kanzō, and Nitobe Inazō" (Ph.D. dissertation, Princeton University 1967), 385–393.

Miyadai Shinji 宮台真司, *Ajiashugi no tenmatsu ni manabe: Miyadai Shinji no han Gurōbaraizēshon Gaidansu* 亜細亜主義の顛末に学べ：宮台真司の反グローバライゼーション・ガイダンス [Learn from the details of Asianism: Miyadai Shinji's guidance to anti-globalization], Warabi: Jissensha 2004.

Miyazaki Tōten 宮崎滔天, "Rikkōho sengen" 立候補宣言 [Declaration of Candidacy], *Miyazaki Tōten Zenshū* 宮崎滔天全集 [Complete Writings of Miyazaki Tōten], vol. 2, ed. Miyazaki Ryūsuke 宮崎龍介 and Onogawa Hidemi 小野川秀美, Tokyo: Heibonsha 1971, without page number.

Miyazaki Tōten 宮崎滔天, "Shōka Manroku" 銷夏漫録 [Essay on Enduring Summer], *Miyazaki Tōten Zenshū* 宮崎滔天全集 [Complete Writings of Miyazaki Tōten], vol. 4, ed. Miyazaki Ryūsuke and Onogawa Hidemi 宮崎龍介, 小野川秀美, Tokyo: Heibonsha 1973, 330–337 (originally in *Shanghai Nichi Nichi Shinbun* 上海日日新聞, 24 July 1918).

Miyazaki Tōten 宮崎滔天, "Tōkyō dayori" 東京便り [Letter from Tokyo], 1 May 1919, *Miyazaki Tōten Zenshū* 宮崎滔天全集 [Complete Writings of Miyazaki Tōten], vol. 2, ed. Miyazaki Ryūsuke 宮崎龍介 and Onogawa Hidemi 小野川秀美, Tokyo: Heibonsha 1971, 126–128.

Mizuno Naoki 水野直樹, "1920 nendai Nihon, Chōsen, Chūgoku ni okeru Ajia ninshiki no ichidanmen: Ajia minzoku kaigi o meguru sangoku no ronchō" 1920年代日本・朝鮮・中国におけるアジア認識の一断面――アジア民族会議をめぐる三国の論調 [One section of Asia consciousness in Japan, Korea, and China in the 1920s: Debates Concerning the Pan-Asian Conferences], *Kindai Nihon no Ajia Ninshiki* 近代日本のアジア認識 [Modern Japanese

Asia Consciousness], ed. Furuya Tetsuo 古屋哲夫, Tokyo: Ryokuin Shobō 1996, 509–548.
Morris-Suzuki, Tessa, "Asia is One: Visions of Asian Community in Twenty First Century Japan", *Okakura Tenshin and Pan-Asianism. Shadows of the Past*, ed. Brij Tankha, Folkestone: Global Oriental 2009, 158–170.
Morris-Suzuki, Tessa, "Invisible countries: Japan and the Asian dream", *Asian Studies Review* 22-1 (1998), 5–22.
Müller, Gotelind, *China, Kropotkin und der Anarchismus: eine Kulturbewegung im China des frühen 20. Jahrhunderts unter dem Einfluss des Westens und japanischer Vorbilder* [China, Kropotkin and Anarchism. A Cultural Movement in China in the early 20th century under the influence of the West and of Japanese Models], Wiesbaden: Harrassowitz 2001.
Müller, Gotelind, "Are We 'Yellow'? And Who is 'Us'? – China's Problems with Glocalising the Concept of 'Race' (around 1900)", *Bochumer Jahrbuch zur Ostasienforschung* 32, 2008, 153–180.
Müller, Gotelind, "Glocalizing 'Race in China: Concepts and Contingencies at the Turn of the Twentieth Century", *Racism in the Modern World. Historical Perspectives on Cultural Transfer and Adaptation*, ed. Manfred Berg and Simon Wendt, New York/Oxford: Berghahn 2011, 236–254.
Müller, Gotelind, "Introduction", *Designing history in East Asian textbooks: identity politics and transnational aspirations*, ed. Gotelind Müller, London: Routledge 2011, 1–6.
Müller, Gotelind, ed., *Designing history in East Asian textbooks: identity politics and transnational aspirations*, London: Routledge 2011.
Murakawa Kengo 村川堅固, "Dai Ajia Kyōkai Sōritsu keika" 大亜細亜協会創立経過 [The progress of the founding of the Greater Asia Association], *Dai Ajiashugi* 大亜細亜主義 [Greater Asianism], 1-1 (May 1933), 62.
Nagai Ryūtarō 永井柳太郎, "Hakka Ron" 白禍論 [On the White Peril], *Shin Nihon* 新日本 [New Japan], 2-3, 1 March 1912.
Nagatomi Morinosuke 永富守之助, "Kyokutō Ajia Renpō no kensetsu" 極東アジア連邦の建設 [The establishment of a Far East Asian Republic], *Gaikō Jihō* 外交時報 [Diplomatic Review] 481 (December 1924), 99–107.
Nagatomi Morinosuke 永富守之助, "Gendai no chōkokkateki rengō undō no ichi shimyaku toshite no han Ajia undō" 現代の超国家的連合運動の一支脈としての汎アジア運動 [The contemporary movement for supranational unions as one branch of the pan-Asian movement], *Kokusai Chishiki* 國際知識 [International Knowledge], October 1926, 2–13.
Nagatomi Morinosuke 永富守之助, "Han Ajia undō ni tsuite" 汎アジア運動について [On the pan-Asian movement], *Gaikō Jihō* 外交時報 [Diplomatic Review] 487 (March 1925), 34–40.
Nakagawa Hidenao 中川秀直, "Atarashii Ajiashugi" 新しいアジア主義 [New Asianism], *Nitchū taiwa* 日中対話 [Japanese–Chinese Dialogue], Tokyo: Genron NPO 2006, 12–19.

Nakajima Takeshi 中島岳志, *Nakamuraya no Bōsu. Indo dokuritsu undō to kindai Nihon no Ajiashugi* 中村屋のボース：インド独立運動と近代日本のアジア主義 [Bose of Nakamura's. India's independence movement and modern Japanese Asianism], Tokyo: Hakusuisha 2005.

Nakamura Shunsaku 中村春作, "Ajiashugi" アジア主義 [Asianism], *Nihon Shisōshi Jiten* 日本思想史辞典 [Encyclopaedia of the History of Japanese Thought], ed. Koyasu Nobukuni子安宣邦, Tokyo: Perikan sha 2001, 7–8.

Nakamura Tadashi 中村義, "Chūgoku kindai o yonda shijin. Kodama Kagai to Son Bun, Chin Kibi, Kō Kō" 中国近代を詠んだ詩人児玉花外と孫文、陳其美、黃興 [Poets who sang China's modernity: Sun Yat-sen, Chen Qimei, Huang Xing], *Nishō Gakusha Daigaku Tōyōgaku kenkyūjoshūkan* 二松學舍大學東洋學研究所集刊 [Collected Publication of the Oriental Research Institute of Nishō Gakusha University], 31 (2001), 111–151.

Nakano Akira 中野光, "Kaisetsu" [Explanation] 解説, *Sawayanagi Masatarō Zenshū* 沢柳政太郎全集 [Complete Writings of Sawayanagi Masatarō], Vol. 9, ed. Sawayanagi Masatarō Zenshū kankōkai 沢柳政太郎全集刊行会, Tokyo: Kokudosha 1977, 542–554.

Nakano Seigō 中野正剛, "Son Bun-kun no kyorai to Ajia undō" 孫文君の去来とアジア運動 [Mr. Sun Yat-sen's passing through and the Asia movement], *Gakan* 我観 [My View], 7 (January 1925), 112–117.

Nakano Seigō 中野正剛, *Kōwa Kaigi o mokugeki shite* 講和会議を目撃して [Having witnessed the Peace Conference], Tokyo: Tōhō Jironsha 1919.

Nakanome Tōru 中野目徹, *Seikyōsha no kenkyū* 政教社の研究 [Research into the Seikyōsha], Kyoto: Shibunkaku 1993.

Nakatani Takeyo 中谷武世, "A kyū Kyokutō Kokusai Gunji Saiban Kiroku" A級極東国際軍事裁判記録 [Records from the Class A Far Eastern International Military Tribunal], No. 122 (JACAR A08071264100).

Nakatani Takeyo 中谷武世, "A kyū Kyokutō Kokusai Gunji Saiban Kiroku" A級極東国際軍事裁判記録 [Records from the Class A Far Eastern International Military Tribunal], No. 156-1 (JACAR A08071270900).

Nakatani Takeyo 中谷武世, "Matsui Taishō to Dai Ajiashugi. Jō ni kaete" 松井大将と大亜細亜主義、序に代えて [General Matsui and Greater Asianism: In place of a preface], *Matsui Iwane Taishō no jinchū nisshi* 松井石根大将の陣中日誌 [General Matsui Iwane's War Diary], ed. Tanaka Masaaki 田中正明, Tokyo: Fuyō Shobō 1985, 4–6.

Nakatani Takeyo 中谷武世, *Shōwa dōranki no kaisō. Nakatani Takeyo kaikoroku* 昭和動乱期の回想：中谷武世回顧録 [Recollections of the upheavals of the Shōwa period. The Memoirs of Nakatani Takeyo], Tokyo: Tairyūsha 1989.

Narangoa, Li, "Japanese Geopolitics and the Mongol Lands, 1915–1945", *European Journal of East Asian Studies*, Vol. 3, No. 1 (2004), 45–68.

Narusawa Muneo 成澤宗男, ed., *Nippon Kaigi to Jinja Honchō* 日本会議と神社本庁 [The Japan Conference and the Association of Shinto Shrines], Tokyo: Kinyōbi 2016.

Naruse Masao 成瀬正雄, "Ajia Minzoku Kaigi ni tsuite" アジア民族会議について [On Asian Peoples Congress], *Ajia Minzoku Kaigi ni tsuite, Jiyū Byōdō Hakuai no hongi, gekken shōrei no yōshi* アジア民族会議について、自由平等博愛の本義、撃剣奨励の要旨 [On the Asian Peoples' Congress, the true meaning of freedom, equality, and philanthropy, and an outline for the promotion of Japanese fencing],Tokyo: Chijin Yūsha 1927, 1–42.

Ngai, Mae M., "Ozawa v. United States", *The American Journal of International Law*, 17-1 (Jan. 1923), 151–157.

Ngai, Mae M., "The Architecture of Race in American Immigration Law: A Reexamination of the Immigration Act of 1924", *The Journal of American History*, 86-1 (1999), 67–92.

Nihon Kindai Bungaku Kan 日本近代文学館 [House of Modern Japanese Literature], ed., *Taiyō Sōsakuin* 太陽. 総索引 [General Index of The Sun], Tokyo: Nihon Kindai Bungaku Kan 1999.

Nihon kindai shiryō kenkyūkai 日本近代史料研究会, ed., *Zasshi 'Nihonjin', 'Nihon oyobi Nihonjin' mokuji sōran* 雑誌「日本人」・「日本及日本人」目次総覧 [Compendium of the Table of Contents of the journals 'Japanese' and 'Japan and the Japanese'], Tokyo: Tōkyō daigaku kyōyōgakubu 1977–1984 (5 volumes).

Ninagawa Arata 蜷川新, "Bukkyō to iwayuru Dai Ajiashugi" 仏教といわゆるアジア主義 [Buddhism and so-called Greater Asianism], *Chūō Bukkyō* 中央仏教 [Central Buddhism], 23-9 (September 1939), 2–6.

Ninagawa Arata 蜷川新, "Monrōshugi no mohō" モンロー主義の模倣 [An imitation of Monroeism], *Gaikō Jihō* 外交時報 [Diplomatic Review], 267 (December 1915), 16–20.

Ninagawa Arata 蜷川新, "Nisshi shin dōmei no seiritsu" 日支新同盟の成立 [The establishment of a new alliance between Japan and China], *Chūgai* 中外 [Home and Abroad], 2-8 (1 July 1918), 14–20.

Ninagawa Arata 蜷川新, "Nisshi shinzen no issaku" 日支親善の一策 [A policy towards Japanese–Chinese friendship], *Gaikō* 外交 [Diplomacy], 3-6 (20 May 1917), 7–10.

Ninagawa Arata 蜷川新, "Sekaijin no Sekaishugi" 世界人の世界主義 [Worldism for worldist people], *Gaikō Jihō* 外交時報 [Diplomatic Review], 309 (15 September 1917), 1–8.

Ninagawa Arata 蜷川新, "Ajia Minzoku to wa nan zo" アジア民族とは何ぞ [What on earth does Asian Peoples mean?], *Tōhō Kōron* 東方公論 [Eastern Review], June 1926, 47–49.

Ninagawa Arata 蜷川新, "Ajia Renmei no kūron" アジア連盟の空論 [Empty theory of an Asian League], *Tōhō Kōron* 東方公論 [Eastern Review], February 1926, 12–17.

Ninagawa Arata 蜷川新, "Kiken naru jinshu byōdō no seikō" 危険なる人種平等の政綱 [Dangerous political plan of racial equality], *Tōhō Kōron* 東方公論 [Eastern Review], July 1927, 20–22.

Ninagawa Arata 蜷川新, "Ugu o kiwametaru Ajia Monrōshugi" 迂愚を極めたるアジアモンロー主義 [Extremely arrogant Asian Monroeism], *Dai Nihon* 大日本 [Greater Japan], 4-7 (1 July 1917), 96–97.

Ninagawa Arata 蜷川新, "Ajiajin hon'i ka Nihon kokumin hon'i ka" 亜細亜人本位か、日本国民本位か [The Standard of the Asians or the standard of the Japanese people?], *Tōhō Kōron* 東方公論 [Oriental Review], 1-1 (January 1926), 37–43.

Nippon Kaigi Jigyō sentā 日本会議事業センター, ed., *Koredake wa shitte okitai Dai Tōa Sensō* これだけは知っておきたい大東亜戦争 [That much one should know about the Greater East Asian War], Tokyo: Meiseisha 2006.

Nippon Kaigi Jigyō sentā 日本会議事業センター, ed., *Dai Tōa Sensō to Ajia no dokuritsu* 大東亜戦争とアジアの独立 [The Greater East Asian War and the Independence of Asia], Tokyo: Meiseisha 2013.

Nish, Ian, *Japanese foreign policy in the interwar period*, Westport: Praeger 2002.

Nohara Shirō 野原四郎, "Dai Ajiashugi" 大アジア主義 [Greater Asianism], *Ajia Rekishi Jiten* アジア歴史事典 [Encyclopaedia of Asian History], Tokyo: Heibonsha 1960, 6–7.

Nohara Shirō 野原四郎, *Ajia no rekishi to shisō* アジアの歴史と思想 [Asian history and thought], Tokyo: Kōbundō 1966.

Nomura Kōichi 野村浩一, "Tachibana Shiraki. Ajiashugi no hōkō" 橘樸、アジア主義の彷徨 [Tachibana Shiraki. Roamings of Asianism], *Rikkyō Hōgaku* 立教法学 19 (1980), 36–116.

Northeast Asian History Foundation, ed., *A Window to the Future of Northeast Asia*, Seoul 2009. http://english.historyfoundation.or.kr/?sub_num=9 (last accessed 16 October 2016).

Oates, Leslie Russell, *Populist nationalism in prewar Japan: a biography of Nakano Seigo*, Sydney & London: Allen & Unwin 1985.

Ogawa Reikō 小川冷光, "Ajia o daiben suru Nihon no warera" 亜細亜を代弁する日本の吾等 [We Japanese as Asia's Proxy], *Nihon oyobi Nihonjin* 日本及日本人 [Japan and the Japanese], 312 (January 1935), 55–58.

Ōishi Masami 大石正巳, "Ajia minzoku no sōdōmei o saku seyo" アジア民族の総同盟を策せよ [Let's plan a general alliance of the Asian peoples], *Taiyō* 太陽 30-7 (July 1924), 106–109.

Ōishi Masami 大石正巳, "Dai Ajiashugi no kakuritsu" 大亜細亜主義の確立 [Establishing Greater Asianism], *Nihon oyobi Nihonjin* 日本及日本人 [Japan and the Japanese] 58-5 (October 1924), 4.

Ōishi Masami 大石正巳, "Tōyō minzoku no tenken" 東洋民族の天権 [The divine right of Eastern peoples], *Tōyō Bunka* 東洋文化 [Eastern Culture], No. 5 (May 1924), 11–14.

Okakura, Kakuzō, *The Awakening of the East*, Tokyo: Seibunkaku 1940.

Okuma, Shigenobu [Ōkuma Shigenobu], "Our National Mission", *Japan to America. A Symposium of Papers by Political Leaders and Representative*

Citizens of Japan on Conditions in Japan and on the Relations between Japan and the United States, ed. Naoichi Masaoka, New York/London: G.P. Putnam's sons 1914, 1–5.

Ono Masaaki 小野雅章, "Kumamoto Eigakkō jiken no tenmatsu to kyōiku kai" 熊本英学校事件の顛末と教育界 [The circumstances of the Kumamoto English School incident and the education world], *Kyōikugaku Zasshi* 教育学雑誌, 28 (1994), 175–190.

Orluc, Katiana, "Decline or Renaissance: The Transformation of European Consciousness after the First World War", *Europe and the Other and Europe as the Other*, ed. Bo Strath, Brussels: Peter Lang 2000, 123–156.

Ōtani Kōzui 大谷光瑞, "Teikoku no kiki" 帝国の危機 [Crisis of the Empire], *Chūō Kōron* 中央公論 [Central Review], 32-3 (March 1917), 1–30.

Ōyama Ikuo 大山郁夫, "Dai Ajiashugi no unmei" 大亜細亜主義の運命 [The fate of Greater Asianism], *Shin Nihon* 新日本 [New Japan], 6-3 (1 March 1916), 18–30.

Ozaki Yukio 尾崎行雄, "Ajia Renmei ni tsuite. Mazu mizukara naka ni yashinae" アジア連盟について、まず自ら中に養え [On an Asian League. Let's first cultivate it ourselves], *Nihon oyobi Nihonjin* 日本及日本人 [Japan and the Japanese] 58-5 (October 1924), 20–22.

Ōzumi Shōfū 大住嘯風, *Shin Shisō Ron* 新思想論 [On New Thought], Tokyo: Rikutō Shuppansha 1913.

Passmore, Kevin, *Fascism. A Very Short Introduction*, Oxford: Oxford University Press 2002.

Payne, Stanley G., *A history of fascism, 1914–1945*, Madison: University of Wisconsin Press 1995.

Policy Report 'The State of the Concept of East Asian Community and Japan's Strategic Response Thereto', ed. Council on East Asian Community, Tokyo 2005.

Qi Qizhang 戚其章, "Riben Da Yaxiya zhuyi tanxi: Jianyu Sheng Banghe Xiansheng shangque" 日本大亚细亚主义探析 — 兼与盛邦和先生商榷 [Exploring Japanese Greater Asianism: A Discussion with Mr. Sheng Banghe], *Lishi Yanjiu* 历史研究 [History Research], March 2004, 132–145.

Reynolds, Douglas R., "Chinese Area Studies in Prewar China: Japan's Toa Dobun Shoin in Shanghai, 1900–1945", *The Journal of Asian Studies*, 45-5 (November 1986), 945–970.

Reynolds, Douglas R., *China 1898–1912: The* Xinzheng *Revolution and Japan*, Cambridge (MA): Harvard University Press 1993.

Ri Saika 李彩華, "Tachibana Shiraki no Ajiashugi. Manshū Jihen ikō no gensetsu o chūshin ni" 橘樸のアジア主義、満州事変以降の言説を中心に [Tachibana Shiraki's Asianism. Focussing on the discourse after the Manchurian Incident], *Nenpō Nihon Shisōshi* 年報日本思想史 [Annuals of Japanese intellectual history], 9 (March 2010), 1–13.

Richard, Paul, "The Unity of Asia", *The Dawn of Asia*, Madras: Ganesh & Co. 1920, 1–10.

Richter, Melvin, "Appreciating a Contemporary Classic: The Geschichtliche Grundbegriffe and Future Scholarship", *The Meaning of Historical Terms and Concepts. New Studies on Begriffsgeschichte*, ed. Hartmut Lehmann and Melvin Richter, Washington: German Historical Institute Washington 1996, 7–19.

Richter, Melvin, "Begriffsgeschichte Today - An Overview", *The Finnish Yearbook of Political Thought*, Vol. 3 (1999), 11–27.

Richter, Melvin, "Pocock, Skinner, and the Geschichtliche Grundbegriffe", *History and Theory*, 19 (1990), 38–70.

Richter, Steffi, ed., *Contested Views of a Common Past. Revisions of History in Contemporary East Asia*, Frankfurt: Campus 2008.

Rōyama Masamichi 蝋山政道, *Nichi-Man kankei no kenkyū* 日満関係の研究 [Research on Japanese-Manchurian Relations], Tokyo: Shibun Shoin 1933.

Saaler, Sven, *Politics, Memory and Public Opinion. The History Textbook Controversy and Japanese Society*, München: Iudicium 2005.

Saaler, Sven "The Construction of Regionalism in Modern Japan: Kodera Kenkichi and his 'Treatise on Greater Asianism' (1916)", *Modern Asian Studies*, 41-6, 2007, 1261–1294.

Saaler, Sven, "Pan-Asianism in modern Japanese history. Overcoming the nation, creating a region, forging an empire", *Pan-Asianism in Modern Japanese History. Colonialism, regionalism and borders*, ed. Sven Saaler and J. Victor Koschmann, London: Routledge 2007, 1–18.

Saaler, Sven, "Pan-Asianism during and after World War I", *Pan-Asianism: A Documentary History 1860–2010*, Vol. 1, ed. Sven Saaler and C.W.A. Szpilman, Boulder: Rowman & Littlefield, 2011, 255–269.

Saaler, Sven, "The Pan-Asiatic Society and the 'Conference of Asian Peoples' in Nagasaki, 1926", *Pan-Asianism: A Documentary History 1860–2010*, Vol. 2, ed. Sven Saaler and Christopher W.A. Szpilman, Boulder: Rowman & Littlefield 2011, 97–105.

Saaler, Sven, *Pan-Asianism in Meiji and Taishō Japan. A Preliminary Framework*, Tokyo: Deutsches Institut fur Japanstudien 2004 (Working Paper 02/4).

Sachsenmaier, Dominic, "Alternative Visions of World Order in the Aftermath of World War I: Global Perspectives on Chinese Approaches", *Competing Visions of world order: global moments and movements, 1880s–1930s*, ed. Sebastian Conrad and Dominic Sachsenmaier, New York: Palgrave Macmillan 2007, 151–178.

Said, Edward W., *Orientalism*, New York: Vintage 1978.

Sakai Saburō 酒井三郎, *Shōwa Kenkyūkai. Aru chishikijin dantai no kiseki* 昭和研究会: ある知識人集団の軌跡 [Showa Research Association. The tracks of a group of intellectuals], Tokyo: Chūō Kōron sha 1992.

Sakai Tetsuya 酒井哲哉, *Kindai Nihon no Kokusai Chitsujo Ron* 近代日本の国際秩序論 [The Debate on Modern Japan's International Order], Tokyo: Iwanami Shoten 2007, 239.

Sanlian shudian bianjibu 三联書店編輯部, ed., *'Dong fang za zhi' zong mu: 1904 nian 3 yue-1948 nian 12 yue* 東方雜誌总目: 1904年3月-1948年12月 [General Table of Contents of the 'Eastern Miscellany' from March 1904 to December 1948], Beijing: Shenghuo dushu xinzhi sanlian shudian 1957.

Sano Manabu 佐野学 and Nabeyama Sadachika 鍋山貞親, "Han Ajiashugi no ippan keisō" 汎アジア主義の一般形相 [The general form of Pan-Asianism], *Nihon Kyōsanshugi undō shi* 日本共産主義運動史 [History of the Japanese Communist Movement], ed. Yamamoto Katsunosuke 山本勝之助 & Arita Mitsuo 有田満穂, Tokyo: Seiki Shobō 1950, 381.

Sarkar, Benoy Kumar, "The Futurism of Young Asia", *International Journal of Ethics*, 28-4 (July 1918), 521–541.

Satō Kazuki 佐藤一樹, "Yohakuran no Ajiashugi. Taishō ki 'Taiyō' no shibunran to Kodama Kagai" 余白欄のアジア主義、大正期太陽の詩文欄と児玉花外 [Asianism of the open columns. The poetry columns of Taiyō in the Taishō period and Kodama Kagai], *Zasshi Taiyō to kokumin bunka no keisei* 雑誌『太陽』と国民文化の形成 [The journal Taiyo and the formation of popular culture], ed. Suzuki Sadami 鈴木貞美, Kyoto: Shibunkaku 2001, 324–348.

Satō Yoshimaru 佐藤能丸, *Meiji Nashonarizumu no kenkyū. Seikyōsha no seiritsu to sono shūhen* 明治ナショナリズムの研究: 政教社の成立とその周辺 [Research into Meiji nationalism. The founding of the Seikyōsha and its environs], Tokyo: Fuyō Shobō 1998.

Sawayanagi Masatarō 沢柳政太郎, "Bunkateki han Ajiashugi o teishō su" 文化的汎アジア主義を提唱す [Proposing Cultural Pan-Asianism], *Shin Nihon* 新日本 [New Japan], 7-3 (1 March 1917).

Sawayanagi Masatarō 沢柳政太郎, "Sengo junbi no kontei" 戦後準備の根底 [Foundation of post-war preparations], *Sawayanagi Masatarō Zenshū* 沢柳政太郎全集 [Complete Writings of Sawayanagi Masatarō], Vol. 9, ed. Sawayanagi Masatarō Zenshū kankōkai 沢柳政太郎全集刊行会, Tokyo: Kokudosha 1977, 258–269 (paper from Sawayanagi's estate, dated 24 July 1917).

Sawayanagi Masatarō 沢柳政太郎/Ebi Saikichi 衣斐サイ吉, *Ri-Hua Gongcun lun* 日華共存論 [On Japanese-Chinese Coexistence], Tokyo (without publisher) 1919.

Sawayanagi Masatarō 沢柳政太郎, "Ajiashugi to Nihon no shimei" 亜細亜主義と日本の使命 [Asianism and Japan's fate], *Taiyō* 太陽 [The Sun], 24-8 (15 June 1918), 41–48.

Sawayanagi Masatarō 沢柳政太郎, "Ajiashugi" 亜細亜主義 [Asianism], *Sawayanagi Masatarō Zenshū* 沢柳政太郎全集 [Complete Writings of Sawayanagi Masatarō], Vol. 9, ed. Sawayanagi Masatarō Zenshū kankōkai 沢柳

政太郎全集刊行会, Tokyo: Kokudosha 1977, 269–275 (originally in *Teikoku Kyōiku* 帝國教育 [Education for the Empire], 422, 1 September 1917).

Sawayanagi Masatarō 沢柳政太郎, "Bunkateki han Ajiashugi o teishō su" 文化的汎アジア主義を提唱す [Proposing Cultural Pan-Asianism], *Sawayanagi Masatarō Zenshū* 沢柳政太郎全集 [Complete Writings of Sawayanagi Masatarō], Vol. 9, ed. Sawayanagi Masatarō Zenshū kankōkai 沢柳政太郎全集刊行会, Tokyo: Kokudosha 1977, 213–226 (originally in *Shin Nihon* 新日本 [New Japan], 7–3, 1 March 1917).

Seaton, Philip A., *Japan's contested war memories: the "memory rifts" in historical consciousness of World War II*, London/New York: Routledge 2007.

Seifert, Wolfgang, "Japan und seine Moderne nach dem Asiatisch-Pazifischen Krieg: Takeuchi Yoshimis Intervention 1948" [Japan and its modernity after the Asian-Pacific War: Takeuchi Yoshimi's Intervention in 1948], *Intervalle 11. Schriften zur Kulturforschung. Japanische Intellektuelle im Spannungsfeld von Okzidentalismus und Orientalismus* [Intervals 11. Writings on Cultural Research. Japanese intellectuals between Occidentalism and Orientalism], ed. Takemitsu Morikawa, Kassel: Kassel University Press 2008, 75–120.

Seifert, Wolfgang, "Japans Systemtransformation in den 1930er Jahren und die 'Asiatisierung' Ostasiens" [Japan's system transformation in the 1930s and the 'Asiatisation' of East Asia], *Ostasien im 20. Jahrhundert. Geschichte und Gesellschaft* [East Asia in the 20th Century. History and Society], ed. Sepp Linhart and Susanne Weigelin-Schwiedrzik, Wien: Promedia Verlag 2007, 45–61.

Seifert, Wolfgang, "seikatsu/seikatsusha", *The Blackwell Encyclopedia of Sociology*, ed. G. Ritzer, Malden & Oxford: Blackwell Publishing 2007, 4150–4154.

Seifert, Wolfgang, *Nationalismus im Nachkriegs-Japan. Ein Beitrag zur Ideologie der völkischen Nationalisten* [Nationalism in Postwar Japan. On the Ideology of Ethnic Nationalists], Hamburg: Institut für Asienkunde 1977 (Reihe Mitteilungen, Bd. 91).

Sheng Banghe 盛邦和, "19 shiji yu 20 shiji zhi jiaode Riben Yazhou zhuyi" 19世纪与20世纪之交的日本亚洲主义 [Japanese Asianism in the Transitional Period from the 19th to the 20th century], *Lishi Yanjiu* 歷史研究 [History Research], March 2000, 125–135.

Shi Jiafang 史桂芳, '*Tongwen tongzu' de pianju. Ri wei Dongya Lianmeng Yundong de Xingwang* "同文同种"的骗局:日伪东亚联盟运动的兴亡 [The fraud of 'same culture, same race'. The rise and fall of Japan's fake East Asian League movement], Beijing: Shehui Kexue wenxian Chubanshe 2002.

Shiga Shigetaka 志賀重昂, "Mikomi naki Ajia Renmei" 見込みなきアジア連盟 [Hopeless Asian League], *Nihon oyobi Nihonjin* 日本及日本人 [Japan and the Japanese] 58–5 (October 1924), 26–30.

Shimazu, Naoko, "The Japanese attempt to secure racial equality in 1919", *Japan Forum* 1–1 (April 1989), 93–100.

Shimazu, Naoko, *Japan, race, and equality: the racial equality proposal of 1919*, New York: Routledge 1998.
Shindō Eiichi 進藤栄一, "Ajia haken ka kyōchō ka" アジア覇権か強調か [Asian hegemony or harmony], *Asahi Shinbun* 朝日新聞, 14 October 2010, 8.
Shindō Eiichi 進藤栄一, *Higashi Ajia Kyōdōtai o dō tsukuru ka* 東アジア共同体をどうつくるか [How to build an East Asian Community?], Tokyo: Chikuma shobō 2007.
Shūgiin/Sangiin 衆議院、参議院 [Lower and Upper Houses], ed., *Gikai seido hyakunenshi* 議会制度百年史 [One hundred years of parliamentary system], Vol. 12, Tokyo: Ōkura shō insatsukyoku 1990.
Smith, Craig A., *Constructing Chinese Asianism: Intellectual Writings on East Asian Regionalism (1896–1924)*, PhD dissertation (University of British Columbia), 2014.
Snyder, Louis L., *Macro-Nationalisms. A History of the Pan-Movements*, Westport: Greenwood Press 1984.
So Wai-Chor [Su Wei Chu/So I Sho] 蘇維初, "Ō Seiei to Dai Ajiashugi" 汪精衛と大亜細亜主義 [Wang Jingwei and Greater Asianism], *Shōwa Ajiashugi no jitsuzō. Teikoku Nihon to Taiwan, 'Nan'yō', 'Minami Shina'* 昭和・アジア主義の実像：帝国日本と台湾・「南洋」・「南支那」 [The true picture of Asianism in the Shōwa era. Imperial Japan and Taiwan, the Southern Islands, and Southern China], ed. Matsuura Masataka 松浦正孝, Kyoto: Mineruva Shobō 2007, 182–204.
Son Bun [Sun Yat-sen] 孫文, "Chū-Nichi wa tagai ni teikei subeshi" 中日は互いに提携すべし [China and Japan must cooperate] (15 February 1913), *Chūgokujin no Nihonjinkan 100nen shi* 中国人の日本人観100年史 [A History of one hundred years of Chinese views of the Japanese], ed. Kojima Shinji et al. 小島晋治, Tokyo: Jiyū Kokuminsha 1974, 151.
Son Bun [Sun Yat-sen] 孫文, "Dai Ajiashugi no igi to Nisshi shinzen no yui'itsu saku" 大亜細亜主義の意義と日支親善の唯一策 [The significance of Greater Asianism and the singular policy of Japanese-Chinese friendship], *Kaizō* 改造 [Reconstruction], January 1925, 213–228.
Spira, Ivo, *A Conceptual History of Chinese –Isms. The Modernization of Ideological Discourse, 1895–1925*, Leiden: Brill 2015.
Stalker, Nancy, "Suicide, Boycotts and Embracing Tagore: The Japanese Popular Response to the 1924 US Immigration Exclusion Law", *Japanese Studies*, 26-2 (September 2006), 153–170.
Stegewerns, Dick, "The dilemma of nationalism and internationalism in modern Japan: national interest, Asian brotherhood, international cooperation or world citizenship?", *Nationalism and Internationalism in Imperial Japan: Autonomy, Asian Brotherhood, or World Citizenship?*, ed. Dick Stegewerns, London: Routledge 2003, 3–16.
Stegewerns, Dick, *Adjusting to the New World. Japanese Opinion Leaders of the Taishō Generation and the Outside World, 1918–1932* (Unpublished Ph.D. dissertation, Leiden University, 2007).

Stolte, Carolien and Harald Fischer-Tiné, "Imagining Asia in India: Nationalism and Internationalism (ca. 1905–1940)", *Comparative Studies in Society and History*, 2012, 54(1), 65–92.

Stolte, Carolien, "'Enough of the Great Napoleons!' Raja Mahendra Pratap's Pan-Asian projects (1929–1939)", *Modern Asian Studies*, 2012, 46-2, 403–423.

Storry, Richard, *The Double Patriots. A Study of Japanese Nationalism*, London: Chatto and Windus 1957.

Stuurman, Siep, "The Canon of the History of Political Thought: Its Critique and a Proposed Alternative", *History and Theory* 39 (May 2000), 147–166.

Sugita Teiichi 杉田定一, "Dai Ajia Gasshō Ron" 大亜細亜合従論 [On the United States of Greater Asia], *Tōyō Bunka* 東洋文化 [Eastern Culture], 8 (September 1924), 7–13.

Sugita Teiichi 杉田定一, "Kō A Saku" 興亜策 [Raising Asia Policy], *Sugita Junzan-ō* 杉田鶉山翁 [The honourable Mr. Sugita Junzan], ed. Saiga Hakuai 雜賀博愛, Tokyo: Junzan Kai 1928 (1883), 543–551.

Sugita Teiichi 杉田定一, "Waga Gaikō to Tōa Renmei" 我外交と東亜連盟 [Our foreign policy and an East Asian League], *Nihon oyobi Nihonjin* 日本及日本人 [Japan and the Japanese], 674 (February 1916), 25–30.

Sun Chunri 孙春日, "Dongya guojia gongtong dizhi cuowu shiguan" 东亚国家共同抵制错误史观 [East Asian countries jointly reject erroneous historical views], *Renmin Ribao* 人民日报, 9 July 2014.

Sun Ge 孫歌, "Yazhou yiwei zhe shenme" 亞洲意味著什麽? [What does Asia mean?], *Taiwan Shehui Yanjiu Jikan* 台灣社會研究季刊 [Taiwan: A Radical Quarterly in Social Studies], No. 33 (March 1999), 1–64.

Sun Ge 孫歌, "Ajia to wa nani o imi shite iru no ka" アジアとは何を意味しているのか [What does Asia mean?], *Shisō* 思想 [Thought] 986 (June 2006), 48–74 and 987 (July 2006), 108–129.

Sun, Ge, "How does Asia mean?", *The Inter-Asia cultural studies reader*, ed. Kuan-Hsing Chen and Chua Beng Huat, London: Routledge 2007 (2000), 9–65.

Sun, Ge, "The predicament of compiling textbooks on the history of East Asia", *Designing history in East Asian textbooks: identity politics and transnational aspirations*, ed. Gotelind Müller, London: Routledge 2011, 9–31.

Sun Ge 孫歌/Baik Young-Seo 白永瑞/Chen Kuan-Hsing 陳光興, ed., *Posuto 'Higashi Ajia'* ポスト〈東アジア〉 [Post-'East Asia'], Tokyo: Sakuhinsha 2006.

Sun, Yat-sen, "Pan-Asianism", *China and Japan: Natural Friends, Unnatural Enemies*, ed. Tang Liangli, Shanghai: China United Press 1941, 141–151.

Sun Zhongshan [Sun Yat-sen] 孫中山, "Da Yaxiya zhuyi" 大亞細亞主義 [Greater Asianism], *Xin Yaxiya* 新亞細亞 [New Asia], 1-1 (October 1930), 1–7.

Sun Zhongshan [Sun Yat-sen] 孫中山, "Dao Li Liejun dian" 到李烈鈞电 [Telegram to Li Liejun] (13 October 1924), *Sun Zhongshan Quanji* 孫中

山全集 [Complete Writings of Sun Yat-sen], ed. Guangdong sheng Shehui Kexueyuan Lishi Yanjiushi et al. 广东省社会科学院历史研究室, Beijing: Zhonghua Shuju 1986, Vol. 11, 180.

Sun Zhongshan [Sun Yat-sen] 孫中山, "Zhongguo Cunwang Wenti" 中國存亡問題 [The Question of China's Life or Death], *Sun Zhongshan Quanji* 孫中山全集 [Complete Writings of Sun Yat-sen], ed. Guangdong sheng Shehui Kexueyuan Lishi Yanjiushi et al. 广东省社会科学院历史研究室, Beijing: Zhonghua Shuju Chuban 1985, Vol. 4, 39–99 (originally May 1917).

Sun Zhongshan [Sun Yat-sen] 孫中山, *Sanmin Zhuyi* 三民主義, Taipei: Cheng Chung Books 1988.

Suyematsu, Baron [Suematsu Kenchō], *The Risen Sun*, London: Archibald Constable 1905.

Suzuki Masahisa 鈴木将久, "Hajime ni" 初めに [Introduction], *Takeuchi Yoshimi Serekushon* 竹内好セレクション [Takeuchi Yoshimi Selection], Vol. 2, ed. Marukawa Tetsushi 丸川哲史 and Suzuki Masahisa 鈴木将久, Tokyo: Nihon Keizai Hyōronsha 2006, 7–16.

Suzuki Shizuo 鈴木静夫/Yokoyama Michiyoshi 横山真佳, *Shinsei kokka nihon to ajia: senryō ka no han'nichi no genzō* 神聖国家日本とアジア：占領下の反日の原像 [Holy country Japan and Asia: The original image of anti-Japanese resistance under occupation], Tokyo: Keisō Shobō 1984.

Suzuki, Tadashi, "Profile of Asian Minded Man IX: Tōkichi Tarui", *The Developing Economies*, 6-1 (March 1968), 79–100.

Swale, Alistair, "Tokutomi Sohō and the 'Asiatic Monroe Doctrine', 1917", *Pan-Asianism: A Documentary History 1860–2010*, Vol. 1, ed. Sven Saaler and C.W.A. Szpilman, Boulder: Rowman & Littlefield, 2011, 279–286.

Szpilman, Christopher W.A., *Kindai Nihon no Kakushinron to Ajiashugi: Kita Ikki, Ōkawa Shūmei, Mitsukawa Kametarō ra no shisō to kōdō* 近代日本の革新論とアジア主義：北一輝、大川周明、満川亀太郎らの思想と行動 [Modern Japan's Reform Debate and Asianism: the thought and behavior of Kita Ikki, Ōkawa Shūmei, Mitsukawa Kametarō and others], Tokyo: Ashi shobō 2015.

Szpilman, Christopher W.A., "Miyazaki Tōten's Pan-Asianism, 1915-1919", *Pan-Asianism: A Documentary History 1860–2010*, Vol. 1, ed. Sven Saaler and C.W.A. Szpilman, Boulder: Rowman & Littlefield, 2011, 133–139.

Szpilman, Christopher W. A., "Paul Richard: *To Japan*, 1917, and *The Dawn Over Asia*, 1920", *Pan-Asianism: A Documentary History 1860–2010*, Vol. 1, ed. Sven Saaler and C.W.A. Szpilman, Boulder: Rowman & Littlefield, 2011, 287–295.

Szpilman, Christopher W.A., "Ōkawa Shūmei: 'Various Problems of Asia in Revival', 1922", *Pan-Asianism: A Documentary History 1860–2010*, Vol. 2, ed. Sven Saaler and Christopher W.A. Szpilman, Boulder: Rowman & Littlefield 2011, 69–74.

Tachibana Shiraki 橘樸, "Ajia Renmei to Nisshi Kankei" アジア連盟と日支関係 [An Asian League and Japanese-Chinese Relations], *Manshū Hyōron* 滿洲評論 [Manchurian Review] 4–14, April 1933, 2–5.

Tachibana Shiraki 橘樸, "Han Ajia Undō no shin riron" 汎アジア運動の新理論 [The new theory of the Pan-Asian movement], *Manshū Hyōron* 滿洲評論 [Manchurian Review] 5-2, July 1933, 14–21.

Tachibana Shiraki 橘樸, "Han Ajia Undō" 汎アジア運動 [The Pan-Asian movement], *Manshū Hyōron* 滿洲評論 [Manchurian Review] 4-11, 18 March 1933, 9–10.

Tachibana Shiraki 橘樸, "Son Bun no Tōyō bunka kan oyobi Nihonkan" 孫文の東洋文化観及び日本観 [Sun Yat-sen's views of Eastern culture and of Japan], *Tachibana Shiraki Chosakushū* 橘樸著作集, ed. Tachibana Shiraki Chosakushū kankō iinkai 橘樸著作集刊行委員会, Tokyo: Keisō shobō 1966, Vol. 1, 360–399 (originally in *Gekkan Shina Kenkyū* 月刊支那研究 [China Research Monthly], 1–4, March 1925).

Tadokoro Teruaki 田所輝明, "Ajia Gasshūkoku Ron" アジア合衆国論 [On United States of Asia], *Nihon Kokumin* 日本国民 [Japanese People], June 1932, 219–234.

Takatsuna Hirofumi 高綱博文, "Nitchū kankeishi ni okeru Son Bun no Dai Ajiashugi. Senzen hen" 日中関係史における孫文の大亜細亜主義、戦前編 [Sun Yat-sen's Greater Asianism within the history of Japanese–Chinese relations. Prewar section], *Chikaki ni arite* 近きにありて [Being Nearby], 32 (November 1997), 58–78.

Takeuchi Masashi 竹内正志, *Sengo no Nihon oyobi Shina* 戦後の日本及支那 [Postwar Japan and China], Tokyo: Hakubunkan 1919.

Takeuchi Yoshimi 竹内好 and Hashikawa Bunzō 橋川文三, ed., *Kindai Nihon to Chūgoku* 近代日本と中国 [Modern Japan and China], ed., Vol. 1 & 2, Tokyo: Asahi Sensho 1974.

Takeuchi, Yoshimi, "Was bedeutet die Moderne? Der Fall Japan und der Fall China" [What is modernity? The case of China and the case of Japan], *Japan in Asien. Geschichtsdenken und Kulturkritik nach 1945* [Japan in Asia. Historical Thought and Cultural Critique after 1945], ed. and translated by Wolfgang Seifert and Christian Uhl, München: Iudicium 2005, 9–54.

Takeuchi, Yoshimi, "Der japanische Asianismus" [Japanese Asianism], *Japan in Asien. Geschichtsdenken und Kulturkritik nach 1945* [Japan in Asia. Historical Thought and Cultural Critique after 1945], ed. and translated by Wolfgang Seifert and Christian Uhl, München: Iudicium 2005, 121–189.

Takeuchi, Yoshimi, "Profile of Asian Minded Man X: Ōkawa Shūmei", *The Developing Economies*, 7-3 (September 1969), 367–379.

Takeuchi Yoshimi 竹内好, "Ajiashugi no tenbō" アジア主義の展望 [The prospect of Asianism], *Ajiashugi* アジア主義 [Asianism], ed. Takeuchi Yoshimi 竹内好, Tokyo: Chikuma Shobō 1963, 7–63.

Takeuchi Yoshimi 竹内好, "Chūgoku no Kindai to Nihon no Kindai" 中国の近代と日本の近代 [China's Modernity and Japan's Modernity], *Nihon to Ajia* 日本とアジア [Japan and Asia], Tokyo: Chikuma Shobō 1993 (1948), 11–57.

Takeuchi Yoshimi 竹内好, "Hōhō toshite no Ajia" 方法としてのアジア [Asia as method], *Nihon to Ajia* 日本とアジア [Japan and Asia], Tokyo: Chikuma Shobō 1993 (1961), 442–470.

Takeuchi Yoshimi 竹内好, "Waga Ishibashi hakken" 我が石橋発見 [My discovery of Ishibashi], *Takeuchi Yoshimi Zenshū* 竹内好全集 [Complete Works of Takeuchi Yoshimi], Vol. 8, ed. Nunokawa Kakuzaemon 布川角左衛門, Tokyo: Chikuma Shobō 1980, 199–203.

Takeuchi Zensaku 竹内善作, "Meiji makki ni okeru Chū-Nichi kakumei undō no kōryū" 明治末期における中日革命運動の交流 [Exchanges of the Chinese and Japanese Revolutionary Movements in the late Meiji Period], *Chūgoku Kenkyū* 中国研究 [China Research], No. 5 (September 1948), 74–95.

Tanaka Masaaki 田中正明, ed., *Matsui Iwane Taishō no jinchū nisshi*. 松井石根大将の陣中日誌 [General Matsui Iwane's War Diary] Tokyo: Fuyō Shobō 1985.

Tanaka, Stefan, *Japan's Orient: Rendering Pasts into History*, Berkeley: University of California Press 1993.

Tang, Liangli, ed., *China and Japan: Natural Friends, Unnatural Enemies*, Shanghai: China United Press 1941.

Taoka Reiun 田岡嶺雲, "Tō-A no Dai dōmei" 東亜の大同盟 [Great Alliance of East Asia], *Ajia to Kindai Nihon. Han shinryaku no shisō to undō* アジアと近代日本：反侵略の思想と運動 [Asia and modern Japan. Anti-invasionist thought and movement], ed. Itō Teruo 伊東昭雄, Tokyo: Shakai Hyōronsha 1990, 54–59.

Tarui Tōkichi 樽井藤吉, "Dai Tō Gappō Ron" 大東合邦論 [Great Alliance of the East], *Ajiashugi* アジア主義 [Asianism], ed. Takeuchi Yoshimi 竹内好, Tokyo: Chikuma Shobō 1963 (Gendai Nihon Shisō Taikei, 9 現代日本思想大系9), 106–129.

Terasaki Hidenari 寺崎英成, "Shōwa Tennō no dokuhaku hachi jikan: Taiheiyō Sensō no zenbō o kataru" 昭和天皇の独白八時間、太平洋戦争の全貌を語る [The Shōwa Emperor's eight-hour monologue: Telling the full story of the Pacific War], *Bungei Shunjū* 文藝春秋, Vol. 12 (1990), 94–144.

Tipton, Elise K., *The Japanese Police State: the Tokko in Interwar Japan*, Sydney & Honolulu: Allen and Unwin & University of Hawaii Press 1990.

Tōgō Kazuhiko 東郷和彦/Hatano Sumio 波多野澄雄, ed., *Rekishi Mondai Handobukku* 歴史問題ハンドブック [Handbook of History Problems], Tokyo: Iwanami 2015.

Tokutomi Iichirō [Sohō] 徳富猪一郎 [蘇峰], *Shōrai no Nihon* 将来之日本 [Future Japan], Tokyo: Keizai Zasshi Sha 1886.

Tokutomi Sohō 徳富蘇峰, "Jo" 序 [Preface], Gotō Shinpei, *Nihon Bōchō Ron* 日本膨張論 [On Japan's Expansion], Tokyo: Dai Nihon Yūbenkai 大日本雄弁会 1913, 1–9.

Tokutomi Sohō 徳富蘇峰, *Sekai no henkyoku* 世界の変局 [The World in emergency], Tokyo: Minyūsha 1915.

Tokutomi Sohō 徳富蘇峰, *Taishō no seinen to teikoku no zento* 大正の青年と帝国の前途 [The young generation of Taishō and the future of the empire], Tokyo: Minyūsha 1916.

Tokutomi, Sohō, *The Future Japan*, ed. and translated by Vinh Sinh, Edmonton: University of Alberta Press 1989.

Tomioka Kōichirō 富岡幸一郎, *Shin Daitōa Sensō Kōteiron* 新大東亜戦争肯定論 [New Affirmation of the Greater East Asian War], Tokyo: Asuka Shinsha 2006.

Tongū Yutaka 頓宮寛, "Iwayuru Ajia Renmei zehi" 所謂亜細亜連盟是非 [The Pros and Cons of an Asian League], *Shanghai Jiron* 上海時論 [Shanghai Times] 1-8, August 1926, 2–6.

Townsend, Susan C., *Yanaihara Tadao and Japanese colonial policy: redeeming empire*, London: Routledge 2000.

Tōyama Kōsuke 頭山興助, "Kikan 'Yume Dai Ajia' no sōkan wo iwatte" 季刊夢・大アジアの創刊を祝って [Congratulating the start of the quarterly 'Dream – Greater Asia'], *Yume Dai Ajia* 夢・大アジア [Dream – Greater Asia], 2014, No. 1, 14–16.

Toynbee, Arnold J., *The World After the Peace Conference*, London: Oxford University Press 1925 (1920), 44.

Tsuchiya Mitsuyoshi 土屋光芳, "Ō Seiei [Wang Jingwei] no 'Heiwa undō' to 'Dai Ashū shugi'" 汪精衛の平和運動と大亜州主義 [Wang Jingwei's 'Peace Movement' and 'Greater Asianism'], *Seikei Ronsō*, 政經論叢 [Essay Collection in Politics and Economy], 61-2 (1992), 105–140.

Tsurumi Yūsuke 鶴見祐輔, *Seiden Gotō Shinpei. Mantetsu jidai 1906–1908 nen* 正伝後藤新平 満鉄時代: 1906–1908年 [Real Biography of Gotō Shinpei, the times at the Manchurian Railway Company, 1906–1908], Tokyo: Fujiwara Shoten 2005.

Tsurumi, Yusuke [Tsurumi Yūsuke], *Present Day Japan*. New York: Columbia University Press 1926.

Uchida Rōan 内田魯庵, "Gakujutsuteki Han Ajiashugi" 学術的汎アジア主義 [Academic Pan-Asianism], *Taiyō* 太陽 [The Sun], 23-14 (1 Dec 1917), 65–75.

Uhl, Christian, *Wer war Takeuchi Yoshimis Lu Xun? Ein Annäherungsversuch an ein Monument der japanischen Sinologie* [Who was Takeuchi Yoshimi's Lu Xun? An Attempt at Approaching a Monument of Japanese Sinology], München: Iudicum 2003.

Uhl, Christian, "Takeuchi Yoshimi: 'Japan's Asianism', 1963", *Pan-Asianism: A Documentary History 1860–2010*, Vol. 2, ed. Sven Saaler and Christopher W.A. Szpilman, Boulder: Rowman & Littlefield 2011, 317–326.

Ukita Kazutami 浮田和民, "Shin Ajiashugi. Tōyō Monrōshugi no shin kaishaku" 新アジア主義、東洋モンロー主義の新解釈 [New Asianism. A new interpretation of Asian Monroeism], *Taiyō* 太陽 [The Sun], 24-9 (September 1918), 2–17.

Usher, Roland G., *Pan-Americanism. A Forecast of the inevitable clash between the United States and Europe's Victor*, New York: The Century 1915.

Vollmer, Klaus, "The Construction of 'Self' and Western and Asian 'Others' in Contemporary Japanese Civic and Ethics Textbooks", *Designing history in East Asian textbooks: identity politics and transnational aspirations*, ed. Gotelind Müller, London: Routledge 2011, 60–84.

Wafula, Richard, "Language and Politics in East African Swahili Prose: Intertextuality in Kezilahabi's Dunia Uwanja Wa Fujo 'The World, A Playground of Chaos'", *Surviving through obliqueness: language of politics in emerging democracies*, ed. Samuel Gyasi Obeng & Beverly Hartford, Hauppauge: Nova 2002, 19–29.

Wakamiya Unosuke 若宮卯之助, "Dai Ajiashugi wa nan zo ya" 大亜細亜主義は何ぞや [What is Greater Asianism?], *Chūō Kōron* 中央公論 [Central Review], 32-4 (April 1917), 1–14.

Wang Hui 汪晖, "Yazhou Xiangxiang de puxi" 亚洲想象的谱系 [The genealogy of Imagining Asia], *Shijie* 视界 [Horizons] (8) 2002.

Wang, Hui, "The politics of imagining Asia. A genealogical analysis", *The Inter-Asia cultural studies reader*, ed. Kuan-Hsing Chen and Chua Beng Huat, London: Routledge 2007 (2005), 66–102.

Wang, Jingwei, "Foreword", *China and Japan. Natural Friends, unnatural enemies*, ed. Tang Liangli, Shanghai: China United Press 1941, ix–x.

Wang Jingwei 汪精衛, "Minzu zhuyi yu Da Yazhou zhuyi" 民族主義與大亞洲主義 [Nationalism and Greater Asianism], *Da Yazhou zhuyi* 大亞洲主義 [Greater Asianism], 1-4 (November 1940), 1–5.

Wang Ping 王屏, *Jindai Riben de Yaxiya zhuyi* 近代日本的亚细亚主义 [Modern Japanese Asianism]. Beijing: Shangwu Yinshuguan 2004.

Wang Xiangyuan 王向远, "Cong 'he bang', 'yi ti' dao 'da yaxiya zhuyi': Jindai Riben qinhua lilun de yi zhong xingtai" 从"合邦"、"一体"到"大亚细亚主义"— 近代日本侵华理论的一种形态 [From 'merged states', 'an integral whole' to 'Greater Asianism': A theoretical form for Japanese invasion of China in modern times], *Huaqiao Daxue Xuebao* 华侨大学学报 [Bulletin of Huaqiao University], February 2005, 77–84.

Wang Yi 王毅, "Sikao Ershiyi shiji de Xin Yazhou zhuyi" 思考二十一世纪的新亚洲主义 [Considering Neo-Asianism in the twenty-first century], *Waijiao Pinglun* 外交评论 [Foreign Affairs Review], June 2006, No. 89, 6–10.

Watanabe Kōki 渡辺洪基, "Kō A Kai sōritsu taikai ni okeru enzetsu" 興亜会創立大会における演説 [Speech to the great founding assembly of the Kō A Kai] (1880), *Ajia to Kindai Nihon: han shinryaku no shisō to undō* アジアと近代日本: 反侵略の思想と運動 [Asia and modern Japan: Anti-invasionist thought and Movement], ed. Itō Teruo 伊東昭雄, Tokyo: Shakai Hyōronsha 1990, 20–22.

Weber, Torsten, "Remembering or overcoming the past? 'History politics', Asian identity, and visions of an East Asian Community", *Asian Regional Integration Review*, ed. Tsuneo Akaha, Tokyo: Waseda University 2011, 39–55.

Weber, Torsten, "Nanjing's Greater Asianism: Wang Jingwei and Zhou Huaren, 1940", *Pan-Asianism: A Documentary History 1860–2010*, Vol. 2, ed. Sven Saaler and Christopher W.A. Szpilman, Boulder: Rowman & Littlefield 2011, 209–219.

Weber, Torsten, "The Greater Asia Association and Matsui Iwane, 1933", *Pan-Asianism: A Documentary History 1860–2010*, Vol. 2, ed. Sven Saaler and Christopher W.A. Szpilman, Boulder: Rowman & Littlefield 2011, 137–147.

Weber, Torsten, "Wang Yi: 'Neo-Asianism' in 21st Century China", *Pan-Asianism: A Documentary History 1860–2010*, Vol. 2, ed. Sven Saaler and Christopher W.A. Szpilman, Boulder: Rowman & Littlefield 2011, 359–370.

Weber, Torsten, "'Unter dem Banner des Asianismus': Transnationale Dimensionen des japanischen Asianismus-Diskurses der Taishō-Zeit (1912–26)" ['Under the banner of Asianism': transnational dimensions of Japanese Asianism discourse in the Taishō period], *Comparativ*, 18–6 (2008), 34–52.

Weigelin-Schwiedrzik, Susanne, "Ist Ostasien eine europäische Erfindung? Anmerkungen zu einem Artikel von Wang Hui" [Is East Asia a European invention? Notes on an article be Wang Hui], *Ostasien im 20. Jahrhundert. Geschichte und Gesellschaft* [East Asia in the 20th Century. History and Society], ed. Sepp Linhart and Susanne Weigelin-Schwiedrzik, Wien: Promedia Verlag 2007, 9–21.

Wells, Audrey, *The political thought of Sun Yat-Sen: development and impact*, New York: Palgrave 2001.

Wilbur, C. Martin, "The Nationalist Revolution: from Canton to Nanking, 1923–28", *The Cambridge History of China, Vol. 12: Republican China, 1912–1949, Part 1*, ed. John K. Fairbank, Cambridge: Cambridge University Press 1983, 527–720.

Yabuta Kenichirō 藪田謙一郎, "Kenkyū nōto: Miyazaki Tōten no 'Ajiashugi' to Daiichiji Sekai Taisen go no Sekai shichō" 研究ノート、宮崎滔天のアジア主義と第一次世界大戦後の世界思潮 [Research note: Miyazaki Tōten's 'Asianism' and ideas of a new world order after the First World War], *Dōshisha hōgaku* 同志社法學 [Doshisha law review], 48-1 (1996), 277–377.

Yamada Bukichi 山田武吉, "Nihonshugi to Ajiashugi" 日本主義とアジア主義 [Japanism and Asianism], *Nihon oyobi Nihonjin* 日本及日本人 [Japan and the Japanese], May 1933, 11–16.

Yamada Fuhō 山田芙峰, "Kōdō to Ōdō no hikari o hanate" 皇道と王道の光を放て [Having set free the rays of the Imperial and Kingly Ways], *Nihon oyobi Nihonjin* 日本及日本人 [Japan and the Japanese], 259 (October 1932), 21–22.

Yamada Fuhō 山田芙峰, "Nihon chūshin no Ajiashugi" 日本中心のアジア主義 [Japan-centrist Asianism], *Nihon oyobi Nihonjin* 日本及日本人 [Japan and the Japanese], 258 (October 1932), 22–23.
Yamamoto Hideo 山本秀夫, *Tachibana Shiraki to Chūgoku* 橘樸と中国 [Tachibana Shiraki and China], Tokyo: Keisō Shobō 1990.
Yamamoto, Hideo, "Profile of Asian Minded Man III: Shiraki Tachibana", *The Developing Economies*, 4–3 (September 1966), 381–383.
Yamamuro Shin'ichi 山室信一, *Kimera: Manshūkoku no shōzō* キメラ：満洲国の肖像 [Chimera: A Portrait of Manchukuo], Tokyo: Chūō Kōronsha 1993.
Yamamuro Shin'ichi 山室信一, *Shisō Kadai toshite no Ajia* 思想課題としてのアジア [Asia as a matter of thought] Tokyo: Iwanami Shoten 2001.
Yamamuro, Shin'ichi, *Manchuria under Japanese dominion*, translated by Joshua A. Fogel, Philadelphia: University of Pennsylvania Press 2006.
Yamamuro Shin'ichi 山室信一, "Daiichiji Sekai Taisen: Shiten toshite no jūdaisei" 第一次世界大戦、始点としての重大性 [The First World War: Its significance as a starting point], *Asahi Shinbun* 朝日新聞, 24 March 2008, 13.
Yamanouchi Masayuki 山内昌之, "Nēshon to wa nani ka?" ネーションとは何か [What is the nation?], *Minzoku, Kokka, Esunishiti* 民族・国家・エスニシティ [Nation, State, Ethnicity], ed. Inoue Shun 井上俊et al., Tokyo: Iwanami Shoten 1996.
Yasukawa Junosuke 安川寿之輔, *Fukuzawa Yukichi no Ajia ninshiki. Nihon kindai shizou o toraekaesu* 福沢諭吉のアジア認識：日本近代史像をとらえ返す [Fukuzawa Yukichi's Asia consciousness. Responding to the image of modern Japan's history], Tokyo: Kōbunken 2000.
Ye Chucang 葉楚傖, "Da Yaxiya zhuyi lun" 大亞細亞主義論 [On Greater Asianism], *Minli Bao* 民立報 [Independent People's Paper], 15 March 1913, 3.
Yin Rugeng 殷汝耕, "Dai Ajiashugi wa nan zo ya" 大亜細亜主義は何ぞや [What is Greater Asianism?], *Nihon oyobi Nihonjin* 日本及日本人 [Japan and the Japanese] 58-5 (October 1924), 5–16.
Yin Weilian 印维廉, "Yaxiya Minzu yundong zhi jinzhan" 亞細亞民族之進展 [The progress of the Asian peoples movement], *Xin Yaxiya* 新亞細亞 [New Asia], 1-1 (October 1930), 91–97.
Yonehara Ken 米原謙, *Tokutomi Sohō. Nihon Nashonarizumu no Kiseki* 徳富蘇峰．日本ナショナリズムの軌跡 [Tokutomi Sohō. Tracks of Japanese Nationalism], Tokyo: Chūō Kōron Shinsha 2003.
Yonetani Masafumi 米谷匡史, *Ajia/Nihon* アジア/日本 [Asia/Japan], Tokyo: Iwanami Shoten 2006.
Yoshino Sakuzō 吉野作造, "Jinshuteki sabetsu teppai undōsha ni atau" 人種的差別撤廃運動者に与ふ [To the activists for the abolition of racial discrimination], *Chūō Kōron* 中央公論 [Central Review], March 1919.

Yoshino Sakuzō 吉野作造, "Nichi-Ro kyōyaku to Shina no saigi" 日露協約と支那の猜疑 [Japanese-Russo Agreement and Chinese suspicions], *Shinjin* 新人 [New Man], 17-8 (1 August 1916), 5–7.

Yoshino Sakuzō 吉野作造, "Wagakuni no Tōhō keiei ni kansuru sandai mondai" 我国の東方経営に関する三大問題 [Three paramount problems our country is facing regarding the management of the East], *Tōhō Jiron* 東方時論 [Eastern Review], 3-1 (January 1918), 42–68.

Young, Louise, *Japan's total empire: Manchuria and the culture of wartime imperialism*, Berkeley: University of California Press 1998.

Yu Jingyuan 于静远, "Dai Ajiashugi to sono jissen" 大亜細亜主義とその実践 [Greater Asianism and its practice], *Manshūkoku to Kyōwakai* 満洲国と協和会 [Manchukuo and the Concordia Association], ed. Koyama Sadatomo 小山貞知, Dalian: Manshū Hyōronsha 1935, 135–138.

Yu Xingwei 于兴卫, "Renqing Riben 'Da Yazhou zhuyi' de Junguo zhuyi shizhi" 认清日本"大亚细亚主义"的军国主义实质 [Recognizing the militaristic essence of Japan's 'Greater Asianism'], *Renmin Ribao* 人民日报, 25 August 2015.

Zachmann, Urs Matthias, "Blowing Up a Double Portrait in Black and White: The Concept of Asia in the Writings of Fukuzawa Yukichi and Okakura Tenshin", *Positions: East Asia Cultures Critique*, 15-2 (Fall 2007), 345–368.

Zachmann, Urs Matthias, *China and Japan in the Late Meiji Period. China Policy and the Japanese Discourse on National Identity, 1895–1904*, London: Routledge 2009.

Zachmann, Urs Matthias, "The Foundation Manifesto of the Kōakai (Raising Asia Society) and the Ajia Kyōkai (Asia Association), 1880–1883", *Pan-Asianism: A Documentary History 1860–2010*, Vol. 1, ed. Sven Saaler and C.W.A. Szpilman, Boulder: Rowman & Littlefield, 2011, 53–60.

Zachmann, Urs Matthias, "The Foundation Manifesto of the Tōa Dobunkai (East Asian Common Culture Society), 1898", *Pan-Asianism: A Documentary History 1860–2010*, Vol. 1, ed. Sven Saaler and C.W.A. Szpilman, Boulder: Rowman & Littlefield, 2011, 115–120.

Zarrow, Peter, *China in war and revolution, 1895–1949*, London & New York: Routledge 2005.

Zhang Yiguo 章益国, "Yazhou kongjiangan de fangfa lun yiyi" 亚洲空间感的方法论意义 [The significance of the methodology of a spatial sentiment of Asia], *Shanghai Caijing Daxue Xuebao* 上海财经大学学报 [Journal of Shanghai University of Finance and Economics], Vol. 10, No. 1 (February 2008), 15–21.

Zhang Yufa 張玉法, *Qingji de geming tuanti* 清季的革命團體 [Revolutionary groups in the Qing period], Taibei: Zhongyang Yanjiuyuan Jindaishi Yanjiusuo 1992 (2nd edition).

Zhou Bin 周斌, "Yaxiya Minzu Huiyi yu Zhongguo de fandui yundong" 亚细亚民族会议与中国的反对运动 [The Asian Peoples' Congress and the Chinese opposition movement], *Kang-Ri Zhanzheng Yanjiu* 抗日战争研究 [Studies of China's War of Resistance against Japan], 2006 (3), 128–159.

Zhou Huaren 周化人, "Da Yazhou zhuyi yu Sanmin Zhuyi" 大亞洲主義與三民主義 [Greater Asianism and the Three People's Principles], *Da Yazhou zhuyi* 大亞洲主義 [Greater Asianism], 1-2 (September 1940), 11–15.

Zhou Huaren 周化人, "Dai Ajiashugi to Sanmin shugi" 大亜細亜主義と三民主義 [Greater Asianism and the Three People's Principles], *Dai Ajiashugi* 大亜細亜主義 [Greater Asianism], No. 92 (December 1940), 16–19.

Zhou Huaren 周化人, "Sanmin shugi to Dai Ajiashugi" 三民主義と大亜細亜主義 [The Three People's Principles and Greater Asianism], *Kokusai Bunka Kyōkai Kaihō* 國際文化協會會報 [Bulletin of the International Culture Association], No. 126 (December 1940), 137–148.

Zöllner, Reinhard, "Alternative Regionalkonzepte in Ostasien" [Alternative regional concepts in East Asia], *Leitbild Europa? Europabilder und ihre Wirkungen in der Neuzeit* [Europe as Model? Views of Europe and their impact in modern times], ed. Jürgen Elvert and Jürgen Nielsen-Sikora, Wien: Franz Steiner 2009, 295–303.

Index

A
Afghanistan, 78, 111, 118, 236, 240, 262n39
Africa, vii, 76, 138, 185, 193, 332
aite to sezu, 280
Aizawa Incident (1935), 298
Aizawa Saburō, 298, 339
Aizawa Seishisai, 64, 339
Ajia (journal), 74, 75
Ajia kaiki (return to Asia), 41, 341
Ajia Kyōkai, 69
Ajia Monrōshugi. *See* Asian Monroe Doctrine
Ajia Renmei. *See* Asian League
Alaska, 138
All Asia Association, 165n144, 214n1, 232, 234, 241, 249, 253, 260n21, 345
All Germanism. *See* Pan-Germanism
All Slavism. *See* Pan-Slavism
American Monroeism. *See* Monroe Doctrine (US)
Amō Declaration (*Amō Seimei*), 278, 287, 310n33, 341
Amō Eiji, 310n33, 339
Anti-Asianism, 40, 50, 51, 66, 83, 96n11, 117–119, 121, 135, 136, 149, 156n33, 181, 190, 241, 244–246, 255, 267, 287, 301, 303, 304
Anti-foreignism (*jōi*), 41, 343
Anti-Westernism, xii, 12, 16, 37, 64, 87, 91, 109, 117, 119, 122, 131, 133, 140, 168, 176, 180, 199, 209, 222n94, 232, 233, 242, 244, 252, 255, 283, 295, 319, 323
Aoki Kazuo, 287, 312n61, 339
April 16th Incident (1929), 268
Arao Sei, 80, 298, 339
Ariyoshi Akira, 152
Asahi Shinbun (newspaper), 78, 91, 104n97, 130, 208, 330
ASEAN, 331
Asia Development Board (*Kō A In*), 70, 291, 343
'Asia for the Asians', 39, 40, 80, 109, 120, 122, 123, 128, 171, 213, 242, 305, 322
'Asia for the Japanese', 123

392 INDEX

Asian Exclusion League, 179
Asianism *passim*
  and canons, xiii, 22, 31, 32, 44, 45, 47–49, 320
  'Classical' Asianism, 19–20, 324, 325
  and dichotomies, vii, 22, 31, 42, 43, 49, 51, 320
  as discourse, viii–ix, xi–xiii, 1–10, 12–13, 15–17, 20–22, 34, 37–38, 46–49
  in encyclopedia, 35, 37, 39–43, 45–46, 56n13
  "from above", 2, 22, 23n5, 53, 70, 230, 303, 306, 322
  "from below", 2, 22, 23n5, 170, 230, 257, 322, 331
  and "great thinkers", 6, 14, 46, 48, 320
  as 'inclination', 14, 27n40, 32, 34, 46, 54, 343
  as invasion, 14–16, 19, 32–33, 35, 36, 42–44, 52–54, 89, 123, 125, 127, 145, 169, 214n5, 238, 324, 328, 344
  as practice, 2, 4–6, 18, 40, 52, 82, 186, 257, 287, 302, 303
  as 'principle of Asia', 71, 222n88, 319, 320
  'self-acclaimed', 15, 42, 53
  as solidarity, 3, 4, 14–17, 19, 32, 42–44, 52–54, 85, 112, 123, 130–132, 169, 175, 181, 187, 214n5, 231, 259n12, 267, 274, 289, 303, 320, 323, 329–332, 344
  as 'thought', 5, 14, 15, 18–20, 31–35, 40–41, 44, 47–48, 74, 93, 107, 110, 131, 135–136, 153, 169, 174, 192, 255, 257, 288, 290, 320, 323

Asianist moments, 21–22, 169, 230, 257, 319, 320
Asian League, 39, 40, 109, 111, 112, 115, 129, 171, 175, 176, 182, 188, 189, 194, 195, 199, 213, 232, 235, 236, 241, 244, 246, 248, 252, 256, 257, 263n49, 295, 296, 298, 303
Asian Monroe Doctrine, 78, 83, 84, 94, 109, 110, 118, 121–125, 137–141, 144, 147, 148, 153, 251, 258n2, 310n33, 341, 346
Asian values, 20, 41, 329
Asiatic Asia (journal), 295, 300
Asiatic Humanitarian Brotherhood, 69–70
Atami, 300
Attila, 141, 148
Austria, 142, 163n119, 298
Aydin, Cemil, xii, 290, 306

B

Badao. *See* Rule of Might
Baik Young-seo, 331–332
Balkan, 85
Ball, Terence, 9, 10, 25n17, 230
Bao Guancheng, 303–304
Beasley, William G., 20–21, 30n69
'Befriending the far away to attack the nearby', 177, 342
Begriffsgeschichte. *See* Conceptual History
Beifa (Northern Expedition), 240, 269, 345
Beijing, 145, 149, 150, 198, 199, 234, 253, 298, 337
Berlin, 249
Blood Pledge Corps (*Ketsumeidan*), 268, 343
Bolshevism, 176, 244, 252

Bose, Rash Behari, 47, 110, 155n13, 191, 196, 222n81, 236, 240, 241, 244, 290, 308n13
Bose, Subhas Chandra, 294
Bowman, Isaiah, 108, 110
Britain, 76, 83, 111–112, 116, 128, 167, 183, 189, 202, 209, 225n119, 242. *See also* England
Buddhism, 93, 111–112, 126, 156n33, 184, 187, 192, 220n66, 304
Bulgaria, 85
Burma (Myanmar), 78, 161n95

C

Cai Xiaobai, 263n55, 340
California, 90–91, 103n87, 104n88, 105n100, 179, 181, 218n43
California Alien Land Law (1913), 90, 103n87, 179
Canons, 6, 22, 31, 45–46, 48–49, 320
 Democratic critique, 6, 45, 48–49
 Methodological critique, 45–46, 49
Canton, 86, 198
Capitalism, 113, 128, 289, 305, 313, 324, 328, 330
Caucasian, 51, 179, 185, 220n61
Chadourne, Marc, 294–295
Chen Duxiu, 171–172, 175–176
Chen Gongbo, 312n56, 340
Chen Kuan-Hsing (Chen Guangxing), 327, 330
Chiang Kai-shek (Jiang Jieshi), 145, 240, 267–270, 272, 275–276, 279–281, 284, 299, 310n41
'China Problem' (*Shina mondai*), 84, 110
Chinese Communist Party (CCP), 145, 171, 270, 280, 310n41, 328
Chinese Exclusion Act (1882), 179

Chinese Revolution (1911), 78–80, 144, 280
Chirol, Valentine, 3, 89–94, 208
Chongqing, 272, 280–281
Christianity, xi, 51, 73, 117, 156n27
Christian Youth Association, 87
Chūō Kōron (journal), 132
Civilization, 20, 37, 41, 50, 65–66, 74, 83, 87–88, 92, 94, 109, 116–117, 122, 127–128, 131, 133, 139, 141, 146, 150, 160n83, 168, 175, 186, 196–197, 202–204, 208, 211, 213, 217n36, 232–233, 236, 293, 303, 319, 324, 330
Cohen, Paul A., 207, 225n126
Concepts, xi–xiii, 1–5, 7–10, 14, 71, 74, 230, 305–306
 and conceptions, 7, 9, 16, 25n14, 107, 132, 190, 230, 244, 246, 319, 321
 contestable concepts, 8, 9, 26n19
 contested concepts, 9, 26n19
 functions of concepts, 10, 153, 230, 257, 319, 322
 political concepts, 3, 5, 9–10, 24n8, 26n19, 38, 44, 51, 55n3, 63, 65, 153, 162n104, 167, 174, 188, 192, 196, 210, 213, 230
 universal concepts, 33–34
Conceptual contest, 53, 320
Conceptual history, 6–7, 46, 53, 320
Confucianism, 20, 41, 50–51, 127, 184, 187, 192, 210, 220n66, 239, 270, 274, 306, 325, 328–331, 336n43
Coolidge, Calvin, 179
Coudenhove-Kalergi, Richard, 250–253, 255, 264n67, 298, 325
Council on East Asian Community (*Higashi Ajia Kyōdōtai Hyōgikai*), 326, 333n14

Council on Foreign Relations, 108
Cuong De, 290

D

Da Dongya (journal), 284
Dai Ajia Kyōkai. See Greater Asia Association
Dai Ajiashugi (journal), 291, 293–295, 297, 312n56, 338
Daidō danketsu, 183, 258n6
Dai Jitao, 88–89, 110, 145, 150–151, 200–202, 270–272, 282, 338
Daisan Teikoku (journal), 83–84
Das, Taraknath, 110
Datsu A (Leaving/Dissociating from Asia), 17, 40, 44, 49–52, 66–67, 77, 96n11, 96n13, 162n104, 197, 342
Da Yaxiya zhuyi lun (1912 article/'pamphlet'), 2, 79, 101n59, 101n64, 112, 321
Da Ya Zazhi/The Asiatic Review (journal), 337
Da Yazhou Zhuyi (journal), 283, 312n56
Da Yazhou Zhuyi yu Dongya Lianmeng (journal), 283
Democracy, xi, 25n17, 26n19, 33–35, 41, 90, 117, 147, 150, 285
Democratic Party of Japan (DPJ), 325
Dictionaries, 33, 35, 37–38, 40, 45, 72, 174–175, 193
Dirlik, Arif, 11–12
Discourse
  and conceptual history, 7–10
  defined, 4–5, 7–8
Dōbun dōshu. See same script, same race
Doihara Kenji, 277, 309n31, 339
Dongfang wenming. See Eastern civilization
Dongfang Zazhi (journal), 137, 145, 149–150

Dongfang zhuyi. See Orientalism
Dongya Gongtongti. See East Asian Community
Dongya Lianmeng. See East Asian League
Dönhoff, Marion Gräfin, 207
Dōshisha University, 118, 136
Dōshu dōkon (same race, same roots), 125, 342
Dōshū dōshu (same continent, same race), 173, 342
Duara, Prasenjit, 269, 274, 301, 322, 324
Dutch Studies. See *rangaku*
Du Yaquan, 150, 341

E

East Asian Community, 22, 230, 255, 265n87, 325–327, 330, 342, 345
East Asian League, 152, 170, 254, 283, 312n56
Eastern civilization, 128, 146, 324, 345
Ebina Danjō, 117, 156n27, 339
Endō Ryūkichi, 71–72
England, 128, 163n119
Esperanto, 238–239
Eurasia, 76
'Euro-Americanism', 5, 73–74, 116
'Euro-America', 13, 16, 18, 35, 39, 43–44, 50, 74, 85, 87, 91, 113, 127, 138, 153, 155n12, 176, 189, 208, 213, 216n24, 238, 244–245, 302, 305, 324, 344
Europeanism, 74, 116, 193

F

Far East Asian Republic (*Kyokutō Ajia Renpō*), 249, 251–252, 254, 343
Fascism, 23n5, 28n41, 35, 43, 47, 52, 56n18, 109, 226n137, 327

Fazheng Xuebao (journal), 150
Feng Yuxiang, 198, 341
Foucault, Michel, 8
France, 83, 190, 242, 260n21, 298
Fremdheitserlebnis, 142, 216n24
Fujii, Shōzō, 43
Fukuchi Ōchi (Gen'ichirō), 71, 98n35, 339
Fukuoka, 3, 209
Fukuzawa Yukichi, 49, 50, 66–67, 69, 77, 96n11, 96n13, 99n35, 162n104, 221n72
Furuhata Mototarō, 259n11, 339
Furuya Tetsuo, 16–17, 29n51, 84, 219n52
Fuse Tatsuji, 188, 221n68

G
Gaikō Jihō (journal), 157n33, 298
Gallie, W. B., 8–9, 26n19
Gao, Yuan, 150–151
Gaus, Gerald F., 9
Geneva, 40, 118, 172, 236, 245, 252, 298
Genghis Khan, 76, 141, 175
Gentlemen's Agreement (1907/08), 103n87, 181
Genyōsha (Dark Ocean Society), 3, 28n41, 39, 47, 53, 56n12, 331, 342
Germany, 35, 51, 56n18, 75, 82, 110, 124, 142, 150, 163n119, 180, 209, 242
Ge Zhaoguang, 12, 341
Globalization, 323–324, 331
Gotō Shinpei, 81–83, 89, 101n60, 101n64, 116, 118, 121–122, 125, 132, 142, 146, 157n42, 163n119, 200, 219n51, 300
Gozoku Kyōwa (harmonious cooperation of five races). See *wuzu xiehe*

Gozoku Kyōwa (Republic of Five Races). See *wuzu gonghe*
Greater Asia Association, 2, 259n14, 269, 289–297, 300, 302, 312n56, 314n74, 315n88, 322, 338, 341
Greater East Asia Conference (*Dai Tōa Kaigi*), 231, 257, 342
Greater East Asia Joint Declaration (1943), 43
Greater East Asia Ministry (*Dai Tōa Shō*), 287, 342
Greater East Asian Co-Prosperity Sphere (*Dai Tōa Kyōeiken*), 19, 35, 43, 231, 255–256, 327, 328, 342
'Greater East Asian War' (*Dai Tōa Sensō*), 55n8, 181, 312n56
Greater Japanism, 125, 145, 151, 157n42, 217n37
Greater Japan Raise Asia Alliance (*Dai Nihon Kōa Dōmei*), 297, 342
Great Kantō Earthquake (1923), 199
Greece, 85
Guangdong (province), 275, 280, 297
Guomindang (GMD), 145, 192, 199, 202, 235, 240, 268–269, 273, 280, 322
Gushima Kanesaburō, 39–40, 56n18

H
Hadō. See Rule of Might
Hakka. See White Peril
Hakkō ichiu (imperial rule over the eight corners of the earth), 328, 342
Hakuai (philanthrophy/fraternity), 73, 251, 342
Hakujin. See Whites
Han (ethnic group), 12, 65, 274, 301
Han Ajia Gakkai (Pan-Asia Study Society), 289, 338

Hanjian (traitor), 192, 281, 345
Hankou, 298
Hanoi, 281
Harada Katsumasa, 14–15
Hara Fujirō, 130
Hasegawa Nyozekan, 287, 313n63
Hashikawa Bunzō, 29n49, 60, 97n16
Hashimoto Sanai, 41, 339
Hatoyama Yukio, 325
Hatsuse Ryūhei, 42, 44, 58n35
Hayashi Fusao, 60n59
Hegemony, xi–xiii, 1, 2, 4, 8, 12, 26n29, 37–38, 53, 113, 175, 185, 193, 204, 210, 251, 269, 274, 289, 302, 307, 319–320, 323, 326, 329
He Ruzhang, 69, 341
Heywood, Andrew, 9, 26n24
Higashi Ajia Kyōdōtai. See East Asian Community
Hiraishi Naoaki, 17
Hirakawa Hitoshi, 253
Hirano Ken'ichirō, 41
Hirano Kuniomi, 64, 339
Hirano Yoshitarō, 53, 339
Hirota Kōki, 277, 287, 290, 314n74, 339
Historical reconciliation, xii, 323, 325–327, 332
Historical revisionism, xii, 49, 60n59, 291, 323, 327–328, 334n22
History problems, 22, 326–327, 334n22
Hokkaidō, 66
Honda Toshiaki, 41, 339
Hong Kong, 198, 242, 277, 281, 336n40
Horii Kōichirō, 41–42
Horinouchi Tsuneo, 304
Horiuchi Bunjirō, 124–125
Hōsei University, 280, 291
Hoston, Germaine A., 148
Hotta, Eri, xii, 24n7, 307n4

Huang Chun-chieh, 330
Huang Gongsu, 240, 259n16, 337
Huang Xing, 143–144
Hughes, William Morris, 178
Hu Hanmin, 270, 271, 275–279, 288, 309n25
Hu Jintao, 325, 341
Humanitarianism, 117, 135, 204, 284
Hyōgo (prefecture), 249

I
Ibuka Hikosaburō, 79–80, 100n55, 339
Imaoka Jūichirō, 294, 314n74
Imazato Juntarō, 121, 234, 240, 241, 244–246, 253, 259n12, 262n40, 337
Immigration Act of 1924, 179–181, 185, 188, 196, 199, 200, 204
Immigration legislation, 22, 38, 105n100, 111, 181, 182, 184, 187–188, 203, 213, 230, 231, 249, 251
Imperialism, xii, 1, 5, 10, 15, 18–19, 28n41, 36, 38, 43, 44, 49–50, 52–54, 60n59, 65, 68, 70, 76, 82, 84, 87, 107, 109, 121–125, 131–132, 135–136, 139, 143, 146–147, 151, 167, 171–172, 176, 178, 190, 208–209, 230–231, 234–235, 238, 242, 251, 255, 257, 272–273, 276, 278, 284, 287–288, 293–294, 304–306, 320–323, 327–328
Imperial Rescript on Education (1890), 73, 343
Imperial Way (*kōdō*), 301, 303, 305–306
India, 6, 15–16, 47, 69, 85, 110, 112, 118, 128–129, 131, 134, 139, 161n95, 171, 175, 182–184, 186–187, 191, 193–196,

220n60, 222n94, 235–236, 239–240, 242, 245, 247–248, 253–254, 263n55, 290, 294, 302, 305, 308n13
Inoue Kiyoshi, 15, 339
Interdependency, 42, 68, 70, 83, 152, 243, 344. *See also shinshi hosha*
International Academic Society for Asian Community, 330–331
Internationalism, 1, 3, 5–6, 15, 17, 70, 107, 110, 112, 114, 120, 136, 148, 169, 209, 210, 213, 214n6, 257, 271, 277, 287, 309n28, 320
International Military Tribunal for the Far East (Tokyo Trial), 291, 299, 309n31
Inukai Tsuyoshi, 75, 183, 268, 288, 339
Iran, 290
Iriye, Akira, 169
Ishibashi Tanzan, 59n49, 217n37
Ishida Tomoji, 84, 339
Ishihara Shintarō, 20, 30n65, 339
Ishiwara Kanji, 210
Islam, 112, 211
Isobe Hisashi, 130
Itagaki Taisuke, 172
Itō Hirobumi, 101n64
Itō Teruo, 16
Iwakura Mission, 69, 99n35
Iwasaki Isao, 234, 337

J

Jansen, Marius B., 86, 183, 198, 279
Japan Conference (*Nippon Kaigi*), 328
Japanese Communist Party, 268
Japanism, 5, 73–74, 113, 125, 134, 145, 147, 157n42, 188, 217n37, 244, 269, 277, 301, 303–304, 322
Jeong Yeon-kyu, 221n78, 341

Jiangxi (province), 199
Jin Kemin, 263n55, 341
Jinshuteki Sabetsu Teppai Kisei Taikai. See Taikai
Jiyū Minken Undō (Movement for Freedom and Civil Rights), 14, 48, 69, 214n1, 343
Jiyūtō (party), 67, 172
Joffe, Adolf, 205
Johnson–Reed Act (1924). *See* Immigration Act of 1924

K

Kagami, Mitsuyuki, 41–42
Ka-I (thought), 41, 343
Kaizō (journal), 207, 224n112, 225n128, 312n56
Kajima Morinosuke. *See* Nagatomi Morinosuke
Kamiizumi Tokuya, 125
Kaneko Kentarō, 92, 340
Kang Youwei, 3, 66, 75, 144, 341
Kan Naoto, 336n42
Karl, Rebecca E., 65
Katō Takaaki, 188
Katsu Kaishū, 64, 69, 184, 340
Katsurajima Nobuhiro, 41, 44
Kawai Eijirō, 288, 313n65
Kawashima Shin, 66, 101n57, 275
Kayahara Kazan, 84, 340
Kenseikai (party), 188, 209
Kiautschou (Jiaozhou), 75
Kiki ishiki (consciousness of crisis), 41, 65–66, 124, 343
Kingly Way. *See* Rule of Right
Kishi Nobusuke, 291, 340
Kita Ikki, 28n41, 109
Kō A (Raising Asia), 3, 40, 44, 47, 49–50, 52, 60n59, 67–70, 93, 170, 197, 300, 328, 342
Kō A Kai (Raising Asia Society), 33, 49, 50, 69, 343

Kobe, 3, 22, 36, 38, 42, 145, 197, 203, 206–209, 212, 223n99, 223n103, 270–271, 276, 279, 282, 307n8, 321, 329
Kōbe Shinbun (newspaper), 200
Kodaira Kunio, 305
Kodama Kagai, 130–132, 135, 159n75, 175
Kodera Kenkichi, 16, 29n49, 140–145, 147–149, 155n13, 163n119, 163n122, 163n125, 164n132, 173, 175, 189–190, 216n21, 216n24
Kohn, Hans, 294
Koizumi Jun'ichirō, 325–326, 340
Kōka. See Yellow Peril
Kokugaku (National Learning), 64, 343
Kokuryūkai (Black Dragon Society), 3, 28n41, 39, 48, 56n12, 214n11, 331, 343
Kokutai (national polity), 73, 134, 343
Komazawa University, 118
Kondō Renpei, 92, 340
Konoe Atsumaro, 19, 69–70, 163n119
Konoe Declaration. See New Order in East Asia (1938)
Konoe Fumimaro, 280, 287, 290, 297, 314n74, 340
Korea, 6, 35, 48, 66–67, 73, 78–79, 94, 118, 149, 168, 169, 171–172, 176, 187, 221n78, 235–236, 238, 242, 254, 261n24, 267, 272, 287, 293, 297, 301, 304, 324, 331, 334n17
Koschmann, J. Victor, xii, 9, 230
Koselleck, Reinhart, 7, 10, 25n16
Kōtoku Shūsui, 28n46, 69
Kubota Yoshirō, 75–78, 80, 95, 129
Kumamoto, 73, 136

Kwangju, 268
Kwantung Army (Guandong Army), 267–268, 277, 286, 302

L
Lansing–Ishii Agreement (1917), 110, 180
League for the Promotion of the Abolishment of Racial Discrimination. See *Taikai*
League of Nations, 22, 39–40, 111, 155n12, 169–170, 172, 178, 186–187, 209, 229, 236–237, 244, 252–253, 268, 286–287, 294, 296, 298, 300, 305–306, 310n33, 313n68
Lee Gyeongseog, 123
Lenin, W.I., 108–109
Liang Qichao, 3, 66, 75, 143–144, 341
Liaodong Peninsula, 75
Liberal Democratic Party (LDP), 325–326
Liberal Party. See *Jiyūtō*
Li Dazhao, 16, 36, 42, 47–48, 110, 120, 137, 145, 149, 150–151, 155n13, 164n132, 164n136, 172, 176, 178, 190–191, 238, 286
Li Liejun, 199
Lin Bosheng, 312n56, 341
Liu Shipei, 69, 341
London, 38, 89
Lytton Report, 300

M
Mahan, Alfred Thayer, 3, 89, 94, 104n97, 208
Mahan–Chirol controversy, 3, 89–94, 208

Mainichi Shinbun (newspaper), 172, 177, 206–209, 223n103, 225n123, 225n128
Mainland adventurer (*tairiku rōnin*), 69, 210, 298, 344
Manchukuo, 2, 22, 127, 255, 262n40, 268–269, 287, 290, 293, 300, 303, 305–306, 307n4, 316n100, 328, 343
  Manchukuo Concordia Association, 301, 343
Manchuria, 2, 22, 24n6, 36, 81–82, 125, 127, 200, 210, 240, 267–268, 277, 286–287, 291, 293–294, 296, 298, 300–305, 313n63, 322
  Manchurian Incident (1931), 2, 22, 23n3, 209, 210, 267, 275, 280, 286–287, 293–294, 296, 300, 309n31
Manila, 297
Manshū Hyōron (journal), 210, 294, 313n68
Manzhouguo. *See* Manchukuo
Mao Zedong, 280
March 15th Incident (1928), 268
March First Movement (1919), 169
Marco Polo Bridge Incident (1937), 279
Maruyama Masao, 23n5, 29n49
Matsuda Kōichirō, 65
Matsui Iwane, 267, 277–279, 287, 290–291, 295, 297–300, 310n36, 314n74, 316n95, 338
Matsumoto Saburō, 66
Matsuoka Yōsuke, 313n68, 340
Matsuura Masataka, xiii, 262n40
May 15th Incident (1932), 268, 288
May Fourth Movement (1919), 145, 152, 169, 177
Meiji (era, 1868–1912), 2, 10, 14, 26n28, 31, 36, 41, 47–48, 56n12, 64–66, 70, 77, 114, 137, 160n85, 174, 185, 197, 210, 322, 343
Meiji Constitution (1889), 243
Meiji Emperor, 73
Meiji Restoration (1868), 65, 86, 117, 131, 134, 181, 184, 197, 243
Meiji University, 130
Meishu (leader), 35, 38, 115, 141, 161n92, 168, 184, 194, 253, 300, 305, 325, 331
Militarism, 5, 52, 56n12, 60, 126–127, 145, 147, 150–151, 172, 305, 313n65, 322–324, 327
Minbao (journal), 36, 143, 163n126, 270, 280
Minguo Ribao (newspaper), 207, 225n128
Ministry of Education's General Education Office, 304
Minli Bao (newspaper), 79–80, 83, 94, 101n55, 101n59, 219n51
Minzoku. See race
Minzu. See race
Mito School, 64, 344
Mitsukawa Kametarō, 290, 314n74
Mitter, Rana, 269, 279
Miura Tetsutarō, 217n37
Miyadai Shinji, 323, 333n3
Miyake Setsurei, 74, 99n43, 340
Miyazaki Tōten, 17, 28n41, 47, 129–131, 135, 138, 159n74, 171, 175–178, 217n36
Modernity, 26n29, 51, 108, 109, 233, 239, 329
Modernization, viii, 18, 44, 60n56, 71, 75, 78, 86, 90, 121, 185, 197, 322, 328
Mongolia, 36, 82, 125, 240, 301, 313n63, 328

Monroe Doctrine (US), 77, 80–81, 100n50, 118, 123–124, 126, 138–139, 147, 151, 172, 177, 208, 251–252
Monroe, James, 77
Moscow, 275
Murakawa Kengo, 290, 314n74

N
Nabeyama Sadachika, 288–289, 313n68
Nagai Ryūtarō, 163n119
Nagasaki, 36, 39, 56n18, 98n35, 121, 230, 231, 235–239, 244–246, 249, 254, 255, 257, 259n12, 260n21, 261n23, 263n55, 321, 336n40
Nagata Tetsuzan, 298, 340
Nagatomi Morinosuke, 229, 230, 249–257, 264n64, 264n66, 264n67, 296, 298, 325
Nagoya, 297
Nakagawa Hidenao, 325
Nakamura Shunsaku, 41, 43, 44
Nakano Seigō, 154n12, 209–212, 226n132, 226n134
Nakasone Yasuhiro, 291, 340
Nakatani Takeyo, 290, 291, 295, 297, 314n72, 314n74, 315n83, 338
Nanjing, 2, 192, 240, 267–269, 272, 275, 281, 285, 297–299, 311n51, 312n56, 338, 345
Nanjing Decade, 268, 269
Nanking. *See* Nanjing
Naruse Masao, 155n12, 261n30
Nationalism, 1, 3, 5, 6, 15, 20, 21, 24n12, 28n41, 52, 60n59, 70, 73, 74, 86, 93, 99, 107, 112–122, 131, 136, 139, 146, 148, 149, 161n93, 168, 169, 174, 176, 188, 190, 196, 197, 209, 220n66, 221n70, 224n114, 230, 231, 240, 241, 244, 247, 254, 256, 257, 263n57, 271, 274–277, 279, 284–286, 291, 296, 301, 307, 313n65, 320, 321, 327
Nation state, 17, 23n4, 63, 66, 89, 94, 174, 229, 253, 263n49, 274, 285, 326, 329, 343, 345
Nehru, Jawaharlal, 33
Neo-liberalism, 324
New Order in East Asia (1938), 280, 284, 286, 294
New York Times (newspaper), 39, 92
Nichi–In Kyōkai (Japanese–Indian Association), 134
Nihonjin (journal), 75
Nihon oyobi Nihonjin (journal), 181, 182, 186, 188, 190, 191, 195, 196, 219n50, 231, 301
Ninagawa Arata, 118–121, 156n33, 190, 241–247
Nippon Kaigi. *See* Japan Conference
Nisshin bōeki kenkyūjo (Japan-Qing Trade Research Institute), 80
Nisshin Teikei Ron (Japan-Qing cooperation thesis), 64, 344
Nitobe Inazō, 219n46
Nohara Shirō, 35–37, 40–43, 45, 47, 55n5, 56n10, 56n12, 56n13, 177
Northeast Asian History Foundation, 334n17
Northern Expedition. *See* Beifa
Nyū Ō (enter Europe), 51, 66, 344

O
Ōbei. *See* 'Euro-America'
Occidentalism, 11, 12, 330, 346
Ōdō. *See* Rule of Right
Ogawa Heikichi, 170, 259n11, 340
Ogawa Reikō, 301

Ōi Kentarō, 46, 68, 340
Ōishi Masami, 167, 183–188, 195, 196, 213, 214n1, 219n51, 219n52, 220n66
Okakura Tenshin, 1, 23n2, 28n41, 29n46, 46, 47, 49, 50, 58n45, 171
Ōkashugi (Europeanizationism), 67, 344
Ōkawa Shūmei, 28n41, 28n46, 47, 48, 171, 340
Ōki Enkichi, 170, 340
Okinawa (Ryūkyū), 66, 68, 272
Ōkuma Shigenobu, 92, 178, 183, 216n24, 340
Okumura Teijirō, 73, 340
Opium War, 64, 65, 284
Orientalism, 10–13, 24n8, 27n30, 58n45, 64, 180, 219n47, 320, 324, 330, 345, 346
Osaka, 87, 261n34
Ōsugi Sakae, 69, 100n47, 340
Ōtani Kōzui, 116, 126–128, 132, 147
'Othering', 11, 239
Ōyama Ikuo, 13, 84–86, 112–114, 117, 121, 136, 149
Ozaki Hotsumi, 28n41, 47, 48, 226n137, 340
Ozaki Yukio, 92, 188, 221n68
Ozawa Takao, 185, 220n60
Ōzumi Shōfū, 93–95

P

Pacifism, 135
Pan-Africanism, 20
Pan-Americanism, 74, 100n50, 139, 142, 193, 251, 254, 257, 299
Pan-Anglo movement, 257
Pan-Asian Conferences (1926, 1927), 14, 36, 39, 40, 47, 121, 229–231, 235–245, 247, 254–257, 258n8, 262n39, 262n40, 263n55, 286
Pan-Europe, 193, 249, 298, 325
Pan-Germanism, 21, 33, 93, 113, 115, 193
Pan-Islamism, 33
Pan-ism, 20, 34, 55n6, 81, 142, 147, 165n142
Pan-Serbism, 113
Pan-Slavism, 20, 21, 33, 93, 94, 113, 216n28, 294
Paraguay, 252
Paris, 93, 118
Paris Peace Conference, 22, 38, 107, 109–111, 140, 152, 167, 169, 170, 172, 178, 180, 184, 213, 233, 236. *See also* Versailles
Peking University, 145
People's Daily (newspaper), 19
People's Republic of China (PRC), 15, 324
Persia, 78, 118, 161n95
Philanthropy, 73, 123, 135, 251, 291, 342
Philippines, 75, 126, 139, 244, 302
Pocock, John, 45, 46
Pratap, Mahendra, 240, 261n34
Principle (*shugi/zhuyi*), 1, 3, 5, 9, 15, 24n9, 37, 39, 71–74, 76, 78, 81–83, 95, 107, 121, 129–130, 132, 147, 149, 161n93, 175, 178, 193–195, 271, 273, 285, 319, 320, 322, 332. *See also* Asianism as 'principle of Asia'
Public Security Preservation Law (1925), 268, 341
Puyi, 280, 301, 341

Q

Qing (dynasty, 1644-1912), 64, 65, 86, 192, 280, 324, 344
Qingdao, 124

R

Race, vii, 37–40, 50, 65, 67, 68, 76, 80, 81, 90, 91, 93, 112, 113, 125, 139–142, 167, 168, 171–175, 182, 198, 203, 204, 208, 209, 214n3, 216n24, 220n61, 231, 232, 233, 236, 243, 245, 289, 301, 342, 345
   racial discrimination, 40, 123, 167, 168, 170, 175, 176, 178, 179, 181, 187, 213, 218n43, 231, 232, 236, 245, 259n12, 321
   racial equality proposal (1919), 40, 111, 168–172, 178, 181, 186, 213, 321
Rangaku (Dutch Studies), 41, 64
Red Cross, 118, 119
Reform Movement of 1898, 65, 78
Regionalism, 18, 20, 21, 22, 33, 68, 70, 72, 74, 77, 81, 82, 117, 174, 249, 251, 253, 255, 256, 258n4, 295, 296, 299, 313n63, 319, 323, 324, 327
   regional integration, 21, 324–327, 329, 332
   regionalization, 22, 229–230, 257, 321, 330
Richard, Paul, 171, 175, 176, 215n15
Rikken Dōshikai (party), 183
Rikken Kokumintō (party), 75
Rikken Minseitō (party), 209
Rikken Seiyūkai (party), 79, 100n55, 130, 188, 234
Rōdō Nōmintō (party), 84
Rome, 249
Rōyama Masamichi, 230, 255, 265n87, 287, 313n63
Rule of Might *(badao/hadō)*, 36–38, 40, 43, 50, 127, 128, 147, 197, 204, 206, 209, 225n124, 282, 293, 330, 331
Rule of Right *(wangdao/ōdō)*, 36, 38, 40, 43, 50, 127, 204, 206, 211, 225n124, 267, 270, 276, 282, 288, 293, 301, 303, 306, 330, 331, 344
ōdō rakudo/wangdao letu (paradise of the Kingly Way), 301, 302, 344, 345
Russia, 21, 71, 75, 76, 78, 112, 113, 116, 139, 183, 202, 203, 205, 207, 209, 216n28, 224, 242, 251, 252, 257, 294, 296, 305
Russian Revolution (1917), 110, 125, 146, 147, 240
Russo-Japanese War (1904/05), 71, 138, 140, 194, 202, 210, 217n36, 296, 297

S

Saaler, Sven, xii–xiii, 21, 160n86, 214n11, 258n8
Said, Edward, 10, 11, 13, 26n29, 27n30, 27n32, 64, 219n47, 239, 324
Saigō Takamori, 184
Sakai Toshihiko, 69, 100n47, 340
Sakuma Shōzan, 28n46
'Same script, same race', 3, 40, 70, 72, 77, 89, 93, 115, 141, 189, 216n24, 342, 345
Sanmin Zhuyi (journal), 275, 278
Sanmin Zhuyi. *See* Three People's Principles
Sano Manabu, 288–289, 313n68
Satō Nobuhiro, 41, 340
Sawayanagi Masatarō, 135, 136, 138, 145, 160n86, 161n92, 161n93, 161n95
Seclusionism, 114, 136, 137, 143, 174
Seifert, Wolfgang, 15, 20

INDEX   403

Seikyōsha, 74, 75, 80, 99n43, 99n44, 188
Self-determination, 39, 40, 80, 81, 88, 109, 124, 126, 148, 149, 153, 172–174, 213, 343
Self-Orientalism (*ziwo Dongfang zhuyi*), 12, 24n8, 346
Self-Orientalization, 10–12, 320, 322, 330
Seoul, 297
Serbia, 85, 252
Shandong, 82, 110, 167, 180, 267
Shanghai, 36, 39, 69, 80, 137, 144, 145, 152, 155n15, 164n131, 198, 205, 207, 230, 231, 234, 235, 239, 240, 246–248, 254, 256, 257, 263n55, 264n59, 272, 278–281, 295, 298, 321, 337
Shastri, H.P., 263n55, 337
Sheng Banghe, 18–20
Shenyang (Fengtian), 267
Shidehara Kijūrō, 234, 259n13, 340
Shiga Shigetaka, 74, 99n43, 188–190, 192, 221n70
Shimazu, Naoko, 168
Shimonaka Yasaburō, 289–291, 314n74, 338, 340
Shina (China), 60n59, 84, 210
    Shina Bunkatsu Ron (China partition thesis), 70
    Shina Hozen Ron (China preservation thesis), 70
Shin A Sha (Rouse Asia Society), 19
Shina tsū, 309n31, 344
Shindō Eiichi, 331, 336n41
Shinjin (journal), 115, 117
Shin Nihon (journal), 84
Shinshi hosha (relations of interdependence), 68, 141, 243, 344. *See also* interdependency
Shizuoka (city/prefecture), 118, 234, 300

Shōwa (era, 1926-1989), 2, 14, 47–48, 344
Shōwa Emperor (Hirohito), 181
Shōwa Kenkyūkai, 297, 315n88
Shugi. *See* principle
Siam (Thailand), 300, 302
Siberia, 125, 139, 242
Siberian Expedition, 125
Sichuan (province), 82, 102n64
Singapore, 278, 336n40
Sinocentrism, xii, 5, 88, 89, 150, 273, 274, 325
Sino-Japanese cooperation, 42, 82, 83, 88, 111, 129, 132, 141, 143, 144, 151, 152, 172, 175, 190, 194, 205, 216n24, 234, 270, 277, 278, 282, 284–286, 288, 302, 312n56, 324, 325, 336n42
Sino-Japanese Treaty of Amenity (1871), 68
Sino-Japanese War, First (1894-95), 65, 75, 79, 142
Sino-Japanese War, Second (1937-1945), 269, 299
Sinophilism, xi, 28n41, 29n49, 115, 117, 130, 136, 138, 140, 144, 189, 190, 210, 226n137, 255
Skinner, Quentin, 45, 46, 49, 63, 95
Socialism, 6, 28n41, 33–35, 47, 69, 84, 100n47, 107, 109, 110, 130, 131, 188, 210, 226n137, 268, 277, 287, 313n64
Son Bun. *See* Sun Yat-sen
Sone Toshitora, 49
Sonnō Jōi Undō (Revere the Emperor, repel the barbarians movement), 41, 344
South America, viii, 77
Southeast Asia, 42, 75, 291, 331, 338
South Manchurian Railway Company, 81
Sovietism, 205, 257, 270

Soviet Union, 198, 205, 251, 299
Special Higher Police (*Tokubetsu Kōtō Keisatsu*), 268, 345
Spencer, Herbert, 183
Spengler, Oswald, 109, 294
Stalker, Nancy, 222n94
Stegewerns, Dick, 133
Stoddard, Lothrop, 203, 224n116
Straits Times (newspaper), 278
Stuurman, Siep, 45, 46, 48, 49
Suematsu Kenchō, 71, 340
Suetsugu Nobumasa, 290, 314n74, 340
Suez Canal, 124, 202
Sugimori Kōjirō, 294
Sugita Teiichi, 47, 49, 67–69, 97n17, 111–113, 170, 178, 215n12
Sun Ge, 328–330
Sun Yat-sen, 2, 3, 16, 22, 28n46, 33, 36, 38, 40, 42, 43, 47, 48, 53, 56n16, 72, 78, 80, 86–89, 101n55, 101n59, 102n80, 110, 127, 131, 132, 143–145, 150–152, 155n13, 176, 190, 196–213, 216n24, 223n99, 223n103, 224n112, 225, 227n142, 232, 235, 241, 245, 247, 263n57, 291, 293, 297, 298, 301, 306, 307n7, 307n8, 308n9, 308n19, 309n24, 311n51, 312n56, 321, 322, 327–331, 336n40, 336n42, 336n43
  and Kobe speech, 3, 22, 36, 38, 42, 145, 197–198, 200–203, 206–209, 212, 223n99, 270, 271, 276, 279, 282, 307n8, 321, 329
Sun Zhongshan. *See* Sun Yat-sen
Supranationalism, 80, 111, 113–115, 220n66, 251, 254, 255
Suzuki Teiichi, 291, 314n74, 340
Switzerland, 35, 142, 163n119
Szpilman, Christopher W.A., xiii, 130

T
Tachibana Shiraki, 28n46, 210–212, 226n137, 227n142, 294, 295, 307, 313n68
Tadokoro Teruaki, 287, 313n64
Tagore, Rabindranath, 132, 160n78, 196–198, 210, 222n93, 222n94, 223n96, 232
Taikai (League for the Abolition of Racial Discrimination), 170, 171, 178, 179, 214n11, 230, 234, 343
Taishō (era, 1912-1926), 2, 14, 15, 28n42, 36, 48, 63, 84, 95, 181, 212, 213
Taishō Democracy, 84, 115, 131, 135, 344
Taishō Restoration (*Taishō Ishin*), 184, 344
Taishō no Seinen to Teikoku no Zento (book), 122, 137, 140
Taiwan, 6, 68, 75, 81, 149, 160n83, 176, 242, 243, 268, 287, 293, 297, 304, 311n44, 327, 330, 335n31
Taiyō (journal), 70, 130, 132, 137, 145, 185, 186
Takatsuna Hirofumi, 207, 226n129, 277, 278
Takebe Tongo, 147, 165n144, 340
Takeuchi Masashi, 172–174, 215n21, 216n24, 216n28
Takeuchi Yoshimi, 14–16, 18, 21, 22, 24n10, 26n29, 27n40, 28n41, 28n42, 29n49, 31–37, 40–49, 52–54, 56n12, 58n45, 59n47, 60n56, 61n60, 96n14, 159n74, 320, 324, 327, 329, 332
Takeuchi Zensaku, 69
Taki Masao, 287, 313n62, 340
Tamerlane, 76
Tanaka, Stefan, 12–13, 26n28, 27n38, 226n137
Tanaka Giichi, 240, 340

Tanaka Masaaki, 291
Tanaka Memorandum, 240
Tanaka Zenryū, 215n13, 259n11
Taoka Reiun, 97n19
Tarui Tōkichi, 28n41, 29n46, 43, 47, 58n45, 67, 68, 96n13, 97n19
Tennōism, 36, 134
Terasaki Hidenari, 219n49
Three People's Principles, 72, 263n57, 270, 271, 273–274, 285, 308n19, 345
Tianjin, 198, 297
Times (newspaper), 38, 89–91
Tōa Dōbunkai (East Asia Common Culture Association), 19, 69, 134, 163n119, 166n157, 313n62, 344
Tōa Dōbun Shoin (East Asia Common Culture Study Institute), 28n46, 69, 345
Tōa Renmei. See East Asian League
Tōgō Heihachirō, 202, 224n114
Tōhō Kōron (journal), 241
Tōjō Hideki, 209
Tokugawa (era, 1603-1868), 98n35, 137, 143
Tokutomi Sohō, 1, 10, 11, 17, 109, 116, 121–126, 132, 137, 138, 140–142, 146–148, 150, 155n13, 157n41, 157n42, 163n119, 290, 297, 300, 314n74, 324
Tokyo, 2, 20, 69, 76, 84, 91, 100n47, 101n60, 130, 136, 145, 170, 180, 192, 199, 231, 232, 235, 247, 249, 253, 259n12, 264n59, 272, 280, 290, 291, 299, 301, 303, 308n13, 309n31, 312n56, 337, 338
Tokyo Nichi Nichi Shinbun (newspaper), 91, 99n35
Tokyo University, 118, 165n144, 249, 290

Tongmenghui (Revolutionary Alliance), 36, 143, 280, 345
Tongū Yutaka, 247, 248, 256, 257, 263n55, 263n58, 272, 308n13
Tongwen tongzhong. See 'same script, same race'
Tōyama Mitsuru, 28n46, 47
Toynbee, Arnold J., 108
Tōyō Kyōkai (Oriental Association), 134, 160n83
Tōyō Shakaitō (party), 67
Triple Intervention (1895), 75
Tsurumi Yūsuke, 102n64, 180, 185, 219n46, 219n47
Turkey, 85, 111, 118, 224n114, 290, 294
Twenty-One Demands (1915), 82, 84, 110, 120, 146, 152, 169, 188, 237

U

Uchida Rōan, 134, 160n83
Uchida Ryōhei, 28n46, 48, 340
Uchimura Kanzō, 73, 340
Ueki Emori, 46, 69, 340
Ukita Kazutami, 17, 120, 135–141, 143, 145, 146, 148–150, 155n13, 162n104, 163n119, 175, 204, 209, 210, 217n36, 299
Umeya Shōkichi, 331, 336n40, 336n42
Unequal Treaties, 200, 202, 212
United Kingdom. *See* Britain
United States, viii, 22, 38, 75, 77, 79, 81, 84, 90, 92, 104n87, 105n100, 108, 110, 111, 116, 118, 123, 124, 126, 128, 138, 139, 142, 147, 151, 152, 163n119, 167, 179, 180, 183, 184–189, 196, 197, 199, 203, 208, 218n43, 219n46,

220n60, 222n94, 243, 249, 251, 252, 260n21, 321. *See also* Immigration Act of 1924; Monroe Doctrine (US)
Ural Mountains, 124
Usher, Roland G., 142
'Using one barbarian to check another' (*yi yi zhi yi*), 86, 177, 276, 342
Utopia, 6, 35, 107, 139, 211

V

Versailles, 108, 111, 133, 167–171, 177, 178, 180, 212, 213, 232, 236, 237, 243, 244, 246, 296, 321
Vietnam, 78, 118, 139, 161n95, 194, 236, 290
Vladivostok, 202

W

Wakamiya Unosuke, 107, 127–129, 132, 146
Wangdao. *See* Rule of Right
Wang Hui, 329–330, 336n34
Wang Jingwei, 42, 47, 48, 192, 224n112, 270, 271, 275, 276, 279, 280, 282–283, 306
Wang Ping, xii, 18–20, 324, 325
Wang Tao, 69, 341
Wang Yi, 324–326, 336n43
Waseda University, 84, 136, 145, 192, 209, 259n12
Washington Conference (1921/22), 180, 184, 234
Watanabe Kōki, 69
Westernization, viii, 18, 44, 60n56, 75, 90, 109, 116, 197, 247, 322
Whampoa Military Academy, 270
Whig history, 45–46, 58n42

White Peril, 3, 16, 51, 93, 133, 140, 141, 160n83, 163n119, 173, 203, 342
Whites, vii, 37, 43, 50, 91–92, 120–123, 133, 138, 140, 141, 143, 147, 172–176, 179, 184, 187, 191, 193, 202, 209, 213, 216n24, 220n61, 231, 232, 243, 245, 248, 259n10, 274–275, 302
Wilson, Woodrow, 108, 109, 139, 174, 178, 232, 304
Worldism, 5, 73, 107, 113, 114, 120, 136, 139, 276, 277, 309n28
World War One, 16, 17, 22, 29n51, 56n14, 63, 68, 85, 95, 107–111, 118, 122, 124, 128, 131, 135, 139, 145, 147, 151, 153, 159n76, 167, 175, 181, 195, 197, 212, 213, 217n36, 233, 251, 296, 298, 304, 319–321
World War Two, 27n29, 31, 43, 44, 48, 52, 54, 58n35, 84, 108, 118, 130, 191, 250, 301, 323, 326
Wu Peifu, 198
Wushe Incident (1930), 268
Wuzu Gonghe (Republic of the Five Races), 301, 346
Wuzu xiehe (harmonious cooperation of five races), 301, 328

X

Xenophobia, 114, 133, 143, 180
Xiandai Pinglun (journal), 238, 261n31
Xi Jinping, 328, 341
Xin Guomindang (party), 276
xing Ya. *See* Kō A
Xin Yaxiya (journal), 272, 273, 275, 308n19, 338, 346
Xi'an Incident (1936), 279, 280, 310n41

Xin Yaxiya Xuehui (New Asia Study Society), 272, 346
Xu Xue'er, 80, 341

Y
Yamada Shōji, 15, 340
Yamada Yoshimasa, 47
Yamamuro Shin'ichi, xii, 17, 18, 60n54, 108, 110
Yanaihara Tadao, 218n37
Yano Jin'ichi, 290, 294, 314n74, 340
Yasukuni Shrine, 299
Yaxiya Mengluo zhuyi. *See* Asian Monroe Doctrine
Yaxiya Minzu Da Tongmeng (Great Alliance of Asian Peoples), 234, 337, 346
Yazhou Minzu Xiehui (Asian Peoples' Association), 247, 337, 346
Yellow (race/people), 39, 67, 68, 76, 112, 120, 131, 133, 141, 142, 168, 172, 173, 181, 204, 231, 232, 243, 257, 331
Yellow Peril, 13, 16, 27n30, 38, 50, 51, 65, 71, 83, 91, 92, 110, 140–142, 160n83, 173, 203, 260n21, 343
Yin Rugeng, 182, 191–196, 219n51, 222n82
Yomiuri Shinbun (newspaper), 78

Yorozuchōhō (newspaper), 93
Yoshida Shōin, 41, 340
Yoshino Sakuzō, 114–115, 117, 132, 136, 138, 143, 175–176, 217n33
Yuan Shikai, 87, 88, 110, 131, 341
Yu Jingyuan, 302–303

Z
Zachmann, Urs Matthias, 70
Zen Ajia Kyōkai. *See* (All Asia Association)
Zhang Binglin, 66, 69, 341
Zhang Ji, 69, 341
Zhang Shizhao, 150, 341
Zhang Xueliang, 310n41, 341
Zhang Yiguo, 12
Zhang Youshen, 199, 200, 223n107, 341
Zhang Zhenzhi, 272, 275, 338
Zhang Zhidong, 65
Zhang Zuolin, 145, 149, 267, 302, 341
Zhonghua Fazheng Daxue (Chinese Law and Politics University), 272
Zhou Fohai, 281, 312n56, 341
Zhou Huaren, 285–286, 312n56
Zhuyi. *See* principle
Zongli. *See* Sun Yat-sen

CPSIA information can be obtained
at www.ICGtesting.com
Printed in the USA
LVHW082137060619
620471LV00006B/376/P